Logistics and Supply Chain Management in the Globalized Business Era

Lincoln C. Wood
University of Otago, New Zealand

Linh N.K. Duong
University of the West of England, Bristol, UK

A volume in the Advances in Logistics, Operations, and Management Science (ALOMS) Book Series

IGI Global
PUBLISHER of TIMELY KNOWLEDGE

Published in the United States of America by
IGI Global
Business Science Reference (an imprint of IGI Global)
701 E. Chocolate Avenue
Hershey PA, USA 17033
Tel: 717-533-8845
Fax: 717-533-8661
E-mail: cust@igi-global.com
Web site: http://www.igi-global.com

Library of Congress Cataloging-in-Publication Data

Names: Wood, Lincoln C., editor. | Duong, Linh Nguyen Khanh, 1985- editor.
Title: Logistics and supply chain management in the globalized business era / Lincoln C. Wood, and Linh Nguyen Khanh Duong, editors.
Description: Hershey, PA : Business Science Reference, 2022. | Includes bibliographical references and index. | Summary: "This publication covers both strategic and operational level elements of logistics and supply chain research, providing a comprehensive overview of the field with particular attention to new technologies, digitization, and optimization as applied in the era of globalized business"-- Provided by publisher.
Identifiers: LCCN 2021024400 (print) | LCCN 2021024401 (ebook) | ISBN 9781799887096 (hardcover) | ISBN 9781799887102 (paperback) | ISBN 9781799887119 (ebook)
Subjects: LCSH: Business logistics. | Strategic planning. | Management--Technological innovations.
Classification: LCC HD38.5 .L6144 2022 (print) | LCC HD38.5 (ebook) | DDC 658.5--dc23
LC record available at https://lccn.loc.gov/2021024400
LC ebook record available at https://lccn.loc.gov/2021024401

This book is published in the IGI Global book series Advances in Logistics, Operations, and Management Science (ALOMS) (ISSN: 2327-350X; eISSN: 2327-3518)

British Cataloguing in Publication Data
A Cataloguing in Publication record for this book is available from the British Library.

For electronic access to this publication, please contact: eresources@igi-global.com.

Advances in Logistics, Operations, and Management Science (ALOMS) Book Series

John Wang
Montclair State University, USA

ISSN:2327-350X
EISSN:2327-3518

Mission

Operations research and management science continue to influence business processes, administration, and management information systems, particularly in covering the application methods for decision-making processes. New case studies and applications on management science, operations management, social sciences, and other behavioral sciences have been incorporated into business and organizations real-world objectives.

The **Advances in Logistics, Operations, and Management Science** (ALOMS) Book Series provides a collection of reference publications on the current trends, applications, theories, and practices in the management science field. Providing relevant and current research, this series and its individual publications would be useful for academics, researchers, scholars, and practitioners interested in improving decision making models and business functions.

Coverage

- Finance
- Networks
- Production Management
- Computing and information technologies
- Political Science
- Risk Management
- Organizational Behavior
- Information Management
- Marketing engineering
- Services management

IGI Global is currently accepting manuscripts for publication within this series. To submit a proposal for a volume in this series, please contact our Acquisition Editors at Acquisitions@igi-global.com or visit: http://www.igi-global.com/publish/.

The Advances in Logistics, Operations, and Management Science (ALOMS) Book Series (ISSN 2327-350X) is published by IGI Global, 701 E. Chocolate Avenue, Hershey, PA 17033-1240, USA, www.igi-global.com. This series is composed of titles available for purchase individually; each title is edited to be contextually exclusive from any other title within the series. For pricing and ordering information please visit http://www.igi-global.com/book-series/advances-logistics-operations-management-science/37170. Postmaster: Send all address changes to above address.

Titles in this Series

For a list of additional titles in this series, please visit: www.igi-global.com/book-series

Managerial Issues in Digital Transformation of Global Modern Corporations
Thangasamy Esakki (Poompuhar College (Autonomous), India)
Business Science Reference • © 2021 • 323pp • H/C (ISBN: 9781799824022) • US $195.00

Reviving Businesses With New Organizational Change Management Strategies
Nuno Geada (College of Business Administration, Polytechnic Institute of Setúbal, Portugal) and Pedro Anunciação (College of Business Administration, Polytechnic Institute of Setúbal, Portugal)
Business Science Reference • © 2021 • 356pp • H/C (ISBN: 9781799874522) • US $225.00

Handbook of Research on Decision Sciences and Applications in the Transportation Sector
Said Ali Hassan (Cairo University, Egypt) and Ali Wagdy Mohamed (Cairo University, Egypt)
Business Science Reference • © 2021 • 419pp • H/C (ISBN: 9781799880400) • US $285.00

Handbook of Research on Management Techniques and Sustainability Strategies for Handling Disruptive Situations in Corporate Settings
Rafael Perez-Uribe (Universidad Santo Tomas, Bogotá, Colombia) David Ocampo-Guzman (EAN University, Colombia) Nelson Antonio Moreno-Monsalve (EAN University, Colombia) and William Stive Fajardo-Moreno (EAN University, Colombia)
Business Science Reference • © 2021 • 616pp • H/C (ISBN: 9781799881858) • US $295.00

Digitalization of Decentralized Supply Chains During Global Crises
Atour Taghipour (Normandy University, France)
Business Science Reference • © 2021 • 254pp • H/C (ISBN: 9781799868743) • US $225.00

Advances in Intelligent, Flexible, and Lean Management and Engineering
Carolina Machado (University of Minho, Portugal) and J. Paulo Davim (University of Aveiro, Portugal)
Business Science Reference • © 2021 • 295pp • H/C (ISBN: 9781799857686) • US $225.00

The Role of Islamic Spirituality in the Management and Leadership Process
Mahazan Abdul Mutalib (Universiti Sains Islam Malaysia (USIM), Malaysia) and Ahmad Rafiki (Universitas Medan Area, Indonesia)
Business Science Reference • © 2021 • 254pp • H/C (ISBN: 9781799868927) • US $195.00

IGI Global
PUBLISHER of TIMELY KNOWLEDGE

701 East Chocolate Avenue, Hershey, PA 17033, USA
Tel: 717-533-8845 x100 • Fax: 717-533-8661
E-Mail: cust@igi-global.com • www.igi-global.com

Table of Contents

Detailed Table of Contents

The challenges facing procurement managers across industries and public services are quite important. Businesses need to take care of the bottom line while public services need to manage tight budgets. This is aggravated by difficult economic environments such as the one that has come with COVID-19. Reducing procurement costs means less funds and working capital. Such is achieved by means of adequate negotiation processes. Technology procurement is a field with long acquisition lifecycles, where negotiations span over considerable periods of time, and where the features of technology may impact negotiations, including the technology inherent obsolescence speed. Such negotiations occur in an environment where demanding technical requirements abound alongside economic rationality and where negotiations are conducted by teams of managers and engineers, addressing the distinct dimensions. An approach to technology procurement negotiation is presented with viewpoints for reflection on how procurement and negotiations shall be addressed for technology procurement purposes.

The purpose of this chapter is to explore the role of trust or confidence through the managerial lens. The chapter aims to acquire empirical evidence regarding the importance of factors that play a role in fostering trust during procurement decision making exemplified through a New Zealand-owned company, ContainerCo. This exploratory study scrutinises trust as perceived by SME managers in the supply chain of logistics and procurement in New Zealand. It uses the repertory grid analysis and is based on two interviews conducted through the repertory grid technique, a semi-structured method. Although different in every company and country, trust plays a major role during the selection of suppliers. Factors such as reliability and value are regarded as the most important ones for choosing the right supplier in the case of ContainerCo.

It seems that the COVID-19 pandemic, which started in December 2019, will have longer and more profound consequences on our lives than initially foreseen. Among the most obvious are everyday decisions about the mode of transport. From related research, it can be seen that the most affected transport mode is public transport, which had the greatest decline. The reason for lesser use of public transport is in complete closure of public transport in some parts of the world. However, where this measure has not been applied, the reason for the reduction is people's fear of infection when using public transport or any shared modes of transportation. The fear stems from the fact that the COVID-19 virus is spreading extremely fast in densely populated rooms. All these changes are affecting the changes in city mobility. Related research shows a decrease of mobility in general and an increase in the use of individual modes of transportation. Distinct changes can be observed in different environments as compared to previous travel behaviour.

Container terminals play an important role in linking regional and continental areas for the exchange of goods. Port authorities have to provide their services under competitive prices and service levels to customers. This increasing competition pushes feeder ports to improve their processes. The goal is to increase the port capacity to deal with the increasing demand for containers and, at the same time, to reduce the environmental impact and operative costs. The authors address the gap in the literature regarding alternatives for feeder ports. They analyse best practices adopted in international terminals and evaluate the implementation in feeder ports. They apply a quantitative approach using the simulation software AnyLogic. The model uses market data to analyse the vessel unloading process at the berth. Moreover, an alternative to reduce the CO2 emissions for diesel equipment is presented. A flowchart for the vessel unloading and loading operations is proposed that includes the strategies to increase capacity and efficiency of operations and the utilisation of equipment.

The goal of this research was to measure the cost of road freight transport in the 20 European countries with the highest recorded quantity of tonne-kilometres and assess their competitiveness. Cost competitiveness was measured by four main cost categories: fuels, drivers' wages, tyres and tolls, and the results show large cost variances between countries. The countries with the lowest road freight transport cost were Bulgaria, Poland, and Romania, and those with the highest costs were Norway, Austria, and the UK. The largest differences in costs were met in tolls and other road taxes, followed by drivers' wages, fuels, and finally, tyres.

The COVID-19 pandemic has greatly magnified supply challenges in all industries, and virus waves continue to cause an extraordinary amount of variation in both the demand for and the availability of necessary products. This uncertainty has also forced many organizations including container liner shipping to redesign their supply chain. Feeder services from hub ports are essential chain of shipping networks. This chapter addresses the design of feeder networks under consideration of demand fluctuations over the year. For this purpose, a perturbation-based variable neighbourhood search approach is developed in order to determine the feeder ship fleet size and mix, the fleet deployment, service routes, and voyage schedules to minimize operational costs. In the case study investigation, the authors consider the feeder network design problem faced by a feeder shipping company as a sample application. The performance of alternate network configurations is compared under dynamic demand conditions. Numerical results highlight the advantage of dynamic and flexible design of feeder service networks.

An efficient supply chain management helps to increase the productivity of a business. Use of information technology and concepts like artificial intelligence, blockchain, and cloud computing have integrated the different aspects of supply chain with its stakeholders. Published literature in the field of SCM, IT, and the pharmaceutical industry has been reviewed, and different aspects of innovation, technique, risks, advancements, factors, and models have been taken into consideration to form a comprehensive chapter focusing on the role of information technology in the supply chain management of the pharmaceutical industry. The chapter finds that IT has made a significant impact in improving the efficiency of SCM. But its successful implementation and collaboration with other firms is the key to success for an efficient SCM. Within each category, gaps have been identified.

This empirical research investigates the reverse logistics practices adopted by a leading pharmaceutical company in Egypt, the drivers behind the applied reverse logistics activities, and the barriers affecting the application of reverse logistics. The methodological approach of interpretive structural modeling (ISM) is applied to study the mutual influences across barriers listed by a preliminary case analysis, and to identify the "driving" barriers which may worsen other barriers, and "dependent" barriers influenced by the driving barriers. A key finding of the analysis is that lack of regulation enforcement and lack of public awareness regarding the importance of reverse logistics are the most driving barriers influencing the rest of the identified barriers.

system. A bi-objective model is then proposed to combine the two objectives mentioned previously using LP-metric method. To solve big instances of the problem in reasonable time, an approximate approach is proposed using the rolling horizon-based fix and relax heuristic. Finally, computational results are presented to compare the solutions obtained by both approaches.

Demand forecasting and production planning are challenging issues when working to supply perishable goods to fulfil supermarket requirements as opposed to dry goods that can be manufactured and have a fixed storage life. The focus of this report is on the improvement of resource utilisation through better forecasting, planning, and information flow. There is a fluctuation for labour demand within the processing function; controlling the number of staff daily is vital to the efficient running of production and waste reduction. It is the belief for the management that left unchecked the production planners can tend to overorder staff as a contingency.

Retail is one of the most important industries that is continuously improving around the world and in particular in Turkey. Competitive advantages owned by firms keep businesses one step ahead of their competitors. The main objectives of this chapter are determination of the main competitive advantages and capabilities for firm performance, determination of competitive advantages and capabilities which are relatively important for firm performance, and determination of competitive advantages and capabilities that are mainly used under the effects of environmental dynamism for firm performance in the Turkish retail industry. In this chapter, retailers are evaluated into two groups as organized and traditional. Totally, 50 competitive advantages and capabilities were identified in the research. The results of the study would be beneficial both for retail literature and retail business life.

Further scientifically finding of total logistics costs model during execution the cement projects in Indonesia, the consecutive further tasks are how to examine the best logistics' provider to perform the logistics' works. This is the ultimate goal of this chapter. The methodology developed is by case study, elaborate techniques of focus group discussion (FGD), expert judgment (EJ), and enriched by the analytical hierarchical process (AHP) to obtain the best decision. The finding is the total costs of ownership (TCO) as the best tool to examine several considerations to select the best provider's candidates can be applied. Data as sources of this chapter are consolidated from the cement projects in Indonesia from

2010 to 2018. During the period, cement projects in Indonesia were rampant, and certainly, it demanded logistics providers. The TCO in practical fits during procurement-processes, it is also valuable during the selection of the logistics' providers. The TCO is fair enough as the best tool to build governance during procurement to avoid miss-discrimination-treated.

Preface

We have witnessed a significant expansion of the global supply chain since the last decades of the twentieth century, especially in the automobile, food, and textile industries. For example, by turning over Adidas or Nike shoes in stores in London or New York, we can see that they are made in China, Bangladesh, or Vietnam. This growth of the globalized business era brings both challenges and motivation for researchers and practitioners for interests in logistics and supply chain management. The supply chain has become longer and more complex. Another example comes from the recent disruption due to the spread of Covid-19. To stop the spread of the new Covid-19 variant, the French government decided to stop the channel between France and the United Kingdom without notice. This action caused a long queue of trucks waiting to cross the channel, a temporary shortage of food products in the United Kingdom, and many trucker drivers could not arrive home for Christmas. Thus, logistics and supply chain management are crucial topics, and the globalized business era just brings more challenges to the topics. When a company decides to work with foreign partners, it is necessary to understand and coordinate the entire supply chain. They need to share the forecast data with their suppliers. They need to know the shipment status and where it is. These are some of the functionalities that are essential in all industries and services.

This book aims to provide an introduction and up-to-date knowledge in the logistics and supply chain management field. It provides readers with some case studies and methodologies. This book can be used in core and advanced classes. Therefore, it is targeted at a wide range of readers, including researchers, professionals, and laypersons. The book focuses on applying theory into practice. The book provides both quantitative and qualitative methods for decision-makers in making their decisions. In addition, because of the significant development of digitalization, information technology, and optimization techniques, this book will pay particular attention to these topics.

The target audience for this book are business managers, logistics managers, analysts, research scholars, and advanced postgraduate students – and each group would use the book in different ways. The book tackles several pressing practical issues from broad strategic and geopolitical perspectives, such as issues in the Turkey retail industry or challenges in transportation due to the COVID-19 pandemic. The book may be of interest to logistics research scholars and technical analysts or technically-minded logistics managers; it provides greater insight into using different methods and their value. In this way, the book can serve as a valuable supplement to a more management-oriented postgraduate class. It will benefit businesses and practitioners as they seek to understand how to apply new technologies and approaches or evaluate suggestions or business proposals within their own company. Instructors of undergraduate courses might find chapters relevant as a supplement to their teaching where they can use a chapter as a solution to a particular problem or as a starting point to lead the class in a discussion of a particular challenge.

The book starts with a discussion on procurement management. The globalized business era leads to high competitiveness; thus, outsourcing has become a common business strategy (de Araújo et al., 2017). Suppliers have significant effects on the success of buyers. Selecting a qualified supplier improves a buyer's confidence and performance. For example, the collapse of the Rana Plaza building, a house of several garment factories in Bangladesh, increases the awareness of the risks and costs of outsourcing from low-cost countries. Following the Rana Plaza disaster, there was a negative reaction on the stock market for major retailers who source garments significantly in Bangladesh (Jacobs & Singhal, 2017). In this context, excellent procurement management has a vital role in any company. Therefore, the first two chapters in this book focus on the procurement process and strengthening relationships among supply chain partners.

Agua et al. (Portuguese Naval Academy, Portugal) focus on the negotiation and negotiation process and pinpoints some critical "post-negotiation" issues that typically arise within the context of technology acquisition. Because most agreements implementation does not develop exactly as negotiated or expected, there is a permanent need to negotiate during the delivery or implementation stages. Besides the need for an integrative approach to negotiation, as opposed to competitive ones, such issues involve several typical steps and are discussed within the context of this chapter. The chapter is written from the viewpoint of the purchasing side procurement. Such raises a different set of questions when compared with the selling side point of view. Each side or party takes its particular perspective, where sellers want to maximize their profits. In contrast, buyers want to reduce acquisition costs, which, together with the always present asymmetry of information among the parties, will raise friction and damage the procurement effectiveness during or after the main negotiation stage. This kind of procurement, where technology is involved, points toward cooperative modes of negotiation, where the long-term relationship between suppliers and purchasing companies shall be taken care of. Regardless of the benefits of such long-term relationships and the involved collaborative approaches, there is also a negative side. Such negative side arises from the following issues: (i) since procurement managers will have the attention focused on fewer suppliers, they may be missing some new emerging technologies and solutions, (ii) long term relationships have the potential to feed the vicious cycle where another potential supplier will not present themselves to the procuring companies, because they may believe that there is a barrier related to the long-term relationships, already in place, with current vendors, and (iii) there may be some installed inertia on the procurement departments, with procurement managers and officers getting accustomed to the usual suppliers, and where the current sellers, despite less competition, may have the tendency to increase their products or solutions prices, even not developing new innovative products. Some human skills issues accompany the explanation, but such will be referred to throughout the chapter.

Since the past two decades, supply chain management (SCM) has been many efforts in eliminating inefficiencies and ineffectiveness in the procurement process. The contractual relationship in SCM primarily relies on monitoring and control methods and sometimes could be described as 'hard' management systems. It is also inflexible in resolving unforeseen circumstances, rendering it myopic and inactive in times of dire need. Therefore, there is a need to strengthen relationships among supply chain partners and increase flexibility in dealing with uncertainties. Kripanshu Vora (Otago University, New Zealand) highlights the importance of trust in supply chain relationships, especially procurement management. The author investigates the case of a New Zealand company and aims to understand how staff perceives their trust (or confidence) in suppliers during the procurement process and its role in procurement decisions. The results show that trust is perceived through criteria that inform the senior staff members of the trusting factor in their suppliers. Companies should focus on principle constructs such as the reliability of value, the physical location, the point of contact, the eagerness of a supplier, the duration of their dyadic relationship, the speed of delivering goods or services, the flexibility of contracts, the quality of service, the adaptability of the supplier, a trickle-up and down communication, the work orientation of the supplier, the origin of the supplier, and the supplier's goods or service fit to the company's requirements.

With the increasing globalization, transportation has gained importance in business and the economy. However, the volatility in fuel prices and surging demand have shown that transportation is vulnerable and critical for global supply chains. Recently, many countries and regions have implemented strict transportation rules due to the COVID-19 pandemic. This leads to challenges in managing transportation and how to ensure the movement of products. The following four chapters dedicate the discussion regarding transportation, especially, chapter 3 discusses challenges in transportation due to the COVID-19.

The pandemic caused by the SARS-CoV-2 (COVID-19) pandemic impacts every aspect of our lives and represents the unique situation in the last few decades. Many regions have implemented strict transportation regulations. This leads to challenges in making decisions about the mode of transport. From related research, it can be seen that the most affected transport mode is public transport, which had the most significant decline. The reason for lesser use of public transport is incomplete closure of public transport in some parts of the world. However, where this measure has not been applied, the reduction is people's fear of infection when using public transport or any shared modes of transportation. The fear stems from the fact that the COVID-19 virus is spreading extremely fast in densely populated rooms. All these changes are affecting the changes in city mobility. Related research shows a decrease in mobility in general and an increase in individual modes of transportation. Furthermore, distinct changes can be observed in different environments as compared to previous travel behaviour. To successfully adjust city mobility according to the new conditions due to COVID-19, Šinko et al. (University of Maribor, Slovenia) analyze the differences in city mobility before and during the COVID-19 pandemic. The authors use the transport simulation using a microscopic open-source road traffic simulation package SUMO (Simulation of Urban Mobility) to show the urban transport system changes due to the pandemic. The chapter aims to elaborate on the reported changes due to the COVID19 situation in Slovenia. The study is a novelty because there is no such simulation of the effect of COVID19 on city mobility. The process described in the chapter could be used for different cities worldwide, and the results could help city policymakers adjust the traffic situations.

Container terminals play an essential role in linking regional and continental areas for the exchange of goods. Port authorities must provide their services under competitive prices and service levels to customers. This increasing competition push feeder ports to improve their processes. The goal is to increase the port capacity to deal with the increasing demand for containers and, at the same time, to reduce the environmental impact and operative costs. It is noted that transportation is responsible for 1% of the global carbon dioxide (CO_2) emissions. Therefore, the implementation of innovative solutions will have a positive effect on company performance. Londono-Bernal et al. (Curtin University, Australia) addresses the gap in the literature regarding alternatives for feeder ports. The authors analyze best practices adopted in international terminals and evaluate the implementation in feeder ports. The chapter focuses on developing an understanding of the process flows for feeder ports and mapping this process rather than solving for a particular business case. A flowchart for the vessel unloading and loading operations is proposed, including strategies to increase operations capacity, efficiency, and equipment utilization. Moreover, an alternative to reduce the CO2 emissions for diesel equipment is presented.

At a European level, freight transport has recorded a remarkable increase in the last decades. Among freight transport methods, road transport was responsible for more than half of total freight transport across Europe, followed by shipping, trains and other transport means. However, as the quantity of Road Freight Transport (RFT) differs from one European country to the next, similar differences can be recorded in RFT cost due to variances in cost factors such as fuels, wages, insurance, taxation, tolls, maintenance, repairs, tyres, parking space etc. Even though scarce, previous research on the topic has pointed out such differences. In this context, Kotsios and Folinas (Greece) aim to measure and compare RFT cost competitiveness in the 20 European countries with the highest recorded quantity of traveled tonne-kilometres and examine cost differences between their size and size the factors that create them. Cost competitiveness was measured using four main cost categories: fuels, drivers' wages, tires, and tolls. This examination and its conclusions can be helpful for European transport policy designers that wish to harmonize commercial road transport procedures and costs across European Union countries.

Driven by the ever-increasing loading capacity of containerships, hub-and-spoke networks became the most economical mode of organizing global container shipping. In this network, hubs are connected to the main intercontinental sea routes while small and medium-sized feeder ships serve regional ports with low transport demand. The connections from the hub ports to the regional ports constitute the feeder network which provides the global containership liners access to local transportation markets and avoids the megaships' calling at too many ports. Global liner shipping and feeder service require significant capital investment for the fleet of containerships and involve substantial operational costs. High utilization of the fleet capacity is needed to secure the desired return on investment. Principally, the revenue of container shipping is affected by the transported container volume, which depends on the development of the world economy and world trade. Specifically, there are close relationships to regional economic developments for feeder services, which strongly affect the transportation demand of export and import goods and raw materials. In addition to volume, the balance between import and export containers at ports is a critical factor. Theoretically, a feeder ship could carry up to twice its slot capacity in a cyclic route if it departs from the hub port with all the import containers, delivers them to regional ports, simultaneously picks up export containers, and returns to the hub port loaded with export containers. When the trade is imbalanced at the ports, slots remain idle during the journey of the ship. In particular, trade imbalance in certain regions makes it difficult for feeder services to fully utilize the capacity of feeder ships operating in the network. Therefore, the design of feeder services plays a crucial role in maritime logistics. Polat (Pamukkale University, Turkey) considers the feeder network design problem of a Turkish short-sea shipping company because of the opening of a new port. The cost performance of different feeder network configurations serving the Black Sea region is evaluated under unstable demand conditions. The various configurations are determined according to the forecasted container transportation volume of the terminals in the region during a 52-week sailing season. The results of the numerical study show that the total costs of the service network can be significantly reduced if unstable demand conditions are considered in the network design.

The following four chapters discuss issues relating to pharmaceutical supply chains and the healthcare system. The complexity of the pharmaceutical industry stretches worldwide as all countries are part of this supply chain (Rossetti et al., 2011). Moreover, due to high investment in developing pharmaceutical products, its supply chain relies on only a few manufacturers. For example, there are only a few companies that can develop and manufacture COVID-19 vaccines. This leads to challenges in how to work with influential partners in the pharmaceutical supply chain. The following four chapters review the literature and business practices in this industry.

Saha et al. (Sikkim Manipal Institute of Technology, India) conducted a literature review on the use of information technology in supply chain management of the pharmaceutical industry. An efficient Supply Chain Management helps to increase the productivity of a business. The use of information technology and concepts like artificial intelligence, blockchain, cloud computing has integrated the different aspects of the supply chain with its stakeholders. Published literature in the field of SCM, IT, and the pharmaceutical industry has been reviewed, and different aspects of innovation, technique, risks, advancements, factors, and models have been taken into consideration to form a comprehensive paper focusing on the role of information technology in the supply chain management of the pharmaceutical industry. The chapter finds that IT has made a significant impact in improving the efficiency of SCM. Nevertheless, its successful implementation and collaboration with other firms is the key to an efficient SCM. Within each category, gaps have been identified.

Reverse logistics is one of the most critical aspects of any business related to manufacturing, distribution, service, and support. It is practiced in different industries, including steel, commercial aircraft, computers, automobiles, appliances, chemicals, and medical items. Its increasing popularity underscores the importance of reverse logistics in both business and academic communities since the last decade. Reverse logistics is essential in the pharmaceutical industry, not only from the economic point of view but also from the environment and the regulatory points of view. In addition, the application of reverse logistics in this industry is more challenging than in other industries, as most pharmaceuticals get destroyed when they are recalled or returned; they are seldom repaired or resold. As a result, reselling expired pharmaceuticals in Egypt is an increasing problem with severe consequences. It is estimated that EGP 600 million (approximately $US 76.6 million) worth of counterfeit and expired drugs in the Egyptian market, constituting two percent of the country's total annual pharmaceutical sales. Elbelehy and Abdelsalam (Arab Academy for Science, Technology and Maritime Transport, Egypt) explore the reverse logistics drivers, practices, and barriers at Pharco Pharmaceuticals, a leading pharmaceutical manufacturer in Egypt. Next, the authors apply the ISM methodology to explore the mutual influences between the identified barriers affecting the implementation of reverse logistics practices at the case company. The research revealed that the application of reverse logistics at Pharco is mainly regulatory-driven. However, the interviews with the company management showed a lack of full compliance to the imposed regulations, as around 90 percent of the total pharmaceutical waste is destructed in a non-approved disposal site by MOH.

Multidisciplinary cooperation of participating health care professionals, use of common standards in diagnostics, and clinical pathways in the treatment of vascular patients should provide for a higher-quality clinical practice. The aging population, increase of chronic diseases, increasing people's demands for new, more complex diagnostic and therapeutic methods, and lack of health providers lead the way towards the introduction of new health services based on new process models and advanced information and telecommunications solutions. E-health services promise a better health service for the future, being more effective than existing, established healthcare models. By applying the telemedical approach, an efficient, equally personalized, but faster multidisciplinary specialist treatment can be introduced into clinical practice. On the other hand, its introduction raises data security issues. Data in electronic form are easy to access, track and archive, and travel very fast – properties facilitating data abuse. Gumzej and Fošnarič (University of Maribor, Slovenia) provide a model of patient-telemonitoring after revascularization procedures in the lower extremities is presented. A protocol for proper authentication and authorization to access medical equipment and patient's medical records has been introduced. The associated clinical study has shown that trained nurses can successfully perform most post-operative follow-up examinations. Hence, improvements to healthcare logistics, mainly due to shortening waiting times for specialist treatment and the reduction of follow-up examinations on the secondary healthcare level, can be achieved using telemedicine. The main benefit of this approach is that patients can be treated in their local environment. The waiting times for initial visits at the angiology department can be reduced. Consequently, more time can be allotted to patients undergoing vascular surgery procedures. By minimizing the number of follow-up appointments with vascular surgeons also the cost of their medical treatment can be reduced. In addition, by safe and secure telemedical and telediagnostic applications, the patients would gain trust in personalized telehealth systems and the notion of a better health service due to shorter waiting times and the reduced need for travel to obtain specialist treatment.

Safeguarding the supply of drugs and satisfying the needs of patients when it comes to quantity, quality, cost, and accessibility is a strategic priority of any health care system priorities. Pharmaceuticals represent a large portion of the costs in the healthcare industry due to the high costs of these products and their storage and control requirements. The pharmaceutical supply chain is subject to many threats leading to deteriorating treasured resources and the disruption of available drugs, resulting in shortages. Drug shortage is a condition in which the supply of all clinically alternative versions of controlled drugs is insufficient to meet the current or estimated demand at the user levels, which are patients. In many healthcare practice settings, the shortage is prevalent and affects nearly all the classes, with the most critical ones being surgical and being affected the most. Moreover, the quality use of medicines is a crucial factor in achieving positive health outcomes. A drug shortage is a deficiency in the supply of medicines or products that affects the ability of a patient to get the necessary treatment in due time. The roots of drug shortages are multifaceted and varied. The problem can either be due to supply or demand. However, the situation affects almost every stakeholder in the health care system, so collaboration is required to handle or reduce shortages. It can also affect the amount of work, important decisions, and financial impact if not anticipated on time. Public expectation of quality healthcare and the burgeoning costs of more sophisticated and expensive medical interventions has been a significant cause of worry and deliberation the world over. Baporikar (University of Science and Technology, Namibia & University of Pune, India) focuses on drug delivery issues in Namibia, a country situated in the southern part of Africa. The efficient functioning of Namibia's public pharmaceutical management system, one of the central support systems, is critical to the success of the health sector. This chapter analyzes the causes of drug supply shortages and determines strategies to address and handle the shortage crisis from a contemporary perspective. The results indicate disruptions in the supply chain, lack of raw materials, management inefficiencies, increasing demand, improper inventory system, manufacturers delay, being causes of drug supply shortage in Katutura hospital. Lack of integration and collaboration between the procurement function and distribution function and the expiry date of drugs are factors causing drug supply shortages.

Presently, in the economic context, the relationship between the customer and the supplier has significantly progressed, establishing the need for customization of products and services, minimizing delivery delays, multiplication of delivery channels, and satisfaction rates. This led industrial companies to search for new methods to improve their performances and answer the greater degree for customers' expectations. Facing these goals, those companies need to set new planning all along the supply chain network to optimize their processes. Zeddam et al. (University of Tlemcen, Algeria) address the Production Routing Problem (PRP), which makes part of the noted integration problems. In such a problem, the aim is to simultaneously optimize the production decision, the inventory, and the distribution. The

PRP is an NP-hard problem because it jointly optimizes many decisions that are: setup, production, inventory, delivery amounts, and routing decisions, which makes the problem hard to be solved, seeing that the various decisions may be conflicting, and finding the compromised solution with multiple decision variables under various categories of constraints presents the complexity of the problem. The PRP may arise within a supply chain composed of a manufacturing factory that produces goods and delivers them to a set of customers or warehouses. According to the literature, the PRP aims to find the optimal production and distribution schedule in a multi-period planning horizon to minimize the whole system costs. However, most of the papers dealing with the PRP consider only the total costs minimization (setup, production, inventory, and transportation costs) while energy, an important aspect, has not yet been considered. Therefore, the authors propose including energy into the PRP definition in a multi-objective method to address this gap. They provide a MILP approach that considers both classical and energy-minimizing PRP versions to deal with such a problem. The results show a significant reduction of the computational time, which depends on the Observation Window (OW) size; each time the OW size is smaller, the computational time is smaller. Besides, the best objective value is obtained by the higher OW size in terms of the solution quality.

Demand forecasting and production planning are challenging issues when working to supply perishable goods to fulfill supermarket requirements. Supplying soft fruit such as grapes has many additional factors that must be considered, such as significant seasonal variation and uncertain demand at the store level. Coulthard et al. (University of Lincoln, United Kingdom) focus on improving resource utilization through better forecasting, planning, and information flow. There is a fluctuation in labor demand within the processing function; controlling daily staff is vital to efficient production and waste reduction. The research runs packing trials using both fruits packed into punnets at source and lose fruit that requires packing into punnets on-site and used fruit with both good and poorer quality product to measure the packing speeds. The staff used will also be controlled per job using either core or agency staff to pack the same fruit into the same job types. Data from the trials completed showed a significant difference when work requiring any level of grading was conducted by core staff compared to the agency. The results also indicate the difference in the packs per minute that can be expected when using differing grades/ quality of raw material. The trial also highlighted that when completing production runs where grading of the product was not required, there was no significant difference between the core and agency staff. The result of these trials has provided the basis to provide not only an accurate and reliable forecast but also a powerful tool that can be interrogated to produce metrics that can be used as a point of discussion between the pack-house manager and the business concerning run-rates, staff levels, job management and planning and efficient use of labor resources.

Retail is one of the most essential industries continuously improving around the world, particularly Turkey. Competitive advantages owned by firms provide one step ahead of their competitors. Bülend Avcı (Bahçeşehir University, Turkey) determines the main competitive advantages and capabilities for firm performance. The author also determines competitive advantages and capabilities mainly used under the effects of environmental dynamism for firm performance in the Turkish Retail Industry. In this chapter, retailers are evaluated into two groups as organized and traditional. There are 50 competitive advantages and capabilities in the Turkish retail industry. Nineteen competitive advantages were identified as main competitive advantages, 19 as relatively critical competitive advantages, and 12 as mainly used competitive advantages under the effects of environmental dynamism for firm performance in the Turkish retail industry.

Subiyanto and Effnandya (Widya Mandala Surabaya Catholic University, Indonesia) investigate the total logistics costs model during the cement projects in Indonesia and examine the best logistics providers to perform the logistics works. The authors adopt a case study, elaborate techniques of focus group discussion (FGD), expert judgment (EJ), and the analytical hierarchy process (AHP) to obtain the best decision. The finding is that the total costs of ownership (TCO) as the best tool to examine several considerations to select the best provider's candidates can be applied. Data as sources of this paper is being consolidated from the cement projects in Indonesia from 2010 to 2018. During the period, cement projects in Indonesia were rampant, and indeed, they increased the demand for logistics providers. The TCO is in practical fits during procurement processes, but it is also valuable when selecting the logistics providers. Therefore, the TCO is a suitable tool to enhance governance during procurement to avoid miss-discrimination-treated to the suppliers.

We hope that the readers of this volume find value in the collection of chapters and can improve their management or research as a result.

Lincoln C. Wood
University of Otago, New Zealand

Linh N. K. Duong
University of the West of England, Bristol, UK

REFERENCES

de Araújo, M. C. B., Alencar, L. H., & de Miranda Mota, C. M. (2017). Project procurement management: A structured literature review. *International Journal of Project Management*, *35*(3), 353–377. doi:10.1016/j.ijproman.2017.01.008

Jacobs, B. W., & Singhal, V. R. (2017). The effect of the Rana Plaza disaster on shareholder wealth of retailers: Implications for sourcing strategies and supply chain governance. *Journal of Operations Management*, *49–51*(1), 52–66. doi:10.1016/j.jom.2017.01.002

Rossetti, C. L., Handfield, R., & Dooley, K. J. (2011). Forces, trends, and decisions in pharmaceutical supply chain management. *International Journal of Physical Distribution & Logistics Management*, *41*(6), 601–622. doi:10.1108/09600031111147835

Acknowledgment

This has been another fun and enjoyable project working with my old friend and past Ph.D. student. While Linh and I shared the load, taking on different tasks at different times, I am grateful that he supported the project in the end while we were preparing the final manuscripts. I am forever thankful to my wife, Penelope, for her endless support and encouragement. While she was in need at the end of this project (with a broken leg), the early part of the project benefitted from her constant support. Finally, I would like to acknowledge my children. In the words of our three-year-old Ella, she "likes it when I smile!" Abigail, Eleanor, and Fionnlagh bring great joy and brightness to my life between the numerous tasks and jobs. Thank you to my lovely children and wife – thank you for all the smiles you help me find in life!

In my professional life, I have benefitted from a range of mentors and senior scholars at various universities who have helped me to acclimatize and find success in new environments. On a day-to-day basis, I have received significant support from my departmental and divisional colleagues, particularly my Head of Department, Associate Professor Fiona Edgar. In addition, my professional life would be less colorful and enjoyable without the constant support and encouragement from my friend and colleague at Curtin University, Dr. Torsten Reiners. Finally, I am grateful for the support from the *International Journal of Applied Logistics* Editorial team and authors. I have developed some long-term relationships and friendships over the years due to my involvement at the journal.

Together, the support from my colleagues, friends, and family has enabled me to undertake my projects with success.

Lincoln C. Wood

We would like to thank the reviewers for their valuable feedback and the tremendous support from the IGI publishing team.

I want to thank Dr. Lincoln Wood, co-editor of this book, and my Ph.D. supervisor, for the opportunity to work with him on this project.

My biggest appreciation is for my wife, Huong, and our baby, May. Without their support, I would not have quite the time to finish this book.

Linh N. K. Duong

Chapter 1
Strategic Procurement Negotiation

Pedro B. Agua
https://orcid.org/0000-0003-1886-9938
CINAV-Portuguese Naval Academy, Portugal

Anacleto Correia
https://orcid.org/0000-0002-7248-4310
CINAV-Portuguese Naval Academy, Portugal

Armindo S. Frias
https://orcid.org/0000-0003-1298-4273
CINAV-Portuguese Naval Academy, Portugal

ABSTRACT

The challenges facing procurement managers across industries and public services are quite important. Businesses need to take care of the bottom line while public services need to manage tight budgets. This is aggravated by difficult economic environments such as the one that has come with COVID-19. Reducing procurement costs means less funds and working capital. Such is achieved by means of adequate negotiation processes. Technology procurement is a field with long acquisition lifecycles, where negotiations span over considerable periods of time, and where the features of technology may impact negotiations, including the technology inherent obsolescence speed. Such negotiations occur in an environment where demanding technical requirements abound alongside economic rationality and where negotiations are conducted by teams of managers and engineers, addressing the distinct dimensions. An approach to technology procurement negotiation is presented with viewpoints for reflection on how procurement and negotiations shall be addressed for technology procurement purposes.

DOI: 10.4018/978-1-7998-8709-6.ch001

INTRODUCTION

"If you know the weaknesses and capabilities of yourself and your competition and are familiar with the specific environmental culture (the terrain), you cannot fail." - Sun Tzu, 544 B.C.

Complex technological procurement managers have to manage for technology acquisition, both products and associated services. Products may include hardware components, systems and platforms, but also software. As for services, there is a considerable range as well, from consulting, engineering, maintenance, software programming, even financial ones. Besides the technical concerns, the economic rational shall always be taken care of, and the 'value for money equation' must be always present in mind within the procurement context. These issues demand some care in addressing procurement negotiation. The value of equation (1) must always be greater than one, that is, the value attributed to the functionalities associated with the good or service being purchased, plus the perception of future returns, must be higher than the value paid plus the risks associated with the business (Huet).

$$Value\,for\,money = \frac{Functionality + feelings}{Price + insecurities + doubts} \tag{1}$$

For example, when considering the procurement of telecommunications equipment and systems, purchases involve hardware and software acquisition processes related to categories such as radio relay links, networking devices, cable infrastructure, management information systems, geographic information systems, planning tools, as well as a considerable set of services, from design and installation to maintenance. Procurement managers must have equation (1) always in mind as a sort of navigation compass.

This chapter has a special focus on the negotiation and negotiation process and pinpoints some critical "post-negotiation" issues that typically arise within the context of technology acquisition. Because most agreements implementation does not develop exactly as negotiated or expected, there is a permanent need to carry on negotiating during the delivery or implementation stages, a concept oftentimes referred to as "post-settlement settlements" (Mendenhalt, 1996; Raiffa, 1982). Besides the need for an integrative approach to Negotiation, as opposed to competitive ones, such issues involve several typical steps and will be discussed within the context of this chapter.

This chapter is written from the viewpoint of the purchasing side procurement. Such raises a different set of questions when compared with the selling side point of view. Each side or party takes its particular perspective, where sellers want to maximize their profits. In contrast, buyers want to reduce acquisition costs, which, together with the always present asymmetry of information among the parties, will raise friction and damage the procurement effectiveness during or after the main negotiation stage.

This kind of procurement, where technology is involved point toward cooperative modes of Negotiation, where long-term relationship between suppliers and purchasing companies shall be taken care of. Regardless of the benefits of such long-term relationships and the involved collaborative approaches, there is also a negative side. Such negative side arises from the following issues: (i) since procurement managers will have the attention focused on a fewer supplier, he may be missing some new emerging technologies and solutions, (ii) long term relationships have the potential to feed the vicious cycle where other potential supplier will not present themselves to the procuring companies, because they may believe that there is a barrier related to the long-term relationships, already in place, with current vendors, and (iii) there may be some installed inertia on the procurement departments, with procurement managers and officers getting accustomed to the usual suppliers, and where the current sellers, in spite of less competition, may have the tendency to increase their products or solutions prices, even not developing new innovative products, something which is critical in Hi-Tec businesses (Rosseti & Choi, 2005). There are also some human skills issues accompanying the explanation, but such will be referred to throughout the chapter.

Besides this introduction, this chapter is composed of four main sections. Section one addresses the general procurement process in Hi-Tec sector. Section two deals with negotiation preparation. Section three has a focus on the negotiation development itself. Section four addresses the critical issues of Negotiation close and lessons learned as a key issue for organizational learning and an asset for the future.

GENERAL PROCUREMENT PROCESS IN HI-TEC SECTOR

When a company develops a new business strategy, it begins to compare the gap between the "as is" business paradigm and comparing it with the "as should be" paradigm ("where are we … and where we want to be"). From this comparison, the business creates a strategy conducting to a specific goal or a set of goals. To reach such goals, some needs and conditions must be satisfied, thus often conducting a procurement process.

A procurement process within companies or public services organizations starts after a need has been identified. Such gap by its side comes from an identified problem, defined as a difference between a desirable future situation and the current one. After such problem has been clearly delimited, one can plan how to reduce such difference to zero to solve the problem. This involves implementation and feedback as a control mechanism, where one is permanently seeking to close the gap between the desired reality and the perceived current one by acting on the current fact (Figure 1).

Figure 1. A systems thinking approach to "reducing the gap" cycle.

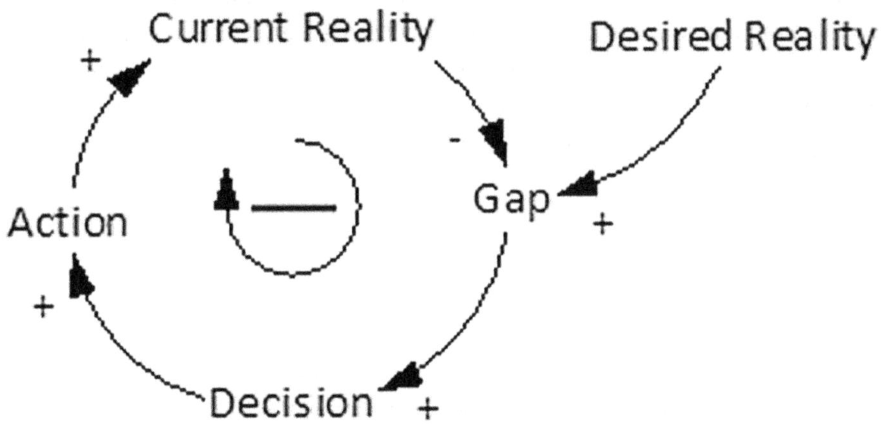

As such, the acquisition process starts with operational requirements, which drive the need for technical requirements to implement the required solution. In practice, such technical requirements can usually be reached by means of a procurement process, which starts by supplier's capabilities research. After that, a company in need for technological solutions sends a *Request for Information* (RFI) to a selected subset of suppliers (Figure 2).

Figure 2. General procurement process in Hi-Tec business

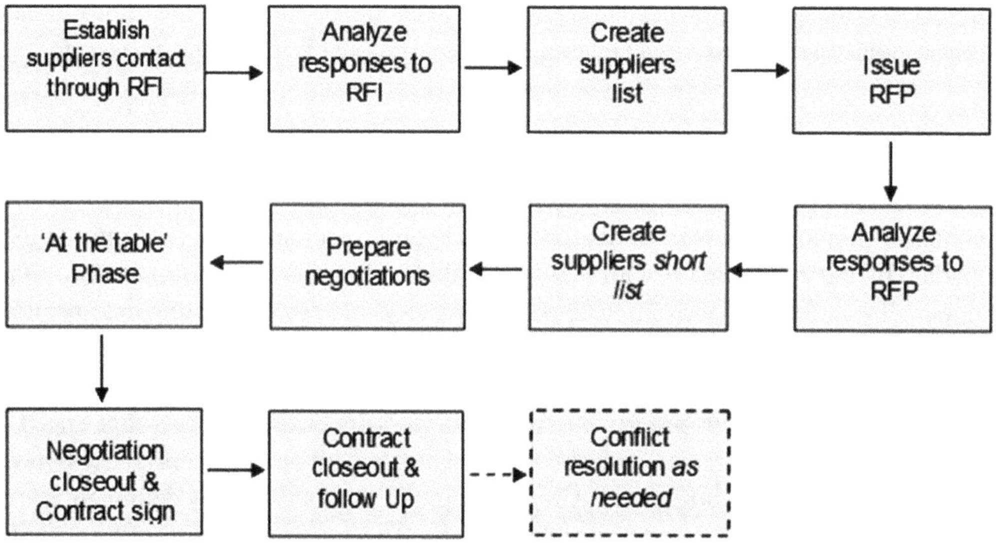

After close analysis of the several suppliers' responses to the issued RFI, purchasing companies eliminate suppliers who do not fully comply with requirements or have weaker solutions, creating a short list of potential suppliers to send then a *Request for Proposals* (RFP). The analysis of the potential suppliers' responses to the issued RFP usually signals the start of the negotiation preparation phase. From this point, both organizations, seller and buyer, try to estimate the other party's Best Alternative to a Negotiated Agreement (BATNA). As the Sun Tzu saying goes, the situational assessment is normally accomplished by doing a strengths and weaknesses analysis, among other techniques, scenario generation and general pre-negotiation planning (Lax & Sebenius, 2003). To achieve the best result, preparation of the negotiation process is essential.

NEGOTIATION PREPARATION

This section focuses on the critical subject of negotiation preparation. It will introduce the following subjects: (i) establishing negotiation goals, (ii) structuring objectives, (iii) establishing a strategy to optimally reach procurement goals, (iv) estimation of both parties bargaining power, (v) estimation of both parties BATNAs, (vi) Intelligence process and BATNA, and (vii) use of a preparation checklist.

Establishing Negotiation Goals

Every experienced procurement manager knows the critical importance of establishing clear goals regarding the different specific acquisition initiatives. Negotiation outcomes are better attained when one has clearly established goals. Having a clear set of goals present in mind during the whole procurement negotiation process, as a reference frame, is an effective way to protect against 'giving in' too early or giving in at all where otherwise would be undesirable. This is also related to mind traps as the known "anchoring effect" (Hammond et al., 2006). The anchoring effect belongs to a set of biases of the mind where a negotiator confronted with, for example, an unexpected opening demand from the other party, may prompt the former to adjust his own asking position just because of such unexpected demand from the other party. Preparation is, of course, a good way to counter such bias.

Whenever a procurement manager has a fuzzy goal, a not that clearly defined goal, but instead a broad and not well defined one, the manager may be at odds ding the negotiation development phase. This fuzzy or general goal will make such procurement negotiators feel uncomfortable and always on the risk line, affecting the power balance between the parties and potentially making more concessions than needed.

After estimating the openings, which are closely related to the negotiation goals, the procurement negotiator shall evaluate the relative 'negotiation bandwidths', perhaps supported by spreadsheet calculations or using a Negotiation Support Systems (NSS), typically a computerized assistance tool based on some Multi Criteria Decision Making (MCDM) tool. MCDM support tools are useful to help procurement negotiators visualize and keep track of the established set of negotiation goals. Clemen and Reilly (2013) present a reasonable description of MCDM techniques and algorithms. A clear evaluation of this negotiation ranges also helps in graphically visualize the agreement "bandwidth" or interval where the negotiation closeout agreement will set (Lax & Sebenius, 1986). This range or bandwidth is sometimes referred to as the Zone Of Possible Agreement or ZOPA (Figure 3).

Figure 3. Negotiated outcomes must occur inside the agreement bandwidth.

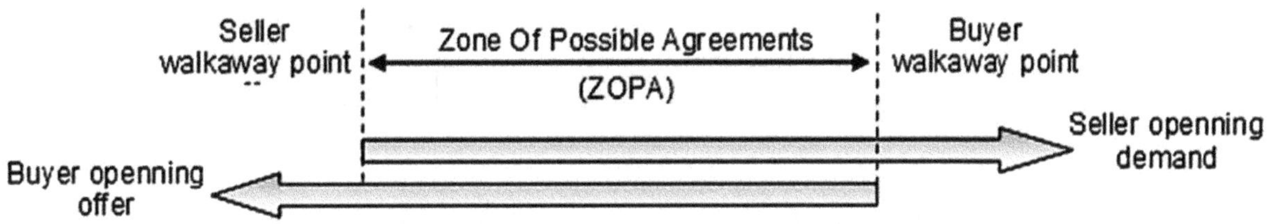

Only by having a reference frame constituted by the negotiation goals can one make adequate concessions and manage corrections during the bargaining phase of Negotiation. With a clear set of goals one can easily establish:

- The price that one will pay for what needs to be purchased
- Identify negotiation limits, also known as walkaway points
- Determine alternatives, i.e., equivalent concessions within a Pareto frontier
- Decide what concessions are reasonable and can be made during negotiations in order to reach an agreement

During a negotiation process, one is faced with adversities that need addressing and sometimes a correction effort. Such adversities may challenge triggered by the other party or from incorrect estimations originated from our planning. With a clear set of goals, even in the face of opposing demands, one can always compare our current position toward our elected destination (our negotiation goal) and make the adequate corrections viable. This negotiation stage resembles like a blend between science and art, and a few authors have been calling attention to this fact (Raiffa, 1982).

Structuring Objectives

Structuring objectives is a process of organizing objectives to facilitate the establishment of boundaries and clarify our set of goals. Structuring objectives end up at a visual aid that results in overall clarification and may be helpful at the negotiation planning phase. When considering technology acquisition, be it hardware or software, it may resemble the following structure (Figure 4).

Figure 4. Structuring objectives help in planning negotiations.

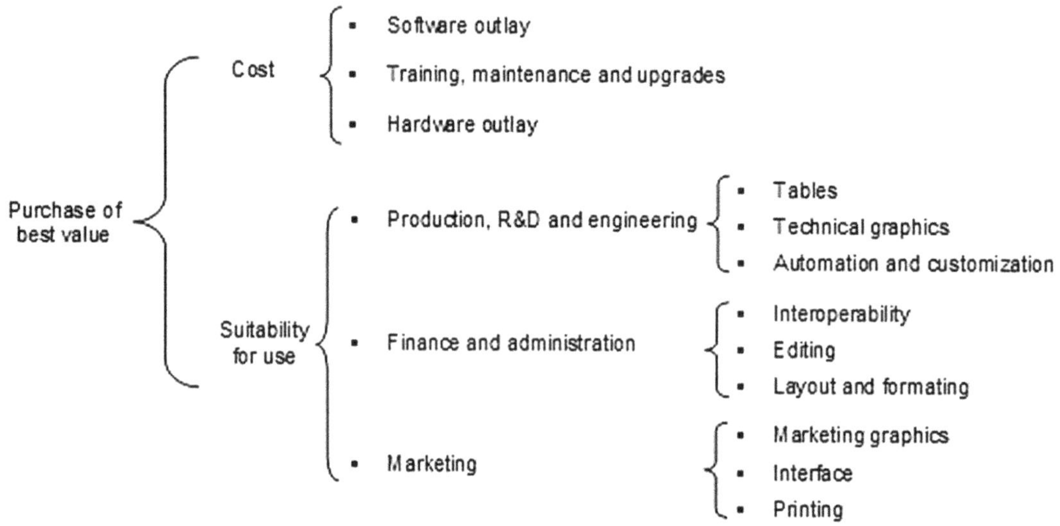

Objectives structuring diagrams can also be used as an aid for the following contexts:

- *A guide for information collection.* When one has a clear picture of what is critically important for the procurement objectives, then one is more focused on which information to collect in the preparation step of Negotiation.
- *Help in identifying alternatives.* In preparing a negotiation where alternatives are initially not clearly specified, having such diagrams is a basis to design alternatives. When one knows what is one trying to achieve than one can start generating alternatives.
- *Facilitate communication.* Many negotiations involve teams, several stakeholders and a broad set of technical issues. These diagrams help in communication and manage discussions. In situations involving controversy, a common understanding about what is important helps provide a better

understanding for compromises and consensus regarding selecting alternatives, sometimes internally to one's own organization.

- *Help in evaluating alternatives.* An important issue resulting from these diagrams is the fact they are helpful in evaluating the different alternatives.

Furthermore, formalizing objectives forces procurement managers to think about what is wanted, why such is wanted, and what are they willing to give in return for concessions asking.

Establishing a Strategy to Optimally Reach Procurement Goals

Having established a clear set of negotiation goals, it is then necessary to develop several alternative ways to attain them. Because some opposition is expected from the other party, it is advisable to plan upfront for potentially different negotiation development paths. Considering various different paths, one is better prepared to deal with the other party's arguments and counter arguments. Scenario generation and planning are recommendable mental frameworks for managing such dynamics (Wollenberg, Edmunds, & Buck, 2000), (Figure 5).

Figure 5. It is useful to consider multiple strategies when planning a negotiation.

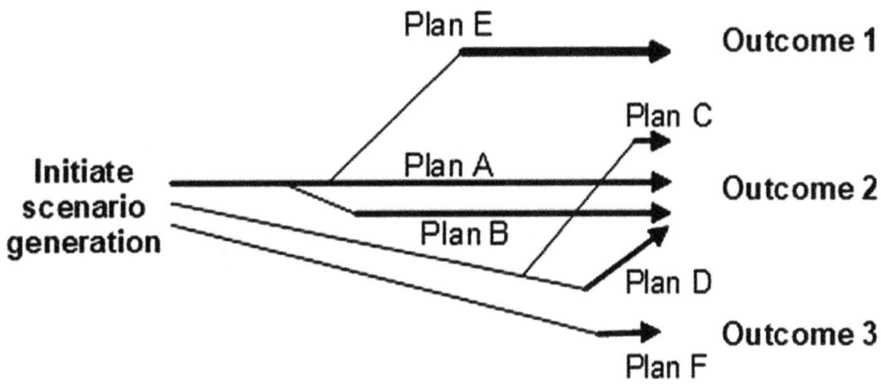

Scenario generation and planning is a technique used to plan for possible future outcomes and design some contingency plans. As such, it can be useful during the negotiation planning stage as well. As suggested by Schwartz (1996), this technique may be composed of eight steps;

Step 1: Identify the focal issue
Step 2: Be aware of the key surrounding forces
Step 3: Be aware of the driving forces
Step 4: Rank forces by importance and uncertainty
Step 5: Selecting scenario logics
Step 6: Fleshing out the scenarios
Step 7: Implications
Step 8: Selection of leading indicators

During the negotiation planning phase and considering scenarios generation as an aiding tool, it is possible to foresee potential obstacles and conflicts arising during the face-to-face negotiation phase, at 'the table'. Such conflict can be diverse, ranging from technical misunderstandings and uncompromising positions dur to financial constraints. One effective technique that may be used for dealing with conflicts during the course of procurement negotiations is a kind of conflict resolution diagram, where it is possible to make both parties' requirements explicit (Dettmer, 2014; Goldratt, 1999). However, as each requirement have prerequisites which are generally in conflict, it is sometimes wise to investigate the true nature of the prerequisites and look for creative solutions in order to try to satisfy both parties ending at a win-win negotiation closeout (Figure 6).

Figure 6. Conflict resolution diagram

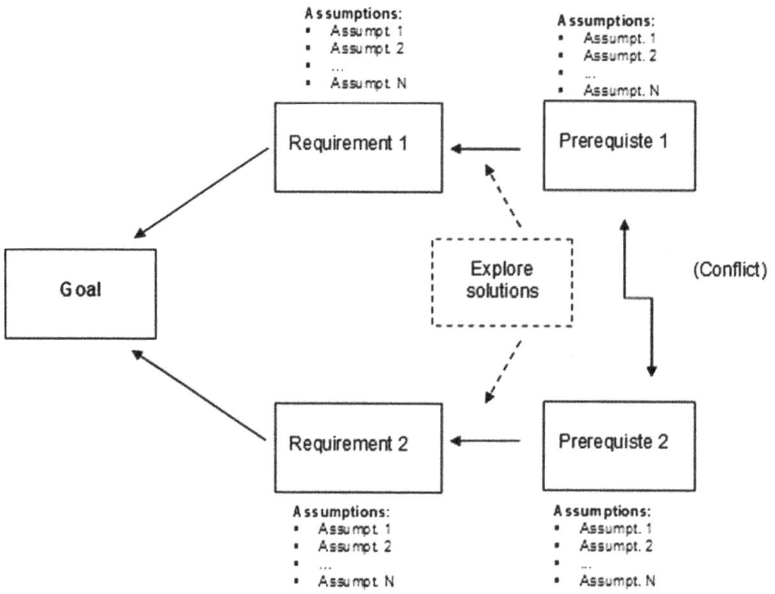

These conflict assessment and resolution diagrams should ideally be used at the preparation stage, combined with several potential scenarios, identified before and even during negotiation interactions between the involved parties. These diagrams can even be used for the purpose of trying to low negotiation pressure in *quasi*-deadlock situations. They can further be used as a persuasion tool involving communication with the other party during a win-win search for fair solutions in order to reach a mutual agreement. More specifically, this diagram may be of help in several the following situations:

- In confirming that a conflict really exists, and where is it located (assumptions)
- In-depth understanding of why a problem or conflict exists (assumptions)
- Identifying major root causes for conflict by analyzing assumptions, and hence proactively prevent them
- Create solutions in which both parties may win by checking their assumptions
- Help in resolving conflict between the negotiation parties, which may be further complicated when negotiating technology solutions.

Estimation of Both Parties Bargaining Power

Another assessment that must be done carefully is the relative power assessment of each party involved in the negotiation. This concerns not only organizational power, but also each negotiator personal power, which have multidimensional facets. A negotiator is a person, and despite the power and authority its organization poses on him, he may be more or less skilled, so a procurement negotiator may have different formal or informal power levels. Galbraith (1983) suggest several different types of power, useful in understanding the several dimensions that power may exhibit and a critical issue whenever complex negotiations are at play.

As soon as one is conscious about the specific person or team on the 'other side of the table', one must proceed with such power assessment, which calls for some intelligence. At least the following points should be taken care of:

- Intelligence about the other party's company and negotiators
- Intelligence on the relationship history, past drawbacks and successes?
- Intelligence on specific strategic and market constraints? What is the current and near-term outlook for the other party's business?
- How important is this Negotiation to the other party?
- What is the overall financial impact of the specific deal under consideration?

Estimation of Both Party's BATNA

A critical concept in Negotiation and closely related with power is the *Best Alternative to Negotiation Agreement* (BATNA). BATNA has a critical effect over each party's confidence and how each one feels about personal power during negotiations development because BATNA is the single highest source of power. If one has a good BATNA, he or she can just walk away from the Negotiation. A good BATNA doesn't exist on itself. It must be developed. Procurement negotiators should not rest on their initial alternatives but should try to find new ones and pursue them by building a good BATNA. For example, one way of building a good BATNA is by having a broad pool of suppliers instead of just one or a few of them. Actually, better deals may be achieved when considering a broad list of suppliers, because the procurement negotiator does not feel under as high pressure for making concessions, as in the case of few existing suppliers. By having just one or two suppliers, procurement negotiators generally end at one-dimension Negotiation – price. And having just one negotiation dimension does not allow for trade-offs. This is not an absolute truth when dealing with the purchasing of hi-tec systems due to the need to negotiate over a broad set of technological requirements, which spans from guarantees and manufacturers technical assistance to additional features not envisioned in the initial RFI or even the RFP.

Having a wide range of competing suppliers reinforces the purchaser BATNA. The drawback was that procurement personnel have to analyze much more information, sometimes spanning well into the thousands of technical and commercial documentation pages. They have to cautiously verify each technical characteristic, additional features not previously aware of, logistics and delivery times, among other criteria. Typically, MCDM tools are adequately supporting in these cases, as it helps structure technical and non-technical objectives, where the price is just one of them. Such complexity considerably differentiates Negotiation over high-technology and systems from other more common goods, for example, commodities, where purchasing managers negotiate essentially over price. But such technological complexity usually helps in building a better BATNA, because there is more room for creativity in terms of potential conceivable solutions.

However, even in commodities procurement, it is possible to improve the purchasing party's BATNA, my means of, for example, increasing the" purchase volume". The same concept can also be used within technological industries. For example, a telecommunications service provider with multinational operations can gather similar technology requirements and needs from several countries' subsidiaries, thus increasing total purchasing volume. With such coordinated effort a procurement manager improves his or her BATNA. From their side, the suppliers, in face of a potential opportunity to make a bigger sale, fall into a position of less relative power, in short, a weaker relative BATNA.

Additionally, it should be said that purchasing optimal technical solutions are a distinct matter from purchasing the most complete or performing system. An example from some years ago, that can be brought at, was a procurement for a large network infrastructure project within a Telco company that despite an existing supplier with a more performing product, the choice was for a lesser performing one, but with a reasonable obsolescence horizon, and a much lower price. Hence, reinforcing the idea that in high-technology procurement, price or performance are neither the only negotiation dimensions nor always the decisive ones. And this usually misleads the vendors in estimating technology procurement negotiator's BATNA.

Let us consider an illustrative example of this kind of trade-off that may even be applied to daily life in general. Let´s say some company of purchaser wants to purchase a set of printers, where it has to choose between a system with a lower acquisition cost (investment) but with a higher operating cost (also known as variable cost) and a more expensive system, but with lower operating cost. In such cases, a cross-over analysis approach is of help. It allows us to determine at which production volume point one should switch from one solution to a competing option and take advantage of such in managing negotiations. Here how to deal with it, by means of an example (not the true names):

Printer PH printing solution (per unit):

Acquisition cost = 1000€ with 3 Cents per copy to operate.

Printer CONAN printing solution:

Acquisition cost = 800€ with 4 Cents per copy to operate.

To accomplish a crossover analysis, one must use the formula:

$$N = \frac{AC2 - AC1}{VC1 - VC2} \tag{2}$$

N = crossover point
AC1 = Acquisition cost for printer 1
AC2 = Acquisition cost for printer 2
VC1 = Variable cost for printer 1
VC2 = Variable cost for printer 2

$$N = \frac{800 - 1000}{0.03 - 0.04} = \frac{-200}{-0.01} = 20000 \text{ Copies}$$

"N", is the point of indifference, known as the crossover point. If one estimates of taking more than 20000 copies per year, the printer with the more expensive acquisition cost should be chosen. This example call attention to some cautions that must be taken when negotiation technology acquisition, a situation in which concerns to the total cost of ownership, i.e., acquisition cost plus operating costs, shall be clear. Oftentimes, technology vendors do not understand the purchasing organizations' operations, volumes or business model, which may help the purchasing organization shape a robust BATNA when negotiating over alternative solutions.

Intelligence Process and BATNA

When estimating both parties BATNAs, one should take an intelligence process approach similar to the general four-step framework used by intelligence agencies (Figure 7).

Figure 7. The intelligence process.
Based on Rustmann, (2002).

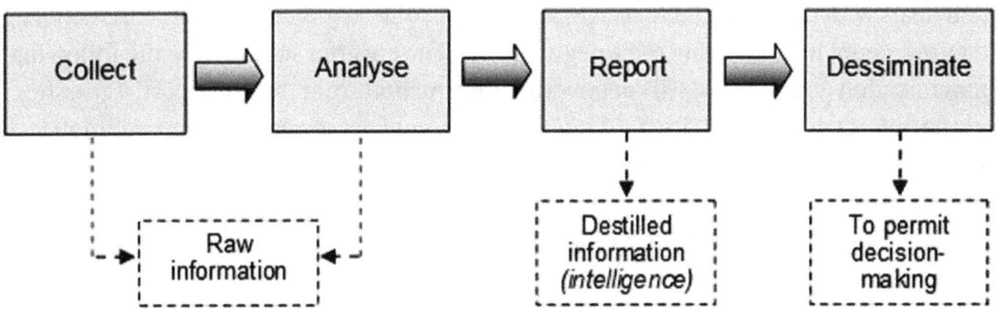

In the first step, *collect*, the available raw information about the solutions under Negotiation, as well potential supplier's characteristics (capabilities, history, track record, quality standards, conflicts) shall be addressed. Secondly, *analyze* such collected information to produce distilled or structured information, i.e., intelligence, ending at reports for own use (step 3) or to disseminate (step 4) to interested parties within the purchasing organization to better prepare for the negotiation phase.

Despite this general process being shared within the negotiation team, it is advisable to just share information on a "need to know" basis. The "need to know" term is well familiar within the intelligence, security and military communities and is intended to be a way to minimize the risk of unwanted information leaks. Therefore, minimizing the chances of "information leakage", is critical when dealing with high technology purchases, involving sometimes hundred million contracts. Therefore, once more, a trade-off exists, in this case between best practices for increasing information sharing across organizations (enhancing overall company skills) and a need for secrecy, demanding some restrain on the information. There are people in opposite sides of businesses that meet due to a panoply of reasons, such as belonging to that same engineering association, alumni networks, or even community church. Caution with information sharing is of the essence whenever one is in the business of technology procurement negotiation.

Use of a Preparation Checklist

A negotiation aiding tool quite helpful in preparing a negotiation is the use of a structured negotiation sheet, or at least a checklist. Shell (2000) suggest a comprehensive yet expedite one, which is included in the Appendix. The systematic use of a negotiation planning sheet has several advantages, as it helps in:

- Systematically structure information about one's goals and other party's goals
- Better assessment of our and other party's BATNA, bringing in clarity
- Better assessment of our and other party's power and leverage points

Above all it allows an overall holistic overview about the whole frame within which the Negotiation will develop.

Fisher and Ertel (1999), and Gosselin (2007), also suggest alternative negotiation preparation sheets. The later checklists might be combined with the one proposed by Shell (2000), however there is a compromise between detail and utility. Hence the proposed one is enough for an adequate preparation.

NEGOTIATION DEVELOPMENT STAGE

This section deals with the 'at the table' stage, and covers some key issues that procurement negotiators shall take into account in conducting their negotiations. The covered subjects are the following: (i) personal communication and protocol, (ii) uncovering information from the other part – Questioning; (iii) joint development of win-win scenarios, (iv) dealing with conflict in negotiations over high technology, and (v) real time negotiation and "damage control".

Personal Communication and Protocol

A technology supplier is someone a purchasing company should ideally see as almost an ally, as far as the relationship is based on fairness. As such, procurement negotiators shall care their overall communication dynamics with their suppliers or even potential ones. Care about such communication dynamics should imply attention to the three communication modes generally present when considering negotiation relationships: (i) writing, (ii) speaking, and (iii) non-verbal communications. Care for such communication modes demands more than just the advice to 'use a neutral tone of voice and be calm'.

If the goals imply long-term relationships, then the procurement negotiator shall be cordial and fair with the seller. Procurement negotiators and managers should provide comfortable facilities when receiving supplier's negotiators. Usually, negotiations take place at purchasers' premises, but may also happen at supplier premises or in a neutral place (e.g., a hotel). In any case old 'hard-nose' negotiation tactics, used by some "Die-hard bargainers", where one party tries to make the other side uncomfortable by pre-arranging the meetings set up are not advised if the objective is to build a win-win long term relationship between suppliers and the procurement organizations (Field, 2003; Parker, 2003). A number of negotiation manoeuvres aim to make the other party discomfortable, be it physically or emotionally, aiming at taking advantage and disorienting a potential seller during the negotiation interaction. Such approaches should definitely not be used within the context of Hi-Tec procurement negotiations, because it damages the critical and needed long-term relationships between the negotiating parties.

Several experts within the field of Negotiation suggest that the negotiation bargaining phase should start by establishing credibility by opening the Negotiation with a reasonable and justifiable opening position, or making a counteroffer that is reasonable and defendable (Galinsky, 2004; Fisher, Ury,& Patton, 2011). A good practice is to make such offer (or counteroffer) conditional in terms of concessions exchange and an attached deadline if viable. Offer incentives for prompt acceptance may be a way to close efficiently.

Despite both party's awareness there is sometimes the possibility that one party (most often the purchasing party) may change the decision maker, just to try to start demanding additional concessions from the seller. Similarly, such tactic has a high potential to damage the needed long-term relationships because the use of such "unfair" tactics may increase the number of potential conflicts between them and undermine the mutual thrust.

Uncovering Information From the Other Part- Questioning

Good decision-making needs adequate information. However, one rarely has all the desirable information when entering a procurement negotiation process. Therefore, one possible way to get more information from the other party is throughout questioning. Despite being an important and critical step when Hi-Tec systems acquisition is at stake, it also supports empathy building. There are two broad categories of questions: closed questions and open questions. Open questions are preferable within the context of trying to uncover information from sellers or suppliers. It is not that closed questions are not useful during negotiations. They are, especially as the procurement negotiators approach the negotiation closeout, however, close questions are classified as "closed" as they only provide one of two answers: 'yes' or 'no'. There is a lot of questions one can put forward during a negotiation interaction, but it depends mostly from the issue under discussion at a specific stage of the negotiation interaction. There is, however one particular question that may be used by any procurement negotiator when negotiating with potential suppliers: *"What differentiates you, Mr. supplier, from your competitor?"*

This is probably one of the most useful questions a procurement negotiator may place during the negotiation interaction, not to discover what differentiates them from their competitors. With such question, the suppliers generally disclose who their competitors are. Then the procurement negotiator can research such competitors and their products, thus facilitating the procurement work. This question, however, is so demanding that the supplier's negotiator usually feels psychologically obligated to offer more information, as for example:

- Giving comparative analysis between their products and those of their competitors
- Potentially disclose some price issues
- Disclose hidden costs, as total cost ownership is more than just initial acquisition costs

Sometimes it happens that a supplier faced with such question makes a further concession.

Above all, this one question is fair and ethical and not a negotiation trick. This is why it is always advisable to use it whenever a procurement negotiator finds himself at the negotiation table. Moreover, procurement negotiators shall ask questions that require facts to be supplied as part of the answers and not just opinions. Potentially such questions may be preceded by a series of "soft" questions first, for such question to appear as natural.

Effective procurement negotiators use silent as an effective move during negotiation interactions to uncover further information from the other party. Many people disregard silent as a valuable negotiation tool by itself. Faced with silent, oftentimes the other party speaks when they did not want to, and perhaps something wonderful happens for the procurement negotiator, ranging from getting confessions to getting concessions.

Sometimes it happens that procurement negotiators just get vague answers to the placed questions. In such cases, the following techniques may be useful:

- Procurement negotiators should repeat the answer and then ask for further clarification
- Procurement negotiators may ignore the unsatisfying answer at first, and raise the same question again later on at an unexpected moment during the negotiation interaction
- Procurement negotiators shall not feel intimidated if the other party gets angry, which may be a negotiation tactic.
- After all the purchasing organization has usually the power to walk away, unless there are a sole supplier or a few ones for the procured technology solutions.

Joint Development of Win-Win Scenarios

Conducting negotiations involving the procurement of large technological systems have a distinguishing characteristic from negotiating simpler equipment, as it may give place to the analysis of hundreds of different features. These technical requirements richness contribute to a cooperative mode of Negotiation (Fisher & Ury, 2011), because the negotiators will become more focused on the adequate coverage of systems overall technical requirements, alongside guarantees and maintenance features. Therefore, the technological endeavour may indirectly make it easy to look for more dimensions for trade-off within the Negotiation.

The use of "What if…?" questions in jointly developing scenarios with the other party (the seller or supplier) is highly advisable, because it build trust, which helps the other party become more fearless of being caught into a bad decision.

Once the other supplier is open to a joint analysis over suggested alternatives, he or she would feel less competitive and more prone to enter into a more cooperative mode, a commitment that might break at any time, for which it is important to be cautious with the chosen words, verb tenses and nonverbal communication, while being persuasive at the same time (Conger, 2000). If the other party does not seem to cooperate, it may be useful to use some of the following approaches:

- Ignore ultimatums
- Consider other alternatives
- Remembering the other party, that they have a competitor.

This is a delicate stage and care should be taken for the dynamics arising from the tension between empathy and assertiveness, because too much assertiveness may raise emotions and pass the perception of inflexibility, while too much empathy may convey a perception of the possibility for giving in (Mnookin et al., 1996).

Dealing With Conflict in Negotiations Over High Technology

When dealing with Hi-Tec procurement this may lead sometimes to technical bargaining, i.e., bargaining over technical requirements or systems requirements solely. At this point, engineers are usually involved and despite their specialized knowledge, they may unintentionally add some "stress" to the bargaining dynamics, motivated by an over detailed focus on technical requirements, oftentimes contributing to a stalemate situation (Sander, 2004; Simpson, 2003).

Negotiation is a political process and sometimes it is better to establish a negotiating team in order to reach better agreements, while avoiding deadlocks. However, such negotiation team' members shall have a clear understanding about who will be speaking and when; when to disclose information and what are the roles of each one in such negotiation team, always taking care of lies (Shell, 1991).

Teams may become more effective in Negotiation when compared with sole negotiators, because teams can gather more information, broaden the knowledge base, and create more alternative scenarios for conducting the negotiations. Additionally, some team members may assist the main negotiator in terms of keeping the objectivity of a clear set of goals during the "hot" phase of the negotiation process. In this phase it may help to consider the following traits:

- Supporting one's arguments with documentation, technical or otherwise
- Avoid using excessive hype or unfounded claims
- Ensuring one's words and actions are in agreement
- Bringing in technology experts to support one's own position.

The other party may use tactics as well. Tactics are designed to throw the other party off balance and divert their thoughts away from the substantive negotiation issues and set of goals. When facing adversary tactics, the first step in order to counter them is to recognize them, and then act accordingly (Table 1). Recognition of the opponent's different tactics is not an easy task to accomplish, and demands specific training and practice. Sometimes, however, just naming the tactic is quite effective for the neutralization of its intended effect, as it raises at least some confidence on the side being impacted by the tactic.

Table 1. Some typical negotiation tactics and potential responses.

Tactic	Response
Intimidation	Ignore it, as a general rule.
Lying	Ask for supporting evidence.
Deadlines	Ignore them.
Ultimatums	Ignore them.
Threats	Challenge them.
Bluffs	Call them to avoid being victimized.

Real Time Negotiation and "Damage Control"

One shall always try to concede the least possible during a negotiation, but this advice shall be observed just up to the point of avoiding excessive deadlocks, which might be overcome by conceding in minor issues (Sander, 2004; Sebenius, 2002). In complex technology purchases, it is advisable to offer a "fair" split to the supplier or seller, as one approaches the end of the Negotiation, but only in case the seller have been conceding fairly during the overall negotiation development. Otherwise "splitting the difference" may not benefit the buyer.

It sometimes occurs that a seller surprises the procuring organization with unexpected information about the subject of Negotiation. If such occurrence provokes a negotiation deadlock, one does not need to deal with such right at that moment. One can always ask for a negotiation break in order to get more time to deal with such issue. This should not be viewed as a weakness but a fair right of each party. This is a moment in a negotiation to take a break and pick the right tools to analyze the Negotiation in face of such new issue. In general, a negotiation over technology acquisition may have a large and diverse set of criteria, beyond the sole price, and one such tool could be a multicriteria decision support tool mentioned above. There is some commercial software for decision support, but because in technology acquisition there are usually people with strong mathematical background, they can easily build a spreadsheet with some multicriteria decision making algorithms for helping visualize scenarios in quantitative terms and support better decision-making. After all, always look for fair (win-win) arguments when negotiating over technological product purchases. Here the rational is to build *de facto* partnerships, as this is critical in Hi-Tec supplier-client relationships. The Information and Communication Technologies (ICT) businesses being just an example of such endeavours.

NEGOTIATION CLOSEOUT AND LESSONS LEARNED

This section addresses the critical subject of negotiation closeout and the too often overlooked subject of lessons learned to build organization assets derived from past negotiation experience. The covered subjects are the following: (i) preparing the negotiation closeout, (ii) after the close - Tasks due for the parties, (iii) negotiation analysis, also known as post-mortem analysis, and (iv) relevant recordings.

Preparing the Negotiation Closeout

When negotiations develop within an integrative or cooperative mode, the negotiation close is a natural step, that starts with technical requirements checking and ends at a fair price. Obviously, some sellers may try to close at higher than fair price. A measure of fair price may be done by comparing that supplier's product price against competitors or substitute products' prices. On such closing technique is the "split the difference" close. As suggested by Karrass (1994), one should be cautious about splitting the difference to close. Many times, the other party – seller or supplier – concedes almost nothing or concedes only in minor issues during the whole Negotiation and then may try a "lets split the difference "close.

This is a dangerous point which shall be avoided or take with care, because if, let's say negotiation openings began with purchaser A offering 2 and seller B asking for 8, if A further offers 4 and B only concedes 1 (dropping from 8 to 7), if a "lets split the difference" comes into play, it will happen that the difference is (7-4)/2=3/2=1,5 which makes party A pay 4+1,5=5,5 to party B. If before the occurrence of the "lets split the difference", both parties had conceded equal amounts, let's say, party A concedes from 2 to 4 and party B concedes from 8 to 6 (both parties conceded two units) than splitting the difference would make for (6-4)/2=2/2=1, so party A (the purchaser) would pay 4+1=5, which is better than the previous 5,5 situation.

After the Close – Tasks Due to the Parties

There is a strong reason why one shall try to be the one preparing the written contract, as the party that writes it, control what goes into it. After reaching a successful negotiation outcome, there is a need for contract sign-off and afterwards compliance of such contract. Something that must be clearly clarified in the written contract is the responsibilities and tasks due to each party. Some mandatory points to be covered are:

- The specifics of performance requirements for both parties
- Detailed payment provisions, including any condition under which payment may be delayed or withheld
- How and under what conditions the agreement can be modified as well as any agreed upon procedure for dispute resolution
- Any provision option and the specifics of any performance incentives
- Necessary administrative procedures to implement the agreement as well any legal requirements
- Definitive starting and completion dates (unless some form of flexibility should be built in).

Despite the existence of written and signed-off contracts, experience shows that one always faces some "after negotiation misunderstandings" of diverse severity. A buyer (or procurement negotiator) for complex Hi-Tec systems and equipment, must oftentimes continue to negotiate at a post-contract stage, in order to implement the solution adequately. Such is, however, more of a conflict resolution interaction than a real negotiation as such. Sometimes, a procurement negotiator must set or design a lateral project to manage conflicts that arise at implementation or during the delivery phase.

Negotiation Analysis

Nowadays, and perhaps due to the competitive economic environment, everybody has less time to sit and calmly analyze the resulting outcomes from the perspective of "lessons learned" within the context of procurement negotiations. However, it pays to do so (Craver, 2012). In fact, it is one of the more effective ways for improving negotiation skills, beyond formal training. It does not constitute a huge effort, and typically just involves personal reflections and recordings about how the negotiations developed, which may be done by using some questions:

How far from the goals did the parties ended?

- *Focus on quantitative and qualitative goal discrepancies*

What went wrong during the "hot" moments of the negotiation process (bargaining dynamics)?
Communication issues:

- *Focus on good/bad communication practices, intimidating postures, body language issues.*

Lost opportunities:

- *Why did we miss it?*

What relevant signals were recognized during the negotiation dynamics?

- *Focus on other party ability to close. Threat of leaving negotiation table.*

What were the "estimated" relevant levels of negotiation expertise of the other party and how did this affect the negotiation process?

- *Focus on organizational and communication skills.*

It seems like this would be critical information to be familiar with before the negotiation phase initiated. However, since one may negotiate again with the same person (or team) regarding future acquisitions, it is relevant to record relevant analyses and lessons learned in order to map such person(s) in a "supplier's negotiators" file. In a centralized procurement department, such information should ideally be available to every individual negotiator within the company to prepare them against the negotiation skills of the person they may face when negotiating again.

Relevant Recordings

Sometimes when doing procurement involving some specific supplier or set of suppliers, one should pose some relevant questions before engaging in in-depth Negotiation:

- Are we using such supplier technology elsewhere in the company or organization?
- Are we using similar products?
- Is there a partnerships history with such supplier?
- Past issues (good and bad)?
- Did it occur any past conflicts with them?

Since long term relationships with suppliers are the rule in Hi-Tec industries, as the ICT ones, it is recommendable to keep a database of past negotiations for each of the relevant suppliers. It is also advisable to keep the MCDM and analyses recordings from each past Negotiation for a reasonable time horizon, alongside with discussed scenarios. When a negotiation with a specific supplier fails, a company has the tendency to eliminate all historic recordings from such Negotiation. However, there is a lot to learn from failed negotiations. Perhaps we can learn more from a failed negotiation then from successful ones.

One shall always make *post-mortem* negotiation analyses to improve negotiation skills and not fall on the same trap, if any, as before. Hence, it is advisable to organize a database by supplier, then by successful and unsuccessful negotiations, as one never knows when such information may be relevant as a source of data for future negotiations with those suppliers or even with similar ones.

Moreover, one can learn what negotiation techniques have been effective, disseminate it across the department or organization's negotiators and apply it in future negotiations. The rational here is to share Negotiation best practices among other procurement negotiators within the organization, thus improving overall negotiation skills of the organization's procurement department.

CONCLUSION

Negotiations related with Hi-Tec procurement seem to be a clear mixture between science and art. One may have the help of analytical and mathematical tools, but also has to deal with a bigger complexity – the human nature – which involves communication, verbal and non-verbal. As suggested by Danny Ertel (1999), procurement department managers and leaders would gain a true edge if they turn Negotiation into a true capability within such departments.

The domains covered here relates to rules of procurement and purchasing of large systems for technology-based business as would be the case of the ICT industry involving big and Small and medium-sized enterprises (SMEs) as suppliers of hardware and software. These negotiations involve a high level of technical expertise as well as negotiation skills. Sometimes the weakness is not the technical expertise, and because that an effort shall be made in learning and improving soft skills: communication, assertiveness, and empathy.

Procurement of technology is a different field when compared, for example, with commodities trading, where there is not a strong need to keep long term relationships with the other party, and where one is typically negotiating over just one dimension – usually price. This chapter provided a brief description of typical procurement practices and procedures involved in procuring high-technology systems and solutions, focusing on the negotiation process.

This is a field that deserves further research, specifically the need for a systems think approach, w in order to model the structure of the structure of the underlying system, identifying the relevant variables at play. Only determinism ensures causality, so no statistical studies will bring true insight into the field. An approach that would bring insight into this field would be a systems approach, something that would benefit, for example, from a system dynamic modelling. Statistical analysis can show what is happening, but what would bring true value would be to harness what are the structures behind the how and whys, hence the appropriateness of systems dynamics modelling.

REFERENCES

Clemen, R. T., & Reilly, T. (2013). *Making Hard Decisions with Decision Tools* (3rd ed.). Cengage Learning.

Conger, J. (2000). The Necessary Art of Persuasion. *Harvard Business Review*, *76*, 84–97. PMID:10179656

Craver, C. B. (2012). *The Benefits to Be Derived from Post-Negotiation Assessments.* GW Law Faculty Publications & Other Works. 464.

Dettmer, H. W. (2014). *The Logical Thinking Process: A Systems Approach to Complex Problem-Solving* (8th ed.). ASQ Quality Press.

Ertel, D. (1999). Turning Negotiation into a Corporate Capability. *Harvard Business Review, 77*(3), 55–56. PMID:10387578

Field, A. (2003). How to negotiate with a Hard-Nosed Adversary? *Harvard Management Update, 8*(3), 1–3.

Fisher, R., Ury, W. L., & Patton, B. (2011). *Getting to yes: Negotiating agreement without giving in*. Penguin Books.

Fisher, W., & Ertel, D. (1995). *Getting Ready to Negotiate: The Getting to Yes Workbook*. Penguin Books.

Fisher, W., & Ury, W. (2011). *Getting to Yes: Negotiating agreement without giving in* (3rd ed.). Penguin Books.

Galbraith, J. K. (1983). The Anatomy of Power. *The Challenge (Karachi), 26*(3), 26–33. doi:10.1080/05775132.1983.11470852

Galinsky, A. D. (2004). Should you make the first offer? *Negotiation., 7*, 1–4.

Goldratt, E. M. (1999). *What Is This Thing Called Theory of Constraints and how should it be implemented?* North River Press.

Gosselin, T. (2007). Practical Negotiating. Tools, Tactics & Techniques. John Wiley & Sons.

Hammond, J. S., Keeney, R. L., & Raiffa, H. (2006). The Hidden Traps in Decision Making. *Harvard Business Review, 84*(1), 1–9. PMID:10185432

Huete, L. M. (1997). *Servicions & Beneficios*. Ediciones Deusto.

Karrass, C. (1994). The Negotiation Game: How to get What You Want (7th ed.). Harper Collins Publishers.

Lax, D. A., & Sebenius, J. K. (1986). *The Manager as a Negotiator: Bargaining for Cooperation and Competitive Gain*. The Free Press.

Lax, D. A., & Sebenius, J. K. (2003). 3-D Negotiation. Playing the whole game. *Harvard Business Review, 81*(11), 64–74. PMID:14619152

Mendenhalt, R. W. (1996). Post-Settlement Settlements: Agreeing to Make Resolutions Efficient. *Journal of Dispute Resolution*, 81.

Mnookin, R. H., Peppet, S. R., & Tulumelo, A. S. (1996). The Tension Between Empathy and Assertiveness. *Negotiation Journal, 12*(3), 217–230. doi:10.1111/j.1571-9979.1996.tb00096.x

Parker, S. G. (2003). Block That Tactic. *Harvard Management Communication Letter, 6*(9), 3–5.

Raiffa, H. (1982). *The Art and Science of Negotiation: How to resolve conflicts and get the best out of bargaining*. Harvard Business Press.

Rossetti, C., & Choi, T. Y. (2005). On the dark side of strategic sourcing: Experiences from the aerospace industry. *The Academy of Management Perspectives, 19*(1), 46–60. doi:10.5465/ame.2005.15841951

Rustmann, F. W. (2002). *CIA, Inc.: Espionage and the Craft of Business Intelligence*. Brassey´s, Inc.

Sander, F. A. (2004). *How to break a stalemate*. Academic Press.

Schwartz, P. (1996). *The Art of the Long View: Planning for the Future in an Uncertain World*. Doubleday.

Sebenius, J. K. (2002). Six Habits of Merely Effective Negotiators. *Harvard Business Review*. PMID:11299696

Shell, R. (1991). When is it legal to lie in negotiations? *Sloan Management Review*, *32*(3), 93–101.

Shell, R. (2000). *Bargaining for Advantage: Negotiation Strategies for Reasonable People*. Penguin Publishing Group.

Simpson, L. (2003, April). Get around resistance and win over the other side. *Harvard Management Communication Letter*, 1–5.

Wollenberg, E., Edmunds, D., & Buck, L. (2000). Using scenarios to make decisions about the future: Anticipatory learning for the adaptive co-management of community forests. *Landscape and Urban Planning*, *47*(1-2), 65–77. doi:10.1016/S0169-2046(99)00071-7

ADDITIONAL READING

Carnegie, D. (1936). *How to Win Friends and Influence People*. Simon and Schuster.

Kennedy, G. (1994). *Field Guide to Negotiation: A Glossary of Essential Tools and Concepts for Today's Manager*. Harvard Business Review Press.

Lewicki, R. J., Bruce Barry, B., & Saunders, D. M. (2016). *Essentials of Negotiation* (6th ed.). McGraw-Hill Education.

Menkel-Meadow, C., & Wheeler, M. (2004). *What's fair: Ethics for Negotiators*. Jossey-Bass.

Mnookin, R., Susskind, L. E., & Foster, P. C. (1999). *Negotiating on Behalf of Others: Advice to Lawyers, Business executives, Sports Agents, Diplomats, Politicians, and everybody Else*. Sage Publications.

Rackham, N. (1988). *SPIN Selling*. McGraw-Hill Education.

Salacuse, J. W. (1991). *Making Global Deals: negotiating in the International Marketplace*. Houghton Mifflin.

Schelling, T. C. (1960). *The Strategy of Conflict*. Harvard University Press.

Steven, C. (2002). *Negotiating Skills for Managers*. McGraw-Hill Education.

Stone, D., Patton, B., & Heen, S. (2010). *Difficult Conversations: How to Discuss What Matters Most*. Penguin Books.

Watkins, M. (2002). *Breakthrough Negotiations*. John Wiley & Sons.

Watkins, M. (2006). *Shaping the Game. The New Leader's Guide to Effective Negotiating*. Harvard Business School Press.

KEY TERMS AND DEFINITIONS

BATNA: Best Alternative to a Negotiated Agreement. The term would better describe its meaning if it was renamed as solution away from the table, because the "best alternative to the considered negotiated agreement" might be another negotiated agreement.

Collaborative or Integrative Negotiations: One of the two main types of Negotiation. Usually characterized by a true attempt to reach a win-win situation for both parties in a negotiation.

Die-Hard Bargainers: People to whom every Negotiation is a battle.

Distributive Negotiations: This is one of the two main types of Negotiation and typically characterized by competitive approaches, where long-term relationships are not a concern.

Framing: How one understands and tries to describe a situation. The way one party frames a proposal or solution will affect the way the other party will behave.

Interests: The 'must have' goals a party will try to achieve during a negotiation.

Negotiation: A process involving planning and discussion aimed at reaching an agreement.

Positions: What the parties to a negotiation will be asking for. A bad initial positional may become a very expensive mistake.

Procurement: Concentrates on the strategic process of product or service sourcing, which typically involves researching, Negotiation and planning. procurement is not the same as just purchasing.

Reservation Price: A concept similar to the walkaway point, i.e., that point in a negotiation range that when reached the negotiator abandons the Negotiation. In this case, reservation price relates to the actual price involved in the potential purchasing.

Scenario: An initial set of conditions and timeline of significant events imposed on trainees to achieve exercise objectives.

Strategy: Defined typically as a planned sequence on how one intends to approach a negotiation.

Tactics: This refers to the specific methods, and sometimes processes, to implement a strategy.

Trade Off: To substitute or bargain one issue for another. A move typically found in many selling vs. purchasing actions.

Walkaway Point: A concept similar to the reservation price, however it may consider variables other than price, as would be the case of the reservation price concept, which is a particular case of the walkaway point concept.

ZOPA: The acronym for "Zone of Possible Agreement," which defines the ranges along which an agreement may be closed. Each party walkaway point defines the boundaries of the ZOPA. The ZONE gives a graphical visualization of the superposition between both parties' negotiation ranges.

APPENDIX

Table 2. Negotiation preparation sheet

<table>
<tr><td colspan="2">1. The Problem
Problem statement I must negotiate with (person) to solve (the problem)</td></tr>
<tr><td colspan="2">2. Specific Goals</td></tr>
<tr><td>My specific, High expectation:</td><td>Target decision-maker:</td></tr>
<tr><td>Bottom line:</td><td>Relationship background:</td></tr>
<tr><td colspan="2">3. Interests (Shared / Conflicting)</td></tr>
<tr><td>Mine:</td><td>Theirs:</td></tr>
<tr><td colspan="2">4. Leverage</td></tr>
<tr><td>■ If no deal, my BATNA is:
■ Can I improve this?
■ Leverage favours: Me/Other part/Even?
(Who has the most to lose from "no deal"?)</td><td>■ If no deal, their alternative is:
■ Can I affect their alternatives or make their status quo worse?</td></tr>
</table>

Adapted from Shell (2000).

Chapter 2
Trust in Procurement Decisions of New Zealand SMEs:
A Repertory Grid Analysis

Kripanshu Vora
University of Otago, New Zealand

ABSTRACT

The purpose of this chapter is to explore the role of trust or confidence through the managerial lens. The chapter aims to acquire empirical evidence regarding the importance of factors that play a role in fostering trust during procurement decision making exemplified through a New Zealand-owned company, ContainerCo. This exploratory study scrutinises trust as perceived by SME managers in the supply chain of logistics and procurement in New Zealand. It uses the repertory grid analysis and is based on two interviews conducted through the repertory grid technique, a semi-structured method. Although different in every company and country, trust plays a major role during the selection of suppliers. Factors such as reliability and value are regarded as the most important ones for choosing the right supplier in the case of ContainerCo.

INTRODUCTION

Since the past two decades, supply chain management (SCM) has been put in the limelight of research as it has gained considerable attention. One particular aspect of this research was to focus on eliminating inefficiencies and ineffectiveness in the procurement process. However, it has been found through experimental work that many supply chain members tend to deviate from the optimized decisions that literature provides. This highlights the fact that there is something more to relationships in the supply chain than just the economic exchange (Ebrahim-Khanjari et al., 2012).

Traditionally, SCM is based on contractual ties, which primarily relied on monitoring and control methods. The traditional theory of management had a 'fixed' view on what can be described 'hard management' systems. This system suffered from various problems (Meng, 2015). A primary concern of this traditional method was its inflexibility to resolve the issues of unforeseen circumstances, render-

DOI: 10.4018/978-1-7998-8709-6.ch002

ing it myopic and inactive in times of dire need. The contract in any project is considered the standard of behaviour; however, the lack of equal information sharing, limited rationality and transactional costs substantiate the project to remain unfinished (Turner, 2004). An unfinished contract snowballs to another old problem that creates uncertainty and disputes between the business partners. Heavy monitoring and control cause another set of issues that turn the relationships sour and adversarial which leads to the 'hurt' party to implement hidden costs (Cheung et al., 2015). Therefore, such traditional practices of management have been an obstacle to the successful completion of large business deals and burgeon substandard performance comprising of postponements of time, higher costs and undesirable quality.

Although they cannot be quantified or contracted on, such non-pecuniary issues are important because they affect businesses (Ebrahim-Khanjari et al., 2012). Uzzi (1996) demonstrated in longitudinal empirical research of buyer-supplier relationships in the textile industry that the economic exchange over time became more rooted in complex relationships that involved investments, friendship, and altruistic attachments. There is sufficient affirmation that business decisions are influenced or impacted by successful relationships amongst business partners (Coughlan, 2002).

The Problem and Research Question

A plethora of studies on SCM viewed trust as the trust between organisations, i.e., inter-organisational trust (Joshi & Stump, 1999). Furthermore, trust is often perceived as collateral to collaboration's constructs such as knowledge sharing and dyadic decision making. Therefore, trust is perceived as one of the key effects of organisational performance (Byoung-Chun et al., 2011).

Although literature has attempted to expand the definitions and factors of trust through synonymous use of trust, literature has not really defined what trust is and how it can be fostered and what are its practical aspects during the purchasing process. Since trust is considered as sentiments and beliefs between people, it is crucial to scrutinise it at an inter-personal level rather than at an organisational level (Mouzas et al., 2007).

This project aims to comprehend the research gap of the underlying factor that builds stronger client-supplier relationships that goes beyond the normal parameters of doing business. Researchers have succeeded in broadly defining the glue that binds such relationships in the supply chain by coining it on 'trust'. To enrich this understanding of what is defined and measured by 'trust' practically, I scope my research based on the organisational setting of ContainerCo. For any decisive changes made in an organisation, it involves the management, especially at the senior level, where the decisions are generated, much like in the case of ContainerCo. With the company willing to make radical changes to expand its business, these senior managers want to go beyond the fiscal gain of the company, by taking society and the environment into account. They intend to venture into delivering their products to their customers in a more efficient, effective and attainable way.

From equating the balance sheet to actually implementing such decisions, the participants of this research, need to "trust" their suppliers before signing the contracts. Therefore this paper will answer the research question: how do staff perceive their trust (or confidence) in suppliers during the procurement process and what role does this have on procurement decisions?

LITERATURE REVIEW

Evolution of Trust in Procurement

As an effect of globalisation, organisations' development and management largely depend on other organisations' relationships. It has increasingly become difficult for organisations to take measures on their own. In order to gain a competitive advantage, they need to cooperate closely with their business partners (Ryciuk & Nazarko, 2020). Therefore, shaping proper relationships in the supply chain is emphasised for its operation. The glue that binds successful sustainable relationships in the supply chain together is a non-pecuniary element called trust (Al-Hakim et al., 2012; Ebrahim-Khanjari et al., 2012). Furthermore, trust benefits a business relationship economically as it alleviates the stress on details in contract monitoring, lowers transactional costs and risks (Gulati, 1995). Partners are to make business decisions and perform activities through trust that mutually benefit both while also being wary of actions that may fragment the relationship.

Being the non-tangible, emotional, subjective, and complex 'ganglion' that it is, trust is the soul and foundation of supply chain management (Zhou et al., 2016). A variety of articles have focused on untangling the relationship between the antecedents, correlates, consequence and predictors of trust. Empirical and conceptual research on trust has increasingly become popular in various disciplines, such as anthropology, psychology, education, health science, political science, sociology, and business and management. Over the past twenty years, researchers have considered trust as a dependent variable to identify its antecedents, with interest in it fostering factors and activities that have accelerated its development, especially in the supply chain. As the literature on trust covers a plethora of subjects, even within the literature of supply chain management (SCM), it is vital to identify what literature is being scrutinised in this review (see Fig. 1).

The triangular cross-section formed of the three circles is the part that this study focuses on.

Within SCM, when it comes to enhancing organisational performance, it is largely dependent on investing in goods and services that will up scale the organisation. This has been put under the umbrella term of 'Procurement' (See Fig. 1 above). Like the proverbial milk stool, procurement is formed of three legs – Organizational Relations, Supplier Selection and Trust. The amalgamation of these three, is the ideal potion to invest in goods and services that will benefit the buyer.

Figure 1. The literature being analysed

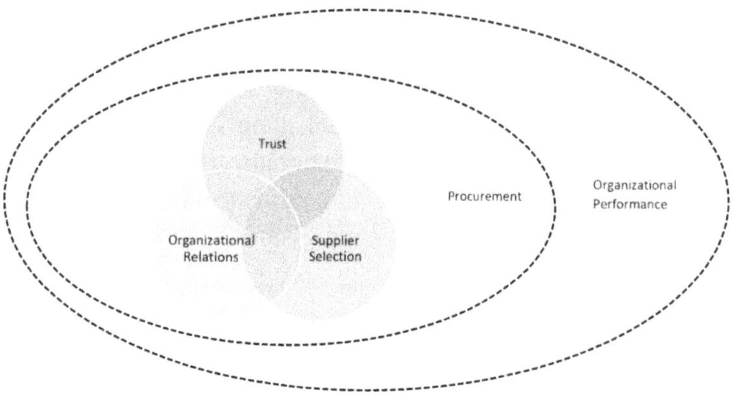

Systematic Literature Review Process

In this paper, I have systematically organised the insights of literature on Trust gained over the past two decades in SCM literature and identified future research avenues. My review is different from previous ones (Hutchinson et al., 2012; McEvily et al., 2017) in a few salient ways. First, included in my analysis are articles on 'Trust' in disciplines such as Management, Psychology, Construction, Agriculture and Supply Chain. While I acknowledge articles from the other mentioned sectors which have often relied on Trust literature, I target mainly the ones within Management and Supply Chain literature. However, as research on trust is deeply rooted in Psychology, Construction and Agriculture, it would not make sense to discard them entirely as that would affect the sampling of my scholarly research. The sample I wish to produce should be broadly representative. It is not necessary to have an exhaustive sample but sufficiently large to let my readers confide to the inferences made in my research (van Weele & van Raaij, 2014; Wood & Wang, 2018). Second, I discuss several fundamental conceptualisations by various researchers of trust literature. By doing so, I identify and analyse the key concepts, similarities and differences.

Furthermore, this allows me to shed light on a space that, despite extensive research and verification of the concepts, it has been limited by its dependence on just these conceptualisations. While preceding reviews have focused only on antecedents and outcomes of trust, my paper has also reviewed articles that mention trust as a moderating factor. This additional feature emphasises research models and analyses that nourish academic literature of the indirect effects of trust. This addition enriches the concepts of 'Trust' beyond its tight-knit boundaries of scholarly literature.

Evolution of Trust in Supply Chain Management

What is meant by trust in an ongoing inter-organisational relationship? Given that trust is important for governance (Gulati, 1995), consequential performance and exchange processes (McEvily et al., 2017), there has been increasing research with a focus on the trust fostering antecedents between exchange partners (Poppo et al., 2008). In the inter-organisational literature, trust is perceived as a relational concept. It is seen as the bond that is jointly held by the two exchange partners. The emphasis on the relational orientation comes from a sociological tradition and extends into the business world where trust is similarly conceptualised as a shared expectation of the involved parties (McEvily et al., 2017). Keeping in mind the deeply rooted sociological foundations, Gulati and Sytch (2007) claim that joint dependence of high level promotes trust that is reciprocated by the business partner.

Uncertainty and the risk of action taken are subdued between the business partners when there is a sense of trust (Morgan & Hunt, 1994). This allows reactions to be more flexible if and when there is a change in the business environment (Cao & Zhang, 2011). Furthermore, the risk of a firm behaving opportunistically along with mechanisms to protect and scrutinise the execution of projects or the necessity to chart out a detailed contract, are softened with trust (Ryciuk & Nazarko, 2020).

Trust is generally considered to be a belief, of the trusting party, of credibility in the promise of a business associate to act in a way that does not lead to negative outcomes (Friman et al., 2002). Morgan and Hunt (1994) and Sahay (2003) state it is a belief that a business partner will be honest, reliable and competent upon the execution of a particular task. The act of trusting an entity means that the trustee believes that the entrusted entity is led by positive intentions and has the ability to meet the expectations set and agreed by both entities (Nannestad, 2008). When an organisation trusts its partner, it expects its partner to fulfil all obligations and commit actions that are beneficial to the trustee (Sahay, 2003).

These trust fostering actions are determined by factors that contribute to the enhancement of cooperation in supply chains, indicated as determinants for the quality of the relationship in a supply chain. For the purpose of this project, I consider the following as synonymous factors to trust: partner qualities, adaptation, cooperation, commitment, organisational capacity, and partnering.

Although these factors are inherently subjective and are continuously being debated and criticized in literature, they provide a set of criteria that can be beneficial to practitioners as well as researchers to either use for understanding the underlying factors and aspects of trust or for selecting studies to review. Such criteria are not readily available for books and book chapters.

Factors of Trust – Partner Qualities

At first, the trust in inter-organisational relationships is mainly assessed with the credibility of the parties, their capabilities, and resources, along with the benefits of collaboration as expected. This is known as calculative and competence trust (Ryciuk & Nazarko, 2020). Having had no past experience or relationship, the supplier's brand, reputation, recommendations from peer business associates who have previously dealt with the supplier are all essential in building trust. This is known as 'transitive trust', where if company X trusts company Y, and if Y trusts company Z, then X can trust Z. The emphasis for trust-building in literature is often on the influence of reputation (Wong & Cheung, 2005). However, achieving a reputable position is expensive in terms of both price and time. Therefore, trusting a well-known company is much easier as it cuts the clutter of risk involved, which could damage that trust. If a company is not reputable or does not have solid reputations in the market, long term engagement and establishment with the company is likely to be low (Schmidt & Wagner, 2019) because if it were a reputable firm the chance of it behaving opportunistically would be unlikely as it would anyway need to protect its reputation in the long run. As a result, this makes a cheaper option that requires fewer monitoring mechanisms (Lui et al., 2009). Products and services of high quality, good market opinions and positive feelings from other companies are what is understood by a good reputation. Additionally, the trustworthiness of a company can be identified by its brand, which separates the company's products from its peer companies as the high quality of the product is assured. A brand is not merely measured by its name, slogan or logo; communication, visual and behavioural elements are to be considered. Furthermore, the financial records of the company can also influence the credibility of the organisation (Ryciuk & Nazarko, 2020).

Adaptation

When supply chain partners modify their resources to improve cooperation through a change or adjustment of their business models, is when adaptation takes place (Powers & Reagan, 2007). Being a consequence of trust, adaptation is expressed when an organisation invests in methods that ameliorate cooperation (Kwon & Suh, 2004). As these investments are dedicated to partnering firms and no other firms, the value is lost upon the termination of that cooperated partnership. Such investments directed at specific asset acquisitions enhance the value of the relationship. Because of the cost of investing in cooperative resources, the risk of opportunistic behaviour is lowered, which in turn, boosts trust (Lui et al., 2009). Contrastingly, these investments fortify the dependence of the investing party on this relationship, thus increasing the risk of the investee's likelihood to behave opportunistically (Langfield-Smith, 2008). That said, the rise in such behaviour also depends on the kind of relationship the investor and investee firms have (Rokkan et al., 2003). The risk of opportunistic behaviour is elevated when it comes to transactional relationships, whereas in cooperative relationships, specific investments fetter the probability of opportunism. Adaptation of activities jointly held and performed by the involved firms can also accrue trust in the relationship (Ryciuk & Nazarko, 2020). Assets that invest in building relationships are often investments in the resources, business processes and people (Lui et al., 2009; Morgan & Hunt, 1994; Yoon & Moon, 2019).

Commitment

Commitment is defined as a conviction of the ongoing relationship with a business partner as beneficial and that continuing the relationship through possible acts of maintenance is justified and reasonable (Chen et al., 2011). It is the extent to which a supplier would feel appreciative to continue collaborating with a particular client, which is one of the factors that lead to long-term corporate relationships (Tanskanen & Aminoff, 2015). Commitment hints at future orientation. This is the reason why it is regarded as a positive behaviour towards creating a conducive atmosphere to extend the relationship while also emanating an intention to maintain and construct the relationship, particularly in scenarios where supply chain partners are dependent on one other (Liu et al., 2017). Emotional commitment is usually linked to an optimistic acknowledgement towards a specific partner. On the other hand, calculative commitment indicates the lack of potentials or expensive substitutes for the specific partner (De Ruyter et al., 2001). The strength of supply chain relationships between business partners is confirmed by the extent to which the partners involve informal ways to maintain their relationships (Sarkar et al., 1998). These bonds are formed over a long period of mutual friendship through interaction. Trust is the main factor that affects the commitment of supply chain partners and is the key factor that binds supply chain management (Chen et al., 2011). It also permits effective and efficient modifications (Morgan & Hunt, 1994).

Cooperation

Generally, cooperation is regarded as an agreed joint activity set to achieve common goals, which would be pricey or unattainable if not performed jointly (Brito et al., 2014). Cooperation is built through various harmonious collaborations, acceptance and understanding of the partner's behaviour and goals (Hutchinson et al., 2012). Jointly resolving through chosen resolution mechanisms also increase cooperation (Ha et al., 2011). In terms of business, relationships cooperation is a consequence of trust (Hausman & Johnston, 2010). Companies are not likely to coordinate or interact with untrusted suppliers as the level of cooperation is affected by trust (Redondo & Cambra Fierro, 2008). The willingness to cooperate is reduced through opportunism; thus, trust is required to enhance cooperation (Ting et al., 2007). If companies want their relationships to succeed collaboratively, a joint effort is crucial to plan and coordinate and sort disputes together (Nyaga et al., 2010).

Collaboration

The success of an organisation is largely dependent on its ability to collaborate with overseas companies (Sako & Helper, 1998) and can enhance its performance by exploring and involving potential business partners instead of forming an eventual roadblock (Al-Hakim & Lu, 2017). The main reason for the failure of initiatives of collaboration is the inability to comprehend the structure and characteristics of collaboration (Busi & Bititci, 2006). Thus, the necessity to be able to identify the key factors that hint at collaboration (Busi & Bititci, 2006). Collaboration has several pointers (Spekman & Carraway, 2006). For example, Fiske (1990) had introduced 'interdependence' as one of the indicators of collaboration. Being based on the concepts of social relationship, this was later supported by other researchers in the literature (Al-Hakim et al., 2012).

The importance of information-sharing within collaboration has come into play three decades ago (Powell et al., 1996) and persists to be highlighted in recent literature as well (Al-Hakim et al., 2014). A mix of internationalisation of firms, the evolution of the internet and other information technologies have birthed and enhanced the adoption of collaboration between organisations (Al-Hakim et al., 2014). Having said that, it does not mean that the availability of resources such as the internet or any other informational and technological source automatically sustain collaboration and promote information sharing; there is a certain level of trust involved (Al-Hakim et al., 2012; Mangel et al., 2010) along with responsibility and commitment (Bititci et al., 2002). The more recent research publications also emphasise on fostering strategic value in collaborative relationships (Mangel et al., 2010) as collaboration will require shared goals of the partners (Verdecho et al., 2009) as well as parallel cultures (Burgess & Singh, 2006), governance control (Bititci et al., 2002), forecasting (Mangel et al., 2010), shared consumption of resources (Rycroft & Kash, 2004) and management of risk (Doukidis et al., 2007). Researchers such as and Burgess and Singh (2006) consider functional coordination as a key requirement for collaboration.

Organisational Capacity

Organisational capacity, more precisely capability, is defined as an organisation's ability to accomplish certain goals in a specific business environment (De Wever et al., 2005). When an organisation is able to succour its strengths in an unpredictable environment, which demands flexibility and responsible organisational activities, it requires behaviours, information, technologies and skills that add to the organisation's performance (Hafeez et al., 2006).

Excellent performance is exemplified through the case of the Japanese car manufacturer, Toyota. They paid more attention to the learning abilities to build strategic alliances, which is essential for any organisation to be open to create, seize and implement all relevant information, experience and skills with the help of physical assets as in benefits of sharing resources (Rycroft & Kash, 2004).

An array of indicators of organisational capacity related to collaboration exists. Dynamic capacity of an organisation is defined as the ability to acquire new resources when the market inflates, subsides, divides, clashes and sometimes dies (Sambharya & Lee, 2014). Innovative capability is when a firm produces, assimilates and can convert a particular technological innovation (Zawislak et al., 2012). Other less moderate organisational capacities that potentially increase collaboration are the capabilities to learn, gain knowledge, operationalise, communicate and solve problems (Sambharya & Lee, 2014).

Partnering

To create more attractive partnering approaches for their clientele, companies must be willing to resolve or adjust to problems such as cultural differences, ongoing stereotypes and accusatorial views of the people involved, as well as novel ways to work strategies (Liu et al., 2004). Research publications have reported of finding clients being obsessive over competitive pricing of bids rather than focus on getting the best value (Beach et al., 2005).

Challender et al. (2016) report in their study that to encourage firms to partner, there needs to be greater coordination, growth, systematisation and mentality to work collaboratively and the aim of obtaining value for money (Tan, 2002). However, in order to clearly communicate and impart knowledge required for complete integration, trust is a fundamental necessity for all members of the supply chain, from the clients to the smallest firms involved (Laeequddin et al., 2012).

RESEARCH DESIGN AND METHODS

Importance of a Balanced Methodology

Research methodology refers to techniques used to collect data and analyse it. It is utilised to answer a specific research question or a particular research problem (Teddlie & Tashakkori, 2009) and guide the study to gain new understandings of the investigated phenomena (Hair, 2009). The two most common methods used in management research are qualitative and quantitative methods. There has been a long-standing tension between their use for conducting research, and this debate has swung back and forth over the last 20 years (Easterby-Smith et al., 2012).

Given the increasing complexity and uncertainty of the environment in which current organisations operate within, it has become a requisite for managers to embrace this convolution and learn how to resolve this uncertainty (Jankowicz, 2001). Aram and Noble (1999) elucidate this well in their management class to their students:

"In times of rapid change and high uncertainty, all organisations need some part of their operations to be at the edge of chaos[...]This implies valuing not only the edifice of knowledge that we need to construct deliberately for our students but also the spaces for "pure" action - acting without a directing image." (Aram & Noble, 1999, p.340)

This highlights the importance of intuition of the action-value, which may not be founded upon proposed principles that are explicit and presentable at the moment of commitment. It also brings to light the requirement to manage such subjective uncertainties that are involved in such scenarios.

Management, almost by definition, is an activity that comes about when there is a lack of a standardised operating rubric (Jankowicz, 2001), and it has been known for a long time that managerial thinking, especially at the senior level in every organisation, requires intuition and the ability to judge subjectively (Lin & Lee, 2004). Nevertheless, as our knowledge of the subject broadens, we seek to manifest a managing system that highlights the making of tacit information into explicit knowledge (Myers, 1996). This complements as an association to newer approaches and reflects the emphasis of researchers interacting with their research participants. As a newer approach, it focuses on investigating fewer sources but with more depth than sampling data from various sources to draw statistical conclusions (Hunter, 1997); or as Reason et al. (1981) explain it to be a systematic search, for truth is objectively subjective.

What Is RGT?

The repertory grid technique, also known as the RepGrid, is an established cognitive technique since its creation 40 years ago by Kelly (1955), a clinical psychologist. In our quotidian lives, we relentlessly attempt to understand how other people and we view the world in order to make decisions and undertake actions that are both meaningful and sensible. We are often unaware of this psychological process, and the repertory grid is a tool through which a researcher can attempt to unfurl and present it in a formal way how people construct their world (Curtis et al., 2008; Easterby-Smith et al., 1996; Zuber-Skerritt & Roche, 2004). In a way, the grid can be thought of as a cognitive "map", which plots a particular aspect of a person's world.

The Use and Components of RepGrid

It is usually challenging to answer questions about things that one has taken for granted for a reasonably long duration. For example, "what is it that makes X a better person than Y?"; "what do you mean by leadership qualities?"; "what do you mean by better at leading?". Such questions often make senior-level managers reply with answers they think they should be knowing rather than answer what they actually think (Tan & Hunter, 2002). Thus, the repertory grid's attempt to dig deeper and deconstruct the theories that managers actually use, in the case of this research.

The RGT comprises four essential components: the topic, the elements, the constructs, and the ratings/links as explained below (Tan & Hunter, 2002).

1. The topic – what the interview in its entirety is based on.
2. Elements – these are examples or objects of attention that depict the topic. These objects consist of people, objects, experiences, events related to the topic. The elements are either preselected or chosen by the interviewee.
3. Constructs/links – this is the most important component in the grid. At this point, the various elements are compared to each other to create statements that describe what the interviewee links the element to the topic.

Each research participant elicits the grid by going through a series of comparisons that result in the bi-polar production of constructs. The participant is asked to compare three elements and indicate to pair the two that are similar according to the participant. Upon doing so, the participant is then asked to justify how they are similar and how they differ from the third and excluded element. What the participant considers as opposing poles (may not be direct opposites), or at least a semblance of distinctive attributes, is brought forth through the comparison (Zuber-Skerritt & Roche, 2004).

One of the core advantages of the RGT is that it avoids interviewer bias (where the interviewer's questions are derived from his or her own set of values), as it allows the interviewees to express their experience in the way they see the world according to their own constructs (Davis & Hufnagel, 2007). With a play of differences and similarities supported with examples, it facilitates teasing out of the interviewee's perspective rather than talking abstractly. This can also be an excellent way to expand the question to its various dimensions (Tan & Hunter, 2002). Additionally, it also uses rating scales that can be presented in statistical analysis; hence it combines both of these methodologies. In terms of epistemology, it presents knowledge as a subjective view in which meaning is often or to a large extent, an individual property (Hunter, 1997).

Why Is RGT the Most Suitable Method?

The interviews were structured and followed a Repertory Grid process, with the aim of learning about the participants' perceptions regarding procurement decisions, with a particular focus on trust or confidence in the supplier. Two Interviews were held by Zoom (depending on resources, participant availability, and travel restrictions), took 40-60 minutes, were recorded and then transcribed by an online transcribing software called 'Otter'. A Repertory Grid method was selected as this process allowed a clear presentation of the interviewee's construction processes, reducing any interviewer inferences. This method was chosen as it allowed the participants' values to clearly be understood and used to understand the trust/confidence in suppliers in the procurement process.

The Repertory Grid method was used by initially asking the participant to write down all the significant procurement decisions they have been involved with, each on separate flashcards/boxes on the screen (if by video conference); prompts were given when the participant got stuck. Then, a series of questions were asked regarding the similarities and differences between the elements (the procurement decision), the participant's reasons for the similarities/differences were used as the constructs.

As it is called, laddering is one of the ways that allows the interviewee to explore the interviewer's understanding more deeply. This later relates to the conceptualising of the constructs. Laddering down is when a participant's particular construct is being investigated in order to get a further understanding. On the other hand, laddering up is used when the researcher asks the participant why a particular construct is important. This often leads the participant to quickly assess and spell out a description of his values (Easterby-Smith et al., 1996).

Constructs are often adjectives (e.g., trustworthy, credible, transparent) or a short descriptive phrase (e.g., not to be trusted, does not communicate meaning clearly) (Curtis et al., 2008). Once the participant stops coming up or has 'dried up' (Easterby-Smith et al., 1996) with new constructs, the interviewer moves on. In scientific terms, this is known as 'minimum context card form' (Curtis et al., 2008; Easterby-Smith et al., 1996; Hair et al., 2009). A two-way protocol table was used so the participant can rate each element in terms of the constructs developed. Various rating methods can be used: dichotomous method, ordinal method, or rating scale. Once the data had been obtained, it was then synthesised through analysing the constructs and elements that had been developed. A qualitative assessment and thematic coding of the interview transcripts provided insight into core concepts in the procurement decision made by the senior staff members of ContainerCo.

The participants' responses were transcribed and were linked to those responses to participants' names in case there arose a need to follow-up with participants or if participants wished to withdraw their responses. However, that information was kept confidential during the data collection. Once the data collection was finalised, all responses were anonymised (i.e., participants' responses were not identifiable). From the transcripts and field notes, the participants' perceptions of procurement and confidence and trust in suppliers were analysed.

Why ContainerCo as a Case Study?

ContainerCo undertakes a range of processes that involve procurement activities from domestic and international suppliers. When procuring from international suppliers, it is often difficult to establish which supplier should be selected and how the concept of 'trust' or 'confidence' is used to help select the suppliers. At the moment, the decision does not explicitly include elements of trust or confidence and focuses on other factors (e.g., economic factors). The company would like to better understand how to make procurement decisions and, therefore, this project aims to develop a model that explicitly includes the trust and confidence in the supplier, allowing the company to better adapt to changing procurement landscapes and circumstances.

What ContainerCo aims to do fits well into the research gap found in the literature review. This is why ContainerCo was selected as a case study as it provides a pathway to directly relate research to practice through this exploratory study.

Recruitment of the participants was based on their experience with international and national sourcing/procurement projects. The potential candidates were identified and were invited to participate using the recruitment email. Two senior staff members of ContainerCo agreed to participate in my project. The interview consisted of one of the top three most experienced operational supervisor in the company (participant 1), the other was the National Fleet Manager of the company (participant 2) and I (the researcher). Two interviews were conducted with staff at ContainerCo. All interview questions solicited the participants' professional opinions. Despite the number of participants is not enough to generalise the data it suffices the need to provide a sample that sets the foundation for future scholarly research and indicates future steps for ContainerCo.

How Was the Data Analysed?

During this phase, the researcher submits completed RepGrid to either quantitative or qualitative analysis. An analysis is crucial because it helps the researcher comprehend the content and the formation of the participants' construct system. Researchers can either analyse the content of the grid, its element and construct labels, or if the researcher intends to quantify the data, he will analyse the grid ratings (Curtis et al., 2008).

Once the RepGrid is created where the elements are rated based on the constructs, the researcher now has a matrix of labels and numbers that result in two areas of analysis, the construct labels and the element-construct ratings. One must know that the element-construct labels themselves are a type of data (Hunter, 1997) that can help the researcher draw qualitative interpretative conclusions on how the research participant viewed the topic in question. A researcher can single-handedly group and analyse these construct labels without the elements being rated in the grid at all. This is done by observing the commonalities between the elements and constructs by analysing the rows and columns to conclude what is valued the least and the most (Easterby-Smith et al., 1996). An analysis of such a kind is called content analysis. Content analysis (Moynihan, 1996) is a qualitative way of analysing which elements and construct labels are placed into common categories in the repertory grid (Feixas et al., 2002) or main issues (Hunter, 1997) and are interpreted to conclude to subjective meaning, as described by the participant (Langan-Fox & Tan, 1997).

Therefore, in this case, content analysis was the chosen method of research as it allowed the researcher to understand the construct labels textually and grasp a more comprehensive meaning of what trust entails for the senior staff members of ContainerCo.

Summary of the Procedure

Participant 1 was asked to name the six most recent procurement projects he was involved in. The participant responded that being in the operational division, he is not involved in procurement projects as that is organised by the head office. However, the participant acknowledged that he interacts with local suppliers as he is in charge of the day-to-day management of operations within the company. In the case of the second participant, being the National Fleet Manager of ContainerCo, his role was to supervise transportation and logistics vehicles, along with maintenance and purchase of new vehicles and large mechanical instruments. So, the topics of both interviews were based on trust in selecting suppliers, which is a key aspect of procurement decisions.

Both participants were asked to name six suppliers that they regularly deal with. Upon doing so, the names of the six suppliers were inserted in the grid under the component 'Elements' on a blank sheet by the researcher.

Once the names and roles of the suppliers were clear, the crux of the interview commenced.

Three of the elements were picked at random by the researcher. The participant was verbally presented with the three names or scientifically known as the 'triad'(Wright & Cheung, 2007). As the objective of this project intends to explore the role that trust plays in procurement decisions, both participants were then asked the Kellian question: "In what way are any two of these similar, but different from the third, when it comes to trust?" After the initial answer, laddering up and down procedures was applied to probe the participants. This method was done to allow both the participants to elaborate and to dissect the link or the constructs they were building for the researcher to get to the core of the answer. The same procedure was repeated until there came a 'theoretical saturation' point at which no further attributes transpired from it.

FINDINGS

In the interest of a parsimonious report, but still provide assurance to the reader of the robustness of my process, a deep dive into a couple of constructs is provided below to demonstrate not just the abstract description of the process in this chapter but an in-depth understanding of how the interviewee's justifications were tabulated as constructs in my RepGrid:

Upon the participant's selection of two similar suppliers from the triad, through a laddering up the question, he was asked to elaborate on what role did trust play when it came to dealing with these suppliers. To which he replied that "both companies" had "bad call centres", which means that the procedure in order to book a complaint or request was to go through a roster every time. This not only took time but also changed the person on the other end of the call. On the other hand, the company he excluded from the triad had a "one to one" contact. Thus, the bipolar construct deduced from the interviewee's response is 'Direct-Indirect contact', where "Indirect contact" was labelled under the negative pole and "Direct contact" was labelled under the positive pole.

One can comprehend the process of tabulating the rest of the constructs in the RepGrid for both interviews upon reading the example stated above. Based on this, I think you can agree with me, reader, that when I get to these constructs, it is grounded on the participants' perceptions.

Elements of Interview 1

The six companies that the participant named were Woodmass Transport, Milton Goughs, BOC Gases, Apparelmaster, Bay Engineers and Fulton Hogan.

In the first interview (see Grid 1), the first round of random elements consisted of 1(i.e., Woodmass Transport),3 (i.e., BOC Gases), and 6 (i.e., Fulton Hogan). The second round had elements that were not covered or selected in the first round. Thus, elements 2 (i.e., Milton Goughs),4 (i.e., Apparelmaster) and 5 (i.e., Bay Engineers).

The participant was requested to explain the roles each company played for ContainerCo with a brief description, as follows:

E1: Woodmass Transport – primary truck company;
E2: Walton Goughs - mobile mechanics;
E3: BOC Gases – secondary transport company;
E4: Apparelmaster - overalls and personal protective equipment (PPE) for engineers;
E5: Bay Engineers - for tools in workshops;
E6: Fulton Hogan – yard maintenance and development and secondary truck company.

The Constructs

After the interview was transcribed, the constructs were summarised in Grid.1. In the first round, the participant selected BOC Gases (E3) and Fulton Hogan (E6) as similar as they are secondary companies. In the second round, the participant considered Walton Goughs (E2) and Bay Engineers (E5) similar as they are both mechanical related companies, whereas Apparelmaster (E4) was not in the same business. The constructs were later filled in the grid based on the transcribed interview.

The constructs created were: C1) value reliability, C2) physical distance, C3) contact point, C4) supplier's interest, C5) relationship duration, C6) delivery time.

Table 1.

Value reliability	Worth the money spent
Physical distance	Geographical location from ContainerCo sites
Contact point	Single representative or contact through call centre
Supplier's interest	If the supplier is proactive in providing service
Relationship duration	Length of knowing the single representative; duration of the bond
Delivery time	Speed and punctuality of delivering goods or services

Elements of Interview 2

In the second interview, the six companies that the participant named were Hyster New Zealand, Kalmar Global, Clark Equipment, Lease Plan, Custom Fleet and Nissan New Zealand.

Similar to the previous interview, the second participant, too, was asked to give a brief description of what kind of companies he deals with. He described that as the national fleet manager, his role revolves around mainly three things: container handlers, terminal tractors and company 'Utes' (utility vehicles).

E1*: Hyster NZ - forklift trucks;
E2: AB Equipment - cargo handlers;
E3: Clark Equipment - 'Omega' forklift trucks;
E4: Lease Plan - car and vehicle leasing company;
E5: Custom Fleet - empty container handlers;

E6: Nissan NZ - company vehicles.

* This element is split in two. The left marking represents when Hyster was owned by Goughs, the second marking represents its ownership by Sime Darby.

In the first round of interview 2, the second participant was randomly given a triad consisting of Hyster NZ (E1), Lease Plan (E4) and Custom Fleet (E5). The second round consisted of the non-selected elements, i.e., Kalmar Global (E2), Clark Equipment (E3), and Nissan NZ (E6).

The Constructs

In the first round of the second interview, the participant recognised Hyster NZ (E1) and Lease Plan (E4) to be similar as the participant deals with these two companies more often, almost on a daily basis. In the second round, the participant labelled AB Equipment (E3) and Nissan NZ (E6) together as, unlike the other combinations mentioned, Clark Equipment (E3) was behind in terms of technological advancements.

Upon transcription of the second interview, the constructs were filled in Grid 2., as follows.

C7) Contractual flexibility, C8) service quality, C9) supplier adaptability, C10) hierarchical communication, C11) work orientation, C12) company ownership, C13) product/service fit.

Table 2.

Contractual flexibility	If flexible the supplier is when it comes to tailoring the contract
Service quality	Overall quality of the service in relation to customer satisfaction
Supplier adaptability	If the supplier is willing to adapt to the buyer's requests
Hierarchical communication	Whether the supplier's decisions have a trickle-down effect, where everybody from the team is implementing that change
Work orientation	Whether the supplier blindly follows a systematic approach or is willing to skip steps if need be
Company ownership	Whether the supplying company is locally owned or overseas
Product/service fit	Whether the product or service meets all the requirements of ContainerCo

Miscellaneous Constructs

Conducting interviews through the repertory grid technique can sometimes divert to a tangent. As was the case, in these interviews. However, these constructs described by the two interviewees are also valuable to this research. Although they could not fit into the grid directly as these constructs were not based on the elements selected by the participants, they will be mentioned in the next chapter to strengthen the understanding of the participants' perceptions.

The following are the miscellaneous constructs not elicited in the grid: C14) Peers with history, C15) Company culture.

Table 3.

Peers with history	Past work experience or known network of people
Company culture	What are the core values / core purpose of the company?

Table 4. Grid 1: RepGrid of interview 1

		Woodmass Transport	**Walton Goughs**	**BOC Gases**	**Apparel-Master**	**Bay Engineers**	**Fulton Hogan**	
	Negative Pole (O)	*E1*	**E2**	*E3*	**E4**	**E5**	*E6*	**Positive Pole (X)**
C1	Value unreliability	X	O	X	X	O	X	Value for money
C2	No service station available	O	X	X	O	O	X	Short distance to the service station of supplier
C3	Indirect contact	X	X	O	X	O	O	Direct contact
C4	Lack of interest from the supplier	X	X	O	X	X	O	Ease of service provided
C5	Short term relationship	X	X	X	O	X	X	Long term relationship
C6	Long waiting time	X	O	O	X	O	O	short waiting time

Italicized columns refer to the first round.

Table 5. Grid 2: RepGrid of interview 2.

		Hyster NZ	**AB Equipment**	**Clark Equipment**	**Lease Plan**	**Custom Fleet**	**Nissan NZ**	
	Negative Pole (O)	*E1*	**E2**	**E3**	*E4*	*E5*	**E6**	**Positive Pole (X)**
C7	Rigid contract	X O	X	X	O	X	X	Flexible contract
C8	Poor service	X O	X	O	X	O	X	Commendable service
C9	One-sided	O	X	X	O	X	X	Open to adjust
C10	Communication only at senior manager level	O	O	O	X	O	X	Communication throughout the staff chain
C11	Going by the book	O	X	X	O	X	X	Following informal procedures
C12	Internationally owned	X O	X	X	O	X	O	New Zealand Owned
13	Not meeting requirements	X O	X	O	X	X	X	Meeting requirement

Italicized columns represent the first round.

DISCUSSION

This project reviewed the scholarly progress made by researchers regarding trust. A comprehensive analysis of how Trust is perceived in supply chains, unravelling various areas for further theorisation and additional empirical evidencing. This paper's research question: 'How do staff perceive their trust or confidence in their suppliers during the procurement process and what role does this have on procurement decisions?' became more prominent in light of what has been found by previous scholars. To further explore and compare what academicians perceive and how it is actually perceived, this study analysed this through a repertory grid analysis.

The literature review defines the various forms through which 'trust' has been enhanced. The studies elucidate the various practices that when implemented, boost the trust or confidence between supply chain organisations. The literature review shows the concepts that build the theoretical foundation of this project. It highlights the key ways that can increase trust in organisations. However, it is important to remember two important factors that trust is an interpersonal trait and that organisations are made up of people. Therefore, organisational trust is the collective trust of the people forming the organisation, especially at the senior management level as they are the decision makers. This expounds how the literature review builds a strong theoretical foundation and discloses a clear research gap of the impacts of trust at personal-level and the effect it has on procurement decisions at organisational levels.

Key Observations of the RepGrids

With a glance at the repertory grids, one can notice patterns formed. In Grid 1, one can see that BOC Gases and Fulton Hogan (i.e., columns E3 and E6) are the same and differ from Woodmass Transport (E1) on three constructs. Both miss out on direct contact, ease of service and have long waiting time.

Looking at the rows, Apparelmaster is the only company that does not have a long-term relationship with ContainerCo as the participant considered it "easily replaceable". As for the length of waiting time, one can see that Woodmass Transport and Apparelmaster are the fastest in delivering their product or service to ContainerCo.

In the second grid's columns, it is obvious that when Hyster NZ was bought over by Sime Darby, an international company, everything went south for the company with ContainerCo. On the other hand, Nissan NZ seemed to offer the best of all constructs despite being an international company.

In terms of rows, there is an obvious similarity between companies that had one-sided contracts were also the ones that purely went by the book, this proved that these companies were not flexible in their actions.

Similarities and Correlation to the Grids' Constructs

When it comes to the selection of a new supplier, the operational advisor (participant 1) said that apart from doing a background check of the supplier, he would also go as far as asking his "peers" and "friends who have had a business history" with the supplier. This confirms Ryciuk and Nazarko (2020)'s theory of calculative and competence trust where the supplier's reputation, brand and recommendations are factors that build trust and appeals to the construct (C14). It also confirms the influential factor of credibility of a good supplier, of seeing the financial factors. This is what the participant meant by "background check". Adaptation was also another important aspect that both participants spoke of. To support this point with an example, the national fleet manager of ContainerCo said that AB Equipment had their machinery on ContainerCo's yards as they "did not own a big enough yard". As these machines were mainly used by ContainerCo, AB Equipment was "not charging" ContainerCo despite having their gear on ContainerCo property. This also made it convenient for AB Equipment's technicians to offer instantaneous service (C2 & C8). For this, they charged ContainerCo only for "working hours" (C4). This is similar to what Fiske (1990) mentioned about the interdependence of firms as part of collaborative measures. This also supports Powers and Reagan (2007) and Lui et al. (2009)'s idea of when supply chain members change their work pattern to improve cooperation (C9), it does assure ContainerCo that AB Equipment is trustworthy. AB Equipment's act of using their assets as a stepping stone (C9) to build a good relationship rather than behaving opportunistically also confirmed the research made by Lui et al. (2009), Morgan and Hunt (1994) and Yoon and Moon (2019).

Understanding the partner's goals also helps in building a cooperative relationship as discussed by Hutchinson et al. (2012). As the fleet manager explained that when it came to working with Lease Plan, it took them "a while to understand" ContainerCo's goals (C4 & C9), but once they did "things went smooth" (C8 & C13). Another interesting confirmation was that of Tan (2002) when the operational supervisor considered leasing machinery which was "value for money" which assured him as a buyer (representative) that he can trust all three trucking companies, Woodmass Transport, BOC Gases and Fulton Hogan for their services (C6) against the price they charge per truck (C1). Such services continued into long term relationship as the participant agreed to have dealt with them for "a long time" (C5).

Theoretical Assumptions of Reputation vs. Practical Outcomes

One main argument that had a contrasting result was that of Schmidt and Wagner (2019). According to them, trusting a well-known company would make it easier to trust and that such highly-reputed companies would not tamper this reputation with opportunistic behaviour. This was not seen in the case of ContainerCo. Here, the moment Sime Darby, a global company, bought the Hyster dealership from Goughs, "things went south" for their business with ContainerCo (C4, C1, C7, C10 & C12). One can see in the second grid that their service turned poor due to their inflexible contract. This made them follow exactly what the contract said and as these lengthy contracts had to be scrutinised by the senior management, the communication did not have a trickle-down effect (C10), thus limiting the understanding only to the top tier of ContainerCo.

Similar to this, is the case of Lease Plan. This company is Australian owned and shared the contractual rigidity of Sime Darby (C12). This made it "frustrating" for the second participant to work with both companies (C7), thus also disproving Sako and Helper (1998). However, regarding their article, one must also consider the time their article was published was probably when globalisation was at its nascent stage. But for their point that a company's success is 'largely dependent' on its ability to work with foreign companies was not true in the case of ContainerCo's success based on the findings of the interview. Among the other examples that the senior managers spoke of, they mentioned having worked with reputed Chinese firms (C12) that manufactured goods at "European standard" (perceived as high quality) in their "past life". After six months of good collaboration and relationship, all of a sudden, the packaging of the products had "unsafe pins" "sticking out", which was a major health hazard. This assures the reader well-known companies may not necessarily be the best choice or fit for purpose (C13).

In general, despite these companies being global and operating in different countries, they were not willing to resolve or adjust disputes at various levels – contractual (C7), cultural (C15) and managerial

(C9). Despite this rigidity of "this is who we are" and "this is what it is" the second participant said that this was how Sime Darby operated all over the world. This was not the way Lui et al. (2009) perceived, stating that reputable companies are more likely to abstain from opportunism, for fear of tarnishing their reputation.

AB Equipment's move was an almost 'courageous' act to enable or expose their assets in the hands of their supplier, this did make them more trustworthy for ContainerCo (C11). However, the idea of behaving opportunistically never occurred to ContainerCo. Instead, they replicated that trust by giving security to their supply chain partner's (biggest) assets. Therefore, this contradicts 's the claim that investee companies are more likely to behave opportunistically, as this was not the case with ContainerCo.

Can Commitment, Cooperation and Trust Be Foreseen?

Although commitment hints at future orientation (Liu et al., 2017) it cannot be perceived beforehand by practitioners. Based on the conversation I had with the two senior managers, commitment cannot be foresighted. In a practitioner's point of view, only upon retrospection of the long-term relationship ContainerCo has had with the majority of the companies, can the loyalty of good service over time (C5, C8 & C9) be considered as commitment. In the sense, that commitment cannot be seen, said, felt from the commencement of a business relationship, but is defined by action over time. Furthermore, for companies like Nissan NZ, and Hyster NZ (when it was owned by Goughs) their level of commitment or the conviction of their commitment rose fast as they were proactively seeking effective measures rather than efficient measures, in other words, value.

Hausman and Johnston (2010) argued that cooperation is a consequence of trust. Although this is true when seen from the observer's 'deck', in the case of ContainerCo, trust was created because there was cooperation emitted from the suppliers. This trust was mirrored by ContainerCo's staff members as this incentivised them to do so. Therefore, it is not necessarily that cooperation is consequential to trust, but possibly vice versa.

Trust is the main factor that affects the commitment of a company (Chen et al., 2011) and is the glue that binds all supply chain partners. This is true from a researcher's perspective, but is not the way practitioners would often describe it as nor would they call it 'trust'. Trust is perceived as an indirect effect of the various factors described above, over time. This was seen by Nissan NZ, Woodmass Transport and AB Equipment in the RepGrids where they seemed to be leaning more on the positive pole.

Getting one's money's worth is of paramount importance. However, in the case of ContainerCo, the operational supervisor said that to him it is more important to "pay a little more for something of that service and reliability" (C8 & C13). This shows that although expenditure of financial resources is a major concern for all companies and not the biggest concern. In this case, value is not based on sheer price over quality, but on reliability as well. Therefore, Tan and Hunter's (2002) proposition of obtaining value for money goes beyond obtaining a pecuniary advantage.

Although 'partnering' is often used as a term for firms to conduct business through collaborative relationships, practitioners do not use this term often. Instead, ContainerCo's senior managers simply call it "doing business".

Conflict Management Resolution

Sarkar et al.'s (1998) findings of measuring strength through the company's informal ways of maintaining relationships were not measured or proven in this paper. Therefore, I am unable to confirm or deny their findings.

There were no conflicts discussed during the interview, as the senior managers did not disclose how they had resolved a conflict. This could mean that conflict resolution comes at a later stage and in case of a conflict, but may not be the primary factors of fostering trust. Thus, Hausman and Johnston's (2010) and Nyaga et. al's (2010) technique of jointly resolving a conflict was not seen as an important factor for the participants' trust perceptions.

Role of Company Culture

Based on the grids, and the interview conversations a significant pattern was observed. Lease Plan and Hyster NZ (or Sime Darby) were both Australian owned, (i.e., C12) and business relationships turned sour for ContainerCo being a New Zealand owned company. However, companies like Nissan NZ which originated from Japan (C12) seemed to meet all of ContainerCo's criteria to call it a trustworthy and reliable company. Although the data collected is a general sample, it does shed light on the aspect of work culture orientation, where company culture such as Nissan's, seem to be providing greater value and reliability to ContainerCo, a New Zealand-owned company.

These findings proved that a majority of themes set by the literature review matched the formations of the trust constructs used by ContainerCo when it came to procurement. Not all constructs and themes went hand in hand. The themes in the literature review are pathways that bind organisational relations, trust and supplier selection during procurement. The RGT constructs were the practical measures exemplified by ContainerCo, that set the parameters for buyers to qualify their suppliers as 'trustworthy'. But the hidden pattern that glued these constructs as a mechanism to set the parameters was not simply the number of constructs or the order of constructs. Similar to the collective trust of people that built the organisational trust, it was the collective value created by these constructs when put together that enhanced the trust or confidence of ContainerCo in its suppliers.

This indicated that the cross-sectional triangle that was formed in Fig.1 by organizational relations, trust and supplier selection was 'value created'. As only when value was created did it generate trust which in turn increased organizational relations for a better selection of suppliers.

CONCLUSION

Through a content analysis of the literature derived from a systematised search and through the repertory grid technique, this paper attempted not to fill a gap in the world of research on trust in the context of supply chain management but to highlight that there is a gap that needs to be explored.

This project set out to answer the research question - how do staff perceive their trust (or confidence) in suppliers during the procurement process and what role does this have on procurement decisions?

The answer to this is that trust is perceived through a set of criteria that inform the senior staff members of the trusting factor in their suppliers, in the case of ContainerCo. These criteria were drawn out from the two senior managers, one being the operational supervisor and the other being the national fleet manager of ContainerCo, by using the repertory grid technique. The results were presented in the form of grids defined by elements, and constructs. The following are the principle constructs derived from the RepGrids 1 and 2: the reliability of value, the physical location, the point of contact, the eagerness of a supplier, the duration of their dyadic relationship, the speed of delivering goods or services, the flexibility of contracts, the quality of service, the adaptability of the supplier, a trickle-up and down communication, the work orientation of the supplier, the origin of the supplier, and the supplier's goods or service fit to ContainerCo's requirements. However, it is essential to note that the perception of trust is not limited to these constructs.

After the findings were discussed and elaborated with the comparison of past literature, new avenues have come to light which will be stated in the following section.

Recommendations – ContainerCo

Based on one of the key trends displayed by RepGrid, one could see that Australian firms generally lacked a number of constructs, all under the umbrella of customer relationship. Whereas, the Japanese company tended to be more proactive and trustworthy due to its commitment to provide all necessary services to its clients. Based on this trend it is safe to say that there seems to be an organisational culture difference. Therefore, I would recommend ContainerCo use an assessment tool that could measure cultural differences for organisations. One probable assessment method could be that of Hofstede's cultural dimensions tool. This could allow them to sift through companies that resembled the Japanese work culture or companies that originated from Japan.

Another key observation was that senior staff members tended to prefer locally owned companies for two reasons. One was that New Zealand-owned companies tended to share the work culture of ContainerCo, and seemed flexible in delivering services that flowed beyond their contractual obligations. The second reason is that local servicing stations are of paramount importance to ContainerCo. Because, in case of technical or mechanical breakdowns, it is best suited when the servicing company is a stone's throw away from the yards.

Lastly, the two companies out of the twelve companies mentioned in the grids that seemed best suited in terms of constructs, are Woodmass Transport and Nissan NZ. In short, a company that offered services or goods that were 'value for money' like Woodmass Transport and proactive nature to provide ContainerCo with an overall smooth experience as that of Nissan NZ, would be the best-suited choice to have a business relationship with.

Recommendations for Managers

While the results of my RepGrids cannot be generalised to all companies, they do provide a rough outline of what companies in New Zealand or companies resembling ContainerCo's business sector and business model would expect from their suppliers. While the underlying factor of doing business is to be financially profitable, some companies such as ContainerCo attempt to go beyond the pecuniary advantage, to create value. The key implication in the case of ContainerCo, is that value can be created when there's a concoction of high-quality service, adaptability and consistency. Therefore, ContainerCo should select suppliers that share the same or similar perspectives on generating value in the supply chain. Based on the findings, Japanese companies like Nissan, seem to fit their criteria when it comes to ease of doing business and creating value proactively for their customers. ContainerCo's ideal suppliers would be those that create value throughout the supply chain, thus creating a value chain.

Recommendations for Researchers --- Limitations and Future Research?

I sought to analyse and synthesize what researchers have learned over two decades of conceptual and empirical research on trust in SCM literature. Despite all my efforts, this project suffers from a few important limitations. First, my selection method of literature only included articles and reviews and left out books and book chapters, conference papers and other sources. I acknowledge that such published studies have recorded interesting findings. Additionally, as the screening process was done at face value, many articles that could potentially look at trust in different business sectors could not be included in the scope of this search, selection and synthesis criteria. Furthermore, Scopus was the sole database through which literature was examined. Gathering articles through different databases could give more depth in particular theoretical domains.

Second, due to the constraint of time of this project and the unavailability of staff members of ContainerCo, it was not possible to gather more data through the RepGrid technique to create a solid data pool to draw conclusions that could be generalised to give fellow researchers a greater depth in understanding the trust fostering criteria involved in procurement decisions of ContainerCo, and ideally of companies based in New Zealand.

Third, although the RepGrid is a semi-structured interview technique, it has some disadvantages too. It is a time-consuming method, lasting up to ninety minutes in some cases. Being an indirect method, it may become frustrating for the participants and direct questions may be more effective and precise. As this technique facilitates exploration of an intellectual domain, it is only a tool to describe and not prescribe that domain. Therefore, other methods would be more effective to generalise the data such as statistical analyses and other data modelling techniques.

Research on trust in SCM is at its adolescence. The construct has been and will continue to be an important and vibrant topic in Supply Chain and Management. Some possible opportunities to be looked at based on this project are the role of organisational culture's impact on trust in SCM. One could also look at larger organisations instead of merely SMEs, to understand the role of trust in megaprojects conducted all over the world. Future research can also elaborate this project by collecting more data and with a longer time frame, optimise the RepGrids with the aid of the participants. It could also examine conflict management which also plays a large role in maintaining trust between staff members.

Another prospective research area could be evaluating the perceptions of managers from various companies to gain a broader understanding of the perception of trust in the value chain.

Knowing the current stage future research should look at the different factors of trust through different modes and as described by previous researchers, which is a step forward in the right direction.

REFERENCES

Al-Hakim, L., Abdullah, N. A., & Ng, E. (2012). The Effect of Inter-Organization Trust and Dependency on E-Procurement Adoption: A Case of Malaysian Manufacturers. *Journal of Electronic Commerce in Organizations*, *10*(2), 40–60. doi:10.4018/jeco.2012040103

Al-Hakim, L., & Lu, W. (2017). The role of collaboration and technology diffusion on business performance. *International Journal of Productivity and Performance Management, 66*(1), 22–50. doi:10.1108/IJPPM-08-2014-0122

Al-Hakim, L., Morgan, M. J., & Chau, R. (2014). An Empirical Evaluation of Information Sharing Between Australia-Singapore Beef Organisations in Light of Trust and ICT Diffusion. *International Journal of e-Collaboration, 10*(3), 1–29. doi:10.4018/ijec.2014070101

Beach, Webster, & Campbell. (2005). An evaluation of partnership development in the construction industry. *International Journal of Project Management, 23*(8), 611-621. doi:10.1016/j.ijproman.2005.04.001

Bititci, U., Carrie, A., & Turner, T. (2002). 11 Integrated performance measurement systems: Structure and dynamics. *Business Performance Measurement*, 174.

Burgess, K., & Singh, P. J. (2006). A proposed integrated framework for analysing supply chains. *Supply Chain Management, 11*(4), 337–344. doi:10.1108/13598540610671789

Busi, M., & Bititci, U. S. (2006). Collaborative performance management: Present gaps and future research. *International Journal of Productivity and Performance Management, 55*(1), 7–25. doi:10.1108/17410400610635471

Byoung-Chun, H., Yang-Kyu, P., & Cho, S. (2011). Suppliers' affective trust and trust in competency in buyers: Its effect on collaboration and logistics efficiency. *International Journal of Operations & Production Management, 31*(1), 56–77. doi:10.1108/01443571111098744

Cao, M., & Zhang, Q. (2011). Supply chain collaboration: Impact on collaborative advantage and firm performance. *Journal of Operations Management, 29*(3), 163-180. doi:10.1016/j.jom.2010.12.008

Challender, J., Farrell, P., & Sherratt, F. (2016). Effects of an economic downturn on construction partnering. *Proceedings of Institution of Civil Engineers: Management, Procurement and Law, 169*(4), 159–167. doi:10.1680/jmapl.15.00033

Chen, J. V., Yen, D. C., Rajkumar, T., & Tomochko, N. A. (2011). The antecedent factors on trust and commitment in supply chain relationships. *Computer Standards & Interfaces, 33*(3), 262-270. doi:10.1016/j.csi.2010.05.003

Cheung, Y.-L., Kong, D., Tan, W., & Wang, W. (2015). Being Good When Being International in an Emerging Economy: The Case of China. *Journal of Business Ethics, 130*(4), 805–817. doi:10.100710551-014-2268-7

Coughlan, A. T. (2002). Channel Management: Structure, Governance, and Relationship Management. In *Handbook of Marketing*. Sage Publications.

Curtis, A. M., Wells, T. M., Lowry, P. B., & Higbee, T. (2008). An Overview and Tutorial of the Repertory Grid Technique in Information Systems Research. Communications of the Association for Information Systems, 23. doi:10.17705/1CAIS.02303

Davis, C. J., & Hufnagel, E. M. (2007). Through the eyes of experts: A socio-cognitive perspective on the automation of fingerprint work. *Management Information Systems Quarterly, 31*(4), 681–703. doi:10.2307/25148816

De Ruyter, K., Moorman, L., & Lemmink, J. (2001). Antecedents of commitment and trust in customer-supplier relationships in high technology markets. *Industrial Marketing Management, 30*(3), 271-286. doi:10.1016/S0019-8501(99)00091-7

De Wever, S., Lievens, A., Martens, R., & Vandenbempt, K. (2005). Developing capabilities through networks: a step-by-step process. In S. Ron & H. Aime (Eds.), *Competence Perspectives on Managing Interfirm Interactions* (Vol. 8, pp. 71–110). Emerald Group Publishing Limited. doi:10.1016/S0749-6826(04)08004-7

Doukidis, G. I., Matopoulos, A., Vlachopoulou, M., Manthou, V., & Manos, B. (2007). A conceptual framework for supply chain collaboration: Empirical evidence from the agri-food industry. *Supply Chain Management, 12*(3), 177–186. doi:10.1108/13598540710742491

Easterby-Smith, M., Thorpe, R., & Holman, D. (1996). Using repertory grids in management. *Journal of European Industrial Training, 20*(3), 3–30. doi:10.1108/03090599610114138

Ebrahim-Khanjari, N., Hopp, W., & Iravani, S. M. R. (2012). Trust and information sharing in supply chains [Review]. *Production and Operations Management, 21*(3), 444–464. doi:10.1111/j.1937-5956.2011.01284.x

Feixas, G., Geldschläger, H., & Neimeyer, R. A. (2002). Content analysis of personal constructs. *Journal of Constructivist Psychology, 15*(1), 1–19. doi:10.1080/107205302753305692

Fiske, A. (1990). Relativity within Moose ("Mossi") Culture: Four Incommensurable Models for Social Relationships. *Ethos (Berkeley, Calif.), 18*(2), 180–204. doi:10.1525/eth.1990.18.2.02a00040

Friman, M., Gärling, T., Millett, B., Mattsson, J., & Johnston, R. (2002). An analysis of international business-to-business relationships based on the Commitment–Trust theory. *Industrial Marketing Management, 31*(5), 403–409. doi:10.1016/S0019-8501(01)00154-7

Gulati, R. (1995). Does familiarity breed trust? The implications of repeated ties for contractual choice in alliances. *Academy of Management Journal, 38*(1), 85–112. doi:10.5465/256729

Gulati, R., & Sytch, M. (2007). Dependence asymmetry and joint dependence in interorganizational relationships: Effects of embeddedness on a manufacturer's performance in procurement relationships. *Administrative Science Quarterly, 52*(1), 32–69. doi:10.2189/asqu.52.1.32

Ha, B., Park, Y., & Cho, S. (2011). Suppliers' affective trust and trust in competency in buyers: Its effect on collaboration and logistics efficiency. *International Journal of Operations & Production Management, 31*(1), 56–77. doi:10.1108/01443571111098744

Hafeez, K., Hooi Keoy, K., & Hanneman, R. (2006). E-business capabilities model: Validation and comparison between adopter and non-adopter of e-business companies in UK. *Journal of Manufacturing Technology Management, 17*(6), 806–828. doi:10.1108/17410380610678819

Hair, N., Rose, S., & Clark, M. (2009). Using qualitative repertory grid techniques to explore perceptions of business-to-business online customer experience. *Journal of Customer Behaviour, 8*(1), 51–65. doi:10.1362/147539209X414380

Hausman, A., & Johnston, W. J. (2010). The impact of coercive and non-coercive forms of influence on trust, commitment, and compliance in supply chains. *Industrial Marketing Management, 39*(3), 519–526. doi:10.1016/j.indmarman.2009.05.007

Hunter, M. G. (1997). The use of RepGrids to gather interview data about information systems analysts. *Information Systems Journal, 7*(1), 67–81. doi:10.1046/j.1365-2575.1997.00005.x

Hutchinson, D., Singh, J., Svensson, G., & Mysen, T. (2012). Inter-relationships among focal dimensions in relationship quality: A quantitative and exploratory approach. *International Journal of Procurement Management, 5*(2), 229–252. doi:10.1504/IJPM.2012.045651

Joshi, A. W., & Stump, R. L. (1999). The contingent effect of specific asset investments on joint action in manufacturer-supplier relationships: An empirical test of the moderating role of reciprocal asset investments, uncertainty, and trust. *Journal of the Academy of Marketing Science, 27*(3), 291–305. doi:10.1177/0092070399273001

Kwon, I. W. G., & Suh, T. (2004). Factors affecting the level of trust and commitment in supply chain relationships. *The Journal of Supply Chain Management, 40*(1), 4–14. doi:10.1111/j.1745-493X.2004.tb00165.x

Laeequddin, M., Sahay, B. S., Sahay, V., & Abdul Waheed, K. (2012). Trust building in supply chain partners relationship: An integrated conceptual model. *Journal of Management Development, 31*(6), 550–564. doi:10.1108/02621711211230858

Langan-Fox, J., & Tan, P. (1997). Images of a culture in transition: Personal constructs of organizational stability and change. *Journal of Occupational and Organizational Psychology, 70*(3), 273–293. doi:10.1111/j.2044-8325.1997.tb00648.x

Langfield-Smith, K. (2008). The relations between transactional characteristics, trust and risk in the start-up phase of a collaborative alliance. *Management Accounting Research, 19*(4), 344–364. doi:10.1016/j.mar.2008.09.001

Liu, A. M. M., Fellows, R., & Ng, J. (2004). Surveyors' perspectives on ethics in organisational culture. *Engineering, Construction, and Architectural Management, 11*(6), 438–449. doi:10.1108/09699980410570193

Liu, Y., Luo, Y., Huang, Y., & Yang, Q. (2017). A diagnostic model of private control and collective control in buyer-supplier relationships. *Industrial Marketing Management, 63*, 116–128. doi:10.1016/j.indmarman.2016.11.003

Lui, S. S., Wong, Y.-y., & Liu, W. (2009). Asset specificity roles in interfirm cooperation: Reducing opportunistic behavior or increasing cooperative behavior? *Journal of Business Research, 62*(11), 1214–1219. doi:10.1016/j.jbusres.2008.08.003

Luiz, A. L. B., Eliane, P. Z. B., & Hashiba, L. H. (2014). What type of cooperation with suppliers and customers leads to superior performance? *Journal of Business Research, 67*(5), 952-959. doi:10.1016/j.jbusres.2013.07.015

McEvily, B., Zaheer, A., & Kamal, D. K. F. (2017). Mutual and exclusive: Dyadic sources of trust in interorganizational exchange. *Organization Science, 28*(1), 74–92. doi:10.1287/orsc.2016.1102

Meng, X. (2015). The role of trust in relationship development and performance improvement. *Journal of Civil Engineering and Management, 21*(7), 845–853. doi:10.3846/13923730.2014.893923

Morgan, R. M., & Hunt, S. D. (1994). The commitment-trust theory of relationship marketing. *Journal of Marketing, 58*(3), 20–38. doi:10.1177/002224299405800302

Mouzas, S., Henneberg, S., & Naudé, P. (2007). Trust and reliance in business relationships. *European Journal of Marketing, 41*(9/10), 1016–1032. doi:10.1108/03090560710773327

Moynihan, T. (1996). An inventory of personal constructs for information systems project risk researchers. *Journal of Information Technology, 11*(4), 359–371. doi:10.1177/026839629601100409

Nannestad, P. (2008). What have we learned about generalized trust, if anything? *Annual Review of Political Science, 11*(1), 413–436. doi:10.1146/annurev.polisci.11.060606.135412

Nyaga, G. N., Whipple, J. M., & Lynch, D. F. (2010). Examining supply chain relationships: Do buyer and supplier perspectives on collaborative relationships differ? *Journal of Operations Management, 28*(2), 101–114. doi:10.1016/j.jom.2009.07.005

Poppo, L., Zhou, K. Z., & Ryu, S. (2008). Alternative origins to interorganizational trust: An interdependence perspective on the shadow of the past and the shadow of the future. *Organization Science, 19*(1), 39–55. doi:10.1287/orsc.1070.0281

Powell, W. W., Koput, K. W., & Smith-Doerr, L. (1996). Interorganizational collaboration and the locus of innovation: Networks of learning in biotechnology. *Administrative Science Quarterly, 41*(1), 116–145. doi:10.2307/2393988

Powers, T. L., & Reagan, W. R. (2007). Factors influencing successful buyer-seller relationships. *Journal of Business Research, 60*(12), 1234–1242. doi:10.1016/j.jbusres.2007.04.008

Redondo, Y. P., & Cambra Fierro, J. J. (2008). Educational level as moderating element of long-term orientation of supply relationships. *Journal of Marketing Management, 24*(3-4), 383–408. doi:10.1362/026725708X306158

Rokkan, A. I., Heide, J. B., & Wathne, K. H. (2003). Specific investments in marketing relationships: Expropriation and bonding effects. *JMR, Journal of Marketing Research, 40*(2), 210–224. doi:10.1509/jmkr.40.2.210.19223

Ryciuk, U., & Nazarko, J. (2020). Model of trust-based cooperative relationships in a supply chain. *Journal of Business Economics and Management, 21*(5), 1225–1247. doi:10.3846/jbem.2020.12829

Rycroft, R. W., & Kash, D. E. (2004). Self-organizing innovation networks: Implications for globalization. *Technovation, 24*(3), 187–197. doi:10.1016/S0166-4972(03)00092-0

Sahay, B. S. (2003). Understanding trust in supply chain relationships. *Industrial Management & Data Systems, 103*(8), 553–563. doi:10.1108/02635570310497602

Sako, M., & Helper, S. (1998). Determinants of trust in supplier relations: Evidence from the automotive industry in Japan and the United States. *Journal of Economic Behavior & Organization, 34*(3), 387–417. doi:10.1016/S0167-2681(97)00082-6

Sambharya, R., & Lee, J. (2014). Renewing Dynamic Capabilities Globally: An Empirical Study of the World's Largest MNCs. *MIR. Management International Review*, *54*(2), 137–169. doi:10.100711575-013-0199-7

Sarkar, M., Aulakh, P. S., & Cavusgil, S. T. (1998). The strategic role of relational bonding in interorganizational collaborations: An empirical study of the global construction industry. *Journal of International Management*, *4*(2), 85–107. doi:10.1016/S1075-4253(98)00009-X

Schmidt, C. G., & Wagner, S. M. (2019). Blockchain and supply chain relations: A transaction cost theory perspective. *Journal of Purchasing and Supply Management*, *25*(4), 100552. doi:10.1016/j.pursup.2019.100552

Spekman, R. E., & Carraway, R. (2006). Making the transition to collaborative buyer-seller relationships: An emerging framework. *Industrial Marketing Management*, *35*(1), 10–19. doi:10.1016/j.indmarman.2005.07.002

Tan, F. B., & Hunter, M. G. (2002). The Repertory Grid Technique: A Method for the Study of Cognition in Information Systems. *Management Information Systems Quarterly*, *26*(1), 39–57. doi:10.2307/4132340

Tan, K. C. (2002). Supply chain management: Practices, concerns, and performance issues. *The Journal of Supply Chain Management*, *38*(4), 42–53. doi:10.1111/j.1745-493X.2002.tb00119.x

Tanskanen, K., & Aminoff, A. (2015). Buyer and supplier attractiveness in a strategic relationship—A dyadic multiple-case study. *Industrial Marketing Management*, *50*, 128–141. doi:10.1016/j.indmarman.2015.04.011

The SCM Journal List. (n.d.). http://www.scmlist.com/

Ting, S., Chen, C., & Bartholomew, D. E. (2007). An integrated study of entrepreneurs' opportunism. *Journal of Business and Industrial Marketing*, *22*(5), 322–335. doi:10.1108/08858620710773459

Turner, J. R. (2004). Farsighted project contract management: Incomplete in its entirety. *Construction Management and Economics*, *22*(1), 75–83. doi:10.1080/0144619042000186077

Uzzi, B. (1996). The Sources and Consequences of Embeddedness for the Economic Performance of Organizations: The Network Effect. *American Sociological Review*, *61*(4), 674–698. doi:10.2307/2096399

van Weele, A. J., & van Raaij, E. M. (2014). The future of purchasing and supply management research: About relevance and rigor. *The Journal of Supply Chain Management*, *50*(1), 56–72. doi:10.1111/jscm.12042

Verdecho, M. J., Alfaro, J. J., & Rodriguez-Rodriguez, R. (2009). Foundations for collaborative performance measurement. *Production Planning and Control*, *20*(3), 193–205. doi:10.1080/09537280902721001

Wood, L. C., & Wang, J. X. (2018). The Event Study Method in Logistics Research: Overview and a Critical Analysis. *International Journal of Applied Logistics*, *8*(1), 57–79. doi:10.4018/IJAL.2018010104

Wright, R. P., & Cheung, F. K. K. (2007). Articulating appraisal system effectiveness based on managerial cognitions. *Personnel Review*, *36*(2), 206–230. doi:10.1108/00483480710726118

Yoon, J., & Moon, J. (2019). The moderating effect of buyer purchasing strategy on the relationship between supplier transaction-specific investment and supplier firm performance. *Journal of Business Research*, *99*, 516–523. doi:10.1016/j.jbusres.2017.08.022

Zawislak, P. A., Cherubini Alves, A., Tello-Gamarra, J., Barbieux, D., & Reichert, F. M. (2012). Innovation capability: From technology development to transaction capability. *Journal of Technology Management & Innovation*, *7*(2), 14–27. doi:10.4067/S0718-27242012000200002

Zhou, G., Fei, Y., & Hu, J. (2016). The analysis of vertical transaction behavior and performance based on automobile brand trust in supply chain. *Discrete Dynamics in Nature and Society*, *2016*, 1–13. Advance online publication. doi:10.1155/2016/4793851

Chapter 3

Use of Traffic Simulation to Analyze the Changes in City Mobility During the COVID-19 Pandemic

Simona Šinko
University of Maribor, Slovenia

Bojan Rupnik
University of Maribor, Slovenia

Roman Gumzej
https://orcid.org/0000-0002-2646-217X
University of Maribor, Slovenia

ABSTRACT

It seems that the COVID-19 pandemic, which started in December 2019, will have longer and more profound consequences on our lives than initially foreseen. Among the most obvious are everyday decisions about the mode of transport. From related research, it can be seen that the most affected transport mode is public transport, which had the greatest decline. The reason for lesser use of public transport is in complete closure of public transport in some parts of the world. However, where this measure has not been applied, the reason for the reduction is people's fear of infection when using public transport or any shared modes of transportation. The fear stems from the fact that the COVID-19 virus is spreading extremely fast in densely populated rooms. All these changes are affecting the changes in city mobility. Related research shows a decrease of mobility in general and an increase in the use of individual modes of transportation. Distinct changes can be observed in different environments as compared to previous travel behaviour.

DOI: 10.4018/978-1-7998-8709-6.ch003

INTRODUCTION

The pandemic caused by the SARS-CoV-2 (COVID-19) pandemic impacts every aspect of our lives and represents the unique situation in the last few decades (de Haas, Faber & Hamersma, 2020). All the consequences caused by the virus are not seen yet when the spreading is not entirely stopped at the time (Award- Núñez, Julio, Gomez, Moya- Gómez & González, 2021).

The beginning of the spread of the virus dated to 2019 when it was detected in the Chinese city of Wuhan. However, due to the rapid spread, the first cases of the disease around the world were soon detected, so on January 30, 2020, the World Health Organization (WHO) declared COVID-19 as an international public health concern, and on March 11, 2020, declared a pandemic (WHO, 2020).

The virus impact is also noticeable in people's activity patterns, the workplace (many people started to work from home, where this is possible), and how they travel (de Haas et al., 2020). The outbreak of the virus has caused lead not only to work from home but also higher unemployment (De Vos, 2020). Different measures have been taken to prevent the spread of the virus worldwide (Fisher & Wilder-Smith, 2020; Sohrabi et al., 2020; Wilder-Smith & Freedman, 2020; Zhang et al., 2020). The measures taken are labelled as "social distancing" measurements (Wilder-Smith & Freedman, 2020). They are very suitable for preventing the infection with the viruses transmitted by exhaled droplets and requiring a certain closeness of people to transmit like COVID-19. Social-distancing measures, case isolation, and shielding have been used to limit transmission of the virus and protect the most vulnerable groups (Chen, Yang, Yang, Wang, & Bärnighausen, 2020; Tian et al., 2020). Human mobility is considered the primary driver of the virus spreading in several parts of the world. So the many restrictions were just in the field of mobility (Li et al., 2020). Several studies based on comparing the mobility data before the virus outbreak and the first wave have shown that mobility had undergone a significant change (Oliver et al., 2020). The first studies focused on mobility trends, and their most important finding is the noticeable reduction in mobility. A decrease in mobility depends on the countries and measures taken, but the reduction is seen everywhere (Gao et al., 2020; Lee et al., 2020; Pepe et al., 2020). Furthermore, the first studies also noticed the importance of demographic characteristics on reactions to the virus situation (Van Dorn, Cooney, & Sabin, 2020). For example, people with higher socioeconomic status are more likely to avoid the city (Coven & Gupta, 2020).

Mobility restrictions were taken on different levels. Some of them were taken on a local or regional level. The most common was limiting the length of walking or motorized movements from home. On an international level, the most common was the closure of entire regions or counties (Cereda et al., 2020). Such rigorous measures were taken mainly were because the burden on COVID-19 patients in hospitals was very high.

In many countries, mobility restrictions have proved to be an effective way to reduce the spread of the virus (Nouvellet et al., 2021). But to apply measures in the future and add some new one, it is important to understand their effects in detail (Schlosser et al., 2020).

The first important fact that need to be mentioned is a general reduction in the number of trips caused by the mentioned measures. This reduction is the consequence of e-learning, remote working and cancelling the cultural and sporting events and other social events (Shi et al., 2019). In France, the study has shown that reduction is most noticeable in the usual rush hours because of the school closing and working from home (Pullano, Valdano, Scarpa, Rubrichi & Colizza, 2020). Some other study reveals reduced grocery shopping trips (de Haas et al., 2020). The grocery shopping trips reduction might be the consequence of increased ordering of the grocery with home delivery (Shi et al., 2019).

The effects may continue to be visible after the spread of the COVID-19. The changes may be seen in the people's interaction with each other and their travel habits. Although measures related to social distance may no longer be mandatory, people will still be inclined to avoid close contact. De Vos (2020) argues that people will travel less in the future and avoid trips with public transportation. With the expected lower use of public transport, it is also expected to avoid using sharing systems like car-sharing and bike-sharing. Vehicle sharing systems are also expected to have a greater chance of transmitting the virus (Hensher, 2020).

Car owners may also decide to drive independently more often than before the outbreak of the virus because of the fear of infection. However, because of the reduced travel demand (remote work and remote school), their decisions may not cause greater distances driven by car. Because of this, no major road congestion and greater traffic congestion are expected than was the case before the virus outbreak. Many countries observe reduced car traffic, resulting in a noticeable reduction in air pollution (De Vos, 2020).

On the other hand, the expected trend is in the greater use of walking and cycling with own bikes (Schewdhelm et al., 2020), which represent active transport mode. The trend is seen based on the research that shown the increased number of trips by bike (Aloi et al., 2020; Huang et al., 2020). With walking and cycling, social contact could be completely eliminated or reduced to a minimum (De Vos, 2020), so these two modes are suitable for reducing the chances of infection. The increase in the use of walking and cycling may also be due to a decrease in the possibilities for outdoor recreation and entertainment, so more people are opting for them than in the past, when much more outdoor activities were allowed (De Vos, 2020).

The reduction of personal trips was seen in every part of the world. The most significant was the reduction of public transport use (Aloi et al., 2020; Bucsky, 2020; de Haas, Faber, & Hamersma, 2020). In Germany, for example, 25% of people participating in the survey claim that they totally stopped using public transport and 17% claim that they reduce the number of trips done with public transport (ADAC, 2020).

For many years, public transport has been regarded as a sustainable and green mode of transport. Today operators of public transport are facing challenges in keeping their customers despite the presence of a virus (Faass, Greenberg, & Lowrie, 2013). According to many studies, public transport represents the greatest potential for virus transmission among all means of transportation (Sirkeci & Yucesahin, 2020). One possible solution to maintain the minimum level of public transport users is to develop and invest in biosecurity measures (Faass et al., 2013).

An interesting fact is revealed by the (König & Dreßler, 2021) research. People were asked how their transport habits have changed, and their answers show different results than objective measurements of transport.

BACKGROUND – THE CITY OF MARIBOR

With a population 110,461 (2020 data), Maribor is the second-largest city in Slovenia. The city is the seat of the Municipality of Maribor. It is considered the economic, financial, administrative, educational, cultural, commercial and tourist centre of the whole of north-eastern Slovenia. The city's plan shows a mostly rectangular network of roads and buildings along with them in a north-south and west-east direction (Maribor, n. d.). Among the larger cities in Slovenia, Maribor is the city with the highest share of the elderly population and has the highest ageing index (Horvat, 2019).

In Šinko and Gumzej (2021), we showed that road closures might negatively affect the city transport system if all the people who have driven cars do not choose any other transport mode. At the time of writing before mentioned work and writing the continued version, one of the main traffic roads in the city was closed for the transport completely (the road is marked with red colour on the map) except for small buses that have citywide access.

Figure 1. Map of the sample city from the OSM web wizard

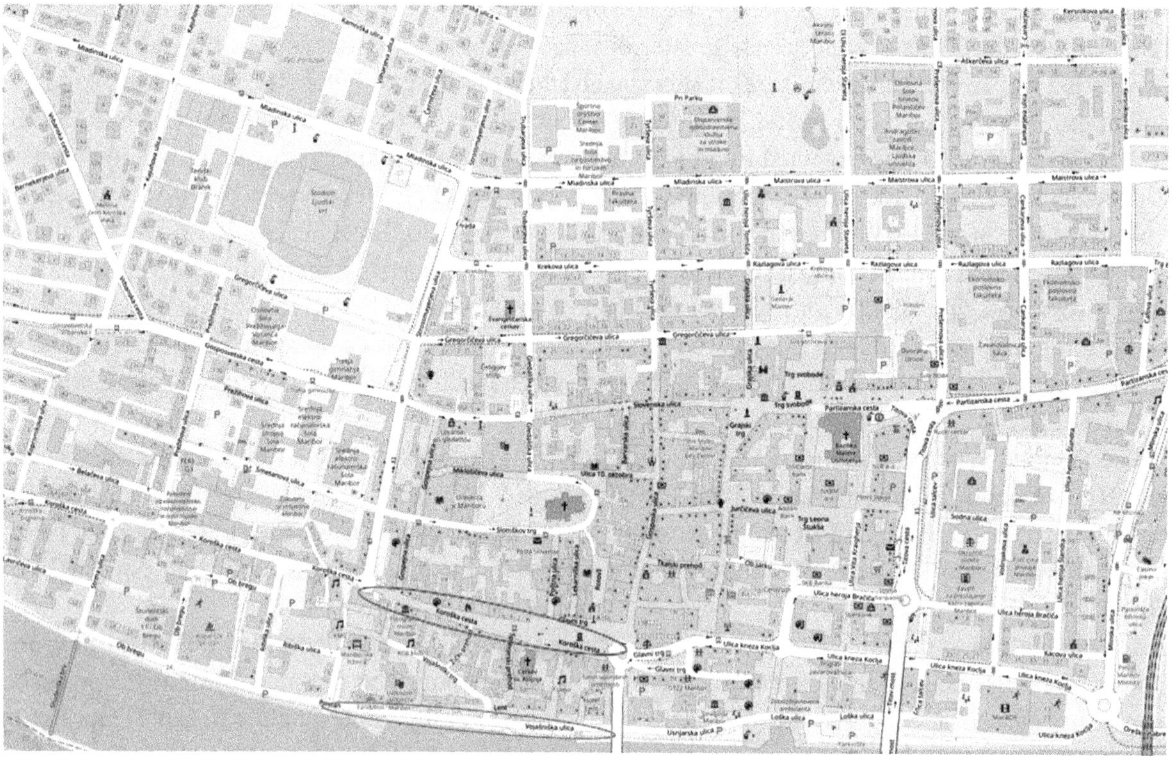

With the closing of such important road for the city, more than half of the road traffic was diverted to the road along the river (marked green on map). According to measurements, this alternative road is a part of a protected area of the city and due to the closure of Koroška cesta, according to measurements, as many as 10,000 vehicles drive here daily. The planned comprehensive renovation of Lent, which is expected to begin in 2021, will also temporarily close this transport connection (Klipšteter, 2020). Of course, this number would be even higher if people did not opt for a different mode of transport due to changes in traffic regulations. Traffic measurements used to monitor changes due to road closures in the run-up to the epidemic show that some people have already opted for a different mode of travel. If the municipality continues to promote walking, cycling and other forms of active mobility and optimize public transport, the need for infrastructure for cars will be reduced. Even more, residents will opt for travel modes that positively impact health and the environment and contribute to a more pleasant life in the city (Inštitut za politike prostora, 2021).

After the outbreak of COVID-19, there is concern that public transport will decrease and people will use car transport more. As seen in the introductory part, the measures taken worldwide were also aimed at reducing close contact between people, i.e., reducing the use or abolishing the use of public transport altogether.

The Municipality of Maribor also adopted a decision on the complete cessation of urban passenger traffic in Maribor in March and April (Mariborinfo, 2020) to curb the spread of coronavirus infection.

The Slovenian Consumers' Association conducted a survey, which shows that the use of public transport in Slovenia fell by 16%. The use of other modes of transport also decreased slightly (walking by 3%, car use by 2%, car use as a passenger decreased by 9% and bicycle use by 5%) (Zveza potrošnikov Slovenije, 2020). The use of public transport in Slovenia decreased the most among students who were primarily public transport users before the outbreak of the virus. The decrease is because, since the beginning of October 2020, the study has primarily taken place online. The share of respondents who take a taxi at least occasionally also dropped, and in October, there were slightly fewer of those who walk or cycle. The results are similar in other countries, but the share of cyclists has increased somewhat. The general reduction in the use of various means of transport is a consequence of the country's measures in October. One of the most important reasons for reducing the use of public transport is certainly people's fear of infection. The survey, conducted by the Consumers' Association of Slovenia, fears as many as 70% of participants fear infection when using public transport, 51% when using taxis and 35% when using a car from the rental system. Fear of other ways of sharing vehicles was expressed by 26% of respondents (Zveza potrošnikov Slovenije, 2020).

METHODOLOGY

We used a simulation to show the impact of the COVID-19 epidemic on city traffic flows. Simulations models are useful to show the behaviour of different systems and play a significant role in four steps (Baudrillard, 2018):

1. Scientific understanding
2. system development in technology
3. system management
4. development planning.

Shannon (1975) wrote that simulation is "the process of designing a model of a real system and conducting experiments with this model for the purpose either of understanding the behavior of the system or of evaluating various strategies (within limits imposed by a criterion or set of criteria) for the operation of the system."

Traffic simulations are capable of emulating the time variability of traffic phenomena because they capture the complexity of traffic systems (Krajzewicz, 2010). For the purpose of our research, we use the SUMO environment. SUMO refers to "Simulation of Urban Mobility" and is a microscopic road traffic simulation ("Simulation of Urban Mobility," 2019). SUMO is open-source software and is suitable for the simulation of road transport traffic of the size of a city, not for bigger networks (Krajzewicz, 2010).

Microscopic road traffic simulation means that each vehicle or other participant in the transport is modelled individually. All entities have a certain place and speed (Krajzewicz, 2010; Krauss, 1998). Besides microscopic simulation, there are macroscopic (where simulation bases on average vehicle dynamics), mesoscopic (which is a mixture of macroscopic and microscopic model) and sub microscopic (where each function inside the vehicle is explicitly simulated) simulations (Krauss, 1998).

SUMO's most important advantage is derivation of the safety gap vehicles must maintain to prevent collision with the vehicle in front of it. Another important advantage of the SUMO is that assumption that drivers are not perfect in realizing the desired speed. The driver imperfection is implemented by the stochastic deceleration (Lopez et al., 2018). The routes through the network are computed using Dijkstra routing algorithm (Dijkstra, 1959).

From the OpenStreetMaps (OSM), which is the part of SUMO package, we downloaded the map of the sample city area of Maribor (Figure 1). In the section for vehicles, we formed the randomized traffic demand (cars, trucks, buses, motorcycles, bicycles and pedestrians) for simulation based on certain probability distribution, which depends on the Through Traffic Factor and Count parameter. The formula to calculate the count parameter is presented below (Equation 1). Count parameter (Sumo, 2019a): "defines how many vehicles are generated per hour and lane-kilometre".

Count factor:

$$count\ parameter = \frac{number\ of\ vehicles\ in\ one\ hour}{length\ of\ roads} \tag{1}$$

For the number of vehicles was used the numbers described in Šinko and Gumzej (2021), the length of roads was obtained from SUMO.

OSM online wizard randomly selects the departure and arrival edge for each vehicle in the system. The Through Traffic Factor determines how many times the selected edge is more likely to be at the boundary of the simulation area compared to the edge that is entirely within the simulation area. The high value of the traffic flow factor means that many vehicles leave and arrive at the simulation area boundary, which corresponds to a scenario with a lot of traffic flow (Sumo, 2019a).

The traffic network in SUMO-context is a directed graph. The network shows the part of the city map that is related to traffic. It includes roads and intersections on which simulated vehicles drive. The network includes following information about all streets and roads (presented as a collection of lines, with the information of its position, shape and speed limit), all junctions (with the traffic rules in force), traffic light logics, all nodes, districts, roundabout (Sumo, 2019a).

The trips for vehicles in a simulation are defined in an additional file and are presented in Table 1.

Simulation in SUMO is based on Krauss(1998) car-following model. The parameters used in the model are presented in Table 2. The primary model assumption is that vehicles could drive as fast as possible while maintaining safety.

Vehicles are wary of pedestrians. When some pedestrians cross the road, the vehicle is forced to stop. If pedestrians and vehicles are on the same lane, the vehicle will do everything to avoid a collision (Sumo, 2019b).

Table 1. Definition of the individual parts of the command for trips

	Definition
id	uniquely identification number of the vehicle in the simulation which consist of type and generated number
type	defines the type of the vehicle in the simulation
depart	defines the trip star time
departLane	defines the lane on which the vehicle shall start
from	origin point on the map
to	destination point

Source: Sumo, 2019b

Table 2. The parameters used in the Krauß car following model

Parameter	tau	accel	decel	minGap	impatience	sigma	maxSpeed
Value	1.45	2.78-3.25	4.5	2	0.5	0	100

Source: Bjärkvik et al., 2017

The safety speed for vehicle is calculated by the formula (Song et al., 2014ši):

$$v_{safe} = v_l(t) + \frac{g(t) - v_l(t) \cdot t_r}{\frac{v_l(t) + v_f(t)}{2b} + t_r}$$

where v_l is the speed of leading vehicle in queue, $g(t)$ is the gap between the specific vehicle and the leading one, t_r is the reaction time of driver and b is a maximum deceleration of the vehicle.

In the simulation we used 6 different type of traffic participants. The specific values for their traffic behaviour are defined in Table 3.

Table 3. Specific values for participants in simulation

Type	minGap [m]	Accel $\left[m/s^2\right]$	Decel $\left[m/s^2\right]$	Emergency Decal $\left[m/s^2\right]$	maxSpeed $\left[km/h\right]$	Seats	emissionClass
Pedestrian	0.25	1.5	2	5	5.4	-	zero
Bicycle	0.5	1.2	3	7	20	1	zero
Motorcycle	2.5	6	10	10	200	2	LDV_G_EU6
Car	2.5	2.9	7.5	9	180	5	LDV_G_EU4
Truck	2.5	1.3	4	7	130	3	HDV
Bus	2.5	1	4	7	130	2	HDV

Souce: Sumo, 2019b

The outputs give the information about number of vehicles in the system, time the participants need from starting point to their destination, reasons for lane change, length of queue, speed of all participants in every second, gap between vehicles in the queen and environmental indicators like amount of CO_2, CO, HC, NO_X, PM_X, noise and fuel consumption.

Scenarios

As already pointed out, the emergence of COVID-19 has changed many aspects of life. One of the more noticeable changes is also the perception of mobility and the choice of means of transport. It is essential to understand the impacts of changes on transport activity in cities. Only by detailed analysis and understanding of traffic events is it possible to plan cities' further development and mobility.

To show the changes caused by the pandemic in traffic flows around the city, we took the example of the city centre of Maribor (Slovenia) and formulated three different scenarios:

- Pre-COVID-19 situation
- The situation with strict measures
- The situation with milder measures

Pre COVID-19 situation is based on the scenario from (Šinko & Gumzej, 2021), where we took into account the regular use of means of transport. We partly considered the foreseen road closure we mentioned in chapter two, so the results are not the same as in the aforementioned article.

The situation with strict measures considers the time during the pandemic when all social activities were cancelled, public transport did not operate, students were educated from home, and most of the work, where possible, took place from home, crossings between municipalities were prohibited, except for a small number of exceptions.

In the situation with milder measures, the restrictions and measures are still present, but life returns to normal. Social activities are possible with certain limitations. Public transport is operational, however there is a limit on the number of people who can travel together. Safety distances between people need to be maintained, even on public transport. Wearing a mask is mandatory, and in most cases, people have returned to their workplaces, schools, and colleges.

RESULTS

In this chapter, the results of the three scenarios described in the previous chapter will be presented.

Number of Vehicles

To observe the changes in traffic situation because of the outbreak of COVID-19 virus, we use the facts about the pandemic situation in Slovenia described in the second chapter and the final participants in the different scenarios are presented in the different scenarios Table 4.

The situation with strict measures represents the time where the measures imposed staying at home, except in exceptional cases (the economy was still operating). Hence, the number of traffic participants in this scenario is lower than prior to COVID-19. Only the number of trucks is larger, because the ordering of household products and other necessities from home increased during the pandemic. In situation with milder measures, fewer people opt for public transport, so the frequency of their operation is slightly lower. More people than before the virus outbreak use a car, a bicycle and motorcycle, representing the modes of transport reducing the contacts with others, and hereby the chances of transmitting the infection are smaller. Because of the decisions of residents who used public transport before and now travel alone, the total number of vehicles in the last scenario has increased.

Table 4. Number of participants in the different transport situations

Type of Transport Mode/Number of Vehicles	Pre COVID-19 Situation	Situation With Strict Measures	Situation With Milder Measures
Automobile	3021	2322	3307
Motorcycle	163	128	269
Truck	75	96	94
Bus	82	0	34
Bicycle	417	128	612
Total	**3758**	**2604**	**4316**

Average Journey Time

The critical factor besides the number of vehicles in the system is the time spent on the journey from the start point to the destination point, depending on various factors. The most crucial factor is the density of road users. The average time spent in the system, divided according to the type of road users, is presented in Table 5.

As a result of the lower traffic density in the city during strict measures, the times required to travel from the starting point to the destination are much shorter. For automobiles, the times have decreased by about 47% and for trucks by about 60%. The situation with milder measures has a greater time-span for cars than prior to COVID-19 (for about 13%). Trucks and buses spent less time on their routes than before the pandemic, but the reduction in time was not very noticeable. In addition to the traffic density, the average time-span in the system also depends on the length of the route taken by additional participants in a situation with milder measures. The shorter times for trucks and buses may therefore be due to the fact that the routes for the new participants were shorter than in the Pre COVID-19 situation.

Table 5. Average time spent in the system

Type of Transport Mode/Time [s]	Pre COVID-19 Situation	Situation With Strict Measures	Situation With Milder Measures
Automobile	651,66	301,93	742,52
Truck	593,54	355,18	572,59
Bus	567,47	/	561,43
Bicycle	489,67	304,43	414,19
Motorcycle	535,65	266,14	540,04

Lane Change

Lane changes could be one of the indicators of driver behaviour in traffic and can significantly impact road safety and characteristics of traffic flow (Sparmann, 1979). The lane changes also can have an impact on traffic capacity (Jin, 2010). The number of lane changes due to the reason for performing change is presented in Table 6.

Table 6. Reasons for lane change

Reason	Pre COVID-19 Situation	Situation With Strict Measures	Situation With Milder Measures
Cooperative	293	230	268
keepRight	583	559	604
SpeedGain	235	170	196
Strategic	370	315	350
Strategic|urgent	3264	2244	2880

Strategic lane changes present the situations when the vehicles need to change the lane in order to reach the next edge on it's way to the destination. Urgent means that lane change was done because of a road's dead end or occupancy at the final destination. SpeedGain presents the situation when the desired lane change cannot be performed due to vehicle locking, the vehicle can adjust its speed to allow successful lane change in later steps. Cooperative means that the driver performs a lane change maneuver with the sole purpose of assisting another vehicle in changing lanes towards his own (Erdmann, 2015).

More important than mere number of shifts is the structure of the causes for lane changes. From the data in the table, we can see that the number of lane changes decreased in pandemic-related scenarios. The structure of the reasons for changes is shown in Figure 2.

Figure 2. The structure of the reasons for lane change

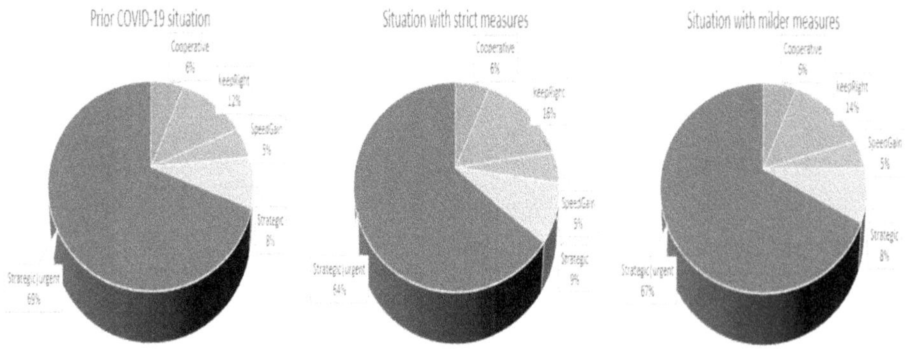

One can observe that the structure of the reasons for the lane change did not change with the change of the scenarios. In all these derived scenarios, the most common reason for changing the road lane is urgent (between 54% and 69%). The following most common reason is keepRight (12% to 14%). The lowest share of lane changes is due to speeding (only 5% in all three scenarios).

Traffic Jams

Another critical performance indicator for traffic analysis and later traffic management are congestions. Table 7 presents some important information about the congestions in different scenarios.

Table 7. Traffic jams

	Pre COVID-19 Situation	Situation With Strict Measures	Situation With Milder Measures
Average waiting time of vehicles due to a queue [s]	86	48,97	88,5
The length from the junction until the final vehicle in line [m]	23,8	15,30	25,9
The length of the queue, thus until the last vehicle with speed lower than 5 km/h [m]	22,38	15,84	23,9

The scenario representing the time before COVID-19 is worse in terms of the average waiting time of vehicles in line as opposed to the times obtained from the simulations in the article, as certain roads in the city were closed for traffic. As expected, the waiting time had almost halved during the period when strict restrictions on movement applied. At the time the regulations were released, it was longer than it before the pandemic. The length of queues has also increased by around 8% when the measures were released. Longer waiting times were due to higher traffic density.

Fuel Consumption

Being another important performance indicator, fuel consumption is considered a part of the emissions simulation output in SUMO. The average fuel consumption results from our simulations are presented in Table 8.

Table 8. Fuel consumption

Type of Vehicle/Fuel Consumption [l/s]	Pre COVID-19 Situation	Situation With Strict Measures	Situation With Milder Measures
Truck	104.30	135.21	182.1
Bus	93.97	0	45.42
Motorcycle	35.31	31.79	72.45
Automobile	912.20	535.45	1004.25
Total	1 145.78	702.45	1304.22

As expected, the fuel consumption in time with strict measures have fallen by about 61% because people stayed more at home than before COVID-19. Also, buses did not operate, as they are large fuel consumers. Higher consumption is detected only in trucks. More trucks and vans on the roads during this time than before the epidemic, so results are expected. On the other hand, higher fuel consumption has been perceived over time with milder measures. Increased use of cars, vans and motorcycles contributed the most to the increase in fuel consumption.

Environmental Impact

The simulation results referring to the environmental impact are listed in Table 9. The table contains the average amounts of specific pollutants that have an important impact on humans health.

Table 9. Amount of specific pollutants in different situations

Type of Emission/Amount [kg]	Pre COVID-19 Situation	Situation With Strict Measures	Situation With Milder Measures
CO_2 [kg]	2724.31	1612.58	3078.47
CO [kg]	82.41	49.51	93.13
HC [kg]	0.67	0.43	0.78
NO_X [kg]	6.05	3.63	6.83
PM_X [kg]	0.36	0.21	0.41

The values of most pollutants are related to the total fuel consumption in each scenario. As the traffic density was lower during the strict measures, individual pollutants' amount of emitted emissions have almost halved. On the other hand, there has been a significant increase in emissions during milder measures.

DISCUSSION

Over the past year, people worldwide have been confronted with a new reality due to the highly contagious COVID-19 virus outbreak. The virus has changed the way we think, act and our daily decisions. Actions have been taken worldwide to prevent the spread of the virus, which have limited daily activities. One of the significant changes could also be seen in the decision on the mode of transport. In some places, public transport has come to a complete halt, while in others they have only limited the number of people that can be driven in a vehicle at a time.

Initial analyzes of transport data obtained using mobile devices have shown that the epidemic in the US has led to a sharp decline in mobility in general (Beck & Hensher, 2020; Lee et al., 2020) because many people no longer travel daily due to distance work and education and back, the virus also prevented visits and vacations.

In some places, they report an 80% reduction in the use of public transport (Bernhardt, 2020; de Haas et al., 2020), in some areas up to 90% (McKinsey & Company Automotive & Assembly, 2020). One of the more substantial reasons for reducing the use of public transport is undoubtedly the fear of contracting the virus (de Haas et al., 2020). However, where public transport operates despite the spread of the virus, public transport operators and users are subject to strict hygiene protocols (wearing a protective mask, conducting medical examinations, maintaining a sufficient distance, limiting the number of passengers) (McKinsey & Company Automotive & Assembly, 2020).

According to research, no such decline in the use of public transport has been detected in Slovenia. In the survey, only 16% of people stopped using public transport (Zveza potrošnikov Slovenije, 2020). In Slovenia, the population is less dependent on public transport and relies more on other modes of transportation. We took this fact into account when designing the simulation scenarios.

CONCLUSION

In this chapter, we wanted to show that simulations of traffic flow at the microscopic level can be helpful in understanding changes due to the virus and its consequences. As noted by the authors before us, one of the positive consequences of the virus outbreak was reducing the use of motorized means and reducing environmental pollution and increasing traffic security. Our results show that the pollution in the city of Maribor, which we took for display, decreased by about 60%, viewed by individual pollutants. Congestion results can confirm the improvement in traffic safety. Congestion in the city has decreased, in line with the reduced traffic density. Traffic was more fluid, waiting in jams was reduced by 50%. According to the Public Transport Agency of the Republic of Slovenia, the number of traffic accidents in 2020 decreased by 21% compared to the previous year due to the measures in force (Javna agencija Republike Slovenije za varnost prometa, 2021).

The results of this work are of great importance for the city administration in their decision-making process for urban traffic planning in the future. Changes in the mobility of people caused by the virus will have to be taken into account in urban traffic planning. For example, to maintain physical distance, some cities, such as Bogota in Colombia, have additionally provided 76 kilometers of bike paths so that residents can maintain physical distance using bicycles. In Oakland, California, 10% of traffic roads have been blocked so that pedestrians and cyclists can easily maintain a sufficient distance (Assembly, 2020). The question arises as to whether these changes will be permanent. What will be the consequences of such changes in the cities when the virus's rapid spread stops? City managers and researchers also face a major challenge in finding a replacement for public transport, which has so far been considered one of the sustainable modes of transport. In many places, road facilities were fully occupied even before the pandemic broke out. What if the number of cars on the roads really increases due to fear of infection? How to reduce the number of vehicles on the roads despite people's fear of infection? Precisely such questions can be answered by simulations as shown in this work.

REFERENCES

ADAC. (2020). *Corona und Mobilität: Mehr Homeoffice, weniger Berufsverkehr.* Retrieved from https://www.adac.de/verkehr/standpunktestudien/mobilitaets-trends/corona-mobilitaet/

Aloi, A., Alonso, B., Benavente, J., Cordera, R., Echániz, E., González, F., ... Mazzei, V. (2020). Effects of the COVID-19 lockdown on urban mobility: Empirical evidence from the city of Santander (Spain). *Sustainability*, *12*(9), 3870. doi:10.3390u12093870

Baudrillard, J. (2018). *Die Simulation*. Akademie Verlag.

Bjärkvik, E., Fürer, F., Pourabdollah, M., & Lindenberg, B. (2017). Simulation and Characterization of Traffic on Drive Me Route around Gothenburg using SUMO. *Proceedings of the SUMO2017-Towards Simulation for Autonomous Mobility*, 1-13.

Bucsky, P. (2020). Modal share changes due to COVID-19: The case of Budapest. *Transportation Research Interdisciplinary Perspectives*, *8*, 100141. doi:10.1016/j.trip.2020.100141 PMID:34171021

Cereda, D., Tirani, M., Rovida, F., Demicheli, V., Ajelli, M., Poletti, P., . . . Barone, A. (2020). *The early phase of the COVID-19 outbreak in Lombardy, Italy*. arXiv preprint arXiv:2003.09320.

de Haas, M., Faber, R., & Hamersma, M. (2020). How COVID-19 and the Dutch 'intelligent lockdown' change activities, work and travel behaviour: Evidence from longitudinal data in the Netherlands. *Transportation Research Interdisciplinary Perspectives*, *6*, 100150. doi:10.1016/j.trip.2020.100150 PMID:34171019

De Vos, J. (2020). The effect of COVID-19 and subsequent social distancing on travel behavior. *Transportation Research Interdisciplinary Perspectives*, *5*, 100121. doi:10.1016/j.trip.2020.100121 PMID:34171016

Dijkstra, E. W. (1959). A note on two problems in connexion with graphs. *Numerische Mathematik*, *1*(1), 269–271. doi:10.1007/BF01386390

Erdmann, J. (2015). SUMO's lane-changing model Modeling Mobility with Open Data. Springer.

Faass, J., Greenberg, M., & Lowrie, K. W. (2013). Defending a moving target: H1N1 preparedness training for the transit industry. *Health Promotion Practice*, *14*(1), 24–29. doi:10.1177/1524839911399432 PMID:21460256

Gao, S., Rao, J., Kang, Y., Liang, Y., & Kruse, J. (2020). Mapping county-level mobility pattern changes in the United States in response to COVID-19. *SIGSpatial Special*, *12*(1), 16–26. doi:10.1145/3404820.3404824

Hensher, D. A. (2020). *What might Covid-19 mean for mobility as a service (MaaS)?* Taylor & Francis.

Horvat, U. (2019). *Prebivalstvo Maribora: razvoj in demografske značilnosti*. Maribor: Univerzitetna založba Univerze v Mariboru.

Huang, J., Wang, H., Fan, M., Zhuo, A., Sun, Y., & Li, Y. (2020). Understanding the impact of the COVID-19 pandemic on transportation-related behaviors with human mobility data. *Proceedings of the 26th ACM SIGKDD International Conference on Knowledge Discovery & Data Mining*. 10.1145/3394486.3412856

Inštitut za politike prostora. (2021). *Mestna občina Maribor spodbuja aktivno in trajnostno mobilnost*. Retrieved from https://ipop.si/2021/03/24/mestna-obcina-maribor-spodbuja-aktivno-in-trajnostno-mobilnost/

Javna agencija Republike Slovenije za varnost prometa. (2021). *Stanje prometne varnosti 2020 – za petino manj mrtvih in poškodovanih, za petino manj prometnih nesreč*. Academic Press.

Jin, W.-L. (2010). Macroscopic characteristics of lane-changing traffic. *Transportation Research Record: Journal of the Transportation Research Board, 2188*(1), 55–63. doi:10.3141/2188-07

Klipšteter, T. (2020). *Tudi na Dravi javni potniški promet.* Retrieved from https://www.dnevnik.si/1042940324

König, A., & Dreßler, A. (2021). A mixed-methods analysis of mobility behavior changes in the COVID-19 era in a rural case study. *European Transport Research Review, 13*(1), 1–13. doi:10.118612544-021-00472-8

Krajzewicz, D. (2010). Traffic simulation with SUMO–simulation of urban mobility Fundamentals of traffic simulation. Springer.

Krauss, S. (1998). *Microscopic modeling of traffic flow: Investigation of collision free vehicle dynamics.* Universität zu Köln.

Lee, M., Zhao, J., Sun, Q., Pan, Y., Zhou, W., Xiong, C., & Zhang, L. (2020). *Human mobility trends during the COVID-19 pandemic in the United States.* arXiv preprint arXiv:2005.01215.

Li, Q., Guan, X., Wu, P., Wang, X., Zhou, L., Tong, Y., ... Wong, J. Y. (2020). Early transmission dynamics in Wuhan, China, of novel coronavirus–infected pneumonia. *The New England Journal of Medicine, 382*(13), 1199–1207. doi:10.1056/NEJMoa2001316 PMID:31995857

Lopez, P. A., Behrisch, M., Bieker-Walz, L., Erdmann, J., Flötteröd, Y.-P., Hilbrich, R., ... Wießner, E. (2018). Microscopic traffic simulation using sumo. *21st International Conference on Intelligent Transportation Systems (ITSC).*

Maribor, M. o. (n.d.). *Lega in podnebje.* Retrieved from https://www.maribor.si/povezava.aspx?pid=3794

Nouvellet, P., Bhatia, S., Cori, A., Ainslie, K. E. C., Baguelin, M., Bhatt, S., Boonyasiri, A., Brazeau, N. F., Cattarino, L., Cooper, L. V., Coupland, H., Cucunuba, Z. M., Cuomo-Dannenburg, G., Dighe, A., Djaafara, B. A., Dorigatti, I., Eales, O. D., van Elsland, S. L., Nascimento, F. F., ... Donnelly, C. A. (2021). Reduction in mobility and COVID-19 transmission. *Nature Communications, 12*(1), 1090. doi:10.103841467-021-21358-2 PMID:33597546

Oliver, N., Lepri, B., Sterly, H., Lambiotte, R., Deletaille, S., De Nadai, M., & Cattuto, C. (2020). *Mobile phone data for informing public health actions across the COVID-19 pandemic life cycle.* American Association for the Advancement of Science.

Pepe, E., Bajardi, P., Gauvin, L., Privitera, F., Lake, B., Cattuto, C., & Tizzoni, M. (2020). *COVID-19 outbreak response: a first assessment of mobility changes in Italy following national lockdown.* MedRxiv; doi:10.1101/2020.03.22.20039933

Schewdhelm, A., Li, W., Harms, L., & Adriazola-Steil, C. (2020). *Cycling during COVID-19 | world resources institute. Biking Provides a Critical Lifeline During the Coronavirus Crisis.* Retrieved from https://www.wri.org/blog/2020/04/coronavirus-bikingcritical-in-cities

Schlosser, F., Maier, B. F., Jack, O., Hinrichs, D., Zachariae, A., & Brockmann, D. (2020). COVID-19 lockdown induces disease-mitigating structural changes in mobility networks. *Proceedings of the National Academy of Sciences of the United States of America*, *117*(52), 32883–32890. doi:10.1073/pnas.2012326117 PMID:33273120

Shannon, R. E. (1975). *Systems Simulation – The Art and Science*. Prentice-Hall.

Shi, K., De Vos, J., Yang, Y., & Witlox, F. (2019). Does e-shopping replace shopping trips? Empirical evidence from Chengdu, China. *Transportation Research Part A, Policy and Practice*, *122*, 21–33. doi:10.1016/j.tra.2019.01.027

Simulation of Urban Mobility. (2019). Retrieved from http://sumo.sourceforge.net/userdoc/Sumo_at_a_Glance.html

Šinko, S., & Gumzej, R. (2021). Towards Smart Traffic Planning by Traffic Simulation on Microscopic Level. *International Journal of Applied Logistics*, *11*(1), 1–17. doi:10.4018/IJAL.2021010101

Sirkeci, I., & Yucesahin, M. M. (2020). Coronavirus and migration: Analysis of human mobility and the spread of COVID-19. *Migration Letters: An International Journal of Migration Studies*, *17*(2), 379–398. doi:10.33182/ml.v17i2.935

Song, J., Wu, Y., Xu, Z., & Lin, X. (2014). Research on car-following model based on SUMO. *The 7th IEEE/International Conference on Advanced Infocomm Technology*. 10.1109/ICAIT.2014.7019528

Sparmann, U. (1979). The importance of lane-changing on motorways. *Traffic Engineering & Control*, *20*(6).

Sumo. (2019a). *Definition of Vehicles, Vehicle Types, and Routes*. Retrieved from https://sumo.dlr.de/docs/Definition_of_Vehicles,_Vehicle_Types,_and_Routes.html

Sumo. (2019b). *Pedestrian Simulation*. Retrieved from https://sumo.dlr.de/docs/Simulation/Pedestrians.html

WHO. (2020). WHO *Director-General's opening remarks at the media briefing on COVID-19 - March 11 2020*. Retrieved from https://www.who.int/dg/speeches/detail/who-director-general-s-opening-remarks-at-the-media-briefing-on-covid 19

Zveza potrošnikov Slovenije. (2020). *Strah pred okužbo s COVID-19 bo zaznamoval mobilnost*. Retrieved from https://www.zps.si/okolje-topmenu-320/trajnostna-mobilnost/10708-strah-pred-okuzbo-s-covid-19-bo-zaznamoval-mobilnost

Chapter 4
Mapping the Process to Improve the Operative and Environmental Performance of Feeder Ports

Daniel Londono-Bernal
Curtin University, Australia

Adil Hammadi
Curtin University, Australia

Torsten Reiners
https://orcid.org/0000-0001-6243-4267
Curtin University, Australia

ABSTRACT

Container terminals play an important role in linking regional and continental areas for the exchange of goods. Port authorities have to provide their services under competitive prices and service levels to customers. This increasing competition pushes feeder ports to improve their processes. The goal is to increase the port capacity to deal with the increasing demand for containers and, at the same time, to reduce the environmental impact and operative costs. The authors address the gap in the literature regarding alternatives for feeder ports. They analyse best practices adopted in international terminals and evaluate the implementation in feeder ports. They apply a quantitative approach using the simulation software AnyLogic. The model uses market data to analyse the vessel unloading process at the berth. Moreover, an alternative to reduce the CO2 emissions for diesel equipment is presented. A flowchart for the vessel unloading and loading operations is proposed that includes the strategies to increase capacity and efficiency of operations and the utilisation of equipment.

DOI: 10.4018/978-1-7998-8709-6.ch004

INTRODUCTION

The increasing number of competitors in the different sectors of the economy are pushing organizations to find ways to become more productive in order to offer products and services at competitive prices, superior quality and lower impact to the environment. As distribution and transportation play an important role, accounting up to 30% of the product price (Hasani Goodarzi and Zegordi 2016, Kaliszewski et al. 2020), ports have a significant position to implement innovative solutions for a positive (regional) impact on the economy and, therewith, the competitive advantage. In addition, it is crucial for ports to reduce their environmental impact as transportation and freight is a major source for global carbon dioxide (CO_2) emissions (Dekker, Bloemhof and Mallidis 2012, Pazirandeh and Jafari 2013). As a key component of transportation activities, feeder ports, smaller ports where large vessels generally cannot berth, serve as a link between regional and intercontinental areas, with the possibility of combining different modes of transportation through the use of standardized containers at the container terminal (specialised area of the port for container handling). The need for innovative and less environmental impacting port operations is emphasized by the large growth of container trade over the past decades World Shipping Council (2021).

Technological advances in the design of containers are one of the factors that contribute to their increasing demand and flow through seaports. According to Dekker, Bloemhof, and Mallidis (2012) the new generation of containers, including cooled (reefers) and temperature data loggers, allows the transportation of time sensitive products via ship, truck and rail to farther locations, including intercontinental areas. These new alternatives reduce significantly the transportation costs compared to the air mode (Dekker, Bloemhof and Mallidis 2012), making viable the demand of these types of products to even thousands of kilometres away, where container terminals work as transhipment points along the way.

Containerization allows the intermodal transportation through multiple modes such as barges, ships, trains and trucks and the changes between them in a single trip, without any manipulation of the freight (Gharehgozli, Roy and De Koster 2016). Loading a container provides security, with lower possibility of losses and damages and reduces the manipulation in intermodal trips, resulting in a faster and more efficient operation. Different sized containers can be handled by straddle carriers (SC), yard trucks (YC), yard cranes (YC) and quay cranes (QC) (Petering et al. 2009).

The key factors that give a competitive advantage to container terminals are their capacity and competitive rates (Gharehgozli et al. 2016). In previous decades it was common to design ports with machinery to handle ships with Panamax capacity (5000 TEU); however, the increasing annual demand is pushing port authorities to provide services at a competitive turn-around time and quality for mega-vessels (Stahlbock and Voß 2008) such as the new Panamax (18000 TEU) (Gharehgozli et al. 2016). However, the investment in machinery should be carefully studied. According to Low (2010) the careful investment in intelligent facilities results in competitiveness for the port, as it is not only the investment in already over-capacitated ports, such as some in Japan, UK and US, will contribute to a greater traffic control for port operators. This decision is more viable for newer container terminals that still need to implement more effective operative strategies and are located in areas that allow an infrastructure expansion. Therefore, solutions such as a new layout, automated vehicles, handling processes and investment in infrastructure (Stahlbock and Voß 2008), can have a greater impact on lower capacity ports. In the following, we investigate some measurements to increase their productivity and reduce the environmental impact of container terminals.

The focus in the seaside operations was motivated also due to the fact that Quay Cranes (QCs) are generally the bottleneck of a container terminal, and their operations set the speed and turn-around time of the vessel at the port (Zeng and Yang 2009). We investigated the literature on feeder ports and its operations (Humang et al. 2021, Al Amien et al. 2020, Sutanto, 2021). We identified several opportunities for improvement in the berthing and QCs operations. The goal is to study ways that a port can operate more efficiently in terms of container handling operations and machinery utilisation. While shorter berth time at feeder ports can increase the interest by shipping lines as an alternative to major ports, it has also a positive environmental impact.

Container terminals are composed of seaside, landside and hinterland operations, each one with determined factors and opportunities for improvement. This chapter will focus in the former (represented as Quay Cranes area in Figure 1), with the purpose of describing best practices from other ports.

Figure 1. Main areas in a Container Terminal. Adopted from Scorpionv6, Container Port, 2018. Source: https://imgbin.com/png/2sfdZ5bt/container-port-container-ship-intermodal-container-png.

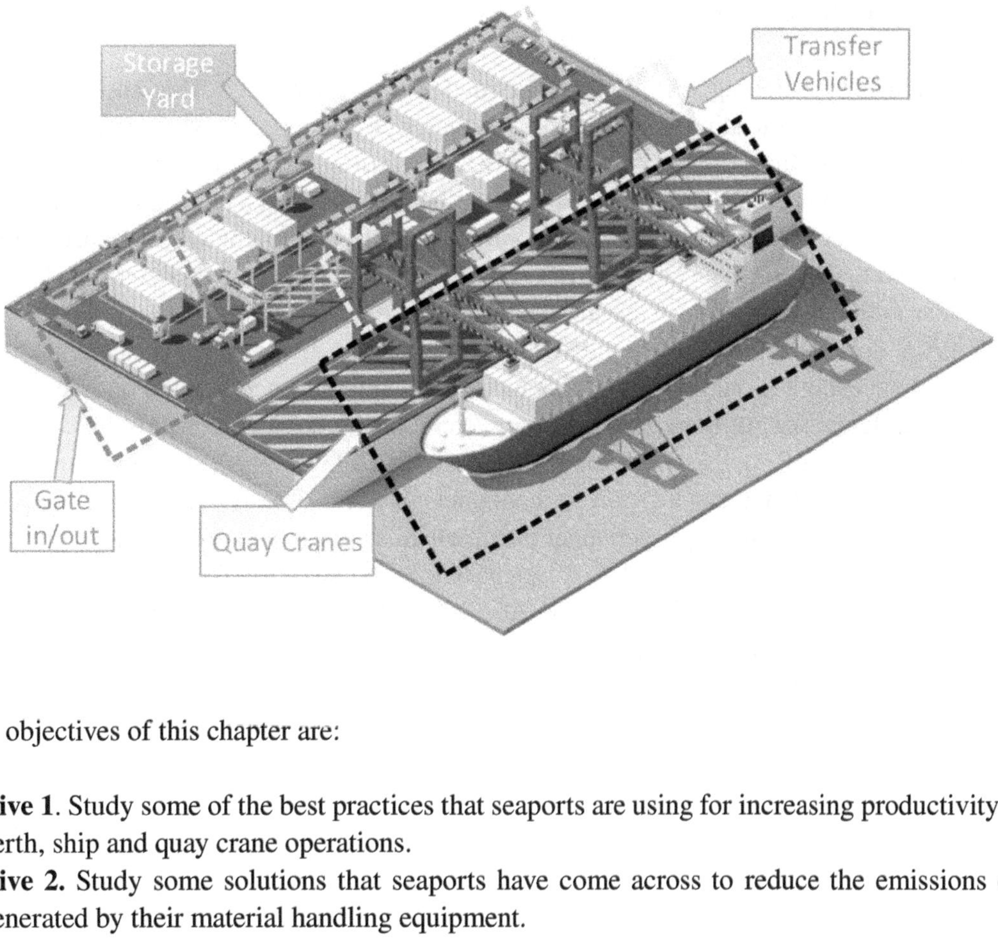

The objectives of this chapter are:

Objective 1. Study some of the best practices that seaports are using for increasing productivity for the berth, ship and quay crane operations.

Objective 2. Study some solutions that seaports have come across to reduce the emissions of CO_2 generated by their material handling equipment.

The research questions are:

Question 1. Are there strategies and methodologies that can help to reduce the waiting time of the vessels, and increase the utilisation of the berths and quay cranes in a container terminal?
Question 2. Are there strategies or new solutions to reduce emissions for current or new container handling equipment, that other ports have evaluated its feasibility?

The literature is, in general, focussed on the larger sea ports and international transhipment terminals with access for deep sea vessels, limiting the research and exposure of smaller feeder ports. Here, we investigate the operational processes at container terminals to identify what is best to apply in feeder ports.

LITERATURE REVIEW

In this section, we provide an overview of the current operations at container terminals. This includes an investigation of currently use equipment, their utilisation, and how those are impacting on the environment.

Container Terminal Layout

Container terminals for shipping vessels can be divided into two interfaces. The seaside, which is responsible for loading and unloading the vessels, and the landside (Hinterland), where internal trucks load or unload the containers from the stacking area and external trucks deliver or receive containers from the customers (Carlo, Vis and Roodbergen 2014; Saeed Nooramin, Reza Ahouei and Sayareh 2011).

The operation of a container terminal can follow different configurations of layouts, concepts to handle the containers and the diverse type of equipment. However, Kemme (2013), has determined a common scheme similar to the seaport used for the study which is represented in Figure 2.

The Ship-to-Shore system is at the seaside where the unloading and loading operation from the vessels are carried out using the quay cranes (QCs). Next, in the interface between the seaside and storage area, is the waterside or seaside horizontal transport . Here, the horizontal transports are carried out by different types of vehicles, such as yard trucks (YTs) and straddle carriers (SCs). Next to the storage area, which serves as a temporary location for containers and it is usually located in close proximity to the QCs, there is usually an empty container depot where shipping lines keep empty containers according to their needs, a station for container freight (CFS) and a section for maintenance and fixing operations. This is part of the landside (Kemme 2013). The last system connects the landside with the hinterland. It is composed by the gate in and gate out facilities, of the infrastructure to change modes of transportation from the rail terminal to yard trucks (YTs) or external trucks (XTs), and the handover area. The coordination of the systems mentioned is critical for the productivity of the terminal. Most important is the equipment and will be covered in the following section.

Container Terminal Equipment

The equipment plays an important role in the operation of a container terminal. The selection of the right type and quantity for the different operations, may not only provide more efficiency in the process but also reduce the environmental impact. This section will cover commonly used equipment for landside and seaside operations.

Figure 2. Basic scheme of a container terminal.
Adopted from (Kemme 2013)

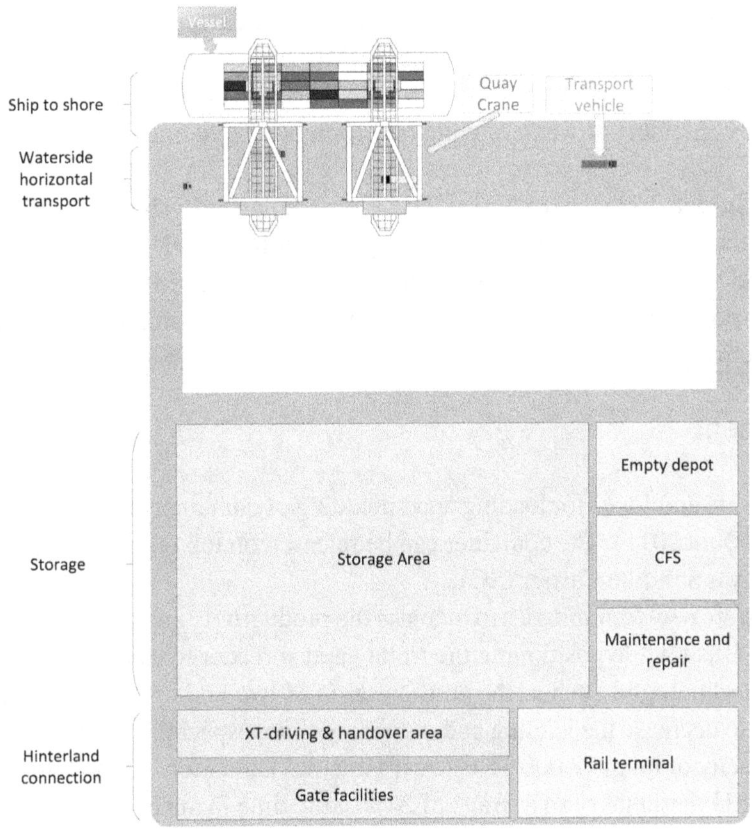

Landside Equipment

In the design and optimisation of a container terminal, the capacity and features of handling equipment should be considered. The most common hoist equipment, used to lift containers on/off at the quayside and stacking area, and popular automatic transfer vehicles, will be described in this section with some of their latest innovations.

- **Rail Mounted Gantry Crane (RMG):** Key component for container terminals that integrates rail and road transportation modes and require a high stacking capacity. Common RMGs are able to stack 1100 TEU/Hectare.
- **Rubber Tyred Gantry (RTG):** Common equipment used for stacking containers in the storage yard, with the capability to lift containers on/off from road transtainers, including trucks, straddle carriers and automated vehicles. They provide high capacity, measured in TEU/Hectare, which allows more flexibility in periods with higher demand of containers without requiring additional space in the storage area (Stahlbock and Voß 2008). An example of an efficient RTG is the one to be implemented in the port of Manila that uses a hybrid of diesel and Li-ion batteries to reduce 40% of CO_2 emissions and 60% fuel. Mitsui, the manufacturer, reveals that this model can stack up to 6 containers wide and 5 up (Port Technology 2021).

- **Straddle Carriers (SCs):** This is a popular and convenient equipment that can lift containers on/off, released from an RMG, RTG or similar crane in the stacking area and transport them horizontally to the QC or vice versa. This versatility eliminates the requirement of trucks and for instance the time required to position the QC or RTG/RMG trolley on top of the vehicle for the lift-on operation and the alignment of the truck with the crane for the lift-off. The SCs are useful as well for reshuffling containers or when moving one container from one slot to another (Stahlbock and Voß 2008).
- **Automated Guided Vehicles (AGVs):** These are unmanned vehicles popular in container terminals since the 90s, with their first models powered by diesel engines and hydraulic systems (Geerlings and van Duin 2011). Their technology had advanced quickly with the development of diesel-electric and then battery-driven vehicles (lead- acid compound) in the early 2000's and 2010's, respectively.

Seaside Equipment

Quay Cranes (QCs) are employed for loading and unloading of containers from different types of vessels (Geerlings and van Duin 2011). The container can be released on top of a truck, AGV or on the floor to be then picked up by a Straddle Carrier (SC).

Nowadays, there are new technologies to increase the productivity and deal with common issues such as the QC swaying effect while positioning the trolley and spreader to catch the container.

The QC lifting technologies such as the configuration of two and up to three trolleys and QCs with shuttles are crucial to decrease the loading and unloading time, especially for the continuous innovation of vessels with capacity of up to 18,000 TEU (Post-Panamax) and more. Gharehgozli et al. (2016) indicate that an 8000 TEU vessel takes an average of 24% of the time in the port, whereas a ship with half of this capacity will take 17%. Although the larger the vessel the more time spent at the berth, the average handling time per container will be reduced for bigger ships and also higher economies of scale can be achieved. If keeping a 2,000 TEU vessel in idle time costs around $20,000 dollars per day (Gharehgozli et al. 2016), imagine the cost for an 18,000 TEU one. That is why port managers are in constant search for new technologies that can reduce the costs significantly and increase the efficiency of the system.

Apart from the transfer vehicles, the components that intervene in the seaside operations are the berth area, in which the vessels are allocated and the quay cranes positioned for the loading and unloading operation.

Operation Research (OR) for Seaports

The quantity of each type of equipment required for a determined container terminal layout and expected capacity are some of the decisions that every container terminal has to make, to keep the competitiveness in the market. Even though this calculation requires an optimisation approach, which is not the focus of this chapter, it is relevant to mention what can be achieved through the application of OR methodologies before presenting some considerations when upgrading equipment.

OR as a Decision-Making Tool

Murty et al. (2005) present a comprehensive supporting system for decision making. The system has the capabilities for determining an effective appointment schedule for external trucks (XTs), the internal routes that minimises the distance travelled and an optimal space allocation. In addition to that, the authors designed an integer programming model to determine the number of yard trucks (YTs) required to reduce the unloading and loading time of the ships (also known as the turn-around time) based on the quay cranes (QCs) efficiency. Murty et al. (2005) estimated savings for the port of Hong Kong of around $6,000,000 dollars per year if this system is implemented.

Evaluating Equipment

The constant necessity to reduce the operative costs and increase the capacity and service level for the port operations motivates managers to evaluate new material handling equipment. Therefore, an analysis of both transfer vehicles (perform horizontal movement) and hoist equipment (for lift on/off operations) is important before studying green and cost-effective alternatives that can be implemented in a seaport.

There are several studies that compare the performance of internal trucks and hoist equipment, and suggest the modes of transportation and the types of equipment to employ for ensuring a greener operation. Solutions such as the intelligent autonomous vehicles (IAVs) evaluated by Kavakeb et al. (2015) in a European port, were cost- effective in terms of the performance achieved and reduction of CO_2 emissions.

Even though the bottleneck in container terminal operations is usually generated in the quayside (Zeng and Yang 2009), when there are upgrades in equipment and methods of work which improve the efficiency for the QCs loading and unloading rate, it is important to consider if extra improvements have to be done for the transfer vehicles and storage yard equipment. The idea is to ensure that the entire import, export and transhipment processes run smoothly with the utilisation of equipment including RMGs, RTGs, SCs, yard trucks (YTs) and/or AGVs at the rate of the QCs. Moreover, checking if a redesign of the yard layout and gate in and out operations, including an analysis of the implications of traffic congestion in the city or region in which the port is located, can help to organise more efficiently the operations at the port and increase the efficiency and service level provided to shipping lines. For more information about the optimisation/simulation models for the right choice of equipment and number please refer to (Goodchild and Daganzo 2007; Yang, Choi and Ha 2004).

Sustainable Solutions for Container Terminals

Overview

The increasing demand of freight transportation has contributed to the sea shipping industry growth, not only in capacity and infrastructure but also in the emissions of pollutants to the environment. This industry is accountable for 1,260 million tons of carbon dioxide (CO_2) per year or 3.9% of the entire carbon emissions, where handling equipment is the key source of emissions in a container terminal (Yang 2017). For instance, it is important to study some sustainable and green practices available in the literature.

Sustainable Container Terminals

A container terminal becomes sustainable when it responds to the three anchors of sustainability: environment, social and economic, and maintain the harmony and link with the surrounding community living in the area, through the implementation of sustainable solutions for the port infrastructure and economic performance (Pedrick 2006). From the environmental perspective, there are studies that focus on calculating CO_2 emissions at ports and present some ways to reduce the contamination. Some solutions are going to be covered in the following section.

Environmental Solutions

Geerlings and van Duin (2011) carried out a study to first determine the carbon emissions and energy consumption of different kinds of equipment employed in the port of Rotterdam. Following their analysis, they suggest alternatives that may reduce the emissions by 70%. Another study in which the energy consumption and CO_2 emissions are calculated per type of equipment is done by Yang and Lin (2013) with information of the terminals located at the port of Kaohsiung, Taiwan. The working time in seconds was registered by the ABC company (which rents 6 wharfs in the port) for each pick/stack system (accounts for 6-9% of the movement time), trolley system (26-28%) and hoist system (53-57%) for the 4 types of equipment: tire transtainers (TTs), rail transtainers (RTs), automatic rail and electric tire transtainers (ARTs) and (E-TTs) respectively, in order to determine their operating efficiency, in moves/hour (Yang and Lin 2013). With the average energy consumption per move, the cost of kWh and the coefficient of CO_2 emission, the authors determined the total cost and emissions for equipment in the year 2010.

Regarding the container handling equipment, there are several innovations that if adopted may increase the productivity and reduce the emissions of feeder and transhipment ports. For example, a yard equipment (Mitsui RTG) powered by a hybrid of Li-ion batteries and diesel engine that generates 40% less carbon emissions and consumes 60% less fuel than the traditional diesel RTG, with the possibility to stack up to 6 containers wide and 5 up (Port Technology 2017). At the seaside, important results can be achieved if a port with high demand of mega-vessels implements a dual trolley crane with twin lift QC. It brings the possibility to lift two 40 ft. containers at the same time, resulting in the ability to handle 80 to 100 containers per hour, compared to a conventional single trolley and spreader 40 to 56 per hour rate (Stahlbock and Voß 2008). Another option, which does not involve changing the diesel equipment, is to mix biofuel with the current diesel at 30% or 20% to reduce approximately 21% or 14% respectively the CO_2 emissions (Geerlings and van Duin 2011).

Seaside Operative Problems and Best Practices

Overview

Identifying the optimal number of berths that will reduce the waiting time for the upcoming vessels, better practices for the quay cranes to increase their loading and unloading efficiency, and evaluating different methodologies to reduce the port turn- around time, are common operative tasks. Moreover, they are financial decisions that container terminals must keep working on to become more competitive. If these types of initiatives are successfully implemented and cost-effective, the port authorities will be able to increase their service level and offer more competitive prices to shipping lines, which is crucial for the continual growth of the business.

The Berth Allocation Problem

This is a common issue in transhipment ports and some feeder ports in peak seasons, where the constant arrival of ships makes it difficult to reduce their waiting time. That happens particularly if the quantity available of berths is not the optimal in terms of expected service level to shipping lines and maintenance costs for the port authorities. This problem will be discussed after introducing some characteristics of indented and conventional berths.

Issues at Indented Berths

There are different ways that quay cranes can be allocated to serve the vessels. It depends on the berth design, its length and the size of the vessels. The indented berth allows a close proximity from the berth to the stacking area. Although it reduces the time to serve a mega-vessel, the total time to serve all the vessels will be longer that in the traditional layout (Stahlbock and Voß 2008). In this layout, the vessels take longer to berth and exit the terminal resulting in longer idle times for trucks, straddle carriers (SCs) and/or automated guided vehicles (AGV) to continue the operation with the next vessel. Unfortunately, one way to reduce the total time, but at higher costs than benefits associated, is by adding more yard vehicles and the equivalent number of QCs and hoist equipment such as RTGs, in order to maintain the operation synchronised at higher rate and avoid making the yard or berth the bottle neck of the operation.

Issues at Conventional Berths

Another problem to consider in berth allocation is the size of the ships that restrict their allocation in berths one next to the other. This is common issue in international transhipment ports where it is crucial to determine if it is more productive to maximise the utilisation of the berths or minimise the waiting time of the vessels (Stahlbock and Voß 2008). However, the only idea of making vessels wait and then assign the berth based on the priority to serve a determined vessel, is not the best way to increase the efficiency. For instance, Henesey (2004) took into account scenarios with vessels arriving sequences, quay and berth lengths analysing the results based on two assignment policies: a) identify berth closest to the stock area and b) minimise the turn- around time. The result from the simulation runs for the two policies indicates that having the information to decide what policy to apply can optimise the SCs utilisation and decrease the turn-around time of the vessel (Henesey 2004).

Scheduling Problem for Berths

The number of berths in a container terminal is one of the critical factors that determines its capacity. However, there is a trade-off between the capacity provided by the port authority and the maintenance and construction costs. If the port decides to increase the number of berths, less waiting time and costs will be incurred by the vessels in the queue (Saeed and Larsen 2016). Nevertheless, this decision will be efficient for the port if the berths are fully utilised during the year, and the associated revenues counteract and exceed the new infrastructure and maintenance costs. This problem has been addressed through an effective tool to solve congestion problems, the queuing theory (Saeed and Larsen 2016). This theory helps to estimate the average of important parameters such as: berth utilisation, queuing lengths, number of vessels and waiting time.

Vessel Loading and Unloading Considerations

The loading operation requires coordination between the yard and the quayside. There should be trucks available to transport the containers from the stacking area to the seaside for the loading operation. This could be done following a pre-planned storage plan. The loading sequence is determined by port of destination, vessel's time of departure and weight (Gharehgozli et al. 2016). For instance, containers with earlier destinations must be loaded at the end, which follows the last in first out (LIFO) method.

However, other variables should be also considered when defining the sequence. The ship stability is a serious thing to consider in order to avoid perils and flip overs. An option to mitigate this problem is by locating heavier containers on the bottom or at least before light ones (Gharehgozli et al. 2016). Moreover, reefer and hazardous material containers have to be positioned on specific locations, with power points and lower risk of explosion respectively. Therefore, the loading operation has a great deal of importance for the turn-around time of vessels and productivity of the seaport as a whole.

Important considerations when unloading a vessel are the stability and storage plan. The containers should be unloaded in the way that the weight of the vessel is equilibrated in the front, back and sides. Therefore, the ship will keep stable and will not suffer container flip overs. Moreover, there should be a storage pre-plan for the yard so the operation runs smoothly in the way that no delays will occur for the trucks/AVGs, when deciding on what slot the container will be positioned.

Double Cycling and Mix Strategy for a QC

One of the alternatives that help to reduce the vessel's turn-around time is double cycling. It is a method that allows the QC handling of an export container and import container in the same cycle, with the condition that both containers are located on the same vessel bay (Zhang, Zeng and Yang 2016). This alternative can be implemented if there is enough availability of YTs/AVGs or equivalent transfer vehicles and they are coordinated at the same efficiency rate as the QCs. The idea is that the transfer vehicle (in this case a YT), which comes with an outbound container to load onto the vessel, receives in the same QC trolley movement or cycle, an import container to be stacked in the yard. Hence, this technique can increase the utilisation of the QC by filling the empty moves with productive ones (Goodchild and Daganzo 2007). The double cycling methodology, apart from improving the QC productivity and YTs utilisation, helps to increase the berth utilisation due to the reduced vessel's turn- around time that the port can use to serve additional vessels in the berths (Goodchild and Daganzo 2007). According to Zhang, Zeng, and Yang (2016) this technique can decrease by 20% the cycles made by a QC and by 10% the operative time.

This type of layout is known as the mix storage strategy. Although this strategy increases more the complexity of the double cycling methodology on account of a more precise coordination between the yard cranes, trucks and quay cranes, Zhang, Zeng, and Yang (2016) determined that when there are less than 10 blocks positioned horizontally in the stack, the distance travelled by the YTs is less than when using the single strategy. As a result of this, the operation will require 16% less YTs and the yard crane operation time will be decreased 26% due to more productive movements from the mix strategy. These results from the methodologies discussed not only contribute to the productivity of the port, but also have a positive effect on the reduction of carbon emissions.

According to Zhang, Zeng, and Yang (2016), the YCs cycle time is still an open question. The truck distance and time depend on the yard layout, the storage block and berth location; for instance, it is important in this case to analyse what could be the effect in the components that are part of the mix storage strategy. In addition to the complexity, double cycling requires significant investment, so it is important to make a feasibility study before implementing it into the container terminal operations.

Vessel Reshuffling Operation

There are two types of vessel reshuffling operations. In the external or conventional method, the containers that are going to be reorganised, known as reshuffles, are unloaded from the ship and put aside until the unloading operation finishes, or there are no more containers to unload from a determined stack and bay to then reload them on top (Liu et al. 2015). For internal reshuffling, the positions on a pre-planned bay (or row), which the reshuffles can be directly assigned to, are considered in order to replace the temporary unloading and loading activity to and from a yard buffer area for the repositioning operation, resulting in an increased utilisation of the QCs. This activity can be done if a stowage plan for the arrival and another for the departure of the vessel are given, since they contain the slots of the containers to proceed with the reshuffling, loading and unloading of export and import containers respectively (Meisel and Wichmann 2010).

PROBLEM IDENTIFICATION

Terminal Layout

The container terminal layout for the study is the model presented in **Figure 3.** The terminal can attend small ships with less than 35,000 DWT and the stacking capacity is up to 300,000 TEUs per year. These numbers are key to classify the container terminal as part of a feeder port.

The current layout is complemented with information of dimensions and capacity of the terminal, which is shown in Table 1.

Table 1. Terminal marine and land facilities information

Facility	Component	Description
Marine	Quay	Length: 270m. Width: 30m Vessel: up to 35,000 DWT (deadweight tonnages)
	Basin	Area: 10,000 m². Depth: 20 m. Quayside depth: 14 m
	Channel	Depth: 13 m. Length: 15 miles. Width: 600 m
	Trestle	Length: 282 m. Width: 10.5 m
Land	Stacking area	Area: 6,000 m². **Capacity: 300,000 TEU/year**
	CFS	1,500 m²
	Workshop	1 unit

The port capacity may compromise the competitiveness in the following years if the demand surpasses the 300,000 TEUs per year. For instance, finding ways to reduce the turn-around time for the vessels unloading and loading operations, and external vehicles delivery and receiving processes, will be crucial for coping with the increasing demand and level of service expected from the shipping lines. This improvement will allow the port to continue growing and keeping their competitive advantage in the region.

Seaside Processes at a Feeder Container Terminal

In this section, we describe the process of unloading and loading operations at a container terminal being part of a feeder port. The process is based on the real-world processes observed for this purpose, see also for further literature on container operations. We discuss changes to increase the number of TEUs handled to deal with the increasing demand, but also will impact in the service level to customers and more power to negotiate contract indexes resulting in higher revenues for the port authorities. Therefore, an analysis of the QC operations through flow charts is the first step to detect problems and then present some suggestions.

3.1.1 Unloading Vessel

The Figure 3 flow chart is explained as follows:

- **Vessel Arrival**: The seaside operation begins with the vessel arriving at the port, where can either move directly to the anchorage area if there is a berth available, or has no option but to wait until the current vessel leaves the port.
- **Availability of Trucks:** Once the vessel has berthed, the yard trucks (YTs) are informed and come one after the other to the quay, so the unloading operation can start.
- **Unlash Container:** The containers are previously lashed to the deck of the ship in order to secure them during the voyage. Therefore, they must be unlashed before they can be unloaded.
- **Unlock Container:** A container is locked with a twist-lock to a container underneath in order to avoid flip overs. Therefore, it should be unlocked before it is lifted vertically with the crane.
- **Position QC Trolley on Top of the Container**: the trolley has a spreader with a reducer casing to lift 20-ft to 45-ft containers and a cabin for the operator. The spreader is moved horizontally and vertically if reaches the top of the container.
- **Align the Spreader**: The swaying effect from the movement of the trolley and spreader has to be controlled by the operator by reaching slowly to the top of the container.
- **Lock the Container**: The spreader usually contains a hydraulic or equivalent system to activate the twist-lock mechanism. The operator should verify if the container is properly locked before starting the lifting activity, otherwise he or she must notify the issue in order to prevent an incident.
- **Lift the Container Vertically**: This operation frees up the container from obstacles around before the trolley is moved horizontally to the wharf side.
- **Travel Horizontally to Wharf**: The QC trolley moves the container from the waterside to the dock or wharf side.
- **Record Data (Tallyman):** A Tallyman records the container movement on a hand-held terminal which is connected to a CTOS system in order to track the operation.
- **Position Container on Truck**: The operator gets close to the truck as aligned as possible.

- **Align Truck to Receive Container**: Often, it is easier to move the truck than the spreader, with the container attached on top, until both of them are aligned.
- **Released Container**: Once the container is aligned with the truck, the container can be released from the spreader and then set the twist-lock.
- **Movement**: Then the truck can start the route to a determined block and slot (or bay) in the stacking area.
- **Repeat Cycle**: The cycle from unlashing the container to it is release on the truck is repeated until the unloading of all the imported containers is finished.

Figure 3. Flow chart of the seaside unloading process

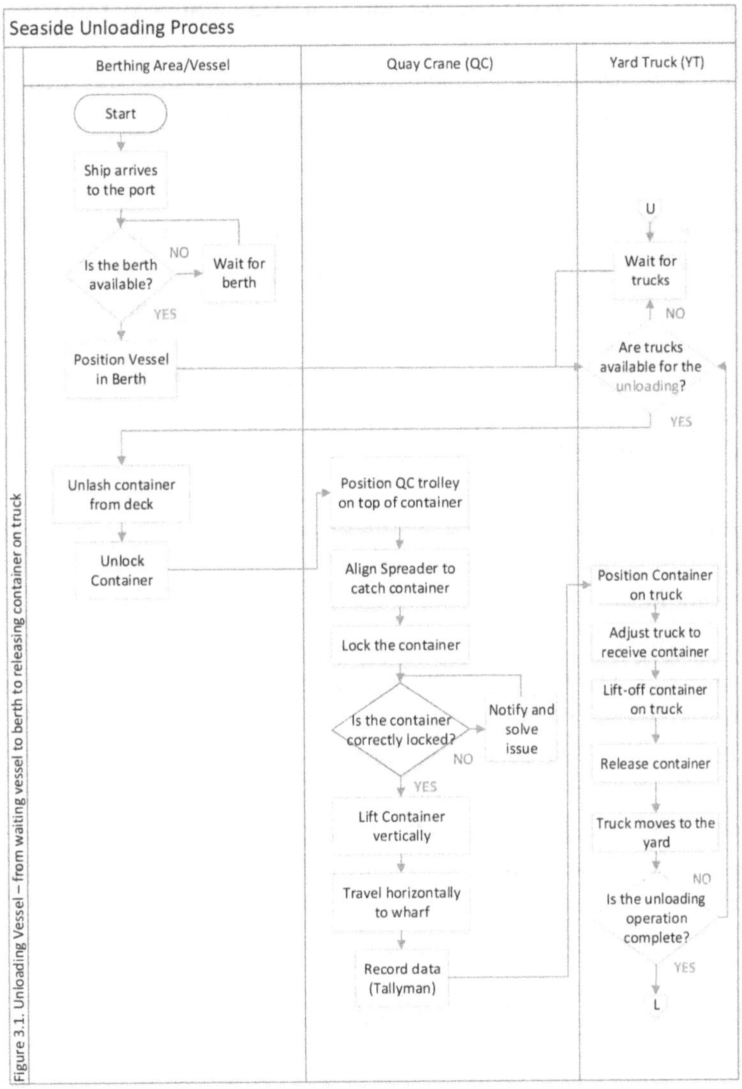

With this complete description of the vessel unloading process, let's move to the loading operation.

Loading Vessel

The Figure 4 flow chart is explained as follows:

- **Vessel Position**: Ensure that the vessel is at the berth to start the loading operation. In most of the occasions a vessel finishes the unloading of containers before starting the loading process. However, it is also considered the cases of an empty ship firstly loaded or that comes from another port for only exporting containers.
- **Availability of Trucks:** In this case, being ready for the loading process means that the yard truck (YT) was informed about the vessel availability, and had already picked up a container from the stacking area to be loaded in the vessel according to the departure plan.
- **Take Container to Dock:** The truck moves the container all the way from the stacking area to the QC for the loading operation.
- **QC Availability:** Confirms if the QC has already served previous trucks in the queue and it is operating correctly to continue with the loading of the next container.
- **Position QC Trolley on Top of Truck**: The spreader is moved horizontally and vertically until it reaches the top of the container carried by the YT.
- **Align the Spreader and Truck to Catch the Container**: The swaying effect from the movement of the trolley and spreader has to be controlled by the operator by reaching the top of the container slowly, where it is often easier to move the truck, than to correct the position with the spreader.
- **Lock the Container**: The operator should verify if the container is properly locked with the twist-lock mechanism, before starting the lifting activity and notify the operations manager if there are issues in the locking system, to prevent an incident.
- **Lift the Container Vertically**: This operation frees up the container from obstacles around it, before the trolley is moved horizontally to the wharf side.
- **Travel Horizontally to Vessel**: The QC trolley moves the container from the wharf side to the position pre-planned on the vessel.
- **Record Data (Tallyman)**: The Tallyman records the container movement on a hand-held terminal which is connected to the CTOS system in order to release the space it was occupying in the yard.
- **Position Container on Vessel**: The operator gets close to a determined row, then align and position the container on top of another container or vessel deck if no containers are in that stack.
- **Released Container**: Once the container is aligned on top of another container or vessel deck, it can be released from the spreader and then the twist-lock is set.
- **Lash and Lock Container**: Once the container is released it can be lashed to the vessel deck and locked to the container underneath in order to avoid movement during the voyage.
- **Repeat Cycle:** The cycle, from verifying the availability of yard trucks until the container is lashed and locked on the vessel, is repeated until the loading of all the containers to export is finished.

Seaside Loading and Unloading Process Analysis

From the flow charts of Figure 3 and Figure 4, some issues were identified, that can be tackled and operations that can be reduced, combined or eliminated. The opportunities for improvement are listed in Table 2.

Figure 4. Flow chart of the seaside loading process

Table 2. Opportunities for improvement - vessel unloading and loading processes.

Activity	Name	Type of Issue and Description
Delay	Availability of trucks unloading - loading	1.1. **Coordination:** If the two QCs loading/unloading rate are not well synchronised with the rate of each one of the RTGs lift-off/lift-on operations, this will generate queues and delays on the trucks that will lower their availability to either load or unload the vessel. 1.2. **Utilisation:** There should be a way to improve the utilisation of the trucks in the way that a container, to be exported (loaded) onto the ship, can be transported from the yard to the quay side in the same trip that the truck receives an import container
Operation	Take container to dock/ container yard	1.3. **Rework:** The YTs follow a queue of other trucks that are also carrying the containers to the dock to be served by the QCs. If both the loading and unloading processes are done separately this queue has to be done twice for each truck resulting in longer vessel turn- around times. Is there any way to combine these operations?
Operation	Reshuffling	1.4. **Additional Requirement:** the unloading and loading operations do not consider how to manage the reshuffling operation for the vessel. This is needed when a container underneath needs to be unloaded. This requires the move of the upper container to the wharf side and then return it when the unloading operation is completed.

SIMULATION

Simulation of Container Terminal Operations

The described operations are implemented using a simulation model. Here, the simulation is used to visualize and demonstrate the operations involved in the vessel unloading and loading process. The intention of the research is on mapping the operations, not about performing an in-depth analysis of the model. The higher-level modelling used here is useful on a managerial level to support decision making, understanding processes, identifying faults in the design or operations at an early stage. For analytical modelling and optimization, more data about the operations as well as advanced mathematical and simulation models are required.

Simulation of Container Terminal Operations

Simulation is an approach that port authorities can adopt in their operations, as it has been proven to be an efficient tool to understand and improve processes. It takes into account relevant information of a process and delivers close estimations and results for different scenarios, including design resources and management rules (Leriche et al. 2015). The efficiency of simulation is recognised in the industry. Important decisions can be made in investments, design and logistics from the outcomes obtained in the validation of different scenarios.

Simulation is used to estimate the optimum number of facilities, such as number of berths and equipment including QCs, RMGs and YTs, in order to increase the port efficiency. For example, Yongqiang et al. (2010) presented an efficient method to improve the utilisation of the equipment at Zhuhai Jiuzhou container terminal in China, through a multi-channel queueing model known as M-M- S, formulated with AnyLogic, and based on data from the terminal which has four QCs, two Berths and works 16 hours per day. For this purpose, the authors firstly validated the probability distribution of the vessel arrival (Poison), and other statistic parameters that were used as input for the simulation model, and as a result of the simulation runs interesting conclusions were drawn. The QCs rate of 41.75 TEUs/hour and 36% utilisation, which is 13% less than the berth occupancy (49%), reflects a coordination problem between the QCs and YTs. A comparison was made between the results of the operation research (OR) method and the ones from the simulation runs. The optimisation model outcome indicates a berth occupancy of 36%, and the simulations runs came up with a proportion of 46.5%, which is much closer to the real operation measurement of 49% (Yongqiang et al. 2010). For instance, the discrete event simulation method was found to be a better predictor of the reality than the OR methodology, being one of the reasons that the latter does not involve, in the experiment, the interaction and coordination between the equipment (such as the QCs with YTs). The simulation runs revealed that in order to increase the QCs utilisation (to 39%), the two current berths occupancy would be reduced to 43%, but this will release some pressure from the YTs (from 76% utilisation to about 48%), as increasing the number of YTs is the most viable alternative, where the optimal ratio of YTs per QC would be 4.7 (Yongqiang et al. 2010).

PROBLEM ANALYSIS AND DISCUSSION

Simulation of a Vessel Unloading Operation

This chapter is demonstrating the simulation of vessels being unloaded at the berth. For this purpose, two methods were utilised to study the interaction between all the relevant components (equipment and operational facilities) to represent a close to real operation at a container terminal. The first method was the design of a prototype using Lego ® bricks, which is a fun way to simulate the operation using physical objects. The second method was based on a computer formulation and modelling of the operation using the simulation software, AnyLogic.

Lego Simulation

The Lego prototype was inspired with the idea that playing is an effective and fun way to learn. The prototype allowed us to interact with the key components of a container terminal, and connect the information previously read about this topic. The layout can be seen in Figure 5.

Figure 5. Layout Lego prototype of a container terminal

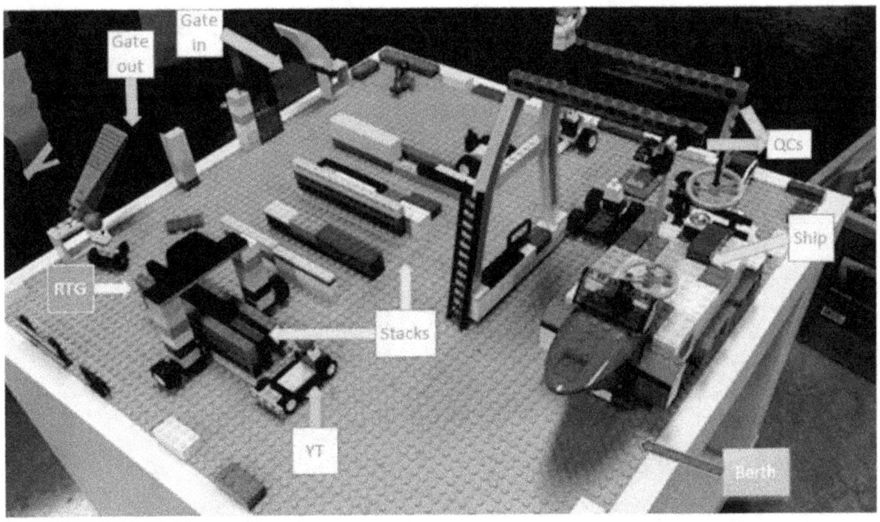

In the Figure 5 the layout is marked with the key facilities and equipment used in a seaport. For the purpose of this study, especial attention is given to the vessel (un)loading processes, from the moment that the vessel arrives to the port and berths to its departure. The container yard, where the stacks are located, including a buffer area for reshuffle containers, is not part of the scope of the study, however, it is only mentioned as that the YT moves to the yard after receiving the import container. Therefore, the key facility in the Lego simulation is the berth and the key equipment - the QCs and YTs. Figure 6 shows the moment where the inbound container is positioned on the truck.

Figure 6. Lego single cycling simulation - positioning inbound container on truck.

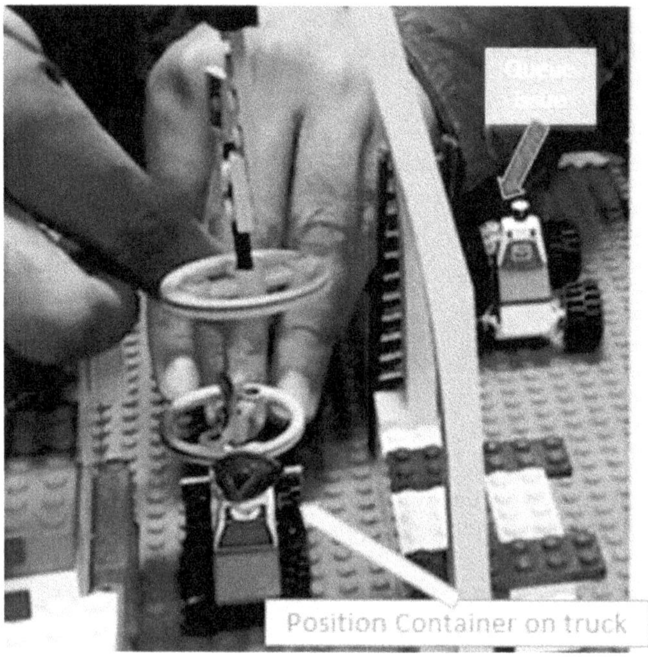

Figure 7. Lego double cycling simulation - outbound container travelling to vessel.

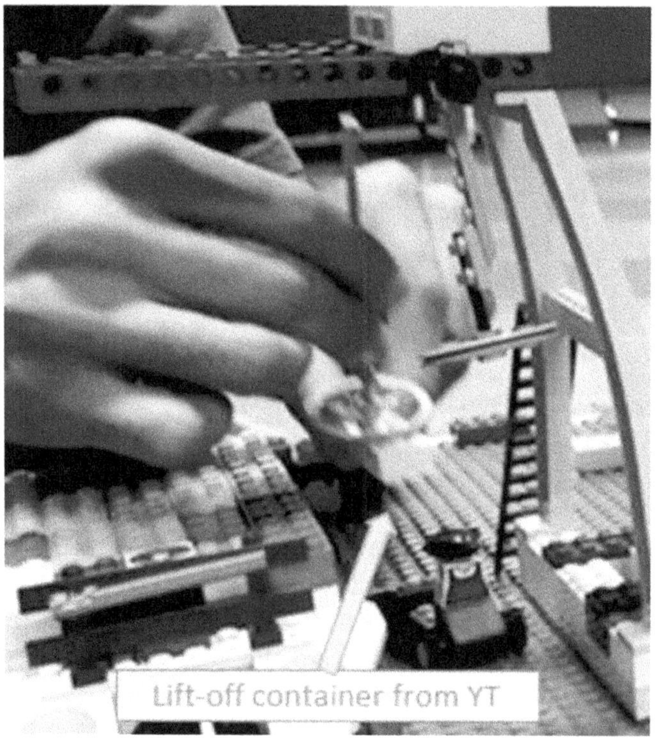

While running the simulation for single cycling (Figure 6), in which both the loading and unloading processes are performed separately, it was identified a queue of YTs waiting to be served by the QCs. This is a common situation in transhipment ports and even feeder container terminals in peak times, which again revalidate Zeng and Yang (2009) findings that the QCs are generally the bottleneck in seaport operations.

The result was different when performing the simulation following the Double Cycling (DC) methodology (Figure 7). The option to carry an outbound container from the yard to the quay side, and receive an inbound container to take it back with the same YT trip, was found more efficient for both the YT and QC productive movements, resulting in higher utilisation of the equipment and lower turn-around time to serve the vessel. It was also perceived the need of less YTs to perform the process and keep the QCs and RTGs synchronised for both the loading and unloading of containers.

The previous results from the Lego simulation may be useful for not only feeder ports operators but also transhipment container terminals. Having the opportunity to build and play with a prototype, is a good way, not only for training new employees, but also to try new alternatives such as the change in the distribution of the layout, number of equipment or even the steps and operations within the process in order to achieve better results.

The computer-based simulation is covered in **Section 5.1.2**. This second simulation option will bring a more logic understanding of the interaction between the components involved in the process.

Discrete Event-Oriented Simulation

The models were implemented using a discrete event-oriented simulation using the Logic 8.1.0 learning edition (Anylogic 2017). Point A, or first event, represents the vessel's arrival, making its first appearance in the simulation (see Figure 8). Point B is when the vessel reaches the berth and positions itself (see Figure 9). Then the unloading of containers is the third event (see Figure 10), and the final event is the vessel's departure after the last container is unloaded (see Figure 11).

Figure 8. Event 1 - vessel arrival to port.

Figure 9. Event 2 - vessel positioned at the berth.

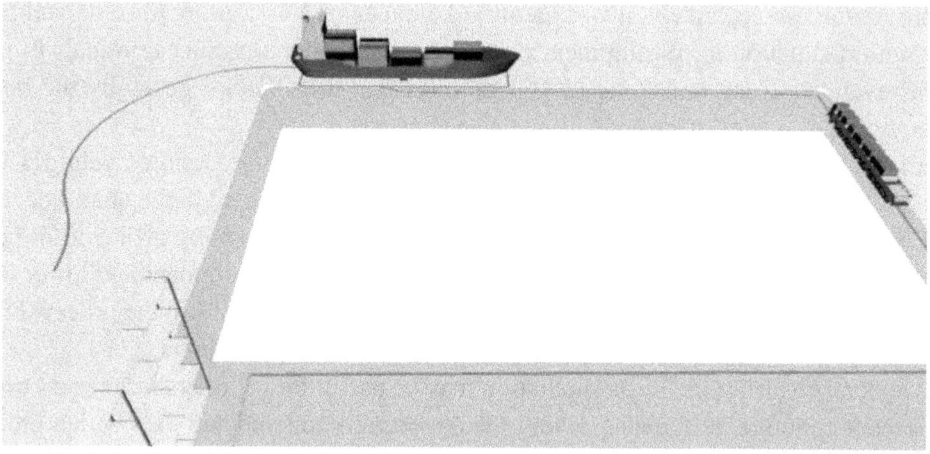

In Figure 10 was identified a queue of trucks waiting to be loaded, which helps port authorities to determine the number of YTs, RTGs and QCs to optimise the operation. The visualisation option makes simulation an easy way to identify problems in the operation. Finally, when the last container is positioned on a truck, the vessel departures.

Figure 10. Event 3 - representation of the vessel being unloaded.

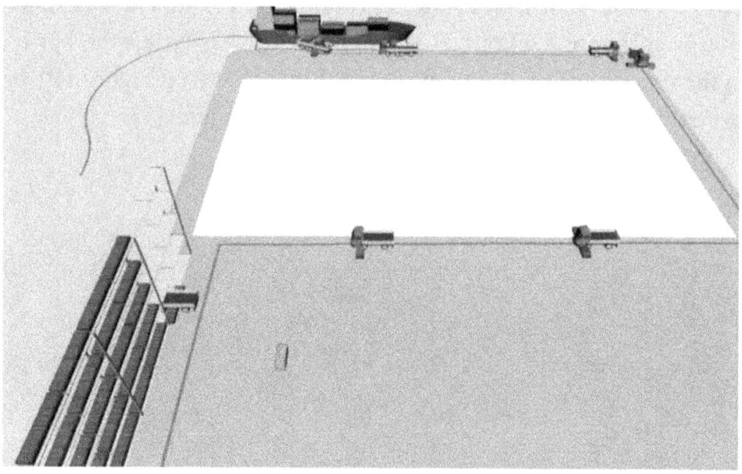

An important observation is that the scope of the simulation is for the unloading operation at the seaside, for instance, not all the attention is put into the visual representation of the yard and the way the containers are lifted on and off. Moreover, the stacking area is emptied each time a vessel departs, assuming that external trucks from customers come to deliver all the containers. This assumption allows the use of only one stack in the yard that triggers the discharge of containers, so the trucks are empty to return for more containers. In summary, the flow of the four discrete events simulated for the unloading operation are shown in Figure 12.

Figure 11. Event 4 - vessel departure.

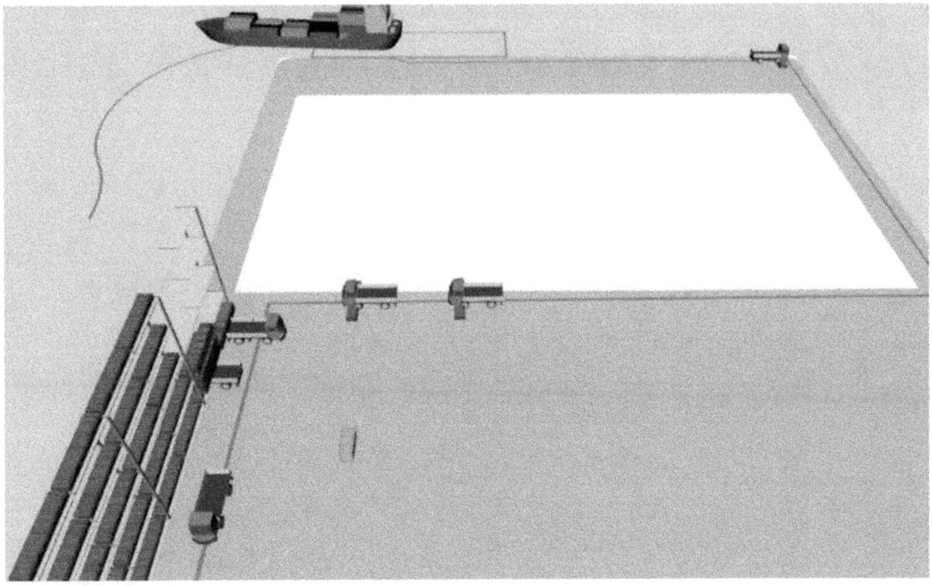

Figure 12. Discrete events for simulation unloading operation.

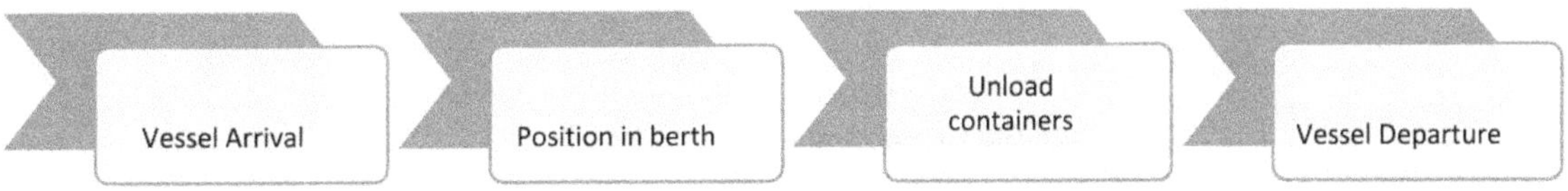

The logic of the events is shown in Figure 13.

With the clear scope of processes and assumptions made for the simulation of the vessel unloading process, the flowchart showing the process, is formulated in AnyLogic, which is presented in Figure 14.

In Figure 14 it can be seen that the first process flow, which begins with **sourceContainers** and end up with **sink**, is in charge of the containers' storage on the stack and their delivery to customers. The second flow manages the sourcing of vessels, their movement to the berth, the waiting time while the containers are unloaded and the vessels departure.

The icon **trucks** is a resource pool that represents the moving vehicles in the simulation, in this case the 16 trucks available at the terminal.

The icon **containerInStorage** represents the queue or waiting time of each container on the stack, and in the second flow **unloading** manages the vessels waiting time while all containers are unloaded before they leave the berth.

With the previous analysis of simulation, as an efficient tool for decision making in container terminals, and the presentation of a basic simulation of container ships unloading process, it is time to cover, in the following subsection, the analysis of the equipment.

Figure 13. Logic of events simulation unloading operation.

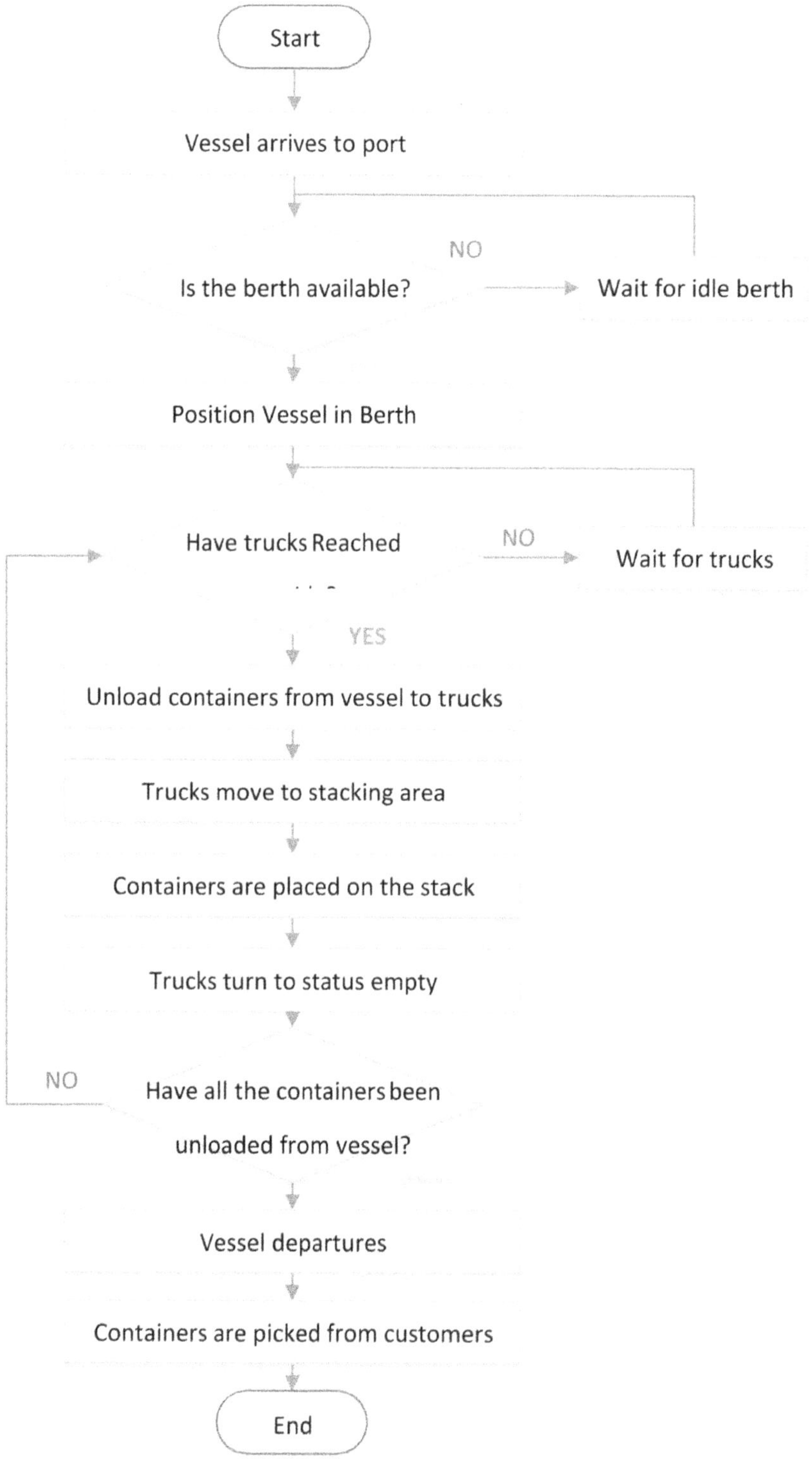

Figure 14. Flowchart vessel unloading in AnyLogic

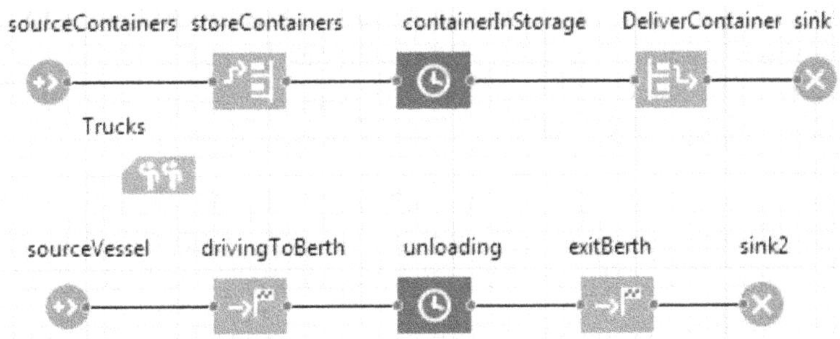

Alternatives to Reduce CO_2 Emissions

There are ways to reduce the carbon emissions from diesel combustion equipment without making significant changes. The first one is to keep the current equipment but to mix biofuel with the already used diesel. The second is to consider moving into rail, electric or battery-powered solutions. That makes the first option easier to implement in a port as a short-term solution. This is the case of the Rotterdam container terminals that achieved a total reduction of 21% in the total CO_2 emissions or from 2.65 kg/l to 1.86kg/l for the diesel-powered equipment with a 30% biofuel mix (Geerlings and van Duin 2011). A similar estimation can be done for other terminals with the information of diesel consumption for their equipment per month. This could be a future research.

Apart from the biofuel alternative, the adoption of new operative methods that may reduce the distances travelled by yard trucks (YTs) and QCs movements, which in the case of the QC double cycling and vessel reshuffling strategies, will reduce by the same proportion, the emissions of carbon emissions into the environment.

Proposed Flowcharts for Seaside (Un)loading Process

The proposed flowcharts may help terminals to handle both the inbound (import) and outbound (export) containers in the same YT trip to Quay side and returning to the yard. The purpose is to optimise the unloading and loading processes.

In Figure 15. the main process flow is presented for managing both inbound and outbound containers, when a stowage plan is available for both the vessel arrival and departure. The operations that change, when comparing to the flowcharts presented in **Subsections 3.2.1** and **3.2.2**, are explained as follows:

- **Availability of Yard Trucks (YTs) to Serve Vessel:** in this case a stowage plan is followed to coordinate the pick-up of a determined outbound (export) container from the yard. Thus, the YT makes a productive movement to the quay side to start the sequence of loading-unloading the vessel in the same trip. With this change, the operation follows the double cycling strategy.
- **Validate if YT comes with Outbound Container:** this decision allows the YT to go empty to the quay side to begin the unloading operations first. This can occur when the outbound container from the yard will take extra time to get ready. Some reasons include: a delay of the RTG reshuffling containers to get the outbound container; when there is not information of its location; or

the double cycling is not possible to execute for this move as it is required to unload a couple of containers from the vessel first, or there are not more containers to load onto the ship.

- **Begin Loading the Container on Vessel:** As mentioned previously the objective of double cycling is to keep the YT occupied carrying an outbound container to the quay side and returning with an inbound container to the yard. Therefore, the **loading** process now becomes a sub-process which is presented in Figure 5.12, it is represented with the "L" **icon ->** L and called again to return to the main flowchart (Figure 5.11) with the same "L" **icon** for their operations.
- **Begin Unloading the Container on Truck:** The **unloading** sub-process can be seen in (Figure 5.13) and out (Figure 5.11) with the "U" **icon ->** U either when: 1) the outbound container carried by the YT to the quay side is picked up by the QC and in the same QC cycle an inbound container is positioned on the YT, 2) the YT goes empty to quay side to pick up an inbound container.

Figure 15. Proposed Flowchart vessel loading and unloading process.

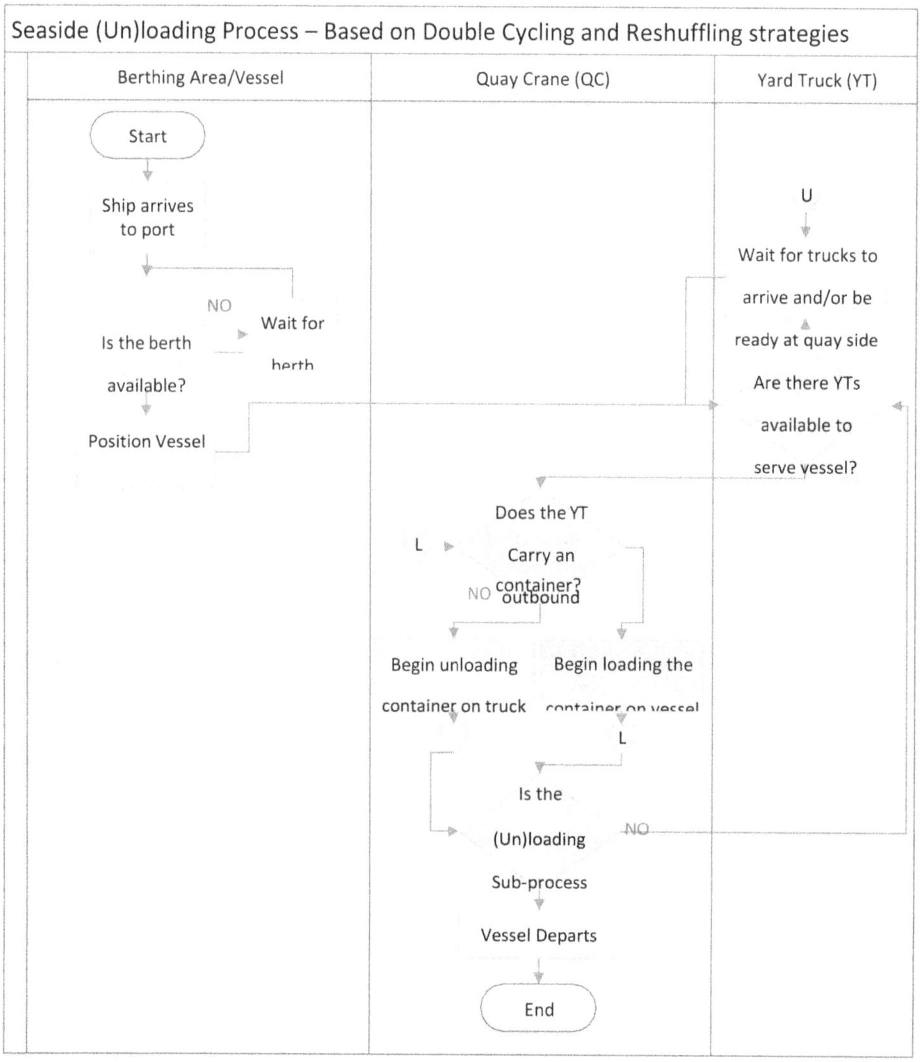

- **Validate if the (Un)Loading Sub-Processes are Complete:** This decision confirms if both the unloading and loading of all containers have been done and if so, allows the vessel to leave the port.

The vessel **loading** and **unloading** sub-processes are shown in **Subsections 5.1.2**, Figures 5.9 and 5.10 respectively with the explanation of their new operations below.

Figure 16. Flowchart loading container on vessel.

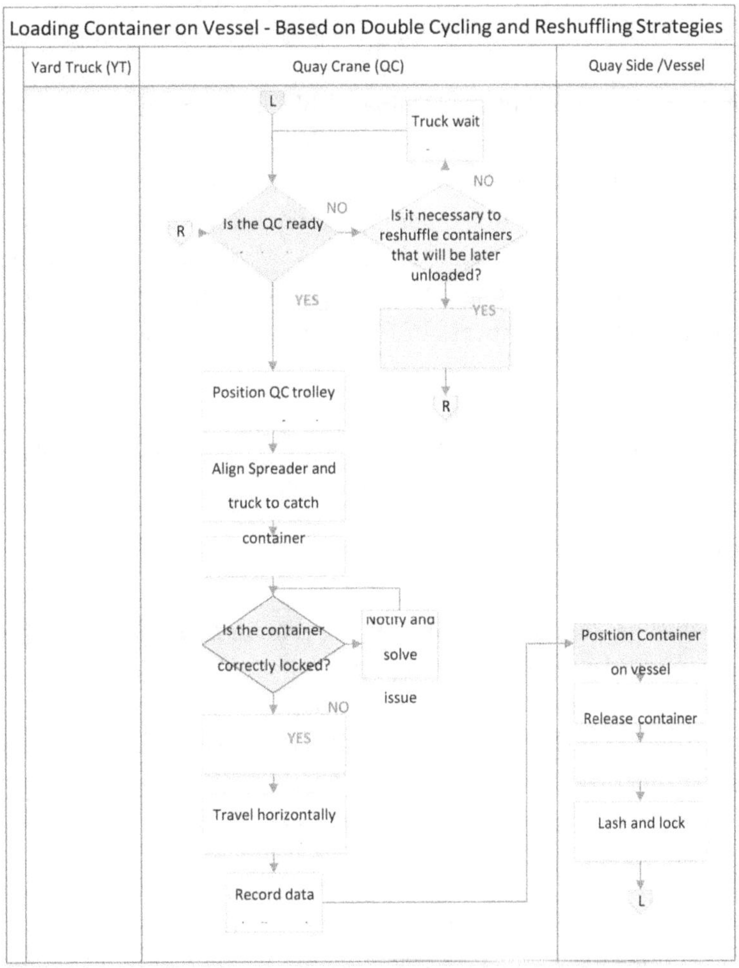

New Vessel Loading and Unloading Sub-Processes

The different operations incorporated into the flowchart of Figure 16, compared with the previous loading vessel flowchart from **Subsection 3.2.2**, Figure 3.2, are explained below:

- **Validate if reshuffling sub-process is needed:** this decision validates if before loading an outbound container – already transported by the YT from the yard -, is necessary to reposition (reshuffle) other inbound containers on the same bay, so they can be reached from the top by the QC without requiring extra reshuffling later. If so the reshuffling sub-process is called with the "**R**" **icon →** R , otherwise the loading sub-process begins (see Figure 5.11).

At the end of the flowchart from Figure 16 the "L" **icon ->** L is called to return to the main flowchart, Figure 15. Here it is validated if the YT carries an outbound container, in this case the answer is No, and then the unloading sub-process of Figure is called with the "U" **icon ->** U . This sub-process will be compared next with the previous unloading vessel process covered in **Section 3.2.1**.

- Validate if it is necessary to reshuffle containers: this decision validates in the same way that for the loading sub-process, if it is necessary to reposition containers to allow the access to the outbound containers. If so, the reshuffling sub-process is called (see Figure 18) with the "**R**" **icon →** R the unloading sub-process starts, otherwise In the same way that the loading sub-process, at the end of the flowchart of Figure 17 the "U" **icon ->** U is called to return to the main flowchart, Figure 15. Here it is validated if the next YT carries an outbound container, in this case the answer is yes, and then the loading sub-process of Figure 16 is called with the "U" **icon ->** U to start the cycle again.

This reshuffling sub-process, which is called by both the loading and unloading sub- processes, can be seen in Figure 17 and it is explained below this flowchart.

Vessel Reshuffling Sub-Process

- **Availability of Stowage Plan and Possibility to Perform Internal Reshuffling**: A stowage plan for both the arrival and departure is key to perform not only the reshuffling sub-process but also the double cycling strategy. Its availability may avoid (in many QC cycles) the necessity to unload the reshuffles to the wharf reshuffling area or transport them to a buffer area in the yard, so they do not block the access to inbound containers. Instead of the external solution, having pre-plan bays will reduce significantly the reshuffling time and increase the QC utilisation. A more complete discussion of the advantages of these strategies is given in **Subsection 5.3.3.**
- **Verify if There are More Reshuffles Blocking Access to Unbound Containers**: this decision allows the cycle to run again until all the reshuffles from the same bay are positioned either on a buffer area or internally on pre-plan bays. This sub-process will allow to continue with the loading or unloading sub-process, depending on which of them call R , letting the seaside processes to be perform in the same QC and YT cycles

Discussion Under the New Seaside Sub-Processes

The new process flows shown in **Figures 5.11** to **5.14** were formulated based on the QC Double cycling and internal reshuffling strategies. According to the literature they are more efficient than the traditional QC single cycle and external reshuffling. For instance, it is expected that a container terminal that implements these alternatives will rise its capacity to serve the increasing demand of TEUs per year, which will surpass the current capacity in the following years. The port capacity is increased when more vessels can be served in less time, which allows as well, to keep a higher rotation of the containers in the yard. This increase of productivity also triggers more external trucks from customers to come for the containers that will be available sooner.

As a result of this, the service level will increase allowing the port authorities to negotiate better prices, and offer the port services to other shipping lines that ask more requirements that can now be met. Therefore, the implementation of these strategies may increase the performance which will bring better opportunities for feeder and also transhipment ports.

Figure 17. Flowchart unloading container on vessel.

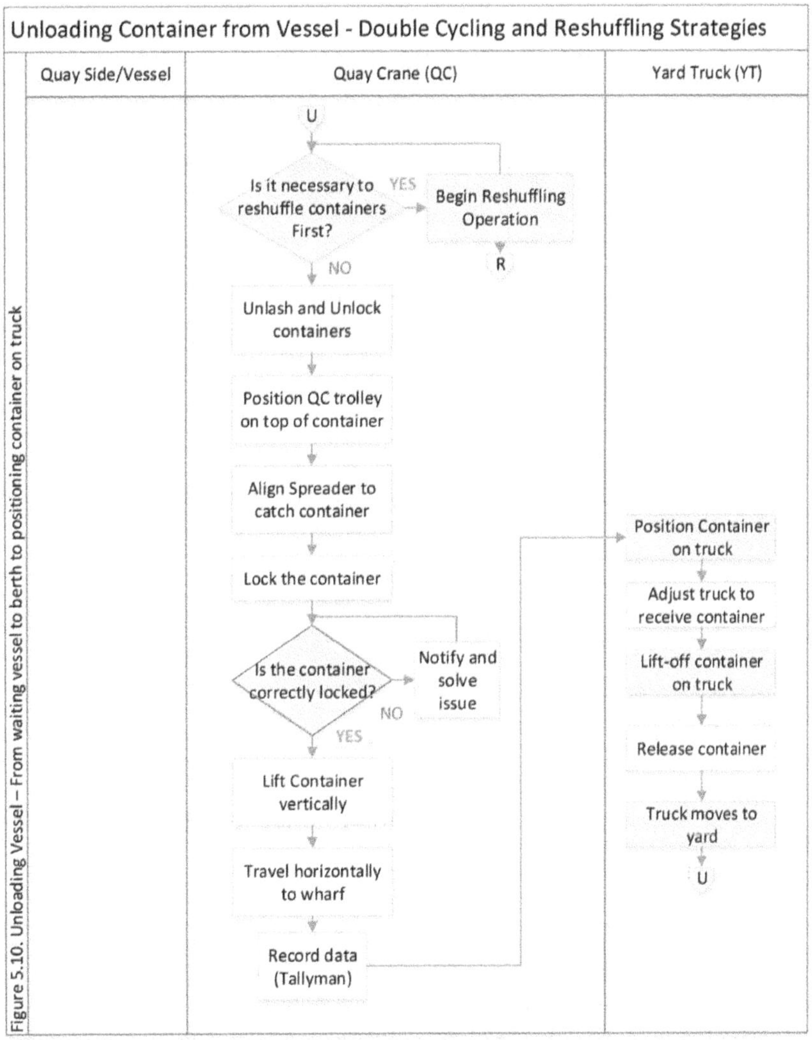

Figure 18. Flowchart vessel reshuffling sub-process

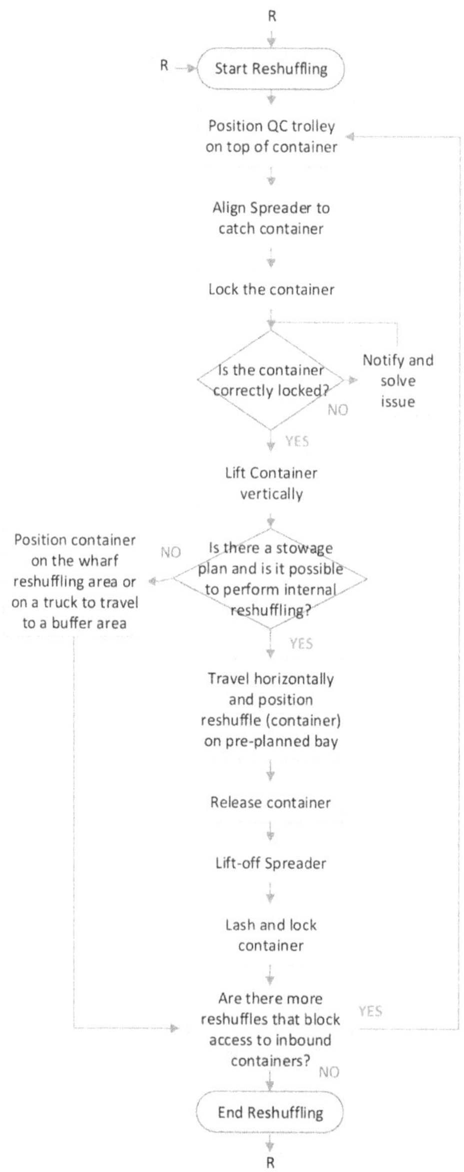

CONCLUSION

The purpose of this chapter is to help port authorities to deal with the increasing demand of containers and the environmental impact from the operations, by finding ways to reduce the material handling time and optimise the utilisation of the equipment. Apart from studying methodologies to reduce the vessel idle time from the arrival to its departure, known as turn-around time, it is assumed that there is a coordination between the container terminals visited on the way to the final destination. This is important for port authorities as they are able to forecast, with some level of accuracy, the arrival time of the vessels. As a result of this, they can coordinate the operations accordingly and offer a competitive service level to shipping lines that will free up time to offer the services to new lines. However, the way to provide a higher service level and be able to handle more containers from new lines is through the increase of the handling capacity. Therefore, this chapter focuses its efforts to present best practices from the literature, with the purpose of reducing the turn-around time of the vessels and the environmental impact of the container terminal operations. The strategies mentioned in this chapter were focused only on the seaside operation, especially the vessel loading and unloading processes.

This chapter explored the operations on a container terminal to improve the overall productivity, with berthing time being one of the main measurements to reduce the cost and increase the attractiveness of the container terminal for shipping lines. Saeed and Larsen (2016) applied the queueing theory and relevant cost information to show that feeder terminals can follow to improve their operation. The double cycling (DC) and reshuffling strategies were found very convenient for a container terminal. According to Meisel and Wichmann (2010) results from a heuristic model 77% of loading and unloading operations can follow DC and 64% of the total reshuffle containers can be repositioned internally. We implemented a simulation model to show how the process improve operations. We propose a new process flow for loading and unloading vessels, which includes the DC and internal reshuffling operations, was formulated. The flowcharts can be used for feeder and transhipment ports as a guide to adopt these strategies, with the final goal of increasing their operative capacity and service level to customers.

Limitations

This study has been the result of the analysis of general market data and the research of relevant literature of container terminals operations, in relation to common issues when unloading and loading vessels. The limitations found during the study are listed below:

- **Environmental Solutions**: During the analysis of the emissions generated by the equipment, it is required to provide the total diesel consumption per year, so the improvements could be estimated if a biofuel mix is adopted.
- **AnyLogic Simulation**: The scope was reduced to analyse only the unloading of inbound containers. This decision allowed for the focus in explaining how the discrete events are formulated, to present the flowchart with the logic of the events, and to explain how the facilities and equipment are programmed to interact with each other.
- **Remote Work**: The container terminal processes were analysed from the perspective of an external consultant, who is given general information of the operations. However, the work has been done remotely, without going to observe in real time the processes which will facilitate the identification of more opportunities for improvement. Moreover, the interaction with container terminal workers on the floor would have been a great opportunity to listen to more specific problems in the operation.

Future Research

The recommendations for future research are based on the limitations and new opportunities identified for container terminals that can be addressed by researchers. They are discussed next:

- **Testing New Operative Strategies with Simulation**: The single cycling scenario run in AnyLogic can be used as a guide to then formulate both the loading and unloading sub-processes using the double cycling (DC) and single cycling methodologies. Comparisons can be done for the turn-around time of the vessel and the utilisation of the YTs and QCs for both scenarios. A similar project can be formulated to integrate DC with mix strategies and reshuffling and compare the results in the simulation runs. This is viable if a terminal operates most of the time based on a stowage plan that allows keeping in the same stack import and export containers. It is expected to increase as well, the utilisation of the RTGs and reduce even more the turn-around time of the vessels if DC is compared with the implementation of the mix strategy.
- **Equipment**: The alternative presented to reduce the emissions of CO_2 (biofuel) did not imply the change of any diesel equipment used by a terminal. For instance, there is an opportunity to evaluate the implications of changing the equipment for their equivalent, powered by a different source of energy, including electric, solar and acid or Li-ion Batteries which will reduce the environmental impact.
- **Cost Analysis**: The cost of the strategies and best practices presented could be estimated by the port authorities taking into account, in the first place, the financial and operative conditions of the terminal. This will allow to determine what budget could be assigned to the project, to then find the specific suppliers, external consultants and construction firms to upgrade the necessary equipment, determine the capacity required and make the necessary changes in layout and processes. Conditions such as the geographical location, intellectual property and cost of ownership of the components acquired should be also considered. Moreover, it is recommended to study the market first and what the different suppliers and consultants are offering before seeking to negotiate the terms and conditions and finally, the price. All these tasks and more, are left for the port operators to take charge, and undergo the necessary research required in order to make cost-effective decisions for seaside operations, taking into consideration their environmental and economic issues. However, the information presented in this document will save considerable time for this undertaking.

REFERENCES

Al Amien, D., Setyani, F. D., & Sihombing, R. (2020, December). Sustainable Port Planning in Future Indonesian Ports: A Case Study of Mafa Port based on UN SDGs. *IOP Conference Series. Earth and Environmental Science*, *618*(1), 012041. doi:10.1088/1755-1315/618/1/012041

Anylogic. (2017). *Discrete Event Modelling*. https://www.anylogic.com/use-of-simulation/discrete-event-simulation/

Carlo, H. J., Vis, I. F. A., & Roodbergen, K. J. (2014). Transport Operations in Container Terminals: Literature Overview, Trends, Research Directions and Classification Scheme. *European Journal of Operational Research*, *236*(1), 1–13. doi:10.1016/j.ejor.2013.11.023

Dekker, R., Bloemhof, J., & Mallidis, I. (2012). Operations Research for Green Logistics – an Overview of Aspects, Issues, Contributions and Challenges. *European Journal of Operational Research, 219*(3), 671–679. doi:10.1016/j.ejor.2011.11.010

Geerlings, H., & van Duin, R. (2011). A New Method for Assessing Co2-Emissions from Container Terminals: A Promising Approach Applied in Rotterdam. *Journal of Cleaner Production, 19*(6), 657–666. doi:10.1016/j.jclepro.2010.10.012

Gharehgozli, A. H., Roy, D., & De Koster, R. (2016). Sea Container Terminals: New Technologies and or Models. *Maritime Economics & Logistics, 18*(2), 103–140. doi:10.1057/mel.2015.3

Goodchild, A. V., & Daganzo, C. F. (2007). Crane Double Cycling in Container Ports: Planning Methods and Evaluation. *Transportation Research Part B: Methodological, 41*(8), 875–891. doi:10.1016/j.trb.2007.02.006

Hasani Goodarzi, A., & Hessameddin Zegordi, S. (2016). A Location-Routing Problem for Cross-Docking Networks: A Biogeography-Based Optimization Algorithm. *Computers & Industrial Engineering, 102*, 132–146. doi:10.1016/j.cie.2016.10.023

Henesey, L. (2004). *Enhancing Container Terminal Performance: A Multi Agent Systems Approach.* Blekinge Institute of Technology Licentiate Dissertation Series, Blekinge Institute of Technology. http://urn.kb.se/resolve?urn=urn:nbn:se:bth-00325

Humang, W. P., Natsir, R., & Fisu, A. A. (2021). Development of a Feeder Port of Tanjung Ringgit Facilities to Support Implementation of Sea Tollway. *Jurnal Penelitian Transportasi Laut, 23*(1), 1–8. doi:10.25104/transla.v23i1.1699

Kaliszewski, A., Kozłowski, A., Dąbrowski, J., & Klimek, H. (2020). Key factors of container port competitiveness: A global shipping lines perspective. *Marine Policy, 117*, 103896. doi:10.1016/j.marpol.2020.103896

Kavakeb, S., Nguyen, T. T., McGinley, K., Yang, Z., Jenkinson, I., & Murray, R. (2015). Green Vehicle Technology to Enhance the Performance of a European Port: A Simulation Model with a Cost-Benefit Approach. *Transportation Research Part C, Emerging Technologies, 60*(Supplement C), 169–188. doi:10.1016/j.trc.2015.08.012

Kemme, N. (2013). Design and Operation of Automated Container Storage Systems. SpringerLink. doi:10.1007/978-3-7908-2885-6

Leriche, D., Oudani, M., Cabani, A., Hoblos, G., Mouzna, J., Boukachour, J., & El Hilali Alaoui, A. (2015). Simulating New Logistics System of Le Havre Port. *IFAC-PapersOnLine, 48*(3), 418–423. doi:10.1016/j.ifacol.2015.06.117

Liu, M., Chu, F., Zhang, Z., & Chu, C. (2015). A Polynomial-Time Heuristic for the Quay Crane Double-Cycling Problem with Internal-Reshuffling Operations. *Transportation Research Part E, Logistics and Transportation Review, 81*(Supplement C), 52–74. doi:10.1016/j.tre.2015.06.009

Low, J. M. W. (2010). Capacity Investment and Efficiency Cost Estimations in Major East Asian Ports. *Maritime Economics & Logistics, 12*(4), 370–391. doi:10.1057/mel.2010.13

Meisel, F., & Wichmann, M. (2010). Container Sequencing for Quay Cranes with Internal Reshuffles. *OR-Spektrum*, *32*(3), 569–591. doi:10.100700291-009-0191-6

Murty, K. G., Liu, J., Yat-wah, W., & Linn, R. (2005). A Decision Support System for Operations in a Container Terminal. *Decision Support Systems*, *39*(3), 309–332. doi:10.1016/j.dss.2003.11.002

Nooramin, S., Amir, V. R. A., & Sayareh, J. (2011). A Six Sigma Framework for Marine Container Terminals. *International Journal of Lean Six Sigma*, *2*(3), 241–253. doi:10.1108/20401461111157196

Pazirandeh, A., & Jafari, H. (2013). Making Sense of Green Logistics. *International Journal of Productivity and Performance Management*, *62*(8), 889–904. doi:10.1108/IJPPM-03-2013-0059

Pedrick, D. (2006). *Green Terminal Design*. Long Beach, CA: CH2M HILL. http://www.fasterfreight-cleanerair.com/pdfs/Presentations/FFCACA2006/Andrew %20Pedrick%20-%20Green%20Terminal%20 Design.pdf

Petering, M. E. H., Wu, Y., Li, W., Goh, M., & de Souza, R. (2009). Development and Simulation Analysis of Real-Time Yard Crane Control Systems for Seaport Container Transshipment Terminals. *OR-Spektrum*, *31*(4), 801–835. doi:10.100700291-008-0142-7

Saeed, N., & Larsen, O. I. (2016). Application of Queuing Methodology to Analyze Congestion: A Case Study of the Manila International Container Terminal, Philippines. *Case Studies on Transport Policy*, *4*(2), 143–149. doi:10.1016/j.cstp.2016.02.001

Stahlbock, R., & Voß, S. (2008). Operations Research at Container Terminals: A Literature Update. *OR-Spektrum*, *30*(1), 1–52. doi:10.100700291-007-0100-9

Sutanto, S. H. (2021). The characteristic, performance, accessibility, and prediction of cargo handling in Probolinggo New Terminal Port. *IOP Conference Series. Earth and Environmental Science*, *649*(1), 012045. doi:10.1088/1755-1315/649/1/012045

Technology, P. (2021). *Ictsi Orders Rtgs from Mitsui for $80 Million Upgrade*. Accessed April 11, 2021, https://www.porttechnology.org/news/ictsi_orders_rtgs_from_mitsui_for_80_million_upgrade

World Shipping Council. (2021). *Top 50 World Container Ports*. Accessed April 01, 2021, https://www.worldshipping.org/about-the-industry/global-trade/top-50-world-container-ports

Yang, C. H., Choi, Y. S., & Ha, T. Y. (2004). Simulation-Based Performance Evaluation of Transport Vehicles at Automated Container Terminals. *OR-Spektrum*, *26*(2), 149–170. doi:10.100700291-003-0151-5

Yang, Y.-C. (2017). Operating Strategies of Co2 Reduction for a Container Terminal Based on Carbon Footprint Perspective. *Journal of Cleaner Production*, *141*(Supplement C), 472–480. doi:10.1016/j.jclepro.2016.09.132

Yang, Y.-C., & Lin, C.-L. (2013). Performance Analysis of Cargo-Handling Equipment from a Green Container Terminal Perspective. *Transportation Research Part D, Transport and Environment*, *23*(Supplement C), 9–11. doi:10.1016/j.trd.2013.03.009

Yongqiang, S., Yang, X., He, Q., Li, Q., & Xu, Q. (2010). Anylogic- Based Simulation Analysis of Queuing System at Container Terminals. *The 2nd International Conference on Information Science and Engineering*. 10.1109/ICISE.2010.5689971

Zeng, Q., & Yang, Z. (2009). Integrating Simulation and Optimization to Schedule Loading Operations in Container Terminals. *Computers & Operations Research, 36*(6), 1935–1944. doi:10.1016/j.cor.2008.06.010

Zhang, X., Zeng, Q., & Yang, Z. (2016). Modeling the Mixed Storage Strategy for Quay Crane Double Cycling in Container Terminals. *Transportation Research Part E, Logistics and Transportation Review, 94*(Supplement C), 171–187. doi:10.1016/j.tre.2016.08.002

Chapter 5
Road Freight Transport Cost:
Differences Between European Countries

Panagiotis Kotsios
International Hellenic University, Greece

Dimitrios Folinas
International Hellenic University, Greece

ABSTRACT

The goal of this research was to measure the cost of road freight transport in the 20 European countries with the highest recorded quantity of tonne-kilometres and assess their competitiveness. Cost competitiveness was measured by four main cost categories: fuels, drivers' wages, tyres and tolls, and the results show large cost variances between countries. The countries with the lowest road freight transport cost were Bulgaria, Poland, and Romania, and those with the highest costs were Norway, Austria, and the UK. The largest differences in costs were met in tolls and other road taxes, followed by drivers' wages, fuels, and finally, tyres.

INTRODUCTION

At a European level, freight transport has recorded a remarkable increase in the last decades. According to the European Commission (2020), the billions of tonne-kilometres (tkm) travelled in the European Union (EU) increased from 2,400 billion in 1995 to 3,353 billion in 2018, an increase of about 40% in a period of 24 years. Among freight transport methods, road transport was responsible for more than half of total freight transport across Europe, followed by shipping, trains and other transport means. As the quantity of Road Freight Transport (RFT) differs from one European country to the next, similar differences can be recorded in RFT cost due to variances in cost factors such as fuels, wages, insurance, taxation, tolls, maintenance, repairs, tyres, parking space etc. Even though scarce, previous research on the topic has pointed out such differences.

DOI: 10.4018/978-1-7998-8709-6.ch005

In this context, the goal of the current research was to measure and compare RFT cost competitiveness in the 20 European countries with the highest recorded quantity of travelled tonne-kilometres and examine if there are cost differences between them, their size and size the factors that create them. Cost competitiveness was measured using four main cost categories: fuels, drivers' wages, tyres and tolls. This examination and its conclusions can be useful for European transport policy designers that wish to harmonize commercial road transport procedures and costs across European Union countries. The research starts with a short literature review about the history of road transport, the categories and the quantity of road transport in Europe and previous investigations on the topic of RFT cost. Next is a description of the applied methodology, followed by the results, their analysis and the conclusions.

LITERATURE REVIEW

Road Transport History

Road transport has developed alongside the development and evolution of humans. The first and most important invention of man related to the development of road transport was the discovery of the wheel 3,500 years ago in Mesopotamia (Britannica, 2018). By using the wheel in combination with the power of domesticated animals (horses, oxen, mules etc.), man was able to carry large quantities of goods across large distances. In order to facilitate the transportation of wagons, he started building roads and rails (Freitag, 1979). The requirements for the movement and distribution of goods by large-scale road transport increased drastically during war periods. Great military leaders of history, such as Alexander the Great, Genghis Khan and Napoleon, relied on the design and implementation of road transport of goods and materials for maintaining their war campaigns. Other important periods for the development of road transport were the British and American industrial revolutions, which supported the expansion or construction of new trade routes, as well as the first and second world wars, which greatly increased the need for logistics in order to meet the needs of combat forces (Erb & James, 2017). One of the most important reasons for the development of transport was also the discovery of the steam engine (Dell, Moseley & Rand, 2014).

In the 20th century, the development of road freight transport was favored further. This growing supremacy stemmed from the growth of cities and the multiplication of private businesses. Especially since the 1970s, significant investments were made in the transport sector. These investments were related to the construction of motorways, better vehicle technology, and computer programs and databases to gather useful information to support road transport services (Banister & Berechman, 1999). Completing the reasons for the development of road transport in the modern world, one should also mention globalization. The term refers to the process of interaction and integration between people, companies and governments worldwide and has grown due to advances in transportation and communication technology. Companies try to benefit from globalization in order to find the best markets for their products and services while securing resources at the lowest cost. The enormous benefits that a company can gain through globalization have played an important role in the development of logistics and road transport in particular (Branch, 2009; Harrison & Hoek, 2012). As for the rest of the world, the road freight transport sector is crucial for Europe.

Road Transport in Europe

The European freight transport sector is of critical importance for the development of the European economy. It fulfils one of the fundamental principles of the Community: the free movement of goods (Giannatos & Andrianopoulos, 1999). The European Union (EU) transport services are divided into several categories and subcategories like sea, air, and land transport. Land transport is inextricably linked to land use, and its main advantages are related to accessibility and cost (Spiekermann & Urban, 2013). Land transport mainly involves rail and road transport, and road transport can be divided into national and international transport. The first category is the national road carriage of goods by the use of a commercial truck from destination A to B. The second category is the carriage of goods by truck from a country of origin to another destination country (Theodoropoulou & Casole, 2014). Road freight transport is the most widespread type of transport because of its flexibility. The road network allows access to more commercial and industrial sites than any other means. Road transport is also used to a significant extent, if not exclusively, in combined transport, such as in cases where the goods are transported either by sea, by the river, by air or by rail or to any other corresponding intermediate infrastructure (Grant, Trautrims & Yew Wong, 2015).

The European Union classifies vehicles as part of emission standards and other vehicle regulations. Passenger cars receive an "M" categorization, while commercial vehicles receive an "N" categorization (Directives 2002/24/EC of 18 March 2002 and 2007/46/EC of 5 September 2007). Category N vehicles are used for the carriage of goods and are divided in the following three categories:

1. N1 - Vehicles for the carriage of goods and having a maximum mass not exceeding 3.5 tonnes,
2. N2 - Vehicles for the carriage of goods and having a maximum mass exceeding 3.5 tonnes but not exceeding 12 tonnes and
3. N3 - Vehicles for the carriage of goods and having a maximum mass exceeding 12 tonnes.

Road transport also includes a large number of different types of freight transport trucks, covering all transport needs (transport of solid, liquid or gas cargo). However, two main categories of freight transport are met on international markets: trucks without a drag (with refrigeration or not) and trucks with a drag (with refrigeration or not). These categories offer the same storage space but have different advantages and disadvantages. In the first case, trucks without a sliding load are suitable for long-distance transport and with as few as possible recipients. The second category, trucks with towed loads - trailers or slings, is suitable for a combination of many and few recipients (Giannatos & Andrianopoulos, 1999).

European Road Freight Transport Statistics

At a European level, freight transport has recorded a remarkable increase in the last decades. According to the European Commission (2020), the billions of tonne-kilometres (tkm)1 travelled in the EU increased from 2,400 b in 1995 to 3,353 b in 2018 (+39.7%)2. Of these, 51% were travelled by road, 29.2% through shipping (within the EU), 12.6% through trains, 4% through inland maritime transport, 3% via pipelines and 0.1% via air. According to official Eurostat statistics, the quantity of goods transported by road in the EU countries is escalating. In terms of tonne-kilometres, European road freight transport increased by 27.2% from 2000 to 2018, with the total recorded quantity of billion tkm reaching 1,708.9 in 2018 (Graph 1). The largest proportion of tkm travelled was for national transport (64%), followed by international transport (24%), cross trade3 (10%) and cabotage4 (2%) (Eurostat, 2019). For 20165, the top 5 countries in road freight transport were Germany, Poland, Spain, the United Kingdom and France, and accounted for 62% of the total tkm travelled in the European Union. The largest increase between 2015 and 2016 in total tkm was recorded in Cyprus (+24.9%), followed by Romania (+23.5%) and Ireland (17.3%) (Eurostat, 2017).

Figure 1. Freight transport in EU27 in billion of tonne-kilometres
Source: European Commission, Statistical Pocketbook 2020, EU Road Transport in Figures

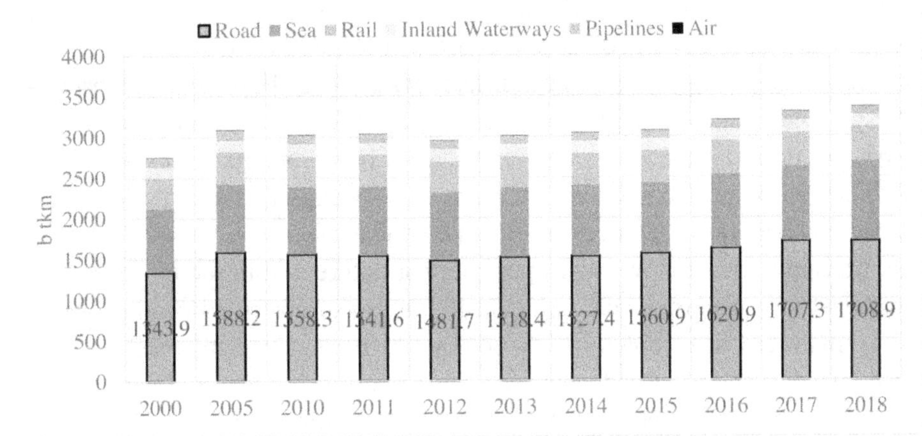

For the provision of the service, in the EU27 in 2017 there were 535.384 road freight transport companies, and most of them were met in Spain (19%), Poland (16%) and Italy (12%). Employment in the RFT sector for the whole of the EU was calculated at 3.06 million employees, and the sector's annual turnover surpassed 324 billion euros (European Commission, 2020). This impressive growth of the European RFT sector can be attributed to several reasons, including the large trade activity between European states, the effort by companies to reduce costs, the need for combined road transport and the fact that it is the most economical and flexible type of freight transport. Last but not least, the preference for this type of transport is mainly due to the fact that the road haulage market is also very competitive and fragmented, with a few large logistics companies and many small transport companies of three or fewer trucks (Harrison & Hoek, 2012).

Cost Comparisons

RFT companies incur a large number of costs in order to provide their services. Leaving aside the initial investment required for setting up a RFT enterprise, the fixed and variable costs for operating it are numerous. These may include the cost of drivers' wages, fuels, tyres, maintenance, repairs, parking space, tolls, road taxes, insurance, administrative expenses, accounting, phone bills, water, electricity, taxes etc. All these cost categories may differ considerably between European countries. However, there is relatively a very small number of researches regarding RFT costs, and some of them will be mentioned in the following lines.

Bina et al (2014) developed a model for comparing unit costs of road and rail freight transport for a sample of selected European countries and found that combined transport (rail and road) can have similar cost advantages under certain infrastructure conditions transport. The European Commission's Directorate-General for Energy and Transport in 1998 funded the project SOFTICE (Survey on Freight Transport Including Cost Comparison for Europe). The project's results showed that drivers' wages were the largest cost factor, followed by fuels, and these factors varied substantially between countries. Total tax costs also varied between countries, ranging from 10% to 25% of the total operating cost of long haulage trucks. For 100km distance, EU prices were between 3 and 8 times higher in Western than in Eastern European countries, but prices were closer for long-distance freight. According to a more recent report by AECOM (2014) for the European Commission, the largest share of the transport cost corresponds to drivers' wages and the cost of fuel. Smaller costs include maintenance, depreciation, taxes, insurance etc. This study also found large cost differences between European countries. A more recent study from Persyn, Díaz-Lanchas and Barbero (2019), on behalf of the European Commission's Joint Research Centre, mentions that drivers' wages represent 42.1% of total road transport costs, fuels 21.2%, vignettes and tolls 5.9%, taxes 0.6%, other time costs (e.g. resting) 17.1% and other distance costs (e.g maintenance, accommodation, insurances) 13.3%. Their analysis of the costs for 268 NUTS 2 regions concluded that transport costs follow a core-periphery structure within the EU, where geographically central regions benefit from shorter trips and reduced fuel consumption. In contrast, peripheral regions tend to benefit from lower wages. Finally, Liakopoulou (2016) analyzed and measured the costs of road transportation companies and proposed a platform for the permanent measurement of these costs at the company level. Lastly, it must be mentioned that the term road transport costs, includes, apart from the monetary, also the environmental ones. Road transport includes environmental impacts that are distinguished by noise and air pollution and the negative impact they have on society and the environment (Milan, 2007). However, the measurement of these costs is not in the goals of the present research.

The literature review has pointed out that road transport is one of the most important means of freight transport in Europe, that it is a growing market and that the quantity of RFT differs significantly from country to country. Moreover, previous research has pointed out considerable differences in RFT cost between countries. In this context, the goal of the current research was to investigate, record, and compare the cost of RFT in different European countries to make comparisons about cost competitiveness between them. The analysis and the conclusions of this research can be useful for European transport policy designers interested in harmonizing commercial road transport procedures and costs across European Union countries.

RESEARCH METHODOLOGY

The methodology that was followed in order to answer the research question was the following: firstly, a sample of 20 countries with the largest RFT quantity measured in tkm was chosen, using open Eurostat data (2017). These countries are shown in Table 1.

Figure 2 presents a map of the travelled tkm for the 20 countries of the sample. From the colors of the map, we can observe that most tkm is travelled in countries of central Europe.[6]

Table 1. Sample of European countries with the largest quantity of RFT

No	Country	Total Million tkm
1	Germany	315,711
2	Poland	290,749
3	Spain	216,997
4	United Kingdom	176,678
5	France	155,843
6	Italy	112,637
7	Netherlands	67,964
8	Czech Republic	50,315
9	Romania	48,176
10	Sweden	42,673
11	Hungary	40,002
12	Slovakia	36,139
13	Bulgaria	35,409
14	Portugal	34,877
15	Lithuania	30,974
16	Belgium	30,865
17	Finland	26,837
18	Austria	25,082
19	Norway	20,932
20	Greece	20,903

Source: Eurostat with processing by the authors

The sum of tkm of RFT in these 20 countries represented 96.3% of the total klm tonnes that were travelled in Europe in 2016. For each of these countries, information was collected regarding four main cost categories: 1) fuels, 2) driver wages, 3) tolls and other road taxes, and 4) tyres. These cost categories were selected because they were included in previous research on the same topic and because of data availability. Each cost category was approximated using the following method:

- **Fuels:** in order to approximate the cost of fuel in each country, the fuel consumption of a truck per 100 klm of highway road was multiplied by the cost of a litre of diesel in each country. The truck type used to estimate fuel consumption was based on information collected a) by asking professional drivers and b) on data about truck sales in Europe. The truck that was pointed out as a very popular type was an 18 tonne, 12,000 cc Mercedes Actros with Euro 5 technology and fuel consumption of 26.5 litres per 100 klm. The information about diesel litre cost was collected from the internet.
- **Driver Cost:** the driver's labour cost was approximated by multiplying the hours that a professional truck driver would require to drive 100 klm of highway road at a speed of 80 klm per hour, by the labour cost per hour. However, from early on in the research it proved very difficult to collect information from companies and freelance drivers about the exact labour hour cost (sal-

ary + social insurance contributions) of a truck driver in each country. As a result, this cost was approximated by using the minimum wage per hour in each country. The minimum wage per hour was used under the assumption that a higher minimum wage means higher driver salaries, while a lower minimum wage means lower truck driver salaries. The minimum wage cost was collected from Eurostat surveys. In cases of countries that do not use minimum wages, the cost was approximated by the typical labour hour cost of an unskilled worker.

- **Tolls and Other Road Taxes:** in order to approximate the cost of tolls, vignette and any other road taxes in each country, the authors estimated this cost for a five axle international truck travelling between each country's two biggest cities by population, and then apportioned this cost on a 100 klm scale.
- **Tyre Cost:** the tyre cost was estimated by finding the tyre consumption of a 5 axle truck for a distance of 100 klm. The estimations were made using the information that truck tyres typically last for about 120,000 klm and a common tyre type that is used for the Mercedes Actros is Michelin 315/70 R 22.5 X Line Energy D2. The authors calculated the cost of 10 tyres (5 axle truck) using prices from local Michelin dealers in each country.

Figure 2. Tkm by country of the sample

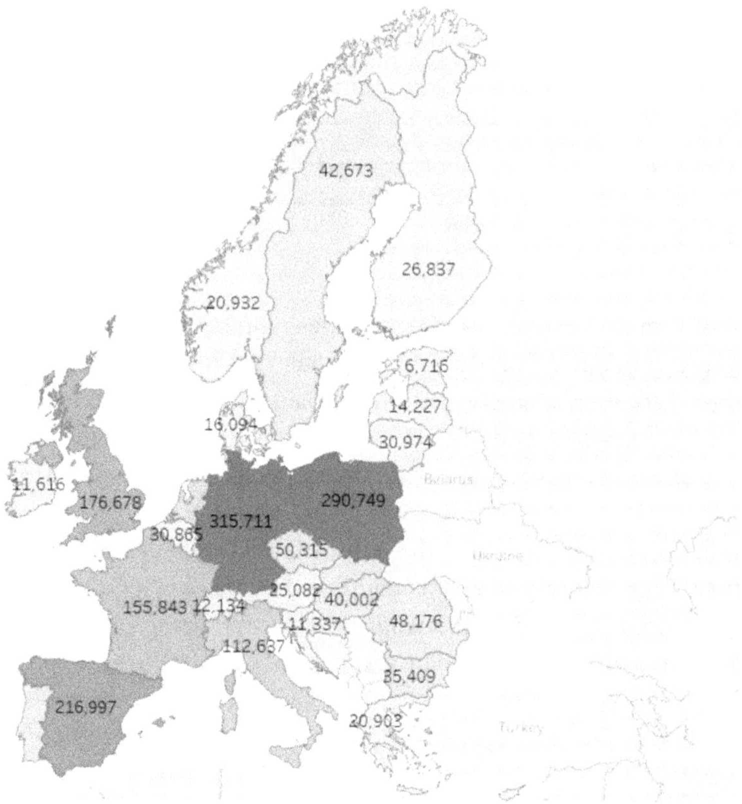

COST CALCULATIONS

Fuel Cost

The cost for the sample truck to travel 100 klm of highway road in each of the 20 European countries is presented in Table 2. The columns present information about the fuel consumption of the sample truck, the price of diesel fuel per litre and the cost in euros (fuel consumption multiplied by the price of a litre of diesel).

In Table 2 considerable variations between countries can be observed. The lowest cost for fuel consumption is noted in Bulgaria (26.50€), followed by Romania (29.15€) and the highest one in Sweden (41.34€), followed by Finland (39.75€). The mean value for the 20 European countries was 34.33€ and 9 countries had values below average and 11 above average. The sample's variance was 18.22 with a standard deviation of 4.27.

Table 2. Fuel cost in 20 European countries

No	Country	Fuel Consumption in Diesel litres per 100 klm	Price of Litre of Diesel Fuel (22/03/21)	Cost in Euros
1	Germany	26.5	1.31	34.72
2	Poland	26.5	1.14	30.21
3	Spain	26.5	1.19	31.54
4	United Kingdom	26.5	1.49	39.49
5	France	26.5	1.39	36.84
6	Italy	26.5	1.44	38.16
7	Netherlands	26.5	1.39	36.84
8	Czech Republic	26.5	1.14	30.21
9	Romania	26.5	1.10	29.15
10	Sweden	26.5	1.56	41.34
11	Hungary	26.5	1.22	32.33
12	Slovakia	26.5	1.17	31.01
13	Bulgaria	26.5	1.00	26.50
14	Portugal	26.5	1.37	36.31
15	Lithuania	26.5	1.13	29.95
16	Belgium	26.5	1.42	37.63
17	Finland	26.5	1.50	39.75
18	Austria	26.5	1.16	30.74
19	Norway	26.5	1.47	38.96
20	Greece	26.5	1.32	34.98

Notes: **a)** the fuel consumption of a 12.000 cc Mercedes Actros with Euro 5 technology was estimated at 26.5 litre per 100 klm (https://www.mercedes-benz.com/en/mercedes-benz/vehicles/trucks/fuel-comparison-tests-in-europe) **b)** the price of diesel fuel was taken from the webpage https://ec.europa.eu/energy/data-analysis/weekly-oil-bulletin_en (Report of 03/22/21)

Drivers' Wages Cost Approximation

As mentioned in the methodology, the labour cost was approximated by multiplying the hours that a professional truck driver would require to drive 100 klm of highway road at a speed of 80 klm/hour, by the minimum wage per hour in each country. Table 3 presents the results.

From Table 3, it can observed that the lowest labour cost is noted in Bulgaria (2.04€) followed by Hungary (2.84€) and the highest one in Norway (23.33€), followed by Sweden (14.15€). The mean value for the 20 European countries was 7.99€, and 9 countries had values above average and 11 below average. The sample's variance was 28.49 and the standard deviation 5.34.

Table 3. Approximation of driver's labour cost in 20 European countries

No	Country	Hours Needed to Travel 100 klm in a Highway With a Speed 80 klm/hour	Minimum Wage per Hour in Euros	Cost in Euros
1	Germany	1.25	8.84	11.05
2	Poland	1.25	3.17	3.96
3	Spain	1.25	4.94	6.18
4	UK	1.25	8.86	11.08
5	France	1.25	9.88	12.35
6	Italy	1.25	7.11	8.89
7	Netherlands	1.25	9.03	11.29
8	Czech Rep.	1.25	2.82	3.53
9	Romania	1.25	2.44	3.05
10	Sweden	1.25	11.32	14.15
11	Hungary	1.25	2.27	2.84
12	Slovakia	1.25	2.50	3.13
13	Bulgaria	1.25	1.63	2.04
14	Portugal	1.25	3.94	4.93
15	Lithuania	1.25	2.45	3.06
16	Belgium	1.25	9.49	11.86
17	Finland	1.25	5.55	6.94
18	Austria	1.25	8.92	11.15
19	Norway	1.25	18.66	23.33
20	Greece	1.25	3.94	4.93

Notes: **a)** the source from the minimum wage value was the report Statutory minimum wages 2018 by Eurofound (https://www.eurofound.europa.eu/sites/default/files/ef_publication/field_ef_document/ef18005en.pdf). **b)** Italy, Sweden, Finland, Austria and Norway do not have minimum wages. For **Italy** the minimum wage per hour was calculated by the monthly unemployment benefit (1,195 euros) divided by the typical workload of 168 working hours per month (4.2 weeks*40 hours) (Source: https://www.eurofound.europa.eu). For **Sweden** it was calculated from the salary of a hotel employee aged 20 and above, with no experience and no education https://www.quora.com/Whats-the-minimum-wage-in-Sweden). For **Finland** the minimum wage must be at least 40 times the basic daily unemployment assistance. Since 1 January 2007 this meant that the paid wages should be at least €956.10 per month, €44.47 per day or €5.55 per hour (Source: https://www.eurofound.europa.eu/publications/report/2009/finland-wage-formation). In **Austria** the minimum wage would be applied in 2020. Its height will be 1,500€ per month (Source: https://www.eurofound.europa.eu). In **Norway** trade unions in each sector bargain different rates. The rate used was taken from unexperienced worked in construction industry (177 krone per hour) (Source: https://www.lifeinnorway.net).

Tolls and Other Road Taxes

In order to approximate the cost of tolls, vignette and any other road taxes in each country, the authors made estimates about a five axle international truck travelling between each country's two biggest cities by population and then apportioned this cost on a 100klm scale. The data are presented in Table 4.

From Table 4, it can observe that the lowest cost is noted in Finland that does not have any tolls, followed by Spain with 5.26€ and the highest one in Austria (41.00€) followed by Norway (30.07€). The mean value for the 20 European countries was 13.34€, and 12 countries had values below average and eight above average. The sample's variance was 87.38, and the standard deviation was 9.35.

Table 4. Calculations of tolls and other road taxes in 20 European countries

No	Country	1st Largest City	2nd Largest City	Distance in klm	Cost in Euros	Reason	Cost for 100 klm in Euros
1	Germany	Berlin	Hamburg	287	44.77	Tolls	15.60
2	Poland	Warsaw	Krakow	360	22.57	Tolls	6.27
3	Spain	Madrid	Barcelona	617	32.45	Tolls	5.26
4	UK	London	Birmingham	126	24.30	Levy cost and tolls	19.29
5	France	Paris	Marseille	773	59.50	Tolls	7.70
6	Italy	Rome	Milan	572	101.40	Tolls	17.73
7	Netherlands	Amsterdam	Rotterdam	95	8.00	Eurovignette	8.00
8	Czech Rep.	Prague	Brno	186	33.93	Tolls	18.24
9	Romania	Bucharest	Iasi	389	11.00	Vignette	11.00
10	Sweden	Stockholm	Goetenberg	468	8.00	Eurovignette	8.00
11	Hungary	Budapest	Debrecen	230	8.00	Eurovignette	8.00
12	Slovakia	Bratislava	Košice	397	73.50	Tolls	18.51
13	Bulgaria	Sofia	Plovdiv	133	11.00	Vignette	11.00
14	Portugal	Lisbon	Porto	312	22.55	Tolls	7.23
15	Lithuania	Vinius	Kaunas	92	11.00	Vignette	11.00
16	Belgium	Antwerp	Ghent	59	7.39	Tolls	7.39
17	Finland	Helsinki	Tampere	178	0.00	No tolls	0.00
18	Austria	Vienna	Graz	195	79.95	Tolls	41.00
19	Norway	Oslo	Bergen	305	91.71	Tolls	30.07
20	Greece	Athens	Thessaloniki	499	77.65	Tolls	15.56

Notes: The information was drawn from the following sources: 1. **Germany** Toll Collect https://www.toll-collect.de/en, 2. **Poland** https://www.tolls.eu, https://www.multiservicetolls.com/, 3. **Spain** https://www.tolls.eu, https://www.viamichelin.com, 4. **UK** https://www.gov.uk/uk-toll-roads, https://www.multiservicetolls.com, 5. **France** http://www.autoroutes.fr, 6. **Italy** https://www.autostrade.it, 7. **Netherlands** https://www.dkv-euroservice.com, 8. **Czech Rep.** http://www.mytocz.eu, 9. **Romania** https://www.untrr.ro, https://www.tolls.eu, 10. **Sweden** https://www.dkv-euroservice.com, 11. **Hungary** https://www.hu-go.hu/, 12. **Slovakia** https://www.dkv-euroservice.com, https://www.emyto.sk, 13. **Bulgaria** https://www.tolls.eu, 14. **Portugal** https://www.portugaltolls.com/, 15. **Lithuania** https://lakd.lrv.lt/en/road-charges-and-tolls/user-charge-vignettes, 16. **Belgium** https://www.viapass.be, 17. **Finland** http://www.highwaymaps.eu/finland, 18. **Austria**, https://www.asfinag.at, 19. **Norway** https://www.fjellinjen.no/private/toll-calculator/, 20. **Greece** http://diodia.com.gr/.

Tyre Cost

The tyre cost was estimated by finding the tyre consumption of a 5-axle truck for a distance of 100 klm. The estimations were made using a tyre type that is common for the Mercedes Actros, the Michelin 315/70 R 22.5 X Line Energy D2. The authors calculated the cost of 10 tyres (5 axle truck) using prices from local Michelin dealers in each country, as provided by the official Michelin European website (Table 5).

The lowest tyre cost is noted in Bulgaria with 4.55€, and the highest one in Norway (6.00€) followed by Finland with 5.99€. The mean value for the 20 European countries was 5.39€, and half of the countries had values below average and the other half above average. The sample's variance was 0.28 and the standard deviation was 0.53.

Table 5. Tyre consumption in euros for 100 klm of highway road for a 5 axle Mercedes Actros.

No	Country	Cost of 1 Tyre	Cost of 10 Tyres	Tyre Duration in klm	Cost for 100 klm in Euros
1	Germany	634.2	6,342	120,000	5.29
2	Poland	680.92	6,809.2	120,000	5.67
3	Spain	708.99	7,089.9	120,000	5.91
4	UK	702	7,020	120,000	5.85
5	France	697.2	6,972	120,000	5.81
6	Italy	693.88	6,938.8	120,000	5.78
7	Netherlands	636.4	6,364	120,000	5.30
8	Czech Rep.	621	6,210	120,000	5.18
9	Romania	558.27	5,582.7	120,000	4.65
10	Sweden	718.37	7,183.7	120,000	5.99
11	Hungary	650	6,500	120,000	5.42
12	Slovakia	573	5,730	120,000	4.78
13	Bulgaria	545.55	5,455.5	120,000	4.55
14	Portugal	708.99	7,089.9	120,000	5.91
15	Lithuania	547.16	5,471.6	120,000	4.56
16	Belgium	636.4	6,364	120,000	5.30
17	Finland	718.37	7,183.7	120,000	5.99
18	Austria	634	6,340	120,000	5.28
19	Norway	720.33	7,203.3	120,000	6.00
20	Greece	550	5,500	120,000	4.58

Total Cost and Variance Analysis

Table 6 presents the total cost of RFT in the sample of 20 European countries.

From Table 6, it can be noticed that the lowest RFT cost is met in Bulgaria with 44.08€, followed by Poland with 46.12€ and Romania with 47.85€. The highest cost is met in Norway with 98.35€, followed by Austria with 88.17€ and the UK with 75.70€. The most important cost category is fuels, keeping in mind that the driver wage cost is an approximation. Regarding the height of each cost category, it is worth noting that a) for Norway, the cost is the highest one in 3 out of 4 categories (except tolls), b) Austria has the second-highest RFT cost mainly because of the cost of tolls - the other cost factors are not far from average and c) Bulgaria has the lowest cost in 3 out of 4 cost categories (except tolls). Table 7 presents basic descriptive statistics about the costs and measurement of standard deviation.

Table 6. Totals of RFT cost for 100 klm of highway road for 20 European countries

No	Country	Fuel Cost	Driver Cost	Tolls	Tyre Cost	Total Cost in Euros
1	Bulgaria	26.50	2.04	11.00	4.55	44.08
2	Poland	30.21	3.96	6.27	5.67	46.12
3	Romania	29.15	3.05	11.00	4.65	47.85
4	Lithuania	29.95	3.06	11.00	4.56	48.57
5	Hungary	32.33	2.84	8.00	5.42	48.58
6	Spain	31.54	6.18	5.26	5.91	48.88
7	Finland	39.75	6.94	0.00	5.99	52.67
8	Portugal	36.31	4.93	7.23	5.91	54.37
9	Czech Rep.	30.21	3.53	18.24	5.18	57.15
10	Slovakia	31.01	3.13	18.51	4.78	57.42
11	Greece	34.98	4.93	15.56	4.58	60.05
12	Netherlands	36.84	11.29	8.00	5.30	61.43
13	Belgium	37.63	11.86	7.39	5.30	62.19
14	France	36.84	12.35	7.70	5.81	62.69
15	Germany	34.72	11.05	15.60	5.29	66.65
16	Sweden	41.34	14.15	8.00	5.99	69.48
17	Italy	38.16	8.89	17.73	5.78	70.56
18	UK	39.49	11.08	19.29	5.85	75.70
19	Austria	30.74	11.15	41.00	5.28	88.17
20	Norway	38.96	23.33	30.07	6.00	98.35

Table 7. Descriptive statistics and variance analysis

No	Fuel Cost	Driver Cost	Tolls	Tyre Cost	Total Cost
Min	26.50	2.04	0.00	4.55	44.08
Max	41.34	23.33	41.00	6.00	98.35
Range	14.84	21.29	41.00	1.46	54.27
Average	34.33	7.99	13.34	5.39	61.05
Standard Dev.	4.27	5.34	9.35	0.53	14.19

From Table 7, it can be noticed that the largest deviation is noted in the tolls and other road taxes cost, while the smallest one is in the tyre cost. The total cost standard deviation from the average value of 61.05€ is 14.19€, and the range from the highest to the lowest total cost is 54.27€. Graph 3 presents a map of the total cost per country of the sample. In this map, the only clear geographical pattern regarding RFT cost is for the lower cost of eastern European countries. In order to examine the geospatial patterns of cost, the authors performed two simple linear regression analyses: one with Total Cost as the dependent variable and total tkm travelled in each country of the sample as the independent one (for the year 2018), and another with Total Cost as the dependent variable and GDP as the independent one (for the year 2018 again). However, in both cases, the results were not statistically significant.

Figure 3. Total cost per country

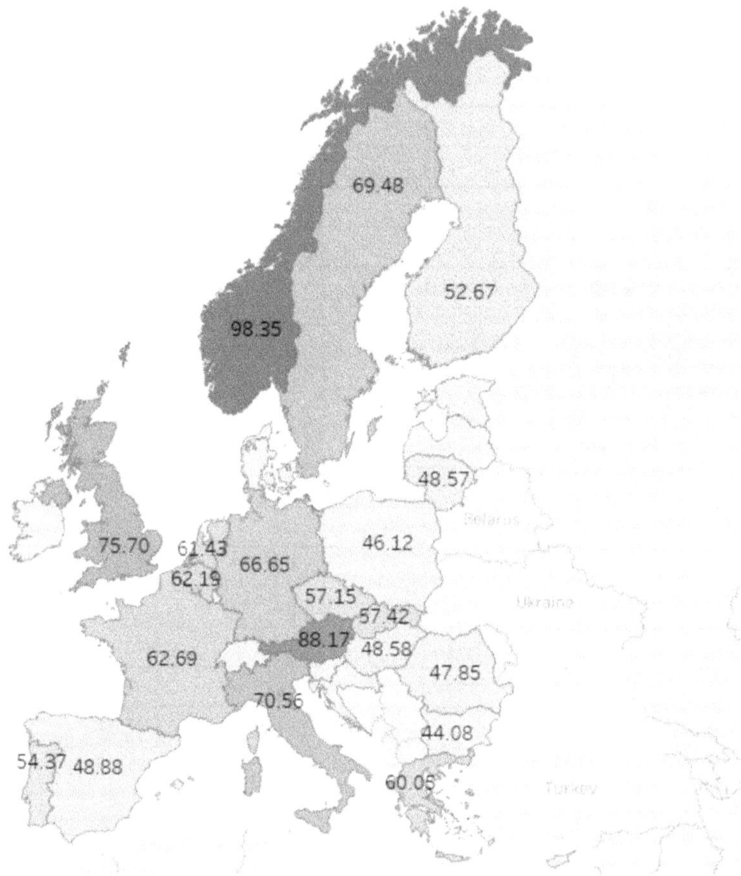

CONCLUSION

As pointed out by the literature review, road transport is one of the most important means of freight transport globally, and the quantity of RFT differs significantly from country to country. The goal of the current research was to investigate, record, and compare the cost of RFT in various European countries to make comparisons between them. The analysis and the conclusions of this research can be useful for

European policy designers, who may wish to harmonize commercial road transport procedures and costs across European Union countries.

The current research results have shown that there are considerable differences in the RFT cost between the 20 European countries of the sample. The countries found to have the lowest RFT cost were Bulgaria, Poland, and Romania, while those with the highest costs were Norway, Austria, and the UK. The largest differences in costs were met in tolls and other road taxes, followed by drivers' wages, fuels and tyres.

Harmonization policies for RFT among EU countries may include the application of common policies regarding the cost of tolls as well as the cost of fuels, which proved to be the most important cost categories. The high standard deviation in the cost of tolls may signal the possibility of designing a common RFT policy across all EU countries. In contrast, the cost of fuels may be harmonized with setting a common tax rate among them. Another proposal would be to promote the development of "greener" commercial tracks, which can be fuelled by electricity produced from renewable energy sources across all EU countries.

It is necessary to mention, though, that the current research has limitations. Two of the most important ones are related to the fact that there are various other cost categories that are not measured in the research and the lack of data on actual drivers' wages, which were found to be the most important cost category in other researches. Further research could shed light on these cost categories and expand the sample to more counties both within and outside the European Union.

REFERENCES

AECOM. (2014). *Report on the State of the EU Road Haulage Market*. European Commission, Directorate General for Mobility and Transport.

Banister, D., & Berechman, J. (1999). *Transport investment and economic development*. Taylor and Francis.

Bína, L., Bínová, H., Březina, E., Kumpošt, P., & Padělek, T. (2014). Comparative model of unit costs of road and rail freight transport for selected European countries. *European Journal of Business and Social Sciences*, *3*(4), 127–136.

Branch, A. (2009). *Global supply chain management and international logistics*. Routledge.

Britannica. (2018). *Wheel*. Retrieved from https://www.britannica.com/technology/wheel

Dell, R., Moseley, P., & Rand, D. (2014). *Towards Sustainable Road Transport*. Academic Press.

Erb, J., & James, S. (2017). *Global logistics for dummies*. John Wiley & Sons.

European Commission. (2020). *EU Transport in Figures 2020*. Author.

Eurostat. (2017). *Road freight transport statistics*. Retrieved from https://ec.europa.eu/eurostat/statistics-explained/index.php/Road_freight_transport_statistics

Eurostat. (2019). *Road freight transport statistics: EU road freight transport continues to grow*. Retrieved from https://ec.europa.eu/eurostat/statistics-explained/index.php/Road_freight_transport_statistics

Freitag, D. (1979). History of wheels for off - road transport. *Journal of Terramechanics*, *16*(2), 49–68. doi:10.1016/0022-4898(79)90001-6

Giannatos, G., & Andrianopoulos, S. (1999). *Logistics, Transport and Distribution*. Tekdotiki.

Grant, D., Trautrims, A., & Yew Wong, C. (2015). *Sustainable Logistics and Supply Chain Management*. Kogan Page Limited.

Harrison, A., & Hoek, R. (2012). *Logistics Management & Strategy*. Rosili.

Liakopoulou, S. (2016). *Cost and pricing in road freight transport: Development of a platform for calculating the cost of transport*. Aristotle University of Thessaloniki Polytechnic School.

Milan, J. (2007). Modelling the full cost of an intermodal and road freight transport network. *Transportation Research Part D, Transport and Environment*, *12*(1), 33–44. doi:10.1016/j.trd.2006.10.004

Persyn, D., Díaz-Lanchas, J., & Barbero, J. (2019). *Estimating road transport costs between EU regions*. JRC Working Papers on Territorial Modelling and Analysis No. 04/2019, European Commission, Seville, JRC114409.

Spiekermann, M., & Urban, W. (2013). *Overview of Country Transport Models*. Regional Section Research Lindemannstrasse.

Theodoropoulou, R., & Kasoli, M. (2014). *Transport and Logistics*. Hellenic General Secretariat for Research and Technology.

ENDNOTES

1. A tonne-kilometre, abbreviated as tkm, is a unit of measure of freight transport which represents the transport of one tonne of goods (including packaging and tare weights of intermodal transport units) by a given transport mode (road, rail, air, sea, inland waterways, pipeline etc.) over a distance of one kilometre.
2. This figure includes intra-EU air and sea transport but not transport activities between the EU and the rest of the world.
3. Cross-trade is international road transport between two different countries performed by a road motor vehicle registered in a third country.
4. Cabotage is road transport by a motor vehicle registered in a country performed on the national territory of another country. Cabotage data are reported by European Union (EU) Member States for hauliers registered in their country.
5. For 2017-18 the Eurostat data have many confidential values that prohibited the extraction of accurate observations.
6. The authors performed a linear regression analysis between the tkm travelled in the top 20 European economies (dependent variable) and their Gross Domestic Product (independent variable) for year 2018, and found a **strong positive relationship** between the two (R=0.739, df=17, F=19.68 at significance level 0.00) (Data source: Eurostat https://ec.europa.eu/eurostat/data/database).

Chapter 6
Designing of Container Feeder Service Networks Under Unstable Demand Conditions

Olcay Polat
Pamukkale University, Turkey

ABSTRACT

The COVID-19 pandemic has greatly magnified supply challenges in all industries, and virus waves continue to cause an extraordinary amount of variation in both the demand for and the availability of necessary products. This uncertainty has also forced many organizations including container liner shipping to redesign their supply chain. Feeder services from hub ports are essential chain of shipping networks. This chapter addresses the design of feeder networks under consideration of demand fluctuations over the year. For this purpose, a perturbation-based variable neighbourhood search approach is developed in order to determine the feeder ship fleet size and mix, the fleet deployment, service routes, and voyage schedules to minimize operational costs. In the case study investigation, the authors consider the feeder network design problem faced by a feeder shipping company as a sample application. The performance of alternate network configurations is compared under dynamic demand conditions. Numerical results highlight the advantage of dynamic and flexible design of feeder service networks.

INTRODUCTION

Driven by the ever-increasing loading capacity of containerships, hub-and-spoke networks turned out to be the most economic mode of organizing global container shipping. In this kind of networks hubs are connected to the main intercontinental sea routes while regional ports with low transport demand are serviced by small and medium-sized feeder ships. The connections from the hub ports to the regional ports constitute the feeder network which provides the global containership liners access to local transportation markets and avoids the megaships' calling at too many ports.

DOI: 10.4018/978-1-7998-8709-6.ch006

Global liner shipping as well as feeder service requires significant capital investment for the fleet of containerships and involves huge operational costs. High utilization of the fleet capacity is needed to secure the desired return on investment (Coskun et al., 2016; Polat & Güngör, 2019). Principally, the revenue of container shipping is affected by the transported container volume which in turn depends on the development of the world economy and world trade (Zachcial & Lemper, 2006). Specifically for feeder services there are close relationships to regional economic developments which strongly affect the transportation demand of export as well as import goods and raw materials. In addition to volume, the balance between import and export containers at ports is a critical factor. Theoretically, a feeder ship could carry up to twice of its slot capacity in a cyclic route if it departs from the hub port with all the import containers, delivers them to regional ports, simultaneously picks up export containers, and returns to the hub port loaded with export containers. When the trade is imbalanced at the ports, slots remain idle during the journey of the ship. In particular, trade imbalance in certain regions makes it difficult for feeder services to fully utilize the capacity of feeder ships operating in the network. Therefore, the design of feeder services plays a crucial role in maritime logistics.

Generally, in maritime transport demand fluctuates over the year with seasonal cycles, peaks at certain times of the year, and unexpected sharp drops and cancelations occur (Schulze & Prinz, 2009). For certain types of goods production and consumption varies over the year, e.g. following the harvest season for fruit or fish. While most of these factors are affecting only a single port or region, other factors like Christmas and Chinese New Year, create peaks in global trade. In addition, unexpected financial and political developments may cause demand fluctuations in intercontinental and regional container shipping. Figure 1 shows the monthly development of container traffic for a number of selected port (The Port of Los Angeles) from 1996 to 2020. The figure not only exhibits the periodic fluctuations but also highlights the impact of the economic crisis.

Figure 1. Monthly total container traffic at the Port of Los Angeles

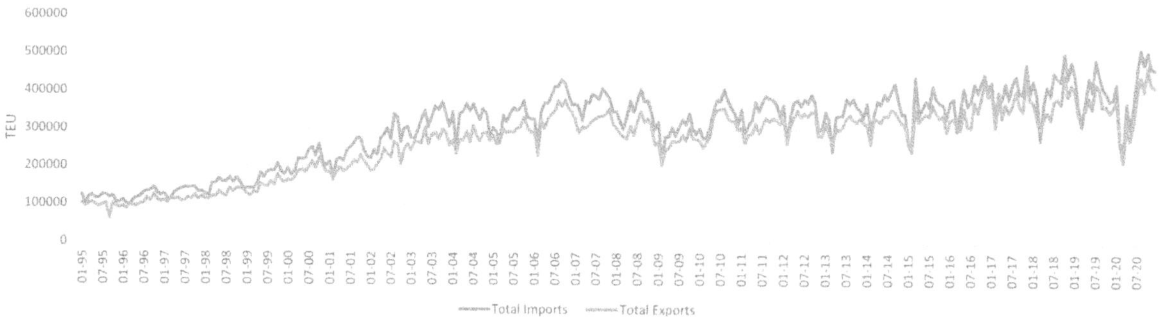

The transportation demand of ports determines the necessary slot capacity for the shipping liners. Since demand is uncertain, shipping liners must carefully consider their capacity decisions. Shortterm fluctuations are further caused by contract conditions which allow shippers to pay for container transportation only when the container is loaded onto a vessel or delivered to its destination. This situation enables shippers to cancel their bookings before loading despite their long term contractual agreements. Hence, demand fluctuations have to be seen as a driving force in the design of service networks. Even small variations in the demand pattern could lead to entirely different service network designs (Andersen,

2010). As we are all very intensely concerned during 2020-2021, the COVID-19 pandemic has greatly magnified supply challenges in all industries. Virus waves continue to cause an extraordinary amount of variation in both the demand for and the availability of necessary products. This uncertainty has also forced many organizations to redesign their supply chain. In the academic literature, the design of feeder service networks under unstable demand conditions has received only little attention. Therefore, the objective of this study is to provide Operations Research based solutions to this challenging problem considering the feeder network design problem faced by a Turkish short-sea shipping company as a sample application.

The remainder of this chapter is structured as follows. First, the relevant literature is briefly reviewed. Then, a mathematical formulation of the feeder network design problem is given. Next, a heuristic solution procedure is proposed. Next part introduces the case study application and presents detailed numerical results. Finally, concluding remarks are given.

BACKGROUND

Recent literature reviews on liner shipping network design, e.g. by (Christiansen et al., 2020; Hoff et al., 2010; Pantuso et al., 2014), revealed that container demand uncertainty and seasonality are rarely addressed in the academic literature. Therefore, this chapter aims to integrate these important aspects into the design problem of feeder service networks. Specifically, shipping liners have to deal with uncertain and seasonal factors like periodic demand variations which impact the necessary number and size of ships and the available capacity of vessels for repositioning empty containers, etc. As mentioned by Meng and Wang (2012) most of the existing studies in the liner shipping literature address the problem of service network design under the assumption of static demand without considering seasonal demand fluctuations which, however, represent a major influencing factor in the maritime shipping industry. Yet there are a number of studies which consider the impact of periodic demand fluctuations in specific problem settings such as slot allocation, empty container repositioning, ship scheduling, and fleet deployment in existing service networks.

Containership deployment is a key issue in the liner shipping industry. A number of recent studies address fleet deployment in service networks by considering uncertain demand patterns, e.g. (Cheaitou et al., 2021; Dong & Song, 2012; Meng et al., 2011; Meng et al., 2012; Wang et al., 2012). The operating efficiency of shipping networks also depends on the appropriate slot allocation of containerships under uncertain demand conditions, which is another important issue in shipping network design (Lu et al., 2010; Zeng et al., 2010; Zurheide & Fischer, 2011, 2012).

Chen and Zeng (2010) present a mixed integer non-linear programming model to maximize the profit for a homogenous ship fleet under seasonally changing demand and freight rates. The proposed model selects cyclic port sequences from a number of candidate ports by declining low profit ports and allocates slots to selected ports. The authors solved a case study from Far East Asia with 10 candidate ports assuming annual and bi-monthly seasonal demand and freight rates by using a bi-level genetic algorithm. Their results show that determining slot allocations under changing demand and freight rates increases total profit 1.41 times and decreases the required slot capacity by 31%. It should be noted that in this study a limiting assumption is that fixed ship sizes for the whole year are assumed despite seasonal demand patterns, whereas slot capacities are allocated to ports according to seasons.

Meng and Wang (2012) investigated a fleet deployment and container routing problem in a liner shipping network with transshipment operations by including weekly origin to destination container demand and maximum transit time durations. The authors first create all possible origin to destination paths by using a space-time network approach subject to the transit time constraints in a-priori determined routes. Then by using a mixed integer linear programming model, the ships are assigned to routes and containers are assigned to paths by considering weekly demand figures in order to minimize total costs. Relaxations are considered in order to solve case study instances from an Asia-Europe-Oceania shipping network consisting of 46 ports and 12 routes with 3 candidate ship types for a 26 week planning horizon. Similar to Chen and Zeng (2010) ship sizes are assumed fixed for the whole year while containers are allocated on different origin to destination paths according to seasons.

In the literature, there are a very limited number of studies that analyze effect of demand fluctuations on the design of container feeder service networks. Polat and Günther (2016) analyzed the effect of unstable economic and political conditions as well as seasonal demand fluctuations on the utilization of feeder service networks. Huang et al. (2020) presented a robust optimization model to reduce the investment risk caused by the uncertainty in the feeder network design.

In this chapter, we propose a mixed-integer linear programming model to simultaneously determine the fleet size and mix, fleet deployment, ship routing and ship scheduling in hub-and-spoke (H&S) networks by minimizing total network costs under seasonal demand fluctuations in a sailing season. A perturbation based variable neighborhood search based approach is proposed to solve this integrated problem. As a practical application, the feeder network design problem faced by a short-sea shipping company is considered. The major contributions of this study to the liner shipping literature are the following. First, it investigates a realistic network design problem for liner shipping under seasonal demand conditions. Second, a mixed integer linear programming model is developed as a comprehensive model formulation. Third, an efficient solution procedure is proposed to support decision makers in their strategic and tactical level service network decisions.

THE FEEDER SERVICE NETWORK DESIGN PROBLEM

Problem Description

Today's shipping networks are characterized by two design challenges: trunk line and feeder service design. Generally, trunk line design determines the routes which a ship sails repeatedly during a sailing season including service frequencies, schedules, fleet composition, and deployment of ships on the individual routes. The ports in the trunk line constitute the hubs which serve as transshipment locations for regional feeder services. Because the regional ports do not have enough cargo demand to fill ships, they cannot attract the main lines to operate a regular service. Hence, feeder services play an irreplaceable role in global shipping networks. In conceptual terms, feeder services simultaneously collect/distribute containers from/to specific regions with small or medium-sized feeder ships and feed/discharge trunk containerships at hub ports so as to avoid their calling at too many regional ports. The connections between the hub port and regional ports are either operated as shuttle service or as cyclic line bundling service containing several feeder ports (Wijnolst et al., 2000). The first service strategy has the lowest transit time but typically requires more and smaller feeder ships. In contrast, bundling services benefit from economies of bigger ship size but incur longer distances and longer transit times.

The majority of feeder service networks are located in the zone of landlocked seas or huge sea gulfs (Jadrijević & Tomašević, 2011). Examples of such networks can be seen in the East Mediterranean area which covers the ports in the Black Sea, the Sea of Marmara and the Aegean Sea via Port Said as hub port. Various sized feeder containerships serve these regional ports with both shuttle and cyclic service routes.

The feeder service network design problem (FSND) can be regarded as a variation of the vehicle routing problem (Andersen, 2010; Lin et al., 2020; Polat, 2017a). It deals with simultaneous pick up of containers from feeder ports and transportation to the hub port and delivery of containers from the hub port to the feeder port. In this problem, feeder liners commonly aim to design their service routes by using a fleet of heterogeneous containerships under ship due date constraints for returning to the hub port at minimum cost. With these specifications the feeder service network design problem fundamentally fits to the vehicle routing problem with simultaneous pickup and delivery with time limit (VRPSPDTL) (Polat et al., 2014).

In most existing studies, container feeder service networks are investigated under the assumption of stable demand at ports during a sailing season. Studies considering demand seasonality and fluctuations are concerned with problems in already designed networks. However, so far none of the published studies has considered the effect of seasonal demand fluctuations on the design of service networks over a complete dynamic sailing horizon. In this paper, we propose a mixed-integer linear programming model to simultaneously determine the fleet size and mix, fleet deployment, ship routing and ship scheduling in H&S feeder service networks by minimizing total network costs under seasonal demand fluctuations. The proposed model allows to periodically adapt the service network design, routes, fleet deployment and schedules according to forecasted demand over a number of periods in a sailing season.

Model Formulation

A mixed integer linear programming (MILP) formulation of the feeder network design problem under unstable demand conditions is presented below by extending the basic FSND formulation of Polat et al. (2014). The new model formulation considers seasonal demand conditions at ports in a given sailing season. In addition to the determination of routes and transportation flows on the arcs of the network, the model reflects decisions on the size and composition of the fleet of containerships including on and off-hire of chartered ships.

Box 1. Indices & sets

$i,j \in N$	The set of ports (0 represents the hub port)
$s \in S$	The set of containership types
$(i,j) \in L$	The set of allowed voyage legs between ports
$g \in G$	The set of allowed network change periods
$r=1,2,\ldots,R$	Routes, where R is the maximum number of routes in a period: R£ $\|N\|$

Box 2. Parameters

f	Service frequency	days
a_g	Duration of period g	days
γg	Number of services in period g	
K	Maximum allowed voyage duration	hours
v_i^s	Vessel set-up duration of ship type s in port i (pilotage, berthing, cleaning etc.)	hours
u^s	Off-hire duration of ship type s	Hours
m^s	Available number of containerships of ship type s for charter-in	ships
sn^s	On hand number of ship type s	ships
q^s	Loading capacity of ship type s	TEU
h^s	Average travel speed of ship type s	Knots
o_i^s	Operation efficiency of port i for ship type s	TEU/hour
w_{ij}	Distance between ports i and j	N.mile
t_{gi}^s	Berthing duration of ship s at port i in period g	Hours
d_{gi}	Container demand (delivery) of port i in period g	TEU/day
p_{gi}	Container supply (pick-up) of port i in period g	TEU/day
α	Main fuel oil price	\$/ton
β	Auxiliary fuel oil price (distillate)	\$/ton
cc^s	Charter-in cost of ship type s	\$/day
cp^s	Charter-out cost of ship type s	\$/day
oc^s	Cost per owned ship of type s	\$/day
fc^s	Operating cost of ship s (administration, maintenance, lubricant, insurance etc.)	\$/day
nf^s	Main fuel consumption of ship type s on sea	ton/n.mile
af^s	Auxiliary fuel consumption of ship type s at berth	ton/hours
bc_i^s	Vessel set-up cost of ship type s at port i	\$/ship

The MILP model formulation is given as follows.

$$\min FC = VC \tag{1}$$

s.t.

$$FC = \sum_{r\in R}\sum_{s\in S}\sum_{g\in G}\left(oc^s + fc^s\right)su_g^{rs}a_g + \sum_{r\in R}\sum_{s\in S}\sum_{g\in G}\left(cc^s + fc^s\right)ci_g^{rs}a_g - \sum_{s\in S}\sum_{g\in G}cp^s co_g^s a_g \tag{2}$$

$$VC = \sum_{i\in N}\sum_{j\in N}\sum_{r\in R}\sum_{s\in S}\sum_{g\in G}\gamma_g w_{ij} m f^s \alpha\, x_{gij}^{rs} + \sum_{i\in N}\sum_{s\in S}\sum_{g\in G}\gamma_g t_{gi}^s a f^s \beta + \sum_{i\in N}\sum_{j\in N/\{0\}}\sum_{r\in R}\sum_{s\in S}\sum_{g\in G}\gamma_g b c_i^s x_{gij}^{rs}$$
$$with\ \gamma_g = \left\lceil \frac{a_g}{f} \right\rceil and\ t_{gi}^s = \frac{\left(p_{gi} + d_{gi}\right) f}{o_i^s} \tag{3}$$

$$\frac{c_g^{rs} + u^s}{f} \le e_g^{rs}\ \forall r \in R, s \in S, g \in G \tag{4}$$

$$\sum_{i\in N}\sum_{j\in N}\left(t_{gi}^s + v_i^s + \frac{w_{ij}}{h^s}\right) x_{gij}^{rs} = c_g^{rs}\ \forall r \in R, s \in S, g \in G \tag{5}$$

$$\sum_{i\in N}\sum_{r\in R}\sum_{s\in S} x_{gij}^{rs} = 1\ \forall j \in N / \{0\}, g \in G \tag{6}$$

$$\sum_{i\in N} x_{gij}^{rs} - \sum_{i\in N} x_{gji}^{rs} = 0\ \forall j \in N, r \in R, s \in S, g \in G \tag{7}$$

$$\sum_{j\in N/\{0\}} x_{g0j}^{rs} \le 1\ \forall r \in R, s \in S, g \in G \tag{8}$$

$$su_g^{rs} + ci_g^{rs} = e_g^{rs}\ \forall r \in R, s \in S, g \in G \tag{9}$$

$$\sum_{r\in R} su_g^{rs} + co_g^s = sn^s\ \forall s \in S, g \in G \tag{10}$$

$$\sum_{r\in R} ci_g^{rs} \le m^s\ \forall s \in S, g \in G \tag{11}$$

$$\sum_{i\in N} y_{gji} - \sum_{i\in N} y_{gij} = p_{gj} f\ \forall j \in N, g \in G \tag{12}$$

$$\sum_{i\in N} z_{gij} - \sum_{i\in N} z_{gji} = d_{gj} f\ \forall j \in N, g \in G \tag{13}$$

$$y_{gij} + z_{gij} \le q^s x_{gij}^{rs}\ \forall i, j \in N, r \in R, s \in S, g \in G \tag{14}$$

$$c_g^{rs} \leq K \; \forall r \in R, s \in S, g \in G \tag{15}$$

$$\sum_{i \in B} \sum_{j \in B} x_{gij}^{rs} \leq \left|B\right| - 1 \; \forall r \in r, s \in S, g \in G, B \in N / 0, \left|B\right| \geq 2 \tag{16}$$

$$\begin{gathered} x_{gij}^{rs} \in \{0,1\} \\ y_{gij}, z_{gij}, e_g^{rs}, su_g^{rs}, co_g^{s}, ci_g^{rs} \in \mathbb{Z}^+ \; \forall i, j \in N, (i,j) \in L, r \in R, s \in S, g \in G \\ c_g^{rs} \geq 0 \end{gathered} \tag{17}$$

Box 3. Decision variables

x_{gij}^{rs}	1, if the arc between ports *i* and *j* belongs to route *r* served by ship type *s* in period *g* (0, otherwise)	Binary
y_{gij}	containers picked up from ports up to port *i* and transported from port *i* to *j* in period *g*	TEU
z_{gij}	containers to be delivered to ports routed after port *i* and transported between port *i* and *j* in period *g*	TEU
e_g^{rs}	Number of employed ships of type *s* on route *r* in period *g*	Ships
c_g^{rs}	Voyage cycle time of route *r* with ship type *s* in period *g*	Hours
su_g^{rs}	Number of owned ships used on route *r* from type *s* in period *g*	Ships
co_g^{s}	Number of charter-out ships of type *s* in period *g*	Ships
ci_g^{rs}	Number of charter-in ships on route *r* of type *s* in period *g*	Ships
FC	Total fixed costs of a sailing season	$
VC	Total variable costs of a sailing season	$

The objective function (1) minimizes total costs of the network for a sailing season. The terms of the objective function consist of fixed and variable costs and are defined in Equations (2) and (3), respectively. The necessary number of ships needed for a service cycle on each route is calculated in (4). Equation (5) determines the cycle time of ships on each route (berthing duration + service duration + voyage duration). Equation (6) ensures that each feeder port is served by only one ship and one route. Equation (7) guarantees that a ship arrives at and departs from each feeder port on each route. Constraint (8) imposes a similar condition for the hub port at which the route starts and ends. Equations (9) and (10) indicate the number of charter-in and charter-out ships, respectively. Constraints (11) represent an upper bound for the number of charter-in ships of each type. Equations (12) and (13) satisfy pick-up and delivery demand of containers at the feeder ports, respectively. Constraints (14) represent the ship capacity and

(15) the maximum voyage duration limits. (16) are the vehicle sub-tour elimination constraints according to Karlaftis et al. (2009). Finally, constraints (17) define the variable domains.

In this study, it is assumed that the service network can be revised at the beginning of every period in response to changes in the demand pattern. Adjustment of the service network may include new routes and schedules as well as chartering in or out ships of different type. In contrast to trunk liners, feeder service providers have the opportunity to update their schedules and routes by means of modified fleet deployment. This study also analyses various scenarios, e.g. in order to study the impact of different seasonal demand estimates, changes in the composition of the ship fleet, or the impact of certain types of costs.

SOLUTION METHODOLOGY

The network design problem presented in the previous section is a highly complex combinatorial optimization problem and thus hard to solve by use of standard optimization software. Even tailor-made exact solution methods are generally not practical for large instances because of the problem complexity. In this study, we propose a perturbation based neighbourhood search (PVNS) algorithm which has shown to be a very efficient heuristic approach for solving both the vehicle routing problem with simultaneous pick-up and delivery with time limit (VRPSPDTL) and the feeder network design problem (Polat et al., 2014).

The proposed PVNS approach applies the Savings Algorithm of Clarke and Wright (1964) in order to gain a fast and effective initial solution. This classic heuristic aims at merging sub-tours based on cost savings which can be achieved by combining two sub-tours to be served by one vehicle. In the literature, some enhancements of the Clarke and Wright savings algorithm have been suggested by adding new terms and parameterizing the savings formula. In our study, we apply the enhanced savings based approach due to Altinel and Öncan (2005). In the next stage, the initial solution is improved with the General Variable Neighborhood Search (VNS) approach proposed by Mladenović and Hansen (1997) and Hansen et al. (2010). VNS is based on the idea of systematically changing the neighborhoods in order to improve the current solution and aims to explore the solution space which may not be searched by a simple local search technique (Hansen et al., 2010). Kytöjokia et al. (2007), Hemmelmayr et al. (2009), Stenger et al. (2013) and Polat (2017b) showed the effectiveness of VNS in VRP applications. *Shaking*, *local search* and *move or not* operators are used in the implementation of the VNS. The shaking operator defines the search direction of the VNS from a set of neighborhoods. The possibility of reaching a global solution increases when combining the shaking operator with local search rather than using a single shaking operator. Therefore, each solution obtained by the shaking operator is further evaluated with the local search operator in order to explore new promising neighborhoods of the current solution. In this study we implemented the Variable Neighborhood Descent (VND) algorithm as the local search operator. If we exclude the randomness in VNS, then the VND is achieved. While this variant of VNS can be used in its original form individually, VND is also useful as a local search within a VNS. The VND aims to combine the set of neighborhoods (*m-max*) in a deterministic order expecting that using more than one neighborhood structure results in better solutions. After each shaking operation, the VND algorithm allows *n-max* trials for maximum possible improvement. At the end of the VND algorithm, if there is an improvement, then the shaking operations start from the first operation. Otherwise, shaking continues with the next operation. After reaching the maximum number of shaking operations (*k-max*), the search procedure continues with the first operation in the new iteration. Shaking and local search operators employed in this study are based on a set of neighborhood structures [*3-opt, swap, insertion, 2-opt, Exchange (m,n), Cross, Shift (0,1), Replace (1,1)*] illustrated in Figure 2.

The temporary solution which is obtained via the shaking and local search operators is compared with the current solution in order to decide whether to *move or not.* In the proposed VNS and VND, the acceptance criterion of the temporary solution is only to accept a solution if there is an improvement. However, this procedure may cause the search to get stuck in a local optimum. Therefore, it is necessary to employ a strategy of accepting non-improving solutions. Perturbation is an effective strategy used to jump out of a local optimum and to search a new promising region. In this study, the current solution is perturbed with a perturbation mechanism (PM) which is called after a number of non-improving iterations counted from the last improving iteration (*p-max*). In the PM, a set of perturbation structures [*double replace, double cross, triple shift, triple replace, and triple cross*] is randomly run whenever the perturbation is called (Polat et al., 2012). In addition to the perturbation move, a local optimization method with the previously defined four intra-route neighborhood structures is applied in order to improve the perturbed solution quality.

Figure 2. Neighborhood structures

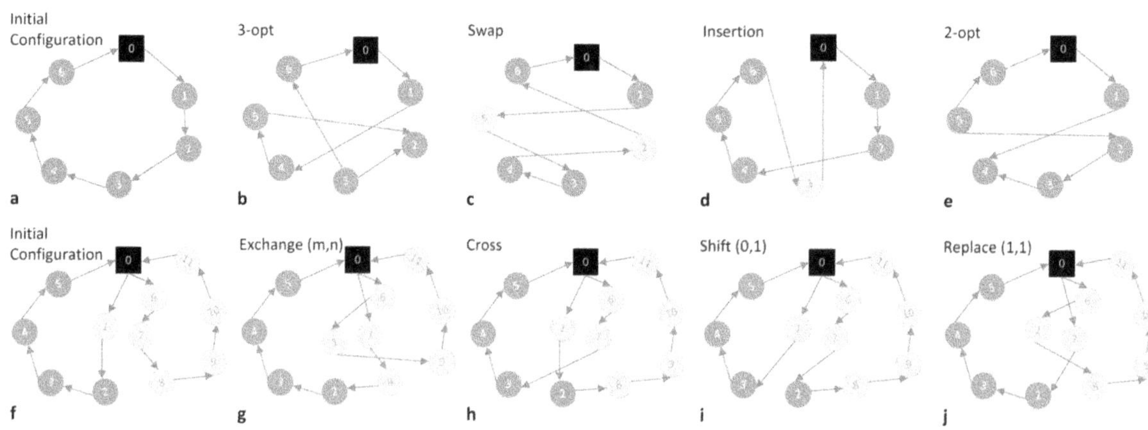

NUMERICAL EXPERIMENTATION

In this section, we consider the Black Sea region as an application example to analyse the design problem of liner shipping networks under unstable demand conditions from the perspective of a feeder shipping company commencing its services from a newly constructed port. The design of the service network is revised at the beginning of each period in response to changes in demand patterns for the upcoming periods. Changes to the service network may include introducing new routes and schedules as well as fleet deployments which may contain chartering in new ships or chartering out unnecessary ships. This section also employs various service scenarios in order to better help decision makers of liner shipping providers. In these scenarios the update frequency of the network design, demand allocation, the numbers of owned ships at the start of sailing season, and ship prices are varied in order to evaluate the ñexibility of decisions under unstable demand conditions.

Case Study

Turkey as a transcontinental country is encircled by the Black Sea, Mediterranean Sea, Adriatic Sea, Ionian Sea, Aegean Sea, and Marmara Sea. In recent years, Turkey and its neighbouring countries have seen a substantial increase in total container traffic. This is mainly caused by the positive economic development in the entire region. Several ports in the Mediterranean Sea are directly connected to the trunk shipping lines between Far East and Europe. With these ports as hubs several regional shipping liners have built up feeder networks which link the hinterland of this region to the global trunk shipping lines. In parallel to the general growth of maritime container traffic an increase in port throughput has also been observed in the regional feeder ports, particularly in the Black Sea region. Hence, the outlook for the maritime transportation market in the region is very promising (Kulak et al., 2013; Varbanova, 2011).

In our numerical experimentation we consider the case of a particular feeder liner who intends to redesign its feeder service network with a hub port at Candarli in Turkey. Since liner shipping is directly affected by financial, political and seasonal conditions, the company regards seasonal demand fluctuations as a major factor to be included in the design of the service network. In the considered region, the concerned feeder liner has 36 contracted container terminals at 26 feeder ports in 12 countries. In the conducted numerical experiments, a four-week service time deadline and seven-day service frequency conditions for a 52-week sailing season are assumed. Because of the limited berth depth at some regional ports and well-known traffic bottlenecks at the Bosporus and Dardanelles straights, ships of three different sizes are considered in the numerical experiment. The major cost parameters for all ship types are shown in Table 1.

Table 1. Parameter values for ship types

Parameter	Unit	Ship Type 1	Ship Type 2	Ship Type 3
Capacity	TEU	4300	2600	1200
Operating speed	(knots)	22.60	19.90	17.40
Fuel consumption (on sea)	(tons/hour)	5.26	2.82	1.51
IFO 180 price (on sea)	($/ton)	647.50	647.50	647.50
Fuel consumption (at port)	(tons/hour)	0.26	0.14	0.08
MGO price (at port)	($/ton)	890.00	890.00	890.00
Chartering costs (charter-in)	($/day)	12772.00	7579.00	5866.00
Amortization costs (on hand)*	($/day)	6386.00	3789.50	2933.00
Rent price (charter-out)**	($/day)	9579.00	5684.25	4399.50
Operating costs	($/day)	11520.00	8887.00	6023.00
Port charges	($/call)	35000.00	29000.00	22000.00
Off-hire time	(hour/call)	28.80	24.00	16.80
Set-up time	(hour/port)	2.00	1.80	1.50
Planning period	Days	364	364	364

Sources: Stopford (2009), VHSS (2013), BunkerIndex (2012),* Amortization cost assumed as 50% of charter-in cost, ** Charter-out price assumed as 75% of charter-in cost.

For the considered region, statistical data on container throughput of the ports are scarce and daily throughput figures are hard to obtain from the port authorities. For this reason, monthly throughput of each container terminals is converted into daily demands based on the judgement of experts from the port and shipping authorities.

Implementation

The candidate networks created by the PVNS according to periodical demand figures are evaluated using a fitness function. Since PVNS is originally intended to solve the VRPSPDTL with homogenous vehicles under the objective to minimize the total travel distance with stable demand in the network, it is necessary to adjust the fitness function of the PVNS according to the unstable demand environment of the FSND problem. In our implementation of the PVNS total operational costs of all routes and all periods for the entire sailing season according to cost functions (2) and (3) of mathematical model are used as the fitness function. The respective procedure for calculating the fitness values is summarized in Figure 3. In the VRPSPDTL application candidate routes are generated with the help of neighbourhood structures. In this step constraints (6) - (17) of the optimization model are checked in order to achieve feasible solutions. The regret value represents the difference between the number of ships available of each type and the actual deployments. The assignment with the highest regret value is selected for the respective route by considering on hand ship numbers. After assigning on hand ships to routes, the remaining empty routes are operated with charter ships. The idle on hand ships are chartered out to the market.

Apart from the network routes the PVNS determines the fleet mix, the number of required ships according to Equation (4) and their deployment to routes in the candidate network under unstable demand conditions for each period. Based on these data the total voyage cycle of a ship on a route is achieved by Equation (5), i.e. considering the related port service times, travel times between ports, off-hire times etc.

Experimental Procedure

The major issue in our experimental study is the effect of demand seasonality on the design of the feeder network. As a first experimental factor the update interval for demand figures is varied. The corresponding update frequency determines how often the design of the feeder network is adapted, e.g. by varying the number of employed ships or by re-defining the ship routes. Table 2 shows the number and composition of update intervals during a season varying from 12 monthly intervals (No. 1) to a full seasonal cycle (No. 6).

Table 2. Definition of update intervals for a one-year sailing season

<table>
<tr><th>No.</th><th>Update Frequency</th><th>Jan.</th><th>Feb.</th><th>Mar.</th><th>Apr.</th><th>May</th><th>Jun.</th><th>Jul.</th><th>Aug.</th><th>Sep.</th><th>Oct.</th><th>Nov.</th><th>Dec.</th></tr>
<tr><td>1</td><td>12</td><td>5</td><td>4</td><td>4</td><td>4</td><td>4</td><td>5</td><td>5</td><td>4</td><td>4</td><td>4</td><td>4</td><td>5</td></tr>
<tr><td>2</td><td>6</td><td colspan="2">9</td><td colspan="2">8</td><td colspan="2">9</td><td colspan="2">9</td><td colspan="2">8</td><td colspan="2">9</td></tr>
<tr><td>3</td><td>4</td><td colspan="3">13</td><td colspan="3">13</td><td colspan="3">13</td><td colspan="3">13</td></tr>
<tr><td>4</td><td>3</td><td colspan="4">17</td><td colspan="4">18</td><td colspan="4">17</td></tr>
<tr><td>5</td><td>2</td><td colspan="6">26</td><td colspan="6">26</td></tr>
<tr><td>6</td><td>1</td><td colspan="12">52</td></tr>
</table>

Figure 3. Calculation of the FSND fitness function

```
procedure: fitness function for ANS
input: candidate network
output: total network costs of candidate network (dNC)
start
  for each route (r) in the candidate network
    initialize a big number for total route cost (RC_r)
    for each ship type (s)
      if (hub and each feeder port departure and arrival loads are feasible for ship type s on
        route r)
        calculate voyage cycle time of route r with ship type s specifications
        if (voyage cycle time is feasible by considering maximum voyage dur. limit)
          calculate required ship number of ship type s for route r
          calculate variable costs for route r operated with ship type s
          calculate fixed costs for route r operated with chartered ship type s
          calculate fixed costs for route r operated with owned ship type s
          calculate total costs of route r operated with chartered ship type s (dRC_rs1)
          calculate total costs of route r operated with owned ship type s (dRC_rs2)
        end if
      end if
    end for
  end for
  create regret value index (variance) matrix between (dRC_rs1) and (dRC_rs2)
  sort rows and columns and rows of the matrix in descending order
  assign on hand ships to routes by considering on hand ship number and regret value
  charter in necessary ships
  charter out unnecessary ships
  calculate total network costs of candidate network (dNC)
end
```

Each container terminal is characterized by its weekly inbound and outbound demand volume. Since an update interval comprises several weeks it is necessary to assign representative inbound and outbound demand figures to each interval. Principally these figures could be oriented towards the maximum or the average demand during the update interval. In our study, we test three different rules for assigning demand figures to update intervals for each terminal (see Table 3 and the numerical example in Table 4). Rule 1 identifies the maximum either inbound or outbound weekly demand value and assumes that week's demand as demand for the update interval of the respective terminal. In the example of Terminal A (Table 4), the maximum inbound value is 47 in week 2 and the maximum outbound value is 32 in week 1. Hence, the inbound and outbound demand values of 47 and 32 are assigned as representative demand for Terminal A. Rule 2 identifies the week in which the maximum either inbound or outbound demand occurs, e.g. week 2 with inbound demand of 47 for Terminal A in Table 4). Both the inbound and outbound demand values of this period are assigned to the update interval for the terminal. Finally, Rule 3 determines the interval demand according to the ceiled average weekly demand of each terminal in the season.

Table 3. Assignment of demand to update intervals

No.	Rule
1	Assigns maximum inbound and maximum outbound weekly demand during the interval
2	Assigns demand values of the week with maximum either inbound and outbound demand during the interval
3	Assigns ceiled average inbound and outbound demand in the interval

Table 4. Example of weekly demand assignment

	Terminal A		Terminal B		Terminal C		Terminal D	
	Inbound	**Outbound**	**Inbound**	**Outbound**	**Inbound**	**Outbound**	**Inbound**	**Outbound**
Week 1	40	32	35	31	34	45	21	12
Week 2	47	30	30	36	28	42	20	16
Week 3	40	20	28	25	25	50	12	8
Week 4	34	24	24	15	30	40	14	10
Rule 1	47	32	35	36	34	50	21	16
Rule 2	47	30	30	36	25	50	21	12
Rule 3	41	27	30	27	30	45	17	12

Another strategic decision concerns the ratio between owned and chartered ships in the fleet. Feeder liners usually operate a small number of owned ships and balance their requirements with chartered ships. This enables them to reduce their capital costs and makes their network more flexible to changes in trade. However, if they face a stable or steadily increasing demand on the market, then operating with a high number of chartered ships would be more costly than operating with owned ships. Therefore, it is crucial for feeder liners to carefully decide on the fleet of owned feeder ships.

In a base configuration (Rule 1) it is assumed that the feeder liner starts with no owned ships and charters in ships in the week when they are needed to cover demand in the network. Table 5 shows the corresponding development of the fleet. To generate alternative configurations of ships owned at the beginning of the planning horizon we apply five additional rules 2 to 6 defined in Table 6. These rules take up the fleet development of Table 5 and determine the initial number of owned ships in different ways. The numerical example of Table 5 is continued in Table 7. For instance, Rule 2 defines the initial fleet of owned ships according to the week with the highest slot demand, i.e. week 3 in Table 5. This rule guarantees that the shipping liner satisfies all demand on the market. However, it can also result in overcapacity. During periods when ships become idle, they can be chartered out. Rule 3 defines the initial number of owned ships according to the maximum number of ships of each type, i.e. 1, 6 and 10, respectively, in the example of Table 5 continued in Table 7. This rule also guarantees satisfaction of customer demand, but possibly impairs the utilization of the owned ships. Rule 4 is similar to Rule 2, except that it selects the ship numbers from the week with the lowest slot demand in the network. This rule does not guarantee complete demand fulfilment of the ports, but increases the utilization of the ships and the number of charter-in ships. Rule 5 is similar to Rule 3 except that it defines the initial fleet of owned ships according to the minimum number of ships of each type, i.e. 0, 3 and 5, respectively, in the example of Table 5 continued in Table 7. This rule also does not guarantee satisfaction of customer demand, but possibly decreases the costs for owned ship by chartering in a greater number of ships in later periods. Rule 6 defines the number of on hand ships according to the ceiled average ship numbers of each ship type resulting from the base configuration. Table 7 summarizes the results.

Table 5. Initial fleet composition with no owned ship

		Ship 1 (4300)		Ship 2 (2600)		Ship 3 (1200)		Slot Capacity
Rule 1	Charter	in	out	in	out	in	out	TEU
	On hand	0		0		0		0
	Week 1	0	0	4	0	10	0	224000
	Week 2	0	0	5	0	5	0	190000
	Week 3	1	0	6	0	9	0	307000
	Week 4	0	0	3	0	6	0	150000

Table 6. Rules for determining the initial fleet of owned ships

No.	Rule
1	No owned ship
2	According to the week with the maximum slot demand in the network
3	According to the maximum number of ships of each type employed in the Rule 1 configuration
4	According to the week with the minimum slot demand in the network
5	According to minimum numbers of ships of each type employed in the Rule 1 configuration
6	According to ceiled average ship numbers from each type in the Rule 1 configuration

Table 7. Example of determining the initial composition of the fleet

Rule	Ship 1 (4300)	Ship 2 (2600)	Ship 3 (1200)	Slot Capacity
2	1	6	9	31900
3	1	6	10	30700
4	0	3	6	15000
5	0	3	5	13800
6	0	5	8	22600

In addition, numerical experiments are conducted in order to evaluate how the general change in ship prices (owning and chartering) impacts the design of the service network configuration. Table 8 shows the investigated increase and decrease levels of ship prices.

In order to evaluate the performance of the specific experimental factors the four test series shown in Table 9 are defined. Test series 1 addresses the impact of the update frequency which is varied according to Table 2 while the other factors remain at constant levels. Test series 2 focuses on the rules for demand assignment as defined in Table 3. Test series 3 investigates the rules for ship ownership defined in Table 6 for different update intervals. Finally, test series 4 consists of experiments which show the impact of changes in ship prices for different rules of ship ownership. For all experiments the PVNS heuristic presented in Section 4 is applied to solve the individual optimization problems for a 52-week sailing season with the forecasted demand values for the case study application.

Table 8. Change in ship prices

No	Approach
1	50% decrease in ship prices
2	25% decrease in ship prices
3	No change in ship prices
4	25% increase in ship prices
5	50% increase in ship prices
6	100% increase in ship prices

Table 9. Test series

Test Series	Update Frequency	Demand Assignment	Owned Ships	Ship Prices
1	1-2-3-4-5-6	2	1	3
2	1-2-3-4-5-6	1-2-3	1	3
3	1-2-3-4-5-6	2	1-2-3-4-5-6	3
4	3	2	1-2-3-4-5-6	1-2-3-4-5-6

Numerical Results

Test Series 1: Number of Update Intervals

In the first test series the update interval takes monthly, bi-monthly, quarterly, tri-semesterly, semi-annually and annually values. Table 10 shows the resulting network-wide costs per year. As expected, decreasing the update frequency causes additional costs due to the reduced flexibility of the feeder network to adapt the configuration to seasonal demand fluctuations.

Table 10. Network-wide costs per year for different update frequencies

No.	Update Frequency	Total Costs (mil $)
1	12	309
2	6	316
3	4	320
4	3	323
5	2	324
6	1	330

Figure 4 shows the slot utilization of the fleet during weeks in the sailing season for different update frequencies. When the number of updates in a sailing season is increased, the utilization ratio of the fleet increases as well. Both costs and utilization figures show the importance of flexible and demand oriented service network design. However, despite the cost advantage of adapting the design of service networks frequently, it is not practical to realize these changes too often. Therefore, adjusting the network configuration quarterly could be seen as the most reasonable option for shipping liners in practice to adapt to demand fluctuations.

Figure 4. Weekly capacity utilization of the fleet depending on the update frequency

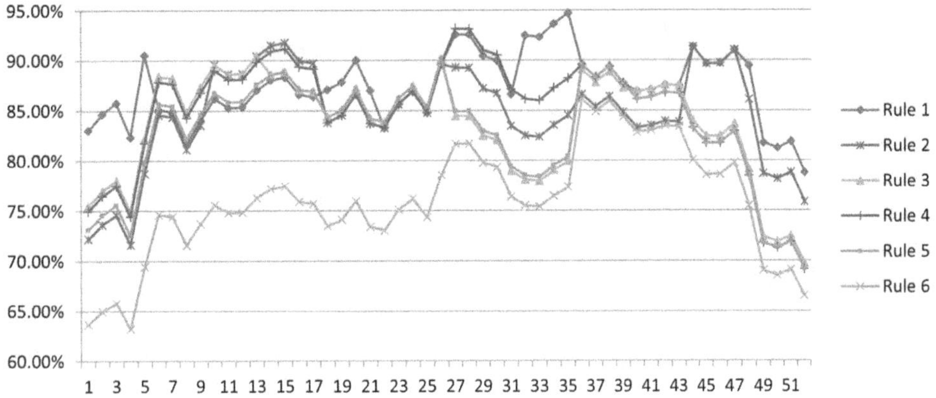

Test Series 2: Demand Assignment

Figure 5 shows the cost results of the second test series which evaluates the dual impact of demand frequency and demand assignment rules. Two observations can be derived from this figure. First, demand assignment rule 3, which is based on average demand figures, outperforms its counterparts for all update frequencies. Second best is demand assignment rule 2 followed by Rule 1, which are both based on maximum demand figures. From these two options Rule 1 builds upon the more optimistic demand expectation. The relatively poor performance of Rules 1 and 2 can be explained by the higher number of ships employed. The second observation is that with decreasing update frequency network-wide costs increase. However, this effect is less pronounced for Rule 3.

Figure 5. Network-wide costs per year for different demand assignment rules under varying update frequencies

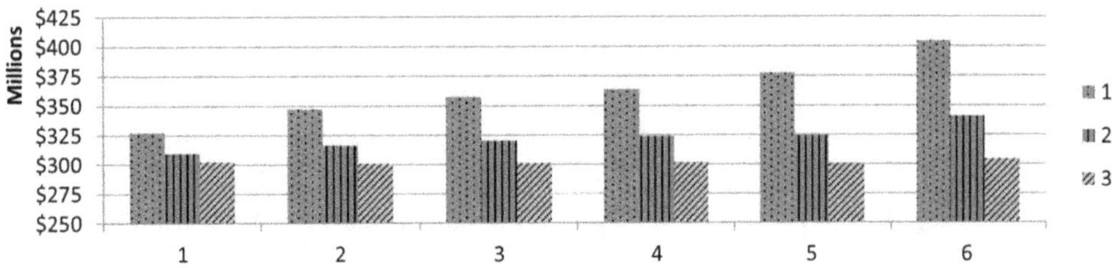

The slot utilization of the ships during weeks in the sailing season is shown in Figure 6 for the case of quarterly update intervals. It can be seen that the utilization rates comply with the relative cost performance of the demand assignment rules, i.e. Rule 3 shows the highest slot utilization rate in the course of the sailing season followed by the two other rules. However, extremely high utilization rates bear the risk of not meeting unexpected demand and being less robust with respect to random demand fluctuations. Therefore, in practice feeder shipping liners usually operate with a capacity utilization of around 90%.

Figure 6. Weekly capacity utilization of the fleet depending on the demand assignment rule for quarterly update intervals

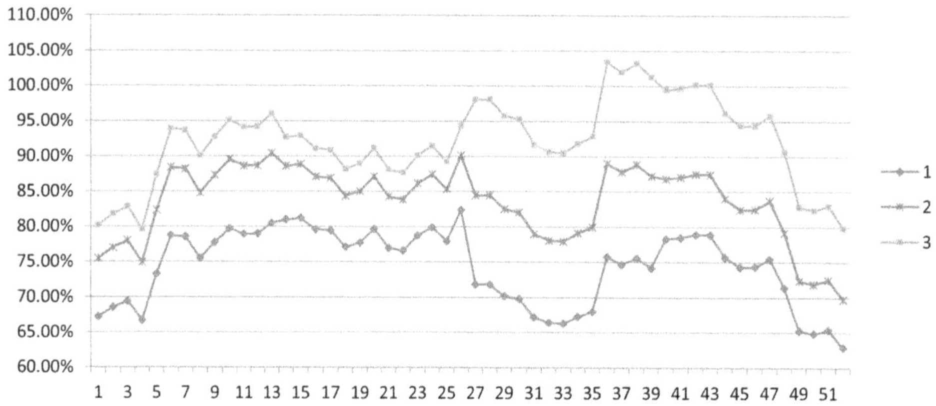

Test Series 3: Owned Ships

The results of the third test series which evaluates the dual impact of different update frequencies and different ship ownership strategies are shown in Figure 7. The displayed results clearly show that under all update frequencies the no owned ship rule has an almost 20% cost disadvantage compared to the other rules. As the update frequency decreases, the impact of the number of owned ships decreases. For the other owned ship number rules, the maximum ship and slot based rules 2 and 3 result in the lowest total network costs. In a practical application, the minimum slot based owned ship rule might be preferred because it requires less capital investment and provides increased flexibility in reacting on seasonal demand fluctuations. It should be noted that the investigated rules assume adequate market conditions for chartering a sufficient number of ships in and out.

Figure 7. Network-wide costs per year for different ship ownership strategies under varying update frequencies

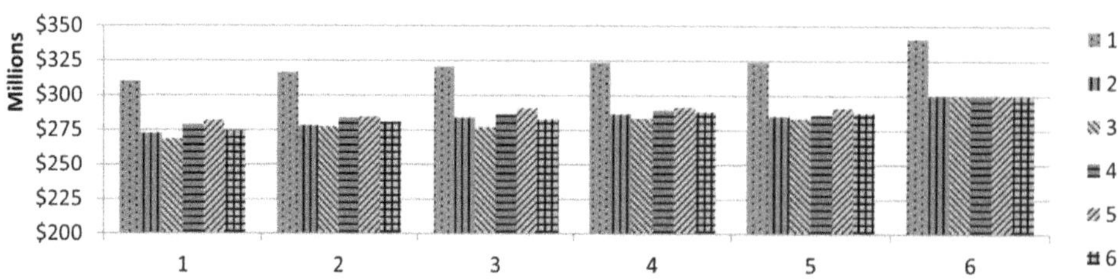

Test Series 4: Ship Prices

Finally, Figure 8 shows the results of the fourth test series which analyzes the dual effect of ship pricing scenarios and ship ownership strategies under varying update frequencies. The obtained results demonstrate that with increasing ship prices total network costs increase accordingly. Obviously, this effect is lowest for an update frequency of four times per year (rule No. 3). With low ship prices total network costs get less ship-cost oriented and the number of owned ships loses its importance. It can also be seen from the figure that update frequency No. 3 (quarterly) performs superior in these experiments.

Figure 8. Impact of ship pricing scenarios on network-wide costs per year under varying update frequencies

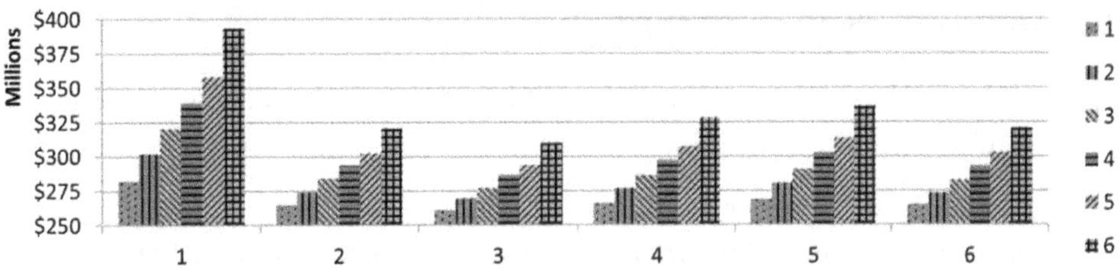

CONCLUSION

Decisions on tactical feeder network design, e.g. on fleet size and mix, fleet deployment, ship routing and scheduling, are usually based on estimates of the container transportation volume in the considered region. However, as it stated by Polat and Günther (2016) transportation volume is highly affected by unstable economic and political conditions as well as seasonal fluctuations. Therefore, the feeder network design is updated repeatedly in the course of the year. As a methodology to solve the underlying combinatorial optimization problem, a perturbation based neighbourhood search approach is employed.

In our case study investigation, we consider the feeder network design problem of a Turkish short-sea shipping company in view of the opening a new port. The cost performance of different feeder network configurations serving the Black Sea region is evaluated under unstable demand conditions. The various configurations are determined according to the forecasted container transportation volume of the terminals in the region during a 52-week sailing season. The results of the numerical study show that total costs of the service network can be greatly reduced if unstable demand conditions are considered in the network design. Parallel to findings of Chen and Zeng (2010), the total slot capacity of the fleet can be reduced and the utilization of the ships increased by quickly adapting the changes in the demand to network designs. As it also indicated by Golan et al. (2020), COVID-19 pandemic show that despite the common goal of all supply chain models are to optimize efficiency and reduce costs, trade-offs of efficiency and leanness with flexibility and resilience are necessary to concentrate. These findings demonstrate the importance of dynamic and flexible feeder service network design without much losing its efficiency. A possible extension of the proposed approach can be seen in the consideration of dynamic freight rate and oil price conditions as well as the integration of decisions on the most economic sailing speed of the ships on their routes.

REFERENCES

Altınel, K., & Öncan, T. (2005). A new enhancement of the Clarke and Wright savings heuristic for the capacitated vehicle routing problem. *The Journal of the Operational Research Society*, *56*(8), 954–961. doi:10.1057/palgrave.jors.2601916

Andersen, M. W. (2010). *Service network nesign and management in liner container shipping applications* [Ph.D. Thesis]. Technical University of Denmark, Lyngby, Denmark.

BunkerIndex. (2012). *South Europe bunker prices*. Retrieved 15.06.2012 from http://www.bunkerindex.com/prices/seurope.php

Cheaitou, A., Hamdan, S., & Larbi, R. (2021). Liner shipping network design with sensitive demand. *Maritime Business Review*. doi:10.1108/MABR-10-2019-0045

Chen, C., & Zeng, Q. (2010). Designing container shipping network under changing demand and freight rates. *Transport*, *25*(1), 46–57. doi:10.3846/transport.2010.07

Christiansen, M., Hellsten, E., Pisinger, D., Sacramento, D., & Vilhelmsen, C. (2020). Liner shipping network design. *European Journal of Operational Research*, *286*(1), 1–20. doi:10.1016/j.ejor.2019.09.057

Clarke, G., & Wright, J. W. (1964). Scheduling of vehicles from a central depot to a number of delivery points. *Operations Research*, *12*(4), 568–581. doi:10.1287/opre.12.4.568

Coskun, S., Ozgur, L., Polat, O., & Gungor, A. (2016). A model proposal for green supply chain network design based on consumer segmentation. *Journal of Cleaner Production*, *110*, 149–157. doi:10.1016/j.jclepro.2015.02.063

Dong, J.-X., & Song, D.-P. (2012). Quantifying the impact of inland transport times on container fleet sizing in liner shipping services with uncertainties. *OR-Spektrum*, *34*(1), 155–180. doi:10.100700291-009-0185-4

Golan, M. S., Jernegan, L. H., & Linkov, I. (2020). Trends and applications of resilience analytics in supply chain modeling: Systematic literature review in the context of the COVID-19 pandemic. *Environment Systems & Decisions*, *40*(2), 222–243. doi:10.100710669-020-09777-w PMID:32837820

Hansen, P., Mladenović, N., & Pérez, J. M. (2010). Developments of variable neighborhood search. *Annals of Operations Research*, *175*(1), 367–407. doi:10.100710479-009-0657-6

Hemmelmayr, V. C., Doerner, K. F., & Hartl, R. F. (2009). A variable neighborhood search heuristic for periodic routing problems. *European Journal of Operational Research*, *195*(3), 791–802. doi:10.1016/j.ejor.2007.08.048

Hoff, A., Andersson, H., Christiansen, M., Hasle, G., & Løkettangen, A. (2010). Industrial aspects and literature survey: Fleet composition and routing. *Computers & Operations Research*, *37*(12), 2041–2061. doi:10.1016/j.cor.2010.03.015

Huang, X., Chen, H., Liu, L., & Chen, J. (2020). Robust Optimization Model of Feeder Lines Routing Based on the Hub Port. *Transportation Journal*, *59*(3), 279–303. doi:10.5325/transportationj.59.3.0279

Jadrijević, N., & Tomašević, M. (2011). *Feeder service development in Mediterranean ports toward more efficient transport technologies.* 14th International Conference on Transport Science – ICTS, Portoroz, Slovenia.

Karlaftis, M. G., Kepaptsoglou, K., & Sambracos, E. (2009). Containership routing with time deadlines and simultaneous deliveries and pick-ups. *Transportation Research Part E, Logistics and Transportation Review*, *45*(1), 210–221. doi:10.1016/j.tre.2008.05.001

Kulak, O., Polat, O., Gujjula, R., & Günther, H.-O. (2013). Strategies for improving a long-established terminal's performance: A simulation study of a Turkish container terminal. *Flexible Services and Manufacturing Journal*, *25*(4), 503–527. doi:10.100710696-011-9128-x

Kytöjoki, J., Nuortio, T., Bräysy, O., & Gendreau, M. (2007). An efficient variable neighborhood search heuristic for very large scale vehicle routing problems. *Computers & Operations Research*, *34*(9), 2743–2757. doi:10.1016/j.cor.2005.10.010

Lin, Y., Wang, X., Hu, H., & Zhao, H. (2020). Research on feeder network design: A case study of feeder service for the port of Kotka. *European Transport Research Review*, *12*(1), 61. doi:10.118612544-020-00450-6

Lu, H.-A., Chu, C.-W., & Che, P.-Y. (2010). Seasonal slot allocation planning for a container liner shipping service. *Journal of Marine Science and Technology*, *18*(1), 84–92. doi:10.51400/2709-6998.1868

Meng, Q., & Wang, S. (2012). Liner ship fleet deployment with week-dependent container shipment demand. *European Journal of Operational Research*, *222*(2), 241–252. doi:10.1016/j.ejor.2012.05.006

Meng, Q., Wang, T., & Gelareh, S. (2011). A linearized approach for the liner containership fleet planning with demand uncertainty. In E. P. Chew, L. H. Lee, & L. C. Tang (Eds.), *Advances in Maritime Logistics and Supply Chain Systems* (pp. 229–256). World Scientific Publishing. doi:10.1142/9789814329866_0011

Meng, Q., Wang, T., & Wang, S. (2012). Short-term liner ship fleet planning with container transshipment and uncertain container shipment demand. *European Journal of Operational Research*, *223*(1), 96–105. doi:10.1016/j.ejor.2012.06.025

Mladenović, N., & Hansen, P. (1997). Variable neighborhood search. *Computers & Operations Research*, *24*(11), 1097–1100. doi:10.1016/S0305-0548(97)00031-2

Pantuso, G., Fagerholt, K., & Hvattum, L. M. (2014). A survey on maritime fleet size and mix problems. *European Journal of Operational Research*, *235*(2), 341–349. doi:10.1016/j.ejor.2013.04.058

Polat, L. Ö., & Güngör, A. (2019). Network Design Problems in E-waste Management. In M. N. V. Prasad & M. Vithanage (Eds.), *Electronic Waste Management and Treatment Technology* (pp. 77–102). Butterworth-Heinemann. doi:10.1016/B978-0-12-816190-6.00004-2

Polat, O. (2017a). An Overview of Feeder Services in the Era of Mega Containerships. In S. Laurence & C. Cécile (Eds.), *Global Intermediation and Logistics Service Providers* (pp. 317–339). IGI Global. doi:10.4018/978-1-5225-2133-4.ch016

Polat, O. (2017b). A parallel variable neighborhood search for the vehicle routing problem with divisible deliveries and pickups. *Computers & Operations Research*, *85*, 71–86. doi:10.1016/j.cor.2017.03.009

Polat, O., & Günther, H.-O. (2016). The impact of seasonal demand fluctuations on service network design of container feeder lines. *Journal of Transportation and Logistics*, *1*(1), 39–58. doi:10.22532/jtl.237886

Polat, O., Günther, H.-O., & Kulak, O. (2014). The feeder network design problem: Application to container services in the Black Sea region. *Maritime Economics & Logistics*, *16*(3), 1–27. doi:10.1057/mel.2014.2

Polat, O., Kulak, O., & Günther, H.-O. (2012). *An adaptive neighborhood search approach for VRPSP-DTL*. The 2nd International Conference on Logistics and Maritime Systems, Bremen, Germany.

Schulze, P. M., & Prinz, A. (2009). Forecasting container transshipment in Germany. *Applied Economics*, *41*(22), 2809–2815. doi:10.1080/00036840802260932

Stenger, A., Vigo, D., Enz, S., & Schwind, M. (2013). An adaptive variable neighborhood search algorithm for a vehicle routing problem arising in small package shipping. *Transportation Science*, *47*(1), 503–527. doi:10.1287/trsc.1110.0396

Stopford, M. (2009). Maritime economics (3rd ed.). Routledge.

Varbanova, A. (2011). Current iIssues in operational planning of general cargo transportation on container feeder lines in the Black Sea region. *The International Virtual Journal for Science, Techniques and Innovations for the Industry Machines, Technologies, Materials*, *2011*(3), 35–38.

VHSS. (2013). *Containership time-charter-rates*. Retrieved 15.06.2012 from http://www.vhss.de/contex_new.php

Wang, T., Meng, Q., & Wang, S. (2012). Robust Optimization Model for Liner Ship Fleet Planning with Container Transshipment and Uncertain Demand. *Transportation Research Record: Journal of the Transportation Research Board*, *2273*(1), 18–28. doi:10.3141/2273-03

Wijnolst, N., Waals, F., Bello, F., Gendronneau, Y., & Kempen, D. v. (2000). *Malacca Max (2) Container Shipping Network Economy*. Delft University Press.

Zachcial, M., & Lemper, B. (2006). Container shipping: An overview of Development Trends. In C. Heideloff & T. Pawlik (Eds.), Handbook of Container Shipping Management (pp. 23-37). Institute of Shipping Economics and Logistics (ISL).

Zeng, Q., Yang, Z., & Chen, C. (2010). Robust optimization model for resource allocation of container shipping lines. *Tsinghua Science and Technology*, *15*(5), 586–594. doi:10.1016/S1007-0214(10)70105-X

Zurheide, S., & Fischer, K. (2011). A Simulation study for evaluating a slot allocation model for a liner shipping network. *Lecture Notes in Computer Science*, *6971*, 354–369. doi:10.1007/978-3-642-24264-9_26

Zurheide, S., & Fischer, K. (2012). A revenue management slot allocation model for liner shipping networks. *Maritime Economics & Logistics*, *14*(3), 334–361. doi:10.1057/mel.2012.11

Chapter 7
Use of Information Technology in the Supply Chain Management of the Pharmaceutical Industry:
A Literature Review

Saibal Kumar Saha
https://orcid.org/0000-0002-7842-698X
Sikkim Manipal Institute of Technology, Sikkim Manipal University, India

Sangita Saha
https://orcid.org/0000-0002-4676-5370
Sikkim Manipal Institute of Technology, Sikkim Manipal University, India

Ajeya Jha
https://orcid.org/0000-0003-0491-5008
Sikkim Manipal Institute of Technology, Sikkim Manipal University, India

ABSTRACT

An efficient supply chain management helps to increase the productivity of a business. Use of information technology and concepts like artificial intelligence, blockchain, and cloud computing have integrated the different aspects of supply chain with its stakeholders. Published literature in the field of SCM, IT, and the pharmaceutical industry has been reviewed, and different aspects of innovation, technique, risks, advancements, factors, and models have been taken into consideration to form a comprehensive chapter focusing on the role of information technology in the supply chain management of the pharmaceutical industry. The chapter finds that IT has made a significant impact in improving the efficiency of SCM. But its successful implementation and collaboration with other firms is the key to success for an efficient SCM. Within each category, gaps have been identified.

DOI: 10.4018/978-1-7998-8709-6.ch007

INTRODUCTION

A digitalized world with Industry 4.0 technologies has set high standards for companies (Kumar et al., 2020). The extensive use of blockchain (Wu et al., 2019), Internet of Things (IoT), Artificial Intelligence (AI) (Kaplan & Haenlein, 2020, Nishant et al., 2020), cloud computing (Lin & Lin, 2019) have changed the dimensions in which business is conducted (Toorajipour et al., 2021) in the 21st century. The synergy between humans and machines has never been better before. The integration of Industry 4.0 with healthcare sustainable supply chain 4.0 is paving the future for a better supply chain network Daú (2019).

An efficient supply chain is essential for increasing organizations' efficiency. The advancements made in Information Technology (IT) helps in improving greening methods (Jarmoszko et al., 2013), demand forecasting (Sarhani and Afia 2014) and connectivity or hyper-connectivity (Linke, 2013). Improvement in coordination (Ghahremani and Tarokh, 2011) and reduction in business risks (Hietajärvi and Karvonen, 2016) is possible with the integration of IT.

The complex nature of the pharmaceutical industry and its importance for an efficient supply chain is essential in distributing and disseminating life-saving drugs to patients at the right time through proper channels. The quality of health care in hospitals can be greatly improved by increasing the efficiency in its supply chain Nsamzinshuti and Ndiaye (2014). This text explores the possibilities of an efficient supply chain in the pharmaceutical industry with the use of integrated IT systems. Published literature in the field of supply chain and information technology have been referred to identify the gaps.

METHODOLOGY

Using the keywords "SCM", "supply chain management", "information technology", "IT", "healthcare", "role of IT", "SCM of pharmaceutical industry", "pharmaceutical industry", "role of IT on SCM" and "role of IT on pharmaceutical industry" in search of databases such as Google Scholar, EBSCO, Scopus and ScienceDirect, resulted in 216 published papers for review. Only papers pertaining to recent developments in SCM were considered, followed by papers involving developments in IT that affected SCM, and finally papers pertaining to pharma. For each of the categories, new technologies and frameworks were investigated, and research gaps were identified. Figure 1 shows the frequency distribution of journals in terms of years:

The published literature has been methodologically categorized into three broad groups: SCM, IT and Pharmaceutical Industry which are further divided into different subgroups and then analyzed accordingly. Research gaps within each category have been identified so that future research could be done in those areas. Table 1 and figure 2 lists the distribution of papers by topic area:

Figure 1. Yearly distribution of journals

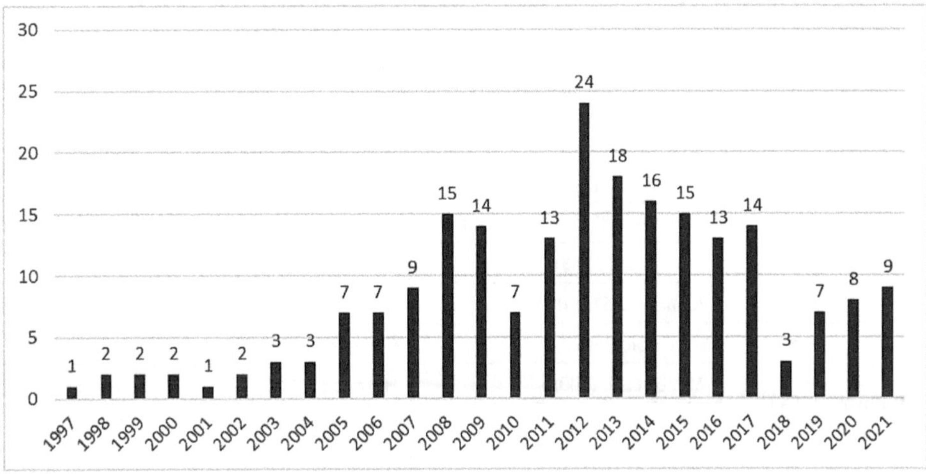

SUPPLY CHAIN MANAGEMENT

The term "supply chain management" (SCM) was coined by Keith Oliver, a Booz Allen consultant, in 1982. Cooper et al. (1997) defined SCM as the management of exchanges of information and materials in the logistics process starting from the purchasing of raw materials to the delivery of products to end customers, linking numerous firms. SCM includes a set of approaches and practices which integrates suppliers, manufacturers, distributors and customers and improves the performance of firms (Chopra and Meindl, 2001). Successful implementation of SCM is possible through information sharing, sharing the risks and benefits (Kwon et al., 2011). Customer value can be increased by enhancing the strategic importance of SCM partners and inter-firm integration, and relationship enabled responsiveness (Kim et al., 2013). By adopting a holistic value chain approach, cumulative value for the customer can be increased exponentially (Woolliscroft et al., 2013). Kumar et al. (2015) identified 13 critical success factors for the implementation of SCM: top management commitment, development of effective SCM strategy, devoted resources for supply chain, logistics synchronization, use of modern technologies, information sharing with SC members, forecasting of demand on the point of sale (POS), trust development in SC partners, developing just in time (JIT) capabilities in the system, development of reliable suppliers, higher flexibility in the production system, focus on core strengths, and long-term vision for survival and growth.

A control model for virtualization of control in a supply chain was proposed by Verdouw et al. (2015). Jin and Hong (2007) explored global supplier-manufacturer relationships. Kundu et al. (2015) reviewed the cross-disciplinary literature from 1934 to 2013 on behavioral operations in supply chain using the Latent Semantic Analysis (LSA) method, while Kamalahmadi and Parast (2015) investigated research developments in the field of supply chain resilience and Bask and Tinnilä (2013) studied the impact of product characteristic on SCM. The study by Wieland (2021) represents SCM as a social-ecological system in which the SCM processes and structures are interlinked with political-economic and planetary phenomena. For increasing the efficiency of SCM, new technologies were adopted and integrated with different SCM functions. Some of these technologies are discussed below.

Table 1. Distribution of papers by topic area.

Topic Area		References		
Supply chain management	SCM	Cooper et al. (1997)	Chopra and Meindl (2001)	Kwon et al. (2011)
		Kim et al. (2013)	Woolliscroft et al. (2013)	Kumar et al. (2015)
		Verdouw et al. (2015)	Jin and Hong, (2007)	Kundu et al. (2015)
		Toorajipour et al., (2021)	Daú (2019)	Wieland (2021)
		Kamalahmadi and Parast (2015)	Bask and Tinnilä (2013).	Wu et al., (2019)
	RFID	Gaukler et al. (2007)	Tajima, (2007)	Sarac et al. (2010)
		Permala et al. (2012)		
	Bullwhip Effect	Stevenson (2007)	Cheng et al. (2010)	Geary et al. (2006)
		Wamba et al. (2008)	Holweg et al. (2005)	Wang et al. (2008)
		Zaharudin et al. (2006)	Buffa and Miller (1979)	Ouyang (2007)
		Ding et al. (2011)	Najafi and Farahani (2014)	Chen et al., (2000)
	JIT	Spekman et al. (1998)	Kros et al. (2006)	(Mehralian et al., 2016)
	Knowledge Management	Chandra and Tumanyan (2007)	Marra et al. (2012)	Crook et al. (2008)
		Cerchione and Esposito (2016)	Wu and Haasis 2013).	
	Collaboration	Melnyk et al. (2014)	Vereecke and Muylle (2006)	Lavie (2006)
		Simatupang and Sridharan (2005)	Tan et al. (2006)	Liu and Wang (2011)
		Jairo et al. (2014)	Nyaga et al. (2010)	Wicher and Lenort (2012).
		Park et.al (2016)	Aris et al. (2016)	Dutta and Hora (2017)
		Mbang (2013)		
	SCM measurement	Galia (2007)	SCC, (2008)	Forslund and Jonsson (2009)
		Cai et al. (2010)	Li et al. (2005)	Fynes et al. (2005)
		Kamalahmadi and Parast (2015)	Biswas and Sengupta (2014)	Delipinar and Kocaoglu (2016)
	SCM Frameworks	Samaddar et al. (2006)	Glock (2017)	Baumann and Genoulaz (2014)
		Al-Shboul, (2017)	Chung and Kwon (2016)	Oliveira et al. (2016)
	Challenges	Krueger (2012)	Ghadge et al. (2012	Pereira et al. 2014)
		Rajeev et.al, (2017)	Busse et al. (2017)F	Modgil & Sharma (2017)

continues on following page

RFID

A Radio-frequency identifier (RFID) is used for processing and sorting goods. The use of RFID has significantly improved inventory management, transportation, logistics, assembly, manufacturing, asset tracking and object location (Gaukler et al., 2007). It also helps for proper visibility of the product throughout the entire supply chain. It increases the reliability of SCM and speeds up operational processes such as checkout, shipping, tracking and counting processes (Tajima, 2007). RFID also helps to reduce inventory losses and speeds up the process by providing accurate information. RFID can be used extensively for dealing with inventory inaccuracy, bullwhip effect and replenishment policies (Sarac et al., 2010). Automated, remote and wireless identification reduces manual work and errors, saving costs, increasing productivity and efficiency (Permala et al., 2012).

Table 1. Continued

Topic Area		References		
Information technology	IT	Li et al. (2009)	Gunasekaran and Ngai (2004)	Ngai et al. (2011)
		Du et al. (2012)	Zhou and Benton, (2007)	Swafford et al. (2008)
		Pereira (2009)	Nath and Standing (2010)	Sahin and Robinson (2005)
		Huang et al. (2003)	Martınez-Olvera (2008)	Helo and Szekely (2005)
		Krishanpillai et al. (2012)	Welker et al. (2008)	Chen et al. (2011)
		Wu and Cheng (2008)	Jain et al. (2009)	Ryu et al. (2009)
		Bayraktar et al., (2009)	Soni and Jain (2011)	Fawcett et al. (2011)
		Bailey and Francis (2008)	Meredig, (2017)	Bag (2017)
		Kumari et al., (2021)	Kumar et al., (2020)	
	SCM IT Frameworks	Ngai et al. (2011)	Smith et al. (2012)	Prajogo and Olhager (2012)
		Colina et al. (2015)	Matani et al. (2012)	Madenas et al. (2014)
		Yu et al. (2010)	Cho and Lee. (2013)	Fawcett et al. (2011)
		Zhu et al. (2011)	Soroor et al. (2009)	Khan et al. (2016)
	Factors affecting SCM collaboration	Hudnurkar et al. (2014)	Mohtadi (2008)	Okano and Marins (2014)
		Prajogo and Olhager (2012)	Sanders and Premus (2002)	Dias et al. (2003)
	ERP	Bylinsky (1999)	Gunasekaran et al. (2004)	Chang et al. (2008)
		Dolci et al. (2017)		
	BIG Data	Manyika et al. (2011)	Strawn (2012)	McAfee and Brynjolfsson (2012)
		Ann Keller et al. (2012)	Gobble (2013)	Wamba et al. (2015)
		Ittmann (2015)	Khan (2013)	Demchenko et al. (2013)
		Megatrend (2014)	Wang et al. (2015)	
	Frameworks for IT implementation in SCM	Sahay & Ranjan (2008).	Chae and Olson (2013)	Waller & Fawcett (2013)
		Yan et al. (2014)	Sohn and Lim (2008)	Bayraktar et al. (2009)
		Jaggi and Kadam (2016)		
	Artificial Intelligence	Kaplan & Haenlein, (2020)	Nishant et al., (2020)	Amisha et al., (2019)
		Klumpp (2018)	Mobarakeh et al. (2017)	(Letheren and Glavas, 2017)
		Van den Broeck et al., (2019)	Kantasa-ard et al., (2019)	
	Cloud Computing	Lin & Lin, (2019)	(Attaran, 2020)	Sundarakani (2019)
		Lin et al., (2020)	Puica (2020)	
	IT Failure	Kumar & Pugazhendhi (2012)		

continues on following page

Table 1. Continued

Topic Area		References		
Pharmaceutical industry	**PI**	Shah (2004)	Papageorgiou (2009)	Yu et al. (2010)
		Laínez et al. (2012)	Nahmias (2011)	Niziolek (2008)
		Schapranow et al. (2011)	Alnaji and Ridha (2013)	Rossetti et al. (2011)
		Narayana et al. (2012)	Ik-Whan et al. (2016)	Burns (2002)
		Johnson (2015)	Dooner (2014)	Mehralian et al., 2015
		Masoumi et al. (2012)	Vila-Parrish and Ivy (2013)	Stecca et al., 2016)
		Shao et al., (2021)		
	Barriers in SCM of pharmaceutical industry	Nachtmann and Pohl (2009)	Elmuti et al. (2013)	Harrington (2015)
		Kwon and Hong (2011)	Hansen and Grunow (2015)	
		Gregor et al., (2021)		(Ahmad, 2021).
	Framework for SCM in pharmaceutical industry	Meiler et al. (2015)	Ryu and Pistikopoulos (2007)	Susarla and Karimi (2012)
		Jetly et al. (2012)	Shah and Ierapetritou (2012)	Mousazadeh et al. (2015)
		Abdelkafi et al. (2009)	Rotstein et al. (1999)	Susarla and Karimi (2012)
		Pishvaee et al. (2012)	Gatica et al. (2003)	Masoumi et al. (2012)
		Rossetti et al. (2011)	Meiler et al. (2016)	Syahrir et al. (2015)
		Pujawan et al. (2009)	Dasaklis et al. (2012)	Gupta et al. (2013)
		Abbas and Routray (2014)	Mehralian et al. (2017)	
	Pharmaceutical reverse supply chain	Bartelt-Hunt et al. (2009)	Weraikat et al. (2015)	Xie and Breen (2012)
		Tat et al., (2020)	Marques et al., (2020)	Ritchie et al., (2000).
		Amaro and Barbosa-Póvoa (2008)	Ali (2017)	Tat et al., (2020)

Figure 2. Topic area and references

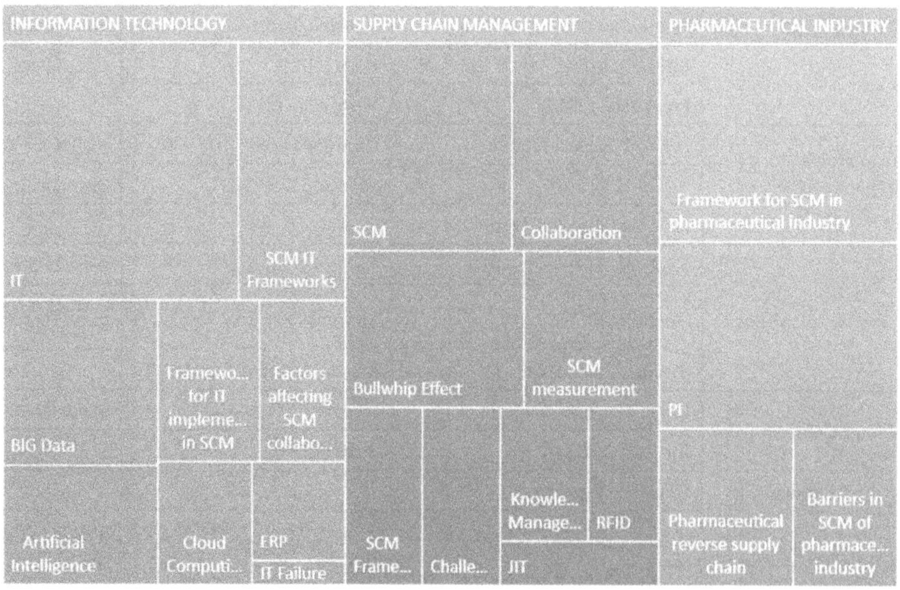

Bullwhip Effect

The bullwhip effect is associated with the demand variations from customers, which become progressively large when they diffuse backwards through the chain (Stevenson, 2007). It is caused due to distortion of demand information while moving from downstream to upstream (Cheng et al., 2010) and is caused due to poor material flow (Geary et al. (2006). By controlling the bullwhip effect, materials and resources could be optimized by decreasing unnecessary locations and safety stocks along the supply chains (Wamba et al., 2008). Forecasting methods can be used to control bullwhip effects (Najafi and Farahani, 2014). Some factors which help in controlling the bullwhip effect are information sharing (Chen et al., 2000), supply chain collaboration and visibility of information flow (Holweg et al., 2005), use of RFID (Wang et al., 2008), use of AUTO-ID technologies and information sharing between all supply chain actors (Zaharudin et al., 2006) and proper planning and control (Buffa and Miller, 1979). The bullwhip effect on market demand can be reduced by sharing customer demand information (Ouyang, 2007) and by motivating retailers (Ding et al., 2011) to share information with other supply chain partners.

JIT

By using the concept of just in time (JIT), firms can reduce inventory storage costs. High productivity is achieved by using the right products at the right time (Mehralian et al., 2016). Hence, JIT is a cohesive set of activities that help achieve high production volumes using minimum raw materials, work in process (WIP), and finished goods (Spekman et al., 1998). In JIT, suppliers must produce and deliver the right quantity at the right time to the manufacturer (Kros et al., 2006), thus reducing the lead-time, inventory, and holding cost.

Knowledge Management

Effectiveness in SCM can be attained by sharing organizational knowledge (Chandra and Tumanyan, 2007; Wu and Haasis, 2013). Marra et al. (2012) showed the importance of measuring the impact of Knowledge Management (KM) in SCM performance by associating IT adoption to the firm's growth. When independent firms share knowledge and collaborate with others, great advantages in terms of SCM can be achieved (Crook et al., 2008). Cerchione and Esposito (2016) divided SCM into different objective systems: economic, productive, strategic, social, and environmental which are affected by different flows of finance, material, information, technology etc., and gave a systematic review of KM in the supply chain.

Collaboration

With the help of information sharing and performance monitoring, potential problems in SCM can be identified (Melnyk et al., 2014). Vereecke and Muylle (2006) empirically tested the connection between supply chain collaboration and performance enhancement using IMSS 2001 data on 374 firms from different engineering and assembly industries from 11 different European countries. Lavie (2006) proposed a prolonged resource-based view model, incorporating the different network resources of interconnected firms. Simatupang and Sridharan (2005) proposed an instrument to measure the degree of collaboration in SCM consisting of both supplier and retailer. A model based on reliability, velocity, and the cost was introduced by Mbang (2013).

The increase in Multi-National Corporations (MNC) has highlighted the effectiveness of global SCM. SMEs also need to be integrated into this SCM to increase efficiency (Tan et al., 2006). An improved understanding of the crisis and causes in collaborative SCM is important for developing better strategies (Liu and Wang, 2011). Information sharing and collaboration strategies on supply chain dynamics help increase its performance (Jairo et al., 2014). Dutta and Hora (2017) categorized SCM partnerships into two types of alliances, upstream (with research universities) and downstream (with large industry incumbents), and found that upstream partnerships had a positive impact on invention success while there was no impact on commercialization success. But the joint effect of both the alliances showed positive success for both invention and commercialization. Collaboration and relationships in SCM can be improved by information sharing, building trusted networks, planning and forecasting (Wicher & Lenort, 2012; Nyaga et al., 2010). Improved forecasting support systems can help in proper information dissemination and inventory management (Aris et al., 2016). Dynamic interactive visual systems can enhance the decision-making processes of the supply chain (Park et al., 2016).

SCM Measurement

Customer relations, supplier relations, production, product development, corporate strategy and corporate structure are the six fields used as assessment tools for evaluating supply chain performance (Galia, 2007). The SCOR model defines five metrics for assessing SCM: reliability, responsiveness, flexibility, costs and asset management (SCC, 2008) and is mostly used in the manufacturing industry (Delipinar and Kocaoglu, 2016). Forslund and Jonsson (2009) identified the different complications in the SCM relationship and operational tools obstructing SCM integration for performance management. The formation of trust and information sharing between buyers and suppliers helps to improve SCM performance (Cai et al., 2010). A six-measurement instrument for SCM practices: strategic supplier partnership, information sharing, information quality, internal lean practices, customer relationship and postponement was proposed by Li et al. (2005). Different aspects like the impact of SCM relationships on quality performance (Fynes et al., 2005) and principles of enterprise and supply chain resilience (Kamalahmadi and Parast, 2015) can bring in more robustness in SCM. Biswas and Sengupta (2014) identified twelve success factors for the execution of total quality management (TQM) principles in SCM: strategic quality management, process quality management, design quality management, education and training, supplier quality management, customer satisfaction, employee empowerment and involvement, business results, information and analysis, benchmarking, impact on society and environment and statistical process control.

SCM Frameworks

Authors have proposed a number of models and frameworks intending to improve SCM processes. Samaddar et al. (2006) provided a theoretical framework to inspect the associations between inter-organizational information sharing and the design of an SCM network. Glock (2017) reviewed decision support models for the management of closed-loop supply chains, which involve returnable transport items (RTIs). Baumann and Genoulaz (2014) proposed a framework for sustainable performance characterization and an analytical model for sustainable performance assessment. Oliveira et al. (2016) developed a meta-analysis about modelling and simulation's relationships and potential perspectives. Chung and

Kwon (2016) proposed an integrated SCM framework based on product perishability. Al-Shboul (2017) examined the role of time to market and delivery dependability on the relation amid the infrastructure framework and supply chain agility and found that infrastructure framework elements do not contribute expressively to support supply chain agility associated with enhanced firm performance.

Challenges

Rajeev et al. (2017) worked to understand the evolution of sustainability issues in SCM by analyzing trends across industries and economies. Sustainability related uncertainties: task uncertainty, source uncertainty and supply chain uncertainty were identified by Busse et al. (2017). Krueger (2012) examined different ethical problems associated with global SCM of multinational companies in developing countries. Some of the major challenges are demand variability, decrease in the product life cycle, varied expectations and requirements of customers (Ghadge et al., 2012; Pereira et al., 2014). SCM can be made efficient with strong backup, accuracy, speed and responsiveness (Modgil and Sharma, 2017).

Gaps in the Literature

1. Detailed industry-based studies can be done on technologies like barcodes and color codes.
2. Multi-level supply chain systems using multiple products can be a scope of study in the future.
3. Considering time as the main dimension, future research could be done for elimination of the bullwhip effect.
4. Future research could be done on methodologies like Six Sigma, Lean Manufacturing, or JIT to check their impact on SCM performance.
5. The impact of proper knowledge management could be studied in greater depth, and the impact on the implementation of customer relationship management (CRM) could be studied.
6. Quality issues in SCM could be measured with the help of historical records with respect to temperature and light conditions.

INFORMATION TECHNOLOGY

IT has changed the scope and dimensions of SCM and has improved its efficiency (Li et al., 2009). It is like a nervous system (Gunasekaran and Ngai, 2004) and plays an important role in aiding organizations' sensing and response abilities (Ngai et al., 2011). For an SCM system to be efficient and effective, information has to be shared between different parties (Du et al., 2012; Zhou and Benton, 2007; Huang et al., 2003)). Firms use information system (IS) practices to achieve agility and increase operational performance (Swafford et al., 2008). Pereira (2009) reviewed different issues and trends in IT-enabled SCM with examples from manufacturing and logistics case studies. Nath and Standing (2010) assessed the IT drivers, patterns and key factors for success. Sahin and Robinson (2005) threw light on the impact of physical flow coordination and information sharing in SCM of make-to-order business. Martınez-Olvera (2008) proposed that by increasing the level of information sharing among supply chain partners, order fulfilment can be managed in a better way. Helo and Szekely (2005) demonstrated that a software application could improve information sharing in manufacturing and service phases and proved that logistics information systems could benefit SCM. Krishanpillai et al. (2012) performed a study to find the impact of information technologies implementation on tourism supply chain performance. With a focus on SMEs, Welker et al. (2008) inspected the impact of business conditions on different internal and external information sharing and the role of information and communications technology (ICT). Chen et al. (2011) examined the role of information availability, information sharing, and information quality in developing commitment and trust in SCM relationships. Wu and Cheng (2008) studied the impact of information sharing on inventory and the probable cost of a three-echelon supply chain. Jain et al. (2009) worked on prevailing information systems that supported supply chain dynamics at strategic and operational levels, focusing on web-enabled collaboration between supply chain partners. Pereira (2009) focused on IT technical issues and their implication for SCM business performance. Bayraktar et al. (2009) established a causal relationship between information systems and SCM practices.

Sharing information can help eliminate additional inventory problems and a lack of service due to uncertainty (Bag 2017; Ryu et al., 2009). Post disruption collaboration and information sharing in SCM can significantly affect the system's ability to deal with future disruptions (Soni and Jain, 2011) and is applicable to all three phases: before, throughout, and after an incident. Decision support models provide guidelines to manage supply chains. They help managers to assess the probable impact of changes to the system beforehand. Still, the study conducted by Fawcett et al. (2011) revealed that managers do not understand the dynamics of trust-building or its nature. Information sharing alone is insufficient (Bailey & Francis, 2008) as demand amplification effects can be seen inside an erudite value chain with collaborative practices and high levels of information transparency. Trends such as cloud computing, open data, Big Data technologies, large-scale materials data and machine learning have led to new industrial opportunities for informatics (Meredig, 2017).

SCM IT Frameworks

The foundation of SCM competence lies in IT competence (Ngai et al., 2011). IT can deliver important benefits to the business (Smith et al., 2012). Integration of information (Colina et al., 2015; Yu et al. 2010) and material flows, inventory management (Matani et al., 2012) between SCM partners helps to increase operational performance (Prajogo and Olhager, 2012). Madenas et al. (2014) analyzed different publications in the field of information flow in SCM, emphasizing the product life cycle. The seasonal effect impacts the supplier's optimal inventory policies based on the information sharing policies of supplier, retailer and customer (Cho and Lee, 2013). With the help of a resource-based view approach, Fawcett et al. (2011) investigated the mechanisms by which SCM performance is influenced by IT. Zhu et al. (2011) calculated the value of information sharing for different inventory policies using mathematical models. Khan et al. (2016) observed that information sharing resulted in better profits with a drop in the buyer's price. Soroor et al. (2009) formulated a framework to organize and develop a wireless web for implementation of a mobile real-time supply chain coordination system through intelligent wireless web (IWW) services.

Factors Affecting SCM Collaboration

Information sharing has a vital role in supply chain collaboration and is the most important factor (Hudnurkar et al., 2014; Prajogo and Olhager, 2012). Based on a study of the food industry supply chain, Mohtadi (2008) inspected the determinants of information sharing between retailers and their suppliers. IT greatly impacts the planning, manufacturing, suppliers and delivery (Okano & Marins, 2014) processes of SCM, also confirmed that IT plays a very important role in SCM. Higher use of IT produces operational benefits in SCM by reducing costs and cycle times (Sanders & Premus, 2002). By using IT in SCM a number of benefits can be achieved: instant information sharing, real-time monitoring of consumer load, sharing of programs for increase operational efficiency, global sales channels development, reduction in inventories and in the creation of more flexibility (Dias et al., 2003).

Types of Data in SCM IT Integration

Data, which is the most vital input for the process of IT, can be obtained from different stages in SCM. This information can be broadly segmented based on the point of their origin and can be further identified as per their nature, as shown in figure 3.

Figure 3. Types of data in SCM IT integration
Source: Author work

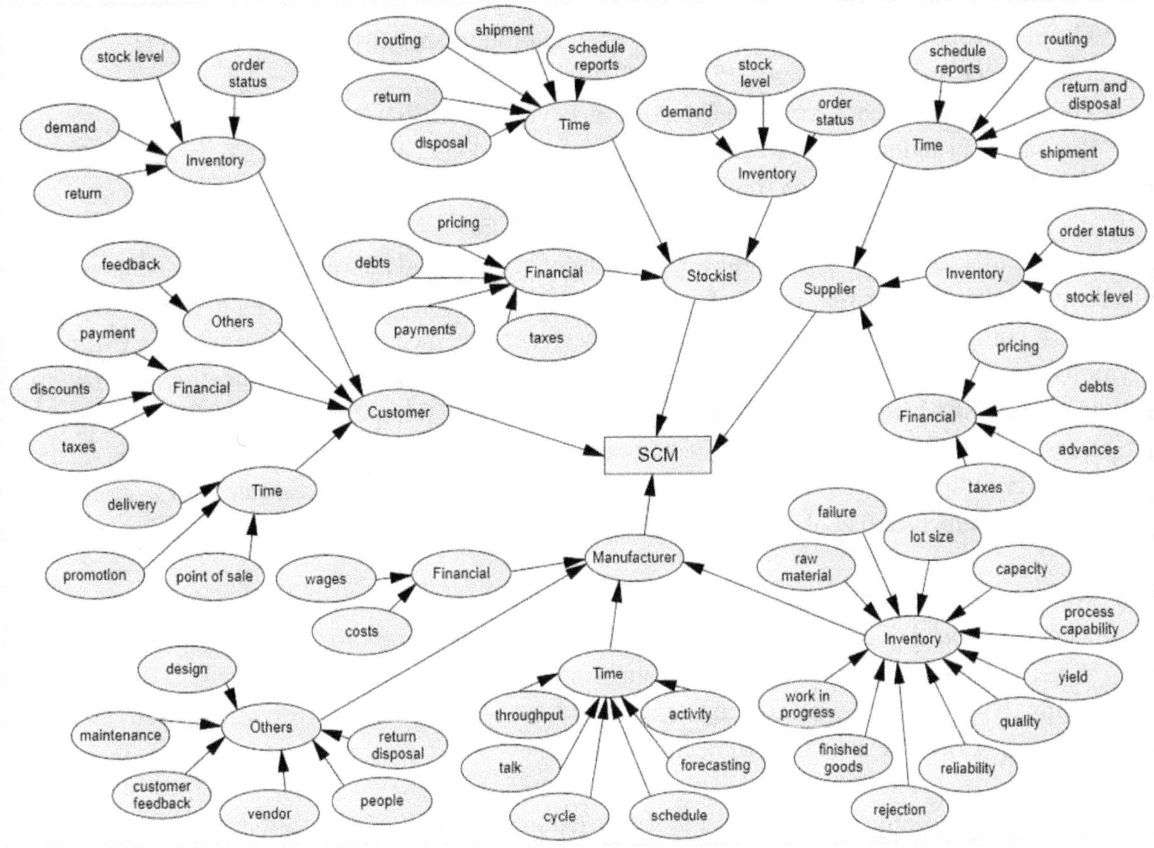

Enterprise Resource Planning

ERP is a software package that integrates a firm's internal information systems (Bylinsky, 1999). It integrates the process of resource planning (purchasing, production, distribution, performance, human resource and reduction of business costs) with E-procurement tools and automated purchase and payments (Gunasekaran et al., 2004). Chang et al. (2008) proposed a neural network evaluation model for ERP performance in SCM, enhancing competitive enterprise advantage. By investing in e-procurement and ERP, companies can achieve more relational governance by integration with their suppliers (Dolci et al., 2017).

Big Data

Big data is a collection of a large amount of data consisting of both structured and unstructured data. It is as large as zettabyte and cannot be managed by a conventional database management system. Big data has been characterized as:

- The next frontier for innovation, competition and productivity (Manyika et al., 2011)
- The fourth paradigm of science (Strawn, 2012)
- The next management revolution (McAfee & Brynjolfsson, 2012)
- Big data is bringing a revolution in science and technology (Ann Keller et al., 2012)
- Next big thing in innovation (Gobble, 2013)

Wamba et al. (2015) investigated the applications of big data and its role in capturing business value. Big data can play a major role in transforming the decision-making process by providing greater visibility of a company's operations and improved performance measurement mechanisms (McAfee & Brynjolfsson, 2012). Adapting big data analytics into the system is one of the critical success factors of next generation SCM (Ittmann, 2015). By tracking and understanding the data generated by the different processes of SCM, useful information can be obtained to operate a smart supply chain. Analytics can play a very important role in designing strategies for enhancing the performance of a supply chain (Khan, 2013). Demchenko et al. (2013) explained Big Data on five 'V' dimensions:

1. Volume - Amount of data generated
2. Velocity - Speed of data generation, accumulation, retrieval and process
3. Variety - Diversification of generated data
4. Value - Usefulness of generated data
5. Veracity - Correctness of data subject to variation

According to Accenture Global Operations: Megatrend (2014), business analytics can help decision-makers improve demand fulfilment by at least 10% faster. The effective reaction time for supply chain issues can reach 41% and supply chain efficiency can be increased by 10% to 36%. There is great scope for research in outsourcing healthcare services, financial services, and telecommunication with respect to recent advances in big data analytics (Wang et al., 2015). The incorporation of consumer welfare into the SCM optimization models is an area which could also be explored. Risk management in service coordination could also be explored in the future.

Frameworks for IT Implementation in SCM

A real-time Business Intelligence (BI) system could be integrated with different management functions for understanding and controlling the operations for predicting future requirements (Sahay & Ranjan, 2008). An analytic supply chain can integrate data management, process management and performance management, which integrates people, processes and organization to forecast and plan for meeting demands in an agile way (Chae & Olson, 2013). Predictive analytics can be used to estimate the level of business process integration, required service level and cost by using both quantitative and qualitative analysis (Waller & Fawcett, 2013). Yan et al. (2014) proposed a cloud-based framework for sharing information on a real-time basis to include agility in the system and promote flexible collaboration and integration. For products with a short life cycle, proper selection of an information-sharing policy and forecasting methods significantly impact supply chain performance (Sohn & Lim, 2008). Bayraktar et al. (2009) created a framework of the impact of information systems and supply chain management practices. Jaggi and Kadam (2016) looked for the advantages of the apache spark framework over the existing Hadoop framework. The study also provided information about how big data analytics and supply chain management are integrated.

Artificial Intelligence

Artificial intelligence has the potential to achieve significant change in the operations of an organization. AI is a system that puts the brain into a machine and gives it the capability to think, behave and perform things like a human being (Amisha et al., 2019). Klumpp (2018) study aimed to differentiate superior and inferior performing human artificial collaboration systems in logistics using a multi-dimensional conceptual framework. Mobarakeh et al. (2017) used AI based methods to estimate demand forecasts accurately. To enhance customer relationships, (Letheren and Glavas, 2017) present an innovative form of marketing communication using AI (Van den Broeck et al., 2019). Kantasa-ard et al., (2019) used AI to forecast the demand for white sugar consumption rate in Thailand. The process of regression and artificial neural network (ANN) was used in the study.

Cloud Computing

As the life cycle of products has decreased and new variants of products are launched at a rapid pace in the market, cloud computing technologies have the potential to enable the companies to capture the pulse of the market and analyze the data to make effective decisions (Attaran, 2020). Sundarakani (2019) proposed a hybrid cloud framework to integrate Industry 4.0 situation and provide a consistent central management system to provide adequate knowledge to optimize its workload placement. To achieve flexibility, better communication, accessibility, and effectiveness of services, Lin et al. (2020) conducted a survey with 223 top 1,000 manufacturing firms in Taiwan. It was found that if the internal resources of an organization were allocated effectively, it has a strong positive effect on external cloud-based supply chain management systems. Puica (2020) found that cloud computing-based information and communication systems positively impact supply chain management. It also helps to maximize economic profitability and social welfare and further helps in minimizing the environmental impact.

IT Failure

Some of the reasons for the failure of proper IT implementation in SCM are poor IT infrastructure, inequality in technological capabilities among SCM partners, information security, lack of trust among SCM partners, unwieldiness of information sharing, risks in information sharing and financial constraints (Kumar & Pugazhendhi, 2012).

Gaps in the Literature

1. In most of the studies, IT implementation is measured in a general context. Technology specific studies could be done in the future and the impact of different technologies could be assessed.
2. Comparative studies could be done for different technologies that have been adapted in SCM.
3. Future study could include the study of consumer behavior due to implementation of IT in SCM.
4. The study of the impact of IT in different stages of SCM could show new insights into the possibilities for integration of different technologies suitable for each stage.
5. Integration of AI and cloud computing with other technologies can be studied in detail.

PHARMACEUTICAL INDUSTRY

The pharmaceutical industry (PI) is a global industry that involves complex processes, operations, and organizations involving discovering, developing, and manufacturing drugs and medications (Mehralian et al., 2015; Shah 2004). Health care logistics optimization is a critical factor for health care services as expenditure must be strictly controlled while maintaining high health care service levels (Stecca et al., 2016). According to Papageorgiou (2009), pharmaceutical drug supply chains need an efficient optimization technique to reduce costs and increase productivity and responsiveness. The challenges and methodologies in the pharmaceutical supply chains were studied by Yu et al. (2010) and Laínez et al. (2012), perishable inventory management systems by Nahmias (2011), drug quality and safety due to perishability with time by Masoumi et al. (2012) and Vila-Parrish and Ivy (2013), shipment strategies in medical drug SCM by Niziolek (2008) and impact of technologies like RFID on operations of pharmaceutical chains was studied by Schapranow et al. (2011). The role of different SCM applications in the pharmaceutical industry was highlighted in the study of Alnaji and Ridha (2013). Rossetti et al. (2011) identified the major forces in pharmaceutical SCM that could revolutionize how biopharmaceutical medications are purchased, distributed, and sold. Different managerial issues in the PI were reviewed by Narayana et al. (2012). Ik-Whan et al. (2016) explored strategic areas of healthcare supply chain which can increase efficiency in terms of cost per patient discharge of healthcare operations and improve the quality of care by reducing the re-admission rate. According to Burns (2002), the quality of products is critical in the healthcare supply chain where there are many regulations. Ik-Whan et al. (2016) confirmed that payments in SCM is made mainly by third parties and the customer is less involved, and planning and forecasting are still in their infancy. Johnson (2015) stated that the logistics cost in healthcare is 38% of total expenses, which is very high compared to 5% for the retail industry and 2% for the electronics industry. The healthcare industry is unable to achieve a cost advantage as they do not use standardized processes (Dooner, 2014). Recent studies are focusing on industry 4.0 to implement across the supply chain (Shao et al., 2021).

Barriers in SCM of the Pharmaceutical Industry

Lack of cooperation from health care supply chain partners (Nachtmann & Pohl, 2009) and lack of implementation of supply chain tools (Elmuti et al., 2013) were identified as the major barriers in the implementation of cost-effective, standardized processes in the healthcare industry. Progress made in exploring and utilizing different tools of SCM for the healthcare sector has been slow (Harrington, 2015). Kwon and Hong (2011) highlighted four critical SCM spots that are vital for the healthcare industry. Hansen and Grunow (2015) conducted a study on planning operations before market launch for balancing time-to-market and risks with respect to pharmaceutical supply chains and identified three areas of risks: the uncertain duration of different authorization processes, risk of a forced label change and uncertain reimbursement levels which result in larger demand variations. The study conducted by Gregor et al., (2021) reveals that the models developed by researchers with respect to SCM have assumptions or abstractions, which do not correctly portray the present pharmaceutical business environment.

Framework for SCM in the Pharmaceutical Industry

Meiler et al. (2015) proposed a pattern-based supply network based on a mixed-integer linear programming model with the continuous representation of time. In order to deal with multi-period supply chain planning problems, Ryu and Pistikopoulos (2007) conceptualized operation policies based on a hierarchical two-stage optimization framework for dealing with the problem complexity. Susarla and Karimi (2012) developed a multi-market, multi-period model for a network of primary and secondary production plants. A multi-agent simulation model was developed by Jetly et al. (2012) to analyze pharmaceutical SCM. Shah and Ierapetritou (2012) created a framework for a supply network with multipurpose batch plants that serve different markets. Mousazadeh et al. (2015) developed a bi-objective mixed-integer linear programming model for a pharmaceutical supply chain network. By using the Bayesian principle to re-evaluate supply strategies over time, Abdelkafi et al. (2009) proposed a method for balancing the risks and costs of supply shortage in the clinical supply chain. With the clinical outcome dependent demand approach, Rotstein et al. (1999) modelled an optimization approach for selecting product development and introduction strategies and investment strategy and capacity planning for a pharmaceutical supply chain. Susarla and Karimi (2012) proposed a mixed integer linear programming model for a pharmaceutical firm. It integrated the different functions of SCM like procurement, production and distribution, material shelf-lives, inventory holding cost, waste treatment, etc. With the objective of total cost maximization, Pishvaee et al. (2012) took an optimization approach to closed-loop supply chain network. Gatica et al. (2003) developed a MILP model and formed a multi-period, multi-stage stochastic optimization model for a pharmaceutical inventory system. Masoumi et al. (2012) developed a supply chain generalized network oligopoly model that handled pharmaceutical product perishability and allowed a firm to minimize discarding cost of wasted and perished medicine and captured product differentiation under oligopolistic competition which included both brands and generics. Rossetti et al. (2011) explored the complexities of pharmaceutical supply chains and gave insights into this industry, including the challenges. Meiler et al. (2016) worked on pattern-based supply network planning for a complex production network with multiple plants of the pharmaceutical industry. They presented a model which generates a comprehensive schedule coordinating the production activities and the campaigns in the network.

Pharmaceutical products are directly related to the quality of life. In certain cases, lack of availability may cause life-threatening situations. They are important to government, companies, healthcare system authorities and societies at large (Mehralian et al., 2017). In the case of natural disasters, proper and timely supply of food, clothing, beverages, medicines, medical equipment, etc. are critical (Syahrir et al., 2015). Pujawan et al. (2009) proposed the principles of SCM for disaster relief operations and proposed a framework to evaluate the handling of logistic operations in relief disaster. Dasaklis et al. (2012) worked on the role of management and logistic operations to control epidemic attack. Gupta et al. (2013) developed models for vaccination programs during epidemic attacks, while Abbas and Routray (2014) developed models for risk assessment at the hospital during a flood disaster. Neutrosophic set, which uses fuzzy and intuitionistic fuzzy sets, is used to optimize multiobjective programming problems for solving problems related to pharmaceutical supply chain (Ahmad, 2021).

Pharmaceutical Reverse Supply Chain

Due to large volumes of production, it is important to gauge the potential severity of using improper or expired drugs, and unsold and unwanted medicines must be recovered (Bartelt-Hunt et al., 2009). Weraikat et al. (2015) investigated a pharmaceutical reverse supply chain. Due to the zero-salvage value of returned medications, firms do not pay much attention to the development of reverse SCM (Xie & Breen, 2012). The authors designed a green pharmaceutical SC model to reduce preventable pharmaceutical waste and to dispose of unavoidable waste. Amaro and Barbosa-Póvoa (2008) presented a model for planning and scheduling of SCM with reverse flows for a pharmaceutical company. Ali (2017) identified 17 reverse logistics barriers for implementing a reverse supply chain for a pharmaceutical company in Egypt. Tat et al., (2020) proposed a buyback policy to gather surplus drugs before they expire. These drugs would then be sold in the secondary market. It will help to curb the wastage and prevent penalties laid by the government. Marques et al., (2020) tried to address the issue based on decision-support challenges and inventory management. Some researchers raised concerns with respect to the environment and tried to address them based on green supply chain to being a drop the wastage levels (Ritchie et al., 2000). Tat et al., (2020) proposed a model for an optimized medicine donation scheme using corporate social responsibility. A take-back plan would give the donation amount in the process of the reverse supply chain.

Gaps in the Literature

1. The research shows that the proportion of study on SCM of the pharmaceutical sector is relatively low. Future research may be done on reverse SCM of medical waste on the consumer side.
2. Specific literature on the impact of IT on SCM of the PI was very limited. Future research could be done in this field. The impact of different technologies on SCM in the pharmaceutical industry could be taken up for future research.
3. The change in purchasing behavior of pharmacy products by consumers due to the impact of IT on SCM could also be studied in future.
4. The quality of pharmaceutical products is critical. The effect of light, temperature and other conditions needs to be regulated throughout the process of manufacturing, transport, storage until consumption. Future in depth research could be done on each of these fields.

5. The effect of temperature, humidity and microbiological control on SCM of pharmaceutical products could be studied in detail with respect to awareness, availability of power, cold chain storage facilities and their proper enforcement.
6. The gaps that exist in quality approach of Good Manufacturing Practices and Good Distribution Practices could be studied with an emphasis on pharmaceutical products.
7. Synchronization of SCM in pharmacy has not been studied, especially with respect to diseases.

Framework of SCM IT Integration for Pharmaceutical Industry

Figure 4 is a framework for SCM of the PI integrated with IT. As found in the literature studied so far, a high level of IT adoption is inevitable for efficiency, quality, cost, time and productivity. Hence, even for the PI, IT can be used effectively to reap the benefits. IT collaboration with suppliers will help get timely information about the requirement for raw materials and check inventory levels. The medicines which leave the factory should be monitored with the help of IT to check for consistency of maintenance of temperature, light, pressure and humidity conditions throughout the journey from the distributor to retailer and then finally to customers. This will make sure that the consumer gets the right medicine in good shape and has all the medicinal properties it should have. In addition to this, IT can also benefit the retailers, distributors and manufacturers to share information about inventory levels, location of goods in transit and payment schedules. IT can benefit each process of SCM. Advanced technologies like RFID, bar codes, and IT-enabled web services could be used to increase the efficiency of the system and improve SCM. Integration of IT with Blockchain has the potential to eliminate the loopholes present in the present system of SCM and deal with problems of expired and fraudulent drugs (Arora et al., 2021), ensuring data security and privacy protection (Kumari et al., 2021).

Figure 4. Framework of SCM of pharmaceutical industry integrated with IT

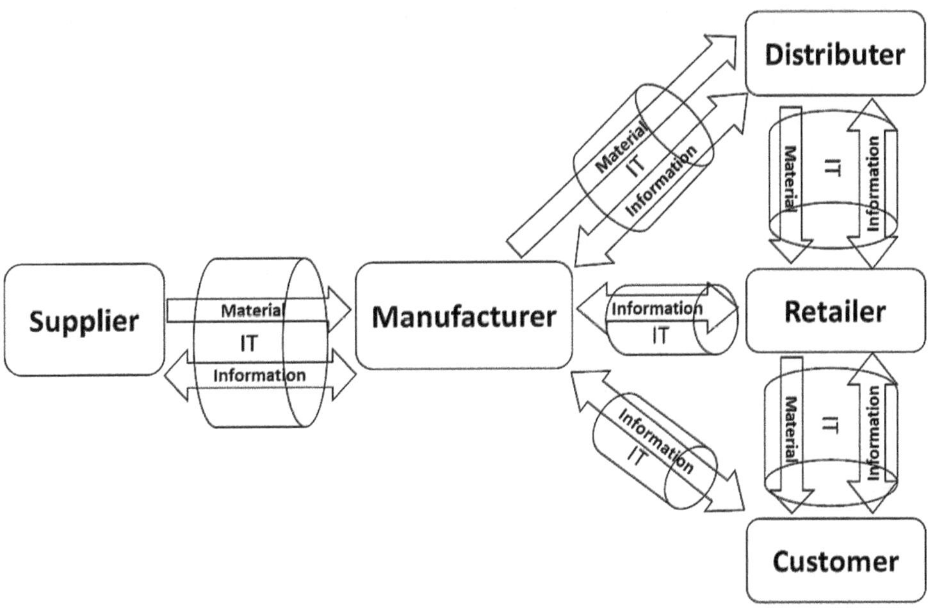

CONCLUSION

The literature reveals that the competitive environment of 21st century demands quality products and services and an efficient SCM to fulfil the customers' needs. An efficient SCM ensures a competitive edge over the competitors and increases customer satisfaction. SCM optimization may be obtained by using knowledge management, information sharing, RFID, bar code, color code, etc. An efficient SCM can help to reduce bullwhip effect. Just in time helps in inventory storage cost reduction. Knowledge management and collaboration with partners increases the overall performance. Future research may be directed towards technologies like RFID, bar code, color code etc. The implication of each of these technologies in different sectors of work, specific to industries and product related studies can be done in the future. There is lack of literature with respect to multi-level supply chain systems and multiple products.

Use of IT solutions in different dimensions of SCM has improved its efficiency. IT greatly reduces problems of additional inventory and shortage of service minimizing uncertainty. Real time information sharing helps to forecast accurate demand and reduce operational costs and cycle time. The evolution of e-commerce and m-commerce have increased customers' expectations which can be met by integrating IT and SCM. Future research can be directed towards consumer behavior based on IT and SCM integration and the impact of IT on different stages of SCM. Comparison of different IT technologies in SCM could also be taken up with respect to IT.

A study conducted by Kayikci et al. (2014) using a hybrid Delphi analytical hierarchy process technique revealed the criteria for forming strategic alignment of heterarchical transport collaboration. Hence, the role of SCM is crucial in the PI. By using the latest techniques of SCM and incorporating IT in pharmaceutical SCM, efficiency can be increased. Literature reveals that specific studies pertaining to the field of pharmaceutical SCM are relatively few. The impact of IT on the SCM of the PI could be an area for future studies. Literature on reverse SCM of pharmaceutical products is also limited. As SCM of pharmaceutical products is greatly affected by external conditions like light, temperature, humidity, handling etc., the research could be conducted on the impact of these factors on the quality of pharmaceutical products. Cullinane and Cullinane (2018) worked on the reverse supply chain of the online clothing industry, identified seven reverse supply chain types, and found that multiple reverse chain types were being used. Multiple reverse chain types could be used for pharma products.

It is evident from the literature reviewed that IT has made a significant impact on supply chain management. The use of IT in SCM has increased its efficiency and helped in the reduction of costs. It has also affected the customers and suppliers. Challenges in technology and hardware compatibility, cost, time, human perceptions, training and security need to be overcome for successful IT implementation. As new technologies like cloud computing, artificial intelligence, blockchain are evolving every day, there is a lot of scope for future research in the field of SCM. Literature on pharmaceutical SCM is limited, and there is scope for more research in this field. The study of the effect of new technologies could be undertaken in the future, and unique models could be developed to improve SCM's efficiency.

REFERENCES

Abbas, H. B., & Routray, J. K. (2014). Assessing factors affecting flood-induced public health risks in Kassala State of Sudan. *Operations Research for Health Care*, *3*(4), 215–225.

Abdelkafi, C., Beck, B. H., David, B., Druck, C., & Horoho, M. (2009). Balancing risk and costs to optimize the clinical supply chain—A step beyond simulation. *Journal of Pharmaceutical Innovation*, *4*(3), 96–106.

Accenture Global Operations. Megatrend Study. (2014). *Big data analytics in supply chain: hype or here to stay?* www.accenture.com/megatrends

Ahmad, F. (2021). Interactive neutrosophic optimization technique for multiobjective programming problems: An application to pharmaceutical supply chain management. *Annals of Operations Research*, 1–35.

Ali, C. M. S. E. (2017). Analyzing Pharmaceutical Reverse Logistics Barriers: An Interpretive Structural Modeling Approach. *International Journal of Applied Logistics*, *7*(1), 16–48.

Alnaji, L., & Ridha, M. (2013). The role of Supply Chain Applications in Jordanian Pharmacies: A case study on Pharmacies in the capital city Amman. *Industrial Engineering Letters*, *3*, 65–71.

Al-Shboul, M. D. A. (2017). Infrastructure framework and manufacturing supply chain agility: The role of delivery dependability and time to market. *Supply Chain Management*, *22*(2), 172–185.

Amaro, A. C. S., & Barbosa-Póvoa, A. P. F. (2008). Planning and scheduling of industrial supply chains with reverse flows: A real pharmaceutical case study. *Computers & Chemical Engineering*, *32*(11), 2606–2625.

Amisha, P. M., Pathania, M., & Rathaur, V. K. (2019). Overview of artificial intelligence in medicine. *Journal of Family Medicine and Primary Care*, *8*(7), 2328. PMID:31463251

Ann Keller, S., Koonin, S. E., & Shipp, S. (2012). Big data and city living–what can it do for us? *Significance*, *9*(4), 4–7.

Arora, P., Sachdeva, C., & Sharma, D. (2021). Securing the Pharma Supply Chain Using Blockchain. *Integration of Cloud Computing with Internet of Things: Foundations. Analysis and Applications*, 343–359.

Attaran, M. (2020, July). Digital technology enablers and their implications for supply chain management. *International Journal (Toronto, Ont.)*, *21*(3), 158–172.

Bag, S. (2017). Key Success Factors of an SME's Multi-Site Organizational Restructuring: A Case Study Approach. *International Journal of Applied Logistics*, *7*(2), 1–20.

Bailey, K., & Francis, M. (2008). Managing information flows for improved value chain performance. *International Journal of Production Economics*, *111*(1), 2–12.

Balfaqih, H., Nopiah, Z. M., Saibani, N., & Al-Nory, M. T. (2016). Review of supply chain performance measurement systems: 1998–2015. *Computers in Industry*, *82*, 135–150.

Bartelt-Hunt, S. L., Snow, D. D., Damon, T., Shockley, J., & Hoagland, K. (2009). The occurrence of illicit and therapeutic pharmaceuticals in wastewater effluent and surface waters in Nebraska. *Environmental Pollution*, *157*(3), 786–791. PMID:19110357

Bask, A., & Tinnilä, M. (2013). Impact of Product Characteristics on Supply Chains: An Analytical Literature Review. *International Journal of Applied Logistics*, *4*(1), 35–59.

Bayraktar, E., Demirbag, M., Koh, S. L., Tatoglu, E., & Zaim, H. (2009). A causal analysis of the impact of information systems and supply chain management practices on operational performance: Evidence from manufacturing SMEs in Turkey. *International Journal of Production Economics*, *122*(1), 133–149.

Bayraktar, E., Demirbag, M., Koh, S. L., Tatoglu, E., & Zaim, H. (2009). A causal analysis of the impact of information systems and supply chain management practices on operational performance: Evidence from manufacturing SMEs in Turkey. *International Journal of Production Economics*, *122*(1), 133–149.

Biswas, S., & Sengupta, G. (2014). A case study on the critical success factors determining the success or failure of TQM implementation in Indian Organizations. International Journal of Management, IT and Engineering, 4(10).

Blossey, G., Hahn, G. J., & Koberstein, A. (2021, January). Managing Uncertainty in Pharmaceutical Supply Chains: A Structured Review. *Proceedings of the 54th Hawaii International Conference on System Sciences.*

Buffa, E. S., & Miller, J. (1979). *Production-Inventory Systems: Planning and Control* (3rd ed.). Irwin.

Burns, L. R., DeGraaff, R. A., Danzon, P. M., Kimberly, J. R., Kissick, W. L., & Pauly, M. V. (2002). *The Wharton School study of the health care value chain. In The health care value chain: producers, purchasers and providers*. Jossey-Bass.

Busse, C., Meinlschmidt, J., & Foerstl, K. (2017). Managing information processing needs in global supply chains: A prerequisite to sustainable supply chain management. *The Journal of Supply Chain Management*, *53*(1), 87–113.

Bylinsky, G. (1999). The challengers move in on ERP. *Fortune*, *140*(10), 306C.

Cai, S., Jun, M., & Yang, Z. (2010). Implementing supply chain information integration in China: The role of institutional forces and trust. *Journal of Operations Management*, *28*(3), 257–268.

Cerchione, R., & Esposito, E. (2016). A systematic review of supply chain knowledge management research: State of the art and research opportunities. *International Journal of Production Economics*, *182*, 276–292.

Chae, B., & Olson, D. L. (2013). Business analytics for supply chain: A dynamic-capabilities framework. *International Journal of Information Technology & Decision Making*, *12*(01), 9–26.

Chandra, C., & Tumanyan, A. (2007). Organization and problem ontology for supply chain information support system. *Data & Knowledge Engineering*, *61*(2), 263–280.

Chang, I. C., Hwang, H. G., Liaw, H. C., Hung, M. C., Chen, S. L., & Yen, D. C. (2008). A neural network evaluation model for ERP performance from SCM perspective to enhance enterprise competitive advantage. *Expert Systems with Applications*, *35*(4), 1809–1816.

Chardine-Baumann, E., & Botta-Genoulaz, V. (2014). A framework for sustainable performance assessment of supply chain management practices. *Computers & Industrial Engineering*, *76*, 138–147.

Chardine-Baumann, E., & Botta-Genoulaz, V. (2014). A framework for sustainable performance assessment of supply chain management practices. *Computers & Industrial Engineering*, *76*, 138–147.

Chen, F., Drezner, Z., Ryan, J. K., & Simchi-Levi, D. (2000). Quantifying the bullwhip effect in a simple supply chain: The impact of forecasting, lead times, and information. *Management Science*, *46*(3), 436–443.

Chen, J. V., Yen, D. C., Rajkumar, T. M., & Tomochko, N. A. (2011). The antecedent factors on trust and commitment in supply chain relationships. *Computer Standards & Interfaces*, *33*(3), 262–270.

Cheng, J. C., Law, K. H., Bjornsson, H., Jones, A., & Sriram, R. (2010). A service oriented framework for construction supply chain integration. *Automation in Construction*, *19*(2), 245–260.

Chengalur-Smith, I., Duchessi, P., & Gil-Garcia, J. R. (2012). Information sharing and business systems leveraging in supply chains: An empirical investigation of one web-based application. *Information & Management*, *49*(1), 58–67.

Cho, D. W., & Lee, Y. H. (2013). The value of information sharing in a supply chain with a seasonal demand process. *Computers & Industrial Engineering*, *65*(1), 97–108.

Chopra, S., & Meindl, P. (2001). *Supply Chain Management*. Prentice-Hall.

Chung, S. H., & Kwon, C. (2016). Integrated supply chain management for perishable products: Dynamics and oligopolistic competition perspectives with application to pharmaceuticals. *International Journal of Production Economics*, *179*, 117–129.

Colin, M., Galindo, R., & Hernández, O. (2015). Information and communication technology as a key strategy for efficient supply chain management in manufacturing SMEs. *Procedia Computer Science*, *55*, 833–842.

Cooper, M. C., Lambert, D. M., & Pagh, J. D. (1997). Supply chain management: More than a new name for logistics. *International Journal of Logistics Management*, *8*(1), 1–14.

Council, S. C. (2008). Supply-chain operations reference-model. *Overview of SCOR Version, 5*(0). Available on: http://supply-chain.org/

Crook, T. R., Giunipero, L., Reus, T. H., Handfield, R., & Williams, S. K. (2008). Antecedents and outcomes of supply chain effectiveness: An exploratory investigation. *Journal of Managerial Issues*, ●●●, 161–177.

Cullinane, S. L., & Cullinane, K. P. (2018). The Reverse Logistics of Cross-Border e-Tailing in Europe: Developing a Research Agenda to Assess the Environmental Impacts. *International Journal of Applied Logistics*, *8*(1), 1–19.

Dasaklis, T. K., Pappis, C. P., & Rachaniotis, N. P. (2012). Epidemics control and logistics operations: A review. *International Journal of Production Economics*, *139*(2), 393–410.

Daú, G., Scavarda, A., Scavarda, L. F., & Portugal, V. J. T. (2019). The healthcare sustainable supply chain 4.0: The circular economy transition conceptual framework with the corporate social responsibility mirror. *Sustainability*, *11*(12).

Demchenko, Y., Ngo, C., & Membrey, P. (2013). Architecture framework and components for the big data ecosystem. *Journal of System and Network Engineering*, 1-31.

Dias, R, Pitassi, C, & Joia, L. (2003). *Integrated management of the supply chain.* Rio de Janeiro: FGV, EBAPE.

Ding, H., Guo, B., & Liu, Z. (2011). Information sharing and profit allotment based on supply chain cooperation. *International Journal of Production Economics, 133*(1), 70–79.

Dolci, P. C., Maçada, A. C. G., & Grant, G. G. (2017). Making Sense of Information Technology Investment on Type of Supply Chain Governance. In Handbook of Research on Technology Adoption, Social Policy, and Global Integration (pp. 258-279). IGI Global.

Dooner, R. (2014). How supply chain management can help to control health-care cost. *Supply Chain Q. Q., 3*, 50–53.

Matani, Tripathi, & Matani. (2012). Information Technology Tools uImproving Supply Chain Management Productivity In Food Processing Industries. *International Journal of Advanced Engineering Technology, 3*(1), 237-238.

Du, T. C., Lai, V. S., Cheung, W., & Cui, X. (2012). Willingness to share information in a supply chain: A partnership-data-process perspective. *Information & Management, 49*(2), 89–98.

Dutta, D. K., & Hora, M. (2017). From Invention Success to Commercialization Success: Technology Ventures and the Benefits of Upstream and Downstream Supply-Chain Alliances. *Journal of Small Business Management, 55*(2), 216–235.

Elmuti, D., Khoury, G., Omran, O., & Abou-Zaid, A. S. (2013). Challenges and opportunities of health care supply chain management in the United States. *Health Marketing Quarterly, 30*(2), 128–143. PMID:23697853

Fawcett, S. E., Wallin, C., Allred, C., Fawcett, A. M., & Magnan, G. M. (2011). Information technology as an enabler of supply chain collaboration: A dynamic-capabilities perspective. *The Journal of Supply Chain Management, 47*(1), 38–59.

Forslund, H., & Jonsson, P. (2009). Obstacles to supply chain integration of the performance management process in buyer-supplier dyads: The buyers' perspective. *International Journal of Operations & Production Management, 29*(1), 77–95.

Fynes, B., Voss, C., & de Búrca, S. (2005). The impact of supply chain relationship quality on quality performance. *International Journal of Production Economics, 96*(3), 339–354.

Galia. (2007). *Evalog: Global Evalog frame of reference*. Academic Press.

Gatica, G., Papageorgiou, L. G., & Shah, N. (2003). Capacity planning under uncertainty for the pharmaceutical industry. *Chemical Engineering Research & Design, 81*(6), 665–678.

Gaukler, G. M., Seifert, R. W., & Hausman, W. H. (2007). Item-level RFID in the retail supply chain. *Production and Operations Management, 16*(1), 65–76.

Geary, S., Disney, S. M., & Towill, D. R. (2006). On bullwhip in supply chains—Historical review, present practice and expected future impact. *International Journal of Production Economics, 101*(1), 2–18.

Gengeswari, K., Bakar, A., & Zaleha, S. (2012). Impact of information technologies (IT) implementation on over\all TSC performance. *Asian Journal of Business and Management Sciences, 1*(11), 100–108.

Ghadge, A., Dani, S., & Kalawsky, R. (2012). Supply chain risk management: Present and future scope. *International Journal of Logistics Management, 23*(3), 313–339.

Ghahremani, F., & Tarokh, M. J. (2013). IT-Based classification for supply chain coordination mechanisms. In *Technological Solutions for Modern Logistics and Supply Chain Management* (pp. 148–162). IGI Global.

Glock, C. H. (2017). Decision support models for managing returnable transport items in supply chains: A systematic literature review. *International Journal of Production Economics, 183*, 561–569.

Gobble, M. M. (2013). Big data: The next big thing in innovation. *Research Technology Management, 56*(1), 64–66.

Delipinar, G. E., & Kocaoglu, B. (2016). Using SCOR model to gain competitive advantage: A Literature review. *Procedia: Social and Behavioral Sciences, 229*, 398–406.

Gunasekaran, A., & Ngai, E. W. T. (2004). Information systems in supply chain integration and management. *European Journal of Operational Research, 159*, 269–295.

Gunasekaran, A., Patel, C., & McGaughey, E. (2004). A framework for supply chain performance measurement. *International Journal of Production Economics, 87*, 333–347.

Gupta, A., Evans, G. W., & Heragu, S. S. (2013). Simulation and optimization modeling for drive-through mass vaccination–A generalized approach. *Simulation Modelling Practice and Theory, 37*, 99–106.

Hansen, K. R. N., & Grunow, M. (2015). Planning operations before market launch for balancing time-to-market and risks in pharmaceutical supply chains. *International Journal of Production Economics, 161*, 129–139.

Harrington, L. (2015). *Solving the talent crisis: Five alternatives every supply chain executive must consider*. Academic Press.

Helo, P., & Szekely, B. (2005). Logistics information systems: An analysis of software solutions for supply chain co-ordination. *Industrial Management & Data Systems, 105*(1), 5–18.

Hietajärvi, A. M., & Karvonen, I. (2016). Management of Risks in Export Networks: The Role of Collaboration. *International Journal of Applied Logistics, 6*(1), 47–63.

Holweg, M., Disney, S., Holmström, J., & Småros, J. (2005). Supply chain collaboration: Making sense of the strategy continuum. *European Management Journal, 23*(2), 170–181.

Huang, G. Q., Lau, J. S., & Mak, K. L. (2003). The impacts of sharing production information on supply chain dynamics: A review of the literature. *International Journal of Production Research, 41*(7), 1483–1517.

Hudnurkar, M., Jakhar, S., & Rathod, U. (2014). Factors affecting collaboration in supply chain: A literature review. *Procedia: Social and Behavioral Sciences, 133*, 189–202.

Ittmann, H. W. (2015). The impact of big data and business analytics on supply chain management. *Journal of Transport and Supply Chain Management*, *9*(1), 1–9.

Jaggi, H. S., & Kadam, S. S. (2016). Integration of Spark framework in Supply Chain Management. *Procedia Computer Science*, 79.

Jain, V., Wadhwa, S., & Deshmukh, S. G. (2009). Revisiting information systems to support a dynamic supply chain: Issues and perspectives. *Production Planning and Control*, *20*(1), 17–29.

Jarmoszko, A. T., D'Onofrio, M., Lee-Partridge, J. E., & Petkova, O. (2013). Evaluating Sustainability and Greening Methods: A Conceptual Model for Information Technology Management. *International Journal of Applied Logistics*, *4*(3), 1–13.

Jetly, G., Rossetti, C. L., & Handfield, R. (2012). A multi-agent simulation of the pharmaceutical supply chain. *Journal of Simulation*, *6*, 215–226.

Jin, Y., & Hong, P. (2007). Coordinating global inter-firm product development. *Journal of Enterprise Information Management*, *20*(5), 544–561.

Johnson, B. (2015). Intermountain healthcare supply chain. *The 2015 Healthcare Supply Chain Conference*.

Kamalahmadi, M., & Parast, M. M. (2016). A review of the literature on the principles of enterprise and supply chain resilience: Major findings and directions for future research. *International Journal of Production Economics*, *171*, 116–133.

Kantasa-ard, A., Bekrar, A., & Sallez, Y. (2019). Artificial intelligence for forecasting in supply chain management: A case study of White Sugar consumption rate in Thailand. *IFAC-PapersOnLine*, *52*(13), 725–730.

Kaplan, A., & Haenlein, M. (2020). Rulers of the world, unite! The challenges and opportunities of artificial intelligence. *Business Horizons*, *63*(1), 37–50.

Kayikci, Y., Stix, V., LeBlanc, L. J., & Bartolacci, M. R. (2014). A Novel Application of a Hybrid Delphi-Analytic Hierarchy Process (AHP) Technique: Identifying Key Success Factors in the Strategic Alignment of Collaborative Heterarchical Transportation Networks for Supply Chains. *International Journal of Applied Logistics*, *5*(1), 52–75.

Khan, M., Hussain, M., & Saber, H. M. (2016). Information sharing in a sustainable supply chain. *International Journal of Production Economics*, *181*, 208–214.

Khan, R. (2013). Business analytics and supply chain performance: An Empirical Perspective. *International Journal of Operations and Logistics Management*, *2*(3), 43–56.

Kim, D., Cavusgil, S. T., & Cavusgil, E. (2013). Does IT alignment between supply chain partners enhance customer value creation? An empirical investigation. *Industrial Marketing Management*, *42*(6), 880–889.

Klumpp, M. (2018). Automation and artificial intelligence in business logistics systems: Human reactions and collaboration requirements. *International Journal of Logistics Research and Applications*, *21*(3), 224–242.

Kros, J. F., Falasca, M., & Nadler, S. S. (2006). Impact of just-in-time inventory systems on OEM suppliers. *Industrial Management & Data Systems*, *106*(2), 224–241.

Krueger, D. A. (2008). The ethics of global supply chains in China–convergences of East and West. *Journal of Business Ethics*, *79*(1-2), 113–120.

Kumar, R. S., & Pugazhendhi, S. (2012). Information sharing in supply chains: An overview. *Procedia Engineering*, *38*, 2147–2154.

Kumar, R., Singh, R. K., & Shankar, R. (2015). Critical success factors for implementation of supply chain management in Indian small and medium enterprises and their impact on performance. *IIMB Management Review*, *27*(2), 92–104.

Kumar, V., Ramachandran, D., & Kumar, B. (2021). Influence of new-age technologies on marketing: A research agenda. *Journal of Business Research*, *125*, 864–877.

Kumari, M., Gupta, M., & Ved, C. (2021). Blockchain in Pharmaceutical Sector. In *Applications of Blockchain in Healthcare* (pp. 199–220). Springer.

Kundu, A., Jain, V., Kumar, S., & Chandra, C. (2015). A journey from normative to behavioral operations in supply chain management: A review using Latent Semantic Analysis. *Expert Systems with Applications*, *42*(2), 796–809.

Kwon, I. W. G., Kim, S. H., & Martin, D. G. (2016). Healthcare supply chain management; strategic areas for quality and financial improvement. *Technological Forecasting and Social Change*, *113*, 422–428.

Kwon, I. W. G., Kim, S. H., & Martin, D. G. (2016). Healthcare supply chain management; strategic areas for quality and financial improvement. *Technological Forecasting and Social Change*, *113*, 422–428.

Kwon, I. W., & Hong, S. J. (2011). Health care supply chain management in the United States: New paradigm for roles of distributors. *International Journal of Health Management and Information*, *2*(2), 73–82.

Kwon, I. W., Hamilton, J., & Hong, S. J. (2011). Trust and transaction cost in supply chain cost optimization: an exploratory study. In *Inter-organizational Information Systems and Business Management: Theories for Researchers*. IGI Global.

Laínez, J. M., Schaefer, E., & Reklaitis, G. V. (2012). Challenges and opportunities in enterprise-wide optimization in the pharmaceutical industry. *Computers & Chemical Engineering*, *47*, 19–28.

Lavie, D. (2006). The competitive advantage of interconnected firms: An extension of the resource-based view. *Academy of Management Review*, *31*(3), 638–658.

Letheren, K., & Glavas, C. (2017). Embracing the bots: How direct to consumer advertising is about to change forever. *The Conversation*.

Li, G., Yang, H., Sun, L., & Sohal, A. S. (2009). The impact of IT implementation on supply chain integration and performance. *International Journal of Production Economics*, *120*(1), 125–138.

Li, S., Rao, S. S., Ragu Nathan, T. S., & Ragu-Nathan, B. (2005). Development and validation of a measurement instrument for studying supply chain management practices. *Journal of Operations Management, 23*(6), 618–641.

Lin, C., & Lin, M. (2019). The determinants of using cloud supply chain adoption. *Industrial Management & Data Systems.*

Lin, M., Lin, C., & Chang, Y. S. (2020). The impact of using a cloud supply chain on organizational performance. *Journal of Business and Industrial Marketing.*

Linke, M. (2013). Impact of global hyperconnectivity and increased smartphone usage on the delivery and structure of IT organizsation in transport logistics. *International Journal of Applied Logistics, 4*(2), 18–33.

Liu, Y., & Wang, S. (2011). Research on collaborative management in supply chain crisis. *Procedia Environmental Sciences, 10*, 141–146.

Madenas, N., Tiwari, A., Turner, C. J., & Woodward, J. (2014). Information flow in supply chain management: A review across the product lifecycle. *CIRP Journal of Manufacturing Science and Technology, 7*(4), 335–346.

Manyika, J., Chui, M., Brown, B., Bughin, J., Dobbs, R., Roxburgh, C., & Byers, A. H. (2011). *Big data: The next frontier for innovation, competition, and productivity.* Academic Press.

Marques, C. M., Moniz, S., de Sousa, J. P., Barbosa-Povoa, A. P., & Reklaitis, G. (2020). Decision-support challenges in the chemical-pharmaceutical industry: Findings and future research directions. *Computers & Chemical Engineering, 134*, 106672.

Marra, M., Ho, W., & Edwards, J. S. (2012). Supply chain knowledge management: A literature review. *Expert Systems with Applications, 39*(5), 6103–6110.

Martínez-Olvera, C. (2008). Entropy as an assessment tool of supply chain information sharing. *European Journal of Operational Research, 185*(1), 405–417.

Masoumi, A. H., Yu, M., & Nagurney, A. (2012). A supply chain generalized network oligopoly model for pharmaceuticals under brand differentiation and perishability. *Transportation Research Part E, Logistics and Transportation Review, 48*(4), 762–780.

Masoumi, A. H., Yu, M., & Nagurney, A. (2012). A supply chain generalized network oligopoly model for pharmaceuticals under brand differentiation and perishability. *Transportation Research Part E, Logistics and Transportation Review, 48*(4), 762–780.

Mbang, J. J. A. (2013). Compound Supply Chain Efficiency Model Application in the Gabonese Supply Chain: The Case of Comilog. *International Journal of Applied Logistics, 4*(1), 60–129.

McAfee, A., Brynjolfsson, E., Davenport, T. H., Patil, D. J., & Barton, D. (2012). Big data: The management revolution. *Harvard Business Review, 90*(10), 60–68. PMID:23074865

Mehralian, G., Moosivand, A., Emadi, S., & Asgharian, R. (2017). Developing a coordination framework for pharmaceutical supply chain: Using analytical hierarchy process. *International Journal of Logistics Systems and Management*, *26*(3), 277–293.

Mehralian, G., Nazari, J. A., Rasekh, H. R., & Hosseini, S. (2016). TOPSIS approach to prioritize critical success factors of TQM: Evidence from the pharmaceutical industry. *The TQM Journal*, *28*(2), 235–249.

Mehralian, G., Zarenezhad, F., & Rajabzadeh Ghatari, A. (2015). Developing a model for an agile supply chain in pharmaceutical industry. *International Journal of Pharmaceutical and Healthcare Marketing*, *9*(1), 74–91.

Meiler, M., Tonke, D., Grunow, M., & Günther, H. O. (2015). Pattern-based supply network planning in the pharmaceutical industry. *Computers & Chemical Engineering*, *77*, 43–58.

Meredig, B. (2017). Industrial materials informatics: Analyzing large-scale data to solve applied problems in R&D, manufacturing, and supply chain. *Current Opinion in Solid State and Materials Science*, *21*(3), 159–166.

Mobarakeh, N. A., Shahzad, M. K., Baboli, A., & Tonadre, R. (2017). Improved Forecasts for uncertain and unpredictable Spare Parts Demand in Business Aircraft's with Bootstrap Method. *IFAC-PapersOnLine*, *50*(1), 15241–15246.

Modgil, S., & Sharma, S. (2017). Information Systems, Supply Chain Management and Operational Performance: Tri-linkage—An Exploratory Study on Pharmaceutical Industry of India. *Global Business Review*, *18*(3), 652–677.

Mohtadi, H. (2008). Information sharing in food supply chains. *Canadian Journal of Agricultural Economics*, *56*(2), 163–178.

Montoya-Torres, J. R., & Ortiz-Vargas, D. A. (2014). Collaboration and information sharing in dyadic supply chains: A literature review over the period 2000–2012. *Estudios Gerenciales*, *30*(133), 343–354.

Mousazadeh, M., Torabi, S. A., & Zahiri, B. (2015). A robust possibilistic programming approach for pharmaceutical supply chain network design. *Computers & Chemical Engineering*, *82*, 115–128.

Nachtmann, H., & Pohl, E. A. (2009). *The state of healthcare logistics: Cost and quality improvement opportunities.* Center for Innovation in Healthcare Logistics, University of Arkansas.

Nahmias, S. (2011). *Perishable inventory systems* (Vol. 160). Springer Science & Business Media.

Najafi, M., & Farahani, R. Z. (2013). New forecasting insights on the bullwhip effect in a supply chain. *IMA Journal of Management Mathematics*, *25*(3), 259–286.

Narayana, S. A., Pati, R. K., & Vrat, P. (2012). Research on management issues in the pharmaceutical industry: A literature review. *International Journal of Pharmaceutical and Healthcare Marketing*, *6*(4), 351–375.

Nath, T., & Standing, C. (2010). Drivers of information technology use in the supply chain. *Journal of Systems and Information Technology*, *12*(1), 70–84.

Ngai, E. W., Chau, D. C., & Chan, T. L. A. (2011). Information technology, operational, and management competencies for supply chain agility: Findings from case studies. *The Journal of Strategic Information Systems*, *20*(3), 232–249.

Nishant, R., Kennedy, M., & Corbett, J. (2020). Artificial intelligence for sustainability: Challenges, opportunities, and a research agenda. *International Journal of Information Management*, *53*, 102104.

Niziolek, L. (2008). *A simulation-based study of distribution strategies for pharmaceutical supply chains* (PhD Thesis). Purdue University.

Nsamzinshuti, A., & Ndiaye, A. B. (2018). Development of a Conceptual Framework for Performance Measurement of Pharmaceutical Supply Chain within Hospital. *International Journal of Applied Logistics*, *5*(2), 32–49.

Nyaga, G. N., Whipple, J. M., & Lynch, D. F. (2010). Examining supply chain relationships: Do buyer and supplier perspectives on collaborative relationships differ? *Journal of Operations Management*, *28*(2), 101–114.

Okano, M. T., & Marins, F. A. (2014). Measuring the Impact of Information Technology (IT) on Supply Chain Management (SCM) Through Indicators: An Exploratory Study. *Journal of Modern Accounting and Auditing*, *10*(5).

Oliveira, J. B., Lima, R. S., & Montevechi, J. A. B. (2016). Perspectives and relationships in Supply Chain Simulation: A systematic literature review. *Simulation Modelling Practice and Theory*, *62*, 166–191.

Ouyang, Y. (2007). The effect of information sharing on supply chain stability and the bullwhip effect. *European Journal of Operational Research*, *182*(3), 1107–1121.

Ozkan, M., & Solmaz, B. (2015). The changing face of the employees–Generation Z and their perceptions of work (A Study Applied to University Students). *Procedia Economics and Finance*, *26*, 476–483.

Papageorgiou, L. G. (2009). Supply chain optimization for the process industries: Advances and opportunities. *Computers & Chemical Engineering*, *33*(12), 1931–1938.

Park, H., Bellamy, M. A., & Basole, R. C. (2016). Visual analytics for supply network management: System design and evaluation. *Decision Support Systems*, *91*, 89–102.

Pereira, J. V. (2009). The new supply chain's frontier: Information management. *International Journal of Information Management*, *29*(5), 372–379.

Permala, A., Rantasila, K., & Pilli-Sihvola, E. (2012). RFID: From closed systems to improving visibility in the manufacturing supply chain. *International Journal of Applied Logistics*, *3*(2), 14–24.

Pishvaee, M. S., Razmi, J., & Torabi, S. A. (2012). Robust possibilistic programming for socially responsible supply chain network design: A new approach. *Fuzzy Sets and Systems*, *206*, 1–20.

Prajogo, D., & Olhager, J. (2012). Supply chain integration and performance: The effects of long-term relationships, information technology and sharing, and logistics integration. *International Journal of Production Economics*, *135*(1), 514–522.

Puica, E. (2020). Cloud Computing in Supply Chain Management and Economic, Environmental and Social Impact Analysis. *Informações Econômicas*, *24*(4), 41–54.

Pujawan, I. N., Kurniati, N., & Wessiani, N. A. (2009). Supply chain management for Disaster Relief Operations: Principles and case studies. *International Journal of Logistics Systems and Management*, *5*(6), 679–692.

Rajeev, A., Pati, R. K., Padhi, S. S., & Govindan, K. (2017). Evolution of sustainability in supply chain management: A literature review. *Journal of Cleaner Production*, *162*, 299–314.

Ritchie, L., Burnes, B., Whittle, P., & Hey, R. (2000). The benefits of reverse logistics: The case of the Manchester Royal Infirmary Pharmacy. *Supply Chain Management*.

Roberta Pereira, C., Christopher, M., & Lago Da Silva, A. (2014). Achieving supply chain resilience: The role of procurement. *Supply Chain Management*, *19*(5/6), 626–642.

Rossetti, C. L., Handfield, R., & Dooley, K. J. (2011). Forces, trends, and decisions in pharmaceutical supply chain management. *International Journal of Physical Distribution & Logistics Management*, *41*(6), 601–622.

Rotstein, G. E., Papageorgiou, L. G., Shah, N., Murphy, D. C., & Mustafa, R. (1999). A product portfolio approach in the pharmaceutical industry. *Computers & Chemical Engineering*, *23*, S883–S886.

Ryu, J. H., & Pistikopoulos, E. N. (2007). Multiperiod planning of enterprise-wide supply chains using an operation policy. *Industrial & Engineering Chemistry Research*, *46*(24), 8058–8065.

Ryu, S. J., Tsukishima, T., & Onari, H. (2009). A study on evaluation of demand information-sharing methods in supply chain. *International Journal of Production Economics*, *120*(1), 162–175.

Melnyk, S. A., Closs, D. J., Griffis, S. E., Zobel, C. W., & Macdonald, J. R. (2014). Understanding supply chain resilience. *Supply Chain Manag. Rev*, *18*(1), 34–41.

Sahay, B. S., & Ranjan, J. (2008). Real time business intelligence in supply chain analytics. *Information Management & Computer Security*, *16*(1), 28–48.

Sahin, F., & Robinson, E. P. Jr. (2005). Information sharing and coordination in make-to-order supply chains. *Journal of Operations Management*, *23*(6), 579–598.

Samaddar, S., Nargundkar, S., & Daley, M. (2006). Inter-organizational information sharing: The role of supply network configuration and partner goal congruence. *European Journal of Operational Research*, *174*(2), 744–765.

Sanders, N. R., & Premus, R. (2002). IT applications in supply chain organizations: A link between competitive priorities and organizational benefits. *Journal of Business Logistics*, *23*(1), 65–83.

Sarac, A., Absi, N., & Dauzère-Pérès, S. (2010). A literature review on the impact of RFID technologies on supply chain management. *International Journal of Production Economics*, *128*(1), 77–95.

Sarhani, M., & El Afia, A. (2014). Forecasting Demand with Support Vector Regression Technique Combined with X13-ARIMA-SEATS Method in the Presence of Calendar Effect. *International Journal of Applied Logistics*, *5*(2), 74–86.

Schapranow, M. P., Zeier, A., & Plattner, H. (2011, January). A formal model for enabling RFID in pharmaceutical supply chains. In *System Sciences (HICSS), 2011 44th Hawaii International Conference on* (pp. 1-10). IEEE.

Shah, N. (2004). Pharmaceutical supply chains: Key issues and strategies for optimization. *Computers & Chemical Engineering*, *28*(6-7), 929–941.

Shah, N. K., & Ierapetritou, M. G. (2012). Integrated production planning and scheduling optimization of multisite, multiproduct process industry. *Computers & Chemical Engineering*, *37*, 214–226.

Shao, X. F., Liu, W., Li, Y., Chaudhry, H. R., & Yue, X. G. (2021). Multistage implementation framework for smart supply chain management under industry 4.0. *Technological Forecasting and Social Change*, *162*, 120354. PMID:33041379

Simatupang, T. M., & Sridharan, R. (2005). The collaboration index: A measure for supply chain collaboration. *International Journal of Physical Distribution & Logistics Management*, *35*(1), 44–62.

Sohn, S. Y., & Lim, M. (2008). The effect of forecasting and information sharing in SCM for multi-generation products. *European Journal of Operational Research*, *186*(1), 276–287.

Soni, U., & Jain, V. (2011, December). Minimizing the vulnerabilities of supply chain: A new framework for enhancing the resilience. In *Industrial Engineering and Engineering Management (IEEM), 2011 IEEE International Conference on* (pp. 933-939). IEEE.

Soroor, J., Tarokh, M. J., & Shemshadi, A. (2009). Initiating a state of the art system for real-time supply chain coordination. *European Journal of Operational Research*, *196*(2), 635–650.

Spekman, R. E., Kamauff, J. W. Jr, & Myhr, N. (1998). An empirical investigation into supply chain management: A perspective on partnerships. *Supply Chain Management*, *3*(2), 53–67.

Stecca, G., Baffo, I., & Kaihara, T. (2016). Design and operation of strategic inventory control system for drug delivery in healthcare industry. *IFAC-PapersOnLine*, *49*(12), 904–909.

Stevenson, W. J., & Hojati, M. (2007). *Operations management* (Vol. 8). McGraw-Hill/Irwin.

Strawn, G. O. (2012). Scientific Research: How Many Paradigms? *EDUCAUSE Review*, *47*(3), 26.

Sundarakani, B., Kamran, R., Maheshwari, P., & Jain, V. (2019). Designing a hybrid cloud for a supply chain network of Industry 4.0: A theoretical framework. *Benchmarking*.

Susarla, N., & Karimi, I. A. (2012). Integrated supply chain planning for multinational pharma-ceutical enterprises. *Computers & Chemical Engineering*, *42*, 168–177.

Swafford, P. M., Ghosh, S., & Murthy, N. (2008). Achieving supply chain agility through IT integration and flexibility. *International Journal of Production Economics*, *116*(2), 288–297.

Syahrir, I., & Vanany, I. (2015). Healthcare and disaster supply chain: Literature review and future research. *Procedia Manufacturing*, *4*, 2–9.

Syntetos, A. A., Babai, Z., Boylan, J. E., Kolassa, S., & Nikolopoulos, K. (2016). Supply chain forecasting: Theory, practice, their gap and the future. *European Journal of Operational Research*, *252*(1), 1–26.

Tajima, M. (2007). Strategic value of RFID in supply chain management. *Journal of Purchasing and Supply Management, 13*(4), 261–273.

Tan, E. N., Smith, G., & Saad, M. (2006). Managing the global supply chain: A SME perspective. *Production Planning and Control, 17*(3), 238–246.

Tat, R., Heydari, J., & Rabbani, M. (2020). A mathematical model for pharmaceutical supply chain coordination: Reselling medicines in an alternative market. *Journal of Cleaner Production, 268*, 121897.

Tat, R., Heydari, J., & Rabbani, M. (2021). Corporate social responsibility in the pharmaceutical supply chain: An optimized medicine donation scheme. *Computers & Industrial Engineering, 152*, 107022.

The World Bank. (2017). *Listed domestic companies.* https://data.worldbank.org/indicator/CM.MKT.LDOM.NO?end=2015&start=1990

Toorajipour, R., Sohrabpour, V., Nazarpour, A., Oghazi, P., & Fischl, M. (2021). Artificial intelligence in supply chain management: A systematic literature review. *Journal of Business Research, 122*, 502–517.

Van den Broeck, E., Zarouali, B., & Poels, K. (2019). Chatbot advertising effectiveness: When does the message get through? *Computers in Human Behavior, 98*, 150–157.

Verdouw, C. N., Beulens, A. J., Reijers, H. A., & van der Vorst, J. G. (2015). A control model for object virtualization in supply chain management. *Computers in Industry, 68*, 116–131.

Vereecke, A., & Muylle, S. (2006). Performance improvement through supply chain collaboration in Europe. *International Journal of Operations & Production Management, 26*(11), 1176–1198.

Vila-Parrish, A. R., & Ivy, J. S. (2013). Managing supply critical to patient care: an introduction to hospital inventory management for pharmaceuticals. In *Handbook of Healthcare Operations Management* (pp. 447–463). Springer.

Waller, M. A., & Fawcett, S. E. (2013). Data science, predictive analytics, and big data: A revolution that will transform supply chain design and management. *Journal of Business Logistics, 34*(2), 77–84.

Wamba, S. F., Akter, S., Edwards, A., Chopin, G., & Gnanzou, D. (2015). How 'big data'can make big impact: Findings from a systematic review and a longitudinal case study. *International Journal of Production Economics, 165*, 234–246.

Wamba, S. F., Lefebvre, L. A., Bendavid, Y., & Lefebvre, É. (2008). Exploring the impact of RFID technology and the EPC network on mobile B2B eCommerce: A case study in the retail industry. *International Journal of Production Economics, 112*(2), 614–629.

Wang, S. J., Liu, S. F., & Wang, W. L. (2008). The simulated impact of RFID-enabled supply chain on pull-based inventory replenishment in TFT-LCD industry. *International Journal of Production Economics, 112*(2), 570–586.

Wang, Y., Wallace, S. W., Shen, B., & Choi, T. M. (2015). Service supply chain management: A review of operational models. *European Journal of Operational Research, 247*(3), 685–698.

Welker, G. A., van der Vaart, T., & van Donk, D. P. (2008). The influence of business conditions on supply chain information-sharing mechanisms: A study among supply chain links of SMEs. *International Journal of Production Economics, 113*(2), 706–720.

Weraikat, D., Zanjani, M. K., & Lehoux, N. (2016). Coordinating a green reverse supply chain in pharmaceutical sector by negotiation. *Computers & Industrial Engineering, 93*, 67–77.

Wicher, P., & Lenort, R. (2012). The ways of creating resilient supply chains. *Proceedings of CLC: Carpathian Logistics Congress*, 688–694.

Wieland, A. (2021). Dancing the supply chain: Toward transformative supply chain management. *The Journal of Supply Chain Management, 57*(1), 58–73.

Woolliscroft, P., Caganova, D., Cambal, M., Holecek, J., & Pucikova, L. (2013). Implications for optimization of the automotive supply chain through knowledge management. *Procedia CIRP, 7*, 211–216.

Wu, H., Cao, J., Yang, Y., Tung, C. L., Jiang, S., Tang, B., . . . Deng, Y. (2019, July). Data management in supply chain using blockchain: Challenges and a case study. In *2019 28th International Conference on Computer Communication and Networks (ICCCN)* (pp. 1-8). IEEE.

Wu, J., & Haasis, H. D. (2013). Integration of Knowledge Management Approach to the Planning Stage of Freight Villages: Towards Sustainable Development. *International Journal of Applied Logistics, 4*(2), 46–65.

Wu, Y. N., & Cheng, T. E. (2008). The impact of information sharing in a multiple-echelon supply chain. *International Journal of Production Economics, 115*(1), 1–11.

Xie, Y., & Breen, L. (2012). Greening community pharmaceutical supply chain in UK: A cross boundary approach. *Supply Chain Management, 17*(1), 40–53.

Yan, J., Xin, S., Liu, Q., Xu, W., Yang, L., Fan, L., ... Wang, Q. (2014). Intelligent supply chain integration and management based on cloud of things. *International Journal of Distributed Sensor Networks, 10*(3), 624839.

Yu, M. M., Ting, S. C., & Chen, M. C. (2010). Evaluating the cross-efficiency of information sharing in supply chains. *Expert Systems with Applications, 37*(4), 2891–2897.

Yu, X., Li, C., Shi, Y., & Yu, M. (2010). Pharmaceutical supply chain in China: Current issues and implications for health system reform. *Health Policy (Amsterdam), 97*(1), 8–15. PMID:20307912

Zaharudin, A. A., Wong, C. Y., Agarwal, V., McFarlane, D., Koh, R., & Kang, Y. Y. (2006). *The intelligent product driven supply chain.* Tech. Rep. 05, AUTO-ID LABS.

Zhou, H., & Benton, W. C. Jr. (2007). Supply chain practice and information sharing. *Journal of Operations Management, 25*(6), 1348–1365.

Zhu, X., Mukhopadhyay, S. K., & Yue, X. (2011). Role of forecast effort on supply chain profitability under various information sharing scenarios. *International Journal of Production Economics, 129*(2), 284–291.

Chapter 8
Investigating the Drivers and Barriers of Reverse Logistics Practices in the Pharmaceuticals Supply Chain:
Interpretive Structural Modeling (ISM) Approach

Chehab Mahmoud Salah Eldin Ali Elbelehy
https://orcid.org/0000-0001-8844-1078
Arab Academy for Science, Technology, and Maritime Transport, Egypt

Alaa Mohamed Attia Abdelsalam
Arab Academy for Science, Technology, and Maritime Transport, Egypt

ABSTRACT

This empirical research investigates the reverse logistics practices adopted by a leading pharmaceutical company in Egypt, the drivers behind the applied reverse logistics activities, and the barriers affecting the application of reverse logistics. The methodological approach of interpretive structural modeling (ISM) is applied to study the mutual influences across barriers listed by a preliminary case analysis, and to identify the "driving" barriers which may worsen other barriers, and "dependent" barriers influenced by the driving barriers. A key finding of the analysis is that lack of regulation enforcement and lack of public awareness regarding the importance of reverse logistics are the most driving barriers influencing the rest of the identified barriers.

DOI: 10.4018/978-1-7998-8709-6.ch008

INTRODUCTION

Reverse logistics is one of the most critical aspects for any business related to manufacturing, distribution, and service and support of any type of product (Donald F Blumberg, 2004, p. 1). It is also practiced in different industries, including those producing steel, commercial aircrafts, computers, automobiles, appliances, and chemicals and medical items (Dowlatshahi, 2000, p. 144). The importance of reverse logistics is underscored by its increasing popularity in both business and academic communities since the last decade (Nikolaou, Evangelinos, & Allan, 2013, p. 173).

Earlier, reverse logistics was often considered as a process that has little effect on enterprises as a whole. However, the evolving financial and competitive pressure, as well as the complexity in environmental regulations, have made it clear that reverse logistics is no longer an option for an organization to meet its goals and increase profitability (Partida, 2011, p. 62).

Deployment of reverse logistics is not free from barriers (Ravi & Shankar, 2005, p. 1012). Some of the most common barriers facing companies implementing reverse logistics in different industries are: Importance of reverse logistics relative to other issues, company policies, lack of systems, competitive issues, management inattention, financial and personnel resources, and legal issues (Dale S. Rogers & Tibben-Lembke, 1998, p. 32). In spite of these barriers, companies are becoming active in reverse logistics for different reasons, including economic reasons, legislative reasons, and corporate citizenship (de Brito & Dekker, 2003, p. 6). Growing concerns relating to environmental issues, coupled with legal regulations, have made organizations responsive to reverse logistics not only in developed countries but also in developing countries (Samir & Rajiv, 2006, p. 525).

Reverse logistics is very important in the pharmaceutical industry—not only from the economic point of view but also from the environmental and the regulatory points of view. In addition, the application of reverse logistics in this industry is more challenging than in any other industries, as most pharmaceuticals get destroyed when they are recalled or returned, they are seldom repaired or resold (Kabir, 2013, pp. 89, 97).

Proper disposal of recalled, unused, and expired pharmaceuticals is an important issue with legal implications, as some of these products contain hazardous chemicals. Also, the sensitive nature of medicines as well as the potential harm from use of expired or non-effective medicines means that pharmaceutical companies must effectively implement reverse logistics to promptly clear their supply chain channels of expired and non-conforming drugs (Shaurabh, Saurabh, & Moti, 2013, pp. 12, 18).

Research Problem

Reselling expired pharmaceuticals in Egypt is an increasing problem with severe consequences (Ramadan, 2014; RASSD, 2015). The head of the chamber of pharmaceutical industries, said recently that the pharmacists syndicate estimated the existence of EGP 600 million (approximately $US 76.6 million) worth of counterfeit and expired drugs in the Egyptian market, constituting two percent of the country's total annual pharmaceutical sales.

Kabir (2013); Kwateng, Debrah, Parker, Owusu, and Prempeh (2014) as well as other recent studies (de Campos et al., 2021b, 2021a; Laganà et al., 2021; Luís et al., 2021, 2021; Manzolillo, 2021; Ribeiro et al., 2021) suggest extended focus on reverse logistics to potentially reduce this problem. There are however several barriers which hinder or prevent the application of reverse logistics in pharmaceutical industry. Accordingly, this research attempt to explore these barriers that hinder or prevent the application of reverse logistics practices at a leading pharmaceutical manufacturer in Egypt.

The methodological approach of Interpretive Structural Modeling (ISM) is applied to study mutual influences across barriers listed by a preliminary case analysis, and to identify the "driving" barriers which may lead to other barriers, and "dependent" barriers influenced by the driving barriers.

Ravi and Shankar (2005) indicate that "we lack a holistic view in understanding the barriers that hinder reverse logistics" (p. 1011), and highlight that the ISM approach allows for a more in-depth understanding of the situation than observing individual barriers in isolation.

Structural modeling was defined by John N. Warfield (1974) as a methodology that employs graphics and words in carefully defined patterns to illustrate the structure of a complex issue or problem. The ISM method can be used to employ a systematic and logical thinking process while approaching a complex issue and then to communicate the results of that process to others (Malone, 1975).

Research Purpose

The purpose of this research is to first explore the reverse logistics drivers, practices and barriers at Pharco Pharmaceuticals, a leading pharmaceutical manufacturer in Egypt. Next, this research applies the ISM methodology to explore the mutual influences between the identified barriers affecting the implementation of reverse logistics practices at the case company.

The research questions to be explored are as follows:

1. Why Pharco implements reverse logistics practices?
2. What are the reverse logistics practices implemented by Pharco?
3. What are the barriers hindering Pharco in implementing reverse logistics?

The above-mentioned research questions are covered by the following set of objectives:

- To identify the drivers for implementing reverse logistics in Pharco.
- To identify the reasons for distribution returns from Pharco's downstream partners.
- To identify the reverse logistics processes implemented by Pharco.
- To identify the reverse logistics activities practiced by Pharco.
- To identify and rank the barriers of reverse logistics in Pharco by using ISM.
- To determine the interaction between the identified barriers by using ISM.
- To discuss the managerial implication based on the analysis results.

THEORETICAL FRAMEWORK: REVERSE LOGISTICS CONCEPT

The concept of reverse logistics is relatively old. Lambert and Stock (1982) provide one of the oldest descriptions of reverse logistics by saying that it is like "going the wrong way on a one-way street because the great majority of products shipments flow in one direction" (p. 19). In the 1980s the field of reverse logistics was only limited to the movement of materials in the opposite direction of the primary flow—i.e. from the customer toward the manufacturer (Rogers & Tibben-Lembke, 2001, p. 129).

Carter and Ellram (1998) provide a summary of the general literature, saying that the concept of reverse logistics came into being in 1970's. However, the focus shifted from recycling toward the effect of environmental issues on logistics management in the 1990's. Hence, Carter and Ellram (1998) defined reverse logistics as "a process that enables companies to become environmentally efficient through recycling, reusing and reducing the amount of materials used" (p. 85).

During the late 1990s Dale S. Rogers and Tibben-Lembke (1998) defined reverse logistics as "[t]he process of planning, implementing, and controlling the efficient, cost effective flow of raw materials, in process inventory, finished goods and related information from the point of consumption to the point of origin for the purpose of recapturing value or proper disposal" (p. 2).

The above-mentioned definition by Dale S. Rogers and Tibben-Lembke (1998, p. 2) was criticized by de Brito and Dekker (2002, p. 3), as returns could be generated at any point in the supply chain before consumption and could be returned to any point of recovery other than the origin. Accordingly, de Brito and Dekker (2002, p. 3) adopted the following definition provided by The European Working Group on Reverse Logistics REVLOG (1998):

The process of planning, implementing and controlling flows of raw materials, in process inventory, and finished goods from a manufacturing, distribution or use point to a point of recovery or point of proper disposal. (p. 3)

This definition clearly illustrates that the concept of reverse logistics focuses on activities with the goal of both value recovery and proper disposal. In this way, a clear distinction between reverse logistics and waste management concept is made, as the latter primarily focuses on waste collection and processing, and thus there is no reuse or recovery of economic value (de Brito & Dekker, 2003, p. 3).

Also, a distinction between reverse logistics and green logistics is that the latter considers the environmental aspects in all logistics activities—specifically, on forward logistics (Bonev, 2012, p. 6).

Figure 1. Difference between reverse and green logistics
Adopted from (Rogers & Tibben-Lembke, 2001, p. 131) and (de Brito & Dekker, 2003, p. 4)

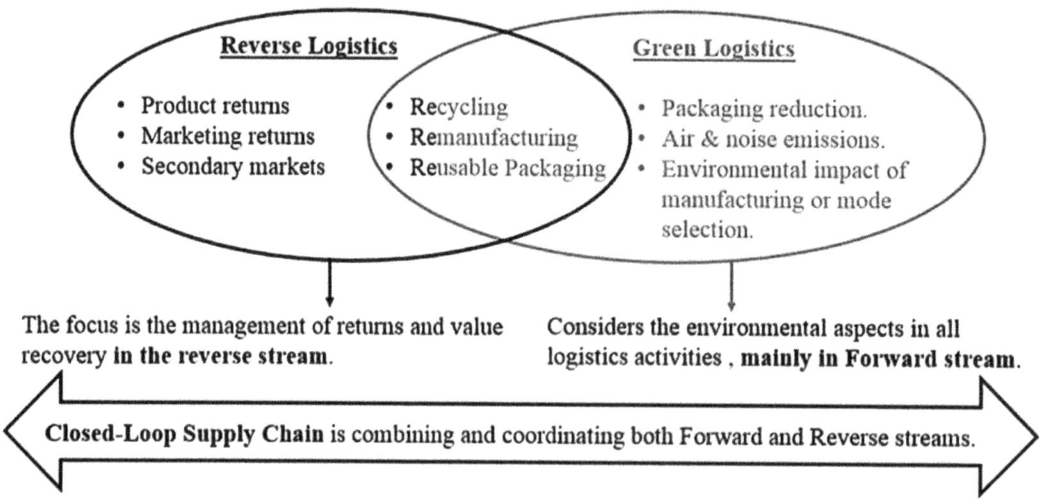

van Hoek (1999, p. 129) differentiates between reverse and green logistics as the latter refers to those practices and activities within the supply chain, which aims to reduce the sources of waste and resources of consumption. However, as shown in Figure 1, there is a number of interrelated activities which can be equally applied in both reverse and green logistics. For example, utilization of reusable packaging in order to eliminate the non-reusable cartoon packaging could be classified as reverse as well as green logistics, while a packaging reduction activity is classified as green logistics activity but not reverse logistics (Rogers & Tibben-Lembke, 2001, p. 130). The holistic view embracing both forward and reverse logistics in a supply chain is the closed loop supply chain concept (de Brito & Dekker, 2003, p. 4).

Therefore, the distinction between waste management, reverse logistics, green logistics, and closed loop supply chain concepts justifies the use of reverse logistics, instead of the other concepts, in the context of this research.

Importance of Reverse Logistics

The evolvement of financial, competitive and customer pressures, as well as the increased complexity regarding the environmental policies and regulations, raised the need for organizations to engage in reverse logistics processes (Partida, 2011, p. 64).

According to Dowlatshahi (2000, p. 144), reverse logistics enables companies to achieve the goal of sustainable development, as it focuses on environmental and economic goals. Hence, reverse logistics aims to maintain the environment and also to generate profits. In addition, effective implementation of reverse logistics can help companies to better compete in an industry characterized by intense competition and low profit margins.

Reverse logistics is also gaining interest in developing countries due to increased competition, market growth, and large numbers of products users. Therefore, the management of product returns in an effective as well as a cost-efficient way has become important as it leads to profitability and elevation of customer service levels, and ensure higher customer retention (Samir & Rajiv, 2006, p. 524).

Reverse Logistics Drivers

As the main driver for forward logistics is to satisfy customer demand at the end of the supply chain, the main drivers in reverse logistics are not that clear (Bonev, 2012, p. 7). Two main parties are involved in reverse logistics: First, the returning party which possesses the product; and second, a receiving party which is interested in capturing value from the product. In this regard, the driving forces from the receiver's perspective are different than those from the returning party's perspective (de Brito & Dekker, 2002, p. 6).

According to de Brito and Dekker (2003, p. 6), Gupta (2013, p. 64), and Samir and Rajiv (2006, p. 524), there are three main drivers that drive companies to receive and accept returns and for other independent companies to be involved in the returns and recovery process, as shown in Figure 2.

The following table 1 summarizes the main drivers for reverse logistics discussed in the literature:

Figure 2. Driving triangle for reverse logistics
Source (de Brito & Dekker, 2003)

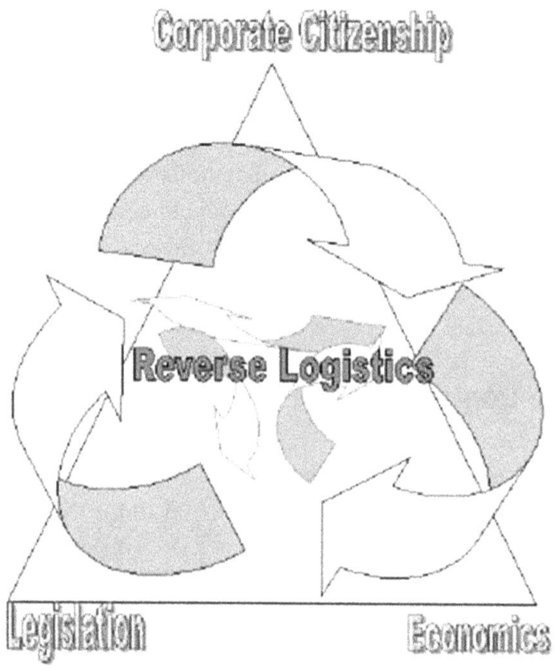

Table 1. Drivers of reverse logistics

Reverse Logistics Drivers	Authors
Economic	(Quesada, 2003; de Brito and Dekker, 2003; Bonev, 2012; C. K. M. Lee and Lam, 2012; Gupta, 2013)
Legislative	(Dale S. Rogers and Tibben-Lembke. 1998; de Brito & Dekker, 2002; de Brito & Dekker, 2003; Quesada, 2003; Schatteman, 2003; Bonev, 2012; Gupta, 2013; Mafakheri & Nasiri, 2013; Rogers, Lembke, & Benardino, 2013)
Corporate Citizenship	(de Brito & Dekker, 2003; Bonev, 2012; Gupta, 2013; Rogers, Lembke, & Benardino, 2013)
Product Recall, commercial returns, stock adjustment and functional returns	(Ronald & Dale, 2002; Dale, Douglas, Keely, & Sebastian, 2002; de Brito and Dekker, 2003; Bonev, 2012)

Product Recall, commercial returns, stock adjustment and functional returns (Ronald & Dale, 2002; Dale, Douglas, Keely, & Sebastian, 2002; de Brito and Dekker, 2003; Bonev, 2012)

Reverse Logistics Barriers

Although the application of reverse logistics practices can result in environmental and economic benefits, it is not free from barriers. The most common barriers in implementing good reverse logistics, according to Dale S. Rogers's and Tibben-Lembke's (1998, p. 32) examination of 300 companies in different industries, are as follows: Importance of reverse logistics relative to other issues, company policies, lack of system, competitive issues, management inattention, financial and personnel resources, and legal issues.

In addition, different studies (Donald F. Blumberg, 1999; Chouinard, D'Amours, & Aït-Kadi, 2005; Cojocariu, 2013; Eric, Thomas, & Lauren, 2010; Gupta, 2013; Ismail et al., 2010; Lau & Wang, 2009; Ravi & Shankar, 2005; Richey, Chen, Genchev, & Daugherty, 2005; Ronald & Dale, 2002) have identified similar barriers as those identified by Dale S. Rogers and Tibben-Lembke (1998, p. 32) as well as other different barriers.

RESEARCH DESIGN

In this empirical research, a mixed approach is applied. The research starts by a qualitative case study, to describe the reverse logistics drivers and the applied practices at the case company and to identify the barriers that potentially hinder their reverse logistics applications. This is followed by Interpretive Structural Modeling (ISM) to explore the interactions among the barriers identified during the case study.

The major benefits of this mixed research approach are that the case study provides in-depth understanding of the problem at hand within its real context, while the ISM analysis helps to structure and analyze the information gathered from the case study in a systematic way.

The mixed research approach is defined by (Johnson & Onwuegbuzie, 2004) as the class of research where the researcher mixes or combines quantitative and qualitative research techniques, methods, approaches, concepts or language into a single study (p. 17). A more detailed explanation is provided by Kelle (2006, p. 309) as a combination of different qualitative and quantitative methods of data collection and data analysis in one empirical research project. The combination of both methods helps the researcher to gain a full picture and deeper understanding of the investigated phenomenon by linking complementary findings to each other. Yin (2009, p. 64) states that a mixed research approach can enable the researcher to address either broader or more complicated research questions than case studies alone. He defines a case study as an empirical inquiry that investigates a contemporary phenomenon in depth and within its real-life context, especially when the boundaries between phenomenon and context are not clearly evident (p. 18).

Hence, the mixed research approach can be used in case studies where quantitative results are expressed in numerical and quantifiable terms, while qualitative results are expressed verbally in order to create an understanding of relationships or complex interactions (M. Ellram, 1996, p. 97).

Sources of Primary Data

In this research, primary data has been collected by using semi-structured and structured interviews in two phases. In the first phase, semi-structured interviews are conducted face-to-face with Pharco's sales manager, health and safety manager, returned products supervisor, and the health and safety supervisor. Each of the interviews with the sales manager and the returned product supervisor lasted two hours on average, while the interviews with the health and safety manager and the supervisor lasted only one hour each.

The interview questions in this phase have been formulated based on the relevant literature of reverse logistics in order to cover the research questions. Thus, one interview guide with three questions sets, in accordance with, the three research questions has been prepared. The purpose of the first set of questions is to understand the reverse logistics drivers from the company's perspective and to obtain knowledge on how Pharco's downstream partners derive the company's reverse logistics practices.

The main purpose of the second set of questions is to determine the current reverse logistics activities and processes applied by Pharco, and then, to understand how the company deals with the returned pharmaceuticals in relation to the imposed regulations. The last set of questions is prepared to investigate the different reverse logistics barriers facing Pharco in implementing reverse logistics.

During the first phase, all the conducted interviews have been audio-recorded and subsequently transcribed prior to data analysis.

In the second phase, structured interviews are conducted electronically and via telephone with the sales manager and the returned products supervisor in order to establish contextual and pairwise relationships among the previously identified barriers in the first phase. Their responses to a set of close-ended questions are the basis in filling the structural self-interaction matrix, which is one of the steps of the ISM analysis as described later in this chapter.

Sources of Secondary Data

Quantitative data is collected from the company in the form of monthly reports for sales and product returns value by distributors for the year 2014. Such data has been useful for the case description. In addition, some relevant information has been collected from Pharco and its distributors' websites, as well as from published reports, and guidelines have been obtained from the Egyptian Drug Authority (EDA) website. Moreover, a significant amount of secondary data has been obtained from scientific articles published in academic journals, which are available through online databases. Also, a number of relevant books and dissertations to this research has been collected and used in the theoretical framework chapter.

Data Analysis Methods

In this research, the ISM methodology is applied to analyze the information gathered from the case study on the barriers hindering Pharco's application of reverse logistics. A brief overview of this method and its steps are provided below.

Interactive Management (IM) is a set of managerial tools invented especially to manage complexity in organizations and to enable them to cope with complex situations whose scopes are beyond the normal type of problem that they can easily solve (John N Warfield & Cárdenas, 1994, p. 1). One such tool is the ISM—it is a methodology designed for use when the researcher desires to employ systematic and logical thinking to approach a complex issue, and then to communicate the results of that thinking to others (Malone, 1975). This technique was developed by Warfield during the period 1972–1974 and published in 1974 (John N Warfield & Cárdenas, 1994, p. 82).

John N. Warfield (1974) defines structural modeling as a methodology which employs graphics and words in carefully defined patterns to illustrate the structure of a complex issue or problem. Thus, in this technique, the intention of the modeler is to embody the geometric rather than the algebraic and to describe form rather than calculating or measuring quantitative output (Lendaris, 1980, p. 807).

Ravi and Shankar (2005, p. 1017) explain ISM as an interactive learning process in which a set of different directly and indirectly related variables affecting the system under consideration are structured into a comprehensive systematic model. This methodology helps to identify order and direction on the complexity of relationships among the elements of a system.

The ISM methodology is interpretive as the judgment of the expert group decides whether and how the variables are related. It is structural on the basis of relationships, and an overall structure is extracted from the complex set of variables. In addition, it is a modeling technique because the specific relationships of the variables and the overall structure of the system under consideration are represented and illustrated in a diagraph model (Ravi & Shankar, 2005, p. 1018). In this regard, the value added by using the ISM methodology is structural and no information is added by the process (Farris & Sage, 1975).

Attri, Dev, and Sharma (2013, p. 5), Luthra, Kumar, Kumar, and Haleem (2011, p. 240), and Ravi and Shankar (2005, p. 1018) explain and summarize the various steps involved in the ISM methodology into eight steps as follows:

1st Step: Identify the variables affecting the system under consideration and which are relevant to the problem. Those variables can be objectives, actions, and individuals etc.

2nd Step: Based on the identified variables in the first step, establish a contextual relationship between the variables with respect to which pairs of elements would be examined.

3rd Step: Develop a structural self-interaction matrix (SSIM) for variables, which would indicate a pairwise relationship among variables of the system under consideration.

4th Step: Develop a reachability matrix from the SSIM and check this matrix for transitivity. The transitivity of the contextual relation is a basic assumption made in ISM. It states that if a variable "A" is related to another variable "B," and "B" is related to "C," then "A" is necessarily related to "C."

5th Step: Partition the reachability matrix obtained in step four into different levels.

6th Step: Based on the relationships given in the reachability matrix, draw a directed graph and remove the transitive links.

7th Step: Convert the resultant directed graph into an ISM-based model by replacing the element nodes with the statements.

8th Step: Review the model to check for conceptual inconsistency and make the necessary modifications. These steps of the ISM are illustrated in Figure 3.

CASE OVERVIEW: PHARCO PHARMACEUTICALS

Pharco Corporation is a group of nine healthcare companies operating in the pharmaceutical field in Egypt since 1987. The corporation specializes in the development, manufacturing, marketing, distribution, and export of a wide range of branded, generic drugs and licensed pharmaceutical products (Pharco Corporation, 2014). Currently, the corporation consists of six manufacturing facilities in Alexandria, Egypt. In addition, there are two trading companies in Egypt while one marketing and distribution Branch in Bucharest, Romania, has been operating in the Romanian market since 1993. Through the nine companies, the corporation employs more than 5,700 employees.

In 2011, the corporation was ranked number one in the Egyptian pharmaceutical market with a market share of 13.2 percent in terms of sales units (345 million units). The corporation is focusing on increasing its product portfolio while improving efficiency and optimizing its processes to provide affordable medication in the Egyptian market.

Pharco Pharmaceuticals is the founder of the corporation and is the second private Egyptian shareholding company. The company is located and headquartered in Alexandria, Egypt, producing and marketing for 237 brands, generics, branded generics and licensed products. Moreover, the company exports to 47 countries (Pharco Pharmaceuticals, 2014).

Figure 3. Flow diagram for preparing the ISM model
Source (Attri et al., 2013, p. 4)

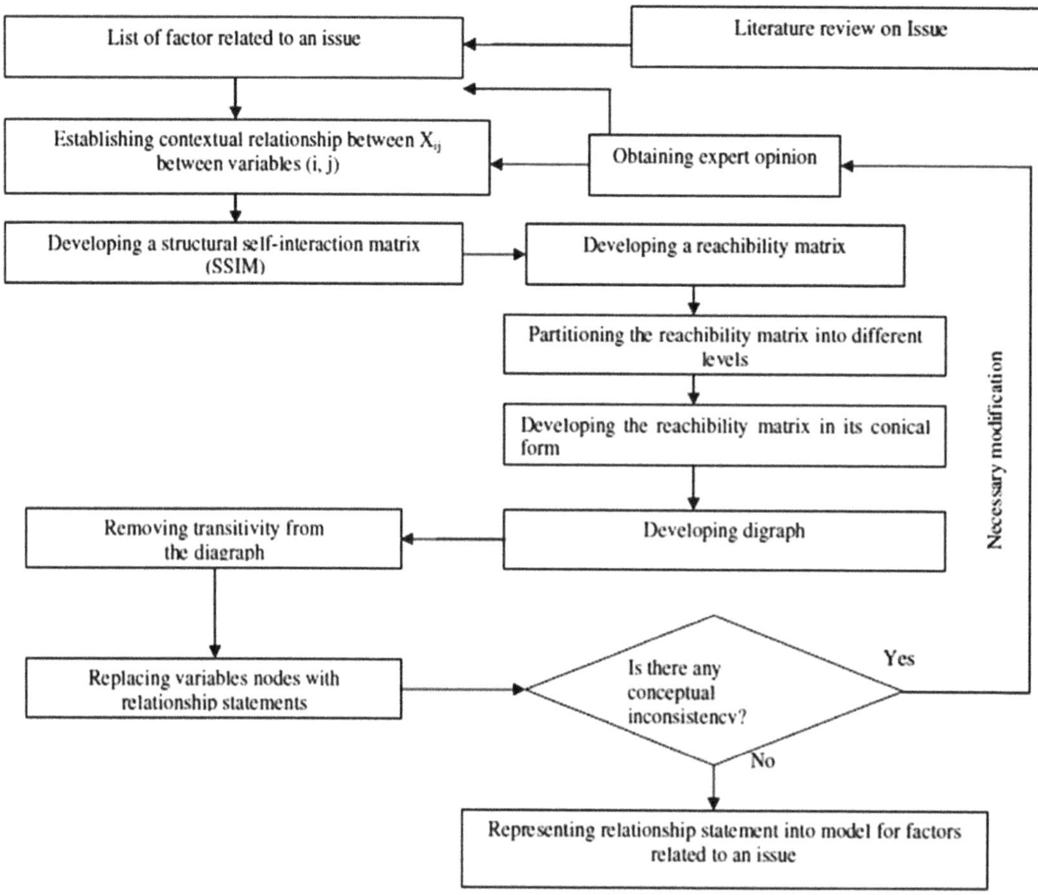

Supply Chain Structure of Pharco Pharmaceuticals

The special nature and high complexity of the pharmaceutical industry in Egypt greatly influence the Pharco supply chain design and objectives. There are two different phases at the Pharco supply chain: the first phase focuses on product development and production (upstream), while the second phase focuses on marketing and selling the product in the market (downstream).

Therefore, Pharco's objectives are different at each of the two phases: In the upstream supply chain the objective is to accelerate the release of the products and the approval of MOH over the production batches, which implies that responsiveness is the main driver shaping the design of the Pharco upstream supply chain.

In the downstream supply chain, the objective is to achieve high product availability in the Egyptian market and the aim is to meet sales targets. In the following sections, the focus will be on the Pharco downstream supply chain and, particularly, the product and information reverse flow.

The company is producing and distributing 237 brands, generics, branded generics and licensed products through 12 authorized distributors and small-sized distributors to pharmacies, hospitals, and private clinics in Egypt. This is illustrated in Figure 4.

Figure 4. Supply chain of Pharco pharmaceuticals

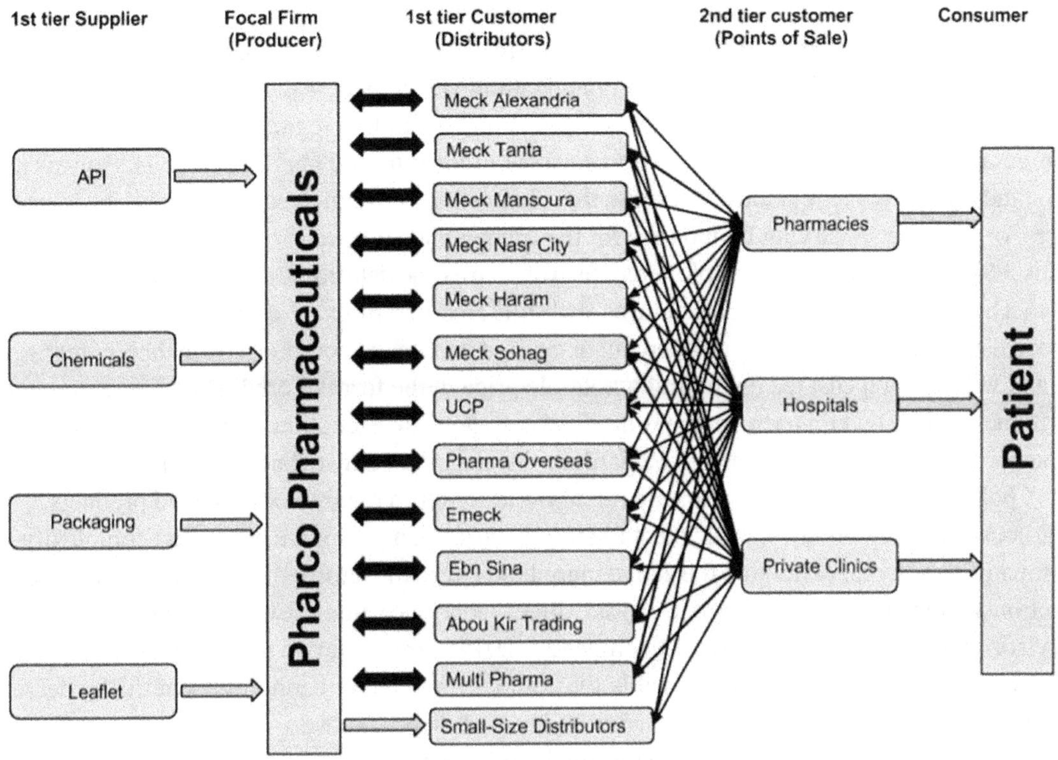

Pharco Supply Chain Downstream Information Flow

Despite the distributors' important role in the forward and reverse product flows, the fragmentation of Pharco supply chain as well as the lack of visibility and transparency between the downstream partners make it difficult to share and transmit timely and precise information to effectively manage the reverse flow. Especially because, neither Pharco nor its downstream partners rely on advanced information systems.

In the forward flow, Pharco's access to its product information, after the products get transferred to distributors, is very limited as distributors control the carried inventory in the chain pipeline. The last information recorded by Pharco regarding its products in the forward flow is the values and volumes of products transferred to each distributor in accordance with their sales orders. Therefore, it becomes very difficult for Pharco to track the amount of inventory carried by distributors on a real-time basis. Moreover, Pharco's control and visibility over the inventory becomes more difficult and complex after the products get distributed to thousands of pharmacies, hospitals, and clinics in Egypt. Consequently, Pharco remains uncertain about the amount of returns until the distributors send them back to the company.

Reverse Logistics Drivers in Pharco Supply Chain

The driving forces stimulating Pharco's implementation of reverse logistics are mainly legislative and regulatory-driven. However, other reasons for product returns from Pharco's downstream partners influence Pharco reverse logistics processes and activities.

- The Receiving Party's Perspective: Pharco Pharmaceuticals

Reverse logistics drivers from Pharco's perspective are legislative in nature, as explained by the Returned Products Supervisor (personal communication, December 24, 2014). This is due to the legal responsibility imposed by MOH and EDA over the company. In this regard, Pharco follows MOH and EDA regulations regarding the collection and disposal of the returned pharmaceuticals. However, there are no standard rules or regulations governing the relationship between the company and its downstream partners, or a decree specifying boundaries for the acceptable percentage of returns.

Thus, Pharco specifies its acceptable percentage of returns and determines the preferable compensation method. The company accepts partial returns with full credit from its 12 authorized distributors—i.e., Pharco's distributors can return up to 2 percent of expired or damaged products from their purchase order value and will be compensated by the full wholesale price in the form of credits for future purchases. It is worth mentioning that this percentage is not final and there are exceptions, depending on the distributor's power in the distribution channel. Regarding the small-sized distributors, Pharco applies the "no returns" policy—i.e., these distributors are not allowed to return expired or damaged products.

The economic driver is not significant at Pharco because the high degree of product complexity limits the company's ability for extracting the active ingredients from the returned products in pharmaceuticals production, thereby making it difficult to capture direct economic value. However, the Returned Products Supervisor (personal communication, December 24, 2014) explained two activities that are performed on an irregular basis. Those activities enable the company to capture economic benefits by decreasing the volume of the destructed returns and hence reduce the disposal costs.

The first activity is relabeling the valid returned products with less than one year of shelf-life as "free medical sample" and using them for marketing purposes. The reason behind the inability of redistributing those valid returns back to the market and capturing their full market value is that distributors are not willing to distribute products with less than one year of shelf-life.

The second activity is donating the returned products with valid expiry date but damaged packages to charitable organizations. The Returned Products Supervisor (personal communication, December 24, 2014) declared that when Pharco gets involved in such activities, the company is exempted from sales taxes over the amounts of donated and free medical samples. He also mentioned that such activities do not generate a significant financial reward for the company, for most products returned by the distributors are past their sell-by dates and only negligible amounts are within valid expiry dates.

- The Returning Party's Perspective: Return Reasons

There are several reasons for pharmaceutical returns in Pharco—the most common being product expiration, followed by damaged packaging and product recalls. One of the uncommon reasons of product returns is the distributor's financial deficit.

According to the pharmaceuticals market standards, Pharco is responsible for accepting returns from the distributors if the product is expired or the remaining shelf-life is two months or less.

Pharco is also responsible for collecting products with damaged packaging during transportation or due to storage activity. Even though the product with damaged packaging remains valid and suitable for consumption, the company does not redistribute them in the market after being returned.

A less frequent reason for return—but when occurring, it is urgent and requires an immediate action—is product recall. When a production batch is defective due to quality issues, Pharco should recall it from

POS through its distributors. In such cases, Pharco distributors are responsible for executing the recall and collection of the defective products from the chain pipeline based on Pharco and CAPA requests. The recall process is executed under CAPA's supervision and it promptly notifies all distributors with the required information to execute the recall—for example, the defective product's batch number, its manufacturing date, and expiration date. Pharco's responsibility is to receive the recalled amount from the distributors and dispose of it in a proper way under CAPA's supervision.

Another uncommon reason for return is the distributor's financial deficit, as some distributors may face a deficit to pay for the purchased orders. In this regard, the distributor will return the purchased products to Pharco. Since the product's remaining shelf-life is longer than one year and the package is not damaged, the company can resell it again to other distributors.

Pharco Reverse Logistics Practices: Processes and Activities

The scope of reverse logistics activities at Pharco depends on the return reasons from downstream partners. Since most of the return reasons take place due to product expiration, the dominant reverse logistics activity at Pharco is disposal by incineration. However, other reverse logistics activities— such as donation to charitable organizations, free medical samples, and redistribution—are practiced but to a lesser extent. Figure 5 maps the process of product return—it is clearly illustrated that the return process is complex as multiple activities and different parties are involved.

Figure 5. Reverse logistics process map of Pharco pharmaceuticals

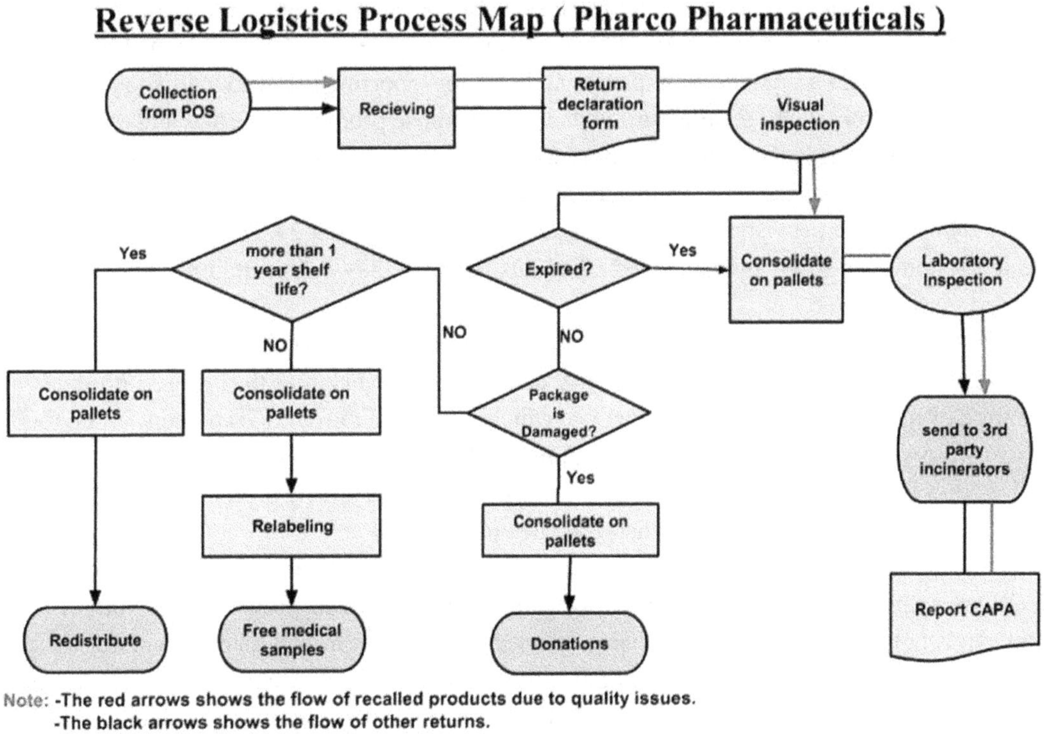

- Collection, Receiving, and Inspection

The product return process starts with the collection activity, as illustrated in Figure 6. The responsible party for collecting returns or recalls from the chain pipeline and POS are Pharco's authorized distributors. Their main task is to collect the returned and recalled products from their central branch warehouses and to transport them back to the Pharco headquarters is in Alexandria.

Then, Pharco receives the returned or recalled products in the finished goods returns warehouse. After receiving, the distributors should manually fill out a standard return declaration form in which they should declare the returned product information by clarifying the returned product's name, returned quantities per product, expiry date, and the main reason for return. After the distributor fills out the declaration form, the company checks the received shipment in correspondence with the document by visual inspection to ensure that the returned products are same as declared in the form. After ensuring that the received products are as declared, the company will check the expiration date in order to determine whether the products are expired and will be disposed of by incineration, or whether they still have a shelf-life and can be donated to charitable organizations or relabeled as free medical samples or redistributed to other distributors for resale. However, the decision to dispose of recalled products by incineration is predetermined due to quality issues, regardless of their expiration dates.

- Disposal by Incineration

If the received products are expired, the company does not have any other option than to destroy them by incineration. Accordingly, the company will consolidate those expired products on pallets along with any recalled products, and the laboratory will randomly check the consolidated shipment before sending them to third-party incinerator companies. The health and safety department is responsible for arranging the disposal activity with incinerator companies and also for reporting the amount disposed of to CAPA.

The disposal of expired and recalled products includes those products' internal and external packaging as well as the product leaflet. Hence, the packaged materials are not separated from those products before the final disposal, as the separation activity is rather time-consuming. Furthermore, according to the Returned Products Supervisor (personal communication, December 24, 2014), it is not economically feasible to separate and resell the packaged materials because they constitute only a small fraction of the returned product value.

The Health and Safety Manager (personal communication, January 10, 2015) explained that the company disposes of around 17 tons of pharmaceutical waste every month. Expired products are the major source of pharmaceutical waste at Pharco, which account for around 70 percent of the total pharmaceutical wastes generated. As illustrated in Figure 5, Pharco disposes of all the recalled and expired returned products as well as other pharmaceutical wastes generated during production stages and product stability testing by incineration at three disposal sites in Egypt.

Two of these sites, namely the Nasreya Hazardous Waste Treatment Center and the United Oil Services (UNICO), are approved by MOH for disposal of pharmaceutical waste. However, the 10th of Ramadan Disposal site is not approved by MOH. Pharco relies on the non-approved disposal site for the disposal of around 90 percent of the total pharmaceutical wastes generated, as the disposal cost is less than half of the cost of the approved sites (Health and Safety Supervisor, personal communication, January 10, 2015).

Figure 6. Disposal activity for pharmaceutical waste of Pharco pharmaceuticals

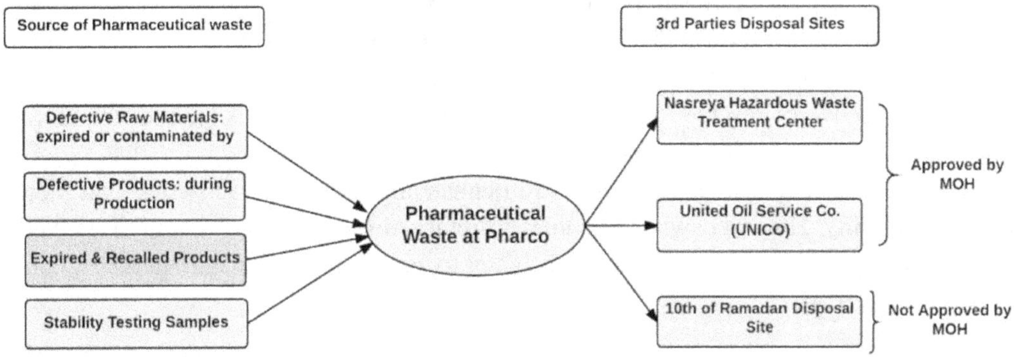

- Donation to Charitable Organizations

If the received products are of valid expiry dates, the company will check whether the product packages are damaged. If damaged, the company will consolidate those products to be donated through charitable organizations in Egypt. Pharco organizes the donation activity in cooperation with the Faculty of Pharmacy Asyut University and the Rotary Club of Alexandria.

- Free Medical Samples

If a product package is in its original form (i.e., not damaged), the company will check the remaining shelf-life of the product—if less than one year is remaining, the company will consolidate the products and re-label them as free medical samples to be used for marketing purposes. Such products are directed free of charge to private clinics to induce medical practitioners to prescribe Pharco products for their patients. The reason behind the inability to redistribute those valid returns back to the market and capture their full market value is that distributors refuse to distribute products with less than one year remaining in shelf-life, as explained before.

- Redistribution

If a product package is not damaged and there is more than one year remaining in the returned product's shelf-life, the product will be redistributed back to the market through distributors and hence the company can capture the full market value from the returned product. However, this activity is rarely performed, as a distributor virtually never returns products with more than one year of shelf-lives (Returned Products Supervisor, personal communication, December 24, 2014).

Reverse Logistics Barriers at Pharco

The following section describes the identified barriers that hinder Pharco in applying their reverse logistics activities and processes and how such barriers are affecting the implementation of reverse logistics.

- Lack of Strategic Planning Resulting in Contradicting Objectives

In Pharco, the sales department is responsible for sales planning and products return planning. The combination of both responsibilities in one department creates a conflict of interest due to the contradicting objectives of each responsibility. The sales department's objective is to achieve the monthly sales targets by selling more units to distributors and by having high product availability in the market. In contrast, the objective of reverse logistics is to accept returned products from distributors, capture economic value from such products, or proper disposal.

Practically, the sales department is interested in enhancing their sales activities as it increases the company's profitability. However, when it comes to returned products, less attention is paid as such products are considered to be an extra cost that is better to avoid (Sales Manager, personal communication, December 24, 2014).

- The Non-existence of Logistics Department in Pharco

Pharco does not have a logistics department responsible for coordinating its logistics activities, and each department works in isolation (Sales Manager, personal communication, December 24, 2014). Consequently, the company neither efficiently nor effectively plans reverse logistics activities, as the real cost of reverse logistics processes and activities is very difficult to estimate due to the lack of awareness regarding the importance of the total logistics cost, including the inbound and outbound transportation, warehousing, handling, storage, and the returned inventory-carrying cost.

- Lack of Advanced Information System

The company does not rely on a database management system and the use of information technology is very limited between Pharco's functional departments. In addition, the sales department does not rely on barcode scanners for counting and sorting returned products.

Consequently, the sales department has to do a lot of paper work regarding products returns, while the manual counting and sorting of returned products are also time-consuming and subject to human error. Moreover, the return declaration form and all the related documents are filled out and transmitted manually by distributors after Pharco receives the returned shipment. This results in several process delays due to manual counting, sorting, and checking (Returned Products Supervisor, personal communication, December 24, 2014).

- Insufficient Performance Metrics

Pharco develops no key performance indicators (KPIs) for measuring reverse logistics performance. The sales department prepares a monthly report showing the percentage of returned products' value from sales by distributors, which is used for internal reporting to the company's top management. However, there are neither performance metrics showing the returned quantities per product groups nor per product type (Sales Manager, personal communication, December 24, 2014).

- Lack of Dedicated Workers and Facilities for Handling Returns

One of the identified barriers confronting Pharco in handling product returns is constituted by limited workers and a small dedicated warehouse for handling returns that prevents Pharco from receiving simultaneous returns from its distributors. Thus, the company is scheduling returns from distributors at separate time intervals in order to avoid creating a buffer of unprocessed returns in the return warehouse.

According to the Returned Products Supervisor (Personal communication, December 24, 2014), some distributors return the expired pharmaceuticals on a quarterly basis rather than a monthly basis. The postponement of returns from one distributor affects the overall receiving plan. This is because when the returned amounts are larger than the usual amount, they requires more processing time and more human efforts due to the limited number of workers handling returns.

- Financial Constraints

As explained by the Sales Manager (personal communication, December 24, 2014), Pharco is facing financial pressure due to three main reasons. First, the cost of reverse logistics activities represents a direct hit on Pharco's profitability since capturing economic benefits from expired products is infeasible. Second, the devaluation of the Egyptian currency relative to the raw materials supplier's currencies during previous years affects the purchasing price of raw materials. As a result, the currency devaluation puts more financial pressure over Pharco, as the company is highly dependent on international suppliers for sourcing the active pharmaceutical ingredients that constitute the greatest portion from the final product total cost. In addition, the retail price of pharmaceuticals is fixed by the Egyptian government, and the application for modifying the existing retail price is a lengthy and complex process.

- Management Did Not Consider Reverse Logistics as a Priority

Reverse logistics at Pharco lacks importance relative to other issues such as production and sales. Pharco's top management perceives reverse logistics as the "cost of doing business." Therefore, they do not take serious actions in order to improve their reverse logistics capabilities and are reactive rather than proactive in solving problems related to product returns (Returned Products Supervisor, personal communication, December 24, 2014).

However, the Sales Manager (personal communication, December 24, 2014) indicated that Pharco's top management is willing to consider any project that would decrease costs, increase revenues, or boost sales.

- Restrictive Return Policy

Although the monthly generated sales by an individual, small-sized distributor was not significant in 2014, the aggregate sales value per month of all small-sized distributors was extremely high compared with any of the other distributors. However, Pharco did not accept returns from small-sized distributors in order to minimize the returned products quantities. Although Pharco did not explicitly specify in formal agreements with distributors the terms and conditions for returns, the Returned Products Supervisor (personal communication, December 24, 2014) declared that it is very important for the top management that product returns do not exceed 2 percent of the company's monthly sales.

- Lack of Workers' Support and Personnel Training

In the sales department the majority of workers resist changes by discouraging their direct manager from modifying their tasks or work standard procedures, as mentioned by the Sales Manager (personal communication, December 24, 2014), and they would like to perform the same task "as it is." Therefore, when the management proposes a modification in the process of handling returns, most of them consider the proposed change as overload and do not support the change. In addition, there is a lack of skilled and trained workers employed in handling returns, as most of training opportunities are dedicated to personnel working in the production and marketing of pharmaceuticals.

- Lack of Information Sharing across the Supply Chain

Pharco is relying on a basic information system that is not capable of integrating the company's internal functional departments or being integrated with the downstream partners for transmitting or sharing information. Similarly, most of its distributors and large chain pharmacies are relying on their own internal information systems which are utilized only for coordinating and planning their sales activities between their own branches (Sales Manager, personal communication, December 24, 2014). Therefore, it is very difficult to share POS data across the supply chain as neither Pharco nor its downstream partners depend on adequate information systems suitable for transmitting the actual sales data or the current valid and expired inventory in the chain pipeline. Consequently, this lack of visibility limits Pharco's ability to estimate returns or to pre-plan for handling returns.

- Lack of Regulation Enforcement

Although the pharmaceutical industry is regulated by MOH and EDA, it is plagued by poor enforcement of regulations (Sales Manager, personal communication, December 24, 2014). According to EDA regulations, it is illegal for pharmacies to purchase pharmaceutical products without a valid invoice, while the production batch number, the expiry date, and the distributor's name are shown clearly on the sales invoice. However, in reality, a number of pharmacies accept shipments without a valid invoice from unauthorized distributors in order to get higher volume discounts than the normal discounts provided by the authorized distributors. Consequently, they face difficulties in returning expired pharmaceuticals, as expired returns without a valid sales invoice are not accepted by most authorized distributors (Sales Manager, personal communication, December 24, 2014).

Moreover, the EDA's role is only supervisory and limited to periodic inspection of the manufacturer's disposal activities, and there is no concrete regulations enforcing Pharco to accept a predefined amount of the expired and damaged products from distributors. In this regard, there is always a debate between Pharco and its distributors over the permissible percentage of expired and damaged returns. At the same time, this debate escalates between distributors and pharmacies, resulting in distributors' reluctance to accept returns from pharmacies (Sales Manager, personal communication, December 24, 2014).

Also, the disposal supervision by CAPA is poor, as the Health and Safety Manager (personal communication, January 10, 2015) declared that the company disposes of on average 17 tons of pharmaceutical waste on a monthly basis. As many as 15 tons of such wastes (around 90 percent) are disposed of in a non-approved disposal site by MOH in order to cut down the disposal cost.

- Lack of Economic Support from Government

The Egyptian government represented in MOH did not provide any economic support to Pharco for handling the returned pharmaceuticals in a better manner. Also, Pharco bears the full responsibility as well as the associated costs of the disposal activity for the expired returns (Returned Products Supervisor, personal communication, December 24, 2014). Therefore, Pharco is unwilling to accept large quantities of expired pharmaceuticals from distributors, as the disposal activity is considered as an extra cost affecting the company's profitability and especially because the company does not capture any economic benefits from the expired returns.

- Lack of Public Awareness Regarding the Importance of Reverse Logistics

The Returned Products Supervisor (personal communication, December 24, 2014) mentioned that patients in Egypt, who can be termed as Pharco's end consumers, are not fully aware of the importance of reverse logistics in protecting the public health and the environment, as their main driver in buying medicines is mainly the price.

In this respect, Pharco is not considering reverse logistics as a source to create a good corporate image. The main objective of Pharco is to provide a pharmaceutical product with an affordable price in the Egyptian market, and this is the main source of its strength in the Egyptian pharmaceutical industry.

- Differences in Supply Chain Partners' Objectives

One of the barriers faced by Pharco is the different goals and objectives of its supply chain partners in reverse logistics, as explained by the Returned Products Supervisor (personal communication, December 24, 2014). Pharco as a producer tries to reduce the amount of returned products and the credits to its distributors over the returned products. Also, the top management will not be satisfied if they figure out that a high percentage from sales is being returned to the company. Accordingly, Pharco has adjusted its return policy to act as an incentive to boost sales volumes through distributors by linking the amount of permissible returned products to the distributors' purchase order value. Consequently, the distributors order unnecessary high volumes from Pharco in order to get volume discounts and to return the most possible amount of expired products based on their purchase order value, without taking into account the actual demand from pharmacies.

Most problems occur when distributors distribute the products to pharmacies. The distributors' objective is to sell large quantities of products to pharmacies and hence they link the credit duration to the quantities purchased—i.e., if the total purchased amount during a month is greater in value than EGP 5000, the credit duration will be 75 days and cash discount 2.75 percent. Consequently, pharmacies are motivated to order larger than needed amounts, while the distributors' return policies are restrictive in order to minimize returns from pharmacies.

Pharmacies aim to minimize their purchase order quantities because they already have unnecessary stock from their acceptance of the distributors' volume discounts offered during previous periods, which will expire in a short time. In spite of this, the only legal solution to return the expired products is by purchasing large volumes of products from the distributors, which simply exaggerates the problem. Such contradicting objectives put pressure on pharmacies to deal with unauthorized intermediaries in order to return their expired products with a deduction from the initial wholesale price. Those unauthorized intermediaries open the gate for counterfeited products in the market, as they modify the expiry date printed on the expired products and redistribute them back to pharmacies as valid.

- Opportunistic Behavior

Some of the distributors are trying to take advantage of Pharco due to the lack of formal return agreements. They are striving to return large amounts of expired products while getting more compensation credits than they should receive, as they have purchased those products based on a volume discount price. Pharco is counteracting such opportunistic behavior by restricting its return policy to safeguard its profits. According to the Returned Products Supervisor (personal communication, December 24, 2014), the traditional standard in the Egyptian pharmaceutical industry for returning expired products is no more than two months prior to the expiration date. However, Pharco is tightening its return policy with all distributors by accepting only products which either will expire at the current month or have already expired.

Furthermore, the supervisor of returned products mentioned that the difference in power between distributors and small-size pharmacies allows the former to behave opportunistically toward pharmacies by being reluctant to accept expired or damaged products.

- Long Processing Cycle Time of Returned Products

Another barrier facing Pharco is the long processing cycle time of returned products—i.e., from receiving returns until final disposal or recovery activity—as the manual preparation of return documents as well as the manual counting, sorting, and inspection of returns require a substantial amount of time and human resources. Moreover, returns might remain unprocessed in Pharco's warehouse for several working days or weeks, in case of conflicts between Pharco and its distributors over the returned quantities, and as a result, the overall receiving plan of returns might be interrupted or delayed (Returned Products Supervisor, personal communication, December 24, 2014).

- Unknown Total Cost of Return Process

According to the Sales Manager (personal communication, December 24, 2014), the total cost of returns at Pharco is composed of the following:

- Value of returned products.
- Transportation cost from POS to warehouses at distributor's branches.
- Transportation cost from distributor's branches to distributor's central warehouse.
- Transportation cost from distributor's central warehouse to Pharco finished goods returns warehouse.
- Returned inventory-carrying cost (warehousing, utilities, and salaries).
- Transportation cost from Pharco finished goods returns warehouse to disposal sites.
- Incineration cost.

As Pharco's responsibility is limited to certain activities in the return process, the company's knowledge about the cost of returns is limited to the value of returned products, transportation cost from their warehouse to the disposal sites, and the incineration cost. However, the cost documentations are only prepared for accounting issues and they are not utilized for the purpose of process improvement or cost reduction (Sales Manager, personal communication, December 24, 2014).

MODEL DEVELOPMENT: ISM

A preliminary list of 17 barriers that hinder the company's implementation of reverse logistics practices have been generated by a literature review and semi-structured interviews with the company management. These are summarized in Table 2 below.

Table 2. Identified barriers of reverse logistics at Pharco Pharmaceuticals

1. Lack of strategic planning resulting in contradicting objectives.
2. The non-existence of a logistics department at the company.
3. Lack of advanced information system.
4. Insufficient performance metrics.
5. Lack of dedicated workers and facilities for handling returns.
6. Financial constraints.
7. Management did not consider reverse logistics as a priority.
8. Restrictive return policy.
9. Lack of workers' support and personnel training.
10. Lack of information sharing across the supply chain.
11. Lack of regulation enforcement.
12. Lack of economic support from the government.
13. Lack of public awareness regarding the importance of reverse logistics.
14. Difference in the supply chain partners' objectives.
15. Opportunistic behavior.
16. Long processing cycle time of returned products.
17. Unknown total cost of return process.

Structural Self-Interaction Matrix

To develop the Structural Self Interaction Matrix (SSIM) with contextual relationships of types "leads to" across the barriers, a set of closed-ended questions were answered by the company managers. The following four symbols are applied to denote the direction of the relationship between the factors (i and j):

- V: barrier i will lead to barrier j;
- A: barrier j will lead to barrier i;
- X: barriers i and j will lead to each other; and
- O: barriers i and j are unrelated.

Table 3 illustrates the SSIM matrix, with the contextual relationship between the 17 barriers.

Table 3. Structural self-interaction matrix (SSIM)

Barriers	17	16	15	14	13	12	11	10	9	8	7	6	5	4	3	2
1. Lack of strategic planning resulting in contradicting objectives.	O	O	O	O	A	A	A	O	V	V	A	A	V	V	O	V
2. The non-existence of a logistics department in Pharco.	V	O	O	O	O	O	O	O	V	O	V	A	V	V	O	
3. Lack of advanced information system.	V	V	O	O	O	O	O	V	O	O	A	A	V	V		
4. Insufficient performance metrics.	A	V	O	O	O	A	O	A	V	O	A	O	O			
5. Lack of dedicated workers and facilities for handling returns.	O	V	O	O	O	O	A	O	O	A	A	A				
6. Financial constraints.	O	O	V	O	O	A	O	V	V	V	V					
7. Management did not consider reverse logistics as a priority.	O	O	V	O	A	A	A	V	V	V						
8. Restrictive return policy.	O	V	X	A	A	A	A	O	O							
9. Lack of workers' support and personnel training.	O	V	O	O	O	A	A	O								
10. Lack of information sharing across the supply chain.	V	V	X	A	O	O	O									
11. Lack of regulation enforcement.	O	O	V	V	A	O										
12. Lack of economic support from the government.	O	O	V	V	A											
13. Lack of public awareness regarding the importance of reverse logistics.	O	O	V	O												
14. Difference in the supply chain partners objectives.	O	V	V													
15. Opportunistic behavior.	O	V														
16. Long processing cycle time of returned products.	O															
17. Unknown total cost of return process.																

The use of the symbols V, A, X, and O in the SSIM are exemplified below:

Barrier 14 leads to Barrier 15. This means that the differences in the company's supply chain partners' objectives lead to opportunistic behavior. Thus, the relationship between Barriers 14 and 15 is denoted by 'V' in the SSIM.

Barrier 13 leads to Barrier 12. This means that the lack of public awareness regarding the importance of reverse logistics (Barrier 13) leads to lack of economic support from the government (Barrier 12), but the opposite relationship—i.e., Barrier 12 leads to Barrier 13—is not assumed. Thus, the relationship between the two barriers is denoted by 'A'.

Barrier 8, "restrictive return policy," and Barrier 15, "opportunistic behavior," lead to each other. Thus, the restrictive return policy adopted by the company leads to opportunistic behavior in the chain and the opportunistic behavior of the chain partners' influences the company's adoption of a restrictive return policy. Thus, the relationship between Barriers 8 and 15 is denoted by 'X'.

No direct relationship exists between the lack of information sharing across the supply chain (Barrier 10) and the lack of regulation enforcement (Barrier 11). Therefore, the relationship between the two barriers is denoted by 'O'.

Reachability Matrix

In this step, the SSIM is converted into a binary matrix (called the initial reachability matrix) by substituting V, A, X, and O by 1 or 0. The rules of substitution of 1s and 0s are as follows:

If the (i, j) entry in the SSIM is V, then the (i, j) entry in the reachability matrix becomes 1 and the (j, i) entry becomes 0.
If the (i, j) entry in the SSIM is A, then the (i, j) entry in the reachability matrix becomes 0 and the (j, i) entry becomes 1.
If the (i, j) entry in the SSIM is X, then the (i, j) entry in the reachability matrix becomes 1 and the (j, i) entry becomes 1.

If the (i, j) entry in the SSIM is O, then the (i, j) entry in the reachability matrix becomes 0 and the (j, i) entry becomes 0.

According to these rules, the initial reachability matrix for the barriers is shown in Table 4.

Table 4. Initial reachability matrix

Barriers	1	2	3	4	5	6	7	8	9	10	11	12	13	14	15	16	17
1	1	1	0	1	1	0	0	1	1	0	0	0	0	0	0	0	0
2	0	1	0	1	1	0	1	0	1	0	0	0	0	0	0	0	1
3	0	0	1	1	1	0	0	0	0	1	0	0	0	0	0	1	1
4	0	0	0	1	0	0	0	0	1	0	0	0	0	0	0	1	0
5	0	0	0	0	1	0	0	0	0	0	0	0	0	0	0	1	0
6	1	1	1	0	1	1	1	1	1	1	0	0	0	0	1	0	0
7	1	0	1	1	1	0	1	1	1	1	0	0	0	0	1	0	0
8	0	0	0	0	1	0	0	1	0	0	0	0	0	0	1	1	0
9	0	0	0	0	0	0	0	0	1	0	0	0	0	0	0	1	0
10	0	0	0	1	0	0	0	0	0	1	0	0	0	0	1	1	1
11	1	0	0	0	1	0	1	1	1	0	1	0	1	1	1	0	0
12	1	0	0	1	0	1	1	1	1	0	0	1	0	1	1	0	0
13	1	0	0	0	0	0	1	1	0	0	1	1	1	0	1	0	0
14	0	0	0	0	0	0	0	1	0	1	0	0	0	1	1	1	0
15	0	0	0	0	0	0	0	1	0	1	0	0	0	0	1	1	0
16	0	0	0	0	0	0	0	0	0	0	0	0	0	0	0	1	0
17	0	0	0	1	0	0	0	0	0	0	0	0	0	0	0	0	1

The final reachability matrix in Table 5 is obtained by adding transitivity, as explained in step four of the ISM methodology. The driving power and dependence of each barrier are also shown.

Table 5. Final reachability matrix

Barriers	1	2	3	4	5	6	7	8	9	10	11	12	13	14	15	16	17	Driving Power
1	1	1	1^{t}	1	1	0	1^{t}	1	1	1^{t}	0	0	0	0	1^{t}	1^{t}	1^{t}	12
2	1^{t}	1	1^{t}	1	1	0	1	1^{t}	1	1^{t}	0	0	0	0	1^{t}	1^{t}	1	12
3	0	0	1	1	1	0	0	1^{t}	1^{t}	1	0	0	0	0	1^{t}	1	1	9
4	0	0	0	1	0	0	0	0	1	0	0	0	0	0	0	1	0	3
5	0	0	0	0	1	0	0	0	0	0	0	0	0	0	0	1	0	2
6	1	1	1	1^{t}	1	1	1	1	1	1	0	0	0	0	1	1^{t}	1^{t}	13
7	1	1^{t}	1	1	1	0	1	1	1	1	0	0	0	0	1	1^{t}	1^{t}	12
8	0	0	0	1^{t}	1	0	0	1	1^{t}	1^{t}	0	0	0	0	1	1	1^{t}	8
9	0	0	0	0	0	0	0	0	1	0	0	0	0	0	0	1	0	2
10	0	0	0	1	1^{t}	0	0	1^{t}	1^{t}	1	0	0	0	0	1	1	1	8
11	1	1^{t}	1^{t}	1^{t}	1	1^{t}	1	1	1	1^{t}	1	1^{t}	1	1	1	1^{t}	1^{t}	17
12	1	1^{t}	1^{t}	1	1^{t}	1	1	1	1	1^{t}	0	1	0	1	1	1^{t}	1^{t}	15
13	1	1^{t}	1^{t}	1^{t}	1^{t}	1^{t}	1	1	1^{t}	1^{t}	1	1	1	1^{t}	1	1^{t}	1^{t}	17
14	0	0	0	1^{t}	1^{t}	0	0	1	1^{t}	1	0	0	0	1	1	1	1^{t}	9
15	0	0	0	1^{t}	1^{t}	0	0	1	1^{t}	1	0	0	0	0	1	1	1^{t}	8
16	0	0	0	0	0	0	0	0	0	0	0	0	0	0	0	1	0	1
17	0	0	0	1	0	0	0	0	1^{t}	0	0	0	0	0	0	1^{t}	1	4
Dependence Power	7	7	8	14	13	4	7	12	15	12	2	3	2	4	12	17	13	152/152

The Driving power of a particular barrier is the total number of barriers, including itself, which it influences. The dependence of a particular barrier is the total number of barriers, including itself, which may influence it.

Those driving power and dependencies shown in Table 5 will be used later to classify barriers into four groups of autonomous, dependent, linkage and independent (driver) barriers in the Driver-Dependence diagram.

Level Partitions

Based on the final reachability matrix, the reachability set and the antecedent set for each barrier is found. The reachability set for a barrier comprises the barrier itself and the other barriers influenced by it. The antecedent set consists of the barrier itself and other barriers that may influence it. The intersection between the reachability and antecedent sets for all barriers determines the intersection set.

The barrier for which the reachability and intersection sets overlap is assigned as a top-level barrier in the ISM hierarchy or Level 1, as shown in Table 6.

Table 6. Iterations summary result 1–10

Barriers	Reachability set	Antecedent set	Intersection set	Level
1	1,2,3,4,5,7,8,9,10,15,16,17	1,2,6,7,11,12,13	1,2,7	**Level 7**
2	1,2,3,4,5,7,8,9,10,15,16,17	1,2,6,7,11,12,13	1,2,7	**Level 7**
3	3,4,5,8,9,10,15,16,17	1,2,3,6,7,11,12,13	3	**Level 6**
4	4,9,16	1,2,3,4,6,7,8,10,11,12,13,14,15,17	4	**Level 3**
5	5,16	1,2,3,5,6,7,8,10,11,12,13,14,15	5	**Level 2**
6	1,2,3,4,5,6,7,8,9,10,15,16,17	6,11,12,13	6	**Level 8**
7	1,2,3,4,5,7,8,9,10,15,16,17	1,2,6,7,11,12,13	1,2,7	**Level 7**
8	4,5,8,9,10,15,16,17	1,2,3,6,7,8,10,11,12,13,14,15	8,10,15	**Level 5**
9	9,16	1,2,3,4,6,7,8,9,10,11,12,13,14,15,17	9	**Level 2**
10	4,5,8,9,10,15,16,17	1,2,3,6,7,8,10,11,12,13,14,15	8,10,15	**Level 5**
11	1,2,3,4,5,6,7,8,9,10,11,12,13,14,15,16,17	11,13	11,13	**Level 10**
12	1,2,3,4,5,6,7,8,9,10,12,14,15,16,17	11,12,13	12	**Level 9**
13	1,2,3,4,5,6,7,8,9,10,11,12,13,14,15,16,17	11,13	11,13	**level 10**
14	4,5,8,9,10,14,15,16,17	11,12,13,14	14	**Level 6**
15	4,5,8,9,10,15,16,17	1,2,3,6,7,8,10,11,12,13,14,15	8,10,15	**Level 5**
16	16	1,2,3,4,5,6,7,8,9,10,11,12,13,14,15,16,17	16	**Level 1**
17	4,9,16,17	1,2,3,6,7,8,10,11,12,13,14,15,17	17	**Level 4**

Level 1 is then, discarded from the other remaining barriers and the iterative procedure is continued until further levels are identified. For complete iterations, see Appendix (A1). The 10 identified levels in Table 6 helps to build the ISM model.

The conical matrix in Table 7 is built on the basis of the partitioned reachability matrix by rearranging the factors in accordance with their levels, which means that factors having the same levels are clustered together.

Table 7. Conical matrix

Clustered levels	Barriers	16	5	9	4	17	8	10	15	3	14	1	2	7	6	12	11	13
Level 1	16	1	0	0	0	0	0	0	0	0	0	0	0	0	0	0	0	0
Level 2	5	1	1	0	0	0	0	0	0	0	0	0	0	0	0	0	0	0
	9	1	0	1	0	0	0	0	0	0	0	0	0	0	0	0	0	0
Level 3	4	1	1	1	1	0	0	0	0	0	0	0	0	0	0	0	0	0
Level 4	17	1	1	1	1	1	0	0	0	0	0	0	0	0	0	0	0	0
Level 5	8	1	1	1	1	1	1	1	1	0	0	0	0	0	0	0	0	0
	10	1	1	1	1	1	1	1	1	0	0	0	0	0	0	0	0	0
	15	1	1	1	1	1	1	1	1	0	0	0	0	0	0	0	0	0
Level 6	3	1	1	1	1	1	1	1	1	1	0	0	0	0	0	0	0	0
	14	1	1	1	1	1	1	1	1	0	1	0	0	0	0	0	0	0
Level 7	1	1	1	1	1	1	1	1	1	1	1	1	1	1	0	0	0	0
	2	1	1	1	1	1	1	1	1	1	1	1	1	1	0	0	0	0
	7	1	1	1	1	1	1	1	1	1	1	1	1	1	0	0	0	0
Level 8	6	1	1	1	1	1	1	1	1	1	1	1	1	1	1	0	0	0
Level 9	12	1	1	1	1	1	1	1	1	1	1	1	1	1	1	1	0	0
Level 10	11	1	1	1	1	1	1	1	1	1	1	1	1	1	1	1	1	1
	13	1	1	1	1	1	1	1	1	1	1	1	1	1	1	1	1	1

ISM-Based Model

The conical matrix helps to generate the structural model from the initial direct relation graph (digraph, Appendix A2). Hence, after removing the transitive links, as described in the ISM methodology, the diagraph is finally converted into the ISM model by replacing nodes with statements, as shown in Figure 7.

The ISM-based model indicates that Barrier 16 – on level 1 – long processing cycle time of returned products has the lowest driving power, and it is strongly dependent on the rest of barriers.

On the other hand, the lack of regulation enforcement from the government (Barrier 11) and the lack of public awareness regarding the importance of reverse logistics (Barrier 13) are very significant barriers hindering the application of reverse logistics at the company. These two barriers form the bottom Level 10 of the model, as they have the highest driving power and the lowest dependence on the rest of the barriers.

Classification of Barriers: MICMAC Analysis

The purpose of the cross-impact matrix multiplication applied to classification, which is known as (MICMAC), is to analyze the drive power and dependence power of barriers. The analysis principle is based on the multiplication properties of matrices.

Figure 7. ISM-based model for barriers of reverse logistics at the case company

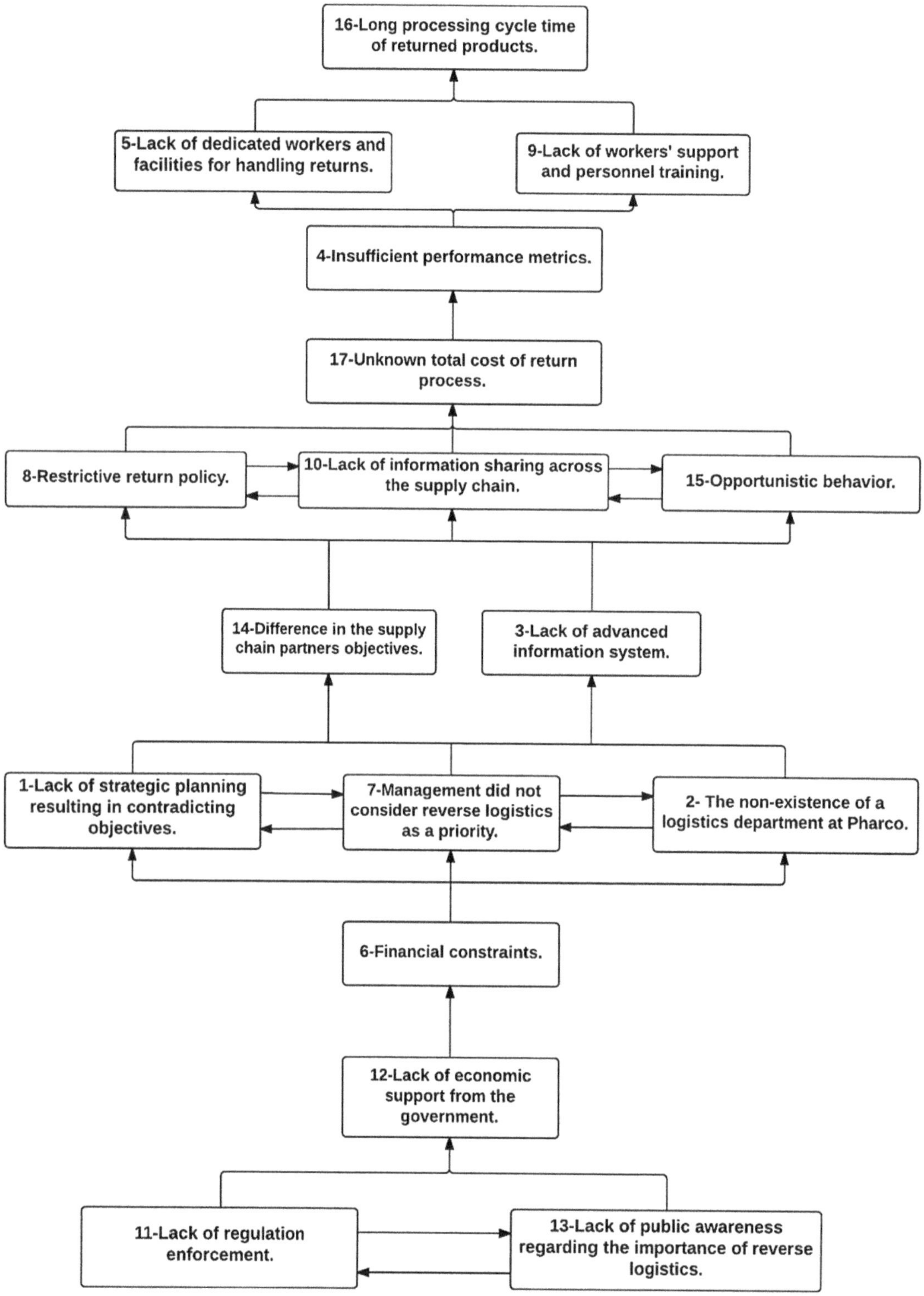

Based on the driving power and dependence power, the barriers have been classified into four categories (Attri et al., 2013, p. 7).

- Autonomous Barriers: These barriers have weak driving power as well as week dependence.
- Linkage Barriers: These barriers have strong driving power as well as strong dependence. They are considered as unstable because any action on these barriers will affect other barriers and result in a feedback effect on themselves.
- Dependent Barriers: These barriers have weak driving power but strong dependence.
- Driver Barriers: These barriers have strong driving power but weak dependence.

The drive-dependence diagram presented in Figure 8 gives a clear picture of the relative importance as well as the interdependencies among the different barriers. The vertical axis reflects the driving power of factors; the horizontal axis reflects their dependence power.

Figure 8. Drive-dependence diagram

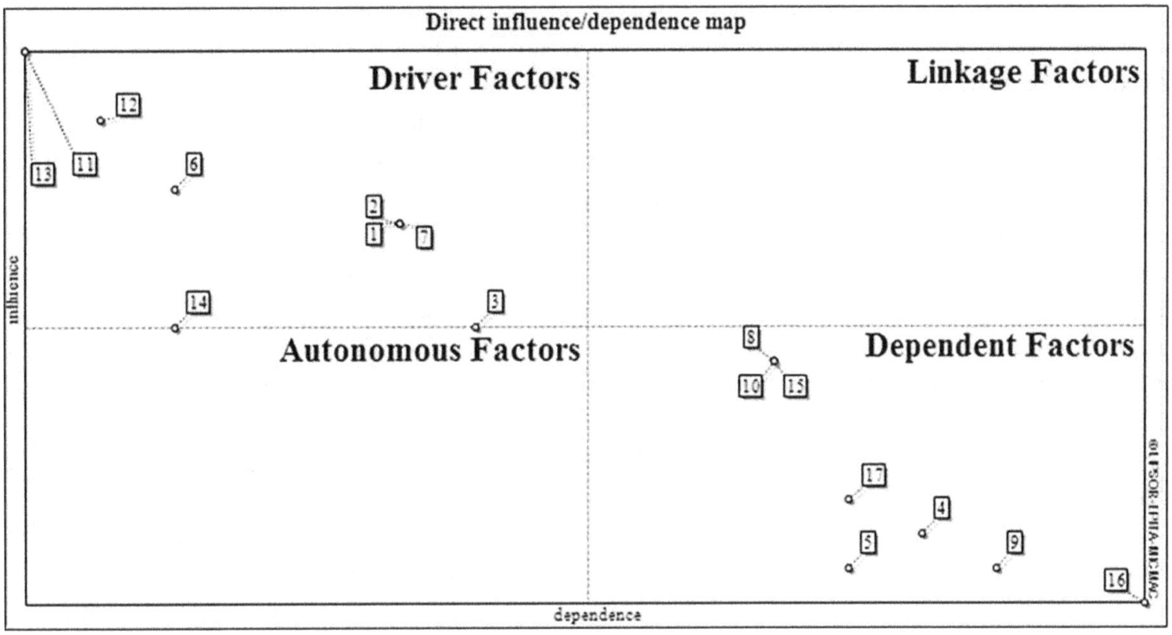

In the MICMAC analysis Figure 8, neither autonomous nor linkage barriers are found. The non-existence of autonomous barriers implies that all the identified barriers affect the reverse logistics application in the company and that all of them are relevant. In addition, the absence of linkage factors under the linkage group implies that no barriers are considered unstable and all of them are either driving or dependent barriers. The dependent barriers have week driving power, but they are highly dependent on the driving barriers. According to the analysis, eight barriers are dependent and represent the undesirable outcome of the nine driving barriers.

MODEL RESULTS AND DISCUSSION

The final results of the ISM can be seen in Figure 6, which depicts the series of influences between the barriers affecting the application of reverse logistics at Pharco. The MICMAC analysis presented in Figure 7 offers directions for dealing with such barriers.

The lower side of the ISM model consists of driving barriers which have very strong driving power and significant influence over the other barriers. These barriers are located in the driver factors' quadrant in the drive-dependence diagram.

Based on the performed analysis, the lack of regulation enforcement and the lack of public awareness regarding the importance of reverse logistics are the most significant barriers hindering reverse logistics application at the company. Also, the ISM model shows that the lack of regulation enforcement and the lack of public awareness regarding the importance of reverse logistics are interrelated, which is similar to the research findings of Donald F. Blumberg (1999, p. 147) and Ismail et al. (2010, p. 51). Their findings indicate that the creation of public awareness is derived from the imposed legislation. In addition, Grabara, Man, and Kolcun (2014, p. 13) state that consumer awareness as well as the imposed legislation are key factors for a successful implementation of reverse logistics, and that the consumer awareness creates legislation which, in turn, leads to a change in consumer behavior.

Therefore, the absence of regulation enforcement negatively affects the application of reverse logistics since the company's main driver in adopting reverse logistics is the imposed regulations by Ministry of Health, as explained earlier. On the other hand, it becomes difficult for the company to make use of reverse logistics in creating a green image if their final consumers lack awareness regarding the importance of reverse logistics in protecting their health as well as the environment.

The absence of economic support from the government is one of the powerful barriers hindering the company implementation of reverse logistics practices, as shown in the power-dependence diagram. The economic support provided by the Egyptian government is essential for the company in order to alleviate the financial pressure resulting from the cost associated with reverse logistics activities. This is especially required when the company cannot capture direct economic value by recycling the expired products that represent a significant amount of returns. The financial constraint has a significant influence on the application of reverse logistics and derives the managers' inattention to the importance of reverse logistics relative to other issues such as sales, marketing, and production activities.

Also, the lack of strategic planning in reverse logistics practices is derived from the financial constraint and is also influenced by the non-existence of a logistics department. This is because the combination of sales and returns activities in the sales department creates a conflict of interest due to the contradicting objectives of each responsibility. Consequently, the company management gives less priority to returned products and reverse logistics activities compared with sales activities. Therefore, the existence of a logistics department for coordinating the multiple reverse logistics activities between the various responsible departments is important for a better application of reverse logistics.

The presence of the previously-mentioned barriers also result in the company's reliance on an outdated information system for handling returns. This is because the developed information system to support reverse logistics requires huge funds (Ravi & Shankar, 2005, p. 1016).

On the fifth level of the ISM model, where the lack of advanced information system is located, the differences in supply chain partners' objectives are located. The presence of the differences in supply chain partners' objectives as a barrier in this position in the ISM model implies that the internal strategic planning and the company's own objectives in handling returns influence the objectives of other chain partners. Thus, setting up of a good internal strategic plan and clear objectives for handling returns might help to align the chain partners' objectives.

The discussed driving barriers are considered key barriers as they have very strong driving power and significant influence over the other barriers. In this regard, the company's management should devote considerable efforts to address such barriers first, as they heavily affect the company's success in implementing reverse logistics.

The upper side of the ISM model consists of barriers which are strongly dependent on the discussed driving barriers. These barriers are located in the dependent factors' quadrant in the drive-dependence diagram.

The appearance of the long processing cycle time of returned products on the top of the ISM model implies that this barrier is derived from the rest of the model barriers. Despite the fact that the lack of dedicated workers and facilities for handling return and also the lack of workers' support and personnel training is a dependent barrier, they have an influence on the processing time of returned products.

Since the company's knowledge about the total cost of return process is limited, the unknown total cost of return process is one of the dependent barriers which limits the company from measuring their reverse logistics performance by establishing performance metrics. Therefore, information sharing between the company and its downstream partners is essential in order to acquire knowledge about the total cost of return process, and develop performance metrics and cost-related KPIs. This is similar to the research findings of Hazen, Overstreet, Hall, Huscroft, and Hanna (2015, p. 7), as they suggest that setting up of clear, specific goals for reverse logistics, combined with information system capabilities (i.e., the ability to receive information within and between organizations) are antecedents to establishing reverse logistics performance metrics.

Opportunistic behavior and restrictive return policy fall in the same sixth level with lack of information sharing in the ISM model. In addition, these three barriers have the same dependence and driving power on the drive-dependence diagram, and they influence each other. Therefore, addressing the three barriers together will be beneficial for the company. The lack of information sharing between the company's partners results in asymmetric information. Togar M Simatupang and Sridharan (2001, p. 4) explain that asymmetric information results from a situation where different supply chain partners have different information regarding resources, cost data, chain operations, performance status, and market condition. Therefore, information asymmetry results in a situation where one partner has private information that other partners in the chain do not possess to make a good decision.

As explained by Togar M. Simatupang and Sridharan (2002, p. 17), supply chain members do not prefer to share private information with each other due to the economic value of that information. Consequently, the supply chain suffers from opportunistic behavior as the existence of asymmetric information allows supply chain partners to hide their private information and increase their willingness to reduce the effort levels by offering incomplete or distorted information. Such behavior was defined by Oliver E. Williamson (1985, p. 47) as opportunism—"self-interest seeking with guile", which includes apparent behaviors such as lying, cheating, and stealing. It also refers to the offering of incomplete and distorted information for the purpose to mislead, confuse, or blind for one's own benefit.

The above clarification for the relationship between information sharing and opportunistic behavior helps to understand the interaction between those two barriers in the ISM model. Therefore, the company's supply chain is vulnerable to opportunism in a situation where each of the supply chain partners tries to maximize individual benefits and avoid reverse logistics costs. This is clearly illustrated in the ISM model as the differences in supply chain partners' objectives leads to the lack of information sharing between partners, thereby paving the way for opportunistic behavior. As a result, the company is adopting a restrictive return policy, known as "zero returns," for small distributors in order to safeguard itself from such opportunistic behavior, as well as a partial return policy (2 percent) of the purchased amount with full credit for the rest of distributors.

Finally, the dependent barriers are heavily influenced by the previously discussed driving barriers, and as the ISM model depicts the influence between barriers and does not provide a road map, the model remains useful even in case where a driving barrier cannot be totally alleviated or is difficult to overcome.

CONCLUSION AND PRACTICAL IMPLICATIONS

This research aimed to investigate the driving forces behind Pharco's implementation of reverse logistics and the reasons for product returns from its downstream partners. It also attempted to understand the interrelation between the different reverse logistics barriers facing Pharco in implementing its reverse logistics practices. In this regard, the research sought to find answers to a set of research questions, of which the first was "Why Pharco implements reverse logistics practices?"

The research revealed that the application of reverse logistics at Pharco is mainly regulatory-driven. However, the interviews with the company management showed a lack of full compliance to the imposed regulations, as around 90 percent of the total pharmaceutical waste is destructed in a non-approved disposal site by MOH.

From the economic point of view, the economic driver is practically unattainable due to the complex nature of pharmaceutical products and the difficulty in extracting direct economic value from returns. The main reasons for returns from Pharco's downstream partners are product expiration, followed by damaged packaging during transportation or storage. Product recalls due to quality issues is a less frequent reason than the previously stated reasons, but when it occurs it is important that the company, its distributors, and also CAPA should respond immediately to execute the recall.

The second research question "What are the reverse logistics practices implemented by Pharco?" was addressed by mapping the process of product return. Multiple parties are involved in the return process. The company's 12 authorized distributors are responsible for the collection activity from thousands points of sale—i.e., pharmacies, hospitals, and private clinics. Pharco is responsible for receiving and inspecting the returned products, as well as for selecting suitable reverse logistics activities in accordance with the returned products' conditions and expiration dates.

In cases where the returned product has not expired or the product package is not damaged, the company will either redistribute those products in the market or will re-label them as free medical samples—the choice depends on the product's remaining shelf-life. Also, in cases where the returned product has not expired but packaging is damaged, the company donates such returns through charitable organizations.

For recalled and expired returns, disposal by incineration through third-party disposal companies is the only suitable activity, and since the most common reason for returns is expired returns, the disposal by incineration is the dominant reverse logistics activity. The only possibility to capture economic value is by separating and reselling the expired or recalled products packaging materials before final disposal. However, such activity is not economically attractive for Pharco and is perceived to be time-consuming, rather than being considered as a source of income.

The last research question was "What are the barriers hindering Pharco in implementing reverse logistics?"

The methodological approach of ISM was applied to study the mutual influences across barriers listed by a preliminary case analysis, and to identify the "driving" barriers which may lead to other barriers, and "dependent" barriers influenced by the driving barriers. Thus, the systematic analysis using ISM approach contributed to a more realistic representation of the complex problem in a visualized and simplified manner and also has provided a deeper understanding of the situation than observing individual barriers in isolation.

A key finding of the analysis is that the "lack of regulation enforcement," "lack of public awareness regarding the importance of reverse logistics," and "lack of economic support from government" form the bottom levels of the ISM model. Thus, those barriers imply high driving power and should be treated as the root cause of the remaining barriers. It was also observed that the "long processing cycle time of returned products," "lack of dedicated workers and facilities for handling returns," and "lack of worker support and personnel training" form the top levels of the model. Those barriers imply high dependence and represent the undesirable outcome of the driving barriers.

Finally, for some of the model barriers, potential actions to alleviate their intensities were discussed. For example, creating effective public awareness campaigns by interest groups and voluntary organizations in Egypt, might raise the public awareness regarding the importance of reverse logistics and yield other benefits, while the imposition of sufficiently deterrent and stringent sanctions by regulatory bodies in Egypt might take steps toward better compliance to reverse logistics regulations. Also, sharing risks and costs of returns equitably between Pharco and its downstream partners might help in aligning their objectives in reverse logistics. Finally, by aligning goals and incentives between Pharco and its downstream partners as well as using explicit and formalized return policy and effective monitoring can facilitate the detection of opportunistic behavior between partners and might help to control opportunism in the Pharco supply chain.

LIMITATIONS AND FUTURE RESEARCH

This research has been limited by the absence of Pharco's key downstream partners' perspectives. Their incorporation would have added more value to the research to understand the problem from a more holistic view. This research used only the ISM approach. However, since the relation among the identified reverse logistics barriers depends on the respondent's knowledge and familiarity with the supply chain of Pharco Pharmaceuticals, its reverse logistics operations, and the pharmaceutical industry in Egypt, there might be a subjective bias affecting the final model due to their judgment. In this regard, the applied ISM methodology should be evaluated in connection with its utility in the research context.

Also, even though the application of ISM approach provides a much better visualization of the complex problem, with directed linkages between the identified reverse logistics barriers, the ISM output is not statistically valid.

This research was carried out within the context of a single case. Hence, further research could extend the investigation to a wider range of companies in the Egyptian pharmaceutical industry. Also, it would be interesting to incorporate the other downstream parties involved in application of reverse logistics in the pharmaceutical industry.

REFERENCES

Attri, R., Dev, N., & Sharma, V. (2013). Interpretive structural modelling (ISM) approach: An overview. *Research Journal of Management Sciences*, *2*(2), 1171.

Blumberg, D. F. (1999). Strategic examination of reverse logistics & repair service requirements, needs, market size, and opportunities. *Journal of Business Logistics*, *20*(2), 141–159.

Blumberg, D. F. (2004). *Introduction to management of reverse logistics and closed loop supply chain processes*. CRC Press.

BMI. (2014). *Egypt Pharmaceuticals & Healthcare Report Q1*. Business Monitor International.

Bonev, M. (2012). *Managing reverse logistics using system dynamics: A generic end-to-end approach*. Diplomica Verlag.

Carter, C. R., & Ellram, L. M. (1998). Reverse logistics: A review of the literature and framework for future investigation. *Journal of Business Logistics*, *19*(1), 85–102.

Chouinard, M., D'Amours, S., & Aït-Kadi, D. (2005). Integration of reverse logistics activities within a supply chain information system. *Computers in Industry*, *56*(1), 105–124. doi:10.1016/j.compind.2004.07.005

Cojocariu, C. R. (2013). The Reverse Gear of Logistics. *Review of International Comparative Management*, *14*(1), 153–164.

Dale, S. R., Douglas, M. L., Keely, L. C., & Sebastián, J. G.-D. (2002). The Returns Management Process. *International Journal of Logistics Management*, *13*(2), 1–18. doi:10.1108/09574090210806397

de Brito, M. P., & Dekker, R. (2002). *Reverse Logistics - a framework*. Erasmus University Rotterdam Econometric Institute Report EI 2002-38.

de Brito, M. P., & Dekker, R. (2003). *A Framework for Reverse Logistics*. Rotterdam School of Management: Erasmus Research Institute of Management (ERIM).

de Campos, E. A. R., Tavana, M., ten Caten, C. S., Bouzon, M., & de Paula, I. C. (2021a). A grey-DEMATEL approach for analyzing factors critical to the implementation of reverse logistics in the pharmaceutical care process. *Environmental Science and Pollution Research International*, *28*, 14156–14176. doi:10.100711356-020-11138-8 PMID:33206293

de Campos, E. A. R., ten Caten, C. S., & de Paula, I. C. (2021b). End-of-use and end-of-life medicines—Insights from pharmaceutical care process into waste medicines management. *Environmental Science and Pollution Research International*. Advance online publication. doi:10.100711356-021-14661-4 PMID:34105077

Dowlatshahi, S. (2000). Developing a theory of reverse logistics. *Interfaces*, *30*(3), 143.

Eric, P. J., Thomas, L. P., & Lauren, S. (2010). Reverse logistics capabilities: Antecedents and cost savings. *International Journal of Physical Distribution & Logistics Management*, *40*(3), 228–246. doi:10.1108/09600031011035100

Farris, D. R., & Sage, A. P. (1975). On the use of interpretive structural modeling for worth assessment. *Computers & Electrical Engineering*, *2*(2–3), 149–174. doi:10.1016/0045-7906(75)90004-X

General Directorate of Pharmaceutical Inspection. (2010). *breaches of pharmaceutical regulation report Code (No. FM-GID-01 Serial: 00001/ 2009)*. Egypt: Ministry of Health. Retrieved from http://www.mohp.gov.eg/pharmacy/DocLib2/Final%20Inspection%20Report%2030-11-2010.pdf

Grabara, J., Man, M., & Kolcun, M. (2014). The benefits of reverse logistics. *International Letters of Social and Humanistic Sciences*, (15), 138–147.

Gupta, S. M. (Ed.). (2013). *Reverse Supply Chains Issues and Analysis*. Taylor & Francis Group.

Hazen, B. T., Overstreet, R. E., Hall, D. J., Huscroft, J. R., & Hanna, J. B. (2015). Antecedents to and outcomes of reverse logistics metrics. *Industrial Marketing Management*, (0). Advance online publication. doi:10.1016/j.indmarman.2015.01.017

Heyes, A. (2000). Implementing Environmental Regulation: Enforcement and Compliance. *Journal of Regulatory Economics*, *17*(2), 107.

Ismail, E., Meltem Nurtanis, V., Funda Sivrikaya, S., Büyüközkan, G., Aras, N., Çakar, N. D., & Aybek, K. (2010). Exploring reverse supply chain management practices in Turkey. *Supply Chain Management*, *15*(1), 43–54. doi:10.1108/13598541011018111

Kabir, M. I. (2013). Reverse Logistics in Pharmaceutical Industry. *International Journal of Supply Chain Management*, *2*(1).

Kwateng, K. O., Debrah, B., Parker, D. V., Owusu, R. N., & Prempeh, H. (2014). Reverse logistics practices in pharmaceutical manufacturing industry: Experiences from Ghana. *Global Journal of Business Research*, *8*(5), 17–26.

Laganà, I. R., Sharifi, S., Khademi, M., Salimi, M., & Ferrara, M. (2021). Analysis of some incentives on two-echelon reverse supply chain with a strategic consumer: The case of unwanted medications in households. *Journal of Multi-Criteria Decision Analysis*. Advance online publication. doi:10.1002/mcda.1736

Lambert, D. M., & Stock, J. R. (1982). *Strategic physical distribution management*. Irwin.

Lau, K. H., & Wang, Y. (2009). Reverse logistics in the electronic industry of China: A case study. *Supply Chain Management*, *14*(6), 447–465. doi:10.1108/13598540910995228

Lendaris, G. G. (1980). Structural modeling a tutorial guide. *Systems, Man and Cybernetics, IEEE Transactions on*, *10*(12), 807–840.

Luís, R. O., Rossoni, H. A. V., & Duarte, N. F. (2021). Systematic review on reverse logistics of drug residues | Revisão Sistemática De Literatura Sobre A Logística Reversa De Resíduos De Medicamentos. *Fronteiras*, *10*, 339–358. doi:10.21664/2238-8869.2021v10i1.p339-358

Luthra, S., Kumar, V., Kumar, S., & Haleem, A. (2011). Barriers to implement green supply chain management in automobile industry using interpretive structural modeling technique-An Indian perspective. *Journal of Industrial Engineering and Management*, *4*(2).

Malone, D. W. (1975). An introduction to the application of interpretive structural modeling. *Proceedings of the IEEE, 63*(3), 397–404.

Manzolillo, B. (2021). Reverse logistics: A solution for medicines disposition at home | Logística inversa: Una solución a la disposición de medicamentos en el hogar. *Gaceta Medica de Caracas, 129*, 13–21. doi:10.47307/GMC.2021.129.1.3

Nikolaou, I. E., Evangelinos, K. I., & Allan, S. (2013). A reverse logistics social responsibility evaluation framework based on the triple bottom line approach. *Journal of Cleaner Production, 56*(0), 173–184. doi:10.1016/j.jclepro.2011.12.009

Partida, B. (2011). Leaders Show Power of Reverse Logistics. *Supply Chain Management Review, 15*(6), 62–64.

Pharco Corporation. (2014). *About Pharco.* Retrieved from https://www.pharco.org/about.aspx

Pharco Pharmaceuticals. (2014). *Pharco Pharmaceuticals.* Retrieved from http://www.pharco.org/Category.aspx?id=711

Ramadan, A. (2014). *Egypt's Deadly Medicines* [Press release]. Retrieved from http://en.arij.net/report/egypts-deadly-medicines/

RASSD. (2015). *The Problem of Pharmaceutical returns and its effect on patients* [Press release]. Retrieved from https://rassd.com/7-127514.htm

Ravi, V., & Shankar, R. (2005). Analysis of interactions among the barriers of reverse logistics. *Technological Forecasting and Social Change, 72*(8), 1011–1029. doi:10.1016/j.techfore.2004.07.002

Ravi, V., Shankar, R., & Tiwari, M. K. (2005). Productivity improvement of a computer hardware supply chain. *International Journal of Productivity and Performance Management, 54*(3–4), 239–255.

Ribeiro, D. P., De Oliveira, U. R., Da Silva César, A., & Aprigliano Fernandes, V. (2021). Evaluation of medicine reverse logistics practices in hospitals. *Sustain., 13*. Advance online publication. doi:10.3390u13063496

Richey, R. G., Chen, H., Genchev, S. E., & Daugherty, P. J. (2005). Developing effective reverse logistics programs. *Industrial Marketing Management, 34*(8), 830–840. doi:10.1016/j.indmarman.2005.01.003

Rogers, D. S., & Tibben-Lembke, R. (2001). An examination of reverse logistics practices. *Journal of Business Logistics, 22*(2), 129–148.

Rogers & Tibben-Lembke. (1998). Going Backwards: Reverse Logistics Trends and Practices. University of Nevada, Reno: Reverse Logistics Executive Council.

Ronald, S. T.-L., & Dale, S. R. (2002). Differences between forward and reverse logistics in a retail environment. *Supply Chain Management, 7*(5), 271–282. doi:10.1108/13598540210447719

Samir, K. S., & Rajiv, K. S. (2006). Managing product returns for reverse logistics. *International Journal of Physical Distribution & Logistics Management, 36*(7), 524–546. doi:10.1108/09600030610684962

Seif, E., Tharwat, B., Naser, A., & Madiha, A. (2010) *The Problem of Pharmaceutical Returns: The Gate for Fake Drugs/Interviewer: M. Reem*. Our country, ON-TV, Egypt.

Shahabadkar, P. (2012). Deployment of Interpretive Structural Modelling Methodology in Supply Chain Management–An overview. *International Journal of Industrial Engineering & Production Research, 23*(3), 195–205.

Shaurabh, S., Saurabh, B., & Moti, K. (2013). Strategic Framework for Reverse Logistics in Pharmaceutical Industry. *Asian Research Journal of Business Management, 1*(1).

Simatupang, T. M., & Sridharan, R. (2002). The collaborative supply chain. *International Journal of Logistics Management, 13*(1), 15–30.

Tibben-Lembke, R. S. (2002). Life after death: Reverse logistics and the product life cycle. *International Journal of Physical Distribution & Logistics Management, 32*(3–4), 223–244.

van Hoek, R. I. (1999). From reversed logistics to green supply chains. *Supply Chain Management, 4*(3), 129.

Warfield, J. N. (1974). Developing Interconnection Matrices in Structural Modeling. *Systems, Man and Cybernetics, IEEE Transactions on, SMC-4*(1), 81–87. doi: . doi:10.1109/TSMC.1974.5408524

Warfield, J. N., & Cárdenas, A. R. (1994). *A handbook of interactive management* (2nd ed.). Iowa State University Press Ames.

APPENDIX 1

Table 8. A1 - iterative procedures for ISM level partitions

Barriers	Reachability set	Antecedent set	Intersection set	Level
1	1,2,3,4,5,7,8,9,10,15,16,17	1,2,6,7,11,12,13	1,2,7	
2	1,2,3,4,5,7,8,9,10,15,16,17	1,2,6,7,11,12,13	1,2,7	
3	3,4,5,8,9,10,15,16,17	1,2,3,6,7,11,12,13	3	
4	4,9,16	1,2,3,4,6,7,8,10,11,12,13,14,15,17	4	
5	5,16	1,2,3,5,6,7,8,10,11,12,13,14,15	5	
6	1,2,3,4,5,6,7,8,9,10,15,16,17	6,11,12,13	6	
7	1,2,3,4,5,7,8,9,10,15,16,17	1,2,6,7,11,12,13	1,2,7	
8	4,5,8,9,10,15,16,17	1,2,3,6,7,8,10,11,12,13,14,15	8,10,15	
9	9,16	1,2,3,4,6,7,8,9,10,11,12,13,14,15,17	9	
10	4,5,8,9,10,15,16,17	1,2,3,6,7,8,10,11,12,13,14,15	8,10,15	
11	1,2,3,4,5,6,7,8,9,10,11,12,13,14,15,16,17	11,13	11,13	
12	1,2,3,4,5,6,7,8,9,10,12,14,15,16,17	11,12,13	12	
13	1,2,3,4,5,6,7,8,9,10,11,12,13,14,15,16,17	11,13	11,13	
14	4,5,8,9,10,14,15,16,17	11,12,13,14	14	
15	4,5,8,9,10,15,16,17	1,2,3,6,7,8,10,11,12,13,14,15	8,10,15	
16	16	1,2,3,4,5,6,7,8,9,10,11,12,13,14,15,16,17	16	Level 1
17	4,9,16,17	1,2,3,6,7,8,10,11,12,13,14,15,17	17	

Table 9.

Barriers	Reachability set	Antecedent set	Intersection set	Level
1	1,2,3,4,5,7,8,9,10,15,17	1,2,6,7,11,12,13	1,2,7	
2	1,2,3,4,5,7,8,9,10,15,17	1,2,6,7,11,12,13	1,2,7	
3	3,4,5,8,9,10,15,17	1,2,3,6,7,11,12,13	3	
4	4,9	1,2,3,4,6,7,8,10,11,12,13,14,15,17	4	
5	5	1,2,3,5,6,7,8,10,11,12,13,14,15	5	Level 2
6	1,2,3,4,5,6,7,8,9,10,15,17	6,11,12,13	6	
7	1,2,3,4,5,7,8,9,10,15,17	1,2,6,7,11,12,13	1,2,7	
8	4,5,8,9,10,15,17	1,2,3,6,7,8,10,11,12,13,14,15	8,10,15	
9	9	1,2,3,4,6,7,8,9,10,11,12,13,14,15,17	9	Level 2
10	4,5,8,9,10,15,17	1,2,3,6,7,8,10,11,12,13,14,15	8,10,15	
11	1,2,3,4,5,6,7,8,9,10,11,12,13,14,15,17	11,13	11,13	
12	1,2,3,4,5,6,7,8,9,10,12,14,15,17	11,12,13	12	
13	1,2,3,4,5,6,7,8,9,10,11,12,13,14,15,17	11,13	11,13	
14	4,5,8,9,10,14,15,17	11,12,13,14	14	
15	4,5,8,9,10,15,17	1,2,3,6,7,8,10,11,12,13,14,15	8,10,15	
17	4,9,17	1,2,3,6,7,8,10,11,12,13,14,15,17	17	

Table 10.

Barriers	Reachability set	Antecedent set	Intersection set	Level
1	1,2,3,4,7,8,10,15,17	1,2,6,7,11,12,13	1,2,7	
2	1,2,3,4,7,8,10,15,17	1,2,6,7,11,12,13	1,2,7	
3	3,4,8,10,15,17	1,2,3,6,7,11,12,13	3	
4	4	1,2,3,4,6,7,8,10,11,12,13,14,15,17	4	Level 3
6	1,2,3,4,6,7,8,10,15,17	6,11,12,13	6	
7	1,2,3,4,7,8,10,15,17	1,2,6,7,11,12,13	1,2,7	
8	4,8,10,15,17	1,2,3,6,7,8,10,11,12,13,14,15	8,10,15	
10	4,8,10,15,17	1,2,3,6,7,8,10,11,12,13,14,15	8,10,15	
11	1,2,3,4,6,7,8,10,11,12,13,14,15,17	11,13	11,13	
12	1,2,3,4,6,7,8,10,12,14,15,17	11,12,13	12	
13	1,2,3,4,6,7,8,10,11,12,13,14,15,17	11,13	11,13	
14	4,8,10,14,15,17	11,12,13,14	14	
15	4,8,10,15,17	1,2,3,6,7,8,10,11,12,13,14,15	8,10,15	
17	4,17	1,2,3,6,7,8,10,11,12,13,14,15,17	17	

Table 11.

Barriers	Reachability set	Antecedent set	Intersection set	Level
1	1,2,3,7,8,10,15,17	1,2,6,7,11,12,13	1,2,7	
2	1,2,3,7,8,10,15,17	1,2,6,7,11,12,13	1,2,7	
3	3,8,10,15,17	1,2,3,6,7,11,12,13	3	
6	1,2,3,6,7,8,10,15,17	6,11,12,13	6	
7	1,2,3,7,8,10,15,17	1,2,6,7,11,12,13	1,2,7	
8	8,10,15,17	1,2,3,6,7,8,10,11,12,13,14,15	8,10,15	
10	8,10,15,17	1,2,3,6,7,8,10,11,12,13,14,15	8,10,15	
11	1,2,3,6,7,8,10,11,12,13,14,15,17	11,13	11,13	
12	1,2,3,6,7,8,10,12,14,15,17	11,12,13	12	
13	1,2,3,6,7,8,10,11,12,13,14,15,17	11,13	11,13	
14	8,10,14,15,17	11,12,13,14	14	
15	8,10,15,17	1,2,3,6,7,8,10,11,12,13,14,15	8,10,15	
17	17	1,2,3,6,7,8,10,11,12,13,14,15,17	17	Level 4

Table 12.

Barriers	Reachability set	Antecedent set	Intersection set	Level
1	1,2,3,7,8,10,15	1,2,6,7,11,12,13	1,2,7	
2	1,2,3,7,8,10,15	1,2,6,7,11,12,13	1,2,7	
3	3,8,10,15	1,2,3,6,7,11,12,13	3	
6	1,2,3,6,7,8,10,15	6,11,12,13	6	
7	1,2,3,7,8,10,15	1,2,6,7,11,12,13	1,2,7	
8	8,10,15	1,2,3,6,7,8,10,11,12,13,14,15	8,10,15	Level 5
10	8,10,15	1,2,3,6,7,8,10,11,12,13,14,15	8,10,15	Level 5
11	1,2,3,6,7,8,10,11,12,13,14,15	11,13	11,13	
12	1,2,3,6,7,8,10,12,14,15	11,12,13	12	
13	1,2,3,6,7,8,10,11,12,13,14,15	11,13	11,13	
14	8,10,14,15	11,12,13,14	14	
15	8,10,15	1,2,3,6,7,8,10,11,12,13,14,15	8,10,15	Level 5

Table 13.

Barriers	Reachability set	Antecedent set	Intersection set	Level
1	1,2,3,7	1,2,6,7,11,12,13	1,2,7	
2	1,2,3,7	1,2,6,7,11,12,13	1,2,7	
3	3	1,2,3,6,7,11,12,13	3	Level 6
6	1,2,3,6,7	6,11,12,13	6	
7	1,2,3,7	1,2,6,7,11,12,13	1,2,7	
11	1,2,3,6,7,11,12,13,14	11,13	11,13	
12	1,2,3,6,7,12,14	11,12,13	12	
13	1,2,3,6,7,11,12,13,14	11,13	11,13	
14	14	11,12,13,14	14	Level 6

Table 14.

Barriers	Reachability set	Antecedent set	Intersection set	Level
1	1,2,7	1,2,6,7,11,12,13	1,2,7	Level 7
2	1,2,7	1,2,6,7,11,12,13	1,2,7	Level 7
6	1,2,6,7	6,11,12,13	6	
7	1,2,7	1,2,6,7,11,12,13	1,2,7	Level 7
11	1,2,6,7,11,12,13	11,13	11,13	
12	1,2,6,7,12	11,12,13	12	
13	1,2,6,7,11,12,13	11,13	11,13	

Table 15.

Barriers	Reachability set	Antecedent set	Intersection set	Level
6	6	6,11,12,13	6	Level 8
11	6,11,12,13	11,13	11,13	
12	6,12	11,12,13	12	
13	6,11,12,13	11,13	11,13	

Table 16.

Barriers	Reachability set	Antecedent set	Intersection set	Level
11	11,12,13	11,13	11,13	
12	12	11,12,13	12	Level 9
13	11,12,13	11,13	11,13	

Table 17.

Barriers	Reachability set	Antecedent set	Intersection set	Level
11	11,13	11,13	11,13	Level 10
13	11,13	11,13	11,13	Level 10

APPENDIX 2: DIRECT INFLUENCE GRAPH AMONG THE BARRIERS AFFECTING PHARCO'S REVERSE LOGISTICS APPLICATION

Figure 9.

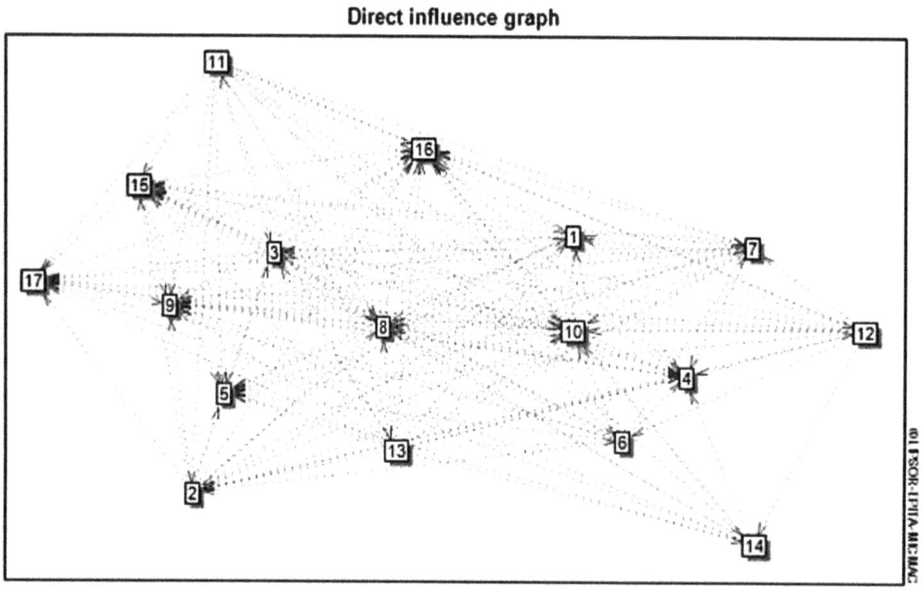

Chapter 9
Patient-Telemonitoring After Revascularization Procedures in the Lower Extremities

Roman Gumzej
https://orcid.org/0000-0002-2646-217X
University of Maribor, Slovenia

Lidija Fošnarič
University of Maribor, Slovenia

ABSTRACT

Multidisciplinary cooperation of participating healthcare professionals, use of common standards in diagnostics, and clinical pathways in the treatment of vascular patients should provide for a higher-quality clinical practice. Using telemedicine, a more efficient way of obtaining specialist treatment is achievable. However, its introduction may raise safety and security issues, which originate from its enabling information technology. In this chapter, a model of patient-telemonitoring after revascularization procedures in the lower extremities is presented. A protocol for proper authentication and authorization to access medical equipment and patient medical records has been introduced. The associated clinical study has shown that most post-operative follow-up examinations can successfully be performed by trained nurses. Hence, improvements to healthcare logistics, mainly due to shortening waiting times for specialist treatment and the reduction of follow-up examinations on the secondary healthcare level, can be achieved using telemedicine.

INTRODUCTION

The worldwide prevalence of lower extremity peripheral artery disease (PAD) is between 3 to 12 percent. In 2010, 202 million people around the world were living with PAD (Fowkes et al., 2013). Due to its epidemic proportions, management of PAD patients represents one of the most challenging problems of contemporary angiology. Since timely diagnostics and strict follow-up examinations play a key role

DOI: 10.4018/978-1-7998-8709-6.ch009

in proper healing, the introduction of telemedicine may be a keystone to a better and more accessible health service for PAD patients.

The ageing of the population, increase of chronic diseases, increasing people's demands for new, more complex diagnostic and therapeutic methods, and lack of health providers lead the way towards the introduction of new health services based on new process models and advanced information and telecommunications solutions. E-health services are promising a better health service for the future, being more effective than existing, established healthcare models.

In current medical practice, patients usually get an appointment at the angiology clinic upon recommendation from their general physician. After waiting in queue for their first interview with the angiologist, they obtain their first diagnosis. Depending on the severity of their medical condition, they are then given some medication or assigned an approximate period for their admission at the angiology clinic. When they are admitted, they are inspected again, and their status is checked. If they need an operation, a bed must be assigned to them, and a team assembled to perform the surgical procedure. After the operation, they are re-examined to determine their further therapy. Usually, they leave the clinic after a few days with an appointment for a follow-up examination at the clinic. The timespan for this whole process varies and may be anything from a couple of weeks to a couple of months. It depends heavily on the capacity of the angiology clinic and the availability of their resident specialists. The documentation on the patient and his/her handling are currently stored in patient's as well as hospital's medical records but are transferred mainly in printed form. Hence, the documentation tends to pile up during the process.

By applying the telemedical approach, an efficient way of equally personalized, but faster multidisciplinary specialist treatment can be introduced into clinical practice. On the other hand, its introduction raises data security issues. Data in electronic form are easy to access, track and archive, and they also travel very fast – properties facilitating the abuse of data (Harrington et al., 2011). While ensuring patient safety is primarily an organizational concern, in e-health and telemedicine, one should also consider information security and make use of the mechanisms provided by the enabling (information) technology. In telemedicine, proper information security management should provide for confidentiality, integrity, and availability of electronic medical records (Harrington et al., 2011). The provision for security should be an integral part of e-health and telemedicine services since the healthcare professionals involved are morally, ethically, and legally responsible for their patients' medical records.

Previous telemedical applications in angiology and vascular surgery featured various partial solutions (e.g., one-/two-tire pre-/post-operative medical consultation via e-mail/teleconference (Schmidt et al. 2014; Polombo et al., 2009), three-tire electronic referral, assessment by a practice nurse, and teleconferencing (Hands et al., 2006). In this chapter, a complete telediagnostic solution for telemonitoring vascular patients after applying revascularization procedures in the lower extremities is presented and empirically evaluated.

METHOD

Electronic Oscillography

The telemonitoring platform uses electronic oscillography to measure fluctuations in blood circulation volume. They can be recorded by infrasonic condenser microphones or electronic receptors. The resulting oscillographic curves are evaluated according to the variations in oscillations on symmetrical parts of the limbs. Important diagnostic evaluation criteria are the periods, amplitudes, and shapes of oscillations (Grochenig, 2012). If the difference in amplitudes of the oscillations is greater than 30%, this is an indication of hemodynamically significant stenosis of the arteries. In combination with visual inspections of the wounds, these criteria are used at follow-up inspections after vascular interventions.

Arterial pressure at the ankle is normally equal to or greater than the brachial pressure. An Ankle Brachial Index (ABI) from 0.91 to 1.3 is considered normal. An ABI of 0.9 or less is an indication of PAD. A lower ABI value suggests a more advanced state of PAD. ABI values below 0.4 indicate critical ischemia, where the absolute value of systolic ankle pressure is lower than 40-50 mmHg. However, a clinical evaluation is necessary to confirm critical ischemia (Norgen et al. 2007; Tendera et al., 2011). If the ABI value is higher than 1.3 (or, according to some data, 1.4), the arteries are considered incompressible (Creager et al., 2012).

Telediagnostics

The telediagnostic platform comprises three categories of telemedicine:

1. Wireless acquisition of ABI measurements from a body sensor network.
2. Transfer, storage and processing of patients' diagnostic data and medical records.
3. Interactive telemedicine – real-time video teleconsultation.

Body Sensor Network

The concept of a wireless juxta-corporal sensor-net on a human body (Body Sensor Network, BSN (Miao et al., 2012)) represents the basis of the telemonitoring platform (Figure 1).

Figure 1. Vascular patients' telemonitoring

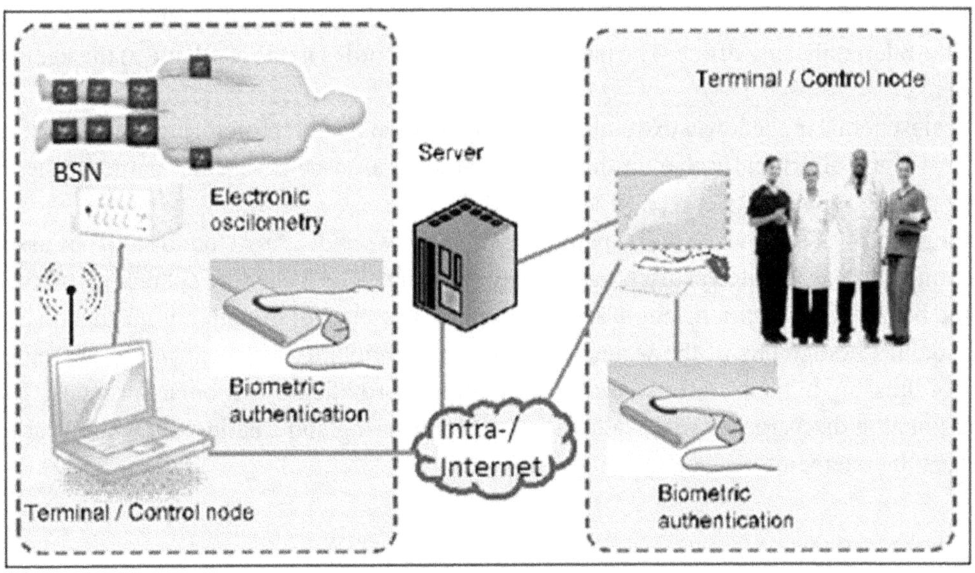

The network consists of diagnostic nodes that gather data on the physical state of patients, being transferred and stored in their medical records on a medical server, and of control nodes that access those data, representing data terminals owned by medical doctors, hospitals' administrative personnel, insurance company clerks etc.

After authentication with the diagnostic device, the operator performs the diagnostic procedure on a patient. The results of performing electronic oscillometry on a patient are acquired by a terminal/ control node attended by the operator. After the diagnostic procedure is complete, the diagnostic data are transferred to the hospital's medical server, where they are stored to be examined by physicians and hospital staff. The access to patient data is restricted to authorized persons, who are granted access by biometric authentication.

By electronic transmission of the diagnostic procedure's results from the primary to the secondary healthcare level, follow-up monitoring after medical interventions, traditionally being carried out at hospitals, can be performed at the primary healthcare level by a trained nurse. Specialist consultations with the attending physician (angiologist), based on diagnostic data inspection, are possible via videoconferencing. Hospital visits can be scheduled immediately in case during the examination they would prove necessary.

Patients with vascular diseases often have associated diseases (diabetes, hypertension, hyperlipidemia), which affect their therapy after applying revascularization procedures in the lower extremities. Hence, in the telemonitoring office, specialist consultations with various medical specialists should be enabled via videoconferencing.

Telemonitoring

The telemonitoring model (Figure 2) features three main decision nodes that facilitate telemedical follow-up examinations:

1. $\downarrow$ABI$\geq$0.20: On the day of discharge from the hospital, a baseline ABI measurement is performed using the Angio Experience Pro8 device. The patient is scheduled for a follow-up appointment with the telemonitoring office. The patient's medical record is made available to the telemonitoring office.
2. Critical ischemia of the lower extremities: The operator at the telemonitoring office must recognize the five signs of critical ischemia that would indicate an urgent vascular surgery: the extremity being painful, pale, pulseless, paraesthetic and paralytic.
3. Healing progression of acute post-operative or chronic wounds: Any wounds must be assessed and electronically documented at discharge from the hospital. The following characteristics of a wound should be recorded: location, length and depth in cm, presence of granular tissue, necrosis, exudate, and odour. Photographs of the wounds should also be included. Clear instructions regarding the type of dressing to be used for wound care should be provided by vascular surgeons. The wound assessment at discharge serves as a baseline for monitoring and treating the wounds at follow-up visits at the telemonitoring office.

Figure 2. Model of telemonitoring of patients after applying revascularization procedures in the lower extremities

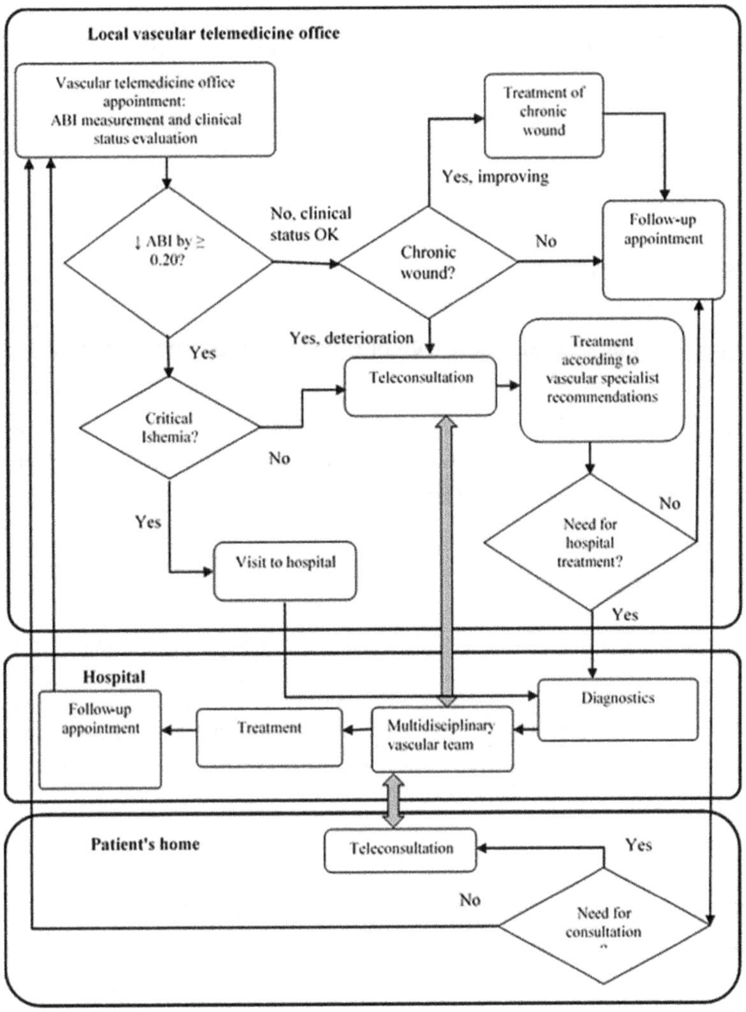

Multifactor Security

The confidentiality of patients' medical records, especially sensitive diagnostic data, produced during medical examinations and treatments, are considered critical. They are accessed by different persons during medical treatments and are managed by persons not involved in medical treatment. On the one hand, the introduction of electronic medical records has benefits for the patients, their doctors and medical insurance companies due to their accessibility. On the other hand, unauthorized accesses to diagnostic reports, correspondence, prescriptions, medical history, and insurance data are possible since these data are often transferred without encryption between patients, doctors, hospital administration and insurance companies.

To provide for security and confidentiality of medical data, especially the following precautions are considered crucial:

- Medical data should always be transferred through secure channels.
- The access to medical data should be protected by appropriate authentication mechanisms (passwords, biometrics etc.).
- A patient's medical data should be verifiable by the patient to detect and correct possible inconsistent data on diagnoses, treatments or prescribed medications and prevent negative consequences for the patient (e.g., ill-treatment and/or ill-medication, changes in medical insurance rate, professional disability etc.)
- Data of patients and medical personnel should be appropriately protected from being misused.

Biometric Authentication

A data security solution must include standardized policies, technologies, and administrative practices to assure data security. According to (Luxton et al., 2012), a successful move towards a standardized data security methodology requires partnerships among consumers, private industry, advocacy groups and governments. The American Telemedicine Association has provided high-level guidance on mHealth security (US DHHS, 2017; Yellowlees et al. 2010). In Table 1 the known authentication methods are listed.

Table 1. Authentication methods

Authentication Category	Methods
Non-biometric (memorized or possessed)	password, personal identification number, pass phrase, mobile device identification number, tokens (key fob), dongle, smart card, radiofrequency identification
Biometric (scanning patterns of the…)	face, fingerprint, hand, iris scan, retina scan, voice print, palm

(USDOHH, 2017)

The biometric approach to authentication is appealing because of its convenience and possibility to provide security with non-repudiation. Often it is not used as specific hardware such as biometric scanners and complex software for feature extraction and biometric template matching are required (Chien, 2011; Yang&Xie, 2012). However, since the required equipment is already present in medical environments and partly being used for diagnostic purposes, the approach can be employed to secure hospital information systems, patients' medical records, and access to sensitive electronic diagnostic devices. Physicians, other medical staff, and administrative personnel are easy and comfortable to use because they always carry their biometric characteristics with them – they cannot lose them, and abuse is much harder to perform.

Security Protocols

To enable secure data interchange among diagnostic/control nodes on one and medical servers on the other side, their mutual authentication and authorization is necessary. The proposed security protocol (Figure 3) reads as follows:

1. Before a node can access any data on the medical server, it needs to be authenticated. In the course of this, it announces its request by sending its entity-identifier to the server.
2. Upon receipt of the authentication request, its plausibility is checked with the server's records, and the connection is refused in case they are not consistent.
3. In case the authentication of the node was successful, the server generates an authorization request and sends it to the requesting node.
4. In response to the authorization request, the node replies with the operator's authorization data. The server compares with the authorization data in its records and authorizes the node and operator access in case they match. Otherwise, it is assumed that the node is being manipulated, and the connection is refused.

Figure 3. Security protocol

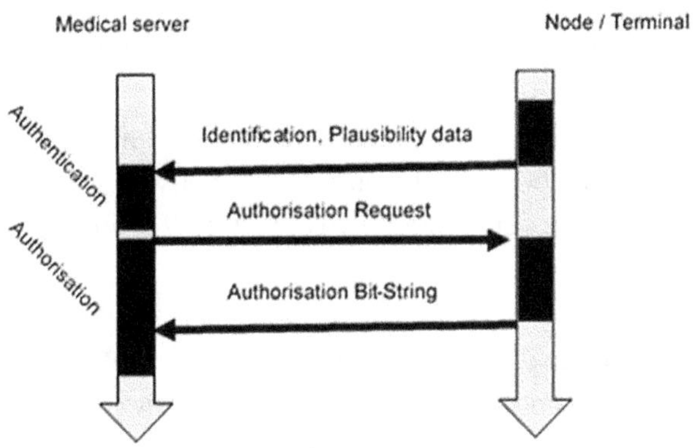

When deploying a node, its producer or despondent seals the unit in a way, which prevents it from being tampered with. In the unit's permanent memory, its identification, as well as operators' digital certificates are stored. Operators' biometric data are stored at the node for authentication and the server for authorization. SSL-encryption is used for secure message interchange among nodes and servers.

Only authenticated operators are allowed to use the node. They are granted access based on their biometric signature or passphrase input. Upon their positive identification the appropriate digital certificate is used to initiate the node's authentication with the server. The node's entity-identifier is formed of the device's identification and the operator's electronic signature.

On the other hand, authorisation is based on the operators' biometric signatures, stored with the server. After receiving appropriate input from the node, the server authorizes the node's access, if they match. Upon successful authentication and authorization, the patient's ID is securely communicated to the server in the form of his/her biometric signature or social security number. As a result of positive patient's identification, the database, containing the patient's medical records is opened for access.

In case the requesting node is a diagnostic node, in the sequel, the database is filled with diagnostic data until the diagnostic procedure is finished and its data stored in the patient's medical record. After that the communication channel is closed. If the communication is interrupted, the connection must be re-established and the data re-sent, following the same protocol.

In case the requesting node is a control node, the communication channel is built up in the same way. Typically, the attending physician or member of hospital administrative personnel uses the terminal to request some diagnostic data from the patient's medical record for evaluation, acknowledges the input of any results from their examination, and closes the connection. In case the communication channel is not closed by the terminal operator, the server needs to close the connection after a certain time interval automatically, to prevent an unattended terminal from being misused by an unauthorized party. For any subsequent requests, the connection needs to be re-established following the same protocol.

RESULTS

The telemonitoring platform was evaluated in a clinical study performed between February and June 2015. The study included 53 patients who either had conventional surgery on the arteries of the lower extremities or an endovascular procedure applied and have given their written consent to be included in the study. The results were analyzed from the perspective of clinical practice and the newly introduced telemedicine office.

34.0% of the patients in the study were women, and 66.0% were men. The highest percentage of patients (22.6%) were aged between 60 to 64.9 years, 18.9% between 65 to 69.9 years, 20.8% were between 55 to 59.9 years, and the same percentage between 70 to 74.9 years. 9.4% of patients were aged 75 years and over.

The detected risk factors for PAD were: 86.8% of the patients involved in the study had hypertension, 47.2% had diabetes mellitus and 90.6% had hyperlipidemia. With respect to smoking, patients were divided into three categories: smoker (24.5%), former smoker (47.2%) and non-smoker (28.3%).

32.1% of the patients had conventional surgery on the arterial system of the lower extremities, with an average claudication distance of 97.1 meters. 67.9% of the patients underwent an endovascular procedure with an average claudication distance of 127.5 meters.

The time intervals between the medical examination at discharge and the first follow-up appointment were determined by the specialists who discharged the patients from the hospital (Figure 4). Patients, who underwent an endovascular procedure and did not have ulcers, were scheduled for a follow-up 21 days after the procedure. Patients, who had conventional arterial surgery and had post-operative or chronic wounds, were scheduled for a follow-up within 10-20 days.

ANALYSIS

At their first follow-up (Figure 5), 64.7% of the patients who had conventional surgery were pain-free while walking, while 35.3% had an average claudication distance of 96.7 meters. 72.2% of the patients, who had undergone an endovascular procedure, had no pain while walking, and 27.8% had an average claudication distance of 269.0 meters. At first follow-up, 35.3% of the patients reported claudication in the treated leg, while 64.7% of the patients reported claudication in the untreated leg.

Figure 4. Time intervals of follow-up examinations

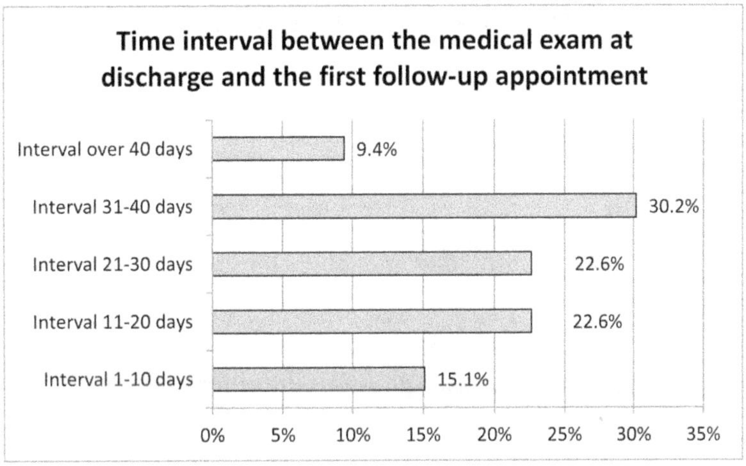

Figure 5. Claudication distance after treatment

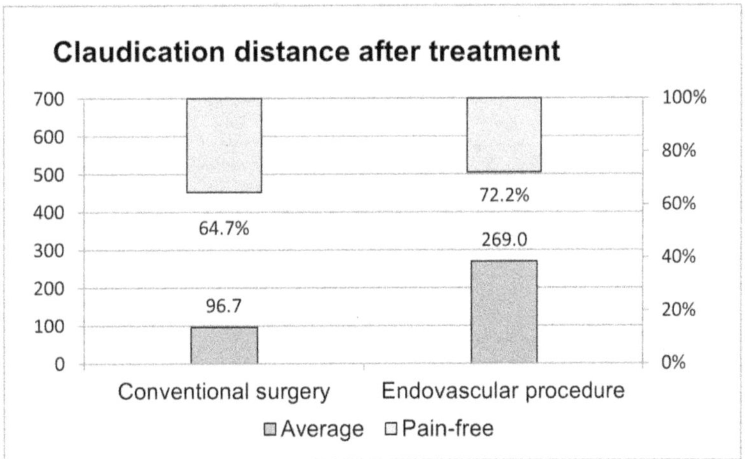

At discharge from the hospital, 60% of the patients were without wounds, 4% had a post-operative wound that healed per primam, and 6% of the patients had a chronic, poorly healing wound. At the first follow-up appointment (Figure 6), 28% of the post-operative wounds had healed, while 2% of the post-operative wounds were healing poorly. Chronic wounds showed improvement with 2% of the patients, while in 4% of the patients the chronic wounds did not progress in terms of healing.

Usually, ABI values are slightly lower with PAD patients than they are with healthy individuals. For this reason, ABI values measured at discharge were used as baseline. At first follow-up (Figure 7) ↓ABI≥0.20 was detected with 3.8% of the patients, ↓ABI between 0.19 and 0.05 was found with 11.3% of patients, ↓ABI≤0.04 to ↑ABI≥0.04 was found with 24.5% of the patients, ↑ABI≥0.05 to ↑ABI≤0.19 was detected with 45.3% of the patients and ↑ABI≥0.20 was detected with 15.1% of the patients. One of the patients, who participated in the study, had critical ischemia, having an ↓ABI value of 0.52 while the extremity was painful, pale, pulseless, paraesthetic and paralytic.

Figure 6. Wound tracking at first follow-up

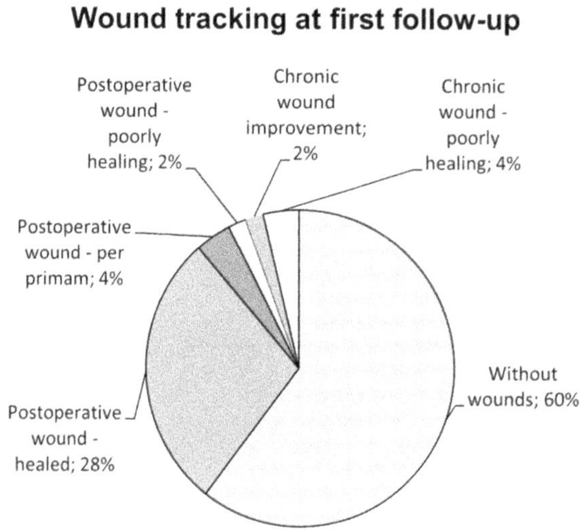

Figure 7. Changes in ABI values found in the treated lower extremity at the first follow-up

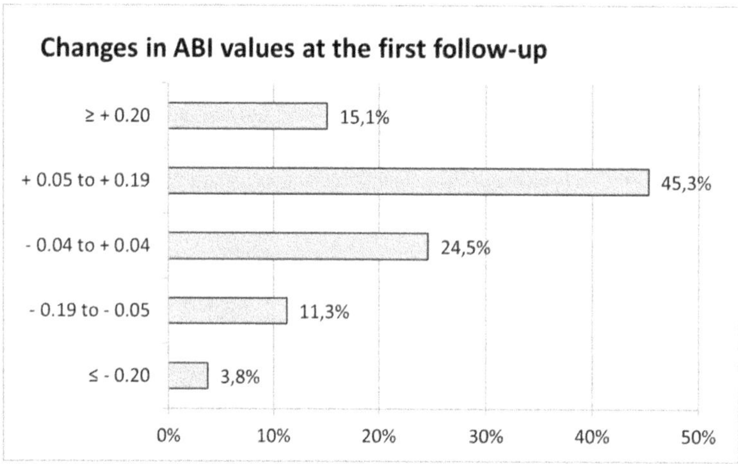

The telemonitoring office processed 53 patients during the 5 months duration of the study (February – June 2015). During this time, only one patient with the indication for critical ischemia needed additional specialist treatment at the hospital. In 18.9% of the cases, a teleconsultation with a vascular specialist was required to determine further diagnostic and therapeutic treatment of patients (Figure 8). The nurse in the telemonitoring office could properly handle other patients until their wounds have healed and they were pain-free while walking.

Figure 8. Need for real time video teleconsultation

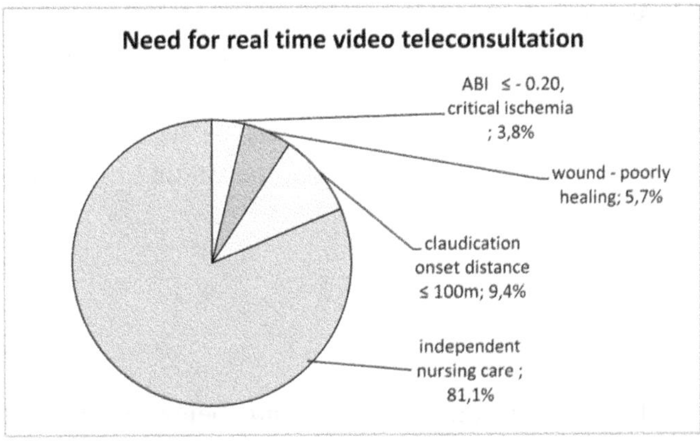

DISCUSSION

By this research, a telemedical approach to treatment and monitoring of vascular patients has been proposed. From best clinical practices a telediagnostic approach has been proposed and by using modern diagnostic equipment a telemedical platform has been designed. They were evaluated in the framework of a clinical study. The proposed approach foresees moving telemonitoring offices closer to the patients, which may be done in the near future. In the framework of the digitization processes in healthcare, implementing new patient-oriented telemedical practices would be easy, since the apparatus and methods, as proposed by the study, are ready to use. In the sequel the experiences from the study are elaborated.

The healing progression of chronic wounds can be effectively monitored by a nurse, provided that detailed records and photographs of the wounds are electronically accessible and clear instructions about appropriate wound dressings are provided by vascular surgeons. The study showed that it is important that both extremities, not only the treated one, are monitored at follow-ups. The decision nodes ↓ABI≥0.20 and Critical ischemia (Figure 2) allow the nurse to effectively identify those patients, who require further treatment by a vascular surgeon. The Angio Experience Pro 8 diagnostic application program should be extended to automatically notify the operator in case of an indication for intervention.

Sharing patients' medical records between a hospital on the secondary and a telemonitoring office on the primary healthcare level is essential for effective telemonitoring of vascular patients. The telemonitoring office should operate daily, following an established schedule with instant reporting of diagnostic results to the secondary level. Vascular surgeons should inspect the incoming diagnostic data at least once a day to efficiently monitor the healing process of the patients and determine their further treatment as well as the time intervals between follow-up examinations.

Mutual multifactor authentication has proven effective in protecting stored diagnostic data to be shared between the telemonitoring office and the hospital information system. Since biometric characteristics are unchangeable and non-detachable, it is impossible to lose and to misuse them. Hence, biometric authentication and authorization of nurses in the telemonitoring office on one side and vascular surgeons at their hospital terminals on the other are considered both secure and effective.

In terms of efficiency, the telemonitoring office can take over most of the follow-up workload. The vascular surgeons are disburdened to be able to focus on new patients' inspections and performing surgery. The doctors on call should be able to examine the diagnostic results from the telemonitoring office and offer teleconsultations during their shifts. Since scheduling operating procedures would only depend on the availability of operating rooms and medical teams as well as the number of free beds at the vascular department, it should be easier to set-up. Consequently, the waiting times for first examinations and procedures could be significantly reduced.

CONCLUSION

By the proposed approach, follow-up examinations, currently being carried out by vascular surgeons at the secondary healthcare level, can be transferred to the primary healthcare level, where trained nurses perform them. The main benefits of this approach are represented by the facts that the patients can be treated in their local environment. The waiting times for initial visits at the angiology department can be reduced. Consequently, more time can be allotted to patients undergoing vascular surgery procedures. By minimizing the number of follow-up appointments with vascular surgeons also the cost of their medical treatment can be reduced. In addition, by safe and secure telemedical and telediagnostic applications, the patients would gain trust in personalized telehealth systems and the notion of a better health service due to shorter waiting times as well as the reduced need for travel to obtain specialist treatment.

ACKNOWLEDGMENT

The Slovenian National Medical Ethics Committee approved the research project in February 2015.

REFERENCES

Chien, L. (2011). *A Survey of Biometrics Security Systems*. https://www.cs.wustl.edu/~jain/cse571-11/ftp/biomet/

Creager, M. A., Belkin, M., & Bluth, E. I. (2012). 2012 ACCF / AHA / ACR / SCAI / SIR / STS / SVM / SVN / SVS Key Data Elements and Definitions for Peripheral Atherosclerotic Vascular Disease: A Report of the American College of Cardiology Foundation / American Heart Association Task Force on Clinical Data Standards (Writing Committee to Develop Clinical Data Standards for Peripheral Atherosclerotic Vascular Disease). *Am Coll Cardiol*, *59*(3), 294–357.

Fowkes, F. G., Rudan, D., & Rudan, I. (2013). Comparison of global estimates of prevalence and risk factors for peripheral artery disease in 2000 and 2010: A systematic review and analysis. *Lancet*, *382*(9901), 1329–1340. PMID:23915883

Grochenig, E. (2012). *Elektronische Oszilographie. Nicht invasive Diagnostik angiologischer Krankheitsbilder* (2nd ed.). ABW.

Hands, L. J., Clarke, M., & Mahaffey, W. (2006). An e-health approach to managing vascular surgical patients. *Telemedicine Journal and e-Health*, *12*, 672–680. PMID:17250489

Harrington, L., Kennerly, D., & Johnson, C. (2011). Safety issues related to the electronic medical record (EMR): Synthesis of the literature from the last decade 2000-2009. *Journal of Healthcare Management*, *56*(1), 31–43. PMID:21323026

Luxton, D. D., Kayl, R. A., & Mishkind, M. C. (2012). mHealth Data Security: The Need for HIPAA-Compliant Standardization. *Telemedicine Journal and e-Health*, *18*(4), 284–288.

Miao, F., Bao, S., & Li, Y. (2012). *New trends and developments in biometrics: Physiological Signal Based Biometrics for Securing Body Sensor Network*. InTech.

Norgen, L., Hiatt, W. R., & Dormandy, J. A. (2007). Inter-society consensus for the management of peripheral arterial disease (TASC II). *International Angiology*, *26*, 81–157.

Palombo, D., Mugnai, D., & Mambrini, S. (2009). Role of interactive home telemedicine for early and protected discharge 1 day after carotid endarterectomy. *Annals of Vascular Surgery*, *23*, 76–80. PMID:18809294

Schmidt, A. P., Schmidt-Weitmann, S. H., Lachat, M. L., & Brockes, C. M. (2014). Teleconsultation in vascular surgery: A 13-year single centre experience. *Journal of Telemedicine and Telecare*, *20*, 24–28. PMID:24352901

Tendera, M., Aboyans, V., & Bartelink, M. L. (2011). ESC guidelines on the diagnosis and treatment of peripheral artery diseases. *European Heart Journal*, *32*, 2851–2906.

U.S. Department of Health and Human Services. (2017). *Health Information Privacy*. https://www.hhs.gov/hipaa/for-professionals/index.html

Yang, J., & Xie, S. J. (2012). *New Trends and Developments in Biometrics*. InTech.

Yellowlees, P., Shore, J., & Roberts, L. (2010). Practice guidelines for videoconferencing-based telemental health. *Telemedicine Journal and e-Health*, *16*(10), 1074–1089.

Chapter 10
Contemporary Perspective on Supply Chain Management Regarding Drug Sourcing Shortages

Neeta Baporikar
https://orcid.org/0000-0003-0676-9913
Namibia University of Science and Technology, Namibia & University of Pune, India

ABSTRACT

Safeguarding the supply of drugs and satisfying the needs of patients is a strategic priority of any healthcare system especially in these pandemic times. The pharmaceutical supply chain is subject to many pressures including non-availability and shortage of requisite drugs. A drug shortage is a deficiency in the supply of medicines or products that affects the ability of a patient to get the required treatment in due time. The roots of drug shortages are multifaceted, varied, and the issue can be due to supply or demand. However, the situation affects almost every stakeholder in the healthcare system, which is why collaboration is a must to deal with drug shortages. Hence, adopting an exploratory and single-case approach of the largest public hospital in the context of Namibia, the objective of this chapter is to provide a contemporary perspective of supply chain management re drug sourcing shortages, analyze the causes of drug shortages, recommend measures to minimize the crisis, and suggest strategies for enhanced efficiency in drug supply.

INTRODUCTION

Safeguarding the supply of drugs and satisfying the needs of patients when it comes to quantity, quality, cost, and accessibility is a strategic priority of any health care system priorities (Abdollahiasl, Nikfar, Kebriaeezadeh, Dinarvand, Abdollahi, Jaberidoost and Cheraghali, 2014). Pharmaceuticals represent a large portion of the costs in the healthcare industry due to the significant costs of these products and their storage and control requirements (Kelle, Woosley, and Schneider, 2012). The pharmaceutical sup-

DOI: 10.4018/978-1-7998-8709-6.ch010

ply chain is subject to many threats leading to deteriorating treasured resources and the disruption of available drugs resulting in the growing problem of shortages. Drug shortage is a condition in which the supply of all clinically alternative versions of controlled drugs is insufficient to meet the current or estimated demand at the user levels, which are patients (Gu, Wertheimer, Brown and Shaya, 2011). In addition, in 2010, 211 newly reported drug shortages tripled the amount in 2006, with almost 75% being sterile injectable (Gu, et al., 2011). In many healthcare practice settings, the shortage is prevalent and affects nearly all the classes, with the most critical ones are surgical and being affected the most (Ventola, 2011). Moreover, the quality use of medicines is a key factor in achieving positive health outcomes. Evidence indicates significant scope for improvement in the use of drugs for hospitalized patients (Dooley, Allen, Doecke, Galbraith, Taylor, Bright, and Carey, 2004). However, drug shortages and supply inefficiencies create obstacles for hospital management and also patients being serviced well. Further, these pandemic times shed light on a number of systemic and organizational challenges linked to supply chain management, including sustainability, supply chain skills and risk management, thus putting much of the taken-for-granted knowledge on supply chain management to the test (Baporikar, 2021; Bals, Schulze, Kelly, and Stek, 2019). Aspects such as sourcing, resilience, public procurement, and sustainable development have emerged as consequential topics for supply chain management (Pettit, Croxton, and Fiksel, 2019), which are critical and relevant to drug sourcing.

A drug shortage is a deficiency in the supply of medicines or products that affect the ability of a patient to get the required treatment in due time (Pauwels, Huys, Casteels and Simeons, 2015). The roots of drug shortages are multifaceted and varied. The problem can either be due to the supply or demand (Bateman, 2013). However, the situation affects almost every stakeholder in the health care system, so collaboration is required to handle or reduce shortages. It is also possible to affect the amount of work, important decisions and financial impact if not be anticipated on time (Pauwels, et al.2015). Burns (2002) examined the healthcare value chain. In addition, Pitta and Laric (2004), provide a model of the healthcare value and supply chains which helps to change the focus from individual transactions to a more comprehensive view of the entire system. This supply chain is not linear or sequential in nature but closely follows the flow of information through the system. Public expectation of quality healthcare and the burgeoning costs of more sophisticated and expensive medical interventions has been a great cause of worry and deliberation the world over (Böhme, Williams, Childerhouse, Deakins and Towill, 2013). Governments worldwide attempt regulation of such services, often through a philosophy of New Public Management which Hood (1995) defines as the lessening of differences between the public and private sectors by shifting the emphasis away from process accountability and towards outcomes.

Namibia, a country situated in the southern part of Africa, comprises a population estimated to be 2.304 million inhabitants from the 14 regions (Namibia Statistical Agency, 2011). Under the Ministry of health and social services (MoHSS), the government ensures the effective and efficient monitoring of the country's health system. The efficient functioning of Namibia's public pharmaceutical management system, one of the central support systems, is critical to the success of the health sector (Ministry of Health and Social Services, 2014). The country uses a classic central medical store (CMS) system. The administration in the CMS and regional stores is not linked; the only relationship between one customer and client. The CMS distributes medicines and supplies to the regional medical store, all hospitals and clinics, both regional and local, are responsible for distributing to other health facilities within their geographic control (World Health Organization, 2013). Hence, there is an issue of supply chain management when it comes to drugs delivery, even as a relief measure in Namibia (Baporikar and Shangheta, 2018). Supply chains have been defined as vertically networked companies extending from raw material production to consumption by end-users (Bask and Tinnilä, 2013). According to one of the first definitions given by Stevens (1989), a supply chain is a connected series of activities involving the planning, coordinating and controlling of materials, parts and finished goods in their journey from the supplier to the customer. It is concerned with two distinct flows – those of material and information – through the organization. Christopher (1992) also includes the service aspect, in which supply chains consist of networked organizations connected by up and downstream linkages, activities and processes to produce value in the form of products and services for ultimate customers. Hence, adopting an exploratory and single-case approach of the largest public hospital, the objective of this chapter is to provide a contemporary perspective of supply chain management re drug sourcing shortages, analyze the causes of drug shortages and recommend measures to minimize the crisis, and suggest strategies for enhanced efficiency in drug supply.

LITERATURE REVIEW

Successful supply chain (SC) management is a significant element of a firm's ability to fill consumer demand in any industry case. It is clear that SC performance may be decreased by disruptive events occurring in the supply chain system. SC disruptions are 'unplanned events that may occur in the supply chain which might affect the normal or expected flow of materials and components' (Svensson 2000). Currently, research interest from academics and practitioners regarding SC disruptions and related issues prevail because SC risks can potentially be harmful and costly for the whole SC (Craighead, Blackhurst, Rungtusanatham and Handfield, 2007). However, challenges in pharmaceutical management in Namibia include the few or few personnel, vague organizational, management structures and procedures, lack of or poor inventory control management systems, and insufficient dispatch and distribution systems. Yet, it is important to distinguish between the quality of product or service offered that is "item" produced by one or more suppliers and quality of service which is achieved between any supplier and customer, not only a consumer, along a supply chain (Gumzej and Gajšek, 2011). Quality of service among supply chain elements is vital for supply chain existence and the source of trust between supply chain elements. All these may result in an inability of the supply system to put up the increased load predicted under the plan to scale up and expand health activities under the MoHSS (Tetteh, 2005).

Drug shortage is a burden on the health care system (McLaughlin, Kotis, Thomson, Harrison, Fennessy, Postelnick and Scheetz, 2013). Globally the efficiency and effectiveness of hospital pharmacies are inextricably linked to the service delivery and the supply of medication to patients (Ventola, 2011). The number of drug supply shortage tripled from 61 types of drugs to 178 between 2005 and 2010, with over 200 reported in 2012 alone. It was reported that from 2014, 754 drug products types remained in shortage (Caulder, Mehta, Bookstave, Sims and Stevenson, 2015). Hence, the problem is pharmacies, and the health authorities responsible for the supply of drugs to patients, cannot attribute the real causes of the increasing drug crisis. In Namibia, there is growing concern about the persistent shortage of drugs in Katutura hospital and other health facilities (Tjitemisa, 2014). The core issue is that Katutura hospital pharmacy is failing to meet the increasing drug demand by patients.

Healthcare does not escape from the general trend towards higher quality demands in an increasingly complex medical environment. The formerly passive patient became an active actor in the treatment process. The active client has other and higher demands, is better informed, and continuously looks for the best care. Most importantly: in healthcare, quality means saving lives (Nsamzinshuti, and Ndiaye,

2014). Hospitals are considered to be one of the most complex players. This complexity is due to the heterogeneity (wide variety of care services offered), professionalism of doctors (they impose requirements and constraints), the human factor (patients induce a high degree of uncertainty) and complex structure (a hospital includes non-primary activities that have to be synchronized with the care providing) (Hammami, 2006). The origin of drug shortages is complex and diverse and the problem can be situated at both the supply and demand sides. Thus, maintaining an inventory of drugs while providing suitable patient care remains a daily challenge for pharmacists in light of national drug shortages.

Overview of Health Care System Supply Chain

It is vital to understand the health care system supply management. The pharmaceutical industry is a scheme of techniques, processes and organizations that are part of the finding, development and creation of drugs and medications. The Pharmaceutical Supply Chain represents the path through which essential pharmaceutical products, including drugs, are distributed to the end-users with the seven rights achieved (Mehralian, 2012). The application of modern logistics and supply chain management practices in the health care sector has trailed behind other industries, which can be due to various reasons. Generally, the supply chain deals with the resources needed to deliver products to consumers. When it comes to health care, the management of the supply chain becomes more complex. To complete the process in this care system, physical goods and information about medical products and services usually go through a number of independent stakeholders, including manufacturers, insurance companies, hospitals, providers, group purchasing organizations, and several regulatory agencies (Belliveau, 2016). This has been attributed to high profits made from patent medicines by pharmaceutical companies and the perceived need for unfailing high service levels that have relegated discussions on supply chain costs (Ouegnimaoua and Savage, 2006).

Shah (2008) addressed a typical pharmaceutical supply chain of low performance and characterized by high pipeline inventory levels, typically ranging from 30 to 90 per cent of annual demand and an inventory turnover rate of 1 and 8 times annually. The healthcare supply chain includes the flow of various product types, with the main aim being to deliver products in a timely manner to fulfil the needs of all the entities involved. Based on their functions, stakeholders in the healthcare supply chain can be divided into three major groups: producers, purchasers, and providers (Kumar, DeGroot and Choe, 2008). Kritchanchai (2012) reviewed literature on the health supply chain and identified major problems as inefficient business processes and data inconsistency among other industry players. Several other researchers have proposed various supply chain strategies, borrowed from other industries to improve the health care supply chain by leveraging opportunities presented by modern information systems. In vendor management inventory, a central production centre (i.e. the vendor) can control the inventory of each retailer according to the optimization of the costs due both to the overfilling/stock-out of the inventories and to the travels required for the deliveries (Bersani and Sacile, 2014).

Nevertheless, significant barriers to the adoption of supply chain management practices in the health care industry exist. Barriers like lack of strategic support, conflicting incentives, need for data collection and performance measurement, limited supply chain education and inconsistent relationship among supply chain partners were identified (Mckone-sweet, Hamilton, and Willis, 2005). Rossetti, Handfield and Dooley (2011) noted a large number of consumption points within hospital settings, the role of the numerous intermediaries, and the long lead times as obstacles to the application of good supply management practices in health care. Others have blamed this inaction on complexity, citing the long pharmaceutical development life cycles, high levels of regulations in the industry and other clinical factors generating unpredictable demand for an extensive range of products (Bhakoo and Chan, 2011). Contained by the healthcare industry, medication is critical in ensuring a high standard of patient care and providing adequate supplies to pharmacies. The supply chain accounts for a high percentage of cost in hospitals operation (Schneller and Smeltzer, 2006). Therefore, this must be properly managed to ensure efficiency in service.

Distribution Concerns: Wholesaler to Hospital

For efficient supply of drugs to the needy patients at hospitals, the distribution channels must be operating smoothly and efficiently. More so, the wholesaler to the hospital channel must be efficient. However, there are various concerns in this channel and the most relevant to the study are briefly discussed below:

Forecasting

It is difficult to predict the exact demand for medicines. One of the issues is the availability of accurate data on consumption. However, the lack of standard language for healthcare products, plus the preferences of clinicians, creates further uncertainties (Lauer, 2004).

Supply Chain Knowledge and Education Deficiency

There is low awareness of the concept of supply chain management, mostly within hospitals (Lauer, 2004). Therefore, managers are less equipped to control the supply of medication. Following this context, a number of creative measures have been carried out to reduce supply chain costs and improve customer service. Preliminary improvements have been based around the implementation of just-in-time (JIT) approaches (Kowalski, 1986). Afterwards, this has been developed further by introducing stockless inventory systems (Wilson, Cunningham and Westbrook, 1992). The JIT and stockless approach both serve to reduce inventory holding costs in the organization while maintaining service levels (Lynch, 1991). More recently, it has been suggested that the stockless system should only be used for high volume products, with a more traditional approach for low volume medical supplies (Rivard-Royer, Landry and Beaulieu, 2002).

Lack and Poor ICT Systems

There is also a lack of proper ICT systems in general, and even if it prevails it is poor. Hence, there is a requirement for improved information and communication technology (ICT) systems to support this and automated processing of orders and suppliers close to the hospital to enable rapid replenishment. The importance of SCM is further emphasized by Mustaffa and Potter (2009), when they noted that poor procurement operations could jeopardize the level of care for patients within the healthcare industry. They contend that effective management of the function can ensure that both service and cost objectives are met. In a similar notion, Kumar et al. (2008) pointed that poor procurement practices affect inventory levels and service provision to patients in the hospital. According to White and Mohdzain (2008), incorrect decisions in supply chain management can end in stock-outs and complete failure of healthcare delivery systems (Mustaffa and Potter, 2009). Accordingly, Kumar et al. (2008) phased vi-ability of inventory elimination in the health care system because medical supplies should always be obtainable for instant use by medical professionals. Thus, Supply Chain Management SCM is a critical part of any business and more so in hospitals. A well-coordinated SCM can improve the efficiency of the business and help in cost reduction. As information technology (IT) is being used widely across all businesses, SCM can benefit largely by the use of IT as it can significantly impact the efficiency of SCM (Saha and Jha, 2018). But its successful implementation and collaboration with other players is the key to efficiency and success. Moreover, supply chain members have to collaborate, sharing information for improving customer's satisfaction (Sadraoui andMchirgui, 2014).

Drug Supply Shortage in Hospital Factors

Healthcare services are known as knowledge-intensive services rendered by knowledge workers (Gu, et al. 2011). After looking at the general supply chain of the health system, it is important to understand that providing such a service requires using some kind of goods which are referred to as pharmaceutical products. Like any other company, hospitals are also striving to make sure that they satisfy their customers, which are referred to as patients. A shortage of products exists in various industries, but when it comes to the health industry, this situation is very critical and needs serious attention with a holistic approach where the logistics in planning procurement for drugs ought to adopt systems thinking (Baporikar, 2020b).

- **Lack of Raw Material***:* Raw materials are essential for the production of all products. Gu et al. (2011) stated that the unavailability of raw materials is a leading factor to shortages of drug supply. He further stated that sub-optimal quality of raw materials might profoundly impact drug shortages, and various factors can contribute to raw material shortage. Supporting the same point, Joel 2010 also alluded that reasons for drug shortages are complex and, despite appearances to the contrary, are generally linked to the laws of supply and demand and raw material shortages. Ventola (2011) also agreed that shortages of raw materials are a major cause of drug shortages in hospitals, and interruptions in the supply of basic materials are normally accountable for drug shortages. These shortages are especially problematic when a primary or sole supplier of the product suspends or ceases production, disturbing other manufacturers. Even when there is more than one manufacturer of a drug, there might be only a single producer of a specific raw material that is vital in the production of a specific drug.
- **Out – Break in Demand:** Demand for products, including drugs, is increasing rapidly. According to Gu et al. (2011), an outbreak in demand can also lead to a shortage of drug supply, especially when there is an outbreak of a new disease. In addition, the authors gave an example of 2009, when the H1N1 pandemic came on the scene; Federal Disease Association amended the original emergency use authorizations (EUAs) for both Tamiflu and Relenza as part of the federal government's responses to the public health emergency. Subsequently, the shortages of Tamiflu were reported everywhere, particularly in paediatric practices (Gu et al., 2011). The issues of supply and demand can also be a leading factor to the shortage of drugs. Ventola (2011) addressed that, sometimes, the demand of a drug can rise above normal prospects or the size of fabrication. This mainly happens when a new medication has been introduced, or an old one needs to be improved. An example was given by the author of 2006 where a shortage of paediatric flu vaccines occurred in the USA. The Centres for disease control and Prevention (CDC) changed its guidelines to include children 6 to 59 months of age. This change in recommendations put pressure on the

suppliers of the only product that the Federal Disease association had approved for use in children 6 to 23 months of age. Unexpected demand for a drug can lead to a shortage when domestic and international supply cannot keep pace. Increases in market demand can result from a new indication for an existing drug, changes to clinical guidelines, or disease outbreaks. These changes can be further exacerbated when the manufacturing process for a drug is lengthy, or the raw materials required to produce it are limited. Ministry of Health and Social Services (2014) identified that; increased demand can also occur when a supplier of a multi-sourced drug experiences a supply disruption or makes a business decision to discontinue the drug. This reduction in supply capacity may drive up demand and deplete the product inventories of the remaining suppliers (Baporikar and Kaloia, 2020).

- **Supplementary Factors:** Apart from lack of raw materials and unexpected demand, there are also other natural and operational factors amounting to the causes of drug supply shortage. The increased consolidation of generic production at a few sites and changes in regulatory standards requiring upgrading of manufacturing plants are all possible reasons for shortages of injectable generic medicines (Gray and Manasses, 2012). Gu et al. (2011) have again identified natural disasters and labor disruptions being factors that lead to a drug supply shortage. Natural disasters may result in a shortage by affecting the raw materials needed by the sole producer of a drug and impose unexpected impairment to manufacturing facilities, and labor disruptions attribute to drug shortages by diminishing the productivity of the manufacturing sector. Other factors contribute to a drug supply shortage, ranging from inefficient distribution networks, inadequate management and external factors, inefficiencies in meeting customer service expectations, and unnecessary logistics costs (Baporikar and Kaloia, 2020). The challenges amounting to this shortage include the lack of proper personnel, unclear organizational and management structures and procedures, inadequate inventory-control management systems, and inadequate dispatch and distribution systems

STRATEGIES TO DEAL WITH DRUG SUPPLY SHORTAGE

The drug supply shortage is a multi- facet, and it requires the collaboration of various stakeholders in order to deal with the situation. Some researchers have written various articles on some strategies and solutions to the drug shortage supply. It is very difficult to effectively address a drug shortage due to the complexity of the supply chain and the difficulty of demand prediction. There are often no obvious and early indications for a shortage (Kohler, 2013). However, in recent years some researchers have attempted to address strategies that can be used to address the worsening situation of drug shortages. The drug shortage situation requires an organizational strategy that includes a focus on client safety. According to Yang, Wu, Cai, Zhu, Shen, Li and Fang, (2016), to help curb the situation of drug supply shortage, it is important to involve the entire care team in some way to help identify strategies to promote client safety and continuity of treatment potential treatment options, most appropriate care provider to manage and minimize wastages of drugs, organization collaboration and management of the issue, making a follow-up of evolving issues from the wastage minimization strategy. Some reports also stated some strategies for dealing with shortages of drug supply.

Ministry of Health and Long Term-Care Report, identifies that, when there is a potential risk of drug shortage supply, strategies of the following nature were identified; developing an inventory of available across care settings based on the availability of supply and how critical the need or demand is, conducting a review on current drug prescription practices, based on the available evidence of clinical efficacy (Baporikar, and Kaloia, 2020). In addition, reducing the wastage of drugs and making use of alternatives medication were also suggested. Kaakeh, Sweet, Reilly, Bush, DeLoach, Higgins and Stevenson (2011) have identified that to deal with the persistent shortage of drug supply, some implementing steps like monitoring, seeking alternatives, and effective communication have to be followed. Similarly, Barlas (2013) alludes that as a solution to the crisis, many hospitals pharmacies make the use of compounded drugs when their usual source of drugs becomes weak. He further discussed that getting an alarm system or records of projected supply data from various suppliers based on demand will enable the health officials, especially the pharmacists and the national health body, for example MoHSS and the Central Medical store in Namibia to know exactly when a certain type of drug will be in short supply, with that information it will be possible to draw up a contingency plan and start looking for alternative suppliers. To add on the above, the author also indicated, the use of incentives payment to the suppliers as a good method of dealing with drug shortage: health bodies need to find suppliers that provide high-quality drug products and be ready to pay them enough so that they can make reasonable profits and can invest in their facilities to increase the production. Sharing the same views with the smart retailing report, Calloway-Sykes (2015) agrees that good communication is a perfect strategy to deal with drug shortage. Working in different sections in the pharmacy, requires some action to compact the issue. Teaching and encouraging the nursing staff to be alert of the types of medication they handle so that they will be able to give prior notification to the pharmacy in case of additional demand required so that it will not delay their therapy is also one of the strategies to deal with the situation. Kahler (2013) indicates that one of the mitigating initiatives by the government of the USA is to establish closer communication ties between the FDA and manufacturers through a notification obligation.

RESEARCH METHODOLOY

The study used a descriptive survey design that used a quantitative approach. The target population is pharmacists, chief pharmacist, hospital superintendent, and nurses in Katutura Hospital. This research adopted non- probability sampling using convenience sampling technique. The research was limited to a group of selected respondents by considering their experience and wards in which they work in the hospital. The sample consisted of 8 pharmacists and 14 nurses that work in different wards. These nurses work in normal wards, surgical wards, theatre and other wards. The total of 22 questionnaires were distributed to pharmacists and nurses in Katutura hospital that are involved directly with the supply of drugs to patients. 22 questionnaires were distributed, and 21 returned, resulting in a response rate of 95%. Both primary and secondary data was collected. Primary data was collected through handing self-administered questionnaires to professionals in Katutura hospital and the Ministry of health and social services. Secondary data was collected from published work, papers, journals, reports of the MOHSS. Thus, the study is regarding the causes of drug supply shortages in Katutura hospital; it will focus more on the pharmacy department because they are the ones that distribute medication to the entire hospital from a supply chain perspective. However, we reckon that the problem of drug shortage is multi-facet and it can even go beyond the supply and distribution management perspective. Further, the study is limited only to the case study of Katutura hospital that may prevent generalization, but since this hospital in Namibia accommodates a large number of patients and health cases, it would certainly represent the other hospitals issues fairly well.

DATA ANALYSIS AND DISCUSSION

This section is about data analysis and discussion to present the findings of the study in relation to research questions and objectives.

Work Sections at Katutura Hospital

The participants were asked to indicate the wards in which they work at the hospital. Options were Pharmacy, Theatre, Normal, Surgical and Others. Different work sections experience distinct shortages, and in order to get information that is concrete and credible, the study took into consideration the work sections of the participants. Table 1 gives the participants work sections at the hospital.

Table 1. Work sections

Serial No.	Work Sections	Percentage
1.	Pharmacy	38
2.	Theatre	33
3.	Normal	24
4.	Surgical Wards	05
5.	Other	00
	Total	100

Source: Research Results

Monthly Drug Supply Shortage (Number of Times per Month)

Participants were asked the number of times they were faced with a drug supply shortage in a month. Figure 1 reflects the drug supply shortage per month which is number of times in a month. Options that were provided are, once a month, 2 to 3 times, 4 to 10 times and lastly, more than ten times. Of the 21 participants, figure 2 above shows that the majority of 52% indicated that they were faces with Drug supply shortage 2 to 3 times a month. 29% of the participants indicated that they were faced with the shortage 4 to 10 times. 19% of the participants indicated that they were faced with a drug supply shortage for more than ten times a month. None of the participants indicated that they were only faced with the crisis of shortage once.

Causes of Drug Supply Shortage

Participants were asked to choose at least 4 important factors that they think cause drug supply shortage. Table 2 gives the identified factors that may be causing shortages in the supply of drugs.

Figure 1. Monthly drug supply shortage (number of times per month)
Source: Research Results

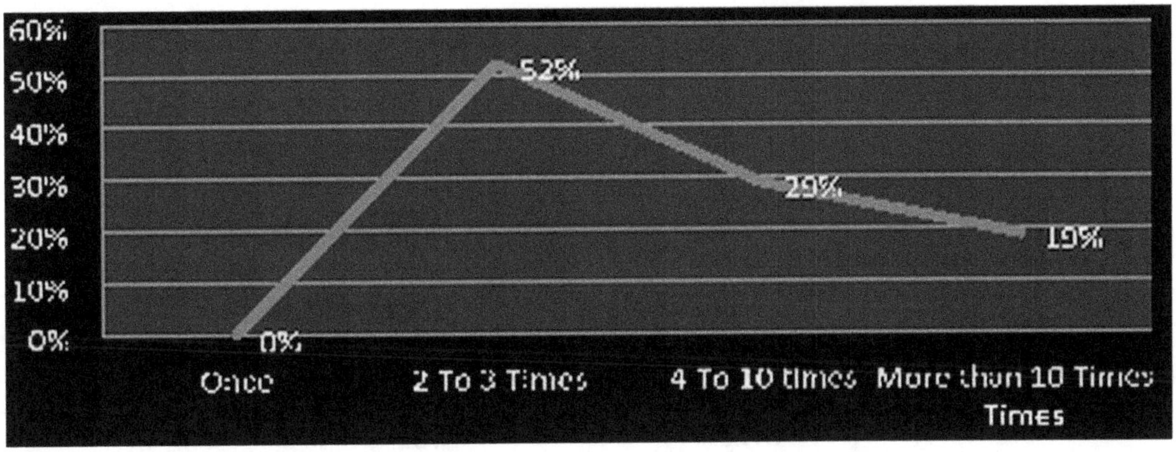

Table 2. Factors causing drug shortage

Serial No.	Factor	Percentage
1.	Supply Chain Disruption	24
2.	Management Inefficiency	23
3.	High Demand	22
4.	Improper Inventory Management System	17
5.	Manufacturers delay	09
6.	Lack of raw Materials	05
	Total	100

Source: Research Results

Shortage of Drugs Type

Participants were asked about the type of drugs that are mostly on shortage in their departments. From the list provided, they were asked to select the most two types. Options were provided such as pain drugs (Paracetamol, Panadol), specific related drugs (insulin, BP, ARVs), generic drugs (Amoxicillin, Lisinopril), emergency operation drugs (furosemide, digoxin) and sedative drugs. Moreover, there was an additional opportunity for other types of drugs that were not provided in the list. Figure 2 below indicates that the most drugs type shortage are pain drugs with 29% and emergency operation drugs with 23%. According to the figure above, the other two types of drugs that are moderately on shortage are generic drugs (19%) and Sedative drugs (17%). Participants indicated the least type of drug on shortage in Katutura hospital is a specific related disease with 12%.

Figure 2. Shortage of drugs type
Source: Research Results

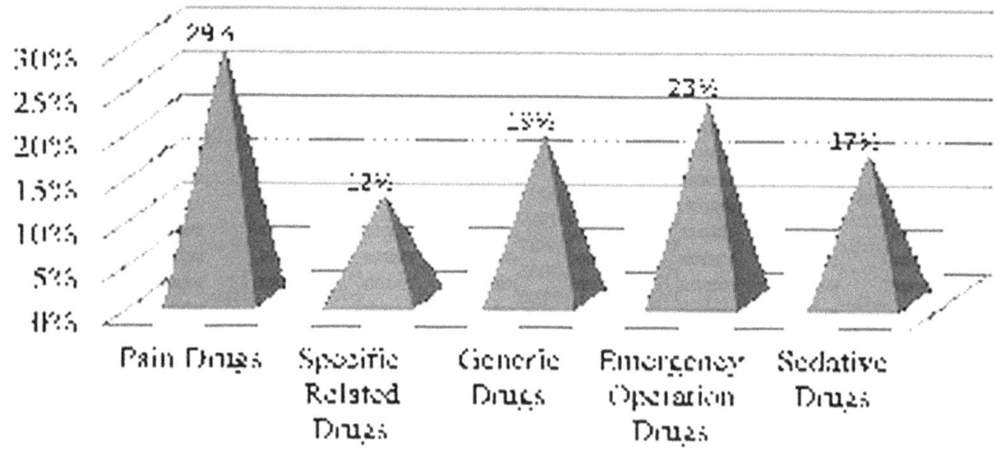

Expiry Date as Factor for Drug Supply Shortage

Participants were asked whether the expiry date of the drugs could be a leading factor in the shortage crisis. Figure 3 below shows that the majority (62%) of the participant agreed that the expiry date or the lifespan of drugs is a leading factor to drug supply shortage. While minority (38%) of the participants disagreed that the expiry date of drugs is a causing factor to supply shortage.

Figure 3. Expiry date as factor for drug supply shortage
Source: Research Results

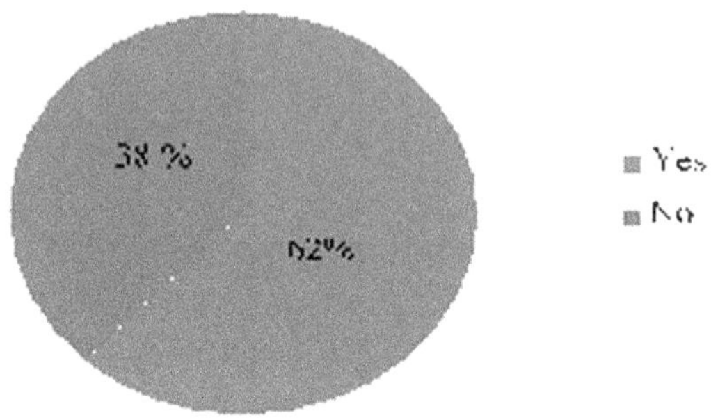

OPERATIONAL FACTORS LEADING TO DRUG SUPPLY SHORTAGE

Patients' Complaints Received due to Drug Shortage

Participants were asked whether they ever received patient complaints on their daily operation as a result of a drug supply shortage. Figure 4 above shows that the majority (90%) of the participant received patient complaints. While minority (10%) of the participants indicated that they never received patient complaints. The study considered this in order for the information to get more credibility, and it shows that the drug supply shortage crisis exists.

Figure 4. Patient complaints due to drug shortage
Source: Research Results

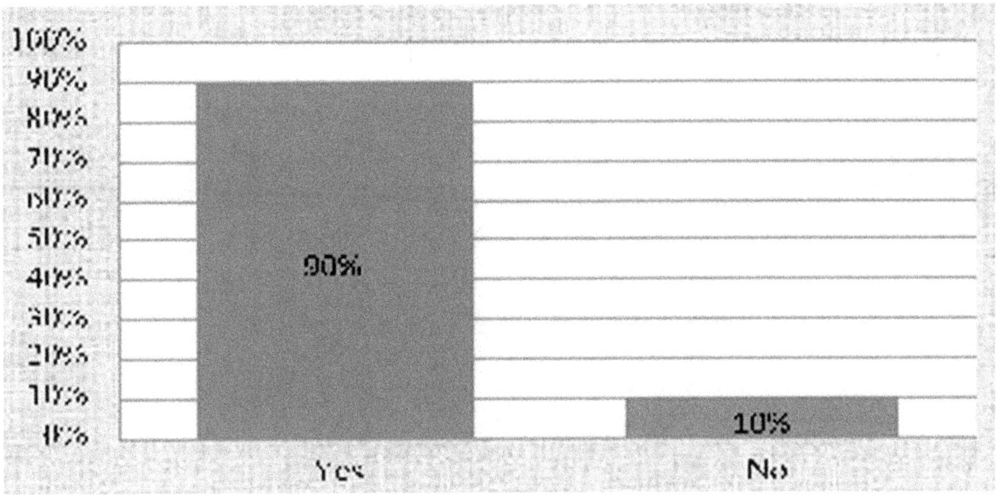

Ordering Frequency of Drugs

Participants were asked to indicate the frequency at which drugs are ordered within their wards in the hospital. Table 3 gives the ordering frequency of the drugs.

Table 3. Ordering frequency of drugs

Serial No.	Ordering Frequency	Percentage
1.	Daily	05
2.	Weekly Once	29
3.	Weekly Twice	38
4.	Monthly Once	00
5.	Others	06

Source: Research Results

Five options were given, such as daily, once a week, twice a week, once a month and others. From the analysis above it is clear that majority of the orders are done twice a week with 38% and next 29% of the orders are done once a week. Only 5% of the orders are done daily, and the other was 6% done every six weeks from the central medical store, while there were no orders made once a month.

Drug Suppliers

Participants were asked to indicate their suppliers of drugs. The options were Central medical store, Internal Pharmacy, Regional medical store and others. Although all the participants work in the same hospital, they have different suppliers. Figure 5 shows that the internal pharmacy is the major supplier of drugs and constitutes 67%. While the central medical store supplies 33% of the drugs. The Regional stores, including other stores that exist, do not supply drugs to Katutura Hospital. The central medical store supplies only to the pharmacy and in turn, the internal pharmacy supplies to all wards and patients.

Figure 5. Drug suppliers
Source: Research Results

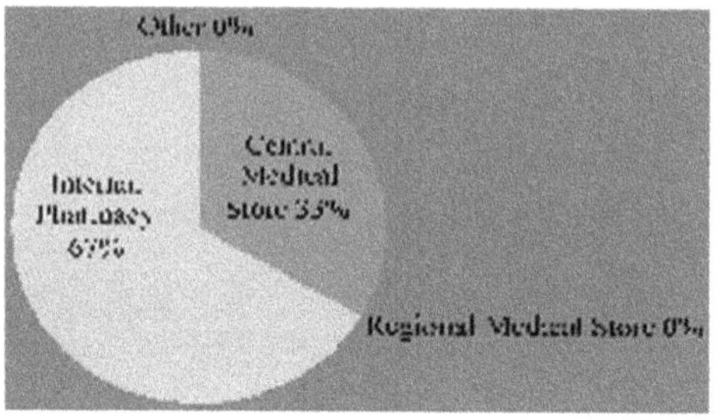

Sharing Drug Shortage Information Medium

Figure 6 shows the medium through which drug shortage information is communicated in the Hospital. Participants were asked to indicate how they communicate information when a shortage arises or how the drug shortage information is communicated to them. Five options were given: emails, newsletter, medical staff committee, return of order forms, and others. Return of order forms is the main media on which drug shortage information is communicated with 71%. Participants also indicated that there are other Media that they use to communicate the information, which was not specified, and this was shown by 24%. Medical staff committee can be said to be the least media used to communicate the drug shortage information with 5%. None of the participants indicated that the use of emails and Newsletter as a media to communicate drug shortage information.

SOLUTIONS TO DRUG SUPPLY SHORTAGE

This part of the discussion on findings addresses the possible solutions to drug supply shortage from a supply chain perspective.

Handling Drug Supply Shortage

Participants were asked to indicate the methods used in handling the drug supply shortage situation in the past.

Figure 6. Sharing drug shortage information medium
Source: Research Results

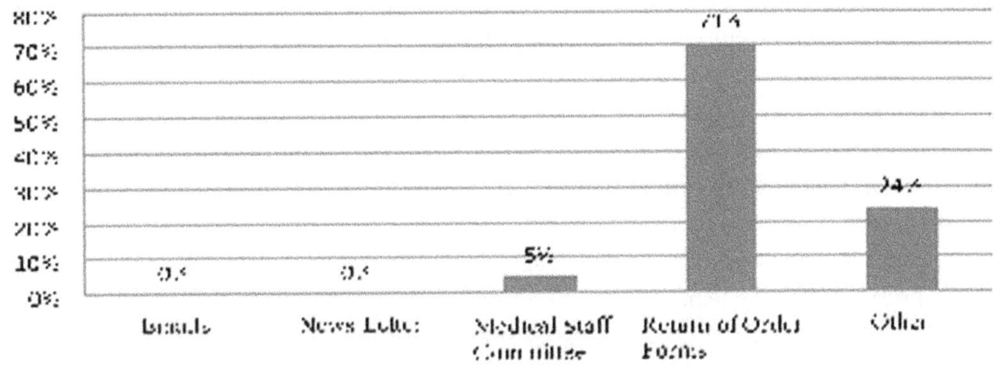

Table 4. Methods used for handling drug supply shortage

Serial No.	Methods Used	Percentage
1.	Alternative Suppliers	66
2.	Extend Space of Pharmacy	00
3.	Introduction of Inventory System	10
4.	Others	24
	Total	100

Source: Research Results

Providing Alternative Medication

Participants were asked whether they provide alternative medication for drugs in short supply to their patients. All the participants indicated that they provide alternative medication to their patients when the prescribed drug is in short supply. Figure 7 shows that 100% provide alternative medication.

Figure 7. Alternative medication
Source: Research Results

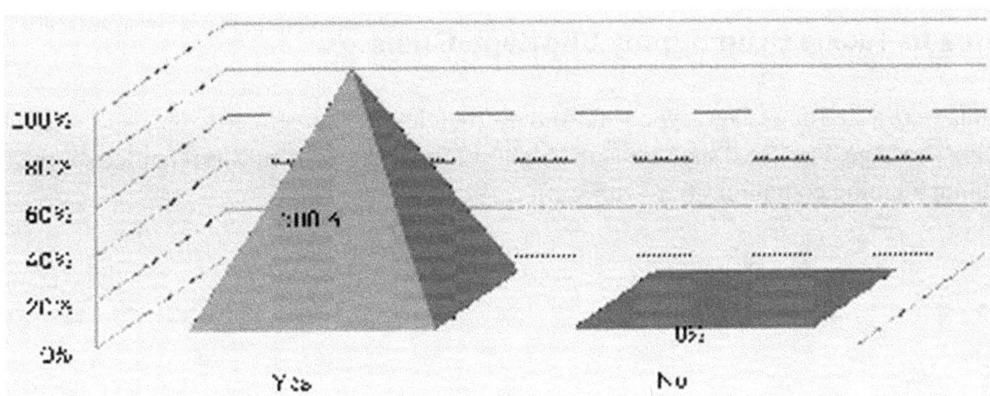

Proper Inventory Management System as Solution

Participants were asked to rate the extent to which a proper inventory management system can serve as a solution to the drug supply shortage in the hospital. Five options were given from 'to a great extent', 'to a certain extent', 'undecided', 'to a small extent', 'not to any extent'. Figure 8 indicates the extent to which participants agree that a proper inventory system is a solution to the shortage crisis. The majority of respondents (66%) indicated that a proper inventory system is a solution to a great extent. 19% of the participants showed that it is only important to a certain extent. 10% showed that a proper inventory system could serve as a solution to a small extent. However, 5% of the participants were undecided as to whether a proper inventory system is a solution to the drug supply shortage. None of the participants showed that a proper inventory management system is not a solution to the drug supply shortage.

Figure 8. Proper inventory management system as solution
Source: Research Results

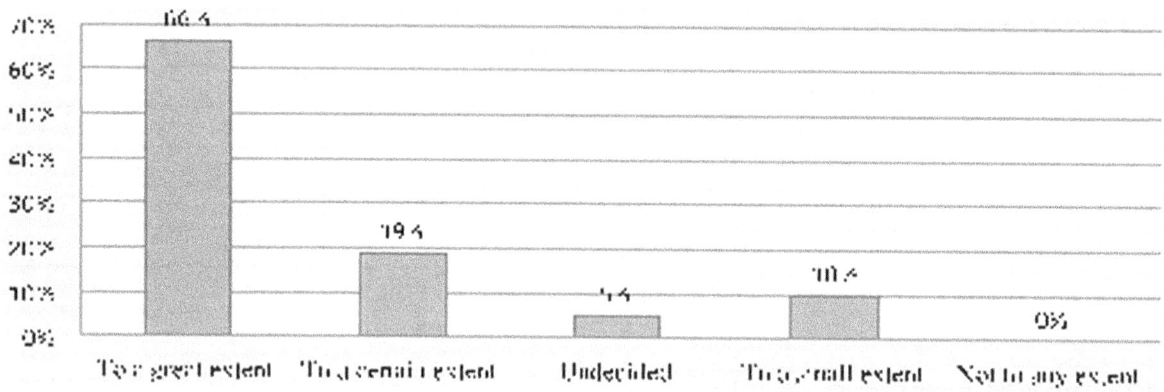

Integration of Procurement and Pharmacy Distribution Function

Participants were asked whether they agree to the statement "close integration of the procurement department with the pharmacy distribution function is a solution to drug supply shortage. Figure 9 below shows that majority of the participants (95%) agreed that close integration of the functions is a solution to drug supply shortage. Only (5%) disagreed with the above.

Measures to Tackle Drug Supply Shortage Crisis

Participants were asked on a Likert-type scale to show their level of agreement to the measures of tackling drug supply shortage. Figure 10 shows that the highest level of agreement was recorded for the measure 'Establishing ongoing communication with staff.

Figure 9. Integration of procurement and pharmacy distribution function
Source: Research Results

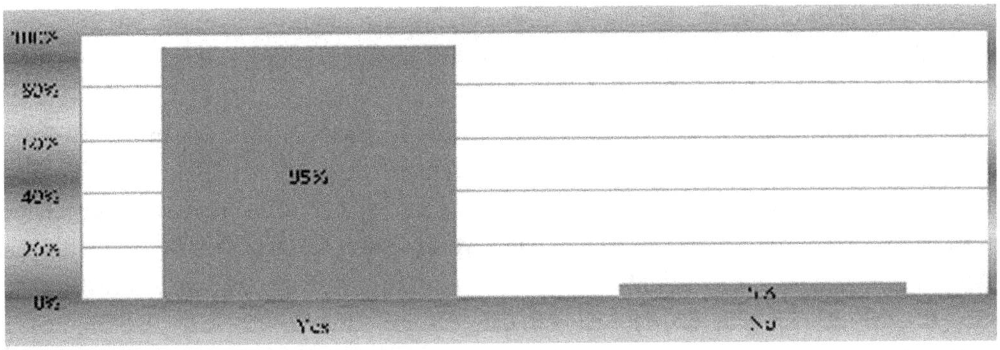

Figure 10. Measures to tackle drug supply shortage crisis
Source: Research Results

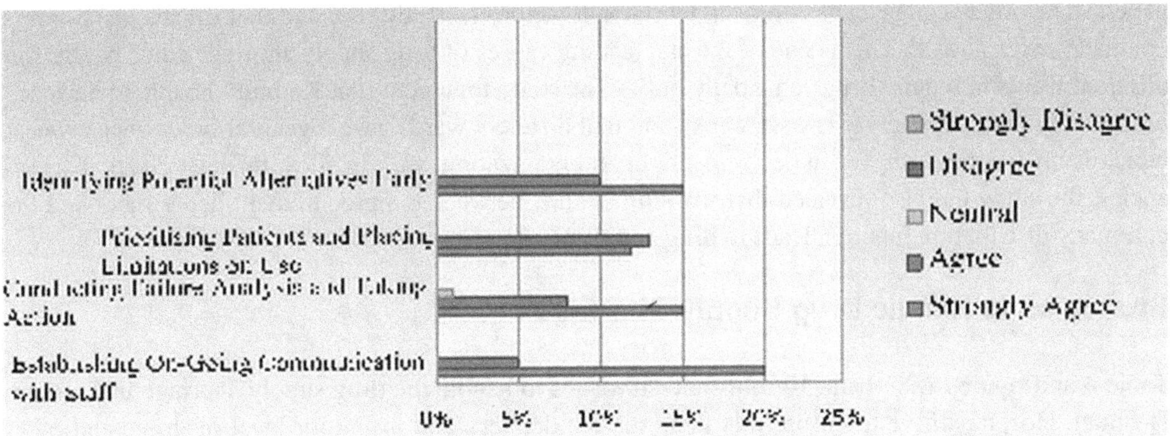

IMPLICATIONS

The study reveals that the shortage of drug supply is not an assumption or perception in Katutura hospital, but a reality and the shortages do occur actually which is line with what is observed by Mclaughlin, Thomson and Poselnick (2013), who state that drug supply shortage is a reality and continues to be a burden in many hospitals around the world. The focus of any business and specifically any national health care institution, is always toward increasing efficiency and reducing costs but ensuring that the supply chains are efficient. This is possible during normal times, but at the cost of being vulnerable to disruptions. From time to time, frequent as well as rare catastrophes also disrupt supply chain operations. Examination of the geographical and chronological distributions of catastrophes provides useful information for all concerned about efficiency in supply chain. Disruptions in supply chain management are usually caused by natural catastrophes (e.g. earthquakes, hurricanes, and floods), man-made threats (e.g. fires, strikes, and terrorism), and severe legal disruptions (e.g. environmental laws) (Ivanov, Dolgui,Sokolov, and Ivanova, 2017). These disruption events might cause structural dynamics in supply chains and have a ripple effect. Further, dynamics of structures and processes is one of the underlying challenges in supply chain management, where multiple dimensions of economic efficiency, risk management and sustainability are interconnected. One of the substantiated issues in supply chain dynamics is resilience. Resilience has a number of intersections with supply chain sustainability (Ivanov, 2018). Supply chain resilience (SCR) manifests when the network is capable to withstand, adapt, and recover from disruptions to meet customer demand and ensure performance (Hosseini, Ivanov, and Dolgui, 2019). According to Ventola (2011), disruptions in the supply chain is a cause to drug supply shortage in the hospitals, which the study also revealed the same reality. It was also found that management inefficiency in hospitals and increased demand and improper inventory systems are causes of drug supply shortages. The number and types of drugs on shortage have been increasing worldwide (Caulder, Mehta, Bookstave and Sims (2015). Although not mentioned in the literature review, the study has found an interesting factor that the expiry date of drugs can be a leading factor to drug supply shortage.

On an operational level, organizations put in place various strategies that can ensure their success, however some daily operation factors lead to them being unsuccessful. Regardless of it not being part of the general objective, the study found out that patients have made numerous complaints due to the fact of drug supply shortage. 90% of the respondents have indicated that they received complaints from patients. As orders can be considered an operational factor, the study revealed that the majority orders are made twice a week. This is one of the can leading causes of drug supply shortage since patients in different wards to require drugs on a daily basis. The study found out that Katutura hospital pharmacy orders from their suppliers every six weeks and that different wards have a general order once a week, which is on Wednesdays. When departments in an organization work in silos, this can create discrepancies, the study has also revealed that working in silos between the procurement department and the pharmacy distribution function leads to drug supply shortage.

Strategies to Handle Drug Supply Shortage

Table 4 and figures 7, 8, 9 and 10; illustrate strategies to handle the drug supply shortage in Katutura Hospital. Hospitals have to ensure that their service delivery and inventory level of drugs and other pharmaceutical products are in an optimum state to ensure that patients' needs are met. However, it is a reality that emergency need arises, and sometimes the current stock cannot meet the demand. To handle supply shortages, the study had revealed that the use of alternative suppliers is a good strategy to deal with the shortages in the hospital (66%). When a shortage arises, providing alternative medicine to patients is a solution to the drugs in short supply (100%). The implementation of a proper inventory management system is also one of the strategies to handle drug supply shortages (66%). Collaboration in any organization is very important. In support of this, the study has indicated a greater level of agreement. The close integration and good communication among different functions or partners in the pharmaceutical supply chain is a strategy that can solve the drug supply shortage.

RECOMMENDATIONS

Based on the analysis and literature review, the following are the recommendations.

- Adopt strategies to enhance SCM robustness: Hospitals can adopt several strategies to increase their robustness to potential supply chain (SC) disruptions. One promising strategy is the use of a cross-functional team with representatives from functional departments to deal and reduce drug shortages. The tacit knowledge sharing this can bring is vital for enhancing efficiency (Baporikar, 2020a). Such a team may facilitate sharing relevant information, enabling the firm to respond effectively to SC disruption warnings. However, despite their potential, cross-functional teams also differ in their ability to respond to SC disruption warnings and to ensure firm robustness (De Vries, Van Der Vegt, Scholten, and Pieter Van Donk, 2021).

- Build micro-level resilience: Micro-level resilience occurs when buyers and suppliers coordinate directly on supply risk prevention and recovery. Macro-level resilience occurs when corporations, including competitors, collaborate with institutions such as government or trade associations to manage or regulate longer-term supply risks (Azadegan and Dooley, 2021).
- *Collaboration:* Katutura hospital pharmacy needs to work more closely with the right partners (central medical store, central hospital and MOHSS) to purchase and deliver all the required medication. This can allow improvement in the effectiveness and expectedness of drug supply shortage response.
- *Early Alert Inventory System:* Proper inventory management is an important way out to drug shortage. Hence, Katutura hospital needs to implement an inventory alert system that will be able to notify them on the level of each drug type left in the pharmacy so that they can order more often and look for alternatives in an earlier stage to avoid and minimize drug shortages.

FUTURE AREAS OF RESEARCH

Comparative studies of private and public hospitals need to be undertaken to get a deeper understanding and analyze the causes of drug supply shortages and challenges. Studies to investigate the impacts of drug supply shortage on patient health care are also another interesting area. The study can also be taken on a national level, for example, the main storage of drugs in the country, the central medical store. Identifying the different players in the SCM is another vital and interesting area since Namibia lacks manufacturing facilities. So is also the need to develop frameworks and models regarding the quality of services with respect to drug delivery to achieve the satisfactory level between any supplier and customer, not only as a consumer but also as a supply chain. Quality of service among supply chain elements is vital for supply chain existence and the source of trust between supply chain elements (Gumzej and Gajšek, 2011). These opportunities pertain to retailers' survival in the face of highly successful e-commerce giants and the mixed-use of robots and human workers. There are also opportunities to share supply chain capacity in distribution and coopetition regarding medically necessary items such as anti-virals or vaccines (Sodhi and Tang, 2020). The growing role of government in supporting business, including creating industry commons, also presents avenues for further research. A well-coordinated SCM can improve the efficiency of the business and help in cost reduction. As information technology (IT) is being used widely across all businesses, SCM can benefit largely from the use of IT as it can significantly impact the efficiency of SCM (Saha and Jha, 2018). Hospitals in Namibia under the aegis of the Ministry of Health must undertake how IT can enhance efficiency and reduce drug shortage supply. However, for its successful implementation and collaboration with other players is the key to efficiency and success, so strategies must be identified and well-crafted to void disappointment and losses as supply chain members collaborate, sharing information to improve customer satisfaction (Sadraoui and Mchirgui, 2014). Finally, adoption of what looks like strategic fast supply-demand chains or network chains: fast because they rapidly settle down and rapidly dismantle (Carvalho, Martins, Ramos and Dias 2014), needs proper studies and investigation, as these arrangements though responsible for several possible and fast relations also contribute to loss of trust, credibility as their partners are already involved with focal companies in stable supply chains.

Last but not least is the issue of inclusivity and sustainability. For that to happen, there is a need to involve traditionally marginalized and silenced or silent voices. More important would be to enhance our understanding of what sustainability and inclusivity mean from those perspectives and the most central concerns. Then work on co-designing an equitable supply chain and design strategies to achieve these in practice while acknowledging the existing power disparities that shape global supply chains currently.

CONCLUSION

Global supply chains (SCs) are increasingly perceived to be at the heart of societal challenges, which places SCs and SCM at the forefront of endeavours to change discourses and practice in light of such wicked problems (Touboulic, McCarthy, and Matthews, 2020). Sickness and diseases are no doubt wicked in nature for human beings and more so for economically weak. Hence, the pharmaceutical supply chain is a field of growing interest in the 21st century. Maintaining the supply of medications and securing the needs of end customers in terms of quantity, quality, and more accessibility of drugs are at the top of any health care system priorities (Abdollahiasl et al., 2014). This chapter analyzed the causes of drug supply shortages and determining strategies to address and handle the shortage crisis from a contemporary perspective. Like many related studies in the literature (Baporikar and Shangheta, 2018), respondents indicated disruptions in the supply chain, lack of raw materials, management inefficiencies, increasing demand, improper inventory system, manufacturers delay, being causes of drug supply shortage in Katutura hospital. Lack of integration and collaboration between the procurement function and distribution function as well as the expiry date of drugs are factors causing drug supply shortages. Hence, to conclude, it important to professionalize the drug procurement and supply chain management, provide alternative medication, do contingencies planning in terms of alternative suppliers, collaborate and integrate strategies to optimize drug supplies effectively.

REFERENCES

Abdollahiasl, A., Nikfar, S., Kebriaeezadeh, A., Dinarvand, R., Abdollahi, M., Jaberidoost, M., & Cheraghali, A. M. (2014). A system dynamics model for national drug policy. *Daru: Journal of Faculty of Pharmacy, Tehran University of Medical Sciences*, *22*(1), 22–34. PMID:24690531

Azadegan, A., & Dooley, K. (2021). A typology of supply network resilience strategies: Complex collaborations in a complex world. *The Journal of Supply Chain Management*, *57*(1), 17–26. doi:10.1111/jscm.12256

Bals, L., Schulze, H., Kelly, S., & Stek, K. (2019). Purchasing and supply management (PSM) competencies: Current and future requirements. *Journal of Purchasing and Supply Management*, *25*(5), 100572. doi:10.1016/j.pursup.2019.100572

Baporikar, N. (2020a). Learning Link in Organizational Tacit Knowledge Creation and Dissemination. *International Journal of Sociotechnology and Knowledge Development*, *12*(4), 70–88. doi:10.4018/IJSKD.2020100105

Baporikar, N. (2020b). Logistics Effectiveness Through Systems Thinking. *International Journal of System Dynamics Applications*, *9*(2), 64–79. doi:10.4018/IJSDA.2020040104

Baporikar, N. (2021). *Handbook of Research on Sustaining SMEs and Entrepreneurial Innovation in the Post-COVID-19 Era*. IGI Global., doi:10.4018/978-1-7998-6632-9

Baporikar, N., & Kaloia, D. S. (2020). Supply Chain Management Perspective on Shortages in Drugs Sourcing. *International Journal of Applied Logistics*, *10*(2), 62–85. doi:10.4018/IJAL.2020070104

Baporikar, N., & Shangheta, L. B. (2018). Challenges Facing Humanitarian Logistics in a Nonprofit Organization. *International Journal of Applied Logistics*, *8*(1), 35–56. doi:10.4018/IJAL.2018010103

Barlas, S. (2013). FDA Strategies to prevent and respond to drug shortages: Finding a better way to predict and prevent company closure. *The Pharmacist and Therapeutics Journal, 38*(5), 261-263.

Bask, A., & Tinnilä, M. (2013). Impact of Product Characteristics on Supply Chains: An Analytical Literature Review. *International Journal of Applied Logistics*, *4*(1), 35–59. doi:10.4018/jal.2013010103

Bateman, C. (2013). Drug stock-outs: Inept supply-chain management and corruption. *South African Medical Journal*, *103*(9), 600–602. doi:10.7196/SAMJ.7332 PMID:24344422

Belliveau, J. (2016). *Exploring the role of supply chain management in healthcare*. Retrieved from http://revcycleintelligence.com

Bersani, C., & Sacile, R. (2014). Optimal Deliveries in a Vendor Managed Inventory Service. *International Journal of Applied Logistics*, *5*(1), 1–14. doi:10.4018/ijal.2014010101

Bhakoo, V., & Chan, C. (2011). Collaborative implementation of e-business processes within the healthcare supply chain: The Monash Pharmacy Project. *Supply Chain Management*, *16*(3), 184–193. doi:10.1108/13598541111127173

Böhme, T., Williams, S. J., Childerhouse, P., Deakins, E., & Towill, D. (2013). Methodology challenges associated with benchmarking healthcare supply chains. *Production Planning and Control*, *24*(10-11), 1002–1014. doi:10.1080/09537287.2012.666918

Burns, L. R. (2002). *Wharton School Colleagues*. The Health Care Value Chain Producers, Purchasers, and Providers.

Calloway-Sykes, K. (2015, February 2). *Strategies for dealing with drug shortages in the hospitals pharmacy settings*. Retrieved from www. Pharmacytimes.com

Carvalho, J., Martins, A., Ramos, T., & Dias, E. (2014). Strategic Fast Supply Demand-Chains in a Network Context: Opportunistic Practices That Can Destroy Supply Chain Systems. *American Journal of Industrial and Business Management*, *9*(4), 123–133. doi:10.4236/ajibm.2014.43019

Caudler, R. C., Mehta, B., Bookstaver, B., Sims, D. L., & Stevenson, B. (2015). Impact of Drug Shortages on Health System Pharmacies in the Southeastern United States. *Journal of Managed Care Pharmacy*, *50*(4), 279–286. PMID:26448658

Christopher, M. (1992). *Logistics and Supply Chain Management*. Pitman Publishing.

Craighead, C. W., Blackhurst, J., Rungtusanatham, M. J., & Handfield, R. B. (2007). The severity of supply chain disruptions: Design characteristics and mitigation capabilities. *Decision Sciences*, *38*(1), 131–156. doi:10.1111/j.1540-5915.2007.00151.x

De Vries, T. A., Van Der Vegt, G. S., Scholten, K., & Pieter Van Donk, D. (2021). Heeding Supply Chain Disruption Warnings: When And How Do Cross-Functional Teams Ensure Firm Robustness? *The Journal of Supply Chain Management*. Advance online publication. doi:10.1111/jscm.12262

Dooley, M. J., Allen, K. M., Doecke, C. J., Galbraith, K. J., Taylor, G. R., Bright, J., & Carey, D. L. (2004). A prospective multicentre study of pharmacist initiated changes to drug therapy and patient management in acute care government funded hospitals. *British Journal of Clinical Pharmacology*, *57*(4), 513–521. doi:10.1046/j.1365-2125.2003.02029.x PMID:15025751

Gray, A., & Manasse, H. R. (2012). Shortages of medicines: A complex global challenge. *Bulletin of the World Health Organization*, *90*(3), 158–158A. doi:10.2471/BLT.11.101303 PMID:22461706

Gu, A., Wertheimer, A. I., Brown, B., & Shaya, T. F. (2011). Drug shortages in the US causes, impacts and strategies. *Innovations in Pharmacy*, *2*(60), 2–6. doi:10.24926/iip.v2i4.243

Gumzej, R., & Gajšek, B. (2011). Introducing Quality of Service Criteria into Supply Chain Management for Excellence. *International Journal of Applied Logistics*, *2*(1), 1–16. doi:10.4018/ijal.2011010101

Hammami, R. (2006). Deniz Kandiyoti. *Development and Change*, *37*(6), 1347–1354. doi:10.1111/j.1467-7660.2006.00530.x

Hood, C. (1995). The new public management in the 1980, s-variations on a theme. *Accounting, Organizations and Society*, *20*(2/3), 93–109. doi:10.1016/0361-3682(93)E0001-W

Hosseini, S., Ivanov, D., & Dolgui, A. (2019). Review of quantitative methods for supply chain resilience analysis. *Transportation Research Part E, Logistics and Transportation Review*, *125*, 285–307. doi:10.1016/j.tre.2019.03.001

Ivanov, D. (2018). Revealing interfaces of supply chain resilience and sustainability: A simulation study. *International Journal of Production Research*, *56*(10), 3507–3523. doi:10.1080/00207543.2017.1343507

Ivanov, D., Dolgui, A., Sokolov, B., & Ivanova, M. (2017). Literature review on disruption recovery in the supply chain. *International Journal of Production Research*, *55*(20), 6158–6174. doi:10.1080/00207543.2017.1330572

Kaakeh, R., Sweet, B. V., Reilly, C., Bush, C., DeLoach, S., Higgins, B., Clark, A. M., & Stevenson, J. (2011). Impact of drug shortages on U.S. health systems. *American Journal of Health-System Pharmacy*, *68*(19), 1811–1819. doi:10.2146/ajhp110210 PMID:21930639

Kelle, P., Woosley, J., & Schneider, H. (2012). Pharmaceutical supply chain specifics and inventory solutions for a hospital case. *Operations Research for Health Care*, *1*(2-3), 54–63. doi:10.1016/j.orhc.2012.07.001

Kowalski, J. C. (1986). Just-in-time for hospitals – so what's new. *Hospital Materials Management*, *11*(11), 6–9. PMID:10317838

Kumar, S., DeGroot, R. A., & Choe, D. (2008). The impact of package design within US hospital supply chain. *International Journal of Physical Distribution & Logistics Management*, *38*(8), 601–615. doi:10.1108/09600030810915134

Lauer, C. (2004). Excellence in supply chain management. *Modern Healthcare*, *34*(50), 29–32. PMID:15631153

Lynch, D. (1991). Just-in-time and stockless programs for hospitals: Fad or trend. *Hospital Materiel Management Quarterly*, *12*(4), 17–21. PMID:10110231

Mckone-sweet, K. E., Hamilton, P., & Willis, S. B. (2005). The ailing healthcare supply chain: A prescription for change. *The Journal of Supply Chain Management*, *41*(1), 4–17. doi:10.1111/j.1745-493X.2005.tb00180.x

McLaughlin, M., Kotis, D., Thomson, K., Harrison, M., Fennessy, G., Postelnick, M., & Scheetz, M. H. (2013). Effects on patient care caused by drug shortages: A survey. *Journal of Managed Care Pharmacy*, *19*(9), 783–788. doi:10.18553/jmcp.2013.19.9.783 PMID:24156647

Mehralian, G. H., Rajabzadeh, A., Reza Sadeh, M., & Reza Rasekh, H. (2012). Intellectual capital and corporate performance in Iranian pharmaceutical industry. *Journal of Intellectual Capital*, *13*(1), 138–140. doi:10.1108/14691931211196259

Ministry of Health and Social Services. (2014). *Annual Report of the Directorate of Tertiary Health Care and clinical support services*. Author.

Mustaffa, N. H., & Potter, A. (2009). Healthcare Supply Chain Management in Malaysia: A case study. *Supply Chain Management*, *14*(3), 234–243. doi:10.1108/13598540910954575

Namibia Statistics Agency. (2011). *Namibia 2011 population and housing Census Main Report*. Author.

Nsamzinshuti, A., & Ndiaye, A. B. (2014). Development of a Conceptual Framework for Performance Measurement of Pharmaceutical Supply Chain within Hospital. *International Journal of Applied Logistics*, *5*(2), 32–49. doi:10.4018/ijal.2014040103

Ouegnimaoua, L., & Savage, C. J. (2008). Restructuring the pharmaceutical and supply chain: An evaluation of distribution networks in Europe. In *Proceedings of logistics network research conference*. University of Newcastle.

Pauwels, K., Simoens, S., Casteels, M., & Huys, I. (2015). Insights into European drug shortages: A survey of hospital pharmacists. *PLoS One*, *10*(3), e0119322. doi:10.1371/journal.pone.0119322 PMID:25775406

Pettit, T. J., Croxton, K. L., & Fiksel, J. (2019). The Evolution of Resilience in Supply Chain Management: A Retrospective on Ensuring Supply Chain Resilience. *Journal of Business Logistics*, *40*(1), 56–65. doi:10.1111/jbl.12202

Pitta, D. A., & Laric, M. V. (2004). Value chains in health care. *Journal of Consumer Marketing*, *21*(7), 451–464. doi:10.1108/07363760410568671

Rivard-Royer, H., Landry, S., & Beaulieu, M. (2002). Hybrid stockless: A case study. *International Journal of Operations & Production Management*, *22*(4), 412–424. doi:10.1108/01443570210420412

Rossetti, L. C., Handfield, R., & Dooley, J. D. (2011). Forces, trends, and decisions in pharmaceutical supply chain management. *International Journal of Physical Distribution & Logistics Management*, *41*(6), 601–622. doi:10.1108/09600031111147835

Sadraoui, T., & Mchirgui, N. (2014). Supply Chain Management Optimization within Information System Development. *International Journal of Econometrics and Financial Management.*, *2*(2), 59–71.

Saha, S. K., & Jha, A. (2018). Role of Information Technology on Supply Chain Management of Pharmaceutical Industry. *International Journal of Applied Logistics*, *8*(2), 39–68. doi:10.4018/IJAL.2018070103

Schneller, E. S., & Smeltzer, L. R. (2006). *Strategic Management of the Health Care Supply Chain* (1st ed.). Wiley.

Shah, N. (2008). Pharmaceutical supply chains: Key issues and strategies for optimization. *Computers & Chemical Engineering*, *28*(6-7), 929–941. doi:10.1016/j.compchemeng.2003.09.022

Sodhi, M. S., & Tang, C. S. (2020). Supply Chain Management for Extreme Conditions: Research Opportunities. *The Journal of Supply Chain Management*.

Ssengonzi, R., & Oginski, P. (2012). *Effective adaptation to global humanitarian challenges* (Master's thesis). Jönköping International Business School, Torpa, Sweden.

Stevens, J. (1989). Integrating the supply chain. *International Journal of Physical Distribution & Materials Management*, *19*(8), 3–8. doi:10.1108/EUM0000000000329

Svensson, G. (2000). A conceptual framework for the analysis of vulnerability in supply chains. *International Journal of Physical Distribution & Logistics Management*, *30*(9), 731–750. doi:10.1108/09600030010351444

Tetteh, G. (2005). *Finalization and Dissemination of the Rapid Assessment of Antimalarial Drug Availability and Use in Nigeria: Rational Pharmaceutical Management Plus program*. Retrieved from http://pdf.usaid.gov

Tjitemisa, K. (2014, June 4). A shortage of essential drugs used in surgery at both public and private pharmacies has sparked panic at leading hospitals in the country. *The Namibian*. Retrieved from http://www.namibian.com.na

Touboulic, A., McCarthy, L., & Matthews, L. (2020). Re-imagining supply chain challenges through critical engaged research. *The Journal of Supply Chain Management*, *56*(2), 36–51. doi:10.1111/jscm.12226

Ventola, L. S. (2011). The Drug Shortage Crisis in the United States. Causes, Impact, and Management Strategies. *Supply Chain Management*, *36*(11), 189–190. PMID:22346307

White, A. D., & Mohdzain, M. B. (2008). An innovative model of supply chain management: A single case study in the electronic sector. *International Journal of Information Technology and Management*, *8*(1), 69–84. doi:10.1504/IJITM.2009.022271

Wilson, J. W., Cunningham, W. A., & Westbrook, K. W. (1992). Stockless inventory systems for the health care provider: Three successful applications. *Journal of Health Care Marketing*, *12*(2), 39–45. PMID:10119212

World Health Organization. (2016). *Pharmaceutical products*. Retrieved from: http://www.who.int

Yang, C., Wu, L., Cai, W., Zhu, W., Shen, Q., Li, Z., & Fang, Y. (2016). Current Situation, determinants, and Solutions to drug shortages in Shaanxi Province, China: A Qualitative Study. *PLoS One*, *11*(10), e0165183. doi:10.1371/journal.pone.0165183 PMID:27780218

Yu, X., Li, C., Shi, Y., & Yu, M. (2010). Pharmaceutical supply chain in China: Current issues and implications for health system reform. *Health Policy (Amsterdam)*, *97*(1), 8–15. doi:10.1016/j.healthpol.2010.02.010 PMID:20307912

Chapter 11
Combining Fix and Relax Heuristic and LP-Metric Method to Solve the Multi-Objective Integrated Production-Routing Problem

Besma Zeddam
https://orcid.org/0000-0003-2282-5030
Manufacturing Engineering Laboratory of Tlemcen (MELT), University of Tlemcen, Algeria

Fayçal Belkaid
https://orcid.org/0000-0003-3531-3931
Manufacturing Engineering Laboratory of Tlemcen (MELT), University of Tlemcen, Algeria

Mohammed Bennekrouf
ESSA-Tlemcen, Algeria

ABSTRACT

Production routing problem is one of the problems of the integrated planning that interests in optimizing simultaneously production, inventory, and distribution planning. This chapter has the purpose of developing two mono-objective models for the production-routing problem: one of them minimizes the total costs which is the classical objective while the other one minimizes the energy consumed by the production system. A bi-objective model is then proposed to combine the two objectives mentioned previously using LP-metric method. To solve big instances of the problem in reasonable time, an approximate approach is proposed using the rolling horizon-based fix and relax heuristic. Finally, computational results are presented to compare the solutions obtained by both approaches.

DOI: 10.4018/978-1-7998-8709-6.ch011

INTRODUCTION

Presently, in the economic context, the relationship between the customer and the supplier has strongly progressed, establishing the need for products and services customization, minimizing the delivery delays, delivery channels multiplication, and satisfaction rates. This led industrial companies to search for new methods to improve their performances and answer the greater degree for customers' expectations. Facing these goals, those companies need to set new planning all along the supply chain network to optimize their processes.

Supply chain management is a huge field that aims to better organize the companies' operations throughout the chain (from the initial suppliers until the distribution of the final product to the final customers) where there are so many issues to deal with. More recently, the focus on the integrated supply chain has become bigger. In fact, its benefits have been proven through the literature, optimizing many activities in a single problem, where its results are better than those of the optimization of each activity independently. For that reason, the operational research community pays more attention and gives more importance to this kind of integrated problem.

The Production Routing Problem (PRP), addressed in this chapter, makes part of the above-mentioned integration problems. In such a problem, the aim is to simultaneously optimize the production decision, the inventory, and the distribution. The PRP is an NP-hard problem because it jointly optimizes many decisions that are: setup, production, inventory, delivery amounts and routing decisions, which makes the problem hard to be solved, seeing that the various decisions may be conflicting, and finding the compromised solution with multiple decision variables under various categories of constraints presents the complexity of the problem. The PRP combines two famous classic problems: the Lot-Sizing Problem (LSP) and the Vehicle Routing Problem (VRP), which was presented by Adulyasak et al. (2015), and both of them have been widely studied. The LSP is the problem of determining the optimal production schedule with the optimal decisions of the amounts to produce and store according to customers' demands. At the same time, the VRP is the problem of determining the optimal vehicle routes either in a term of cost or distance.

The PRP may arise within a supply chain composed of a manufacturing factory that has the role of producing goods and delivering them to a set of customers or warehouses. According to the literature, the PRP aims to find the optimal production and distribution schedule in a multi-period planning horizon to minimize the whole system costs.

Most of the papers dealing with the PRP consider only the total costs minimization (setup, production, inventory and transportation costs) while energy, which is a very important aspect, has not yet been considered. To this fact, and through this work, we propose to include the concept of energy into the PRP definition, and we make a call, in our study, to a multi-objective method. To deal with such a problem, we provide a MILP approach that considers both classical and energy-minimizing PRP versions.

Nowadays, energy consumption has a strong relationship with the worldwide economic development, and because of the limited natural resources, energy has become a critical factor that affects the sustainable development of the industrial and transportation sector. We analyze, in this chapter, the relationship between the cost and the power in the integrated Production-Routing Problem that may be important for production and distribution companies in order to optimally manage their organizations. This chapter contributes to a better understanding of the conflict between the cost and the power consumption, as well as the impact of the power notion on the whole system decisions.

In the rest of this paper, a review of some relevant works from the literature is first presented in section 2, emphasising the proposed resolution approaches for the PRP. In **section 3**, several tabs will be opened. We begin with a description of our problem and strengthen this description by an illustrative example of the classical PRP. Subsequently, we describe the solution procedure followed by a mathematical formulation of the PRP. The mathematical formulation takes into account the cost minimization, the energy consumption minimization, and finally the multi-objective version using an LP-metric method. **Section 4** addresses the efficiency of our model by presenting some small experimental instances. In section 5, the solution approach used to solve the problem is described. Computational results for both exact approach (LP-metric model) and the approximate one (Fix & Relax heuristic combined with LP-metric) are presented in **section 6** then discussed in **section 7**. Finally, **section 8** outlines our approach limitations and opens the door to the perspectives of our study.

LITERATURE REVIEW

The first study on the Production-Routing Problem has been done by Chandra (1993). The author considered the objective of the total costs minimization that combine setup, production, inventory and transportation costs. In (1994), Chandra and Fisher have studied the economic impact of the Production-Routing Problem, where they proved that the implementation of the PRP results in a cost reduction of around 3 to 20% compared to the resolution of the production and the distribution problems each one independently.

Thereafter, many studies have been done on the PRP, treating its different features and proposing the different algorithms and approaches using the different methods to solve it.

The capacited PRP is one of the features of the Production-Routing problem, considering that a capacity limits the production and the storage. Ruokokoski et al. (2010) as well as Bard and Nananukul (2010) treated this feature of the PRP using two different algorithms: Branch & Cut and the Branch & Price, respectively .The same feature has been treated by Absi et al. (2014), where the authors proposed a heuristic algorithm based on a two-phase iterative algorithm: in the first phase the production schedule problem is solved to find the optimal amounts to produce and to store, while in the second phase a set of VRPs and TSPs is solved to determine the vehicle optimal routes.

Regarding close-up solutions (heuristics and meta-heuristics), they are widely used to solve the optimization problems thanks to their ability to explore a big research space in a reasonable time. For example, a GRASP algorithm (Greedy Randomized Adaptive Search Procedure) has been proposed to solve the production-distribution problem by Boudia et al. (2007) through two versions: reactive mechanism process and path relinking process. Brahimi and Aouam (2016) proposed a hybrid heuristic that combines two methods: Relax & Fix and a local search method to solve the PRP. Also a Relax & Fix algorithm has been proposed by Miranda et al. (2018) to solve the PRP in small furniture companies. Differently from papers that consider the classical objective of costs minimization, Darvish et al. (2018) proposed a MILP approach to solving two problems: PRP and IRP, where both cost and carbon emission are minimized. Afra and Behnamian (2021) proposed both MILP model and approximate approach, a Lagrangian heuristic algorithm to solve multi-product PRP with reverse logistics considering the remanufacturing options and the environmental consideration. Zhang et al. (2021) developed a Benders Decomposition approach to solving the production routing problem with multiple vehicles for the distribution, considering the policy of Order-up-to-Level. Liu et al. (2021) proposed a robust optimization approach for the production routing problem of blood products, considering uncertain demand and transhipment.

In the context of sustainability, Galli (2021) discussed environmental sustainability in implementing continuous improvement in manufacturing companies. They presented the most efficient tools and approaches to implement the principles of continuous improvement. Many research papers are interested in solving the production problems that take the energetic aspect into account. For instance, Liu et al. (2014) developed a mathematical model to solve a single-machine production problem. The aim is to minimise energy consumption by minimizing the makespan and greenhouse gas emissions. In their work, a NSGA-II algorithm has been used. In the same context, Yildirim and Mouzon (2011) proposed a mathematical model to minimise both the consumed energy and the makespan using a genetic algorithm. A hybrid flow-shop production system is considered by Bruzzone et al. (2012). They proposed a MILP where the objective is to minimize the total tardiness and the makespan. They integrated power capacity constraints that limit the system's power consumption, using the solver CPLEX and a meta-heuristic called "Randomized Neighborhood Search" to solve the problem. Nedaei (2018) treated the job shop problem and proposed four models in order to study the energy consumption variation and the processing time. This allows showing the conflict between energy consumption and the makespan.

Some other works dealt with the energy aspect in production problems but they considered the energy cost. Moon and Park (2014) developed a set of mathematical models that treat the job-shop problem taking into account the electricity cost variation. They aimed at minimizing the total electricity cost, according to the working time and the state of the machine. The same kind of problems was considered by Zheng and Wang (2015) where they proposed a bi-objective model to minimize the makespan and the carbon emissions that are related to the used energy. Artigues et al. (2013) presented a parallel machines scheduling problem that takes into account two energetic constraints: the maximal and the minimal energy limitation. Bego et al. (2014) proposed a non-linear mathematical model where the objective function included both production and energy costs. In their work, LINGO has been used as a solver. A flow shop scheduling problem has been treated by Ho et al. (2021), where the energetic aspect is considered as a cost to be minimized without increasing the makespan, under the permutation constraints and using Time-Of-Use tariffs. Ahangar et al. (2021) proposed a multi-objective approach for the flexible workshop scheduling problem, with three objectives: minimizing work completion time, work delay time and energy consumption. The problem is solved using multiple algorithms: Epsilon-Constraint, NSGA-II and SFLA meta-heuristic.

Multi-objective optimization is a part of combinatory optimization. It consists of optimizing simultaneously many objectives for the same problem, which are contradictory. It t has been applied to solve various kinds of problems in different domains using different methods. Production problems, in turn, have made extensive use of multi-objective optimization. Sazvar et al. (2014) proposed a new replenishment policy for a centralized supply chain considering deteriorating items and using a bi-objective stochastic programming, minimizing inventory, transportation costs, and greenhouse gas emissions in the same time. Amoozad-Khalili et al. (2010) presented a multi-objective cell formation problem. They considered alternative process routes and machine utilization and fuzzy demand, to minimize jointly the total cell load variation and the total costs using a scatter search algorithm. Bozorgi-Amiri et al. (2013) proposed a stochastic programming model for disaster relief logistics considering the uncertainty. The model aims to minimize the total related costs and, in the same time, to maximize the affected area's satisfaction levels using a multi-objective method which is LP-metric. Dugardin et al. (2012) made a comparative study between some various kinds of multi-objective methods to solve the scheduling problem of reentrant hybrid flow shop, where the objective was to minimize both makespan and the tasks total tardiness. A multi-product advertising billboard location problem has been studied by Lotfi et al. (2017), where a multi-objective model is proposed to solve the small sized problem. The genetic algorithm is then developed to solve the large scale problem. Umarusman (2021) developed a fuzzy Goal Programming to solve multi-objective sustainable supplier selection problems, taking into consideration the economic and the sustainability criteria, using the algorithm of "satisfied optimal supplier design" to increase customer satisfaction.

This study extends the work done by Zeddam et al. (2020), where the authors proposed a MILP approach to solve the production routing problem with energy consideration in a multi-objective context. They introduced the energetic aspect in the integrated production and distribution problem PRP, to show the influence of this side on the PRP, using a bi-objective method: LP-metric, which combines both cost and power minimization objectives. Due to the long computational time of the MILP model to obtain exact results, in this chapter, we propose an approximate heuristic approach that combines Fix & Relax heuristic with LP-metric to solve the same problem, presenting both approaches and comparing their results.

PROBLEM DESCRIPTION AND FORMULATION

The Production-Routing Problem is defined within a supply chain which is composed of a manufacturing plant (factory) that produces and distributes its goods to a set of customers. A central inventory intermediates this chain where the products are stored, considering that each customer has an inventory as well, respecting the storage capacity. The PRP consists in determining, during a given planning horizon that is composed of many periods, the optimal production and the distribution schedule simultaneously, minimizing the total costs of the activities. The PRP aims to optimally determine: the periods when the production should occur, and, if there is a production, the amounts to produce in each period, the amounts to store and to deliver, and finally the vehicle optimal routes.

In the classic PRP, the prime objective is to minimize costs, where those costs (setup, production, inventory and transportation costs) are the major factor to determine the best planning where:

If the **setup cost** is higher in some periods than other ones while the other costs are similar in all periods, the production will occur in the lowest setup cost periods.

If **production cost** is higher in some periods and low for other periods, while the remaining costs are similar in all periods, then the production will occur in the lowest production cost periods.

If the **inventory holding cost** is higher in some periods while low in other ones, then the amounts produced must be delivered in the same periods the production occurred.

If the **transportation cost** is high according to all costs, the number of delivery trips must be minimized to avoid the increase of the transportation cost.

However, the problem is more complicated than what is mentioned previously. The problem should cover all system sides because the costs values cannot be controlled as in the above-mentioned assumptions.

Our approach formulation is set up considering the following assumptions:

- Each period has a fixed length (the same for all periods).
- Each node (production facility and customers) has a limited storage capacity.

- The production capacity is limited with respect to the period's length.
- A single product production and distribution is considered.
- A single vehicle is used for the distribution.
- At the beginning of each production period, the production system must be set up so that a setup time is required.
- The power required for the production is fixed, while the setup power is variable from one period to another.
- The power of two phases (setup and production) must not exceed the maximum power allowed in each period.

Figure 1. The production-routing problem decisions

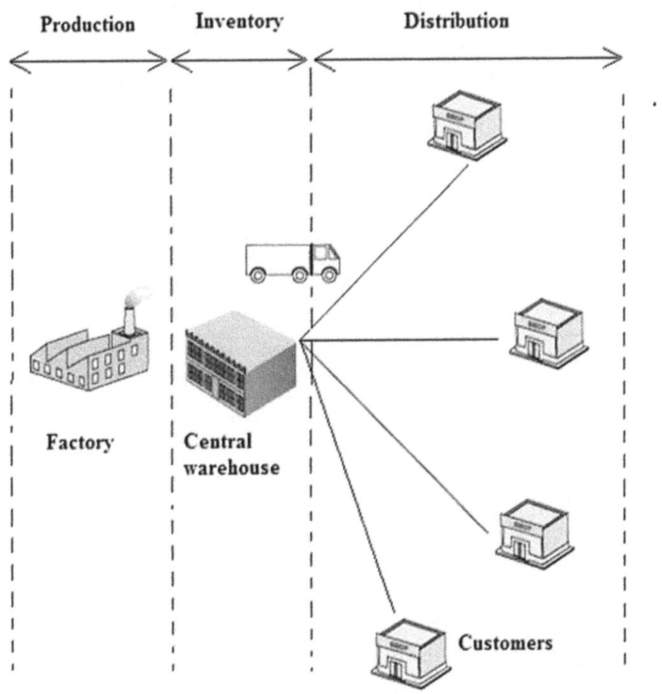

Exact Solution Method

The solution approach proposed in this chapter is based on the Mixed Integer Linear Programming (MILP). Using MILP approach, the problem is formulated through two models, in each of them the objective function aims to minimize the total costs as well as the energy consumed by the production system. Each of the two objectives is optimized independently of the other. Then, they are combined in a single objective using the LP-metric method. The LP-metric method is a rigorous and one of the well-known MCDM methods that are used for the multi-objective optimization problems. It is a rigorous multi- objective technique for making a combined dimensionless objective.

The LP-metric techniquc is intended to make a dimensionless combined objective, i.e. each objective is optimized separately, consequently each model is solved independently, using the same data, then all objective functions are put in the LP-metric function, which is indicated below:

$$Min\ w1\frac{obj1-obj1^{*}}{obj1^{*}}+w2\frac{obj2-obj2^{*}}{obj2^{*}}+...+wn\frac{obj\,n-obj\,n^{*}}{obj\,n^{*}}.$$

obj1, obj2...obj n indicate the objective functions to optimize simultaneously
obj1*, obj2*… obj n*, are the best values corresponding to the functions
w1, w2…wn are the weights granted to the objectives where $0 \leq wn \leq 1$; note that $\Sigma wn=1$.

So to solve the multi-objective model, it is needed to solve each objective separately in order to obtain the objective value that will be used in the LP-metric function. The weights are put according to the decision-maker need. In our study, the possible weights used for each objective are shown in the table below:

Table 1. Possible cases implemented

	W1	W2
Equal weights	0.5	0.5
Different weights	0.7	0.3
	0.3	0.7

The different cases treated in the multi-objective approach are:

- Giving the same importance for each objective, which is represented in the table by equal weights.
- Giving more importance to one objective, so it will be optimized more than the other one. Our study makes different scenarios with different proportions, either giving higher weights to the first or the second objective.

Objective 01: Minimizing Total Costs

Sets:

N: Nodes set of n nodes (one plant and n-1 customers) indexed by i/j ∈ 1,2,..n, where the production plant is presented by node 1. C is a subset of n-1 customers where: C =N–{1}

T: Periods set of m periods indexed by t ∈ 1,2…m.

Parameters:

P_t: Unitary production cost per period t.

h_i: Unitary holding cost for each node i (factory and customers)

S_t: Setup cost for each period t.

CU_t: Vehicle utilization cost per period t.
$Dem_{i,t}$: Demand of customer i in period t.
$CapV$: Capacity of the vehicle.
$CapS_i$: Maximum storage capacity at node i.
$Stock_{i,0}$: Initial inventories at the node i (factory and customers) .
L_t: Length of period t.
$Tprod$: Processing time for one item unit.
$Setup$: Necessary setup time for the production line

Decision Variables

$$Z_t = \begin{cases} 1, \textit{if the production occurs in the plant in period } t \\ 0, \textit{otherwise} \end{cases}$$

R_t: The amount to produce in period t.
$Q_{i,t}$: Quantity of item to deliver to customer i in period t.
$Stock_{i,t}$: Inventory level at node i in period t.
$\alpha_{i,j,t}$: The vehicle loads while travelling the arc (i, j) in period t.

$$Y_{i,t} = \begin{cases} 1, \textit{if node } i \textit{ is visited during period } t \\ 0, \textit{otherwise} \end{cases}$$

$$X_{i,j,t} = \begin{cases} 1, \textit{the vehicle travels from node } i \textit{ to node } j \textit{ during period } t \\ 0, \textit{otherwise} \end{cases}$$

Mathematical Model 01:

$$Min \sum_{i \in N} \sum_{t \in T} h_i * Stock_{i,t} + \sum_{t \in T} CU_t * Y_{1,t} + \sum_{t \in T} S_t * Z_t + \sum_{t \in T} P_t * R_t \tag{1}$$

Subject to:

$$Stock_{1,t} = Stock_{1,t-1} + R_t - \sum_{i \in C} Q_{i,t} \; \forall t \in T \tag{2}$$

$$Stock_{i,t} = Stock_{i,t-1} + Q_{i,t} - Dem_{i,t} \; \forall i \in C, \forall t \in T \tag{3}$$

$$Stock_{i,t} \leq CapS_{i}$$

$$\forall i \in N, \forall t \in T \quad (4)$$

$$Q_{i,t} \leq (CapS_{i} + Dem_{i,t}) * Y_{i,t} \; \forall i \in C, \forall t \in T \quad (5)$$

$$\sum_{i \in C} Q_{i,t} \leq CapV * Y_{1,t} \; \forall t \in T \quad (6)$$

$$\alpha_{i,j,t} \leq CapV * X_{i,j,t} \; \forall i \in N, \forall j \in N, \forall t \in T \quad (7)$$

$$\sum_{j \in N} X_{i,j,t} + \sum_{j \in N} X_{j,i,t} = 2 * Y_{i,t} \; \forall i \in N, \forall t \in T \quad (8)$$

$$\sum_{i \in c} \alpha_{1,i,t} = \sum_{i \in C} Q_{i,t} \; \forall t \in T \quad (9)$$

$$\sum_{j \in N} \alpha_{j,i,t} - \sum_{j \in N} \alpha_{i,j,t} = Q_{i,t} \; \forall i \in C, \forall t \in T \quad (10)$$

$$\alpha_{i,1,t} = 0$$

$$\forall i \in C, \forall t \in T \quad (11)$$

$$\alpha_{i,i,t} = 0$$

$$\forall i \in N, \forall t \in T \quad (12)$$

$$X_{i,i,t} = 0$$

$$\forall i \in N, \forall t \in T \quad (13)$$

$$R_{t} \leq Z_{t} * \sum_{i \in C} \sum_{\substack{t' \in T \\ t' = t}} Dem_{i,t'} \; \forall t \in T \quad (14)$$

$$\sum_{t \in T} Q_{i,t} = \sum_{t \in T} Dem_{i,t} \; \forall i \in C \quad (15)$$

$$\sum_{i \in N} X_{i,j,t} = Y_{j,t} \ \forall j \in N, \forall t \in T \tag{16}$$

$$\sum_{i \in N} \sum_{j \in C} X_{i,j,t} \geq \sum_{j \in C} Q_{j,t} \ / \ CapV \ \forall t \in T \tag{17}$$

$$R_t * Tprod + Z_t * setup \leq L_t$$

$$\forall t \in T \tag{18}$$

$$X_{i,j,t}, Y_{j,t} Z_t \in \{0,1\} \ \forall i \in N, \forall j \in N, \forall t \in T \tag{19}$$

$$\alpha_{i,j,t}, Stock_{i,t}, R_t \geq 0, \forall i \in N, \forall j \in N, \forall t \in T \tag{20}$$

$$Q_{i,t} \geq 0$$

$$\forall i \in C, \forall t \in T \tag{21}$$

The objective function (1) minimizes the total costs of the system including inventory, transportation, production and setup costs, (transportation cost is calculated beside the vehicle utilization cost, every period the vehicle makes a trip, a cost is assigned). Constraints (2) and (3) ensure the inventory balancing at the factory and at the customers. Constraints (4) and (5) indicate that the inventory capacity is respected. Constraints (6) and (7) ensure that the vehicle capacity is not exceeded. Constraint (8) indicates that the vehicle visits a customer and leaves after serving it. Constraints (9) and (10) calculate the vehicle load within the delivered amounts. Constraints (11) and (12) indicate that there is no vehicle load to hold between the node itself nor while returning to the plant. Constraint (13) insures that there is no arc between the node and itself. Constraints (14) and (15) ensure that the amounts produced and delivered are appropriate with customers' demand. Constraint (16) is a route constraint while constraint (17) is the fractional capacity constraint to eliminate the sub-tour. Constraint (18) serves in limiting the amounts produced according to the length of the period. Finally, constraints (19), (20) and (21) indicate the nature of the variables.

Objective 02: Minimizing the Consumed Energy

In this part, another model is introduced. It aims to minimize the energy consumed by the production system, adding to the previous model:

Parameters:

- pow1: required power for the production line while processing.
- $Pow2_t$: required power for the production line during the setup of the production in period t.
- Max_t: maximum amount of power authorized in period t.

Decision Variables

$Cons1_t$: power consumed by the production line during processing in period t

$Cons2_t$: power consumed by the production line during the setup of the production in period t.

E_t: the amount of power to be used in period t.

Mathematical Model 02:

$$Min \sum_{t \in T} Cons1_t * R_t + \sum_{t \in T} Cons2_t * Z_t \tag{22}$$

These constraints are added to model 01 to construct model 02:

$$Cons1_t = pow1 * Tprod \; \forall t \in T \tag{23}$$

$$Cons2_t = pow2_t * setup \; \forall t \in T \tag{24}$$

$$E_t \geq (pow1 + pow2_t) * Z_t \; \forall t \in T \tag{25}$$

$$E_t \leq Max_t \; \forall t \in T \tag{26}$$

The objective function (22) replaces the objective function (1) in the first model, it aims to minimize the total energy consumed by the system in the two phases: setup and production. Constraints (23) and (24) calculate the total power consumed by the production line during production and setup, respectively. Constraint (25) calculates the power used by the line and the constraint (26) serves to limit the power used.

Objective 03: Multi-Objective Case

In this part, we introduce another model that aims to simultaneously minimize the total costs and consumed energy. In our case, the problem formulation will include all the parameters and variables of both of models with:

$$Obj1 = \sum_{i \in N} \sum_{t \in T} h_i * Stock_{i,t} + \sum_{t \in T} CU_t * Y_{1,t} + \sum_{t \in T} S_t * Z_t + \sum_{t \in T} P_t * R_t \tag{27}$$

$$Obj2 = \sum_{t \in T} Cons1_t * R_t + \sum_{t \in T} Cons2_t * Z_t \tag{28}$$

Mathematical Model 03:

Now the mathematical model becomes:

$$Min\ w1\frac{obj1 - obj1^*}{obj1^*} + w2\frac{obj2 - obj2^*}{obj2^*} \tag{29}$$

Subject to: (2) to (21) and (23) to (28) (mentioned previously).

Where (29) is the multi-objective function, w1 and w2 are weights allowing to control the importance of each function. Constraint (27) calculates the objective value of the cost function, and constraint (28) calculates the objective value of the energy function. So this model includes both models' constraints while the objective function is the LP-metric function.

SOLUTION METHOD (ROLLING HORIZON BASED FIX & RELAX HEURISTIC)

Rolling Horizon based Fix & Relax heuristic is an approximate approach that aims to decompose the main problem into a set of sub-problems. The planning horizon is decomposed into three parts and the sub-problems are solved sequentially using the method of Rolling Horizon that serves to browse all the planning horizon. The principle of F&R heuristic is to decompose the planning horizon into three windows:

- **Observation Window:** contains the sub-horizon where the sub-problem is solved, it is generally situated in the beginning of the planning horizon.
- **Approximation Window:** contains the planning horizon removing the observation window. In this window the integer variables are relaxed and become continuous. In our study, this window is not used to avoid obtaining solutions of bad quality in term of gap value.
- **Frozen Window:** is a part of the observation window, it contains the periods where the solution is saved after solving the sub-problem.

Figure 2. Fix and relax principle

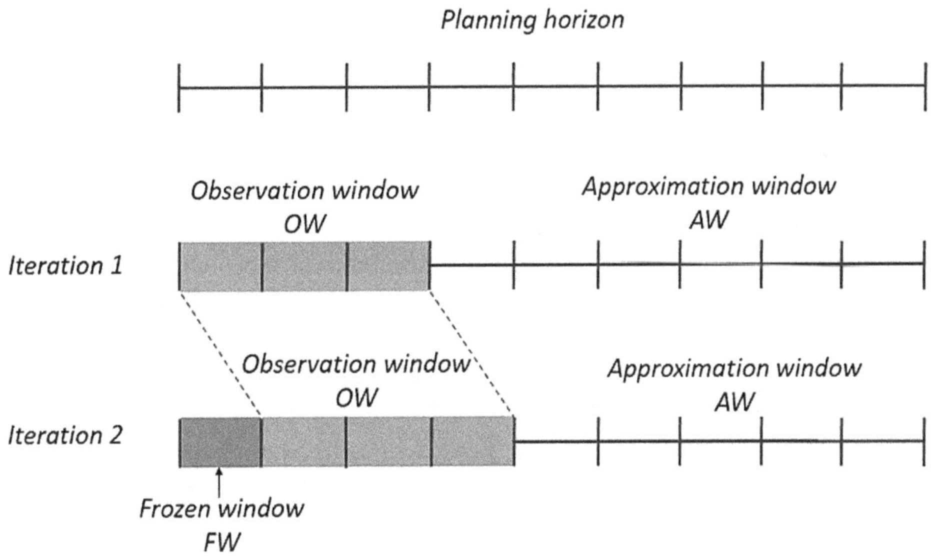

After solving the first iteration sub-problem, the periods in the frozen window are removed from the planning horizon, and using the Rolling Horizon method, the observation window is rolled to start where the frozen window has ended.

In the MILP approach, three models are solved separately: cost minimization, power consumption and LP-metric model. To solve the LP-metric model, the solution of both objectives models should be determined. This presents one of the disadvantages of the LP-metric method.

The F&R heuristic is implemented in JAVA 16 using CPLEX 12.8 libraries to solve the problem (CPLEX JAVA API). The algorithm used in this chapter aims to solve the three models in one JAVA source code that consecutively executes the sub-problems. The values of the objective functions of mono-objective models in each iteration are saved and stored as a non-variable value, so there will be no non-linearity issues in the LP-metric function.

Figure 3. Pseudo-code of the proposed algorithm

PROPOSED SOLUTION ALGORITHM

```
Set: N, OW, FW, i=0;
While i ≤ N-OW do
    For i=i... i+OW  do
        Solve Cost model;
            Save objective function;
        Solve Power consumption model;
            Save objective function;
        Solve LP-metric model;
            Fix variables in i=i... i<i+FW;
    End For
    i=i+FW;
End While
Calculate general solution from fixed variables;
Return solution;
```

Application Example

To better understand the problem treated in this paper, an application example of 5 periods and 5 customers is considered, which presents the first instance treated that will be included in the computational results part. The data are presented in Table 2 and the results are shown in Table 3.

In this example, results of the first model (min cost) show that because the setup cost was lower in periods 1 and 3 then the production occurred in those periods, and the delivery was planned in period 1, 4 and 5 because the of the vehicle utilization cost. The second model gives almost the same results where the production occurred in period 1 and 3 (but with different amounts) where the power consumption was lower, then the distribution happened in all periods because the transportation cost is not taken into consideration in the energy minimization model. In the LP-metric case the objective values of both objectives were exactly the same as in the independent models was close but a little bit higher than the independent function while the value of energy function was exactly the that's why the production decision was in the same periods that to both models, but the amounts like the first model, while the delivery decision was in the same periods as the first model but also with different amounts to optimize the transportation cost. Here the objective functions weights were equal that's the reason why the LP-metric try to satisfy both objectives in the same time with equal proportions.

With the same concept, Fix & Relax heuristic is applied then to reduce the problem complexity, setting the observation window OW=4 and the frozen window FW==1, the main problem then is solved in two iterations: in the first iteration, the sub-problem (from period 1 to period 4) is solved and the solution of the first period is fixed and saved, then in the second iteration, the sub-problem (from period 2 to period 5) is solved, then the solution of all the periods are fixed and saved because there is no more periods. As a result of F&R heuristic, its solution is the same as the solution obtained by the mathematical model.

Table 2. Data of the application example

		P1	**P 2**	**P 3**	**P 4**	**P5**
Demand	**C1**	100	0	200	0	0
	C2	0	300	0	150	0
	C3	50	0	250	0	100
	C4	150	100	0	0	200
	C5	0	200	100	100	0
Max_t		500	200	400	800	600
P_t		2	2	2	2	2
L_t		1000	1000	1000	1000	1000
$Pow2_t$		200	260	250	300	500
S_t		50	30	25	30	50
CU_t		100	200	300	120	200
h_i		**Factory**	**C1**	**C2**	**C3**	**C4**
		0	0	0	0	0
Weights		**W1**		**W2**		
		0.5	0.5			
$CapS_i$	1200	500	500	500	500	500
$S_{i,0}$	400	200	200	200	200	200
Tprod		**Setup**	**Pow1**	**CapV**	**OW**	**FW**
1		10	10	800	4	1

Table 3. Results of the application example

Min cost	**Ob1**	3 695					
	Rt	**P1**	**P2**	**P3**	**P4**	**P5**	
		990	/	610	/	/	
	Q	300	/	/	/	/	**C1**
		250	/	/	/	200	**C2**
		100	/	/	300	/	**C3**
		50	/	/	200	200	**C4**
		100	/	/	300	/	**C5**
Min energy	**Ob2**	20 500					
	Rt	**P1**	**P2**	**P3**	**P4**	**P5**	
		610	/	990	/	/	
	Q	/	210	/	/	90	**C1**
		/	450	/	/	/	**C2**
		/	/	100	300	/	**C3**
		50	/	/	400	/	**C4**
		300	/	/	100	/	**C5**
LP-metric	**LP- ob**	0					
	Ob1	3 695					
	Ob2	20 500					
	Rt	**P1**	**P2**	**P3**	**P4**	**P5**	
		990	/	610	/	/	
	Q	300	/	/	/	/	**C1**
		250	/	/	200	/	**C2**
		100	/	/	/	300	**C3**
		50	/	/	/	400	**C4**
		100	/	/	300	/	**C5**
Fix & Relax	**LP- ob**	0					
	Ob1	3 695					
	Ob2	20 500					
	Rt	**P1**	**P2**	**P3**	**P4**	**P5**	
	Q	990	/	610	/	/	
		300	/	/	/	/	**C1**
		250	/	/	200	/	**C2**
		100	/	/	/	300	**C3**
		50	/	/	/	400	**C4**
		100	/	/	300	/	**C5**

COMPUTATIONAL RESULTS

In this part, computational tests are established to compare results in (Zeddam et al., 2020) obtained by MILP approach with those obtained by the proposed solution method. To test the performance of Fix & Relax, three types of F&R computations are set according to the size of the Observation Window, with fixing the size of the Frozen Window to 1, which means that the variables of the first period in the Observation Window are fixed in each iteration. The computations are made using the same Intel® Core™ i3-2348M CPU @ 2.30 GHz personal computer that performs with 4GB of RAM with a Windows10 operating system, using CPLEX 12.8 and JAVA 16.

Table 4. Results of F and R heuristic with OW size=2 and FW size =1

	Instance	/C/	/T/	MILP (CPLEX)			Fix & Relax: OW=2; FW=1		
				Objective Value 1	Objective Value 2	CPU (s)	Objective Value 1	Objective Value 2	CPU (s)
Small size instances	1	5	5	3 695	20 500	36	3 715	20 550	5
	2			4 075	26 500	29	4 100	26 650	7
	3			32 280	18 500	43	32 480	18 600	7
	4	10	10	7 057	24 685	91	7 075	24 715	28
	5		20	8 912	42 484	177	9 025	42 520	43
	6		30	10 012	67 973	301	10 102	68 280	71
	7		50	16 675	94 054	853	16 715	94 170	137
	8		100	25 943	129 794	2864	26 230	129 830	196
	9		150	58 513	172 545	6094	58 812	172 675	261
Medium size instances	10	20	10	8 134	38 755	229	8 264	38 825	67
	11		20	13 648	55 312	339	13 698	55 450	153
	12		30	16 061	83 019	1661	16 170	83 205	281
	13		50	25 843	102 964	2822	25 920	103 000	302
	14		100	59 628	167 943	5724	59 715	168 003	267
	15		150	CPU for each objective >3600			82 830	211 709	784
Large size instances	16	30	10	11 475	60 410	2701	13 385	61 530	309
	17		20	18 054	77 453	7332	19 023	78 323	512
	18		30	26 839	97 795	9157	27 925	98 992	694
	19		50	45 131	119 891	9904	46 526	121 009	820
	20		100	CPU for each objective >3600			53 584	148 152	1091
	21		150	CPU for each objective >3600			85 475	182 477	1584
	22	40	10	17 103	80 035	4138	18 719	82 104	271
	23		20	31 145	103 144	7245	33 017	104 109	512
	24		30	49 934	133 497	9834	51 224	135 356	1021
	25		50	CPU for each objective >3600			78 574	175 212	1327
	26		100	CPU for each objective >3600			108 278	245 251	1834
	27		150	CPU for each objective >3600			157 412	307 545	2004

Table 5. Results of F and R heuristic with OW size=3 and FW size =1

	Instance	/C/	/T/	MILP (CPLEX)			Fix & Relax: OW=3; FW=1		
				Objective Value 1	Objective Value 2	CPU (s)	Objective Value 1	Objective Value 2	CPU (s)
Small size instances	1	5	5	3 695	20 500	36	3 695	20 500	8
	2			4 075	26 500	29	4 075	26 500	12
	3			32 280	18 500	43	32 280	18 500	9
	4	10	10	7 057	24 685	91	7 070	24 700	34
	5		20	8 912	42 484	177	9 015	42 510	41
	6		30	10 012	67 973	301	10 062	68 190	86
	7		50	16 675	94 054	853	16 705	94 130	129
	8		100	25 943	129 794	2864	26 223	129 805	231
	9		150	58 513	172 545	6094	5 8770	172 625	297
Medium size instances	10	20	10	8 134	38 755	229	8 250	38 812	84
	11		20	13 648	55 312	339	13 672	55 426	197
	12		30	16 061	83 019	1661	16 145	83 195	305
	13		50	25 843	102 964	2822	25 920	102 994	381
	14		100	59 628	167 943	5724	59 702	169 993	696
	15		150	CPU for each objective >3600			82 382	211 415	812
Large size instances	16	30	10	11 475	60 410	2701	12 627	61 324	267
	17		20	18 054	77 453	7332	18 973	78 025	472
	18		30	26 839	97 795	9157	27 528	98 712	661
	19		50	45 131	119 891	9904	46 007	120 609	894
	20		100	CPU for each objective >3600			53 121	147 835	1159
	21		150	CPU for each objective >3600			85 210	182 132	1782
	22	40	10	17 103	80 035	4138	18 622	81 520	183
	23		20	31 145	103 144	7245	32 418	104 230	607
	24		30	49 934	133 497	9834	50 620	134 612	941
	25		50	CPU for each objective >3600			78 315	174 865	1567
	26		100	CPU for each objective >3600			107 865	245 051	1712
	27		150	CPU for each objective >3600			157 184	307 235	2318

The tables 2, 3 and 4 present a comparison of the results of the MILP approach and Fix & Relax heuristic, with different sizes of the Observation Window: 2, 3 et 4 respectively. The comparison is established regarding the value of the objective functions and the total computational time. The computational time in the MILP approach is the sum of the time required to obtain results for each model (cost model, power consumption model and LP-metric model) with a time limit of 3600s (1 hour) for each objective. (See Zeddam et al., 2020)). While in F&R heuristic the results are obtained in only one run.

Table 6. Results of F and R heuristic with OW size=4 and FW size =1

	Instance	/C/	/T/	MILP (CPLEX)			Fix & Relax: OW=4; FW=1		
				Objective Value 1	**Objective Value 2**	**CPU (s)**	**Objective Value 1**	**Objective Value 2**	**CPU (s)**
	1			3 695	20 500	36	3 695	20 500	7
	2	5	5	4 075	26 500	29	4 075	26 500	9
	3			32 280	18 500	43	32 280	18 500	7
	4		10	7 057	24 685	91	70 60	24 658	27
Small size instances	**5**		20	8 912	42 484	177	89 052	42 500	36
	6	10	30	10 012	67 973	301	10 032	68 090	79
	7		50	16 675	94 054	853	16 695	94 130	148
	8		100	25 943	129 794	2864	26 220	129 805	238
	9		150	58 513	172 545	6094	58 765	172 605	327
	10		10	8 134	38 755	229	8 202	38 792	73
	11		20	13 648	55 312	339	13 668	55 412	193
Medium size instances	**12**	20	30	16 061	83 019	1661	16 114	83 173	318
	13		50	25 843	102 964	2822	25 920	102 983	467
	14		100	59 628	167 943	5724	59 685	168 713	518
	15		150	CPU for each objective >3600			82 174	211 101	821
	16		10	11 475	60 410	2701	11 981	61 015	253
	17		20	18 054	77 453	7332	18 619	77 925	488
	18	30	30	26 839	97 795	9157	27 212	98 222	716
	19		50	45 131	119 891	9904	45 823	120 102	917
	20		100	CPU for each objective >3600			52 719	147 533	1352
Large size instances	**21**		150	CPU for each objective >3600			85 001	181 714	2079
	22		10	17 103	80 035	4138	18 029	81 207	192
	23		20	31 145	103 144	7245	31 918	103 830	634
	24	40	30	49 934	133 497	9834	50 328	134 015	1121
	25		50	CPU for each objective >3600			78 112	174 525	1623
	26		100	CPU for each objective >3600			107 432	244 821	2017
	27		150	CPU for each objective >3600			156 689	307 002	2839

The minimization of the total costs requires reducing the inventory level at the depot and at customers, while the minimization of the power consumption aims to make the production in the periods where the required power for the production is smaller but with big amounts in order to eliminate the setup power each time, and this leads to a higher inventory at the depot. The delivery costs (vehicle utilization cost) are also minimized in the first model, the model aims to find the best solution within the storage and the delivery decisions, while in the second model, the distribution routes may not be optimal because the optimization in the second model concerns, not only the production decisions, but also has an influence on the remaining decisions.

The LP-metric method aims to find within the two independent solutions the best compromise with respect to the weights of the objectives. The LP-metric solutions are tendentious to the higher weighted model solution (nearer to the objective that has the higher weight) or exactly the same as it (instances 11, 13, 19, 23 and 24). The computational time increases each time the problem size increases, until it can't be solved within the time limit, which represents a complexity factor for solving the PRP.

It is obvious in the tables 2,3 and 4 that there is a significant reduction in the computational time using F&R heuristic, and this time depends on the size of the observation window, as can be noticed the smaller computational time is obtained in the first table (OW=2), each time size of the observation window is smaller the sub-problem is easier to be solved so the computational time is less. While increasing the size of the OW may result to increase the time to solve the problem. In term of the obtained objective values, the results of the third table (OW=4) are better, (the results are the same to the MILP approach in instances 1, 2 and 3), while the computational time here is higher, this can be explained by the increasing of the complexity of solving the sub-problems comparing to the case of OW=2. In summary for the performance of Fix & Relax heuristic, the greater the size of the observation window, the more complex is the problem, and this will lead to obtaining the best results regarding the objective value, and the longer computational time. While decreasing the observation window size will lead to reducing the complexity of the sub-problems, so the computational time is smaller while the objective value might be farther than the value obtained from the MILP approach.

CONCLUSION

In the present chapter, we studied the integrated production and distribution planning Problem (PRP), which simultaneously optimised production, inventory, and routing decisions. We described a new approach that gathers the economic and the energetic side. We introduced the energetic aspect in our study in order to show the trade-off between the terms: cost and energy. The power consumption expresses the energy in the production phase where the delivery decision is not optimized efficiently while all decisions are taken into account in the classical PRP. The PRP here is treated differently, so that both objectives of the same problem are solved separately using the same data. These objectives are not expressed with the same measure unit and cannot be combined in the same objective, so a multi-objective procedure called: LP-metric is introduced. The LP-metric method is based on assigning weights (importance degree) to each objective. Weights take their values between 0 and 1. Equal weights are used if we want that the final results satisfy the objectives with the same chances.

The proposed MILP approach might give exact solutions for the problem, but when the problem size increases, the computational increases and may lead to some difficulties to obtain results. An approximate solution method is proposed to solve this problem, using Fix & Relax heuristic based on the Rolling Horizon technique. The results of the MILP approach and the proposed heuristic are compared using different sizes of the Observation Window.

Our results showed a significant reduction of the computational time, which depends on the OW size, each time the OW size is smaller the computational time is smaller as well. Besides, in term of the solution quality, the best objective value is obtained by the higher OW size.

Although this chapter presents a dynamic study for the Production-Routing Problem introducing the energetic aspect in this kind of supply chain management problems, many factors are still not considered in our approach. Actually, those limitations provide us with new perspectives and future scopes to enrich our study:

- Our approach treats the PRP where the distribution is done by a single vehicle, this may be good if the vehicle's capacity is huge and it can satisfy all the customers' demands, but if the vehicles' capacity is small, the resolution of the problem might be infeasible. To avoid this problem, we propose to make a complete study considering a fleet of vehicles either homogeneous or heterogeneous.
- The proposed model considers the single item PRP, which might not be the case of the majority of the existing companies. To generalize the proposed approach, a multi-item PRP should be considered, applying this study on a real practical case in order to show the effect of the energetic aspect in the PRP on real case companies. Introducing the traceability as presented by Permala et al. (2012) and Kros et al. (2019) in this kind of study will be also a good contribution.
- Finally, although the proposed heuristic proved its efficiency to solve the problem. Developing another heuristic or metaheuristic to solve the problem would be beneficent (as Multi-Objective Simulated Annealing), either to compare the results or to implement a hybrid approach to solve big instances in less time.

REFERENCES

Absi, N., Archetti, C., Dauzère-Pérès, S., & Feillet, D. (2014). A two-phase iterative heuristic approach for the production routing problem. *Transportation Science*, *49*(4), 784–795. doi:10.1287/trsc.2014.0523

Adulyasak, Y., Cordeau, J. F., & Jans, R. (2015). The production routing problem: A review of formulations and solution algorithms. *Computers & Operations Research*, *55*, 141–152. doi:10.1016/j.cor.2014.01.011

Afra, A. P., & Behnamian, J. (2021). Lagrangian heuristic algorithm for green multi-product production routing problem with reverse logistics and remanufacturing. *Journal of Manufacturing Systems*, *58*, 33–43. doi:10.1016/j.jmsy.2020.11.013

Ahangar, N. K., & Tayebi, H. (2021). The three-objective optimization model of flexible workshop scheduling problem for minimizing work completion time, work delay time, and energy consumption. *Tehnički glasnik*, *15*(1), 76-83.

Amoozad-Khalili, H., Ranjbar-Bourani, M., & Ale-Hashem, S. J. M. (2010). Fuzzy demand consideration in a multi-objective dynamic cell formation problem using a robust scatter search. *J Math Comput SCI-JM*, *1*(4), 321–332. doi:10.22436/jmcs.001.04.09

Artigues, C., Lopez, P., & Hait, A. (2013). The energy scheduling problem: Industrial case-study and constraint propagation techniques. *International Journal of Production Economics*, *143*(1), 13–23. doi:10.1016/j.ijpe.2010.09.030

Bard, J. F., & Nananukul, N. (2010). A branch-and-price algorithm for an integrated production and inventory routing problem. *Computers & Operations Research*, *37*(12), 2202–2217. doi:10.1016/j.cor.2010.03.010

Bego, A., Li, L., & Sun, Z. (2014). Identification of reservation capacity in critical peak pricing electricity demand response program for sustainable manufacturing systems. *International Journal of Energy Research*, *38*(6), 728–736. doi:10.1002/er.3077

Boudia, M., Louly, M. A. O., & Prins, C. (2007). A reactive GRASP and path relinking for a combined production–distribution problem. *Computers & Operations Research*, *34*(11), 3402–3419. doi:10.1016/j.cor.2006.02.005

Bozorgi-Amiri, A., Jabalameli, M. S., & Al-e-Hashem, S. M. (2013). A multi-objective robust stochastic programming model for disaster relief logistics under uncertainty. *OR-Spektrum*, *35*(4), 905–933. doi:10.100700291-011-0268-x

Brahimi, N., & Aouam, T. (2016). Multi-item production routing problem with backordering: A MILP approach. *International Journal of Production Research*, *54*(4), 1076–1093. doi:10.1080/00207543.2015.1047971

Bruzzone, A. A., Anghinolfi, D., Paolucci, M., & Tonelli, F. (2012). Energy-aware scheduling for improving manufacturing process sustainability: A mathematical model for flexible flow shops. *CIRP Annals*, *61*(1), 459–462. doi:10.1016/j.cirp.2012.03.084

Chandra, P. (1993). A dynamic distribution model with warehouse and customer replenishment requirements. *The Journal of the Operational Research Society*, *44*(7), 681–692. doi:10.1057/jors.1993.117

Chandra, P., & Fisher, M. L. (1994). Coordination of production and distribution planning. *European Journal of Operational Research*, *72*(3), 503–517. doi:10.1016/0377-2217(94)90419-7

Darvish, M., Archetti, C., & Coelho, L. C. (2018). Trade-offs between environmental and economic performance in production and inventory-routing problems. *International Journal of Production Economics*.

Dugardin, F., Yalaoui, F., & Amodeo, L. (2012). Hybrid multi-objective methods to solve reentrant shops. *International Journal of Applied Logistics*, *3*(4), 15–32. doi:10.4018/jal.2012100102

Galli, B. J. (2021). How to effectively implement continuous improvement for environmental sustainability. *International Journal of Applied Logistics*, *11*(1), 38–51. doi:10.4018/IJAL.2021010103

Ho, M. H., Hnaien, F., & Dugardin, F. (2021). Electricity cost minimization for optimal makespan solution in flow shop scheduling under time-of-use tariffs. *International Journal of Production Research*, *59*(4), 1041–1067. doi:10.1080/00207543.2020.1715504

Kros, J. F., Liao, Y., Kirchoff, J. F., & Zemanek, J. E. Jr. (2019). Traceability in the supply chain. *International Journal of Applied Logistics*, *9*(1), 1–22. doi:10.4018/IJAL.2019010101

Liu, C., Yang, J., Lian, J., Li, W., Evans, S., & Yin, Y. (2014). Sustainable performance oriented operational decision-making of single machine systems with deterministic product arrival time. *Journal of Cleaner Production*, *85*, 318–330. doi:10.1016/j.jclepro.2014.07.025

Liu, P., Hendalianpour, A., Razmi, J., & Sangari, M. S. (2021). A solution algorithm for integrated production-inventory-routing of perishable goods with transshipment and uncertain demand. *Complex & Intelligent Systems*, 1-17.

Lotfi, R., Mehrjerdi, Y. Z., & Mardani, N. (2017). A multi-objective and multi-product advertising billboard location model with attraction factor mathematical modeling and solutions. *International Journal of Applied Logistics, 7*(1), 64–86. doi:10.4018/IJAL.2017010104

Miranda, P. L., Morabito, R., & Ferreira, D. (2018). Optimization model for a production, inventory, distribution and routing problem in small furniture companies. *Top (Madrid), 26*(1), 30–67.

Moon, J. Y., & Park, J. (2014). Smart production scheduling with time-dependent and machine-dependent electricity cost by considering distributed energy resources and energy storage. *International Journal of Production Research, 52*(13), 3922–3939. doi:10.1080/00207543.2013.860251

Nedaei, M. (2018). Scheduling analysis and strategic service planning for optimum operation of two parallel machines under effect of sequencing: A case study of a manufacturing company in a job-shop environment. *International Journal of Service Science, Management, Engineering, and Technology, 9*(4), 57–72. doi:10.4018/IJSSMET.2018100104

Permala, A., Rantasila, K., & Pilli-Sihvola, E. (2012). RFID: From closed systems to improving visibility in the manufacturing supply chain. *International Journal of Applied Logistics, 3*(2), 14–24. doi:10.4018/jal.2012040102

Ruokokoski, M., Solyali, O. G. U. Z., Cordeau, J. F., Jans, R., & Süral, H. (2010). *Efficient formulations and a branch-and-cut algorithm for a production-routing problem.* GERAD Technical Report G-2010-66.

Sazvar, Z., Mirzapour Al-e-Hashem, S. M. J., Baboli, A., & Jokar, M. A. (2014). A bi-objective stochastic programming model for a centralized green supply chain with deteriorating products. *International Journal of Production Economics, 150*, 140–154. doi:10.1016/j.ijpe.2013.12.023

Umarusman, N. (2021). Fuzzy goal programming with interval type-2 for solving multi-objective sustainable supplier selection problems. In G. Aytekin & Ç. Doğru (Eds.), *Handbook of Research on Recent Perspectives on Management, International Trade, and Logistics* (pp. 164–197). IGI Global. doi:10.4018/978-1-7998-5886-7.ch010

Yildirim, M. B., & Mouzon, G. (2011). Single-machine sustainable production planning to minimize total energy consumption and total completion time using a multiple objective genetic algorithm. *IEEE Transactions on Engineering Management, 59*(4), 585–597. doi:10.1109/TEM.2011.2171055

Zeddam, B., Belkaid, F., & Bennekrouf, M. (2020). An efficient approach for solving integrated production and distribution planning problems: Cost vs. Energy. *International Journal of Applied Logistics, 10*(2), 25–44. doi:10.4018/IJAL.2020070102

Zhang, Z., Luo, Z., Baldacci, R., & Lim, A. (2021). A benders decomposition approach for the multivehicle production routing problem with order-up-to-level policy. *Transportation Science, 55*(1), 160–178. doi:10.1287/trsc.2019.0964

Zheng, H. Y., & Wang, L. (2015). Reduction of carbon emissions and project makespan by a Pareto-based estimation of distribution algorithm. *International Journal of Production Economics, 164*, 421–432. doi:10.1016/j.ijpe.2014.12.010

Chapter 12
Improvement of Resource Utilisation Through Forecasting, Planning, and Information Flow:
An Adoption of Lean Principles

Guy Coulthard
University of Lincoln, UK

Carl Baxter
University of Lincoln, UK

Tu Van Binh
University of Economics Ho Chi Minh City, Vietnam & CFVG, Vietnam

ABSTRACT

Demand forecasting and production planning are challenging issues when working to supply perishable goods to fulfil supermarket requirements as opposed to dry goods that can be manufactured and have a fixed storage life. The focus of this report is on the improvement of resource utilisation through better forecasting, planning, and information flow. There is a fluctuation for labour demand within the processing function; controlling the number of staff daily is vital to the efficient running of production and waste reduction. It is the belief for the management that left unchecked the production planners can tend to overorder staff as a contingency.

INTRODUCTION

Company X (CX) is a privately-owned company whose main business is the service provision of fresh produce for supply to major retailers within the United Kingdom (UK). CX is part of the CX Group whose mission is to develop new apples for commercial release to growers. CX also imports top fruit (apples and pears) and works with British growers of top fruit to supply retailers year-round. It is the

DOI: 10.4018/978-1-7998-8709-6.ch012

largest service provider of top fruit to major supermarkets in the UK. Interests that include joint ventures in table grape production in Greece and Chile pursuing a vertical integration strategy supplies fruit to China and the UK.

The main site in Kent has a state-of-the-art packing facility. Until recently, the focus of the site has been to pack and supply grapes to a single major retailer, delivering around 5.5 million cases of grapes per year. The retailer has decided to streamline its business. They have chosen to move their grape packing to a new bespoke site that will supply several products giving efficiencies of scale that they believe they were lacking. This change has a huge impact on the site in Kent, and for the site to remain a viable going concern CX must find new customers to replace the lost volume.

For the last 15 years, CX has packed fruit either as an importer or a service provider for a single major retailer. During this time CX has prided itself on an exemplary service level of 99.97% and being able to meet the retailers' daily requirements no matter the fluctuation or complexity of the orders in an already complex global supply chain. Delivering these 52 weeks of the year requires flexibility. Although the retailers' sales may be relatively steady throughout the year, table grapes have short seasons and to supply year-round the fruit is imported from a minimum of thirteen countries. Generally, grapes from northern hemisphere countries can be packed and shipped in a relatively short time frame of ten days. This fruit can be packed at source "retail-ready" requiring little or no remedial work prior to onward delivery to the retail customer in the UK. Whereas fruit from the southern hemisphere can arrive upwards of 30 days after packing at source and is generally not packed as "retail-ready", this fruit requires much more work on arrival in the UK to prepare for retail. This is the main factor that determines the demand for labour within the pack-house and imposes the need to employ agency staff within the packing process at CX facility at Orchard Place to complement the core staff at certain times of the year, as the column chart Figure 1 below shows. Core staff are employed year-round as permanent staff members, whereas a third-party labour provider supplies agency staff on a daily shift basis. This way of working optimised to meet the retailers quality requirements has served CX well over time. However, as it seeks to find a new business without the security of the retailers', CX must look inwardly and ensure the business is competitive.

Figure 1 shows that in the period March 2020 to February 2021, agency staff made up to as much as 71% of the pack-house workforce with a high requirement from March through to mid-June when the need for agency staff fell to zero. The requirement for agency staff remains relatively low through the summer and is sporadic through September to January, when the requirement increases once again.

This chapter focuses on the packing facility at Orchard Place. It defines how to improve labour resource utilisation by improving the flow and accuracy of information from the commercial and technical teams at CX to the pack-house manager and planners.

To attract new business, the site must work to improve its efficiencies and prove itself competitive. The site at Orchard Place has around 240 employees, including office, warehouse, and pack-house staff (the packhouse staff work on a four-on-four-off shift pattern; therefore, there are approximately 80 packhouse core staff per shift). To achieve the requirements of new customers efficiently, CX should aim to better control the management of daily workflow and staff levels required.

The Senior Management believes that in meeting the retailers' demanding specification, the pack-house is generally overstaffed and works to Parkinson's Law. The Law proposes that "Work expands to fill the time available for its completion" (Gough, 2011), suggesting that the pack-house will work to complete the daily order cycle in the 12 hours allotted to each shift, without a great incentive to improve efficiency.

Figure 1. Total packhouse weekly staff levels from 20th March 2020 to February 28th, 2021

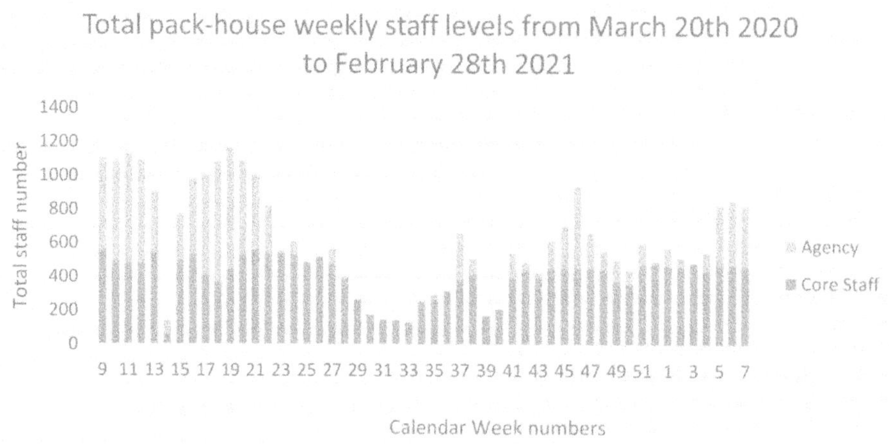

The chapter will explore the inefficiencies within the packing process and investigate how the information coming from CX commercial and technical teams can help the pack-house manager and planners to manage the pack-house labour and the overall pack-house performance better. This will be achieved by creating a forecast with accurate daily information to guide the pack-house planners.

The forecast will incorporate a model to aid with planning and take the fruit quality, labour, and job types required to account. The intention is that this will give greater accuracy when forecasting and allow the analysis of the forecast given. The forecast is expected to produce metrics that can be measured weekly and provide valuable information that, over time will give the business a much clearer picture of where waste is being created. This, in turn, should allow the business to improve the utilisation of labour resources and match the quantity and type of staff to the customer demand.

The expectation is that this information will improve productivity and reduce the perceived over-production. Although the current ways of working have delivered a great service level to The retailers', it is believed to be bringing inefficiencies to the packing process.

Productivity is currently measured in the pack-house using average units of packs per minute (ppm), per direct person-hour (run-rate) for specific activity types. However, the run rate is currently set as a financial benchmark and averages, rather than a calculated rate for individual jobs taking fruit quality and labour into account.

The maximum run rate is determined by the Pro-seal heat-sealer (GT2) speed and the number of staff required to feed it to run at its optimal rate. The manufacturer claims the GT2 capacity to be 120ppm (Pro-seal, 2019). The rate card is calculated using the assumption that the pack-house can consistently run the Pro-seal at 80% capacity (96ppm).

The labour required to achieve this is dependent on the quality status of the fruit, Red, Amber Green (RAG) and the type of packing job required. As seen in Table 1 below, the run rate directly affects capacity and efficiency within the packhouse; running at 4ppm reduces the machine time available, increases the labour cost by 50%, and reduces the operating profit by £871.17.

Table 1. How the ppm effects capacity and run rate

Rate card 0.15p per punnet	Staff	ppm per person (benchmark is 8)	Total PPM	Number of packs required	Labour cost ph	mins required	Total packhouse hours	Direct labour	Chargeable cost	Commision	Total Reveune	Operating Profit
£ 0.15	10	4	40	250000	£ 15.70	6,250.00	10.42	£ 1,635.42	£ 37,500.00	£ 1,500.00	£ 39,000.00	£ 37,364.58
Commsion	10	6	60	250000	£ 15.70	4,166.67	6.94	£ 1,090.28	£ 37,500.00	£ 1,500.00	£ 39,000.00	£ 37,909.72
4%	10	8	80	250000	£ 15.70	3,125.00	5.21	£ 817.71	£ 37,500.00	£ 1,500.00	£ 39,000.00	£ 38,182.29
	10	12	120	250000	£ 15.70	2,083.33	3.47	£ 545.14	£ 37,500.00	£ 1,500.00	£ 39,000.00	£ 38,454.86

The pack-house manager agrees that they often carry additional staff; however, they argue that they need to carry contingency staff as the information coming from the technical team concerning the quality and condition of the fruit is not detailed or accurate enough to allow for better planning. Secondly, they argue that, once the pack-house is running at 60%+ capacity, agency staff must bring in agency staff to complement the core staff. It is suggested that employing agency staff can bring its inefficiencies as grading grapes, which forms most of the work, is a skilled job and having inexperienced staff is believed to directly impact the run rates. The introduction of agency staff takes time and effort due to site inductions and training. Both activities produce waste and put additional financial costs on the business. The product manager believes there is a third aspect that makes the delivery of an accurate forecast challenging. This is the discrepancy between what is expected and what happens based on the fruit quality when it reaches the pack-house. When delivering the forecast, the Product manager may have to make some assumptions from prior knowledge of similar arrivals when setting the forecast for the coming week. This is particularly noticeable when fruit quality is poorer than expected because more staff are required, and the final product takes longer to produce. However, the packhouse management does not consider the type of staff to be as important when allocating labour to job types within the packhouse.

This report will seek to establish the effect of both the fruit quality and the proportion of core to agency staff on the run rate. The report will investigate how the fruit quality and types of "jobs" required daily can be more effectively communicated to the pack-house to give the planners confidence to manage the staff levels in the pack-house.

Currently, the pack-house do not have any firm information concerning the quality of fruit and the expected de-selection (or waste) at packing. This information directly impacts the run rate that the pack-house can operate at to produce the final product. The "run rate" is measured using Yield Control Marco system (YCM); the YCM is an integrated system linked to the packing stations within the packhouse and measures the individual packer productivity, the yield of the product and the overall run rate of each production run (Job). The run rate is set and agreed upon as a financial measure that the packhouse is measured against. The forecast supplied to the pack-house is delivered on a Wednesday for the following week (which starts on Sunday) and does not indicate the daily volumes required. This forecast gives basic information of whether the fruit is Packed at Source (PAS) or loose for packing (Stem up). The forecast does not detail what job types will be required or how much de-selection/waste is expected. The amount of de-selection directly impacts the run rate as if there is a high amount of de-selection, the packer must handle more kilograms to produce the same volume of final product. The job type required has a big impact on the packing time and the number of packing staff required to complete the daily orders. The run rate that the pack-house is set currently is based on a financial figure agreed and is an average for each of the job types. Therefore, if the production is meeting the average, there is no obvious incentive to improve the rate for a given job. Jobs are only investigated when the commercial director alerts the teams that a certain job has cost the business more to produce than they return. This information is not available in a timely manner and can only be used to examine what issues led to the supposed poor performance; this can create a culture of blame and, in the view of the product manager and packhouse planners, is not constructive.

Findings from this chapter provide the packhouse planners with:

A more detailed plan showing how much de-selection the intake quality team expect will be produced from each batch of raw material on arrival. The waste produced directly impacts production because the packers must handle additional raw material to produce the final product.

The expected number of each staff type (core or agency). The planners will use this information to calculate the run rate expected for that job, rather than using the financial run rate that is the base for all jobs. Using the calculated run rate should give the product manager and pack-house manager a basis to discuss where jobs either fall short or exceed expectations.

Set targets using data gathered in packing trials and historical information. Each job will be given a target (the calculated run rate) that the packhouse manager and line leaders can use to monitor production. This target should be calculated using known information, including quality of raw material and type of staff.

Information regarding the quantity of each product required by day and, the job type expected for each of these products (both daily and over a longer period). Thereby detailing by day the volume required by job type. This should allow for better allocation of labour resources within the packing process daily.

Improved monitoring abilities. The planners should be able to monitor jobs in real time using identified metrics to alert the packhouse supervisors when lines are performing below the expected run rate. Giving the packhouse supervisors and product manager metrics that can be checked in real-time during production should alert the team when packing is falling below the calculated run rate. This will allow the product manager to investigate why production is slow. For example, this may lead to the job type being changed due to fruit quality being poorer than the initial inspection suggested. If this is the case, the exporter (whose fruit it is) can be informed in good time and agree to additional packing charges or remove the consignment of fruit.

A better understanding of progress and issues arising on certain jobs. The improved data will allow the planners to carry out interrogation of data on a weekly basis and discuss this at regular management meetings with the pack-house manager, technical manager and product manager to help understanding of the progress made and any issues arising.

More complete information to help safeguard against the implication of future change. As the business seeks to attract new customers, having a clear understanding of the variable cost associated with the packing process should allow the commercial team to have the confidence to bid for new customers and deliver on the costs they propose. The business must realise that new customers will mean a greater variation in the products the pack-house will need to produce. This is likely to result in shorter jobs as new product lines are introduced and will impact negatively on down-time as there will be increased number of packaging and tool changes required.

LITERATURE REVIEW

Benefits of Accurate Forecasting

Demand forecasting and production planning when working with perishable goods are challenging due to many factors, including high volatility of the product due to short storage life, significant seasonal variation and the challenging product demand at the store level (Chen, et al., 2019). In the retail environment, suppliers of perishable consumer goods face the challenge of accurately forecasting demand and managing daily operations. Perishable goods are typically ordered daily with high demand and short shelf-life (Chen, et al., 2019).

The Bullwhip effect can be an important phenomenon in supply chain management which means, as variability increases, the effect is felt more as one moves up the supply chain (Wright and Yuan, 2008). Companies such as Campbells soups and Procter and Gamble have observed that small changes in demand by a retailer can result in higher costs, waste of resources, and loss of market share(Wright and Yuan, 2008). Controlling the impact of the Bullwhip effect through demand forecasting can significantly reduce fluctuation in manufacturing production levels(Wright and Yuan, 2008).

CX has been used to receiving a weekly plan indicating the likely requirement for the next six weeks as a service provider. This plan is updated weekly on a Thursday with more accurate information on the volume required by-product for the coming week, which starts on the following Monday. The actual orders are transmitted on day one for delivery on day two. The pack-house manager and planners need to have enough staff in place to complete the orders daily.

As CX seeks to attract new customers, the variation of products and order fluctuation is likely to increase. Good planning and forecasting will be needed to control costs and waste of resource within production.

How Modelling Can Be Used to Improve Forecasting

As the business works to improve the accuracy of the forecast provided to the planners and business, the use of a model to help predict the labour and hours required to complete packing should prove invaluable. A model is built to mimic or represent a real system, these often use mathematical equations. A model can test hypotheses and assumptions about a systems behaviour (Charumilind, et al., 2020). British statistician George Box states that “all models are wrong, but some are useful”. He refined it by saying, “since all models are wrong, the scientist must be alert to what is importantly wrong. It is inappropriate to be concerned about mice when there are tigers abroad” (Charumilind, et al., 2020) by this Charumilind (2020) is suggesting that by analysing the output of a model and identifying the major contributors that effect the poor running of inefficiencies of a system, these inefficiencies can be targeted for improvement. The Bullwhip effect can be significantly alleviated by choosing an appropriate ordering policy and forecasting model (Wright and Yuan, 2008) (Wright & Yuan, 2008). From the users’ view, the accuracy of any forecasting technique can only play a secondary role and, it is the broader issues that place the forecasting system in context for the organisation (Beard and Fildes, 1992). Data produced from analysing the forecast and how it compares to reality is expected to produce information that will benefit the business by helping it understand where there is greater variation from what is expected. This is expected to produce several metrics that can be measured over time to bring greater understanding and benefits, including financial benefits by way of labour control as well as overall efficiencies. Beard and Filde (1992) argue that the user must define the context of the model's information to forecast and the intended application. For example, inventory control will differ from production control as the same amount of auxiliary material, such as packaging, will be required to produce a finished product irrespective of the quality of the raw material used. Any discussion of effective forecasting must begin with an examination of the data that is intended to be applied (Beard and Fildes, 1992). Forecasting information can come from varying sources, have different levels of importance and make different assumptions about the market (Berry, et al., 2005, p. 28). How well any particular model is working is best assessed through continuous measurement of its performance over time (Beard and Fildes, 1992). Forecasting can be used to support decisions in both long-term and short-term strategies and operations. Among the decisions that require long-term forecasts are capital expansion projects, proposals for new product lines, merger and acquisition opportunities (Berry, et al., 2005, p. 29). Shorter-term models may be more suitable for planning for just-in-time products, such as the perishable goods that are packed at CX. These models can be generated by the operations team weekly or even daily.

Managing Change Within the Pack-House to Refocus the Emphasis Towards Efficient Use of Resource

CX is about to go through a massive upheaval as it loses its main source of income as a service provider to its main customer, who has chosen to consolidate its service providers supply to a single supplier. CX's operation at Orchard Place has been developed and dedicated over the last 15 years to meet the demanding and specific needs of the retailers. CX management's view that the service provision model used to service The retailers will not be effective when seeking new opportunities, even though this model has enabled CX to deliver 99.97% quality service level and 99.98% service level. The tough standards on quality and the ability to deliver big volumes quickly make some aspects of the business inefficient adding cost to the business model. CX must now refocus to show to a potential new business that it is competitive. For change to be effective CX must have the support and buy-in from the Managing director, stakeholders and staff throughout the organisation. When working to bring change, the business must anticipate and overcome employee resistance (Burnes, 2017).

Fisher's theory recognises how people tend to react as they are asked to take on change from initial anxiety to, if managed well, gradual acceptance and moving on. If the change is not managed properly, it can lead to hostility, disillusionment and denial (Duffy, et al., 2016, p. 622). Reality testing can bring employees together to understand the current position of the business and the changes needed to secure the future prosperity of the business. To achieve significant change, constructive and open attitudes must prevail (Carnall and Todnem, 2014).

Being clear that the intention of the management at CX is not to get rid of personnel and that the purpose of the change is to bring efficiencies to the process and make better use of resources it has, whilst working to become less reliant on the use of agency staff. Currently, when the pack-house is running at 60 per cent plus capacity, the core staff levels must be supplemented with agency staff. Agency staff are more costly per hour than the core staff, they are also less skilled in the job and therefore believed to be less productive. The agency staff are often new to the site and need an induction to the site and training on how to carry out the work required. By reducing the overall number of workers required to run at 60% plus capacity, the businesses will reduce their reliance on agency workers. Kotter's change management model provides a tool to aid in the implementation of and sustainability of a change, stating an eight-stage process that must be completed to achieve successful change these are (Kotter, 2012):

- *Establish a state of urgency*
- *Creating the guiding coalition*
- *Developing a vision and strategy*
- *Communicating the change vision*
- *Empowering broad-based action*
- *Generating short term wins*
- *Consolidating gains and producing more change*
- *Anchoring new approaches in the culture*

Employing Lean Principles to Reduce Wastes

The concept of Lean and Lean thinking was originally developed by the Toyota Motor Company's (TMC) founder Sakichi Toyoda and engineer Taiichi Ohno. Sakichi Toyoda set out to eliminate or reduce three main types of waste within their factory (Eaton, 2003, p. 25)

The team that developed Toyota Production System identified three types of activity that were contributing to poor performance and gave them names Muda, Mura and Muri. A brief definition of each is given below:

Muda: any activity that does not add value to your customers is considered Muda. Muda is alternatively called waste or non-value–adding activity.

Mura: variations in the process due to some form of imbalance are considered to be Mura also referred to as unevenness.

Muri: putting unreasonable stress on people, material or equipment is considered to be Muri, another term for which would be overburden.

Toyota's Taiichi Ohno is credited with identifying the seven types of waste associated with Muda, an eighth waste (talent) has been added, these can be attributed as follows:

- **Defects**: Product does not match customers expectation for form, fit or function
- **Extra Processing**: Process includes nonvalue added steps or the processing necessary to correct defective materials or product (rework).
- **Waiting**: Waiting for materials, machines or manpower. Waiting can be reduced by addressing Mura through the use of herjunka and the theory of constraints to remove bottlenecks.
- **Transportation**: Excess movement of product from the poor layout of work cells and overproduction
- **Inventory**: Inefficiencies in process, queue times and push schedules not tied to customer demand create excess inventory.
- **Motion (personal)**:Poor work cell layout without regard to ergonomics contributes to motion waste. Materials must be where they are needed when they are needed.
- **Overproduction**: Producing more than what the customer needs, in either quantity or quality.
- **Talent**: The waste of staff member's expertise

The project manager has identified the following Lean wastes that need to be addressed to improve the overall efficiency and, therefore, competitiveness of the packing operation:

Muda: Overproduction and Extra processing – As the business moves to find new customers, it must move away from the current working environment that focuses on quality and produces products daily to order. This has served CX and the retailers well. However, it has meant production of all products daily in small runs, and this creates downtime with small runs and many product changes throughout the shift. This approach has ensured that CX maintain an exemplary service level with the retailers. However, the belief that a move where possible to batch production, producing enough stock for up to three days orders in a production run without exceeding the quality requirements, will suit other retailers needs whose focus is price based. Processing waste comes from unnecessary processing that does not add value to the item being produced or worked on (Domingo, 2015). This should provide a reduction in processing cost that may help to maintain the oveCXead costs at CX, as adding new smaller customers will bring other variation to the business.

Waiting: This can be attributed to line imbalance or overstaffing (Domingo, 2015). As job types and the number of staff required to complete each job differ, the planners may set up jobs with more staff than necessary without good reliable information of the fruit quality and job types.

Mura: Variation in the process has been noted and may be attributed partly to information either lacking or inaccurate. Variation can be problematic, particularly if communication is not clear and timely. This can lead to sub-optimisation of the workforce, problems with quality and just-in-time delivery, an increase in production cost, delivery and storage and can also lead to a lack of supplier and customer confidence (Griffiths and Margetts, 2000). At CX, this can mean that planners may bring in more staff than needed as "contingency". Once the staff are brought in to work on a particular shift, they must be employed and paid for that shift. Therefore, if the jobs required are poor, the planners may have staff additional to the requirement.

Variation in production runs has been identified as Muda and Mura, as short runs are thought to be less productive than longer runs.

Muri: Work-related stress is a major concern for employees. The HSE figures show that work-related stress, depression or anxiety account for an estimated 12.8 million lost working days per year (Donaldson-Feilder, et al., 2008). As the production team and planners at CX strive to improve efficiency, the Quality Control (QC) team could be put under-stress as they must seek to maintain a high standard of finished product and understand the nuances of each customer and their individual requirements. Managers can avoid putting the team under undue stress by keeping the team informed of what is happening, communicating clear goals and objectives and explaining exactly what is required (Donaldson-Feilder, et al., 2008).

RESEARCH METHODOLOGY

Specific, Measurable, Achievable, Repeatable and Timely (S.M.A.R.T.) Objectives

Specific: Introduce Lean thinking to improve information communicated between the pack-house and the technical team. This will include giving greater guidance to job types required and the underlying quality of the raw material, and expected packing performance. The intention is that this will allow the pack-house planners to regulate cost more closely; this should be achieved by the introduction of a detailed forecast (expected packing plan) for the week that indicates the following attributes:

- Quality of the incoming raw material and the expected de-selection
- The quantities and job types are expected to be required daily and over a longer period
- Targets to achieve at packing (not just the overall average) take into consideration the implication of the percentage of Core or Agency staff available.

Currently, product manager provides the pack-house with a basic weekly forecast, see Table 2.

Table 2. Expected packing for week

TPND	Product	Total Prog	Pre-punnetted	Comment	Cutting	% cutting	Total punnets / bags
10141056	Selection Standard x10	19,045	2,600		16,445	86	190,450
36416762	Jacks Selection pack	94	0		94	100	940
10141319	Selection Express x8	5,547	0		5,547	100	44,376
10140810	Green Standard x10	3,450	3,540		- 90	- 3	34,500
10464899	Green Express x8	7,310	7,310		-	-	58,480
10141400	Red Standard x10	27,387	27,387	Please expect 30% sorting 70% visual checks	-	-	273,870
10520804	Red Express x8	18,422	18,920	Please expect 90% visual checks	- 498	- 3	147,376
12773036	Black Grape Standard x10	6,309	0		6,309	100	63,090
12342902	Black Express x8	0	0		-	#DIV/0!	-
235541	Red Loose 9kg	0	0		-	#DIV/0!	-
209976	White Loose 9kg	0	0		-	#DIV/0!	-
34789222	1kg card tray	0	0		-	#DIV/0!	-
32939339	Selection Pack x8 (800g)	5,577	0		5,577	100	44,616
36416854	Jacks's Red Seedless 500g	140	0		140	100	1,400
37023286	Jaffa Candy Floss 400g	0	0		-	#DIV/0!	-
	Red Standard x20	0			-	#DIV/0!	-
	Green Snack pack x9	0	0		-	#DIV/0!	-
38257261	Red Snack pack x6	0	0		-	#DIV/0!	-
36384049	Finest Vitoria 10x400g	1,298	0		1,298	100	12,980
36384090	Sable Seedless 400g x10	0	0		-	#DIV/0!	-
36384049	Vitoria 400g x 10	1,298	0	No stock expect zero orders!	1,298	100	12,980
	Seeded 700g	0	0		-	#DIV/0!	-
36066150	One Stop Green x10	400	400		-	-	4,000
36065197	One Stop Red x10	400	0		400	100	4,000
36065151	One Stop GSP x10	400	0		400	100	4,000
5743	Green Grape Snack Pot	75	0		75	100	900
6861	Red Grape Snack Pot	75	0		75	100	900
7979	Blueberry Snack Pot	100	0		100	100	1,200
3999	Tomato Snack Pot	50	0		50	100	600
		97,377	60,157		36,920	38	900,658

Table 2 indicates to the pack-house planners the volumes by product that the pack-house is expected to produce for the following week. This gives information as follows:

1. TPND - The product code .
2. Product – Gives description of final product.
3. Total Prog (Program) – indicates the number of cases required to fulfil the program for the week.
4. Pre-punnetted – is the number of cases that are expected to be produced using product that is already packed into punnets as opposed to loose fruit that requires packing into punnets.

5. Comment – Can be used to give the planners additional information concerning the quality of the product to be packed.
6. Cutting – indicates to the planners how many cases require packing from loose.
7. Percentage cutting – Gives a quick overview of the balance between packing from loose and pre-punnetted stock.
8. Total punnets / bags – Indicates to the packaging manager how many new punnets and outers are expected to be used over the week.

This is the only information given to the planners and from this, the planners must decide how many staff they require for the coming week and whether agency staff are required to complement the core staff numbers. It is the belief within the business that the pack-house planners bring additional staff as a contingency to ensure they have enough labour to complete all the jobs. Just two additional staff per shift equates to approximately £134,165 per year. The pack-house manager and planners claim that fruit quality is a major factor that directly impacts the speed of the packing and that without good accurate information, they cannot improve the labour forecast requirement. The intention is to improve the detail and quality of the information to give an accurate forecast of the labour requirement, which is currently lacking.

Having identified the lack of accurate information being provided in a timely manner to allow the planners to assess the staff requirement in advance may be considered a vital step as the business seeks to reduce waste and find efficiencies. As discussed, the main reason for the lack of information provided is that the pack-house planners have historically managed the staff levels in the pack-house and always managed to fulfil the daily orders. Working as a service provider to a single major retailer, this approach appeared to offer benefits to the customer that they were willing to pay for such as, never shorting orders, always being on hand to deliver additional orders and delivering the quality expected.

There are difficulties in providing the required information in advance as the fruit (raw material) has limited storage and shelf-life. At certain times of the year, the fruit will be delivered just one or two days prior to being needed for packing (this is typical for road freight coming from Spain or Greece, for example), at other times of the year fruit will arrive in large batches and required pre-longed storage (typically, from the southern hemisphere such as Chile and South Africa). On arrival, the quality intake team inspected the fruit against the customer specification that is intended for. At this point the arrival will be given an inspection status, Red, Amber or Green (RAG); the RAG is designated following a status decision tree. This gives a good indication of the work or job type required in the pack-house to produce the final product for delivery to the customer and the expected yield. With the information provided from the intake report, the product manager's job is to allocate the fruit to the order of use that the pack-house will use daily to complete that day's packing. To give the pack-house an accurate forecast of the expected packing jobs for the coming week three days in advance (i.e., Friday for the coming weeks packing starting on a Tuesday), the product manager must have good information regarding the recent arrivals. This information is taken from condition tests that are taken on arrival and monitored for signs of deterioration, information from the exporters, knowledge of the seasonal variation and an accurate forecast from the customer.

The new forecast will attempt to consider the quality of the fruit and the mix of the labour required. It is believed that the core staff are more productive than the agency staff, as they are more experienced at packing grapes, which is a skilled task.

To prove these hypotheses and deliver a forecast that is both accurate and reliable, it is the intention to run packing trials using both fruit that is packed in to punnets at source and loose fruit that requires packing in to punnets on site and using both good and poorer quality product to measure the packing speeds. The staff used will also be controlled per job as either core or agency staff will pack the same fruit into the same job types. Initially, there will be eight packing trials consisting of a minimum of one hour per job completed during the morning shift (AM), and the trials will then be repeated in the afternoon (PM). There will be a second round of trials replicating the first, using fruit from a different source. In total, the trail will capture data from 32 packing trials as per Table 4 below, and this will ensure that the data gathered will be statistically significant.

It is imperative that the product manager engages with the pack-house manager and planners at each stage of the process and has the buy-in of the team. To gain this, weekly meetings will be arranged to explain the process and how the forecast and model have been designed to help the planners and give the business a better understanding of the difficulties that they face when planning the labour and jobs.

The trials will measure the four main jobs performed within the pack-house and required to regularly deliver the final product. The job types required have a significant impact on the labour requirement; these job types are:

1. Heat-seal only – The product arrives at Orchard Place pre-packed in punnets and achieves Status Green on arrival. Status green indicates that the fruit is within the tolerances set by the end customer and is suitable to be heat-sealed with the retailer's film and relevant information such as variety, date code, country of origin, class, weight and traceability information. This task requires the fewest number of staff and the lowest skill level as there is no grading required.
2. Visual check - The product arrives at Orchard Place pre-packed in punnets and achieves Status Amber on arrival. Status Amber indicates that the product falls below the customer specification (Amber is set at maximum 20% of punnets out of tolerance for major defects) and requires each punnet to be graded (examined) before being placed on the line to be heat-sealed. Punnets that are seen to be out of tolerance at this stage are returned as stock for re-work.
3. Intrusive sort – Product arrives pre-punnetted with Status Amber or Red and requires every punnet to be emptied. The bunches cleaned using scissors to remove defects and repacked and weighted prior to heat-seal.
4. Cut and Heat-seal – Product arrives packed loose, usually in a nine-kilogram outer for packing into punnets to be heat-sealed. These are also scored Red, Amber or Green (RAG) on arrival according to their condition and appearance. The RAG has a direct impact on the packing speeds and yield that is expected during packing.

Table 3. Packing trials key

Data set	Job type	Labour	Time of day
1	int sort	Core	am
2	c&hs	Agency	pm
	hs		
	vc		

Table 4. Indicates the packing trails to be completed

Trial	Job type	Labour	Time of day
1	int sort	Core	am
1	int sort	Core	pm
1	int sort	Agency	am
1	int sort	Agency	pm
1	c&hs	Core	am
1	c&hs	Core	pm
1	c&hs	Agency	am
1	c&hs	Agency	pm
1	hs	Core	am
1	hs	Core	pm
1	hs	Agency	am
1	hs	Agency	pm
1	vc	Core	am
1	vc	Core	pm
1	vc	Agency	am
1	vc	Agency	pm

Measurable: The result of the packing trials will produce several metrics that the initial plan can be measured directly against. This should provide valuable information to improve the initial planning and enable the pack-house planners to manage staff numbers better. Expected metrics are:

1. Job ratio over the week – This is the number of jobs carried out by the pack-house compared to the number of jobs completed.
2. Percentage of scheduled volume delivered
3. Un-scheduled product – Products that were not expected to be required in that week.
4. Additional job (types) – This can occur when a product needs additional work compare to what was expected at the outset.
5. Labour variance – Hours required compared to hours scheduled
6. Benchmark variance – Cases per hour achieved compared to the expected
7. Waste variance – the percentage waste predicted against the actual
8. Improved monitoring of jobs in real-time, with identified metrics to alert management when lines are performing below expected run rates

Achievable: The expected packing plan (forecast) must be designed in such a way that it is usable for the team to enable it to be completed and shared with the pack-house planners in a timely and understandable format. The plan should then be capable of being easily updated with the results of the weeks packing, taken directly from the Prophet system.

Repeatable: There must be a procedure to ensure the process can be followed and repeated by the planning and commercial teams. The model allows the use of Lean principles to examine the wastes within the pack-house. Giving greater accuracy when forecasting and allow ongoing analysis of the forecast weekly or even daily. The forecast is expected to produce metrics that provide valuable information that can be applied to future planning.

Timely: The aim will be to gather data throughout January 2021, and this will coincide with when the pack-house has the variation in jobs and raw material available to carry out the trials that will be required to collect the data needed to complete the model. Once completed, the model can be trialled and tested over the following six to eight weeks. This should allow the first drafts of the new packing forecast to be delivered to the commercial team and the pack-house planners in mid-March 2021.

Once the model is seen to be producing good information, the project should move to the Plan Check Act Do (PCAD) stage, allowing:

- Interrogation of data with regular management meetings between the pack-house manager, technical and product managers to understand the progress and any issues arising
- Improved monitoring of jobs in real-time, with identified metrics to alert management when lines are performing below expected run rates
- The implication of future change

Data Collection and Analysis

- Each of the trials will take place during "normal" production runs to minimise disruption and additional cost to the business.
- In each case, the fruit to be used will be pre-inspected, and the quality will be suitable for the trial in question.
- The staff type, core or agency, will be arranged in advance with the pack-house manager.
- Productivity for each will be measured using the Marco system, Yield Control Marco (YCM). This is a sophisticated system that allows CX to pack and deliver average weight packs to retail. This not only captures the yield, providing a mass balance but also measures individual packer (operator) performance and overall run rate.
    - Heat-seal and visual check trials will be measured using the Marco check weigher data as the packers are not required to weigh every pack therefore, data on individual performance are not available, the run rate is measured as a team. The figure to determine the packer's overall performance will be the "Total PPM" as seen in the Batch Checkweigher Report, see example Figure 2.
- Intrusive sort and cut and heat seal trials will be measured using the individual operator packs per minute (PPM) data, as seen in Operator Performance data. See example below in Table 5 and Figure 3.
- All trials will use the average PPM recorded by the check weigher and the Batch Summary to measure the yield and the kg processed within each trial. See Figure 4.

Figure 2. Marco batch checkweigher report
(Marco, 2015)

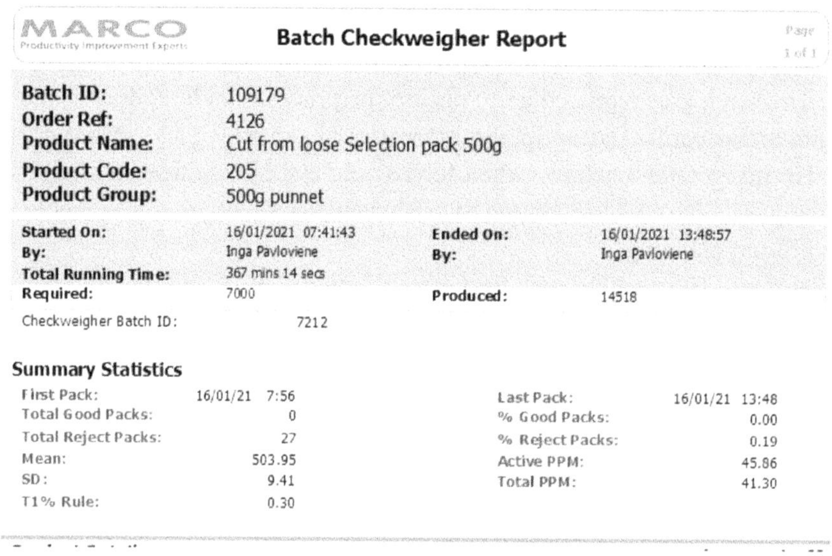
MARCO
Productivity Improvement Experts

Batch Checkweigher Report

Page 1 of 1

Batch ID:	109179		
Order Ref:	4126		
Product Name:	Cut from loose Selection pack 500g		
Product Code:	205		
Product Group:	500g punnet		
Started On:	16/01/2021 07:41:43	**Ended On:**	16/01/2021 13:48:57
By:	Inga Pavloviene	**By:**	Inga Pavloviene
Total Running Time:	367 mins 14 secs		
Required:	7000	**Produced:**	14518
Checkweigher Batch ID:	7212		

Summary Statistics

First Pack:	16/01/21 7:56	Last Pack:	16/01/21 13:48
Total Good Packs:	0	% Good Packs:	0.00
Total Reject Packs:	27	% Reject Packs:	0.19
Mean:	503.95	Active PPM:	45.86
SD:	9.41	Total PPM:	41.30
T1% Rule:	0.30		

Figure 3. Marco operator performance
(Marco, 2015)

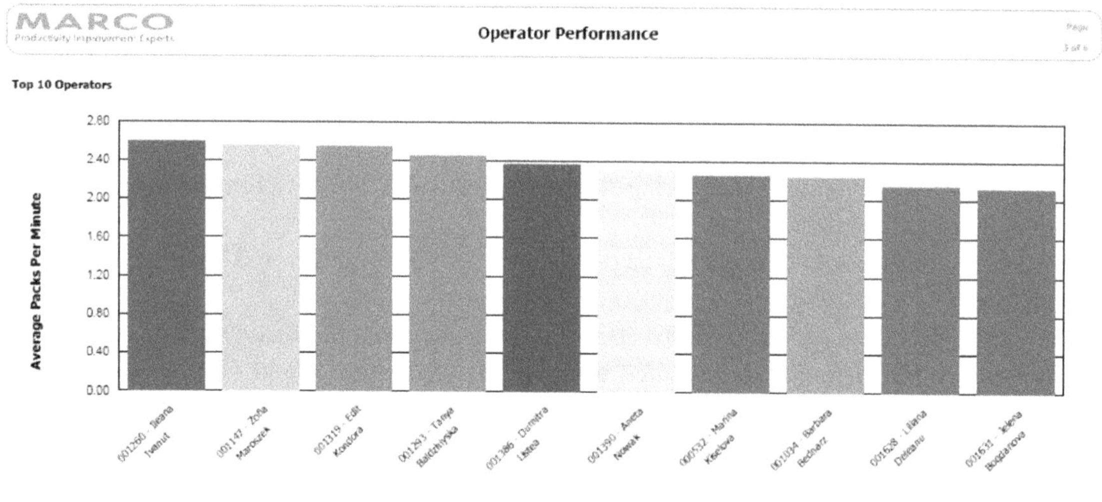

RESULTS

The results generated in the trial have been proven to be statistically valid by the use of the Mann-Whitney U test. This test was chosen as being the most appropriate test following a simple decision tree available on the University of Lincoln Maths and Statistics Help (MASH), page. The Mann-Whitney test can be applied to confirm that results are significant when comparing different tests against one another and when looking for differences in a non-parametric test. The test uses different cohorts to complete trials and different batches of raw material in the second round of trials.

Table 5. Marco operator performance

MARCO
Productivity Improvement Experts

Operator Performance

Page 1 of 6

Batch ID:	109179
Order Ref:	4126
Product Name:	Cut from loose Selection pack 500g
Product Code:	205
Product Group:	500g punnet

Started On:	16/01/2021 07:41:43	**Ended On:**	16/01/2021 13:48:57
By:	Inga Pavloviene	**By:**	Inga Pavloviene
Total Running Time:	367 mins 14 secs		
Required:	7000	**Produced:**	14518
Expected PPM:	2	**No. of Operators:**	25
Packs Per Worker Hour:	95	**Cost Per Pack:**	£0.06
Hourly Rate:	£6.00		

Operator Totals

Operator	Pack Count			Weight	Waste Weight	Waste	Duration	Sessions	Packs Per Minute	Kg Per Hour	Credits	Lock Outs		Packing Efficieny Score
	Lower	Target	Upper	(kg)	(kg)	(%)	(hh:mm:ss)					Under	Over	
001260 - Beana Ivanut	0	813	0	411.72	0.00	0.00	05:14:13	3	2.59	78.62	0.00	0	0	
001147 - Zofia Marczek	0	766	0	388.17	0.00	0.00	04:59:18	6	2.58	77.82	0.00	15	0	
001319 - Edit Kondora	0	812	0	412.31	0.00	0.00	05:19:13	3	2.54	77.50	0.00	1	0	
001293 - Tanya Baldzhiyska	0	464	0	235.47	0.00	0.00	03:09:27	3	2.45	74.57	0.00	3	0	
001386 - Dumitra Listea	0	706	0	358.36	0.00	0.00	04:58:25	8	2.37	72.05	0.00	2	0	
001390 - Aneta Nowak	0	702	0	356.84	0.00	0.00	05:03:41	6	2.31	70.50	0.00	3	0	
000532 - Marina Kiselova	0	671	0	340.31	0.00	0.00	04:57:26	5	2.26	68.65	0.00	10	0	
001034 - Barbara Bednarz	0	675	0	341.57	0.00	0.00	05:00:15	4	2.25	68.26	0.00	5	0	
001628 - Liliana Deleanu	0	405	0	205.77	0.00	0.00	03:08:20	4	2.15	65.56	0.00	1	0	
001631 - Jelena Bogdanova	0	635	0	322.09	0.00	0.00	05:00:08	5	2.12	64.39	0.00	4	0	
001571 - Ionela Fagatianu	0	661	0	335.49	0.00	0.00	05:13:45	4	2.11	64.18	0.00	4	0	
001358 - Silviya Andonova	0	487	0	246.82	0.00	0.00	03:54:06	6	2.08	63.26	0.00	1	0	
001649 - Sofka Kehayova	0	280	0	142.16	0.00	0.00	02:18:19	5	2.02	61.67	0.00	7	0	
001357 - Stanka Georgieva	0	536	0	271.92	0.00	0.00	04:33:04	3	1.96	59.75	0.00	2	0	
001340 - Danuta Nadolska	0	430	0	217.70	0.00	0.00	03:42:56	7	1.93	58.59	0.00	13	0	
001347 - Liliana Marin	0	549	0	278.79	0.00	0.00	04:45:29	8	1.92	58.59	0.00	4	0	
001528 - Elena Belan	0	446	0	226.46	0.00	0.00	03:56:08	4	1.89	57.54	0.00	5	0	

Printed by: Guy Coulthard at VM PC on 16/01/2021 15:49:28 V: 2016.12.02

(Marco, 2015)

Mann-Whitney U Test Results

Trial Data 1 (am) (Figure 6) shows that packs per minute (PPM) for Core staff performing a "Cut and Heat-seal" in the morning (Mdn = 2.10) was higher than the Agency staff PPM (Mdn =1.52). A Mann-Whitney test indicated that this difference was statistically significant. $U(N_{core}=27_{agency}=27)=75.000$. $z=-5.009$. $p<.000$. This result indicates that the core staff are consistently more productive than the agency staff.

Trial Data 2 (am) (Figure 7) shows that PPM for Core staff performing a "Cut and Heat-seal" in the morning (Mdn = 1.39) was higher than the PPM performed by Agency staff (Mdn =1.12). A Mann-Whitney test indicated that this difference was statistically significant. $U(N_{core}=27_{agency}=27)=145.000$. $z=-3.798$. $p<.000$.

Trial Data 1 (pm) (Figure 8) shows that the PPM for Core staff performing a "Cut and Heat-seal" in the morning (Mdn = 2.07) was higher than the PPM achieved by Agency staff (Mdn =1.58). A Mann-Whitney test indicated that this difference was statistically significant. $U(N_{core}=27_{agency}=27)=95.000$. $z=-4.663$. $p<.000$.

Figure 4. Batch Summary
(Marco, 2015)

MARCO
Productivity Improvement Experts

Batch Summary

Page 1 of 3

Batch ID:	109179
Order Ref:	4126
Product Name:	Cut from loose Selection pack 500g
Product Code:	205
Product Group:	500g punnet

Started On:	16/01/2021 07:41:43	**Ended On:**	16/01/2021 13:48:57
By:	Inga Pavloviene	**By:**	Inga Pavloviene
Total Running Time:	367 mins 14 secs		

Required:	7000	**Produced:**	14518
Expected PPM:	2	**No. of Operators:**	25
Autotare Selected:	15g		
Packs Per Worker Hour:	95	**Cost Per Pack:**	£0.06
Hourly Rate:	£6.00		

Checkweigher Results

Batch Number	Nominal	Pass Count	Pass Weight	Mean Between T1	and T2	Below T2 Count	Reject Count	SD
	g		kg	g	%			g
7212	500.00	14557	7336.02	504.0	0.30	6	27	9.41
Summary		14557	7336.02	504.0	0.30	6	27	

Raw Material Usage

Code	Name	Input Weight kg	Output Weight kg	Waste Weight kg	Mass Balance kg
205	Cut from loose Selection pack 500g	7364.75	7358.47	6.28	0.00
		7364.75	7358.47	6.28	0.00

Figure 5. Trial 1 Cut and Heat seal- Core verses Agency staff (am)

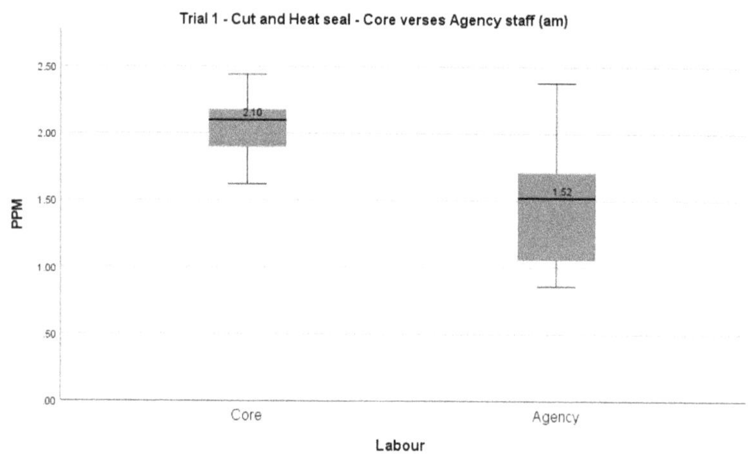

Table 6. Ranks

	Labour	N	Mean Rank	Sum of Ranks
PPM	Core	27	38.22	1032.00
	Agency	27	16.78	453.00
	Total	54		

Table 7. Test statistics[a]

	PPM
Mann-Whitney U	75.000
Wilcoxon W	453.000
Z	-5.009
Asymp. Sig. (2-tailed)	.000
Exact Sig. (2-tailed)	.000
Exact Sig. (1-tailed)	.000
Point Probability	.000

a. Grouping Variable: Labour

Figure 6. Trial data 2 - cut and heat seal- core vs. agency staff (am)

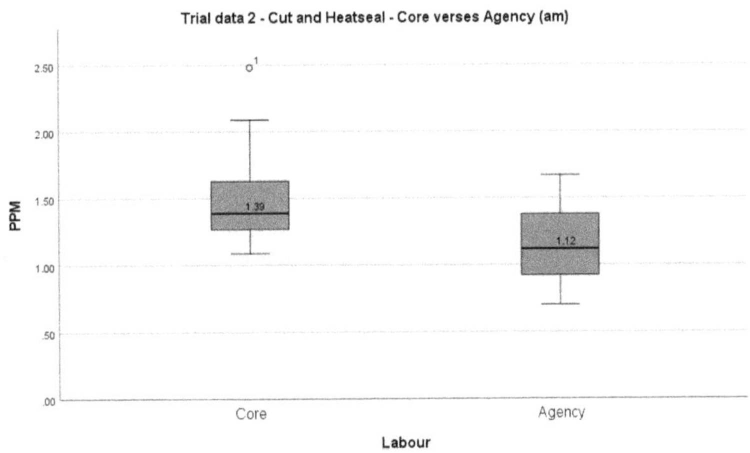

Table 8. Ranks

	Labour	N	Mean Rank	Sum of Ranks
PPM	Core	27	35.63	962.00
	Agency	27	19.37	523.00
	Total	54		

Table 9. Test statistics[a]

	PPM
Mann-Whitney U	145.000
Wilcoxon W	523.000
Z	-3.798
Asymp. Sig. (2-tailed)	.000
Exact Sig. (2-tailed)	.000
Exact Sig. (1-tailed)	.000
Point Probability	.000

a. Grouping Variable: Labour

Figure 7. Trial 1- cut and heat seal – core vs. agency (pm)

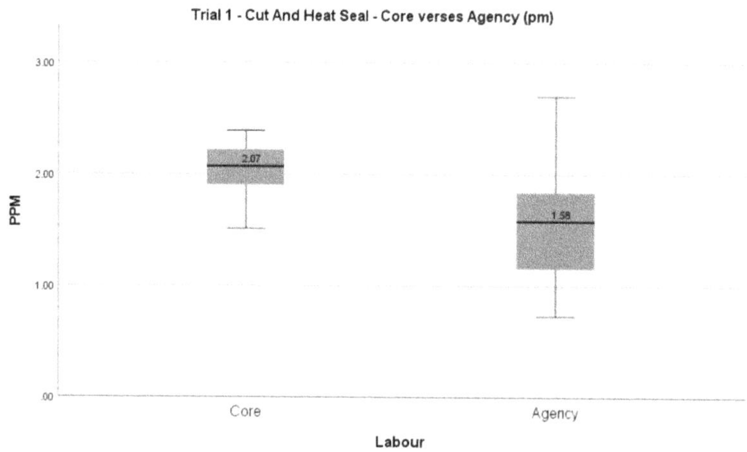

Table 10. Ranks

	Labour	N	Mean Rank	Sum of Ranks
PPM	Core	27	37.48	1012.00
	Agency	27	17.52	473.00
	Total	54		

Trial Data 2 (pm) (Figure 9) shows that PPM for Core staff performing a "Cut and Heat-seal" in the morning (Mdn = 1.59) was higher than the PPM for Agency staff (Mdn =1.24). A Mann-Whitney test indicated that this difference was statistically significant. U(N_{core}=27$_{agency}$=27)=151.500. z=-3.686. *p*<.000. This result indicates that the Core staff are consistently more productive than the agency staff.

Trial Data 1 (am) (Figure 10) shows PPM for Core staff performing a "Intrusive sort" in the morning (Mdn = 1.08) was higher than the PPM for Agency staff (Mdn =0.86) . A Mann-Whitney test indicated that this difference was statistically significant. U(N_{core}=27$_{agency}$=27)=147.500. z=-3.756. *p*<.000. This result indicates that the core staff are consistently more productive than the agency staff.

Table 11. Test Statistics[a]

	PPM
Mann-Whitney U	95.000
Wilcoxon W	473.000
Z	-4.663
Asymp. Sig. (2-tailed)	.000
Exact Sig. (2-tailed)	.000
Exact Sig. (1-tailed)	.000
Point Probability	.000

a. Grouping Variable: Labour

Figure 8. Trial data 2 cut and heat-seal – core vs. agency (pm)

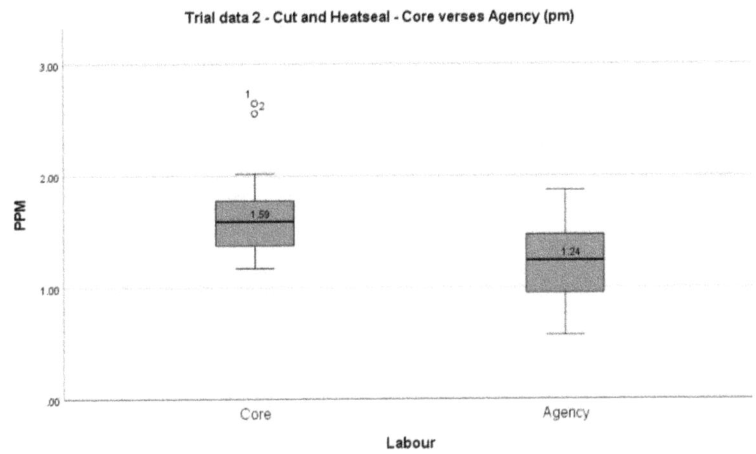

Table 12. Ranks

	Labour	N	Mean Rank	Sum of Ranks
PPM	Core	27	35.39	955.50
	Agency	27	19.61	529.50
	Total	54		

Trial Data 2 (am) (Figure 11) PPM for Core staff performing a "Intrusive sort" in the morning (Mdn = 1.57) and was higher than the PPM for Agency staff (Mdn =0.89). A Mann-Whitney test indicated that this difference was statistically significant. U(N_{core}=27 $_{agency}$=27)=13.500. z=-6073. p<.000. This result indicates that the core staff are consistently more productive than the agency staff.

Trial Data 1 (pm) (Figure 12) PPM for Core staff performing a "Intrusive sort" in the morning (Mdn = 1.23) was higher than the PPM for Agency staff (Mdn =0.92). A Mann-Whitney test indicated that this difference was statistically significant. U(N_{core}=27 $_{agency}$=27)=97.500. z=-4.621 p<.000. This result indicates that the core staff are consistently more productive than the agency staff.

Table 13. Test statistics[a]

	PPM
Mann-Whitney U	151.500
Wilcoxon W	529.500
Z	-3.686
Asymp. Sig. (2-tailed)	.000
Exact Sig. (2-tailed)	.000
Exact Sig. (1-tailed)	.000
Point Probability	.000

a. Grouping Variable: Labour

Figure 9. Trial data 1 – intrusive sort – core vs. agency (am)

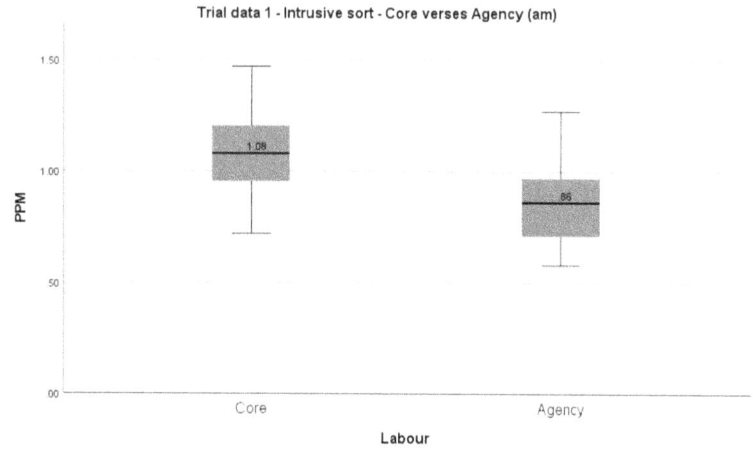

Table 14. Ranks

	Labour	N	Mean Rank	Sum of Ranks
PPM	Core	27	35.54	959.50
	Agency	27	19.46	525.50
	Total	54		

Trial Data 2 (pm) (Figure 13) Packs Per Minute (PPM) for Core staff performing a "Intrusive sort" in the morning (Mdn = 1.62) was higher than the PPM for Agency staff (Mdn =1.02). A Mann-Whitney test indicated that this difference was statistically significant. U(N_{core}=27$_{agency}$=27)=62.500. z=-5.225 *p*<.000. This result indicates that the core staff are consistently more productive than the agency staff.

Trial Data 1 and 2 (Figure 14) combined PPM for Core staff performing a "Visual check" (Mdn = 64.73) and was higher than the PPM for Agency staff (Mdn =41.92). A Mann-Whitney test indicated that this difference was statistically significant. U(N_{core}=8$_{agency}$=8)=.000. z=-2.309 *p*<.014. This result indicates that the core staff are consistently more productive than the agency staff.

Table 15. Test statistics[a]

	PPM
Mann-Whitney U	147.500
Wilcoxon W	525.500
Z	-3.756
Asymp. Sig. (2-tailed)	.000
Exact Sig. (2-tailed)	.000
Exact Sig. (1-tailed)	.000
Point Probability	.000

a. Grouping Variable: Labour

Figure 10. Trial data 2 – intrusive sort – core vs. agency (am)

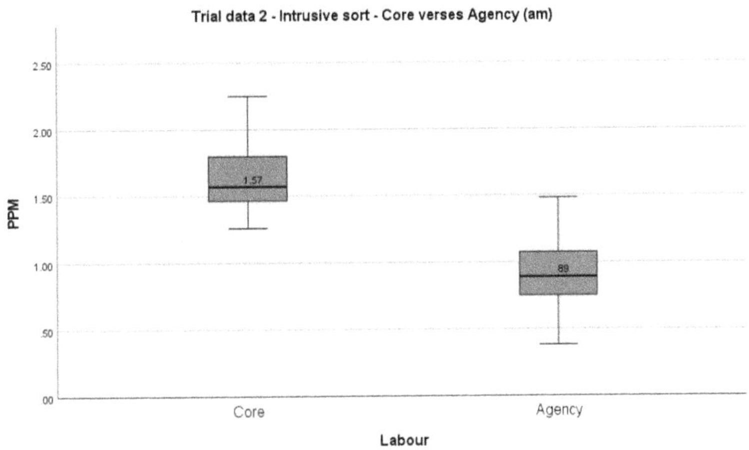

Table 16. Ranks

	Labour	N	Mean Rank	Sum of Ranks
PPM	Core	27	40.50	1093.50
	Agency	27	14.50	391.50
	Total	54		

Trial Data 1 and 2 (Figure 15) combined PPM for Core staff performing a "Heat-seal only" (Mdn = 84.83) and was higher than the PPM for Agency staff (Mdn =79.34). A Mann-Whitney test indicated that this difference was not statistically significant. $U(N_{core}=8_{agency}=8)=7.000$. $z=-0.289$ $p<.100$ This result was not unexpected as this is the least skilled task.

Table 17. Test statistics[a]

	PPM
Mann-Whitney U	13.500
Wilcoxon W	391.500
Z	-6.073
Asymp. Sig. (2-tailed)	.000
Exact Sig. (2-tailed)	.000
Exact Sig. (1-tailed)	.000
Point Probability	.000

a. Grouping Variable: Labour

Figure 11. Trial data 1 – intrusive sort – core vs. agency (pm)

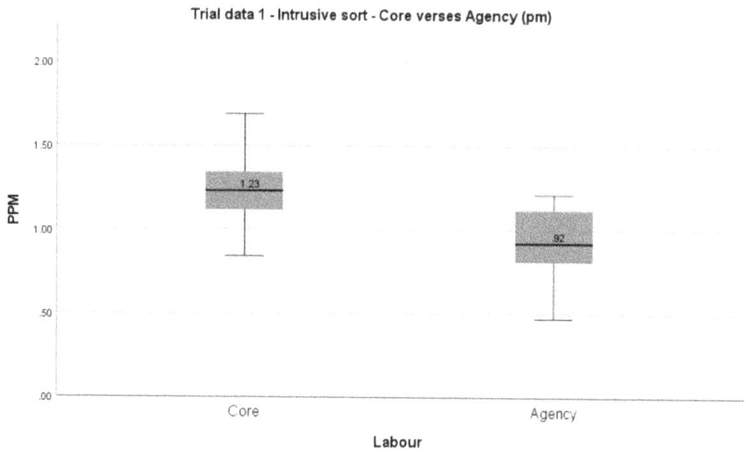

Table 18. Ranks

	Labour	N	Mean Rank	Sum of Ranks
PPM	Core	27	37.39	1009.50
	Agency	27	17.61	475.50
	Total	54		

Results From Packing Trials

For calculations, a single shift will be for an individuals' work taken as 11 hours with a 55-minute hour. This calculation has been arrived at, taking into account one 30-minute break, two 15-minute breaks, plus downtime throughout the shift. Therefore, with 126 packing stations, we can assume the capacity is 11 hours multiplied by 55 minutes and is equal to 1313 available packing hours per shift.

Table 19. Test statistics[a]

	PPM
Mann-Whitney U	97.500
Wilcoxon W	475.500
Z	-4.621
Asymp. Sig. (2-tailed)	.000
Exact Sig. (2-tailed)	.000
Exact Sig. (1-tailed)	.000
Point Probability	.000

a. Grouping Variable: Labour

Figure 12. Trial data 2 – intrusive sort – core vs. agency (pm)

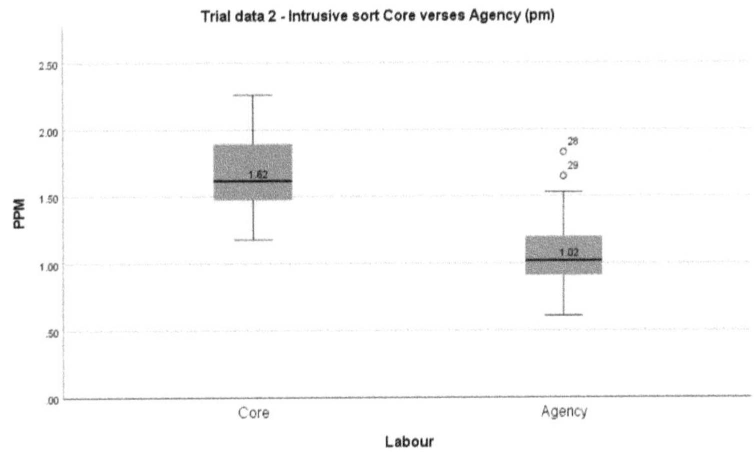

Table 20. Ranks

	Labour	N	Mean Rank	Sum of Ranks
PPM	Core	27	38.69	1044.50
	Agency	27	16.31	440.50
	Total	54		

Pack-house capacity is also restricted by the number of PPM the Pro-Seal heat-seal machines (GT2) can produce; the engineering team advise top speed of 120ppm and recommend running the machines at 80% speed for daily use, therefore 96ppm. The pack house has five machines. (5 x 96) x 605 = 290,400 packs per day (29,400 cases)

Figure 16 indicates that the core staff consistently perform more efficiently that the agency staff.

The bar chart in figure 17 shows trial data 2 which indicates that the core staff consistently perform more efficiently that the agency staff.

Table 21. Test statistics[a]

	PPM
Mann-Whitney U	62.500
Wilcoxon W	440.500
Z	-5.225
Asymp. Sig. (2-tailed)	.000
Exact Sig. (2-tailed)	.000
Exact Sig. (1-tailed)	.000
Point Probability	.000

a. Grouping Variable: Labour

Figure 13. Trial data 1 and 2 combined visual check core vs. agency packs per minute

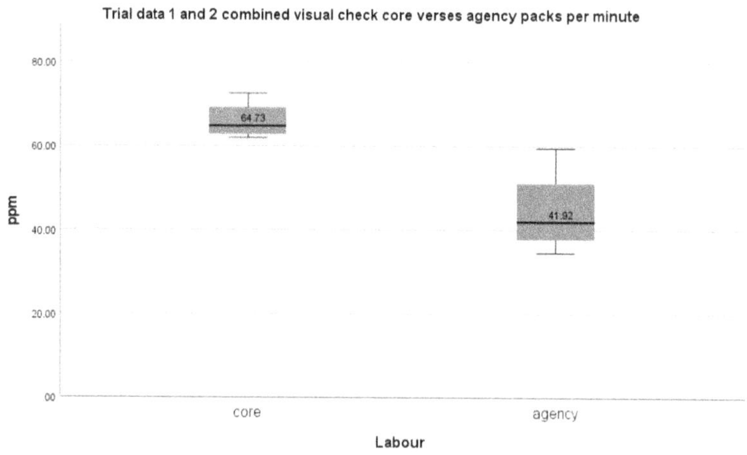

Table 22. Ranks

	Labour	N	Mean Rank	Sum of Ranks
ppm	Core	4	6.50	26.00
	agency	4	2.50	10.00
	Total	8		

The chart in figure 18 indicates waste produced during packing, and this is within the expected range indicated by the incoming inspection of the fruit prior to packing. This suggests the waste produced remains consistent for core and agency staff. The effect of grape quality by job was calculated using additional data taken from Prophet data on 640 packing jobs completed during normal production. Using the result of the experiment combined with the average figures and knowing the quality of the grapes in the test with the selection as a fit parameter in the model indicates that when performing cut and heat seal, intrusive sort and visual check the percentage fruit rejected at packing has a direct impact on the PPM that the staff can achieve. This must be taken into account by Dr R T Carline when building the model that will be used to deliver the forecast to the planners.

Table 23. Test statistics[a]

	PPM
Mann-Whitney U	.000
Wilcoxon W	10.000
Z	-2.309
Asymp. Sig. (2-tailed)	.021
Exact Sig. [2*(1-tailed Sig.)]	.029[b]
Exact Sig. (2-tailed)	.029
Exact Sig. (1-tailed)	.014
Point Probability	.014

a. Grouping Variable: Labour
b. Not corrected for ties.

Figure 14. Trial data 1 and 2 combined visual check core verses agency packs per minute

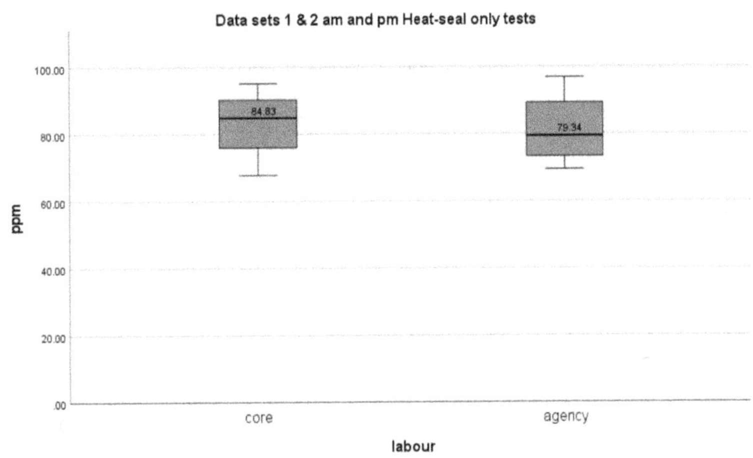

Table 24. Ranks

	Labour	N	Mean Rank	Sum of Ranks
ppm	Core	4	4.75	19.00
	agency	4	4.25	17.00
	Total	8		

The chart in figure 19 sets out the percentage of each job type completed for grape packing in 2020 with cut and heat seals and visual checks making up the main volume. These two jobs also show the greatest difference in efficiency when comparing core and agency staff. See Table 26.

Table 26 shows the difference in the performance of the four trial types, with the data combined from both trial data sets. In all cases, the core staff have been seen to perform more efficiently than the agency staff.

Table 25. Test statistics[a]

	PPM
Mann-Whitney U	7.000
Wilcoxon W	17.000
Z	-.289
Asymp. Sig. (2-tailed)	.773
Exact Sig. [2*(1-tailed Sig.)]	.886[b]
Exact Sig. (2-tailed)	.886
Exact Sig. (1-tailed)	.443
Point Probability	.100

a. Grouping Variable: labour
b. Not corrected for ties.

Figure 15. Bar chart trial data 1 all jobs average ppm core verses agency

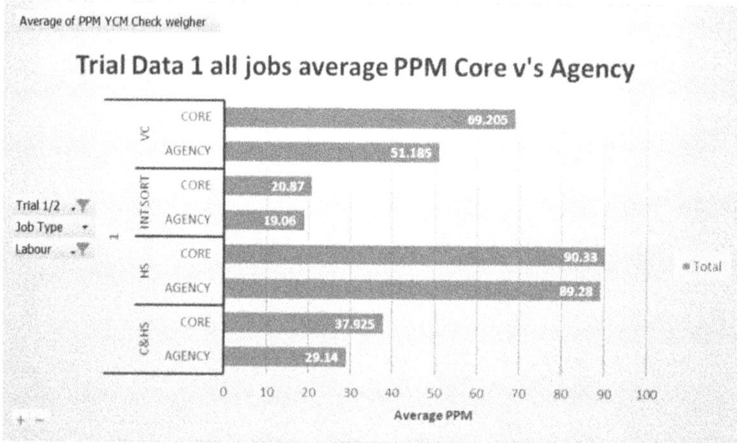

Figure 16. Trial data 2 all jobs average ppm core verses agency

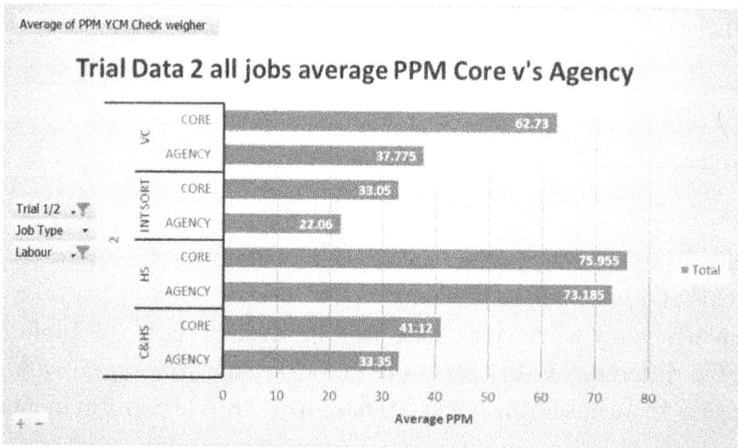

Figure 17. Average percentage reject fruit, by job type (combined trial data)

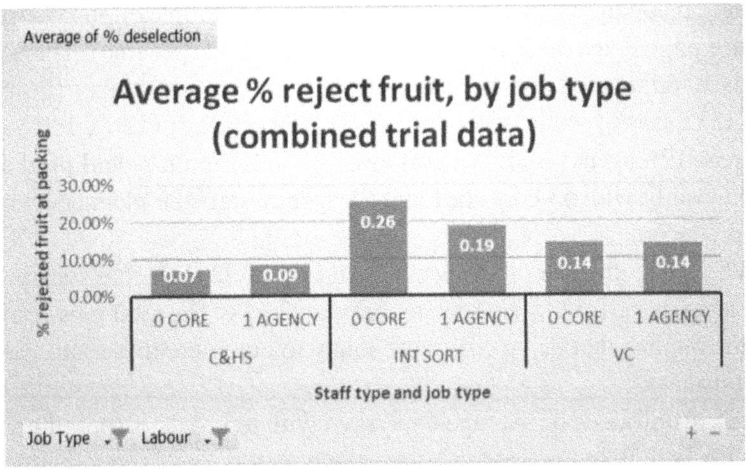

Figure 18. Percentage of job type carried out ot CX Ltd: grape packing for year 2020

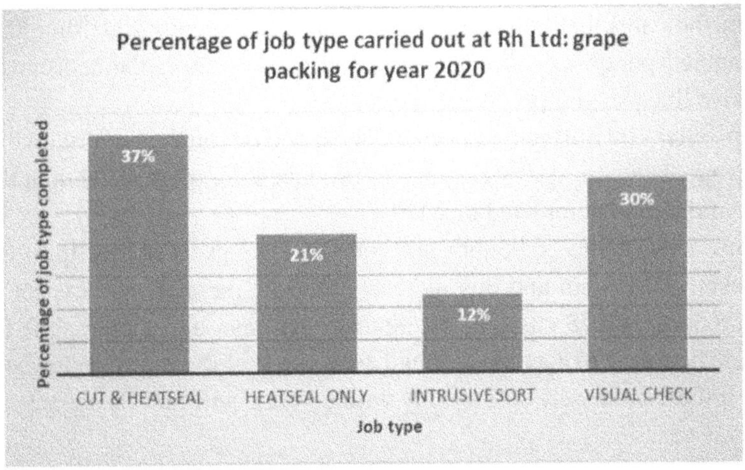

Table 26. Difference in performance of care verse agency across trial types

Labour	C&HS (ppm)	hs (ppm)	INT SORT (ppm)	VC (ppm)	Grand Total (ppm)
Agency	31.25	81.23	20.56	44.48	44.38
Core	39.52	83.14	26.96	65.97	53.90
+/- diff	21%	2%	24%	33%	18%

Cut and Heat-seal (C&HS) - The core staff produce 21% more PPM completing C&HS jobs than the agency workers. These made up the greatest proportion of jobs completed in 2020 at 37%.

Core staff produce on average 39.52ppm hour with 27 packers (per line). Therefore the mean average for one packer is 1.46ppm, and this indicates the planners can expect that 126-core staff should be able to produce 24,153 cases of ten punnets per case in a single shift (126 x 1.46) x 1313=241530/10 24,153 cases. Whereas 126 agency staff with an average of 1.15ppm would produce 19,025 cases. If the labour were split evenly with 63 core staff and 63 agency staff the planners would know to expect 21,589 cases to be produced.

Visual Check (VC) - The greatest difference is seen in the VC with core staff producing 33% more cases per hour than agency staff. VC were seen to make up 30% of the total jobs completed in 2020; see figure 19 above. This implies that using core staff solely to complete these jobs could bring considerable savings to the business.

For VC jobs core staff produce on average 65.97ppm with ten packers (per line), therefore the mean average for one packer is 6.597ppm. This indicates the planners can expect that ten-core staff should be able to produce 3,991 cases of ten punnets per case per line in a single shift. Therefore, planners can expect that 50-core staff working over five lines should produce 19,955 cases. Whereas agency staff produce on average 44.48ppm with ten packers (per line), therefore the mean average for one packer is 4.448ppm and this indicates that the planners can expect ten-agency staff should be able to produce 2,691 cases of ten punnets per case per line in a single shift. Therefore, planners can expect that 50-core staff working over five lines should produce 13,455 cases.

Intrusive Sort (Int Sort) - Int Sort jobs are generally carried out on the poorest quality fruit and require the most remedial work. The core staff were seen to produce 24% more PPM than the agency staff. Int sort jobs were 12% of the total completed in 2020.

Core staff produce on average 26.96ppm per hour with 27 packers (per line) therefore, the mean average for one packer is 0.99ppm and this indicates that the planners can expect that 126 core staff should be able to produce 16,278 cases of 10 punnets per case in a single shift (126 x 0.99ppm) x 1,313=163,783/10. Whereas, 126 agency staff had an average of 0.76ppm agency staff and would produce 12,573 cases. If the labour were split evenly with 63 core staff and 63 agency, the planners would know to expect 14,456 cases.

Heat-Seal Only (HS) - There was only a small difference seen in the HS jobs (this was to be expected as no grading is required). The Mann Whitney U test indicated that there was no significant difference between core and agency staff when performing HS jobs. HS only jobs were seen to make up 21% of the total jobs completed in 2020.

For HS jobs, core staff produce on average 83.14ppm with 6 packers (per line) therefore, the mean average for one packer is 13.85ppm and this indicates that the planners can expect that 6 core staff should be able to produce (83.1ppm x 55min)x11hr =5,027 cases of 10 punnets per case per line in a single shift. Therefore, planners can expect that 30 core staff working over five lines should produce 25,135 cases. Whereas, agency staff produce on average 81.23ppm with 6 packers (per line), therefore the mean average for one packer is 13.53ppm and this indicates that the planners can expect that 6 agency staff should be able to produce (81.2ppm x 55min) x 11hr =4,912 cases of 10 punnets per case per line in a single shift. Therefore, planners can expect that 30 Agency staff working over five lines should produce 24,560 cases.

The data gained is key to ascertaining the number of staff required to complete the daily packing, how the addition of agency staff to the pack-house affects the run-rates and the hours required to complete the orders. The data also shows that when agency staff are needed to complement the core staff deploying workers strategically to ensure they are being used in the most effective manner must be a priority. There is strong evidence that the type of staff allocated to the job type is equally important than the fruit quality in terms of production. For example, a single shift of core staff producing a finished product from visual checks can be expected to produce 19,955 cases with a labour cost of £9,420 to produce the same quantity with agency staff cost £12,434.

In additional to the trial data, Dr R.T. Carline has been provided with further data that has been collated from 640 packing jobs taken over two packing periods, one with good quality and another with poorer quality fruit. The purpose of this is to measure the difference that poorer grape quality and amount of waste produced had on the production rates of the jobs. By doing this it will be possible to calculate the additional cases being handled to produce the final product and the time taken. Dr R.T. Carline has also had detailed discussions with the Technical Director and Product manager to understand what they expect the run rates to be and how they believe this is affected by fruit quality. Both came up with similar figures and the results seen are proving to be very close to those anticipated which is promising for the accuracy of the model.

DISCUSSION

How the Model Is Progressing and Early Benefits/ Results That Have Being Realised

It is not expected that the final version of the model will be completed within the period of the trial as it is expected that the information that can be used and developed will evolve as the model is used and the product manager and planners will learn from the information that is being provided.

Table 27. Expected packing daily with job types

						Delivery day	24/02/2021	25/02/2021	26/02/2021	27/02/2021	28/02/2021	01/03/2021	02/03/2021		
TPND	Product	Total Prog	Job Name	job no	quality	total units	23/02/Tue	24/02/Wed	25/02/Thu	26/02/Fri	27/02/Sat	28/02/Sun	01/03/Mon	benchmark	calculated weekly average benchmark
40	Core staff assumed						0.00%	0.00%	0.00%	0.00%	0.00%	0.00%	0.00%		
63515	GRAPES ALDI SS GRAPE 10X400	3,500	ALD-GP-VIS CHECK & HEATSEAL 10 X 400G	220.0	A	35,000	490	560	560	490	490	455	455	27	27.0
51150	GRAPES ALDI RSG PUN 10X500G	30,400	ALD-GP-HEATSEAL ONLY 10 X 500G	211.0	G	112,000	1,200	1,800	1,800	1,200	1,920	1,640	1,640	44	46.8
	GRAPES ALDI RSG PUN 10X500G		ALD-GP-VIS CHECK & HEATSEAL 10 X 500G	212.0	A	180.000	3,000	3,000	3,000	3,000	2,000	2,000	2,000	27	27.0
	GRAPES ALDI RSG PUN 10X500G		ALD-GP-SORT & HEATSEAL 10 X 500G	213.0	R	12,000	0	400	0	400	0	400	0	6	4.9
51186	GRAPES ALDI WSG PUN 10X500G	15,980	ALD-GP-VIS CHECK & HEATSEAL 10 X 500G	212.0	A	94,800	1,240	1,640	1,640	1,440	1,440	1,040	1,040	27	27.0
	GRAPES ALDI WSG PUN 10X500G		ALD-GP-CUT & HEATSEAL STEM UP 10 X 500G	214.0	G	56,000	800	800	800	800	800	800	800	8	8.9
	GRAPES ALDI WSG PUN 10X500G		ALD-GP-SORT & HEATSEAL 10 X 500G	213.0	R	9,000	300	0	300	0	300	0	0	6	4.9
60513	GRAPES ALDI BSG PUN 10X500G	8,600	ALD-GP-SORT & HEATSEAL 10 X 500G	213.0	R	86,000	1,120	1,200	1,400	1,120	1,320	1,120	1,320	27	27.0
36066150	GRAPES OS GREEN SL GRAPE PA	350	GP-PU-Cut + Heat Seal x10	165.0	G	3,500	200	0	0	150	0	0	0	8	8.9
36065197	GRAPES OS RED SL GRAPE PACK	550	GP-PU-Cut + Heat Seal x10	165.0	G	5,500	400	0	0	150	0	0	0	8	8.9
36065151	GRAPES OS GRAPE SL SELCTION	610	GP-SP-Cut + Heat Seal x10	164.0	G	6,100	400	0	0	210	0	0	0	8	8.9
5743	GRAPES SNACK POT GREEN GRAP	50	SNACK POT - FILL & LID GREEN GRAPE 12X90G	1,500.0	G	600	30	0	0	20	0	0	0	9	9.5
6861	GRAPES SNACK POT RED GRAPE	40	SNACK POT - FILL & LID RED GRAPE 12X90G	1,501.0	G	480	20	0	0	20	0	0	0	9	9.5
7979	BLUEBERRIES SNACK POT BLUEBERRY	70	SNACK POT - FILL & LID BLUEBERRY 12X90G	1,502.0	A	840	40	0	0	30	0	0	0	9	8.6
3999	VEGETABLES SNACK POT TOMATOES	30	SNACK POT - FILL & LID TOMATOES 12X90G	1,503.0	A	360	20	0	0	10	0	0	0	9	8.6
50510416	GRAPES ASDA BLACK GRAPE PUN	1,400	ASDA GP CUT & HS 20 X 400G	401.0	G	28,000	200	200	200	200	200	200	200	4	4.5
11111	GRAPES ALDI EE R 6X500		ALD-GP EE R 6X500 6X500G LABEL X6 CLAMSHEELS	228.0	A	14,040	0	0	0	0	0	1,170	1,170	73	75.8
	GRAPES ALDI EE R 6X500	9,000	ALD-GP - TRANSFER 6X500 + LABEL	276.0	A	39,960	1,260	1,440	1,440	1,260	1,260	0	0	45	45.0
2222	GRAPES ALDI EE W 4X500		ALD-GP – 4X500 + LABEL ONLY	270.0	G	36,000	1,260	1,440	1,440	1,260	1,260	1,170	1,170	110	117.0
		70,580				720,180	10,720	11,040	11,140	10,500	9,730	8,825	8,625		

Figure 19. Job Ratio

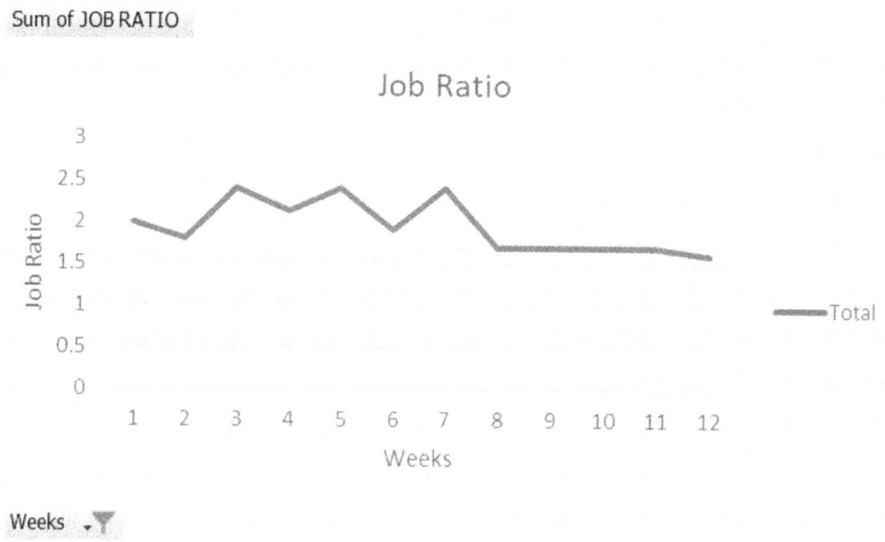

Table 27 provides the business with a greatly improved and detailed expected forecast for the coming week in comparison to the expected packing plan that was being delivered previously (as seen in Table 2 page 24). The new plan indicates the products required and the quantity and job type expected to be carried out for each product daily to fulfil the orders. The plan also indicates the fruit quality R.A.G., the percentage of agency staff expected to be required daily and the calculated benchmark that is dependent on the fruit quality and staff mix, as well as showing the financial benchmark.

How the Information Is Assisting the Planning

In the short term, the model provides good powerful information that can be used effectively to provide daily and weekly forecasts giving the pack-house planners accurate information that they can rely on when planning staff numbers. Early analysis of the model is providing good repeatable information. The product manager has set weekly meetings with the technical and pack-house managers using the data as a tool to discuss the pack-house performance and where efficiencies may be found.

The model is providing information to the planners that were previously lacking, including:

The number of agency staff that the product manager expects to be needed given prior knowledge of the core staff available for the coming week.

The job types expected to be required for each product to be produced on a given day. This information is given by the product manager through knowledge of the raw material on stock and knowledge built over time understanding the product, varieties, and seasonal information.

The quantity that each job type is expected to produce for each product on a given day. As the weekly forecast is being built it is possible for the product manager to see the pinch points in the week and therefore attempt to smooth out the profile of packing jobs to avoid overstretching the pack-house.

The quality of the raw material and the expected de-selection (or waste), using known figures when raw material is on stock and knowledge of the likely quality and condition of arrivals again built over time understanding the product, varieties, and seasonal information.

The calculated benchmark that is expected for the individual jobs, given the fruit quality and mix of staff, rather than the benchmark that has been set by the financial director which is an average benchmark taken from historical data. The calculated benchmark is a product of the model that takes the fruit quality and mix of labour into account and gives the product manager a good indication of when the pack-house should either over or under-perform against the financial benchmark.

The total staff hours required to complete the orders on a given day and whether the forecast is achievable within a standard shift.

Metrics That the Forecast Can Provide for Planning and Productivity Meetings

Using real data from the Prophet Systems Daily Packing Report (DRP) to compare the previous weeks' forecast to what happened is proving to provide good information. This can be used to both analyse where forecasting and planning could be improved. The analysis also highlights packing jobs that exceed or fall below the calculated benchmark, allowing the product manager to investigate individual jobs to understand the causes. The metrics that have been identified are to be used to aid the pack-house and product manager to understand the position as a whole, rather than to be taken in isolation, these are:

Job ratio seen in figure 20 below and percentage of schedule delivered seen in figure 21, is the number of jobs carried out divided by the number of scheduled jobs. In terms of planning, the lower the job ratio the better the planning. A higher ratio may indicate poor or difficult planning. Close monitoring of the job ratio is needed to help manage the bullwhip effect and ensure that the jobs performed to produce a product are kept to a minimum. This will also help reduce variation within the packing, and address Lean wastes "Muda" and "Mura"

Figure 20. % of schedule delivered

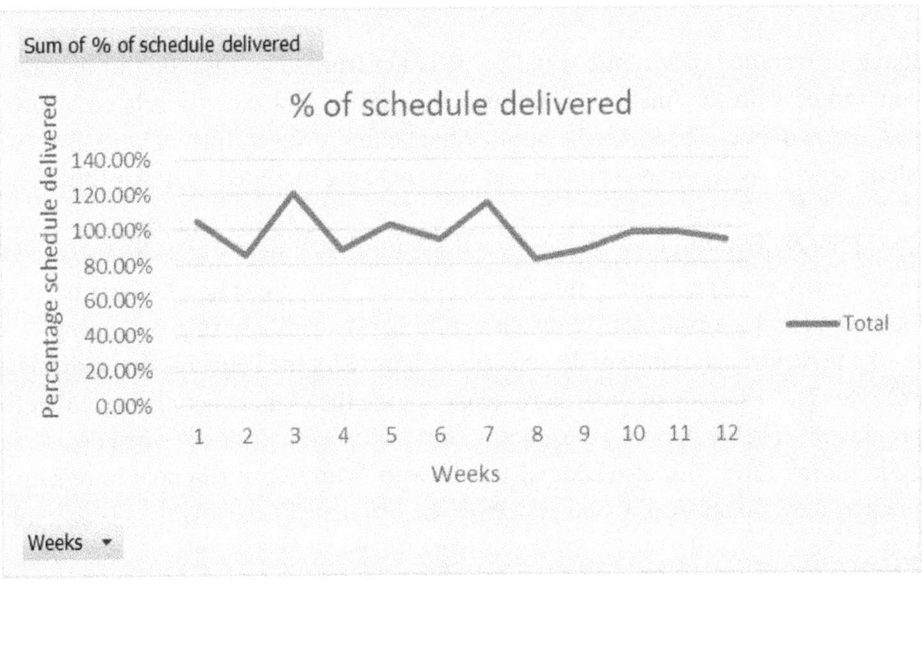

Percentage of unscheduled product seen in figure 21, is the number of packs per product not scheduled divided by the total number of packs for the week. The lower the number, the more accurate the forecast. A large number is likely to be due to customer induced challenges, caused by poor forecasting or unforeseen events

Figure 21. % of un-scheduled product

Percentage of labour variation (figure 23) is the difference between the labour used and labour expected. When productivity is negative this suggests better than expected productivity. This has proven to be a useful metric to open discussions with the pack-house manager and planners and helpful when managing a change of mindset to focus on efficient use of resources.

- Percentage of recorded down time (Figure 23) is not true down time but a financial figure as it has been agreed with the financial director that activities not directly related to production are recorded as down time. The lower the number the better however, further work is required here to understand where savings may be made and what is being recorded as down-time.

Percentage of benchmark variation (figure 24), above the benchmark suggests problem jobs or outliers with large differences. Again, using this figure allows CX to understand why a particular job has performed poorly, allowing a constructive discussion rather than simply finger pointing.

The lower the percentage variance of de-selection (figure 25), the better, as this indicates forecast of quality is accurate. The accuracy of this figure helps to give the planners confidence that the information being provided is reliable because, the amount of waste is a major factor when deciding how many staff to bring in for the shift. This also address Lean waste "Muri" as it can help in reducing the stress for the planners as they are under pressure to deliver the efficiencies the business is working towards.

Figure 22. % of labour variation

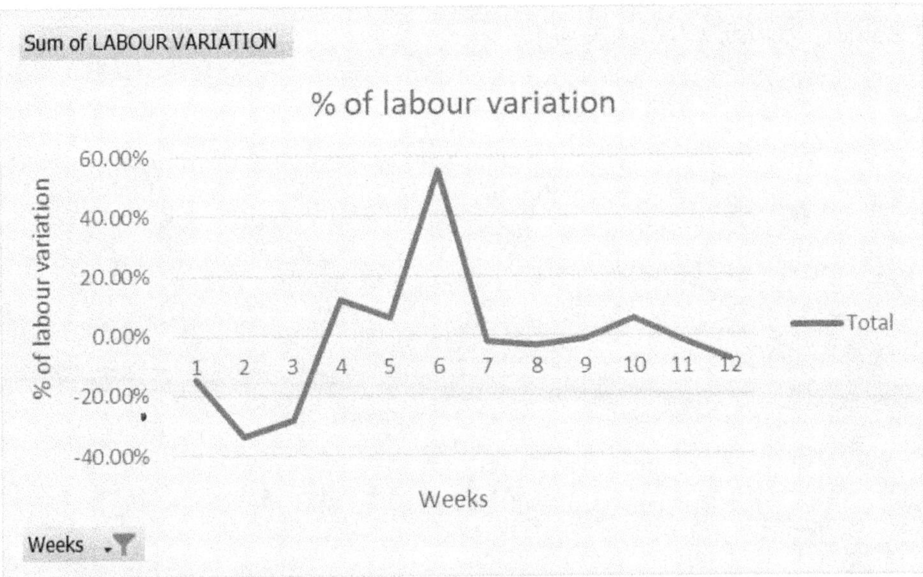

Figure 23. % recorded down time

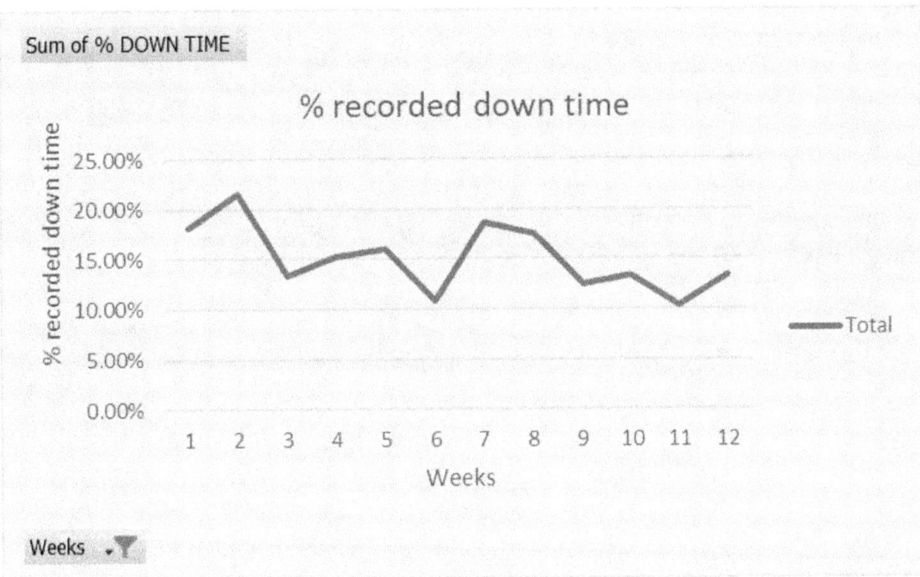

Generally, the higher the percentage packer utilisation (figure 26), the better as this suggests good utilisation of staff however, this is dependent on the quality and job types required. This figure indicates how much of the labour is being used to pack compared to how much is being used to complete ancillary jobs in the pack-house.

Figure 24. % of benchmark variation

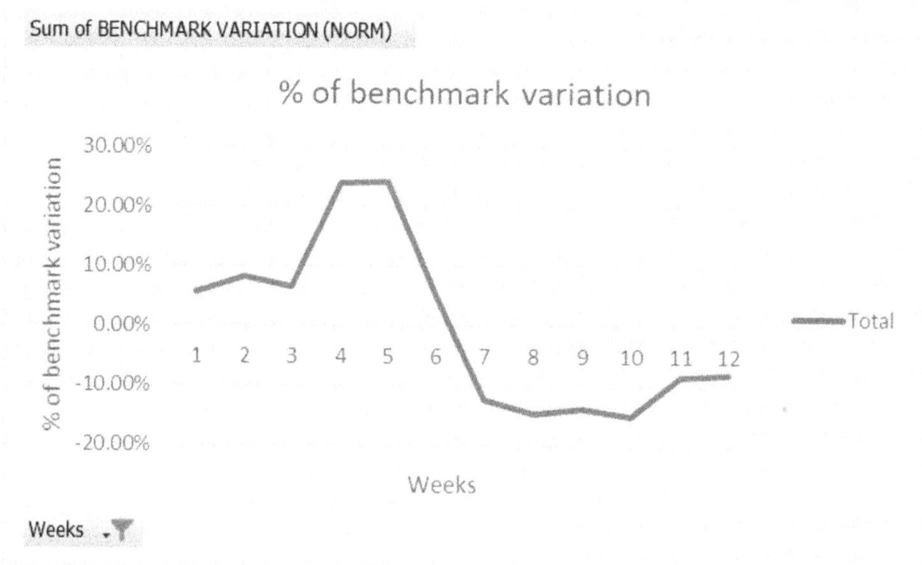

Figure 25. % variance de-selection

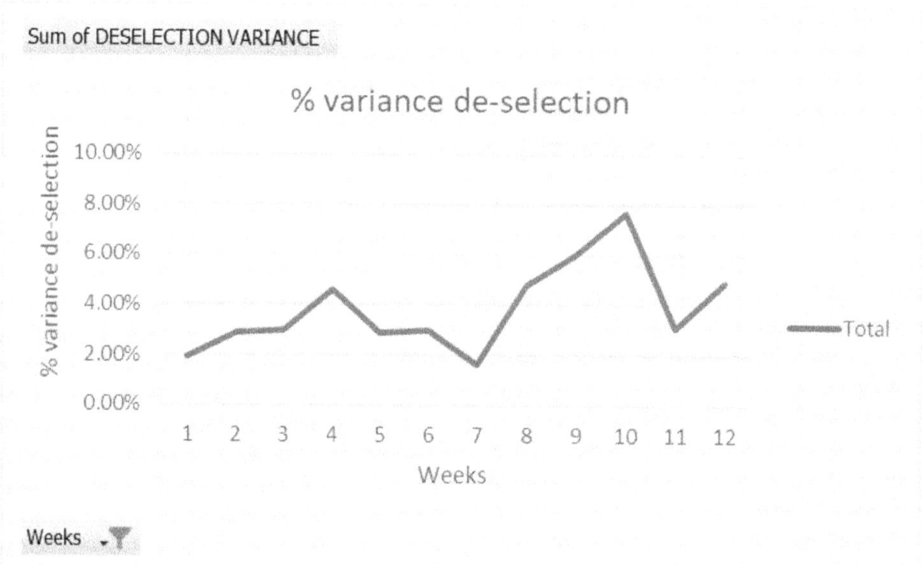

It is not possible to draw a direct comparison to show how the labour resource is being better utilised as following the introduction of the improved forecasting system the profile of customer orders and products has changed significantly. The customers' business has migrated away and CX has begun working with new customers. As predicted the number of products and variation in the daily work profile has increased. In March 2020, CX supplied one main customer. In March 2021 CX has supplied Aldi, Asda, Lidl, One-Stop and Spar.

Figure 26. % packer utilisation

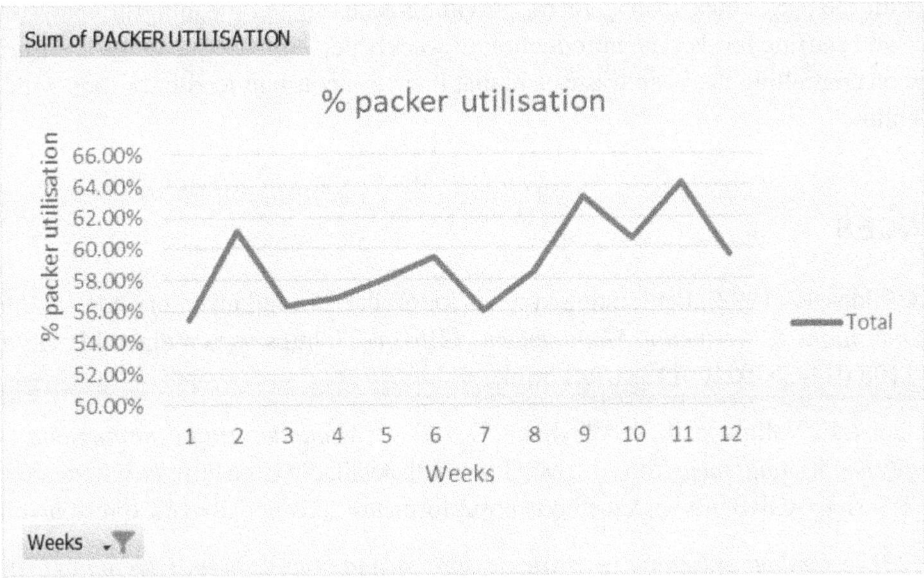

The business can, however, see the benefits of accurate forecasting and utilisation of labour, comparing Week 12 in March 2020 to the same week in 2021. In 2020, the pack-house produced 95,964 finished cases across 16 products for a single retailer and employed an average of 149 staff per day for that week, giving a wage bill of £28,072. In the same week in 2021, the pack-house produced 87,558 finished cases (9% fewer than in 2020), also across 16 products but for five different retailers (bringing greater variation) and employed an average of 82 staff per day for that week giving a wage bill of £15,449, equal to 45% fewer staff. This saving could equate to £656,386 per annum.

CONCLUSION

The introduction of a detailed and accurate forecast to enable better use of labour resource within the packing process at Orchard Place has proven vital to planning and monitoring the packing and labour costs. The information has emphasised the importance of allocating the correct staff type to the correct jobs within the production process and is enabling the pack-house planners to staff the pack-house efficiently and place staff where they will be most effective within the process.

In doing so this has also allowed for the wage bill to be controlled, ensuring that staffing levels are optimised and that planners no longer bring in additional staff as a contingency. Early results show this has the potential to save over £600,000 per year from the pack-house wage bill alone.

This, in turn, has provided support to the commercial team at CX, by proving that the pack-house is working efficiently and can be competitive in the marketplace, as they have sought to bring in new customers.

The forecast and its analysis have improved communication within the business, with constructive discussion with the pack-house management, providing accurate and meaningful analysis of packing performance and staffing levels. The introduction of weekly performance meetings is ensuring that the focus is kept on controlling the Lean wastes and that there is a constant feed-back loop with a Plan-Do-Check-Act culture.

REFERENCES

Beard, C., & Fildes, R. (1992). Forecasting systems for production and inventory control. *International Journal of Operations & Production Management*, *12*(5), 4–27. https://www.emerald.com/insight/content/doi/10.1108/01443579210011381/full/html

Berry, L., Jacobs, F., Vollmann, T., & Whybank, D. (2005). *Manufacturing Planning and Control systems for supply chain managment* (5th ed.). McGraw-Hill. Available from http://www.sidalc.net/cgi-bin/wxis.exe/?IsisScript=AGRIUAN.xis&method=post&formato=2&cantidad=1&expresion=mfn=029246

Burnes, B. (2017). *Managing Change: A strategic approach to organisational dynamics* (7th ed.). Pearson. Available from https://books.google.co.uk/books?hl=en&lr=&id=9J5Ri4xatEMC&oi=fnd&pg=PP11&dq=Managing+Change&ots=q5l5kwpYgV&sig=-AkaW_8aLEQH2WRBpktBDHs9w7s&redir_esc=y#v=onepage&q=Managing%20Change&f=false

Carnall, C., & Todnem, R. (2014). *Managing Change in Organizations* (6th ed.). Pearson Education.

Charumilind, S., Turabi, P., Finn, O., & Usher, A. (2020). *Demystifying modeling: How quantitative models can and cant change the world.* Mckinsey and Company. Available from https://www.mckinsey.com/~/media/McKinsey/Business%20Functions/Risk/Our%20Insights/Demystifying%20modeling%20How%20quantitative%20models%20can%20and%20cant%20explain%20the%20world/Demystifying-modeling-how-quantitative-models-VF.pdf

Chen, C., Wang, Y., Huang, G., & Xiong, H. (2019). *Hierarchical Demand Forecasting for Factory Production of Perishable Goods.* IEEE International Conference on Big Dat. Available from https://ieeexplore.ieee.org/document/9006161

Chen, C., Wang, Y., Huang, G., & Xiong, H. (2019) Demand Forecasting for Factory Production of Perishable Goods. *Big Data,* 188-193. Available from https://ieeexplore.ieee.org/document/9006161

Domingo, T. (2015). *"Identifying and eliminating the seven wastes or muda.* Godina Nepoznata: Asian Institute of Management. Available from http://rtdbiz.com/BMA/MM/SevenWastes.pdf

Donaldson-Feilder, E., Yarker, J., & Lewis, R. (2008). *Ine management competence: the key to preventing and reducing stress at work.* Emeraldinsight. Available from https://www.emerald.com/insight/content/doi/10.1108/14754390810853110/full/pdf?title=line-management-competence-the-key-to-preventing-and-reducing-stress-at-work

Duffy, M., Joakim, V., & Swartout, P. (2016). *Learning DevOps: Continuously Deliver Better Software.* Packt Publishing.

Eaton, M. (2003). *The Lean Practitioner's Handbook.* Kogan Page.

Gough, L. (2011) *Parkinsons's Law.* Infinite Ideas Limited. Available from http://www.infideas.com/books/c-northcote-parkinsons-parkinsons-law/

Graaff, E., & Kolmos, A. (2007) Managemnet of Change. In Management of Change - Implementation of Problem-Based and Project-Based Learning in Engineering. Sense.

Griffiths, J., & Margetts, D. (2000). *Variation in production schedules—implications for both the company and its suppliers. Journal of Materials Processing Technology, 103(1).* https://www.sciencedirect.com/science/article/pii/S0924013600004088

Kotter, J. (2012) *Leading change.* Available from https://books.google.co.uk/books?id=xpGX1EWL_EMC&printsec=frontcover&dq=Kotter%27s+change+model&hl=en&sa=X&ved=2ahUKEwiVkLb19qLrAhUGi1wKHW4oCJkQ6AEwAHoECAkQAg#v=onepage&q=Kotter's%20change%20model&f=false(Boston)

Marco. (2015). *Marco systems YCM reports Version 2.1 Copyright Marco Ltd.* Available from https://www.marco.co.uk/products/#

Mullan, R. (2016). The flying squad. *The Caterer*, *206*(4396), 32–36.

Newton, R. (2020). *The management consultant: Mastering the art of consultancy.* Pearson Education.

Smith, S. (2014). Muda, muri and mura. *Lean & Six Sigma Review, 13*(2), 36-37.

Wright, D., & Yuan, X. (2008). *Mitigating the bullwhip effect by ordering policies and forecasting methods. International Journal of Production Economics, 113(2).* https://www.sciencedirect.com/science/article/pii/S0925527308000340

Chapter 13
Competitive Advantages in the Turkish Retail Industry

Bülend Avcı
Bahçeşehir University, Turkey

ABSTRACT

Retail is one of the most important industries that is continuously improving around the world and in particular in Turkey. Competitive advantages owned by firms keep businesses one step ahead of their competitors. The main objectives of this chapter are determination of the main competitive advantages and capabilities for firm performance, determination of competitive advantages and capabilities which are relatively important for firm performance, and determination of competitive advantages and capabilities that are mainly used under the effects of environmental dynamism for firm performance in the Turkish retail industry. In this chapter, retailers are evaluated into two groups as organized and traditional. Totally, 50 competitive advantages and capabilities were identified in the research. The results of the study would be beneficial both for retail literature and retail business life.

INTRODUCTION

Retail is one of the most important industries continuously improving around the world, particularly in Turkey. Competitive advantages owned by firms provide one step ahead of their competitors. The main objectives of this chapter are the determination of the main competitive advantages and capabilities for firm performance, determination of competitive advantages and capabilities which are relatively important for firm performance and determination of competitive advantages and capabilities that are mainly used under the effects of environmental dynamism for firm performance in Turkish Retail Industry. In this chapter, retailers are evaluated into two groups as organized, and traditional.19 competitive advantages were identified as main competitive advantages, 19 competitive advantages were identified as a relatively important competitive advantage, and 12 competitive advantages were identified as mainly used competitive advantages under the effects of environmental dynamism for firm performance in Turkish retail industry. There are 50 competitive advantages and capabilities in the Turkish retail industry.

DOI: 10.4018/978-1-7998-8709-6.ch013

LITERATURE REVIEW

Theoretical Framework

The nature of firms and activities in business have been changed due to global and tough economic conditions. According to Vibert (2004), theories of the firm, economies, marketing, finance and management have put forward the theoretical frameworks for explaining and predicting the existence of the firms. Firm strategy researchers have been interested in the nature of competition of firms because of the tougher and ever-challenging market environment. Consequently, it leads to economic theories of the firm. While economic efficiency and outcomes of competitions were the most emphasized parameters, most of the economic theories of competition have been focused on competitive advantages for exploring the strategy of firms and competition process actions (Grimm, 2006). In order to investigate determinants of competitive advantage in the retail industry in Turkey, the RA theory of competition and the resource-based theory of firms were reviewed.

Theories of Firm

Theories of the firms were tried to explain the existence of the firms, comparison of the performance of the firms and behaviors of the firms. (Conner, 1991; Vibert, 2004). According to the literature, four different perspectives were proposed for theories of firms (Vibert, 2004).

1. Economic theories.
2. Functional Organization theories.
3. Interpretive and social constructionist theories.
4. Radical humanist and structuralist theories.

Economic Theories of the Firm

The theory is generally discussed in the literature as managerially oriented and functional. (Vibert, 2004). Economic theories of the firm can be classified into seven categories;

1. The neoclassical theory of the firm.

Firms exist in order to produce services and products by using labor and capital. (Conner, 1991; Hunt, 2000; Vibert 2004). In this perspective, all the firms in the market are small and homogeneous.

2. The traditional industrial economics of the firm.

This perspective proposes the Structure-Conduct-Performance (SCP) paradigm (Seth & Thomas, 1994). It means in order to conduct firm performance there is unidirectional causal flow from industry to firm.

3. The new industrial economics of the firm.

This view focuses on theoretical analyses of industry and behavior of firms which include internal organization and market strategy. (Tirole, 1988). This approach relies on game theory's mathematical methodology.

4. The behavioral theory of the firm.

This view rejects the rationality of ''economic man'' instead, according to Simon (1947) rationality have been bounded by individuals. Bounded rationality means that selecting the best possible options in order to provide cost optimization (Ackoff, 1981).

5. The managerial view and resource-based view of the firm.

According to Seth and Thomas (1994) the managerial view of firm came from Berle and Means (1932) who argued that profit maximization may not be the motivation of managers since public firms' managers may pursue activities which are beneficial for themselves rather than public shareholders.

6. Agency theory and the firm.

This view focused on long term wealth maximization of shareholders (Seth & Thomas, 1994). According to this view contractual relationship between managers and shareholders are important since the contractual relationship led to promote actions of shareholder's interest and constrain managerial judgements.

7. The transactions cost framework.

This view was developed by Williamson (1988) and originated by market failure framework which refers to transaction cost become excessive, of Coase's (1937). According to Williamson (1976) cost of consumption over the purchase price defined as transaction cost.

Functional Organization Theories of the Firm

Functional organization theories are similar economic theories in terms of relationship, regularities and management orientation (Gioia & Pitre, 1990). There are also some differences between them, while the economic theories analyze business enterprises, functional organization theories analyze both organizations and business enterprises. Survival and legitimacy are the firm performances with economic measures.

Interpretive and Social Constructionist Perspectives of the Firm

This perspective originated from interpretivism. According to interpretivist view, a member of an organization is an active role makers and under socialized (Vibert, 2004),

Radical Humanist and Structuralist Perspectives of the Firm

This view confronts assumptions, institutions and extant beliefs. (Vibert & Hurst, 2004). According to Gioia&Pitre (1990), this view looks for free members of organization from sources of domination and alienation, so postmodernism, configuration theory and critical theory are the theories that are used for examining the firms from this perspective.

Theories of Competition

Nature of the firm competition, firm strategy roles and getting competitive advantages are the main interests of the competition theories according to literature (Grimm, 2006). According to Grimm (2006) four types of perspectives were identified in the competition theory. These are;

1. Perfect competition from neoclassical economics

According to this view, firm strategy plays a small role because of the perfect information in the competition.

2. The structure-conduct-performance framework from industrial organization economics

This view provide insight for obtaining competitive advantage of firm in the industry structure and sustaining strategies. According to this view there is no attention for internal organization factors and restriction in empirical studies (Grimm, 2006)

3. Game theory from new industrial organization economics

For analyzing competitive advantages and for showing relationship among resources, responses, advantages and competitive moves, this view is very a useful tool. Since the failure to produce practical solutions for many contemporary strategic management problems it is criticized (Singer, 1997).

4. Dynamic competition from Schumpeterian and evolutionary economics

First mover advantage, competitive behavior and innovation insights are very important in this view because of the theory of avoiding sustainability and equilibrium, it is considered applicable for today's and tomorrow's fast-paced competitive environments (Grimm, 2006).

Resource Based View (RBV)

When past 30 years were analyzed, it can be detected that organizations can gather a unique variety of resources that will yield them competitive advantages. RBV is the most important theory in order to explain the differences of firm performance. According to Wernerfelt (1984) and Barney (1991) RBV proposes that in order to gain a sustainable competitive advantage, organizations should invest in resources and capabilities will best assist them in successfully. Barney (1991) proposed VRIN criteria means that, resources should be valuable (V), rare (R), inimitable (I) and non-substitutable (N) in order to generate sustainable competitive advantages. According to Kamasak (2017) RBV has a view of heterogeneity among firms in resources to explain performance differences between firms.

RBV provides an important view about the strategic behavior of organizations for the researchers, so offering an appropriate definition related to RBV important step to understand better. (Rugman&Verbeke, 2002)

From strategic management perspective, the resource-based approach is mainly based on the work of an economist Edith Penrose (1959) "The Theory of the Growth of the Firm," In this study of Penrose (1959), inquiry of the Classical Economic Theory it is proposed that firms were accepted as homogeneous enterprises questions. According to the inquiry Penrose defined the firms as an administrative structure which is a combination of tangible and intangible resources, growing through the use of perceived opportunities.

According to Penrose (1959), competitive advantages that provide growth for firms are directly related to the configuration of the resources that company possess. Apart from the Classical Economic Theory, main point of the study of Penrose (1959) is the effect of the experience of management on the production processes and identifying of critical role of management.

The impressions of the management from company's resources and competitive environment provide unique production opportunities for firms. In other words, the capabilities of management will be catalyst for productive outcome of the company. Capability means repeatedly implemented and initiated organizational changes in order to improve harmony among management, company and environment (Nelson&S., 1982).

Another important study about competition was performed by Birger Wernerfelt (1984) 25 years after the study of Penrose (1959). Birger Wernerfelt used study of Penrose in the effects of resources in formation of companies (Wernerfelt, 1984).

Wernelfelt (1984) proposed in the article that by ''a resourced based view of the Firm' 'companies can grow sequentially via source advantage and a proposed a source product matrix. According to Wernelfelt (1984) balance between the expanding resources that companies possess and developing the new resources are crucial. If the companies manage this strategy, they would be successful in the market.

Another important contribution came from the Barney (1991). According to Barney (1991) in order for companies to provide a sustainable competitive advantage, they needed resources which are valuable, rare, imperfectly imitable and non-substitutable, so in order to create sustainable competitive advantage companies must produce strategy which cannot be copied by the competitors (Barney, 1991).Shown in Figure 1

Figure 1. Resource based view.

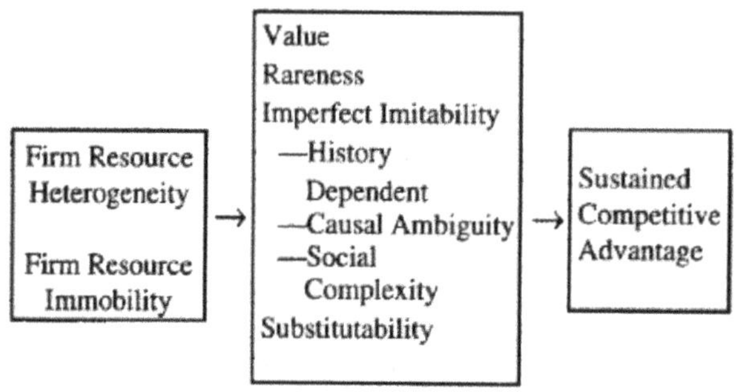

Barney (1991) argued that rare resources were needed in order to create strategy which increases the efficiency and productivity of the companies. The companies can sustain competitive advantages unless the resources can be copied.

There is a relationship between resource heterogeneity and immobility, Value, Rareness, Imperfect İmitability, Sustainability and Sustained Competitive Advantages.

According to Peteraf (1993) a firm leverages various resources, tangible and intangible as shown in Figure 2. Although possessing different types of resources is essential to achieve success, not all resources contribute equally to a firm's achievement of success and competitive advantages.

Figure 2. Resource based view of firms' success.
Source: Peteraf (1993).

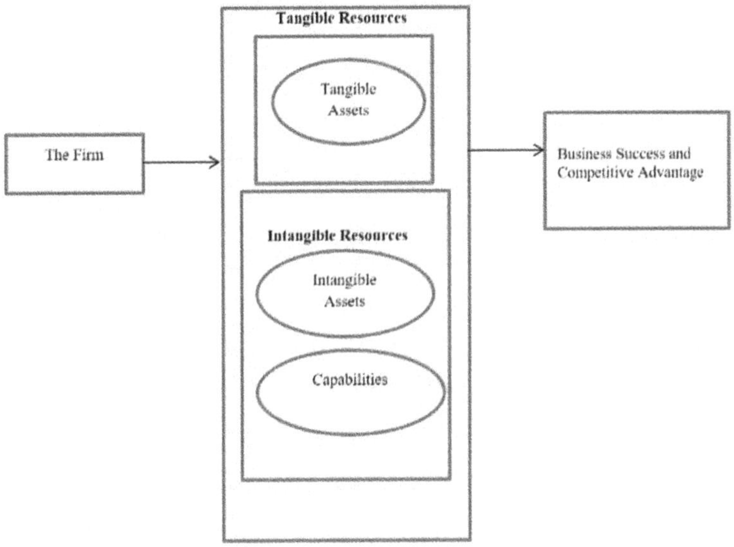

Sousa et al. (2008) proposed that the RBV view of the firm that focuses on the establishment of competitive edge such as assets, knowledge, data, and corporate attributes. According to Cho (2015) RBV and retail marketing literature proposed that there is close relationship among resources, market coverage and performance. Competitive advantage of internal resources can be explained by the RBV. (Wernerfelt, 1984; Barney, 1991). According to Barney and Arikan (2001), resource can be tangible and intangible assets, like routines, materials, routines, and capabilities. According to Peng et al. (2008) competence and capabilities are the high level resources to coordinate routines and materials.

Resource-Advantage Theory of Competition

Resource advantage theory was proposed by Hunt & Morgan (1995) in order to explain dynamic competition among firms. RA theory is the combination of the three theories which are resource based theory, heterogeneous demand theory and theories of dynamic competition. According to RA theory firms try to find unique, costly to copy advantages to secure above normal performance and emphasize heterogeneous and unique resources. (Barney, 1991; Conner, 1991). Moreover, customers are different and they demand different tastes and preferences, so different products and services are needed in order to satisfy customer needs (Alderson, 1957). Consequently, RA theory can be defined as getting superior performance from constant struggle among firms to get comparative advantages which leads to competitive advantage for the market as shown in Figure 3 (Hunt, 2000).

Figure 3. RA theory of competition

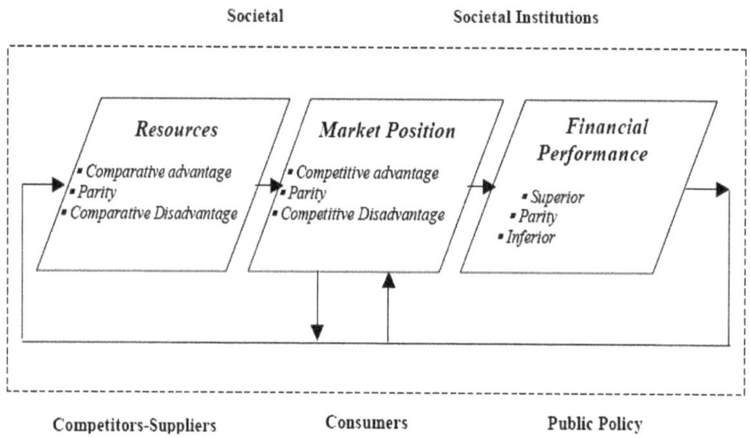

According to resource advantage theory, firms are combiners of heterogeneous resources which are tangible and intangible entities to produce efficiently and effectively for some market segments (Hunt, 2000).

Consequently, resource advantage theory argues that market position of the firm is the outcome of the resource management of the firm as well. Firms have tangible and intangible resources like people, teams, relations and networks. By combination of these resources, firms produce unique strategy in a complex way. Therefore, resource advantage theory is an excellent and realistic explanation in market competition in Turkish retail industry.

Market Environment

One of the major sources of contingencies is external environment that firms need to manage (Hunt, 2000). External environment can be seen as one of the key determinants of decision making in firms (Morris, Shindehutte, & LaForge, 2002). According to neo-classical economic theories firms' environment is stable, homogeneous, static and equilibrium. Provoking that affect firms' performance (Hunt, 2000; Hunt & Arnett, 2003).

Multidimensional Concept of Environment

Dynamism, resource scarcity and complexity are the most widely used dimensions (Sharfman & Dean, 1991). Complexity is the diversity and heterogeneity that firms need to be dealt with in order to take decision (Dess & Beard, 1984; Tung, 1979). Dynamism and instability mean rate of environmental change that is unforeseen (Dess & Beard, 1984). Dynamism consists of routienity, uncertainty and turbulence. Resource availability means the available resources in the environment (Sharfman & Dean, 1991). Resource availability consists of capacity, munificence and hostility.

According to the current literature, characteristics of environment shown in Table 1;

Table 1. Dimensions of the environment

Terms	Definitions
Complexity:	
Complexity	The number of heterogeneity and diversity in the environment for decision making(Dess & Beard 1984)
Turbulence:	
Turbulence	Extent of uncertainty and unpredictability (Dess & Beard 1984)
Dynamism	Unpredictability in environmental change (Dess & Beard 1984)
Routineity	The consistency of variability for organizational units. (Tung 1979)
Uncertainty	Due to lack of information inability to predict environmental elements. (Milliken, 1987)
Resource Availability;	
Hostility	for scarce resources intense competition (Mintzberg, 1979)
Munificence	resource availability for supporting growth.(Dess & Beard 1984)
Acceleration;	
Acceleration	Predictable business cycle speed (Dyer & Ha-Brookshire, in press)

Source: (Dyer, B., & Ha-Brookshire, 2007)

When considering Turkish economy and business environment which is always dynamic, there is no stability. For this reason, it was chosen that Environmental dynamism as a moderating effect.

Firm Performance

Firm performance can be defined as measure of bottom-line by the economic theorists (Viber, 2004). According to Dess &Robinson (1984) performance investigating as an outcome of firms' strategies, is an important part of empirical research. Four perspective of firm performance was examined by Ford and Schellenberg (1982)

1. Goal Approach of Etzioni (1964)
   a. Firm performance was defined in terms of goal attainment.
   b. Assumes pursue ultimate goals for organizations.
2. System Resource Approach of Yuchtman &Seashore (1967)
   a. Firm performance was defined in terms of ability of organizations in order to secure resources.
   b. Organizational and environmental relationship were emphasized.
3. Constituency Approach of Thompson (1967)
   a. Based on fulfillment needs of internal and external constituencies.
4. Process Approach of Steer (1977)
   a. Firm performance was defined in terms of organization participant's behavior.

In addition to above approaches, multiple constituencies has been proposed by Connolly, Conlon and Deutsch (1980). This approach highlights the subjective and multiple evaluative criteria that associates with the firms. According to this view a firm consists of diverse constituencies coalitions that expects different performance.

Firm Performance Measurement

Most researchers used economical and financial parameters in order to measure the firm performance. According to Dess & Robinson, (1984) sales growth and return on assets is the mostly used performance indicator in the literature. Because of the lack of data and complex methodology, performance of private and multi industry firms is hard to evaluate. Moreover, firm performance of privately held smaller firms is hard to measure as well due to the lack of success and failure criteria and problems of getting performance data. (Dess and Beard, 1984).

Retail Performance

Store level and competitor level factors which are important for performance maximization and new entrant's competition.

Store Level Drivers for Performance in Retail

According to Hoch et al (1995) 67% of the price elasticity variation is explained by consumer and competitor factors. On the other hand, when market factors are considered, consumer and competitive factors vanish. Therefore, market factors are more important than all the other factors. The location of the firm is the important determinant for retail performance. (Reinartz and Kumar 1999) but nowadays understanding of retail performance impacts of individual services have shifted retail performance literature towards that way. Research showed that pharmaceutical and floral services (Pauler et al. 2009), and mixed merchandising increase retail sales (Reinartz and Kumar 1999; Kumar and Karande 2000). Moreover, in order to increase store patronage, service quality, assortment breadth and store atmosphere, a low pricing strategy can be used (Pan and Zinkhan 2006). According to Kumar and Karande (2000) non-grocery items affects sales productivity negatively due to higher price.

Competitive Drivers of Retail Performance

According to Arnold et al. (1983) assortment, superior location, customer service initiatives, cleanliness, low pricing strategy and shopping ambience are the important factors in order to obtain competitive advantages. Apart from superior location and low pricing strategy, all other factors produce competitor advantage in the short run. Superior location and low pricing strategy can be leveraged over extended period. According to Ailawadi et al. (2010), for responding to the new Wal Mart entry in the market, increasing prices, decreasing assortments, increasing private label, and changing breadth and depth of promotional campaigns and adapting innovative campaigns in or to attract niche customers are implemented.

Measuring Firm Performance

Different types of performance indicators are used in empirical studies. Some of the indicators are the firm specifics so it is not easy to compare. Most of the authors used profit which is related to sales, equity and assets as indicator. Therefore, return on assets used in most of the empirical studies. (Hatten & Hatten, 1985; Strandskov, 1999). According to Dess and Robinson (1984), return on assets and growth in sales were the most important performance indicator in the literature. Moreover, according to Vorhies & Morgan, (2005) return on assets is a suitable indicator in order to perform comparison within the industry.

Competitive Advantage Theory

The theory framework is based on the study of Porter (1980). The theory of competitive advantage is widely used in most industries in order to secure competitive advantage. According to Porter (1980) competitive advantages are identified over the competitors. There are three types of competitive advantages;

1. Cost Leadership
2. Differentiation
3. Focus

Cost Leadership

Selling price is so important in most of the markets for competing product to get more market share (Porter, 1980). In order to get the cost leadership in the market, distribution and production cost must be lowered to charge minimum cost to the price.

Differentiation

According to Porter (1980) customers are eager to pay higher if the products have superior performance via added value which is called the differentiation strategy. Innovative products, quality products, product improvement and superior customer service are perceived as added value by the customers.

Focus

Focus strategy consist of cost focus and differentiation focus in specific and choosing narrow market segments to gain competitive advantage. Most of the company may prefer to operate in specific markets rather than broad ones.

Competitive Advantages and Capabilities in Retailing

In order to get superior performance, competitive advantages are the important concepts that create relative advantage. Competitive advantages have been evolving year by year because of the change in market information, sophistication in competition, customer, supply chain management, and flow of the goods. (Julie, 2000). Since the evolution of economy differs, competitive advantage emerges.

Value chain is the one of the most important milestones in competitive advantages studies, proposed by Porter (1980). According to Value Chain Approach, there are three important elements which are behavior of a firm, external environment and market results. Firms need to pay attention to their position inside the market and external environment in order to get superior results. There are five competitor forces which are new entrants, competitors, suppliers, and demand and substitute products in the industry. Firms can decide strategies called ''generic competitive strategies'' which include cost leadership, differentiation and focus strategies, according to market environment (Porter, 1985).

Asset and capabilities are the resources to detect market opportunities and threats (Sanchez et al. 1996). There are two types of assets which are tangible and intangible in order to produce, create and offer products to the market. Moreover, according to Srivastava et al. (1998) and Teece et al. (1997), assets can serve both inputs and outputs for the process. Inputs are transformed to output in a greater worth which is defined as capabilities (Amit and Schoemaker 1993; Capron and Hulland 1999; Sanchez et al. 1996). There are some skills of capabilities like technical ability, managerial ability, system development processes or integration processes. So for the retailing, according to literature, three competitive advantages and ten capabilities have been proposed as follows.

1. Differentiation Based Competitive Advantages: The aim of this advantage is creating something unique in the industry (Porter, 1980). According to retailing literature, there are four types differentiation based competitive advantage capabilities including market sensing, brand management, customer service and novel shopping experiences. These are called the sources of differentiation based competitive advantage (Pearce 1989, Day 1994, Frigo 2002, Hulland et al. 2007). According to Pearce (1989) novel shopping experience is used by retailers to create exclusive perception and encourage high profit margin. Moreover, according to Day (1994), retailers use market sense to obtain valuable knowledge and to improve more sustainable programs.
    a. Market Sensing is the collecting, processing and market information (Day 1994).
    b. Customer Service is the providing superior and seamless customer service in order to increase performance of firm (Anderson et al. 2004).
    c. Brand Management is the balancing between maximizing profit and competing brands. (Capron and Hulland 1999; Srivastava et al. 1998).
    d. Novel Shopping Experience is the creating unique formats that produce wow effect on the customers. (Pearce 1989).
2. Cost Leadership Competitive Advantages: The aim of this advantages is maintaining low cost and quality, service and other areas (Dess and Davis 1984). According to literature, there are three types of capabilities including property management, information technology (IT), distribution and logistics operations which belong to the cost leadership competitive advantage (Barney 1991, Bharadwaj 2000, and Wade and Hulland 2004). According to Barney (1991), retailers should strengthen the value chain, minimize stock outs and reduce inventory costs by using IT skills.
    a. Property Management is referring to providing customer convenience, the competence of finding best locations and investing optimal real estates.
    b. Supply Chain Operations is the optimizing transportation organization in order to create cost efficiency.
    c. IT skills Information technology is the IT skills providing cost efficient and convenient system for customers.

3. Balanced-Based Competitive Advantages: The aim of this is to balance competitive forces properly and to respond accordingly by underlining the right set of capabilities. There are three types of capabilities including price-value relationship, inter-functional partnership and buying ability that belong to the Balanced-Based Competitive Advantages.
    a. Price-value relationship is the balancing between profit maximization and fairest price.
    b. Inter-functional partnerships are the improvement of collaboration between stakeholders.
    c. Buying ability is the opportunity for retailers to offer shoppers unique, customized, dominant, and logical assortments of goods (Frigo 2002).

RETAIL INDUSTRY IN TURKISH CONTEXT

Retail in Turkey

When we analyze the historical evolution of retail development of Turkey, we realize that the roots come from the Ottoman Empire period. During that period İstanbul was the trade center between the world and the Ottoman Empire. Retailing process was realized in bazaars, çarsıs, (markets), bedestens (covered bazaars and hans, hostel for traders). Ethnic groups in Ottoman Empire were the most dynamic middlemen among European capitals. After a treaty in 1838 the empire opened to foreign capitals (Tokatli & Boyaci, 1999). Westernization started during the second half of the nineteenth century and some of the European origin stores opened franchises like Louvre, Au Lion, Bon Marche, Au Camelia, Bazar Allemand, Carlmann et Blumberg, Orosdi Back, Au Paon and Baker. This is the first globalization in Turkish history (Geyikdaği&Geyikdaği, 2009).

Till 1970, during the republican period, in addition to bazaars and street sellers, grocers, butchers and small-scale convenience stores were dominant. In 1953 Swiss Migros and Turkish Government performed joint venture to get know-how in food retailing. They started with 20 mobile sales trucks and Migros opened first self-service store in 1957.After Migros, Gima (1956), OYAK (1963) and Tansaş (1973) started their retail operation in urban side of Turkey. All of them were the public investments with local institutions. Apart from Migros case, Central and Eastern European countries have similarities with Turkey in the development of food retailing (Franz et al., 2013). Compared to European countries, Turkey had the lower spatial penetration of supermarket, discounters and hypermarkets in terms of diffusion speed after 1990 (Franz et al., 2013). According to Tokatli&Boyacı (1998) until 1980 retail sector in Turkey showed little changes in international circumstances. Furthermore, the sector was characterized by publicly or privately owned industrial sector which were government dependent. After economic boom was experienced in 1960 and commercial and agrarian capital were converted to industrial capital and importers turn in to industrialists so there was an uncertain line between traders and manufacturers. Turkey faced economic crises in 1970s which showed the necessity in economical restructuring (Tokatli & Boyaci-Eldener, 2002).

Between 1981 and 1993 high rate of economical growth occurred and at the beginning of 1980 Turkey recognized global competition conditions and adopted more outward oriented development strategy (Tokatli & Boyaci, 1998). Country shifted from manufacturing to consumption in the late 1980s' (Tokatli & Erkip, 1998). Increasing privatization and flexibility in regulations of FDI (Foreign Direct Investment) and decreasing control of government led to change in retail sector organization in Turkey as well. Between 1990 and 2000 cash rich retail sector was attracted by the financial sector in a high interest rate economic environment (Ozcan, 2000). Between 1990-2000 globalization in retailing sector started slowly. At the beginning of 1990, the nature of the sector started to change by domestic and transnational corporations and rich consumer market was created by large and organized retail investment (Tokatli & Boyaci, 1998). In 1990s, there was dominantly investment in large scale food retailers in new shopping centers. There were 3 reasons to invest in Turkey;

1. Population was greater than most of the European countries
2. Younger population share was higher
3. Quicker rate of returns when compared to other European countries

Carrefoursa Hypermarkets, ChampiaonSa Supermarket and DiaSa Discount Markets were opened in 1996 with the collaboration between Groupe Carrefour of France and Sabanci Holding. Metro Group opened Metro Grossmarket as a wholesaler in 1990 and opened real hypermarket as a retailer and Praktiker as home improvement and Do It Yourself (DIY) store. In the following years furthermore Corio&ECE (Dutch) and Multimall (German) international investments opened new wave of shopping centers (Ozuduru & Varol, 2011). So, visiting shopping malls became popular activity in urban side of Turkey. Modern retailing in Turkey was changed by rapid urbanization. It increased per capita income and education level, use of technology and young demographics.

Indicators and Retail Expenditures for Turkey and Some European Countries (2008)

During the transformation period, small retailers and groceries did not have enough knowledge and fund in order to deal with the situation. Some of the organized retailers tried to help the small-scale retailers by providing franchising. As an example, Migros partnered with Koç Holding in order to change business strategy via providing know-how in Bakkalım (my bakkal) concept which was more modern and hygienic but resembling the traditional groceries. Proximity to customers was one of the strengths of the independent retailers. You can buy easily daily goods from these retailers and you can buy weekly foods from super/hypermarkets. Central government supported large scale investors because of the tax that can be collected easily. The large capital was supported-because of the economic advantages to shareholders- by Tax Law (1992), the Law of Capital Markets (1994) (Erkip&Ozuduru, 2015). In 1997, to regulate the retail sector, The Turkish Competition Authority was established. As the central government concentrated on large scale foreign capital, small retailers could not be protected properly and retail companies in Turkey started to invest in other countries like Russia and Kazakhstan (Ozcan, 2000).

Between 2000-2010, we can see the high growth rate of the shopping center as shown in Figure 4, in shopping malls. Share of foreign investment increased as well, as shown in Figure 5. This decade was the golden era for shopping malls.

Between 2008-2010 the number of shopping centers increased despite affection of global economic crisis. Between the 2006 and 2013 the number of employees in retail sector increased around 95%. After 2006 because of both political stability and growing purchase power in Turkey investors become more confident so it affects retail sector positively as well. Retail became one of the most profitable sectors when compared to construction, manufacturing and tourism due to the high and quick return on rates so both local and international investors increased their investment in retail in Turkey. In this period the power of retailers increased over government and they also started to shape retail legislation.

Figure 4. Number of shopping centers in Turkey by year.

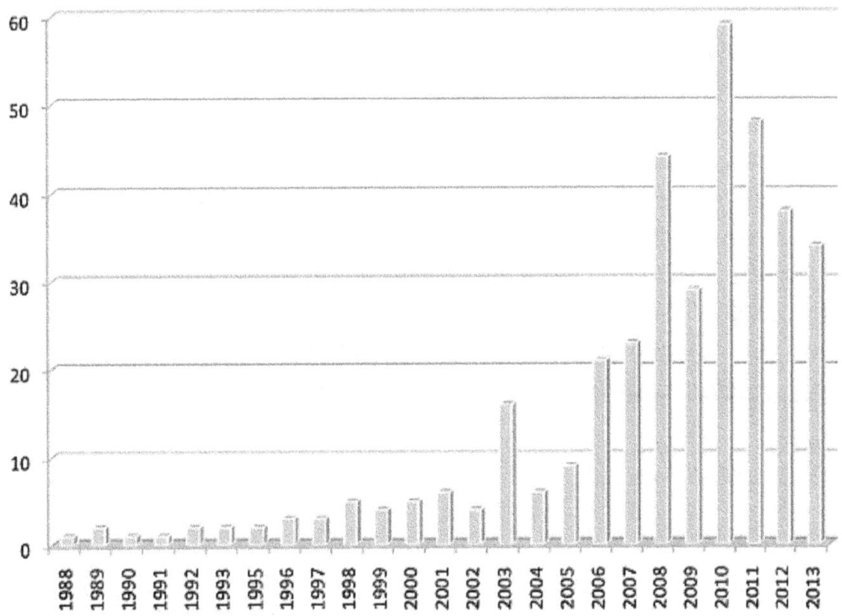

Figure 5. Number of shopping centers by investor type.

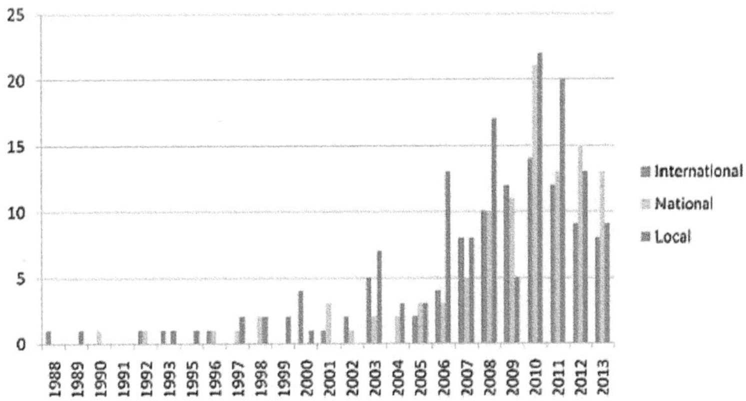

Current Situation in Turkish Retail Industry

When we analyze the retail in Turkey, 67% of the market share belongs to the traditional retail whereas 33% of the market share belongs to the organized retail. Although organized retail has been bounced in the last 20 years, traditional retail keeps the importance in the industry. While the organized retail is increasing, traditional retail is decreasing. There are some reasons behind that fact such as increasing investment in shopping malls, less competitiveness of the traditional retailers, changing of buying behaviors of the customers and technological developments which disrupts habits of the customers. Discount Stores which are growing aggressively against the traditional retail is also another significant factor. Although several important foreign investors have been lost in the past 10 years in the organized retail thanks to local investors, organized retail kept its growth steadily as shown in Figure 6.

Investment in retail in Turkey is still going on, especially discount stores have grown very fast in the last 5 years. They keep accelerating by attracting the A and B segment customers and currently Top 2 discounters reached customers through around 13.000 branches.

Turkish retail industry is in the second rank in terms of employment among industries, according to TUIK as shown in Figure 7. The number of employments reached 1.925.000 people as of September 2017.

We can see the growth trend in yearly basis in unemployment in retail, but especially in the economic recession period industry tend to stop investing in their staff in terms of qualification and improvement. Moreover, it reflects and affects the customer satisfaction badly. Employment turnover is high in retail industry since most of the employee work for minimum salary in Turkey.

Figure 6. Retail turnover in Turkey (billion TL).
Source: (TUIK - Retail Turnover Indexes, Aug 2017)

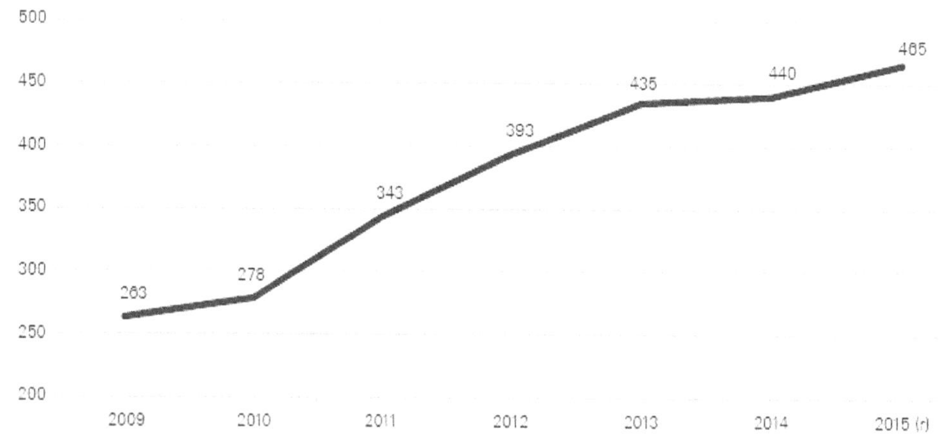

Figure 7. Number of employments in Turkish Retail Industry.
Source: (TUİK)

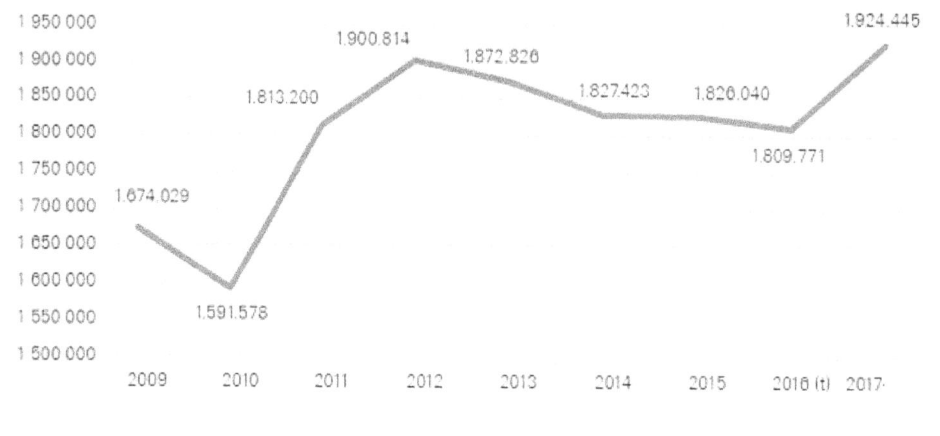

Mall Sector in Turkey

While Turkey had 12 shopping mall in 1995, the expectation in the number of mall is 465 as of 2019, and according to assumptions after 2020 the number will be stable since increasing in the supply did not reflect fulfillment rate of the malls. Fulfillment rate was only %50 for the newly opened malls as of 2017. According to analysis for the last 3 years, while the improvement in malls was 15% in terms of number in 2019, the improvement will only be 1% as shown in Figure 8.

Results obtained from analyzing the investors profile of the malls in Turkey, Show that 73% are local investors which has 8.600.000 m2 rentable area, 23% of the malls belongs the foreign investor which own 2.722.001 m2 rentable area and 4% of the malls belong to the joint venture with local and foreign investors which has 471.750 m2 rentable area (KPMG 2018).

Figure 8. Number of malls in Turkey.
Source: (Eva GYD)

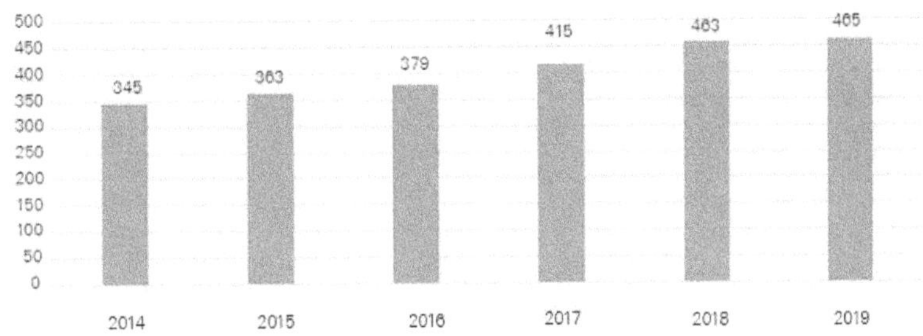

E Commerce in Turkey

Turkey had around 48 million internet users as of 2017. According to analysis of age profile, 95% of the age group between 16-24, 91% of the age group between 25-34, 87% of the age group between 35-44 and 77% of the age group between 45-54 get online at least one time in daily.

According to the survey conducted by Household IT Usage Survey, shopping rate increased 20% in the age group between 16-74 in e commerce.

Category breakdown of the e commerce is as follows;

- 62,3% apparel and sports equipment
- 25,3% household items (furniture, toys, white goods…)
- 24,1% travel ticket, car rent
- 21,9 Food Products
- 19% Consumer electronics (mobile phone, cam, TV…)

Retail game player who gets 97% of total turnover and hold 99% of the employment only perform 30% of the all e commerce turnover in Turkey, so online retailers has 70% of total e commerce turnover. The numbers reflect that brick and mortar retailers should care about omni- channel approach in Turkey.

Important Players in Turkish Retail Industry

The most important player in the Turkish retail industry have become the discounters. Customer demands and disposable income of the customers reshape the retail industry again. Traditional players of organized retail in Turkey tend to open small and boutique concepts due to the high rents, price competitiveness with discounters. Discounters have the biggest share in terms of turnover in Top 10 retailers in Turkey as shown in Figure 9. These two discounters BIM and A 101 have around 13.000 stores and over 80.000 employees. BIM is not only growing in Turkey but also increasing investment in abroad with low cost and unique format strategy. Migros is in 2nd rank position after acquisition of Tesco Kipa and A 101 is in 3rd rank position with the highest number of stores in Turkey. There are 2 wholesalers in the list which are Metro and Bizim Toptan. Teknosa is the one and only company in consumer electronics category in the Top 10 list. LC Waikiki and Koton are the 2 apparel retailers in the list.

Figure 9. The biggest retailers in Turkey as of 2016-year end (sales volume-million TL).
Source: (Fortune, Capital (*) after acquisition of Tesco Kipa)

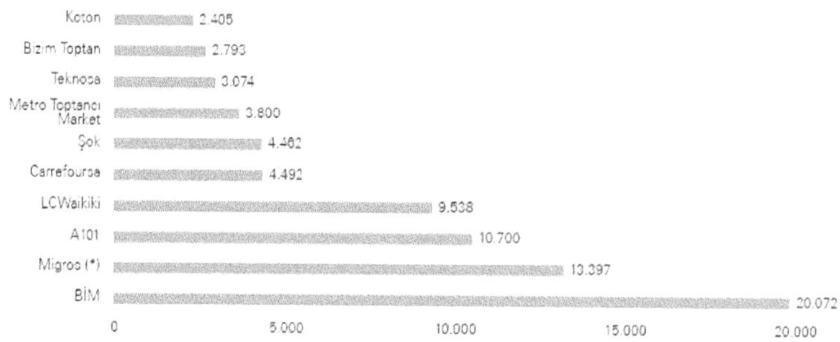

Consumption Patterns of Turkish Consumers

In addition to successful local retailers, global brands also affect Turkish consumers. Beymen Department Store is a good example in terms of brand content selling brands such as Alexander Wang, Armani Collezioni, Balenciaga, Balmain, Givenchy and Gucci. Most brands from all over the world are represented. Since the number of internet user in Turkey has increased, approximately 25 million, brand awareness has increased as well.

The household composition is changing and transforming in Turkey. The nature of family has been changed in past hundred years from agricultural economy. While the children are economic value in agricultural economy, they are cost center in urban mixed economy. Households changed dramatically between 1978-1998 in Turkey because of urbanization. Household shrank from 20% to 10%, and nuclear family household rose from between 62% and 72% to 10%. Divorce rate has tripled, and single adult's households rose from 3% to 5% (Louaragand, 2011), so the figures show that household characteristics of Turkey are transforming to western type. Despite these changes, Turkey still has large households in the Euro Zone. For this reason, this transformation demand for retail services to increase.

Educational attainment is increasing. The youth of Turkey are attending college in greater number; around 13% of high school graduates attend college like in Sweden, Austria and Norway (Louaragand, 2011).

Affluence and income have grown substantially in Turkey. GDP per capita reached around €10,250, according to CIA's The World Factbook. GDP per capita grows 7.6% yearly. Furthermore, according to The Economist Intelligence Unit, private consumption increases more than 5% per year (Louaragand, 2011). Therefore, there is a shift away from traditional retail to modern retail.

Household FMCG expenditures in Turkey rose by 10% in 2015. In Turkey households spend more in neighborhood markets and local chain stores and spend less in local groceries and nationwide discount and supermarket chains. According to Turkstat, (Household Budget Report 2017) when we analyze the consumption pattern of Turkish customers as shown in Figure 10, housing and rental expenses share of household consumption expenditures was 24.7% and food and soft drinks constitute 19.7% of overall spending. The third expenditures are the transportation at 18.7%, furniture, followed by house appliances 6.3%, restaurants and hotels, clothing and footwear 6.2% and 5% respectively, and alcoholic beverages 4.5%. According to reports, households allocate 2.2% and 2.3% for health and education, respectively.

Figure 10. Distribution of household consumption expenditures by expenditure types, 2016, 2017.
Source: (Turkstat-Household Budget Report 2017)

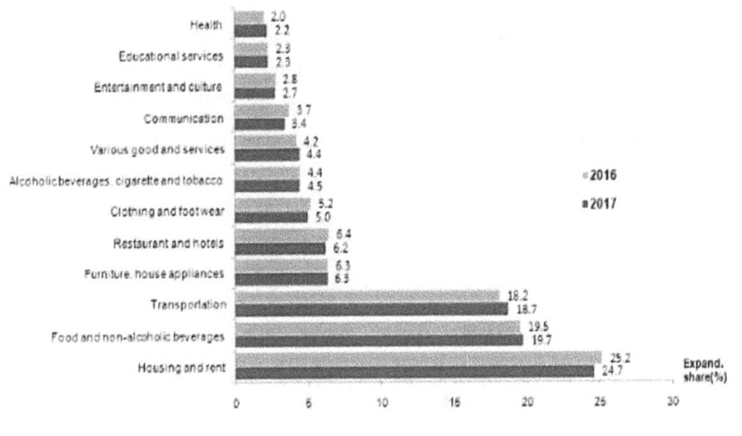

Competition in Turkey

During 1990s, retailers focused on getting financial income instead of operating profit because of the high interest rates. Non-operational profits were so attractive to some of the conglomerates like Sabanci, Dogus and Fiba in retail industry but with the decline in interest rates, the conglomerates started to withdraw from retail industry by selling their retailers to some of the rivals. After this period operational profit became more important with organic growth, acquisition and merger.

In the last 20 years, there has been a transformation in retail industry in Turkey. The number and the dominance of organized retailer have increased with the increase of hypermarkets, chain stores and discount stores causing the market share of the traditional retailers to decline. While the number of organized retailers increased between 1996-2005 the number of traditional retailers decreased dramatically as shown in Table 2.

Table 2. Evolution of store outlets in Turkey, 1996-2005

Number of Retail Outlets	1996	2005
Organised Stores	1.316	5.545
Hypermarkets(>2500 m2)	41	160
Large Supermarkets(1000-2500m2)	91	454
Supermarkets(400-1000m2)	289	1.258
Small Supermarkets(<400m2)	895	3.673
Traditional Stores	175.154	135.473
Market (50-100 m2)	10.755	15.076
Grocery Stores(< 50 m2)	164.399	120.397
TOTAL	176.470	141.018

Source: (ACNielsen, 2004)

When we compare the retail industry of Turkey with the EU countries, Turkey still has great share of traditional retailers which are known as Bakkal. However, their market share is decreasing. Migros, Tansaş and Gima were the first organized local retailers in Turkey. Migros was set up in 1954, Gima was set up in 1956 and Tansaş was established in 1973. During 1990s, some of the important foreign players entered the industry. Metro started their operation in 1990 as a wholesaler and the store used cash and carry concept. Later, it started to operate in the retail format with real hypermarket. Metro was followed by Carrefour and Promodès in 1991 and 1992 respectively in a joint venture of Sabanci. In 2003 Tesco which is the leading UK retail chain entered the market by acquiring Kipa.

2005 was the consolidation year for Turkish retail industry. When Carrefoursa acquired Gima, they took the leadership position in the market. In response, Koç Holding which owned Migros acquired Tansaş and took the leadership position.

CONCLUSION

Summary and Recommendations

The purpose of the qualitative study was to determine competitive advantages and capabilities in Turkish retail industry. The research was determined the competitive advantages and capabilities in terms of organized retailer side and traditional retailer side. Qualitative research method was applied in the research. Focus group study and face to face interviews were performed with 33 retail professionals in Turkey. The competitive advantages and capabilities were determined according to comments, perceptions and experiences of the participants. Participants were chosen based on convenience and purposive sampling approach. All the participants were experienced in Turkish retail industry whose positions ranged from division manager to CEO in organized retailer side and owners from the traditional retailer side. Data was collected via focus group study and semi structured interview.

Core Themes

The main competitive advantages and capabilities for firm performance in Turkish Retail Industry Responses of participants to interview questions resulted in 50 themes in total. Among the 3 research questions, for research question 1, 19 themes were identified for the main competitive advantages and capabilities for firm performance in Turkish Retail Industry as follows;

(1)121 Relationship; (2) Adaptation Speed to Market (3) Buying Power; (4) Cost Advantage; (5) Delivery Service; (6) Easy Shopping (7) HR (8) IT Infrastructure (9) Location (10) Marketing (11) Omnichannel (12) Payment Options (13) Price (14) Product Quality (15) Product Range (16) SCM (17) Trust (18) UF Product Range (19) Working Hours

According to the research results, there are 19 main competitive advantages and capabilities for firm performance in Turkish retail industry. Organized retailer proposed 16 of out of 19 as a main competitive advantage and capabilities, as shown in Table 4.1 and Figure 4.1. According to coding reference count IT Infrastructure is the most referenced competitive advantage in organized side. Data management, CRM, social media usage and adaptation, digitalization, machine learning, artificial intelligence and business intelligence seem to be the most important competitive advantages. In order to create sustained competitive advantages for firms, information technology (IT) has also been evaluated for its possible role (Barney, 1991; Feeny, 1988) Product Range is another most referenced competitive advantages in organized retailers. Width and depth of assortment, exclusive brands, private labels, differentiated products, new and innovative products and the number of sku are the important competitive advantages. Creating right assortment is crucial via close customer focus for strategic competitive advantage of category management (Dupre and Gruen, 2004) .HR is another important competitive advantage which includes, qualified employee, trained employee and investment in employee are the important advantage in the market. According to Chopra (2012), when the firms retained and managed the star performers well, it would create strong competitive advantages in the market. Trust is another important competitive advantage for organized retailers. Brand image and financial power topics are important. Building trust takes time, but the result is worth invested. Trust is an increasing competitive advantage in differentiation in terms of customer satisfaction, customer engagement, confidence in products and services, so it creates competitiveness. (Navickas and Navikaite, 2014). Location includes the number of branches in the country. Being located in shopping malls that have high traffic and first mover advantage when you enter the first to the city or district or being located on high street in the city. One of the main objectives for retailers is sales maximization. For this reason, in order to facilitate customer traffic and growth finding perfect site location is crucial. (O'Malley et al., 1995). Prices are the following main competitive advantages that includes every day best price, sacrificing margin to secure better price, cost efficiency in operations to create better price, reducing COGS (Cost of Goods Sold) for better price, for organized retailers. In 1990s marketers tried to find sustained competitive advantages to overcome turbulent environment to survive. (Czepiel, 1992; Hamel and Prahalad, 1993). At that time industrial buyer recognized that price and combination of price, quality and value as Holy Grail. (Aaker, 1992).

Omnichannel includes giving and getting order via store, phone, web and mobile app. Customers are most demanding currently. They always seek effective shopping experience and entertainment, so this leads to retailers being pushed to provide new technologies to serve the same quality of products and services in different channels (Pantano and Viassone, 2015). Cost Advantage includes cost optimization to secure competitive price and sustainability in business, cost efficiency, minimum service level and high sales, minimum cost in online side. Because of the no inventory cost, no store rent cost, it creates better price in the market. Selling price is so important in most of the market for competing product to get more market share (Porter, 1980). To get the cost leadership in the market, distribution and production cost must be lowered to charge minimum cost to the price. 121 Relationship includes close contact with customers, listening the customer and understanding the problems of the customers, close follow up of the customer data (visit frequency, turnover…etc.), customized solutions for customers, working with customers as a partner. Products and service are two important dimensions for competitive advantages. Furthermore, building close relationship between buyers and suppliers over multiple transaction can give an advantage in terms of one stop shopping (Chatain and Zemsky, 2007)

SCM includes, product availability is key whenever you visit the stores. It creates important mind share, uniqueness and loyalty in the customers. SCM creates important operational cost efficiency if it is implemented correctly. It leads to better stock day, better productivity. If the sustainability is provided in SCM, it also creates better margin in the products. SCM is key in online side. Cargo and logistic firms are the main drivers in online business. You always try to reduce the logistics cost both in supplier and customer's side. You are even trying to provide free of charge delivery to customers most of the time, so cargo and logistics firms are more important in online side. Buckley et.al. (1988) stated that fast and efficiently fast services of customized services and products is the competitiveness all over the world. According to Stadtler (2005) coordinating materials, integrating organizational unit through supply chain to fulfill the customer demands are also important parameters of competitiveness. In order to minimize cost and improve customer service to create competitive advantage logistics operations are key in effective and efficient handling of goods and services. (Christopher, 2006).

Product Quality is another one of the main competitive advantages. Superior product quality provides not only competitive advantage in the market but also protect against the competitors and macroeconomic forces. (Kroll et.al. 1999)

Marketing includes special promotional campaigns, like discount and buy more pay less etc. Well managed of marketing and logistic activities increase efficiency service and price policy, contribute positively to performance and increase the customer satisfaction (Emerson&Grimm, 1996)

Buying Power includes better financial situation, big volume and big sales lead to get the best prices from the suppliers. Bargaining power of supplier and buyer affect competitive advantages according to Porter's generic strategy view

Adaptation Speed to Market includes agility in all processes, fast reaction to customer demand, fast decision making and fast execution in all processes. Agility is one of the competitive advantages under the lean retailing. Especially agility means the ability to become quick, cancelling product lines in order not to do markdowns and operating with a small stock amount. (Vitzthum, 2001).

Payment Options includes using virtual pos in online side to provide easy and secure shopping. Consumers look for the convenient way to perform their daily business in online banking although they have some concerns about, security, accuracy and privacy. So the differentiation and quick adaptation in online banking side will create competitive advantage. (Smith, 2009). Delivery Service, UF Product Range and Working Hours topics couldn't be seen as a competitive advantage or capability from organized side.

Table 3. Organized-main competitive advantages and capabilities for firm performance in turkish retail industry

	Organized
121 Relationship	4
Adaptation Speed to Market	2
Buying Power	2
Cost Advantage	4
Delivery Service	0
Easy Shopping	3
HR	8
IT Infrastructure	19
Location	6
Marketing	2
Omnichannel	4
Payment Options	1
Price	6
Product Quality	2
Product Range	14
SCM	3
Trust	8
UF Product Range	0
Working Hours	0

Figure 11. Organized-main competitive advantages and capabilities for firm performance in Turkish retail industry

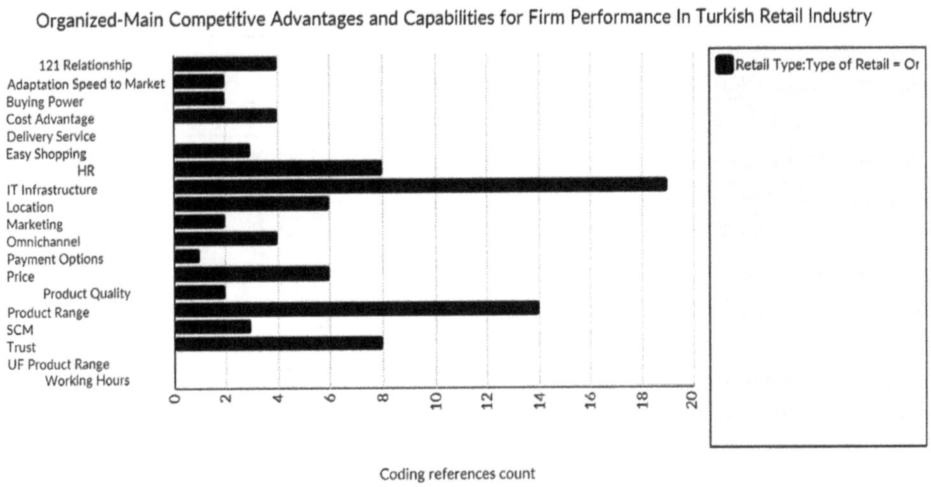

According to research results, there are 19 main competitive advantages and capabilities for firm performance in Turkish retail industry. Traditional retailer proposed 18 of out of 19 as a main competitive advantage and capabilities, as shown in Table 4.2 and Figure 4.2. According to coding reference count Product Range is the most referenced competitive advantage in organized side, A brand product, nonfood products, open and unpacked product, medicines, 121 Relationship is another competitive advantages that is important in traditional side, close relationship with the customers like a family member and neighbor. UF Product Range is another competitive advantage because of the local, fresh and wide variety in fruits and vegetables, meat and cheese products. Assortment and localization in assortment in store level were widely used practice to secure competitive advantages. (Fisher and Vaidyanathan 2014). Adaptation Speed to Market, Price and Trust are the following important competitive advantages in terms of traditional retailer side. Working Hours includes, most of the customers know that as traditional retailers our working hours are longer than the organized, so it creates an advantage for us. Small traditional retailer needs to increase their accessibility, out of the working hours. Neighbors may knock the door for an emergency purchase at night. This is directly related with accessibility and good relationship with the customers. (Litz&Stewart 2000). Extraordinary accessibility is a key competitive advantage for small retailers to compete with organized retailers. They try to use the advantage of natural selection model inspired by biology (Cooper, 2003).

Delivery Service was also seen as a competitive advantage only from traditional side in Turkish retail industry but according to literature, home delivery to consumer can't directly be evaluated as a competitive advantage in grocery retail business since the consumers can't perceive the difference between traditional grocery shopping and home delivery service. (Teller et.al. 2006). Location and HR were also seen as important competitive advantages. Payment Options, Buying Powers, Product Quality, IT Infrastructure, Cost Advantage, Easy Shopping, Marketing and SCM have relatively low code referenced count. Omnichannel topic couldn't be seen as a competitive advantage or capability from organized side.

Table 4. Traditional-main competitive advantages and capabilities for firm performance in Turkish retail industry

	Traditional
121 Relationship	10
Adaptation Speed to Market	9
Buying Power	3
Cost Advantage	1
Delivery Service	8
Easy Shopping	1
HR	7
IT Infrastructure	2
Location	8
Marketing	1
Omnichannel	0
Payment Options	4
Price	9
Product Quality	3
Product Range	12
SCM	1
Trust	9
UF Product Range	10
Working Hours	9

Figure 12. Traditional-Main Competitive Advantages and Capabilities for Firm Performance in Turkish Retail Industry

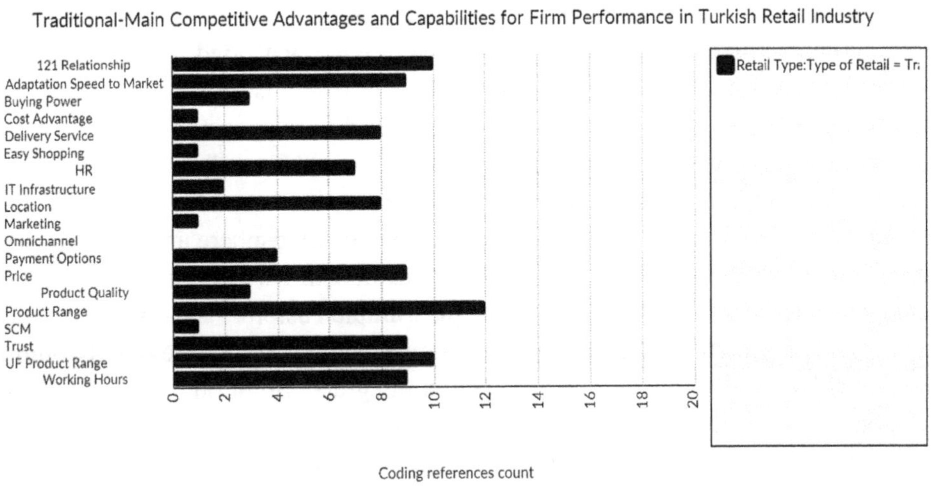

In summary, for research question 1 which is what are the main competitive advantages and capabilities for firm performance in Turkish Retail Industry?

According to research result 19 main competitive advantages and capabilities were identified for firm performance in Turkish retail industry 15 of them were seen as competitive advantages from both organized and traditional retailer side which are; (1) Product Range; (2) IT Infrastructure; (3) Trust; (4) HR ; (5) Price ; (6) 121 Relationship (7) Location; (8) Adaptation Speed to Market; (9) Buying Power; (10) Cost Advantage; (11) Payment Options; (12) Product Quality; (13) Easy Shopping; (14) SCM; and (15) Marketing according to order of code referenced count by the retailer. Omnichannel was only seen as competitive advantage by organized retailer and UF Product Range, Working Hours and Delivery Service were only seen as competitive advantage by traditional retailer. As shown in Table 5.

Relatively Important Competitive Advantages and Capabilities for Firm Performance in Turkish Retail Industry

For research question 2, 19 themes were identified for the relatively important competitive advantages and capabilities for firm performance in Turkish Retail Industry as follows;

(1)121 Relationship; (2) Adaptation Speed to Market (3) Buying Power; (4) Cost Advantage; (5) Delivery Service; (6) HR (7) Integrated Solution to Retail (8) IT Infrastructure (9) Location (10) Marketing (11) Omnichannel (12) Price (13) Product Quality (14) Product Range (15) SCM (16) Store Atmosphere (17) Trust (18) UF Product Range (19) Working Hours

According to research results, there are 19 relatively important competitive advantages and capabilities for firm performance in Turkish retail industry. Organized retailer proposed 17 of out of 19 as a relatively competitive advantage and capabilities, as shown in Table 4.4 and Figure 4.3. According to coding reference count Product Range is the most referenced competitive advantage in organized side, width and depth of assortment, exclusive brands, private labels, differentiated products, new and innovative products and the number of sku are the important competitive advantages.IT Infrastructure is the second relatively important competitive advantages, data management, CRM,social media usage and adaptation, digitalization, machine learning, artificial intelligence and business intelligence topics looks the most important competitive advantages.121 Relationship, emotional bond with the customers, creating loyalty with the customers, customized relationships and offers to customers. HR is another important competitive advantage including qualified employee, trained employee and investment to employee which are the important advantage in the market. Price, Location, Trust, Marketing and Omnichannel are the following relatively important competitive advantages that have almost same code referenced count. Adaptation Speed to Market, Cost Advantage and Store Atmosphere are the following relatively important competitive advantages. Store Atmosphere was new in here and it emerged in the research question 2 and was referenced 3 times. It includes; pleasurable customer experience during shopping, attractive lay out and presentations. Buying Power, Product Quality, SCM, Integrated Solution to Retail and Working Hours have only 1 code referenced count. Integrated Solution to Retail again emerged in research question 2 that includes, integration of health, gastronomy and logistic entities to retail to create synergy and innovative solution. According to literature the purpose of alliance is to get competitive advantages and enhance operational efficiency for future. (Clarke-Hill et al., 1998).

Table 5. Main competitive advantages and capabilities for firm performance in Turkish retail industry

	A: Organized	B: Traditional	Total
Product Range	14	12	26
IT Infrastructure	19	2	21
Trust	8	9	17
HR	8	7	15
Price	6	9	15
121 Relationship	4	10	14
Location	6	8	14
Adaptation Speed to Market	2	9	11
UF Product Range	0	10	10
Working Hours	0	9	9
Delivery Service	0	8	8
Buying Power	2	3	5
Cost Advantage	4	1	5
Payment Options	1	4	5
Product Quality	2	3	5
Easy Shopping	3	1	4
Omnichannel	4	0	4
SCM	3	1	4
Marketing	2	1	3

While the Working Hours was not seen as one of the main competitive advantage in research question 1, it was seen as relatively important competitive advantage in organized side. Delivery Service and UF Product Range were not seen as relatively important competitive advantages in organized side.

According to research results, there are 19 relatively important competitive advantages and capabilities for firm performance in Turkish retail industry. Traditional retailer proposed 14 of out of 19 as a main competitive advantage and capabilities, as shown in Table 4.5 and Figure 4.4. According to coding reference count UF Product Range is the most referenced competitive advantage it includes the fresh and wide variety in fruits and vegetable, meat and cheese products. Product Range is the second most referenced competitive advantage in organized side, A brand product, nonfood products, open and unpacked product, medicines, Location and Working Hours were seen as following relatively important competitive advantages. Delivery Service, HR and Price have the same code referenced count.121 Relationship is another competitive advantage that is important in traditional side, close relationship with the customers like a family member and neighbor. Product Quality, and Trust are other relatively important competitive advantages. Cost Advantage, Marketing, Adaptation to Market and IT Infrastructure were seen as competitive advantages that have less code referenced count. Buying Power, Integrated Solution to Retail, Omnichannel, SCM and Store Atmosphere which includes product range, quality product, creating a pleasant atmosphere for the customers in the store, store concept which also triggers the customer shopping behavior, topics couldn't be seen as a competitive advantage or capability from traditional side. In the literature store atmosphere, defined as ``atmosphere congeniality'' is also directly related to feelings of customers, warmth, ease, acceptance, reputation, reliability and post transaction satisfaction. (Burt&Encinas, 2000)

Figure 13. Organized-relatively important competitive advantages and capabilities for firm performance in Turkish retail industry

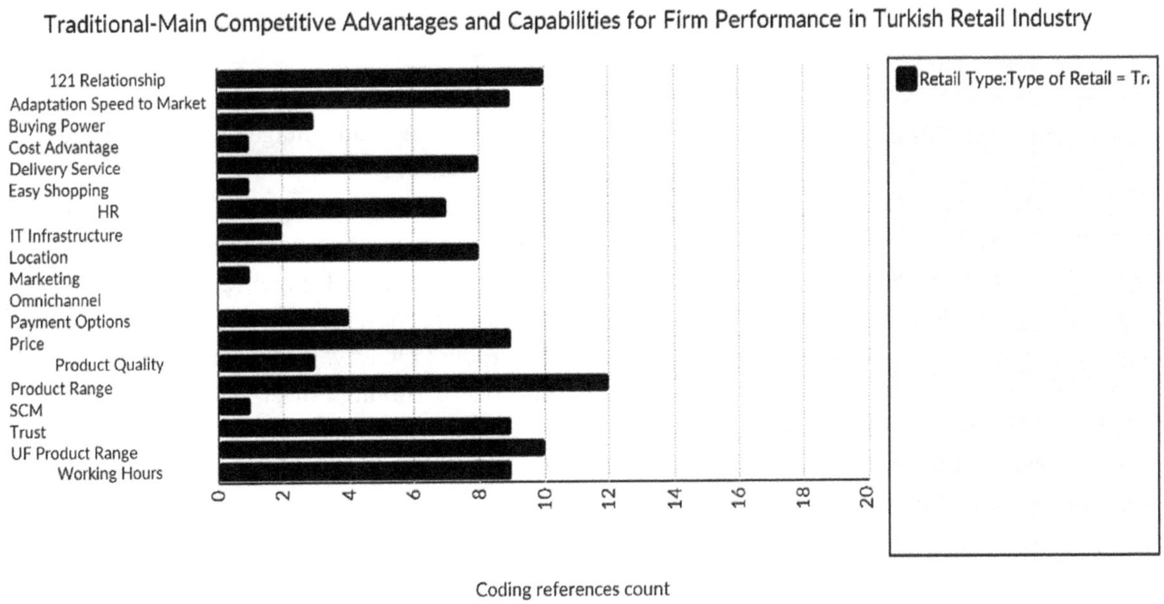

Table 6. Organized-relatively important competitive advantages and capabilities for firm performance in Turkish retail industry

	Organized
121 Relationship	9
Adaptation Speed to Market	3
Buying Power	1
Cost Advantage	3
Delivery Service	0
HR	8
Integrated Solution to Retail	1
IT Infrastructure	15
Location	7
Marketing	5
Omnichannel	4
Price	8
Product Quality	1
Product Range	16
SCM	1
Store Atmosphere	3
Trust	6
UF Product Range	0
Working Hours	1

In summary, for research question 2 which is which competitive advantages and capabilities are relatively important for firm performance in Turkish Retail Industry?

According to research result, 19 relatively important competitive advantages and capabilities were identified for firm performance in Turkish retail industry 12 of them were seen as competitive advantage from both organized and traditional retailer side which are; (1) Product Range; (2) IT Infrastructure; (3) Location; (4) HR; (5) Price; (6) 121 Relationship (7) Trust; (8) Marketing; (9) Working Hours; (10) Cost Advantage; (11) Adaptation Speed to Market; (12) Product Quality. According to order of code referenced count by the retailer, Omnichannel, Store Atmosphere, Buying Power, Integrated Solution to Retail and SCM were seen as competitive advantages by organized retailer and UF Product Range and Delivery Service were only seen as competitive advantage by traditional retailer. As shown in Table 4.6.

Table 7. Traditional-relatively important competitive advantages and capabilities for firm performance in Turkish retail industry

	Traditional
121 Relationship	3
Adaptation Speed to Market	1
Buying Power	0
Cost Advantage	2
Delivery Service	5
HR	5
Integrated Solution to Retail	0
IT Infrastructure	1
Location	7
Marketing	2
Omnichannel	0
Price	5
Product Quality	3
Product Range	8
SCM	0
Store Atmosphere	0
Trust	3
UF Product Range	10
Working Hours	6

Figure 14. Traditional-Relatively important competitive advantages and capabilities for firm performance in Turkish retail industry

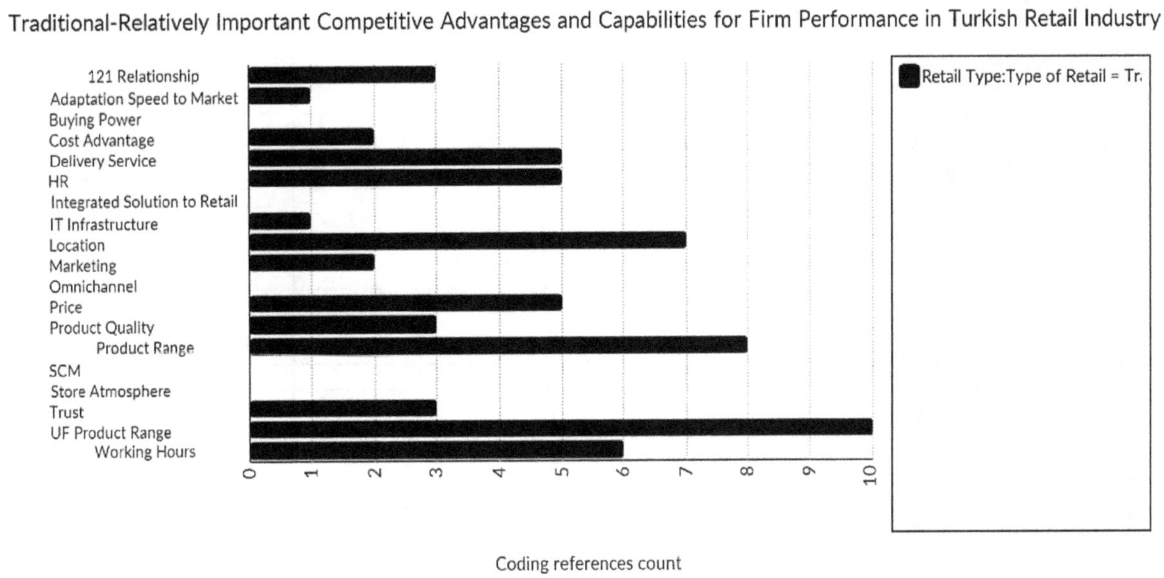

Mainly Used Competitive Advantages and Capabilities for Firm Performance Under the Effects of Environmental Dynamism in Turkish Retail Industry

For research question 3, 12 themes were identified for the mainly used competitive advantages and capabilities for firm performance under the effects of environmental dynamism in Turkish Retail Industry as follows;

(1) Adaptation Speed to Market (2) Cost Advantage; (3) HR (4) IT Infrastructure (5) Location (6) Price (7) Product Range (8) SCM (9) Service Level (10) Trust (11) UF Product Range (12) Working Hours.

According to research results, there are 12 mainly used competitive advantages and capabilities under the effects of environmental dynamism for firm performance in Turkish retail industry. Organized retailer proposed 9 of out of 12 as a mainly used competitive advantage and capabilities, as shown in Table 4.7 and Figure 4.5. According to coding reference count Adaptation Speed to Market, Product Range and Trust are the most referenced competitive advantage in organized side. Price, Cost Advantage and IT Infrastructure are the following mainly used competitive advantage.HR, SCM and Service Level are the others mainly used competitive advantages that have lower code referenced count. Service Level which includes quality in service is one of the competitive advantages during crisis as customers can't give up on you because of the service level. According to literature service and retailing, it is concluded that services are crucial to gain competitive advantage for companies (Gilbert 2003). According to Mitchell (2010) customer service is one of the most important areas in retailing. Location, UF Product Range and Working Hours were not seen as relatively important competitive advantages in organized side.

Table 8. Relatively Important Competitive Advantages and Capabilities for Firm Performance in Turkish Retail Industry

	Organized	Traditional	Total
Product Range	16	8	24
IT Infrastructure	15	1	16
Location	7	7	14
HR	8	5	13
Price	8	5	13
121 Relationship	9	3	12
UF Product Range	0	10	10
Trust	6	3	9
Marketing	5	2	7
Working Hours	1	6	7
Cost Advantage	3	2	5
Delivery Service	0	5	5
Adaptation Speed to Market	3	1	4
Omnichannel	4	0	4
Product Quality	1	3	4
Store Atmosphere	3	0	3
Buying Power	1	0	1
Integrated Solution to Retail	1	0	1
SCM	1	0	1

According to research results, there are 12 mainly used competitive advantages and capabilities under the effects of environmental dynamism for firm performance in Turkish retail industry. Traditional retailer proposed 8 of out of 12 as a mainly used competitive advantage and capabilities, as shown in Table 4.8 and Figure 4.6. According to coding reference count Price is the most referenced competitive advantage in traditional side. Product Range, UF Product Range and Service Level are the following mainly used competitive advantages. Service Level also emerged in traditional side. Cost Advantage, Location, Trust and Working Hours have relatively less code referenced count. Adaptation Speed to Market, HR, IT Infrastructure and SCM were not seen as relatively important competitive advantages in organized side.

In summary; for research question 3 which is which competitive advantages and capabilities are mainly used under the effects of environmental dynamism for firm performance in Turkish Retail Industry?

According research result 12 mainly used competitive advantages and capabilities were identified for firm performance in Turkish retail industry 5 of them were seen as competitive advantage from both organized and traditional retailer side which are; (1) Price; (2) Product Range; (3) Trust; (4) Cost Advantage; (5) Service Level. According to order of code referenced count by the retailer, Adaptation Speed to Market, IT Infrastructure, HR and SCM were seen as competitive advantage by organized retailer and UF Product Range, Location and Working Hours were only seen competitive advantage by traditional retailer. As shown in Table 11.

Table 9. Organized-mainly used competitive advantages and capabilities for firm performance under the effects of environmental dynamism in Turkish retail industry.

	Organized
Adaptation Speed to Market	4
Cost Advantage	2
HR	1
IT Infrastructure	2
Location	0
Price	3
Product Range	4
SCM	1
Service Level	1
Trust	4
UF Product Range	0
Working Hours	0

Figure 15. Organized-mainly used competitive advantages and capabilities for firm performance under the effects of environmental dynamism in Turkish retail industry.

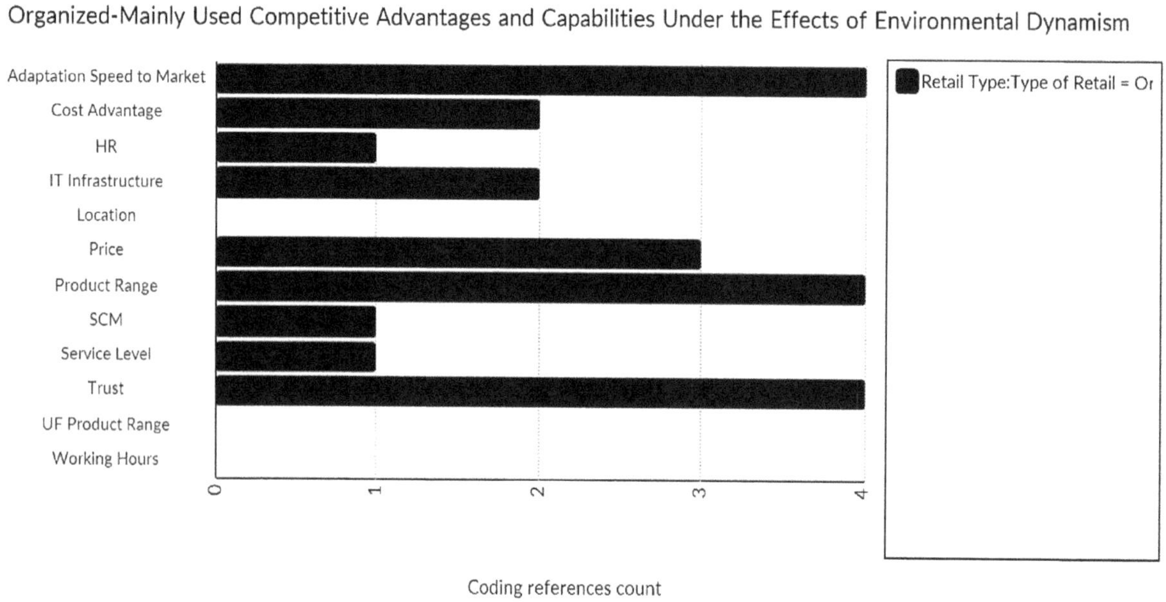

Table 10. Traditional-mainly used competitive advantages and capabilities for firm performance under the effects of environmental dynamism in Turkish retail industry.

	Traditional
Adaptation Speed to Market	0
Cost Advantage	1
HR	0
IT Infrastructure	0
Location	1
Price	8
Product Range	4
SCM	0
Service Level	2
Trust	1
UF Product Range	3
Working Hours	1

Figure 16. Traditional-mainly used competitive advantages and capabilities for firm performance under the effects of environmental dynamism in Turkish retail industry.

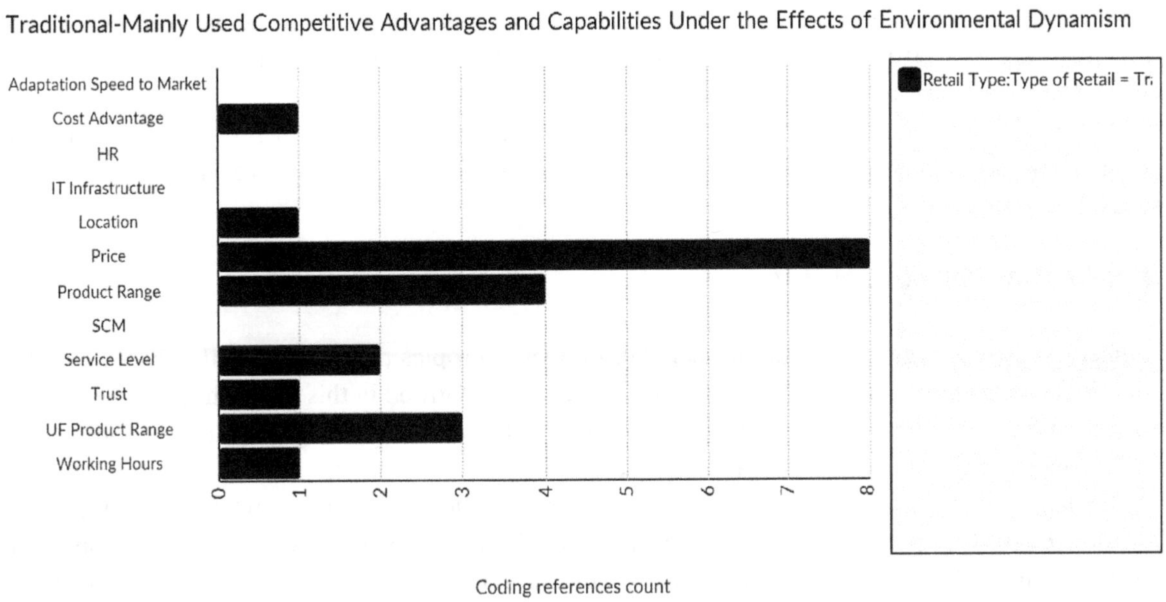

Table 11. Mainly used competitive advantages and capabilities for firm performance under the effects of environmental dynamism in Turkish retail industry

	Organized	Traditional	Total
Price	3	8	11
Product Range	4	4	8
Trust	4	1	5
Adaptation Speed to Market	4	0	4
Cost Advantage	2	1	3
Service Level	1	2	3
UF Product Range	0	3	3
IT Infrastructure	2	0	2
HR	1	0	1
Location	0	1	1
SCM	1	0	1
Working Hours	0	1	1

Theoretical and Business Contribution

In terms of theoretical perspective, the findings of study supported the RBV and RA Theory, moreover findings from the emerged themes for research questions were also supported by the literature. According to research question 1, there are 19 themes which were identified for the main competitive advantages and capabilities for firm performance in Turkish retail industry, and for the research question 2, there are 19 themes which were identified for the relatively important competitive advantages and capabilities for firm performance in Turkish retail industry and finally 12 themes which were identified for research question 3 that is related to the mainly used competitive advantages and capabilities under the effects of environmental dynamism in Turkish retail industry. All are themes were supported by the literature, so findings are consistent with the literature. In addition to that, analysis was performed. According to organized and traditional retailer side in Turkey, it creates the contribution for the business in terms of benchmarking. Apart from the research questions, there are important information about, core competence, relatively weak competitive advantages and capabilities, performance evaluation, future vision and competitive advantages and capabilities that will be important in the near future in Turkish retail industry. This study is also the first study in terms of determination of competitive advantages in Turkish retail industry.

Implications for Leadership

Competitive Advantages and Capabilities are very important topics not only in retail industry but also in all the business environment. Emerged themes that were identified in this research lead to important suggestion for leadership team in Turkish Retail Industry to understand the importance of competitive advantages and capabilities for firm performance.

The data from the research shows organizational leaders who are working in retail environment, the main and relatively important competitive advantages for firm performance and mainly used competitive advantages under the effects of environmental dynamism. Moreover, data also provide weak competitive advantages that need to be invested in.

The findings from the research also show Core Competence of the Turkish retail industries according to comments of retail professionals. Furthermore, the data provide topics about the building and obtaining competitive advantages in Turkish retail environment to organizational leaders.

The data also provide the main performance criteria that are used in Turkish retail industry.

The research findings can help to organizational leaders both in organized and traditional side to understand their competitors well in the market, and by using that they can set their strategy accordingly.

Finally, organizational leaders can find the competitive advantages that would be important and needed to be invested in the near future to be successful in retail business in Turkey.

Recommendations for Retailers

In order to explore the competitive advantages, qualitative research was applied according to experiences and comments of the retail professionals in Turkey, so the following recommendations were presented for leadership team who are working in retailing environment. Recommendations were clustered according to type of retailer as organized and traditional.

For Organized Retailers

1. Buying behavior is also psychological and emotional topic so 121 relationships is always an important competitive advantage especially in Turkey, so they need to pay special attention to reach customers one by one emotionally as well.
2. Price and Pricing Strategies are also important topics for Turkish Customers. Of course, it is changing according profile of customers but most of the customers in Turkey care about price and they are price oriented. They always look for the best price in the market, so price perception is also needed to be invested in the market.

3. SCM is another important topic that is needed to be invested in. Moreover, research result also shows that almost all of the organized retailers agreed that investing in SCM increases customer satisfaction and decreases the cost.
4. IT Infrastructure is an important competitive advantage for organized retailers but in terms of execution, offline retailers need to be fast. When compared with the online retailers the gap is very big in terms of implementation, although they are paying attention to this topic especially different environmental factors, they can't still utilize these competitive advantages.
5. UF Product Range is one the strongest competitive advantage of traditional retailers so organized side couldn't see as a key advantage in this topic, UF Product Range is also important for the customers to create loyalty and traffic.
6. Omnichannel Approach is also future is not only in retailing environment in the world but also in Turkey. Still, most of organized retailers' awareness in not so high on this topic.

For Traditional Retailers

1. Awareness of the importance of IT Infrastructure is so limited. Most of them use smart phones but there is not any intention to invest in that side.
2. Most of them have no future vision about retailing. They all are complaining about the competition and market situation in Turkey. If they worked in this retail industry, they would need to invest in their business in terms of different aspects.
3. Price and Pricing Strategies seem to be one of the big competitive advantages under the effects of environmental dynamism. They can work on different competitive advantages like HR, since they have good 121 relationships with their customers, and IT Infrastructure for some innovative solutions.
4. They have no proper SCM. They have no awareness about the benefits of SCM. Most of them have no proper stock software to follow, over stock, zero stock or availability.

REFERENCES

Aaker, D. (1992). *Strategic Management* (3rd ed.). John Wiley & Sons.

Ackoff, R. L. (1981). The art and science of mess management. *Interfaces*, *11*(1), 20–26. doi:10.1287/inte.11.1.20

Ailawadi, K., Zhang, J., Krishna, A., & Kruger, M. W. (2010). When Wal- Mart Enters: How Incumbent Retailers React and How This Affects Their Sales Outcomes. *JMR, Journal of Marketing Research*, *47*(August), 577–593. doi:10.1509/jmkr.47.4.577

Alderson, W. (1957). *Marketing behavior and executive action*. Richard D. Irwin.

Amit, R., & Schoemaker, P. J. H. (1993). Strategic Assets and Organizational Rent. *Strategic Management Journal*, *14*(1), 33–46. doi:10.1002mj.4250140105

Arnold, S., Oum, T. H., & Tigert, D. J. (1983). Determinant Attributes in Retail Patronage: Seasonal, Temporal, Regional, and International Comparisons. *JMR, Journal of Marketing Research*, *20*(May), 977–1009.

Barney, J. (1991). Firm resources and sustained competitive advantage. *Journal of Management*, *17*(1), 99–120. doi:10.1177/014920639101700108

Barney, J. B., & Arikan, A. M. (2001). The resource-based view: origins and implications. In M. A. Hitt, R. E. Freeman, & J. S. Harrison (Eds.), *Handbook of Strategic Management* (pp. 124–188). Blackwell.

Berle, A. A., & Means, G. (1932). *The modern corporation and private property*. Commerce Clearing House.

Bharadwaj, A. S. (2000). A Resource-based Perspective on Information Technology Capability and Firm Performance: an Empirical Investigation. *MIS Quarterly*, *24*(1), 169-196.

Burt, S., & Encinas, J. (2000). The role of store image in retail internationalization. International Marketing Review, 17(4-5), 433-453.

Capron & Hulland. (1999). Redeployment of Brands, Sales Forces, and General Marketing Management Expertise Following Horizontal Acquisitions: A Resource-based View. *Journal of Marketing*, *63*(April).

Chatain, O., & Zemsky, P. (2007). The Horizontal Scope of the Firm: Organizational Tradeoffs vs. Buyer-Supplier Relationships. *Management Science*, *53*(4), 550–565.

Cho, Y.K. (2015). The relationship between resources and market coverage in small local internet retailing. *International Journal of Retail & Distribution Management*, *43*(7), 597-616. doi:10.1108/IJRDM-12-2013-0220

Chopra, R., & Chopra, A. (2012). Innovative Hr Practices For Competitive Advantage: A Strategic Perspective. *Journal of Organisation & Human Behavior*, *1*(2), 2012.

Christopher, M. (2006), *Logistics and Supply Chain Management*. Financial Times/Pitman.

Clarke-Hill, C. M., Robinson, T. M., & Bailey, J. (1998). Skills and competence transfers in European retail alliances: A comparison between alliances and joint ventures. *European Business Review*, *8*(6), 300–310. doi:10.1108/09555349810241572

Conner, K. R. (1991). A historical comparison of resource based theory and five schools of thought within industrial organization economics: Do we have a new theory of the firm? *Journal of Management*, *17*(1), 121–154. doi:10.1177/014920639101700109

Connolly, T., Conlon, E. J., & Deutsch, S. J. (1980). Organizational effectiveness: A multiple-constituency approach. *Academy of Management Review*, *5*(2), 211–217. doi:10.5465/amr.1980.4288727

Cooper, G. J. (2003). *The Science of the Struggle for Existence: On the Foundations of Ecology*. Cambridge University Press. doi:10.1017/CBO9780511720154

Czepiel, J. (1992). *Competitive Marketing Strategy*. Prentice Hall.

Dess, G. G., & Beard, D. W. (1984). Dimensions of organizational task environments. *Administrative Science Quarterly*, *29*(1), 52–73. doi:10.2307/2393080

Dess, G. G., & Davis, P. S. (1984). Porter's (1980) Generic Strategies as Determinants of Strategic Group Membership and Organizational Performance. *Academy of Management Journal*, *27*(3), 467–488.

Dess, G. G., & Robinson, R. B. Jr. (1984). Measuring organizational performance in the absence of objective measures: The case of the privately-held firm and conglomerate business unit. *Strategic Management Journal*, *5*(3), 265–273. doi:10.1002mj.4250050306

Dupre, K., & Gruen, T. (2004). The use of category management practices to obtain a sustainable competitive advantage in the fast-moving consumer-goods industry. *Journal of Business & Industrial Marketing, 19*(7), 444-459.

Emerson, C. J., & Grimm, C. M. (1996). Logistics and Marketing Components of Customer Service: An Empirical Test of the Mentzer, Gomes and Krapfel Model. *International Journal of Physical Distribution & Logistics*, *26*(8), 29–42. doi:10.1108/09600039610128258

Erkip, F., & Ozuduru, B.H. (2015). *Retail development in Turkey: An account after two decades of shopping malls in the urban scene*. Academic Press.

Etzioni, A. (1964). *Modern organizations*. Prentice Hall.

Feeny, D. (1988). Creating and Sustaining Competitive Advantage with IT. In Information Management: The Strategic Dimension. Oxford University Press.

Fisher, M., & Vaidyanathan, R. (2014). A demand estimation procedure for retail assortment optimization with results from implementations. *Management Science*, *60*(10), 2401–2415. doi:10.1287/mnsc.2014.1904

Ford, J. D., & Schellenberg, D. A. (1982). Conceptual issues of linkage in the assessment of organizational performance. *Academy of Management Review*, *7*(1), 49–58. doi:10.5465/amr.1982.4285450

Franz, M., Appel, A., & Hassler, M. (2013). Short waves of super- market diffusion in Turkey. *Moravian Geographical Reports*, *21*(4), 50–63. doi:10.2478/mgr-2013-0020

Frigo, M. L. (2002). Strategic capabilities of return driven strategy. *Strategic Finance, 83*(12), 6-9.

Gioia, D. A., & Pitre, E. (1990). Multiparadigm perspectives on theory building. *Academy of Management Review*, *15*(4), 584–602. doi:10.5465/amr.1990.4310758

Grimm, C. M. (2006). Strategic paradigms of competitive advantage. Academic Press.

Hamel, G., & Prahalad, K. C. (1993). Strategy as stretch and leverage. *Harvard Business Review*, *71*(March- April), 75–84. PMID:10124635

Hatten, K. J., & Hatten, M. L. (1985). Some empirical insights for strategic marketers: The case of beer. In H. Thomas & D. M. Gardner (Eds.), *Strategic marketing and management* (Vol. 1, pp. 275–292). John Wiley and Sons Ltd.

Hoch, S., & Byung-do Kim, A. L. (1995). Determinants of Store-Level Price Elasticity. *JMR, Journal of Marketing Research*, *32*(February), 17–29. doi:10.1177/002224379503200104

Hunt, S. D. (2000). *A general theory of competition: Resources, competences, productivity, economic growth*. Sage.

Hunt, S. D., & Arnett, D. B. (2003). Resource-advantage theory and embeddedness: Explaining R-A theory's explanatory success. *Journal of Marketing Theory and Practice*, *11*(1), 1–17. doi:10.1080/10696679.2003.11501928

Hunt, S. D., & Morgan, R. M. (1995). The comparative advantage theory of competition. *Journal of Marketing*, *59*(April), 1–15. doi:10.1177/002224299505900201

Kamasak, R. (2017). The contribution of tangible and intangible resources, and capabilities to a firm's profitability and market performance. *European Journal of Management and Business Economics, 26*(2), 252-275. doi:10.1108/EJMBE-07-2017-015

Kroll, M., Wright, P., & Heiens, R. (1999). The Contribution Of Product Quality To Competitive Advantage: İmpacts On Systematic Variance And Unexplained Variance İn Returns Strategic Management. *Journal Strat. Mgmt. J.*, *20*, 375–384.

Kumar, V., & Karande, K. (2000). The Effect of Retail Store Environment on Retailer Performance. *Journal of Business Research*, *49*(August), 167–181. doi:10.1016/S0148-2963(99)00005-3

Litz, R. A., & Stewart, A. C. (2000). The late show: The effects of after-hours accessibility on the performance of small retailers. *Journal of Small Business Management*, *38*(1), 1–26.

Morris, M. H., Schindehutte, M., & LaForge, R. W. (2002). Entrepreneurial marketing: A construct for integrating emerging entrepreneurship and marketing perspectives. *Journal of Marketing Theory and Practice*, *10*(4), 1–19. doi:10.1080/10696679.2002.11501922

Navickas, V., & Navikaite, A. (2014) Competitive Advantage Maximization Through Relation Between Trust And Reputation. *Sociálno-Ekonomická Revue, 4*.

Nelson, R., & S.W. (1982). *An Evolutionary Theory of Economic Change*. Harvard College.

O'Malley, L., Patterson, M., & Evans, M. (1995). Retailing applications of geodemographics: a preliminary investigation. Marketing Intelligence & Planning, 13(2). doi:10.1108/02634509510083482

Ozcan, G. B. (2000). The transformation of Turkish retailing: Survival strategies of small and medium-sized retailers. *Journal of South-ern Europe and the Balkans,* 2(1), 105–120. http://www.cnu.org/node/1360

Ozuduru, B. H., & Varol, C. (2011). *Ankara'daki Alisveris Merkezlerinin ve Alisveris Potansiyelinin Mekansal Dagiliminin Pera- kende Yersecim Modelleriyle Analizi, 108K547 nolu 3501 Uusal Genc Arastirmaci Kariyer Gelistirme Programi tarafindan desteklenen proje raporu, Tubitak*. Sobag.

Pan, Y., & Zinkhan, G. M. (2006). Determinants of retail patronage: A meta- analytical perspective. *Journal of Retailing*, *82*(June), 229–243. doi:10.1016/j.jretai.2005.11.008

Pantano, E., & Viassone, M. (2015). Engaging consumers on new integrated multichannel retail settings: Challenges for retailers. *Journal of Retailing and Consumer Services*, *25*, 106–114. doi:10.1016/j.jretconser.2015.04.003

Pearce, M. R. (1989). Retailers: How to be different from your competitors. *Business Quarterly, 54*(2), 28-33.

Penrose, E. (1959). *The Theory of the Growth of the Firm.* Blackwell Publishing.

Peteraf, M. A., & Bergen, M. E. (2003). Scanning dynamic competitive landscapes: A market-based and resource-based framework. *Strategic Management Journal, 24*(10), 1027–1041. doi:10.1002mj.325

Porter, M. E. (1980). *Competitive Strategy: Techniques for Analyzing Industries and Competitors.* Free Press.

Porter, M.E. (1985). *Competitive Advantage: Creating and Sustaining Superior Performance.* Free Press.

Reinartz, W., & Kumar, V. (1999). Store-, Market-, and Consumer-Characteristics: The Drivers of Store Performance. *Marketing Letters, 10*(Winter), 5–22. doi:10.1023/A:1008011622335

Rugman, A. M., & Verbeke, A. (2002). Edith Penrose's contribution to the resource-based view of strategic management. *Strategic Management Journal, 23*(8), 769–780. doi:10.1002mj.240

Sanchez, R., Heene, A., & Thomas, H. (1996). *Introduction: Towards the Theory and Practice of Competence-based Competition.* Pergamon Press. doi:10.4000/books.pur.47926

Seth, A., & Thomas, H. (1994). Theories of the firm: Implications for strategy research. *Journal of Management Studies, 31*(2), 165–191. doi:10.1111/j.1467-6486.1994.tb00770.x

Sharfman, M. P., & Dean, J. W. Jr. (1991). Conceptualizing and measuring the organizational environment: A multidimensional approach. *Journal of Management, 17*(4), 681–700. doi:10.1177/014920639101700403

Simon, H. A. (1947). *Administrative behaviour.* Free Press.

Singer, A. E. (1997). Game theory and the evolution of strategic thinking. *Human Systems Management, 16*(1), 63–75. doi:10.3233/HSM-1997-16108

Smith A, (2009). Internet retail banking A competitive analysis in an increasingly financially troubled environment. *Information Management & Computer Security, 17*(2), 127-150. doi:10.1108/09685220910964009

Sousa, C. M. P., Martínez-Lopez, F. J., & Coelho, F. (2008). The determinants of export performance: A review of the research in the literature between 1998 and 2005. *International Journal of Management Reviews, 10*(4), 343–374. doi:10.1111/j.1468-2370.2008.00232.x

Srivastava, Shervani, & Fahey. (1998). Market-based Assets and Shareholder Value: a Framework for Analysis. *Journal of Marketing, 62*(1), 2-18.

Stadtler, H. (2005). Supply chain management and advanced planning Basics, overview and challenges. *European Journal of Operational Research, 163*(3), 575588. doi:10.1016/j.ejor.2004.03.001

Strandskov, J. (1999). *Sources of competitive advantage and business performance in the European meat processing industry.* MAPP Working Paper no. 63, Aarhus: Aarhus School of Business.

Teece, Pisano, & Shuen. (1997). Dynamic Capabilities and Strategic Management. *Strategic Management Journal, 18*(7), 509-533.

Teller, C., Kotzab, H., & Grant, D. (2006). The consumer direct services revolution in grocery retailing: an exploratory investigation. *Managing Service Quality, 16*(1), 78-96. doi:10.1108/09604520610639973

Thompson, J. D. (1967). *Organizations in action*. McGraw-Hill.

Tirole, J. (1988). *The theory of industrial organization*. MIT Press.

Tokatli, N., & Boyaci, Y. (1998). The changing retail industry and retail landscapes: The case of post-1980 Turkey. *Cities (London, England), 15*(5), 345–359. doi:10.1016/S0264-2751(98)00030-4

Tokatli, N., & Boyaci, Y. (1999). The changing morphology of commercial activity in Istanbul. *Cities (London, England), 16*(3), 181–193. doi:10.1016/S0264-2751(99)00015-3

Tokatli, N., & Boyaci-Eldener, Y. (2002). Globalization and the changing political economy of distribution channels in Turkey. *Environment & Planning A, 34*(2), 217–238. doi:10.1068/a34113

Tung, R. L. (1979). Dimensions of organizational environments: An exploratory study of their impact on organization structure. *Academy of Management Journal, 22*, 672–693.

Vibert, C. (2004). *Theories of macro-organizational behavior: A handbook of ideas and explanations*. M.E. Sharpe.

Vibert, C., & Hurst, D. (2004). Radical humanist and structuralist perspectives. In C. Vibert (Ed.), *Theories of macro-organizational behavior: A handbook of ideas and explanations*. M.E. Sharpe.

Vitzthum, C. (2001, May 18). Just-in-time fashion: Spanish retailer Zara makes low cost lines in weeks by running its own show. *Wall Street Journal*, p. B1.

Vorhies, D. W., & Morgan, N. A. (2005). Benchmarking marketing capabilities for sustainable competitive advantage. *Journal of Marketing, 69*(1), 80–94. doi:10.1509/jmkg.69.1.80.55505

Wade & Hulland. (2004). Review: The Resource-Based View and Information Systems Research: Review, Extension, and Suggestions for Future Research. *MIS Quarterly, 28*(1), 107-142.

Wernerfelt, B. (1984). A Resource-based View of the Firm. *Strategic Management Journal, 5*(2), 171–180. doi:10.1002mj.4250050207

Williamson, O. E. (1976). *Markets and hierarchies: Analysis and anti-trust implications*. Free Press.

Williamson, O. E. (1988). Corporate finance and corporate governance. *The Journal of Finance, 43*(3), 567–591. doi:10.1111/j.1540-6261.1988.tb04592.x

Yuchtman, E., & Seashore, S. E. (1967). A system resource approach to organizational effectiveness. *American Sociological Review, 32*(6), 891–903. doi:10.2307/2092843

Chapter 14
Applying Total Costs of Ownership (TCO) to Examine the Best Logistics Providers:
Case Study in Indonesia Cement Projects

Effnu Subiyanto
https://orcid.org/0000-0001-7879-2499
Widya Mandala Surabaya Catholic University, Indonesia

Annisa Farahmei Effnandya
Universiti Teknologi Malaysia, Malaysia

ABSTRACT

Further scientifically finding of total logistics costs model during execution the cement projects in Indonesia, the consecutive further tasks are how to examine the best logistics' provider to perform the logistics' works. This is the ultimate goal of this chapter. The methodology developed is by case study, elaborate techniques of focus group discussion (FGD), expert judgment (EJ), and enriched by the analytical hierarchical process (AHP) to obtain the best decision. The finding is the total costs of ownership (TCO) as the best tool to examine several considerations to select the best provider's candidates can be applied. Data as sources of this chapter are consolidated from the cement projects in Indonesia from 2010 to 2018. During the period, cement projects in Indonesia were rampant, and certainly, it demanded logistics providers. The TCO in practical fits during procurement-processes, it is also valuable during the selection of the logistics' providers. The TCO is fair enough as the best tool to build governance during procurement to avoid miss-discrimination-treated.

DOI: 10.4018/978-1-7998-8709-6.ch014

INTRODUCTION

After the concept of total logistics costs had been populated by Subiyanto (2020), further tasks to complete construction projects are going to be increased and detailed. According to Figure 1, three primary elements must be highly concerned. The first is foreign logistics costs; the second is domestic manufacture and the third is domestic logistics costs. All three elements are separated but altogether have directly and indirectly influenced the ultimate goal of the total investment.

Figure 1. Conceptual model populated by Subiyanto (2020)

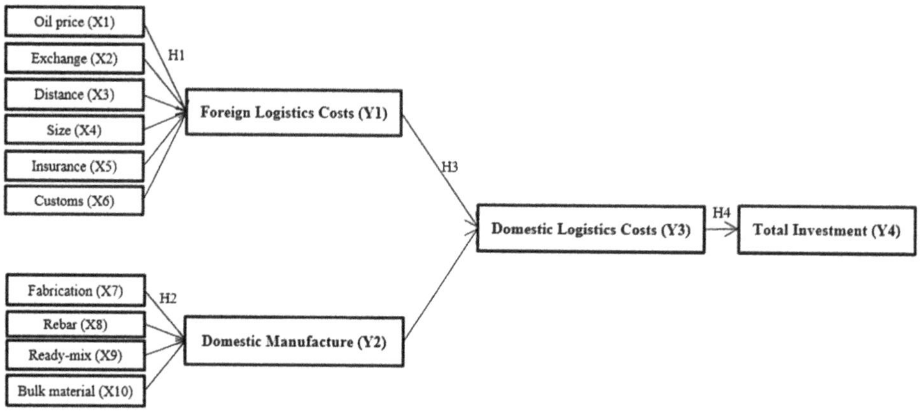

According to the results of Figure 1, variable crude oil prices, exchange rates, distance, sizes, insurance and customs all have a significant impact together but not significantly partially on the foreign logistics costs. Further, variable fabrication, rebar, ready-mix, and bulk material together and partially are significant to the domestic manufacture costs. The next is assessing variable foreign logistics costs and domestic manufacture costs that are significant together but not significant partially on domestic logistics costs. Finally, the domestic logistics costs variable is found to be significant in the total investment.

The recommendation for the cement investors and managers is that they should put high concerns, especially for the foreign logistics costs caused the highest costs contribution than others to the model. Subiyanto (2020) advises that this has an important policy implication for the government, urging that investment in the logistics infrastructure become a high priority to reduce total logistics costs. This suggests that the government should immediately build and develop a chain of logistics infrastructure to lower logistics costs that account for 27% of Indonesia's GDP, which is the highest proportion among countries in the region. These costs would be significantly reduced with better infrastructure.

It is now a knowledge gap that occurred. Theoretical has been developed, but how to make it real and definite to be valuable applied is still questioning.

In general, Figure 2 is ordinary known and widely adopted in procurement stages. At first, the vendors have submitted their proposals in a couple of methods, a technical proposal, and a commercial offer. The further step is evaluation followed by clarification, and the last stage is a negotiation and to be completed by awarding the contract to the winner.

According to Figure 2, every proposal submitted first will be evaluated technically according to technical requirements, and further, when meeting with the minimum technical score, the vendor will enter a commercial evaluation.

Figure 2. General procurement processes applied.
Source: developed by Author (2021)

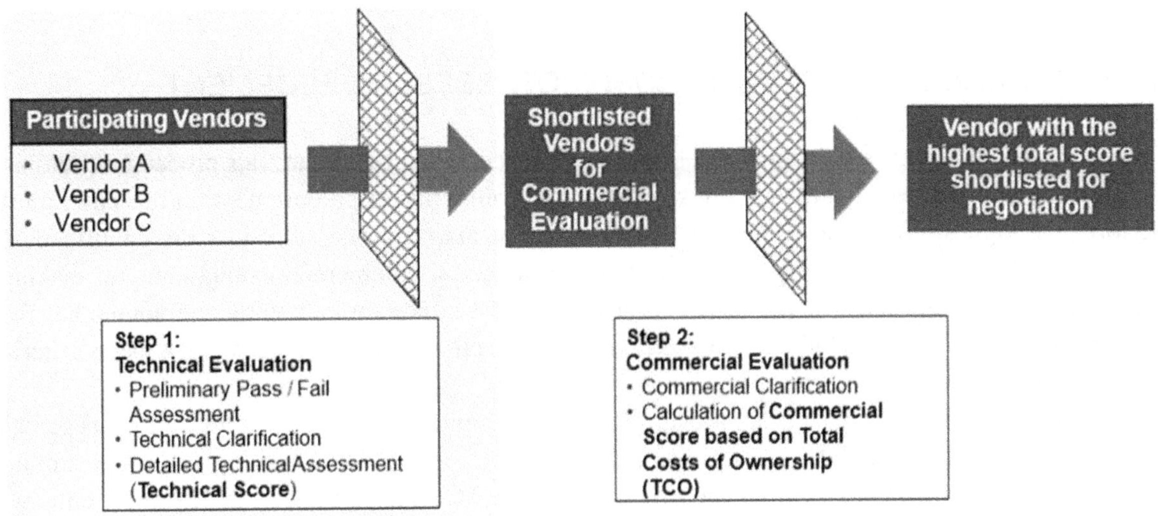

Source: developed by Author (2021)

There are many techniques to perform procurement but many considerations also must be met. The conventional one was based-on a historical technique where the committees are relying on data-based in their archives. The committees have to collect data one-by-one, check appropriateness to accommodate the projects interested, conform to the real market-price at the time of projects taken, and record as the important benchmark material. These steps are quite wasting time, tiring, and most companies or project owners are generally having limited sources of archives, documents, or reliable bank data.

It has the best practical and the same time knowledge-based, proven, and reliable enough to perform better procurement. The author develops a total cost of ownership (TCO) model in applying complex procurements in several cement projects in Indonesia and well-proven in delivering completed and successful projects.

The objects applied came from eight cement projects in Indonesia from 2008 to 2018. The projects were useful in representing complex procurement as considered from the value of projects, duration, scale and scope, impact to the economy, social and environment, and the impact to the governance. The governance, transparency, equal non-discrimination rights for every supplier are basic mandatory understanding to perform procurement in the projects.

This paper investigates how developing the TCO technique affects construction projects. To do so, we employ the expert judgment function to estimate TCO. We then investigate every variable defined, look for to anticipate missing considerations, and then all employ into procurement documents. The selection of cement projects in Indonesia, a complicated project that has ever well-known, is because they face more multi-disciplinary measurements than other projects. They have more difficulties defining every single variable of TCO; simultaneously, the international companies are familiar with these practices and consider TCO as increasingly relevant features in the modern construction project environment.

The rest of this paper is organized as follows. Section 2 reviews the theoretical background and develops hypotheses. Section 3 formulates methods and research techniques. A presentation of results is presented in section 4. The discussion of the results is placed in section 5. Section 6 discusses the concluding remarks.

THEORETICAL BACKGROUND AND HYPOTHESES DEVELOPMENT

Processing procurement is a distinctive task, as governance, equal treatment, fair procedures, and all things must be presented equally and transparently. The committee of procurement, in this case, must perform the highest effort and techniques since invitation bid, vendors' selection, pre-qualification, vendor's evaluation, submission proposal, technical evaluation, commercial evaluation, and making final decision to award the winner of the contract. The most important is how the committee has the best technique to evaluate all bidders' proposals quickly, effectively, and at the same time meets criteria for the owner's interest.

The total costs of ownership (TCO) is originally multidisciplinary knowledge comprised of accounting-engineering-technique that evaluates the total costs of business ownership using a time-consuming activity-based costing procedure (Shabani *et al.*, 2019). The TCO prior was also said as a conventional method outlined by tool-related costs (Brenner *et al.*, 2018), though Tereno *et al.* (2019) have developed into a Building Information Model (BIM) as a tool of lean-approach.

As the first practical goal, the TCO method can help the procurement-process determine the necessary features required to construct complex concepts (Kumar *et al.*, 2014). Following findings of Subiyanto and Suyoto (2020) and Subiyanto (2021), the complex cement construction projects can utilize the TCO method, as also mentioned by Seth and Rastogi (2019) and Fayezi *et al.* (2018). In considering the wide use of the TCO, Mandolini *et al.* (2017), Miller (2020), Letmathe and Suares (2020), Stojčića *et al.* (2020) raised the concerns that the TCO can be said as part of innovation.

Besides simplifying complex procurement processes, the TCO will guarantee governance (Pettersen *et al.*, 2020; Subiyanto, 2020). In many empirical cases worldwide reported, there has been found few illegal practices during procurement-process as such law-violation, miss-discrimination treated due to weakness in control (Melon and Spruk, 2020) as such as ineffective in transaction cost economics, incomplete contracts involving uncertainty and relationship-specific, and in a whole, could practically do more harms for the good governance practices in the industry and in the wider public (Merkert *et al.*, 2018). The point is the TCO technique is highly demanded. To assure governance, otherwise, if it fails to present in well managed, the risks will be against laws and regulations (Hawkins *et al.*, 2014).

To convince earlier, as presented by Goswami and Wettstein (2016), they have revealed that the procurement processes in whole stages found inconsistent with standard as preliminary introduced. The consequence is to find proper of parameters and bidding indicators became hard to be quantified and uncertainty which to be referred by tender participants. Liao and Rittscher (2007) and Handfield *et al.* (2019) found that the unfair processes' procurement generally lies in the section of supplier selection, also during in the determine procurement lot sizing, and during at the stage of commercial negotiation just one step to award the candidate of the winner.

Singh and Modgil (2020) supported Goswami and Wettstein (2016) stated that the key indicators in supplier selection to establish the relationship between available alternatives are not well and clear presented during processes. Hence, simply can be said that the procedure of supplier management as the highest weighted criteria followed by equal information sharing and joint actions are technically violated due to vest-interested. The processes followed by Goswami and Wettstein (2016) according to Liao and Rittscher (2007) that mentioned by Demidova and Yakovlev (2012) as we have known is generally happened in the public procurement. The level that should be respected as the public in nature must strictly follow procedures and governance. In the case, there is required an urgent tool to face the massive situation.

Recently, the TCO techniques can be deemed as an electronic procurement (Boer *et al.,* 2020), or a tool in the corporate strategy (Oyegoke *et al.,* 2009; Kalaitzi *et al.,* 2019; Subiyanto, 2020; Guarnieri and Gomes, 2019), also as smart methodology (Debono, 2019) to get lean procurement (Suresh and Nathan, 2020), and a guaranteed purchase contract timely, clean and clear (Rafiei *et al.,* 2019).

To sum-up according literatures, much benefits of applying TCO as like to expedite procurement processes, simplify, and at the same time follows strictly procedures, meet in aspect of governance and laws. Ahmed (2019) has measured that the TCO is one of the techniques to maintain the performance-based contracting, one of the scheme to determine of the key performance indicators (KPIs). The TCO was also useful to help closer relationship between buyer-supplier that separated by the geographical distance (Wiengarten and Ambrose, 2017). Specifically, before implementing TCO, if the buyer and supplier are located in the same country, tactical and relational procurement have a positive impact on operational performance. Ironically, in cases where they are situated in different countries, none of the procurement tools seems to significantly improve relationship. The TCO offers an improvement to build a different climate and different geography worldwide.

Besides, in recent industries, suppliers play a crucial role in manufacturing supply chains, and firms are dependent on identifying and managing them to help well in operations. Even more, industry generation 4.0 has also relied on suppliers (Salam, 2019). Previous research concerns the more transactional than relationship-oriented between purchaser-supplier, therefore, the TCO could be a non-financial performance measure in supporting true value co-creation between purchaser and supplier (Jääskeläinen and Thitz, 2018).

METHODS AND RESEARCH TECHNIQUES

To achieve the identified research aim, a descriptive focus group study (FGD) method was built to summarize expert judgments. The number of experts had been invited to participate in the study consists of 30 experienced experts consist of consultants, contractors and experience employees. All of them were selected considering their expertise in the cement projects or operations within the group of PT Semen Indonesia (Persero) Tbk in Indonesia. The experts who can be considered in the cases are senior management level, project managers who have worked on projects in the same scope, an expert in business or projects in industry groups, and consultant professional associations, and technicians.

The period taken was 2010 to 2018; the time when Indonesia has experienced eight cement projects due to previously declared would be a shortage.

According to Khosravi *et al.* (2020), at first to be measure is making list of risk identifications and classifications for the projects. As point-out in Figure 3, in particular, the implemented method has followed these steps:

Risk categorization as results from FGD and expert judgment (EJ); and

Risk clarification based-on conclusion by the analytical hierarchy process (AHP).

Figure 3. Framework of methodology

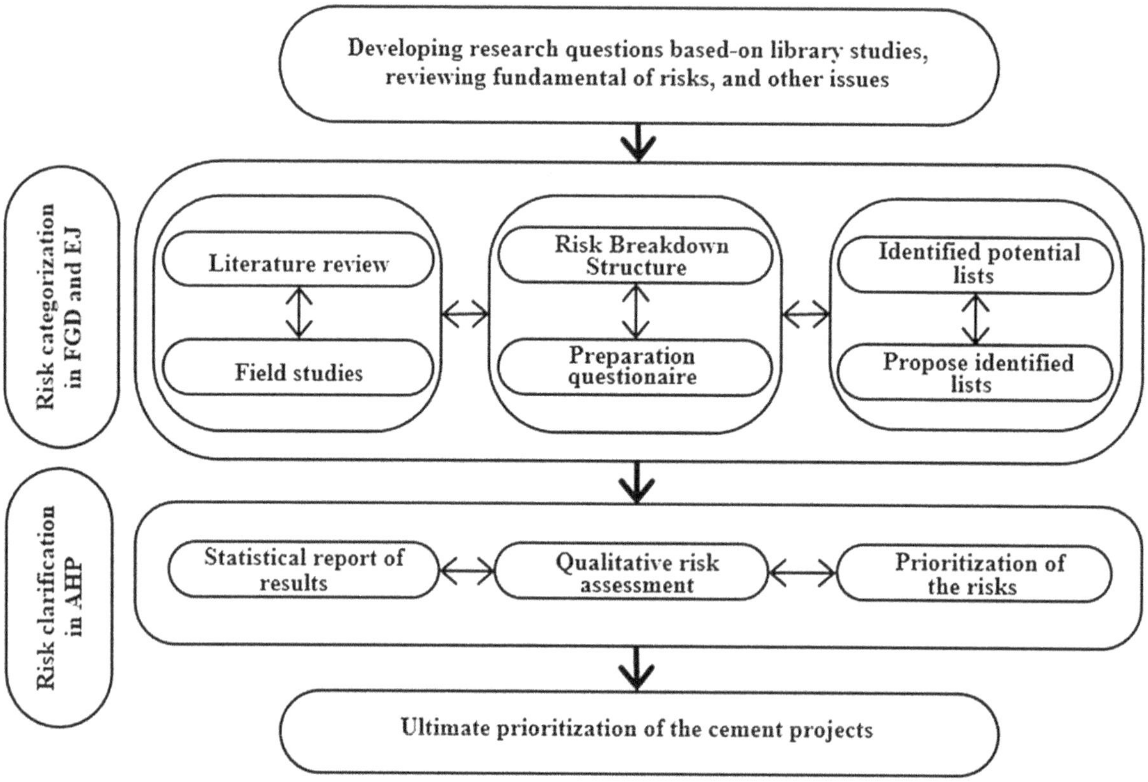

Source: developed Author (2021)

The EJ is one of the tool and technique used in the risk management to assess inputs and processes which aiming to develop a project charter. It can provide input to plan and estimate important activities on the project (Kumar *et al.*, 2018). The technique to ensure comprehensive risk management plan requires consideration of groups, professionals, or individuals with specialized training or knowledge in a specific subject area.

The EJ's approach turns out to not only save time during planning but also pay attention to risks that should be taken into consideration when executing plans. So that it can improve the quality of the estimate and provide an accurate estimate. Risk identification in this case is the most important part that must be done at the beginning of the project cycle. Risks that are not identified properly are a threat to project success. It should be noted that all risk management activities only begin after the process of identifying potential risks in a project.

In its application, the EJ is used for situations that require expert judgment by completing, validating, interpreting, and integrating available data, assessing the impact of changes that occur on the processes and organization, predicting future events and the consequences of each decision, determining the current state, providing the elements needed for an appropriate decision-making process (Leontaris *et al.*, 2019).

To convince this research, a technique of AHP was applied to clarify findings of the prior method of the EJ. According to Ong and Chew (1996), the AHP is a technique in complex decision problems based-on multi-criteria decision analysis that incorporating both qualitative and quantitative factors with the purpose of ranking, select, evaluate, optimize and predict decisions approach. Mukeshimana *et al.* (2021) have applied the techniques in seeking the best biogas dissemination in Rwanda, while Kumar *et al.* (2018) have utilized the approach during project construction, likewise had done in Singapore (Ong and Chew, 1996).

From group of people who play an important role in an organization that has been mentioned above, the role of these experts is needed during the planning and risk identification process. This process is very important because it depends on the success of the project, especially on large or complex scale projects, thus making the project manager take steps to seek experts from external to the organization to help make unbiased and in accurate decisions.

RESULTS AND DISCUSSION

To construct total costs probably occurred in a complicated logistics work in cement projects must be simulated based-on business processes. Following suggest Figure 3, the first step taken by group of experts are developing project questions. Hundreds of literatures must be reviewed and discussed, empirical and cases were reverted again to simulate the real needs of the cement projects. Following Table 1 shows the tabulation questions resulted from the EJ and FGD after several meetings have been organised.

In accommodating voices and suggestions by group of experts as sump-up in Table 1, these are simply clear that a change in procurement process somewhat urgently to be changed. Four group of experts are not proposing something certain ideas, two group others propose package-model and lump-sum model. The main point all groups have pointed out that the change's responsibility must be bear to the procurement's team.

Table 1. Questions collection from 30 experts invited

Group of Experts	No's	Issues Risen	Advise	Responsible to
Procurement	5	Difficult procurement process	Change to a new system	Procurement
Finance/accounting	5	Lack in presenting evidence for payment	Change to a new system	Procurement
Engineering/mechanical/electrical	5	Uncertainty procurement procedure	Propose package model	Procurement
Construction	5	Biased to define volume of construction	Propose lump-sum model	Procurement
Project control	5	Violation governance due to procedures	Change to a new system	Procurement
Supporting	5	Difficult proses	Change to a new system	Procurement

Further round of meetings have been conducted to accommodate the AHP's techniques. In the meeting, all group of experts are invited to propose methodology or techniques that deemed practicable and efficient. The advices are freely without being interfered by other opinions, the statement is based-on their own profession, though, the meetings set at the same time, open, and directly expressed. The result of AHP is sump-up to the Table 2 and the results showed that all experts suggest in order new methods should be immediately applied. All of them advise to apply the technique of total costs of ownership (TCO) as the technique meets almost comprehensive requirements. The TCO has considered aspects of governance and transparency, engineering and construction have been accommodated, operation and maintenance have been assessed, finance and project control's interest.

Considering the FGD has been conducted further sharpened by the EJ of Table 1 and the AHP by Table 2; the important issue that should be immediately addressed is urgently needed a new method to tackle procurement processes. Several experts suggest adopting a new method or technique and their recommendations to apply the TCO technique.

Table 2. Result of AHP discussing the procurement technique

Group of Experts	No's	Suggestions	Technique Advices	Time to Apply
Procurement	5	New methods should be applied	Total costs of ownership (TCO)	Urgent
Finance/accounting	5	New finance methods should be applied	Total costs of ownership (TCO)	Urgent
Engineering/mechanical/electrical	5	New procurement methods should be applied	Pass/fail and further the total costs of ownership (TCO)	Urgent
Construction	5	New procurement methods should be applied	Pass/fail and further the total costs of ownership (TCO)	Urgent
Project control	5	New methods should be applied	Total costs of ownership (TCO)	Urgent
Supporting	5	New methods should be applied	Total costs of ownership (TCO)	Urgent

Applying TCO

The tasks of logistics are completed by two route scenarios both by foreign and domestic logistics as previous designed by Figure 1. Costs for foreign logistics incurred due to six variables that must be performed from origin ports to the destination ports in Indonesia. Different to foreign logistics, the domestic logistics is only covering within Indonesia and probably situated in one island only as the location project in Rembang, the central of Java's island.

The number of providers' invited were given to plan design by their own state-of-art of their proposal to situate scope of the works and being given opportunity to submit proposal both in technical and commercial. The committee of procurement further must develop the best TCO technique to evaluate and analysis every proposal submitted fairly and transparently.

Based-on FGD, EJ and AHP previously built and developed, several variables chosen as deemed important factors to examine providers' fit are determined as follows:

- Sea-freight scope,
- Domestic inland scope,
- Customs clearance, and
- Domestic's obstacles

To combine many expertise are unavoidably needed to take-part in the cement projects. Every invited provider is expected to have professional practices and knowledge in the scope of international freights, having experience to the geography of Indonesia, well understanding the nature of Indonesia's customs clearance and having skill and knowledge to anticipate domestic obstacles.

For the sea-freight scopes might probably not a serious matter for logistics providers, but understanding domestics' issues in Indonesia is a matter of challenging. For providers originated in Indonesia, these matters are well-known and understandable but it will totally different for providers from outside Indonesia. The domestics related to Indonesia is geography, international sea routes in Indonesia, map logistics between islands, understanding inland routes, nature of Indonesian culture, and how to deal with obstacles.

A survey is about activity that mandatory must be done at first. The survey enables providers to collect information and data, do evaluate and make the situation as real as possible, and do simulation on how to describe Indonesia's domestics better. The best technique to do by the survey is following the direction of the goods first after being unloaded from the vessels. Make careful notes since from the ports, how to deal during customs clearance, finding inland trucks, feel quality and know Indonesia's road and to know obstacles as long as the road.

The most important during the survey is mitigating risks relating to the quality of inland roads and bridges. About 20% total volume imported for cement machinery has been qualified as heavy-lift equipment. It means the goods cannot be separated or it must be delivered in assembled. These are due to regarding quality and related with a guarantee of machines. It has been considered no available experts or proper workshop in Indonesia to assemble the machines; therefore, machines are delivered in the assembled method. These are certainly making the goods will be said as heavy-lifts which meant heavy in weight and over-dimension in terms of size.

Regulations regarding goods deliveries in Indonesia are about conservative. The highway in Indonesia has public consensus that the max-width of goods should not over than 3.3 meters while max high is 4.7 meters from the ground. Planning of delivery should be carefully checked and re-check since goods in the country of origin. However, there are many opportunities not to use Indonesia's highway instead but using regular roads are more flexible with adequate technical adjustments.

After providers had been invited to submit their proposals, as following results are compiled and inserted in the TCO's spread-sheet. The following data is shown in Table 3. There are four sections being calculated and evaluated which are sea freight main equipment, inland main equipment, customs clearance, and bridge's enforcement.

According to Table 3, four bidders have interested to submit proposals consecutively VUDS, BSA, Bertling and DFDS. After their proposals had been key-in in the TCO spreadsheets, the results showed that BSA has the highest score in the section of sea freight main equipment, while VUDS shows the best proposal for the section in domestic of Indonesia.

The possibilities might come to couple of alternatives, BSA will be the winner for the sea freight main equipment and VUDS as the winner for domestic's tasks. But the considerations come to the sequence logistics and final decision can be different. The problem later then how to manage domestics well while upstream in managing sea freight is taken by other parties. For these reasons, the way to get better decision by summarize all of them and counted. As the result is following:

BSA proposed US$ 6.04 million for sea freight main equipment while VUDS proposed US$ 6.26 million for the same section. For the domestics' logistics of Indonesia, BSA proposed Rp 75.49 billion while VUDS offered Rp 23.56 billion. Gap value for sea freight accounted only for US$ 212.96 or equal to Indonesia's currency of Rp 3.07 billion. The gap is far below than domestic's gap reached to Rp 51.93 billion for the best offer of VUDS. Considering to prepare Indonesia's logistics that more complicated than the better managing international routes, therefore, the winner decision has been granted to VUDS.

For the benefiting decision to prefer choosing VUDS is said as the procurement is state-of-art previous stated. Working into detail is advised but understanding other factors might change the evaluation during procurement. In the case, VUDS wins the efforts given.

All four mentioned above are logistic's provider in Indonesia, well-enough-known in aspect of performance and reputation

The score given the highest of 100 for the lowest proposal, and the others are given score proportional comparing to the lowest.

For example: Based-on Table 1, VUDS is giving the lowest proposal in the section of domestic's logistics for Rp 23.56 billion. In the case VUDS will be given score 100. Due to BSA to offer higher for Rp 75.49 billion for same section, therefore, score for BSA should be 23.56/75.49 or 31.21.

The same step is applied to other proposal and the results can be seen in Table 1.

Sea-Freight Main Equipment

This sea-freight scope is the most important in every project in Indonesia. It is certainly the total volumes imported must be organized and delivered to one of Indonesia's ports destination. Total volume of import procured for the cement projects are generally less than 10% to total volume of the projects but the values are frequently surprising. In the case of the cement projects in Indonesia, the total value is generally over than 30% of the total costs of the project. Table 4 shows estimating volume imported in generally cement projects.

The most challenging for tender's participants is how to calculate procurement contract into volume of cargo to make reservation the space in vessels. In the case understanding the nature of cement plants is highly required. Participants can optimize the session of field visit to asks, discussions, and clarify several issues that un-familiar during the session.

Project code: RBG (Rembang), IDRG (Indarung), P14 (Citeureup), Tbn#2 (Tuban #2), Train #1 (Tabalong), Byms (Banyumas), Bayah (Bayah), Maros (Maros)

One of following un-familiar above said is how to dealing with heavy-lift equipment. By collecting primary data for the cement projects in Indonesia, Table 5 is a list for heavy machineries in which cannot be separated in generally well-known logistics' packages. These heavy-lift's popularly said are impossible to be inserted in any type and size of regular containers. Therefore, there parts should be considered as breakbulk in which demanded requiring tramper charter vessels or multi-purpose vessels. The consequence to deal these machineries are increasing logistics' tarrif.

Table 3. TCO for Rembang's project

No	Section	VUDS	BSA	Bertling	DFDS				
		Rp	US$	Rp	US$	Rp	US$	Rp	US$
1	Sea Freight Main Equipment (US$)		6,256,585.38		6,043,622.48		6,689,003.87		16,723,722.86
2	Inland Main Equipment (Rp)	21,677,302,221.62		48,553,640,000.00		21,262,909,864.06		30,859,848,096.40	
3	Custom Clearance (Rp)	1,046,395,073.03		23,106,401,000.00		4,852,814,821.50		2,928,462,371.44	
4	Bridge's enforcement (Rp)	840,000,000.00		3,829,300,000.00		2,350,000,000.00		3,973,580,627.58	
	Grand Total Costs	23,563,697,294.65	6,256,585.38	75,489,341,000.00	6,043,622.48	28,465,724,685.56	6,689,003.87	37,761,891,095.42	16,723,722.86
	Score	100.00	96.60	31.21	100.00	82.78	90.35	62.40	36.14

Source: data gathered by Author when involved at the projects. VUDS is Varia Usaha Dharma Segara. BSA is Bima Sepaja Abadi. Bertling is original name Bertling. DFDS is original name DFDS. Rp is Indonesia's currency rupiah.

Table 4. Estimating total volume imported

Projection	Name of Cement Projects							
	RBG	IDRG	P14	Tbn#2	Bayah	Byms	Maros	Train#1
Volume Import (Ton)	14,703	15,254	27,335	13,800	12,665	8,883	10,857	7,770
Volume (FRT)	40,164	43,200	72,372	38,988	35,374	22,551	26,980	16,186

Source: collected and organized by author (2021)

Table 5. Lists of heavy-lift equipment

No	Description	Qty	Weight (ton)		Dimension (meter)			Equip no
			Gross	Net	Length	Width	Height	
1	Table Casting	1	114.00	112.00	6.65	6.65	3.66	321.RM100
2	Rotor for fan type DHRV 45S-2500/K-10	1	33.10	28.00	7.48	4.45	4.50	321.FN400
3	Rotor for fan type DHRV 71N-3150/K-10	1	34.39	28.00	8.80	4.12	4.45	331.FN400
4	FOR 1 Live ring 6880-680 Include the following	1	61.32	60.32	7.18	7.18	0.98	431.KL100
5	FOR 1 Live ring 6970-910 Include the following	1	66.45	65.45	7.18	7.18	1.07	431.KL100
6	FOR 2 Supporting roller, shaft and thrust collars 2200-1100 Include the following	1	39.20	38.79	3.70	2.30	2.35	431.KB102
7	ROLLER ASSEMBLY	1	50.80	50.80	3.00	2.70	3.10	321.RM100
8	ROLLER ASSEMBLY	1	50.80	50.80	3.00	2.70	3.10	321.RM100
9	ROLLER ASSEMBLY	1	50.80	50.80	3.00	2.70	3.10	321.RM100
10	Heavy Kiln Shell section I composed by:	1	59.40	58.75	7.00	5.75	5.85	431.KL100
11	Heavy Kiln Shell Section II composed by:	1	74.80	74.08	7.20	5.90	5.94	431.KL100
12	Heavy Kiln Shell Section III composed by:	1	89.20	88.48	11.70	5.75	5.85	431.KL100
13	Gearbox WPU-302/C	1	147.00	146.00	5.16	5.11	3.35	321.MD140
14	Grinding table LM 59.3+3	1	105.00	103.00	6.35	6.35	3.12	541RM01
15	Grinding table LM 59.3+3	1	105.00	103.00	6.35	6.35	3.12	542RM01
16	Roller cpl. modul 83 with tire	1	42.50	40.00	3.27	3.00	3.80	541RM01
17	Roller cpl. modul 83 with tire	1	42.50	40.00	3.27	3.00	3.80	541RM01
18	Roller cpl. modul 83 with tire	1	42.50	40.00	3.27	3.00	3.80	541RM01
19	Roller cpl. modul 83 with tire	1	42.50	40.00	3.27	3.00	3.80	542RM01
20	Roller cpl. modul 83 with tire	1	42.50	40.00	3.27	3.00	3.80	542RM01
21	Roller cpl. modul 83 with tire	1	42.50	40.00	3.27	3.00	3.80	542RM01
22	Gear Box KMPP size 751	1	109.85	105.00	5.06	4.11	3.40	541RM01
23	Gear Box KMPP size 751	1	109.85	105.00	5.06	4.11	3.40	542RM01

The challenge to manage heavy-lifts hasn't over at the sea freight, but it is continuing to the inland domestics in Indonesia. The difficult starts since unloading from the vessels at the destination ports, stay in ports as the highest charges may incurred. Further challenge will be dealing to do customs clearance, planning to bring out from customs area, choosing appropriate heavy trucks, decision to select proper inland roads or probability to choose water transport to short-cut land barriers, and finally to unloading at the project site.

Following Figure 4 is to show how dealing during inland transport due to limited road's infrastructure. Special heavy truck is required to be able carrying 210 tons of main equipment table mill. Road clearance must be anticipated as like crossing electrical cables, telephone wire, billboards, or any obstacles might installed. Costs for certainly must be directly prepared in advance.

Figure 4. Delivering heavy-lift via inland regular roads

Inland Main Equipment

This scope is purposed to deal with the domestic matter in Indonesia. In principle, roads built in Indonesia are capable to bear regular packages on the trailers. So, if goods can be managed in to standard containers, meant everything can be assured as plan. Table 6 shows total number of packages generally for normal cement projects. The packages are divided in to two type of containers for 20" and 40". Besides, breakbulk type are also present but it relatively manageable transported through regular trailers.

Customs Clearance

This section is set in managing communication and coordination with an official in Indonesia. This mandatory needs to meet state's regulation regarding official documents and for paying taxes. There are three types of taxes of value added tax (VAT), duty and luxury import tax. After taxes mandatory had been accomplished, the customs and concise department issued release and clear notification for the goods. The formal letters will be important paper to process further steps in ports' warehousing or later probably the goods might be field inspection by official state.

Table 6. Total packages in standard containers anticipated

Name of Cement Projects	Number of Standard Containers		Number of General Packages	Total Packages
	20 *Feet*	40 *Feet*		
Rembang	202	397	2,120	2,719
Indarung	214	348	1,923	2,485
P14 Citeureup	412	504	1,964	2,880
Tuban #2	260	321	911	1,492
Bayah	122	270	856	1,248
Banyumas	128	255	771	1,154
Maros	169	260	600	1,029
Train #1 Tabalong	125	235	551	911

Source: Author (2021)

Figure 5. A-24 axles trailer

Domestic's Obstacles

This section anticipates domestic's obstacles due to limitation of quality and capacity of infrastructure. This case especially regarding bridges of roads. Standard capacity of Indonesia's bridges have been designed to bear of maximum 10 tons for every axle. It means to transport for heavy-lift of 210 tons of table mill demanded for 24 axles. If every axle has length for 5 meters then total length will reach for 120 meters.

The critical factor is when total length of bridges more than 120 meters meant all weight of goods and weight of trailer are perfectly ever experiencing at the surface of bridge completely. This is a dangerous ever situation as the bridges are potentially collapse as frequently happened in Indonesia at the period of time. To prevent such accident, based on Table 3, the additional costs to make-up strength of every bridge is about at least Rp 840 million according estimation proposed VUDS. The construction to enforce bridges showed by Figure 6.

Figure 6. Construction to enforce bridges

There is an alternative way to strengthen capacity of bridges by applying a fly over bridge. This mechanical construction will be made in certain design to cover all surface of bridges, but the costs are more expensive than erect mechanical beams according Figure 6. Fly over bridge in Indonesia's logistics cases are not frequently applied due to costs considerations.

CONCLUSION AND FUTURE WORK

Working in the aspect of total logistics costs is covering in broad spectrums and vast. It is not only seeking scientific foundation but also how the model found will be benefiting in every business activity in real business. After the concept of total logistics costs have been formulated, there is now waiting the model can be applied for the selection process to determine the right agents as logistics' provider.

The model can be treated as anchor or reference for procurement officers to give warning or alarm, when procurement-process was out-scope then the direction can be adjusted to the right way. But the real projects are expected to contribute in aspect of empirical findings to develop knowledge. If there is found unusual evidence but rigorous interfere to the model, an important note should be noticed to get attention to the scholars.

Based on problems identified and solution given in this paper, utilizing the total costs of ownership (TCO) is the best method applied during procurement-process in selection logistics providers. The considerations are based on four determinants as empirically found in Indonesia consecutively (1) sea-freight scope; (2) inland; (3) customs clearance; and (4) domestic obstacles. TCO is also state-of-art knowledge and discipline, there is not only considering numbers and values but also measuring other aspects might probably occurred to be anticipated.

ACKNOWLEDGMENT

Author gratitude and thanks for the cement projects in Indonesia were visited and welcoming author and very help and cooperate to share ideas or solution to deal at the subject of this paper. The author has visited the Padang's project, Tonasa project, Tuban project, Rembang project, and Baturaja project.

REFERENCES

Ahmed, M. (2019). The use of performance-based contracting in managing the outsourcing of a reliability-centered maintenance program: A case study. *Journal of Quality in Maintenance Engineering*, *26*(4), 526–554. doi:10.1108/JQME-02-2018-0007

Barrad, S., Gagnon, S., & Valverde, R. (2020). An Analytics Architecture for Procurement. *International Journal of Information Technologies and Systems Approach*, *13*(2), 73–98. doi:10.4018/IJITSA.2020070104

Boer, L., Harink, J., & Heijboer, G. (2002). A conceptual model for assessing the impact of electronic procurement. *European Journal of Purchasing & Supply Management*, *8*(1), 25–33. doi:10.1016/S0969-7012(01)00015-6

Brenner, D., Weber, C., Lenz, J., & Westkaemper, E. (2018). Total Tool Cost of Ownership Indicator for Holistical Evaluations of Improvement Measures within the Cutting Tool Life Cycle. *Procedia CIRP*, *72*, 1404–1409. doi:10.1016/j.procir.2018.03.164

Brooks, M. R., Mccalla, R., Pallis, A. A., & Lugt, L. M. (2010). Coordination and Cooperation in Strategic Port Management: The Case of Atlantic Canada's Ports. *Canadian Journal of Transportation*, *18*(4), 28–42.

Ceran, Y., Alagoz, A., & Ortakarpuz, M. (2013). Incoterms Costs in International Marketing and Their Effects on Product Pricing. In *8th Annual London Business Research Conference*. London: Imperial College.

Debono, P. (2019). Transforming Public Procurement Contracts Into Smart Contracts. *International Journal of Information Technology Project Management*, *10*(2), 16–28. doi:10.4018/IJITPM.2019040103

Demidova, O., & Yakovlev, A. (2012). State-Business relations and participation of firms in public procurement in Russia: An empirical study. *Journal of Public Procurement*, *12*(4), 547–592. doi:10.1108/JOPP-12-04-2012-B004

Fayezi, S., Zomorrodi, M., & Bals, L. (2018). Procurement sustainability tensions: An integrative perspective. *International Journal of Physical Distribution & Logistics Management*, *48*(6), 586–609. doi:10.1108/IJPDLM-01-2017-0013

Gekara, V., & Chhetri, P. (2013). Upstream Transport Corridor Inefficiencies and the Implications for Port Performance: A Case Analysis of Mombasa Port and the Northern Corridor. *Maritime Policy & Management*, *40*(6), 559–573. doi:10.1080/03088839.2013.776716

Goswami, M. P., & Wettstein, D. (2016). Rational bidding in a procurement auction with subjective evaluations. *International Journal of Industrial Organization*, *44*, 60–67. doi:10.1016/j.ijindorg.2015.10.001

Guarnieri, P., & Gomes, R. (2019). Can public procurement be strategic? A future agenda proposition. *Journal of Public Procurement*, *19*(4), 295–321. doi:10.1108/JOPP-09-2018-0032

Handfield, R., Jeong, S., & Choi, T. (2019). Emerging procurement technology: Data analytics and cognitive analytics. *International Journal of Physical Distribution & Logistics Management*, *49*(10), 972–1002. doi:10.1108/IJPDLM-11-2017-0348

Hawkins, T., Nissen, M., & Rendon, R. (2014). Leveraging strategic sourcing and knowledge management to improve the acquisition of knowledge-based services. *Journal of Public Procurement*, *14*(2), 215–251. doi:10.1108/JOPP-14-02-2014-B003

Hussein, A. M., Abdullah, K. O., Faraj, K. A., & Hamamin, D. F. (2018). Radon Concentration in the Work Atmosphere of Cement Plants in the Sulaymaniyah Area, Iraq. *ARO-The Scientific Journal of Koya University*, *4*(1), 7–12. doi:10.14500/aro.10329

Iannone, F., & Thore, S. (2010). An economic logistics model for the multimodal inland distribution of maritime containers. *Rivista Internazionale di Economia dei Trasporti*, *37*(3), 281–326.

Jääskeläinen, A., & Thitz, O. (2018). Prerequisites for performance measurement supporting purchaser-supplier collaboration. *Benchmarking*, *25*(1), 120–137. doi:10.1108/BIJ-08-2016-0121

Kalaitzi, D., Matopoulos, A., Bourlakis, M., & Tate, W. (2019). Supply chains under resource pressure: Strategies for improving resource efficiency and competitive advantage. *International Journal of Operations & Production Management*, *39*(12), 1323–1354. doi:10.1108/IJOPM-02-2019-0137

Khosravi, M., Sarvari, H., Chan, D., Cristofaro, M., & Chen, Z. (2020). Determining and assessing the risks of commercial and recreational complex building projects in developing countries: A survey of experts in Iran. *Journal of Facilities Management*, *18*(3), 259–282. doi:10.1108/JFM-02-2020-0010

Kim, C. B. (2016). Impact of exchange rate movements, global economic activity, and the BDI volatility on loaded port cargo throughput in South Korea. *Asian Journal of Shipping and Logistics*, *32*(4), 243–248. doi:10.1016/j.ajsl.2016.12.008

Kumar, & Clemens, & Keller. (2014). Supplier management in a manufacturing environment: A strategically focussed performance scorecard. *International Journal of Productivity and Performance Management*, *63*(1), 127–138. doi:10.1108/IJPPM-12-2012-0137

Kumar, A., Pal, A., Vohra, A., Gupta, S., Manchanda, S., & Dash, M. (2018). Construction of capital procurement decision making model to optimize supplier selection using Fuzzy Delphi and AHP-DEMATEL. *Benchmarking*, *25*(5), 1528–1547. doi:10.1108/BIJ-01-2017-0005

Leontaris, G., Nápoles, O., Dewan, A., & Wolfert, A. (2019). Decision support for offshore asset construction using expert judgments for supply disruptions risk. *Automation in Construction*, *107*, 102903. Advance online publication. doi:10.1016/j.autcon.2019.102903

Letmathe, P., & Suares, M. (2020). Understanding the impact that potential driving bans on conventional vehicles and the total cost of ownership have on electric vehicle choice in Germany. *Sustainable Future, 2*, 100018. Advance online publication. doi:10.1016/j.sftr.2020.100018

Liao, Z., & Rittscher, J. (2007). Integration of supplier selection, procurement lot sizing and carrier selection under dynamic demand conditions. *International Journal of Production Economics, 107*(2), 502–510. doi:10.1016/j.ijpe.2006.10.003

Mandolini, M., Marilungo, E., & Germani, M. (2017). A TCO Model for Supporting the Configuration of Industrial Plants. *Procedia Manufacturing, 11*, 1940–1949. doi:10.1016/j.promfg.2017.07.339

Manzanero, L. D., & Krupp, K. J. (2009). *Forecasting Container Freight Rates. An Econometric Analysis*. Academic Press.

Melon, L., & Spruk, R. (2020). The impact of e-procurement on institutional quality. *Journal of Public Procurement*. . doi:10.1108/JOPP-07-2019-0050

Merkert, R., Mulley, C., & Hakim, M. (2018). Trade-offs between transaction cost, operation cost and innovation in the context of procurement and asset specificity – The example of the bus industry. *Research in Transportation Economics, 69*, 173–179. doi:10.1016/j.retrec.2018.07.015

Miller. (2020). The innovation impacts of public procurement offices: The case of healthcare procurement. *Research Policy, 49*(7). . doi:10.1016/j.respol.2020.104075

Mukeshimana, M., Zhao, Z., Ahmad, M., & Irfan, M. (2021). Analysis on barriers to biogas dissemination in Rwanda: AHP approach. *Renewable Energy, 163*, 1127–1137. doi:10.1016/j.renene.2020.09.051

Muscatello, J. R., Parente, D. H., & Swinarski, M. (2018). Aligning Supply Chain Logistics Costs via ERP Coordination. *International Journal of Information System Modeling and Design, 9*(2), 24–43. doi:10.4018/IJISMD.2018040102

Oyegoke, A. S., Dickinson, M., Khalfan, M. M., McDermott, P., & Rowlinson, S. (2009). Construction project procurement routes: An in-depth critique. *International Journal of Managing Projects in Business, 2*(3), 338–354. doi:10.1108/17538370910971018

Pettersen, I. J., Nyland, K., & Robbins, G. (2020). Public procurement performance and the challenge of service complexity – the case of pre-hospital healthcare. *Journal of Public Procurement*. . doi:10.1108/JOPP-01-2020-0002

Rafiei, S., Mohammadi-ivatloo, B., Asadi, S., Goldani, S., & Falaghi, H. (2019). Bi-level model for generation expansion planning with contract pricing of renewable energy in the presence of energy storage. *IET Renewable Power Generation, 13*(9), 1544–1553. doi:10.1049/iet-rpg.2019.0074

Ramberg, J. (2011). *ICC Guide to Incoterms® 2010: Understanding and Practical Use*. ICC.

Salam, M. (2019). Analyzing manufacturing strategies and Industry 4.0 supplier performance relationships from a resource-based perspective. *Benchmarking: An International Journal*. . doi:10.1108/BIJ-12-2018-0428

Selviaridis, K. (2020). Effects of public procurement of R&D on the innovation process: evidence from the UK small business research initiative. *Journal of Public Procurement*. . doi:10.1108/JOPP-12-2019-0082

Seth, D., & Rastogi, S. (2019). Application of vendor rationalization strategy for manufacturing cycle time reduction in engineer to order (ETO) environment: A case study. *Journal of Manufacturing Technology Management, 30*(1), 261–290. doi:10.1108/JMTM-03-2018-0095

Shabani, A., Visani, F., Barbieri, P., Dullaert, W., & Vigo, D. (2019). Reliable estimation of suppliers' total cost of ownership: An imprecise data envelopment analysis model with common weights. *Omega, 87*, 57–70. doi:10.1016/j.omega.2018.08.002

Singh, R., & Modgil, S. (2020). Supplier selection using SWARA and WASPAS – a case study of Indian cement industry. *Measuring Business Excellence, 24*(2), 243–265. doi:10.1108/MBE-07-2018-0041

Stojčića, N., Srhoja, S., & Coad, A. (2020). Innovation procurement as capability-building: Evaluating innovation policies in eight Central and Eastern European countries. *European Economic Review, 121*, 103330. Advance online publication. doi:10.1016/j.euroecorev.2019.103330

Subiyanto, E. (2020). Assessing Total Logistics Costs: Case Study during the Execution of Cement Projects in Indonesia. *International Journal of Applied Logistics, 10*(2), 45–61. doi:10.4018/IJAL.2020070103

Subiyanto, E. (2021). Investigating the logistics costs model: Recent update in Indonesia. *Journal of Science and Technology Policy Management, 12*(2), 331–350. doi:10.1108/JSTPM-03-2020-0034

Subiyanto, E., & Rini, H. P. (2020). Developing Model of Logistics Costs in Indonesia's Cement Projects: A Literature and Empirical Study Approach. *Journal of Economics and Business, 3*(2), 697–718. doi:10.31014/aior.1992.03.02.232

Subiyanto, E., & Suyoto, Y. T. (2020). Determining Value of Logistics Costs in Projects; Empirical Findings based-on Executing Several Cement Projects in Indonesia. *Heliyon, 6*(7), e04352. Advance online publication. doi:10.1016/j.heliyon.2020.e04352 PMID:32695900

Suresh, M., & Nathan, A. (2020). Readiness for lean procurement in construction projects. *Construction Innovation, 20*(4), 587–608. doi:10.1108/CI-07-2019-0067

Terreno, S., Asadi, S., & Anumba, C. (2019). An Exploration of Synergies between Lean Concepts and BIM in FM: A Review and Directions for Future Research. *Buildings, 9*(147), 147. Advance online publication. doi:10.3390/buildings9060147

Wiengarten, F., & Ambrose, E. (2017). The role of geographical distance and its efficacy on global purchasing practices. *International Journal of Operations & Production Management, 37*(7), 865–881. doi:10.1108/IJOPM-09-2015-0556

Compilation of References

Aaker, D. (1992). *Strategic Management* (3rd ed.). John Wiley & Sons.

Abbas, H. B., & Routray, J. K. (2014). Assessing factors affecting flood-induced public health risks in Kassala State of Sudan. *Operations Research for Health Care*, *3*(4), 215–225.

Abdelkafi, C., Beck, B. H., David, B., Druck, C., & Horoho, M. (2009). Balancing risk and costs to optimize the clinical supply chain—A step beyond simulation. *Journal of Pharmaceutical Innovation*, *4*(3), 96–106.

Abdollahiasl, A., Nikfar, S., Kebriaeezadeh, A., Dinarvand, R., Abdollahi, M., Jaberidoost, M., & Cheraghali, A. M. (2014). A system dynamics model for national drug policy. *Daru: Journal of Faculty of Pharmacy, Tehran University of Medical Sciences*, *22*(1), 22–34. PMID:24690531

Absi, N., Archetti, C., Dauzère-Pérès, S., & Feillet, D. (2014). A two-phase iterative heuristic approach for the production routing problem. *Transportation Science*, *49*(4), 784–795. doi:10.1287/trsc.2014.0523

Accenture Global Operations. Megatrend Study. (2014). *Big data analytics in supply chain: hype or here to stay?* www.accenture.com/megatrends

Ackoff, R. L. (1981). The art and science of mess management. *Interfaces*, *11*(1), 20–26. doi:10.1287/inte.11.1.20

ADAC. (2020). *Corona und Mobilität: Mehr Homeoffice, weniger Berufsverkehr*. Retrieved from https://www.adac.de/verkehr/standpunktestudien/mobilitaets-trends/corona-mobilitaet/

Adulyasak, Y., Cordeau, J. F., & Jans, R. (2015). The production routing problem: A review of formulations and solution algorithms. *Computers & Operations Research*, *55*, 141–152. doi:10.1016/j.cor.2014.01.011

AECOM. (2014). *Report on the State of the EU Road Haulage Market*. European Commission, Directorate General for Mobility and Transport.

Afra, A. P., & Behnamian, J. (2021). Lagrangian heuristic algorithm for green multi-product production routing problem with reverse logistics and remanufacturing. *Journal of Manufacturing Systems*, *58*, 33–43. doi:10.1016/j.jmsy.2020.11.013

Ahangar, N. K., & Tayebi, H. (2021). The three-objective optimization model of flexible workshop scheduling problem for minimizing work completion time, work delay time, and energy consumption. *Tehnički glasnik, 15*(1), 76-83.

Ahmad, F. (2021). Interactive neutrosophic optimization technique for multiobjective programming problems: An application to pharmaceutical supply chain management. *Annals of Operations Research*, 1–35.

Ahmed, M. (2019). The use of performance-based contracting in managing the outsourcing of a reliability-centered maintenance program: A case study. *Journal of Quality in Maintenance Engineering*, *26*(4), 526–554. doi:10.1108/JQME-02-2018-0007

Ailawadi, K., Zhang, J., Krishna, A., & Kruger, M. W. (2010). When Wal- Mart Enters: How Incumbent Retailers React and How This Affects Their Sales Outcomes. *JMR, Journal of Marketing Research*, *47*(August), 577–593. doi:10.1509/jmkr.47.4.577

Al Amien, D., Setyani, F. D., & Sihombing, R. (2020, December). Sustainable Port Planning in Future Indonesian Ports: A Case Study of Mafa Port based on UN SDGs. *IOP Conference Series. Earth and Environmental Science*, *618*(1), 012041. doi:10.1088/1755-1315/618/1/012041

Alderson, W. (1957). *Marketing behavior and executive action*. Richard D. Irwin.

Al-Hakim, L., Abdullah, N. A., & Ng, E. (2012). The Effect of Inter-Organization Trust and Dependency on E-Procurement Adoption: A Case of Malaysian Manufacturers. *Journal of Electronic Commerce in Organizations*, *10*(2), 40–60. doi:10.4018/jeco.2012040103

Al-Hakim, L., & Lu, W. (2017). The role of collaboration and technology diffusion on business performance. *International Journal of Productivity and Performance Management*, *66*(1), 22–50. doi:10.1108/IJPPM-08-2014-0122

Al-Hakim, L., Morgan, M. J., & Chau, R. (2014). An Empirical Evaluation of Information Sharing Between Australia-Singapore Beef Organisations in Light of Trust and ICT Diffusion. *International Journal of e-Collaboration*, *10*(3), 1–29. doi:10.4018/ijec.2014070101

Ali, C. M. S. E. (2017). Analyzing Pharmaceutical Reverse Logistics Barriers: An Interpretive Structural Modeling Approach. *International Journal of Applied Logistics*, *7*(1), 16–48.

Alnaji, L., & Ridha, M. (2013). The role of Supply Chain Applications in Jordanian Pharmacies: A case study on Pharmacies in the capital city Amman. *Industrial Engineering Letters*, *3*, 65–71.

Aloi, A., Alonso, B., Benavente, J., Cordera, R., Echániz, E., González, F., ... Mazzei, V. (2020). Effects of the COVID-19 lockdown on urban mobility: Empirical evidence from the city of Santander (Spain). *Sustainability*, *12*(9), 3870. doi:10.3390u12093870

Al-Shboul, M. D. A. (2017). Infrastructure framework and manufacturing supply chain agility: The role of delivery dependability and time to market. *Supply Chain Management*, *22*(2), 172–185.

Altınel, K., & Öncan, T. (2005). A new enhancement of the Clarke and Wright savings heuristic for the capacitated vehicle routing problem. *The Journal of the Operational Research Society*, *56*(8), 954–961. doi:10.1057/palgrave.jors.2601916

Amaro, A. C. S., & Barbosa-Póvoa, A. P. F. (2008). Planning and scheduling of industrial supply chains with reverse flows: A real pharmaceutical case study. *Computers & Chemical Engineering*, *32*(11), 2606–2625.

Amisha, P. M., Pathania, M., & Rathaur, V. K. (2019). Overview of artificial intelligence in medicine. *Journal of Family Medicine and Primary Care*, *8*(7), 2328. PMID:31463251

Amit, R., & Schoemaker, P. J. H. (1993). Strategic Assets and Organizational Rent. *Strategic Management Journal*, *14*(1), 33–46. doi:10.1002mj.4250140105

Amoozad-Khalili, H., Ranjbar-Bourani, M., & Ale-Hashem, S. J. M. (2010). Fuzzy demand consideration in a multi-objective dynamic cell formation problem using a robust scatter search. *J Math Comput SCI-JM*, *1*(4), 321–332. doi:10.22436/jmcs.001.04.09

Andersen, M. W. (2010). *Service network nesign and management in liner container shipping applications* [Ph.D. Thesis]. Technical University of Denmark, Lyngby, Denmark.

Ann Keller, S., Koonin, S. E., & Shipp, S. (2012). Big data and city living–what can it do for us? *Significance*, *9*(4), 4–7.

Anylogic. (2017). *Discrete Event Modelling.* https://www.anylogic.com/use-of-simulation/discrete-event-simulation/

Arnold, S., Oum, T. H., & Tigert, D. J. (1983). Determinant Attributes in Retail Patronage: Seasonal, Temporal, Regional, and International Comparisons. *JMR, Journal of Marketing Research, 20*(May), 977–1009.

Arora, P., Sachdeva, C., & Sharma, D. (2021). Securing the Pharma Supply Chain Using Blockchain. *Integration of Cloud Computing with Internet of Things: Foundations. Analysis and Applications*, 343–359.

Artigues, C., Lopez, P., & Hait, A. (2013). The energy scheduling problem: Industrial case-study and constraint propagation techniques. *International Journal of Production Economics, 143*(1), 13–23. doi:10.1016/j.ijpe.2010.09.030

Attaran, M. (2020, July). Digital technology enablers and their implications for supply chain management. *International Journal (Toronto, Ont.), 21*(3), 158–172.

Attri, R., Dev, N., & Sharma, V. (2013). Interpretive structural modelling (ISM) approach: An overview. *Research Journal of Management Sciences, 2*(2), 1171.

Azadegan, A., & Dooley, K. (2021). A typology of supply network resilience strategies: Complex collaborations in a complex world. *The Journal of Supply Chain Management, 57*(1), 17–26. doi:10.1111/jscm.12256

Bag, S. (2017). Key Success Factors of an SME's Multi-Site Organizational Restructuring: A Case Study Approach. *International Journal of Applied Logistics, 7*(2), 1–20.

Bailey, K., & Francis, M. (2008). Managing information flows for improved value chain performance. *International Journal of Production Economics, 111*(1), 2–12.

Balfaqih, H., Nopiah, Z. M., Saibani, N., & Al-Nory, M. T. (2016). Review of supply chain performance measurement systems: 1998–2015. *Computers in Industry, 82*, 135–150.

Bals, L., Schulze, H., Kelly, S., & Stek, K. (2019). Purchasing and supply management (PSM) competencies: Current and future requirements. *Journal of Purchasing and Supply Management, 25*(5), 100572. doi:10.1016/j.pursup.2019.100572

Banister, D., & Berechman, J. (1999). *Transport investment and economic development.* Taylor and Francis.

Baporikar, N. (2020a). Learning Link in Organizational Tacit Knowledge Creation and Dissemination. *International Journal of Sociotechnology and Knowledge Development, 12*(4), 70–88. doi:10.4018/IJSKD.2020100105

Baporikar, N. (2020b). Logistics Effectiveness Through Systems Thinking. *International Journal of System Dynamics Applications, 9*(2), 64–79. doi:10.4018/IJSDA.2020040104

Baporikar, N. (2021). *Handbook of Research on Sustaining SMEs and Entrepreneurial Innovation in the Post-COVID-19 Era.* IGI Global., doi:10.4018/978-1-7998-6632-9

Baporikar, N., & Kaloia, D. S. (2020). Supply Chain Management Perspective on Shortages in Drugs Sourcing. *International Journal of Applied Logistics, 10*(2), 62–85. doi:10.4018/IJAL.2020070104

Baporikar, N., & Shangheta, L. B. (2018). Challenges Facing Humanitarian Logistics in a Nonprofit Organization. *International Journal of Applied Logistics, 8*(1), 35–56. doi:10.4018/IJAL.2018010103

Bard, J. F., & Nananukul, N. (2010). A branch-and-price algorithm for an integrated production and inventory routing problem. *Computers & Operations Research, 37*(12), 2202–2217. doi:10.1016/j.cor.2010.03.010

Barlas, S. (2013). FDA Strategies to prevent and respond to drug shortages: Finding a better way to predict and prevent company closure. *The Pharmacist and Therapeutics Journal, 38*(5), 261-263.

Barney, J. (1991). Firm resources and sustained competitive advantage. *Journal of Management, 17*(1), 99–120. doi:10.1177/014920639101700108

Barney, J. B., & Arikan, A. M. (2001). The resource-based view: origins and implications. In M. A. Hitt, R. E. Freeman, & J. S. Harrison (Eds.), *Handbook of Strategic Management* (pp. 124–188). Blackwell.

Barrad, S., Gagnon, S., & Valverde, R. (2020). An Analytics Architecture for Procurement. *International Journal of Information Technologies and Systems Approach, 13*(2), 73–98. doi:10.4018/IJITSA.2020070104

Bartelt-Hunt, S. L., Snow, D. D., Damon, T., Shockley, J., & Hoagland, K. (2009). The occurrence of illicit and therapeutic pharmaceuticals in wastewater effluent and surface waters in Nebraska. *Environmental Pollution, 157*(3), 786–791. PMID:19110357

Bask, A., & Tinnilä, M. (2013). Impact of Product Characteristics on Supply Chains: An Analytical Literature Review. *International Journal of Applied Logistics, 4*(1), 35–59.

Bateman, C. (2013). Drug stock-outs: Inept supply-chain management and corruption. *South African Medical Journal, 103*(9), 600–602. doi:10.7196/SAMJ.7332 PMID:24344422

Baudrillard, J. (2018). *Die Simulation.* Akademie Verlag.

Bayraktar, E., Demirbag, M., Ko-h, S. L., Tatoglu, E., & Zaim, H. (2009). A causal analysis of the impact of information systems and supply chain management practices on operational performance: Evidence from manufacturing SMEs in Turkey. *International Journal of Production Economics, 122*(1), 133–149.

Beach, Webster, & Campbell. (2005). An evaluation of partnership development in the construction industry. *International Journal of Project Management, 23*(8), 611-621. doi:10.1016/j.ijproman.2005.04.001

Beard, C., & Fildes, R. (1992). Forecasting systems for production and inventory control. *International Journal of Operations & Production Management, 12*(5), 4–27. https://www.emerald.com/insight/content/doi/10.1108/01443579210011381/full/html

Bego, A., Li, L., & Sun, Z. (2014). Identification of reservation capacity in critical peak pricing electricity demand response program for sustainable manufacturing systems. *International Journal of Energy Research, 38*(6), 728–736. doi:10.1002/er.3077

Belliveau, J. (2016). *Exploring the role of supply chain management in healthcare.* Retrieved from http://revcycleintelligence.com

Berle, A. A., & Means, G. (1932). *The modern corporation and private property.* Commerce Clearing House.

Berry, L., Jacobs, F., Vollmann, T., & Whybank, D. (2005). *Manufacturing Planning and Control systems for supply chain managment* (5th ed.). McGraw-Hill. Available from http://www.sidalc.net/cgi-bin/wxis.exe/?IsisScript=AGRIUAN.xis&method=post&formato=2&cantidad=1&expresion=mfn=029246

Bersani, C., & Sacile, R. (2014). Optimal Deliveries in a Vendor Managed Inventory Service. *International Journal of Applied Logistics, 5*(1), 1–14. doi:10.4018/ijal.2014010101

Bhakoo, V., & Chan, C. (2011). Collaborative implementation of e-business processes within the healthcare supply chain: The Monash Pharmacy Project. *Supply Chain Management, 16*(3), 184–193. doi:10.1108/13598541111127173

Bharadwaj, A. S. (2000). A Resource-based Perspective on Information Technology Capability and Firm Performance: an Empirical Investigation. *MIS Quarterly, 24*(1), 169-196.

Bína, L., Bínová, H., Březina, E., Kumpošt, P., & Padělek, T. (2014). Comparative model of unit costs of road and rail freight transport for selected European countries. *European Journal of Business and Social Sciences*, *3*(4), 127–136.

Biswas, S., & Sengupta, G. (2014). A case study on the critical success factors determining the success or failure of TQM implementation in Indian Organizations. International Journal of Management, IT and Engineering, 4(10).

Bititci, U., Carrie, A., & Turner, T. (2002). 11 Integrated performance measurement systems: Structure and dynamics. *Business Performance Measurement*, 174.

Bjärkvik, E., Fürer, F., Pourabdollah, M., & Lindenberg, B. (2017). Simulation and Characterization of Traffic on Drive Me Route around Gothenburg using SUMO. *Proceedings of the SUMO2017-Towards Simulation for Autonomous Mobility*, 1-13.

Blossey, G., Hahn, G. J., & Koberstein, A. (2021, January). Managing Uncertainty in Pharmaceutical Supply Chains: A Structured Review. *Proceedings of the 54th Hawaii International Conference on System Sciences.*

Blumberg, D. F. (1999). Strategic examination of reverse logistics & repair service requirements, needs, market size, and opportunities. *Journal of Business Logistics*, *20*(2), 141–159.

Blumberg, D. F. (2004). *Introduction to management of reverse logistics and closed loop supply chain processes*. CRC Press.

BMI. (2014). *Egypt Pharmaceuticals & Healthcare Report Q1*. Business Monitor International.

Boer, L., Harink, J., & Heijboer, G. (2002). A conceptual model for assessing the impact of electronic procurement. *European Journal of Purchasing & Supply Management*, *8*(1), 25–33. doi:10.1016/S0969-7012(01)00015-6

Böhme, T., Williams, S. J., Childerhouse, P., Deakins, E., & Towill, D. (2013). Methodology challenges associated with benchmarking healthcare supply chains. *Production Planning and Control*, *24*(10-11), 1002–1014. doi:10.1080/09537287.2012.666918

Bonev, M. (2012). *Managing reverse logistics using system dynamics: A generic end-to-end approach*. Diplomica Verlag.

Boudia, M., Louly, M. A. O., & Prins, C. (2007). A reactive GRASP and path relinking for a combined production–distribution problem. *Computers & Operations Research*, *34*(11), 3402–3419. doi:10.1016/j.cor.2006.02.005

Bozorgi-Amiri, A., Jabalameli, M. S., & Al-e-Hashem, S. M. (2013). A multi-objective robust stochastic programming model for disaster relief logistics under uncertainty. *OR-Spektrum*, *35*(4), 905–933. doi:10.100700291-011-0268-x

Brahimi, N., & Aouam, T. (2016). Multi-item production routing problem with backordering: A MILP approach. *International Journal of Production Research*, *54*(4), 1076–1093. doi:10.1080/00207543.2015.1047971

Branch, A. (2009). *Global supply chain management and international logistics*. Routledge.

Brenner, D., Weber, C., Lenz, J., & Westkaemper, E. (2018). Total Tool Cost of Ownership Indicator for Holistical Evaluations of Improvement Measures within the Cutting Tool Life Cycle. *Procedia CIRP*, *72*, 1404–1409. doi:10.1016/j.procir.2018.03.164

Britannica. (2018). *Wheel.* Retrieved from https://www.britannica.com/technology/wheel

Brooks, M. R., Mccalla, R., Pallis, A. A., & Lugt, L. M. (2010). Coordination and Cooperation in Strategic Port Management: The Case of Atlantic Canada's Ports. *Canadian Journal of Transportation*, *18*(4), 28–42.

Bruzzone, A. A., Anghinolfi, D., Paolucci, M., & Tonelli, F. (2012). Energy-aware scheduling for improving manufacturing process sustainability: A mathematical model for flexible flow shops. *CIRP Annals*, *61*(1), 459–462. doi:10.1016/j.cirp.2012.03.084

Bucsky, P. (2020). Modal share changes due to COVID-19: The case of Budapest. *Transportation Research Interdisciplinary Perspectives*, *8*, 100141. doi:10.1016/j.trip.2020.100141 PMID:34171021

Buffa, E. S., & Miller, J. (1979). *Production-Inventory Systems: Planning and Control* (3rd ed.). Irwin.

BunkerIndex. (2012). *South Europe bunker prices*. Retrieved 15.06.2012 from http://www.bunkerindex.com/prices/seurope.php

Burgess, K., & Singh, P. J. (2006). A proposed integrated framework for analysing supply chains. *Supply Chain Management*, *11*(4), 337–344. doi:10.1108/13598540610671789

Burnes, B. (2017). *Managing Change: A strategic approach to organisational dynamics* (7th ed.). Pearson. Available from https://books.google.co.uk/books?hl=en&lr=&id=9J5Ri4xatEMC&oi=fnd&pg=PP11&dq=Managing+Change&ots=q5l5kwpYgV&sig=-AkaW_8aLEQH2WRBpktBDHs9w7s&redir_esc=y#v=onepage&q=Managing%20Change&f=false

Burns, L. R. (2002). *Wharton School Colleagues*. The Health Care Value Chain Producers, Purchasers, and Providers.

Burns, L. R., DeGraaff, R. A., Danzon, P. M., Kimberly, J. R., Kissick, W. L., & Pauly, M. V. (2002). *The Wharton School study of the health care value chain. In The health care value chain: producers, purchasers and providers*. Jossey-Bass.

Burt, S., & Encinas, J. (2000). The role of store image in retail internationalization. International Marketing Review, 17(4-5), 433-453.

Busi, M., & Bititci, U. S. (2006). Collaborative performance management: Present gaps and future research. *International Journal of Productivity and Performance Management*, *55*(1), 7–25. doi:10.1108/17410400610635471

Busse, C., Meinlschmidt, J., & Foerstl, K. (2017). Managing information processing needs in global supply chains: A prerequisite to sustainable supply chain management. *The Journal of Supply Chain Management*, *53*(1), 87–113.

Bylinsky, G. (1999). The challengers move in on ERP. *Fortune*, *140*(10), 306C.

Byoung-Chun, H., Yang-Kyu, P., & Cho, S. (2011). Suppliers' affective trust and trust in competency in buyers: Its effect on collaboration and logistics efficiency. *International Journal of Operations & Production Management*, *31*(1), 56–77. doi:10.1108/01443571111098744

Cai, S., Jun, M., & Yang, Z. (2010). Implementing supply chain information integration in China: The role of institutional forces and trust. *Journal of Operations Management*, *28*(3), 257–268.

Calloway-Sykes, K. (2015, February 2). *Strategies for dealing with drug shortages in the hospitals pharmacy settings*. Retrieved from www. Pharmacytimes.com

Cao, M., & Zhang, Q. (2011). Supply chain collaboration: Impact on collaborative advantage and firm performance. *Journal of Operations Management, 29*(3), 163-180. doi:10.1016/j.jom.2010.12.008

Capron & Hulland. (1999). Redeployment of Brands, Sales Forces, and General Marketing Management Expertise Following Horizontal Acquisitions: A Resource-based View. *Journal of Marketing*, *63*(April).

Carlo, H. J., Vis, I. F. A., & Roodbergen, K. J. (2014). Transport Operations in Container Terminals: Literature Overview, Trends, Research Directions and Classification Scheme. *European Journal of Operational Research*, *236*(1), 1–13. doi:10.1016/j.ejor.2013.11.023

Carnall, C., & Todnem, R. (2014). *Managing Change in Organizations* (6th ed.). Pearson Education.

Carter, C. R., & Ellram, L. M. (1998). Reverse logistics: A review of the literature and framework for future investigation. *Journal of Business Logistics, 19*(1), 85–102.

Carvalho, J., Martins, A., Ramos, T., & Dias, E. (2014). Strategic Fast Supply Demand-Chains in a Network Context: Opportunistic Practices That Can Destroy Supply Chain Systems. *American Journal of Industrial and Business Management, 9*(4), 123–133. doi:10.4236/ajibm.2014.43019

Caudler, R. C., Mehta, B., Bookstaver, B., Sims, D. L., & Stevenson, B. (2015). Impact of Drug Shortages on Health System Pharmacies in the Southeastern United States. *Journal of Managed Care Pharmacy, 50*(4), 279–286. PMID:26448658

Ceran, Y., Alagoz, A., & Ortakarpuz, M. (2013). Incoterms Costs in International Marketing and Their Effects on Product Pricing. In *8th Annual London Business Research Conference*. London: Imperial College.

Cerchione, R., & Esposito, E. (2016). A systematic review of supply chain knowledge management research: State of the art and research opportunities. *International Journal of Production Economics, 182*, 276–292.

Cereda, D., Tirani, M., Rovida, F., Demicheli, V., Ajelli, M., Poletti, P., . . . Barone, A. (2020). *The early phase of the COVID-19 outbreak in Lombardy, Italy*. arXiv preprint arXiv:2003.09320.

Chae, B., & Olson, D. L. (2013). Business analytics for supply chain: A dynamic-capabilities framework. *International Journal of Information Technology & Decision Making, 12*(01), 9–26.

Challender, J., Farrell, P., & Sherratt, F. (2016). Effects of an economic downturn on construction partnering. *Proceedings of Institution of Civil Engineers: Management, Procurement and Law, 169*(4), 159–167. doi:10.1680/jmapl.15.00033

Chandra, C., & Tumanyan, A. (2007). Organization and problem ontology for supply chain information support system. *Data & Knowledge Engineering, 61*(2), 263–280.

Chandra, P. (1993). A dynamic distribution model with warehouse and customer replenishment requirements. *The Journal of the Operational Research Society, 44*(7), 681–692. doi:10.1057/jors.1993.117

Chandra, P., & Fisher, M. L. (1994). Coordination of production and distribution planning. *European Journal of Operational Research, 72*(3), 503–517. doi:10.1016/0377-2217(94)90419-7

Chang, I. C., Hwang, H. G., Liaw, H. C., Hung, M. C., Chen, S. L., & Yen, D. C. (2008). A neural network evaluation model for ERP performance from SCM perspective to enhance enterprise competitive advantage. *Expert Systems with Applications, 35*(4), 1809–1816.

Chardine-Baumann, E., & Botta-Genoulaz, V. (2014). A framework for sustainable performance assessment of supply chain management practices. *Computers & Industrial Engineering, 76*, 138–147.

Charumilind, S., Turabi, P., Finn, O., & Usher, A. (2020). *Demystifying modeling: How quantitative models can and cant change the world.* Mckinsey and Company. Available from https://www.mckinsey.com/~/media/McKinsey/Business%20 Functions/Risk/Our%20Insights/Demystifying%20modeling%20How%20quantitative%20models%20can%20and%20 cant%20explain%20the%20world/Demystifying-modeling-how-quantitative-models-VF.pdf

Chatain, O., & Zemsky, P. (2007). The Horizontal Scope of the Firm: Organizational Tradeoffs vs. Buyer-Supplier Relationships. *Management Science, 53*(4), 550–565.

Cheaitou, A., Hamdan, S., & Larbi, R. (2021). Liner shipping network design with sensitive demand. *Maritime Business Review*. doi:10.1108/MABR-10-2019-0045

Chen, C., Wang, Y., Huang, G., & Xiong, H. (2019) Demand Forecasting for Factory Production of Perishable Goods. *Big Data,* 188-193. Available from https://ieeexplore.ieee.org/document/9006161

Chen, J. V., Yen, D. C., Rajkumar, T., & Tomochko, N. A. (2011). The antecedent factors on trust and commitment in supply chain relationships. *Computer Standards & Interfaces, 33*(3), 262-270. doi:10.1016/j.csi.2010.05.003

Chen, C., Wang, Y., Huang, G., & Xiong, H. (2019). *Hierarchical Demand Forecasting for Factory Production of Perishable Goods.* IEEE International Conference on Big Dat. Available from https://ieeexplore.ieee.org/document/9006161

Chen, C., & Zeng, Q. (2010). Designing container shipping network under changing demand and freight rates. *Transport, 25*(1), 46–57. doi:10.3846/transport.2010.07

Chen, F., Drezner, Z., Ryan, J. K., & Simchi-Levi, D. (2000). Quantifying the bullwhip effect in a simple supply chain: The impact of forecasting, lead times, and information. *Management Science, 46*(3), 436–443.

Chengalur-Smith, I., Duchessi, P., & Gil-Garcia, J. R. (2012). Information sharing and business systems leveraging in supply chains: An empirical investigation of one web-based application. *Information & Management, 49*(1), 58–67.

Cheng, J. C., Law, K. H., Bjornsson, H., Jones, A., & Sriram, R. (2010). A service oriented framework for construction supply chain integration. *Automation in Construction, 19*(2), 245–260.

Chen, J. V., Yen, D. C., Rajkumar, T. M., & Tomochko, N. A. (2011). The antecedent factors on trust and commitment in supply chain relationships. *Computer Standards & Interfaces, 33*(3), 262–270.

Cheung, Y.-L., Kong, D., Tan, W., & Wang, W. (2015). Being Good When Being International in an Emerging Economy: The Case of China. *Journal of Business Ethics, 130*(4), 805–817. doi:10.100710551-014-2268-7

Chien, L. (2011). *A Survey of Biometrics Security Systems.* https://www.cs.wustl.edu/~jain/cse571-11/ftp/biomet/

Cho, Y.K. (2015). The relationship between resources and market coverage in small local internet retailing. *International Journal of Retail & Distribution Management, 43*(7), 597-616. doi:10.1108/IJRDM-12-2013-0220

Cho, D. W., & Lee, Y. H. (2013). The value of information sharing in a supply chain with a seasonal demand process. *Computers & Industrial Engineering, 65*(1), 97–108.

Chopra, R., & Chopra, A. (2012). Innovative Hr Practices For Competitive Advantage: A Strategic Perspective. *Journal of Organisation & Human Behavior, 1*(2), 2012.

Chopra, S., & Meindl, P. (2001). *Supply Chain Management.* Prentice-Hall.

Chouinard, M., D'Amours, S., & Aït-Kadi, D. (2005). Integration of reverse logistics activities within a supply chain information system. *Computers in Industry, 56*(1), 105–124. doi:10.1016/j.compind.2004.07.005

Christiansen, M., Hellsten, E., Pisinger, D., Sacramento, D., & Vilhelmsen, C. (2020). Liner shipping network design. *European Journal of Operational Research, 286*(1), 1–20. doi:10.1016/j.ejor.2019.09.057

Christopher, M. (2006), *Logistics and Supply Chain Management.* Financial Times/Pitman.

Christopher, M. (1992). *Logistics and Supply Chain Management.* Pitman Publishing.

Chung, S. H., & Kwon, C. (2016). Integrated supply chain management for perishable products: Dynamics and oligopolistic competition perspectives with application to pharmaceuticals. *International Journal of Production Economics, 179*, 117–129.

Clarke, G., & Wright, J. W. (1964). Scheduling of vehicles from a central depot to a number of delivery points. *Operations Research, 12*(4), 568–581. doi:10.1287/opre.12.4.568

Clarke-Hill, C. M., Robinson, T. M., & Bailey, J. (1998). Skills and competence transfers in European retail alliances: A comparison between alliances and joint ventures. *European Business Review*, *8*(6), 300–310. doi:10.1108/09555349810241572

Clemen, R. T., & Reilly, T. (2013). *Making Hard Decisions with Decision Tools* (3rd ed.). Cengage Learning.

Cojocariu, C. R. (2013). The Reverse Gear of Logistics. *Review of International Comparative Management*, *14*(1), 153–164.

Colin, M., Galindo, R., & Hernández, O. (2015). Information and communication technology as a key strategy for efficient supply chain management in manufacturing SMEs. *Procedia Computer Science*, *55*, 833–842.

Conger, J. (2000). The Necessary Art of Persuasion. *Harvard Business Review*, *76*, 84–97. PMID:10179656

Conner, K. R. (1991). A historical comparison of resource based theory and five schools of thought within industrial organization economics: Do we have a new theory of the firm? *Journal of Management*, *17*(1), 121–154. doi:10.1177/014920639101700109

Connolly, T., Conlon, E. J., & Deutsch, S. J. (1980). Organizational effectiveness: A multiple-constituency approach. *Academy of Management Review*, *5*(2), 211–217. doi:10.5465/amr.1980.4288727

Cooper, G. J. (2003). *The Science of the Struggle for Existence: On the Foundations of Ecology*. Cambridge University Press. doi:10.1017/CBO9780511720154

Cooper, M. C., Lambert, D. M., & Pagh, J. D. (1997). Supply chain management: More than a new name for logistics. *International Journal of Logistics Management*, *8*(1), 1–14.

Coskun, S., Ozgur, L., Polat, O., & Gungor, A. (2016). A model proposal for green supply chain network design based on consumer segmentation. *Journal of Cleaner Production*, *110*, 149–157. doi:10.1016/j.jclepro.2015.02.063

Coughlan, A. T. (2002). Channel Management: Structure, Governance, and Relationship Management. In *Handbook of Marketing*. Sage Publications.

Council, S. C. (2008). Supply-chain operations reference-model. *Overview of SCOR Version, 5*(0). Available on: http://supply-chain.org/

Craighead, C. W., Blackhurst, J., Rungtusanatham, M. J., & Handfield, R. B. (2007). The severity of supply chain disruptions: Design characteristics and mitigation capabilities. *Decision Sciences*, *38*(1), 131–156. doi:10.1111/j.1540-5915.2007.00151.x

Craver, C. B. (2012). *The Benefits to Be Derived from Post-Negotiation Assessments.* GW Law Faculty Publications & Other Works. 464.

Creager, M. A., Belkin, M., & Bluth, E. I. (2012). 2012 ACCF / AHA / ACR / SCAI / SIR / STS / SVM / SVN / SVS Key Data Elements and Definitions for Peripheral Atherosclerotic Vascular Disease: A Report of the American College of Cardiology Foundation / American Heart Association Task Force on Clinical Data Standards (Writing Committee to Develop Clinical Data Standards for Peripheral Atherosclerotic Vascular Disease). *Am Coll Cardiol*, *59*(3), 294–357.

Crook, T. R., Giunipero, L., Reus, T. H., Handfield, R., & Williams, S. K. (2008). Antecedents and outcomes of supply chain effectiveness: An exploratory investigation. *Journal of Managerial Issues*, •••, 161–177.

Cullinane, S. L., & Cullinane, K. P. (2018). The Reverse Logistics of Cross-Border e-Tailing in Europe: Developing a Research Agenda to Assess the Environmental Impacts. *International Journal of Applied Logistics*, *8*(1), 1–19.

Curtis, A. M., Wells, T. M., Lowry, P. B., & Higbee, T. (2008). An Overview and Tutorial of the Repertory Grid Technique in Information Systems Research. Communications of the Association for Information Systems, 23. doi:10.17705/1CAIS.02303

Czepiel, J. (1992). *Competitive Marketing Strategy*. Prentice Hall.

Dale, S. R., Douglas, M. L., Keely, L. C., & Sebastián, J. G.-D. (2002). The Returns Management Process. *International Journal of Logistics Management, 13*(2), 1–18. doi:10.1108/09574090210806397

Darvish, M., Archetti, C., & Coelho, L. C. (2018). Trade-offs between environmental and economic performance in production and inventory-routing problems. *International Journal of Production Economics.*

Dasaklis, T. K., Pappis, C. P., & Rachaniotis, N. P. (2012). Epidemics control and logistics operations: A review. *International Journal of Production Economics, 139*(2), 393–410.

Daú, G., Scavarda, A., Scavarda, L. F., & Portugal, V. J. T. (2019). The healthcare sustainable supply chain 4.0: The circular economy transition conceptual framework with the corporate social responsibility mirror. *Sustainability, 11*(12).

Davis, C. J., & Hufnagel, E. M. (2007). Through the eyes of experts: A socio-cognitive perspective on the automation of fingerprint work. *Management Information Systems Quarterly, 31*(4), 681–703. doi:10.2307/25148816

de Brito, M. P., & Dekker, R. (2002). *Reverse Logistics - a framework.* Erasmus University Rotterdam Econometric Institute Report EI 2002-38.

de Brito, M. P., & Dekker, R. (2003). *A Framework for Reverse Logistics.* Rotterdam School of Management: Erasmus Research Institute of Management (ERIM).

de Campos, E. A. R., Tavana, M., ten Caten, C. S., Bouzon, M., & de Paula, I. C. (2021a). A grey-DEMATEL approach for analyzing factors critical to the implementation of reverse logistics in the pharmaceutical care process. *Environmental Science and Pollution Research International, 28*, 14156–14176. doi:10.100711356-020-11138-8 PMID:33206293

de Campos, E. A. R., ten Caten, C. S., & de Paula, I. C. (2021b). End-of-use and end-of-life medicines—Insights from pharmaceutical care process into waste medicines management. *Environmental Science and Pollution Research International.* Advance online publication. doi:10.100711356-021-14661-4 PMID:34105077

de Haas, M., Faber, R., & Hamersma, M. (2020). How COVID-19 and the Dutch 'intelligent lockdown' change activities, work and travel behaviour: Evidence from longitudinal data in the Netherlands. *Transportation Research Interdisciplinary Perspectives, 6*, 100150. doi:10.1016/j.trip.2020.100150 PMID:34171019

De Ruyter, K., Moorman, L., & Lemmink, J. (2001). Antecedents of commitment and trust in customer-supplier relationships in high technology markets. *Industrial Marketing Management, 30*(3), 271-286. doi:10.1016/S0019-8501(99)00091-7

De Vos, J. (2020). The effect of COVID-19 and subsequent social distancing on travel behavior. *Transportation Research Interdisciplinary Perspectives, 5*, 100121. doi:10.1016/j.trip.2020.100121 PMID:34171016

De Vries, T. A., Van Der Vegt, G. S., Scholten, K., & Pieter Van Donk, D. (2021). Heeding Supply Chain Disruption Warnings: When And How Do Cross-Functional Teams Ensure Firm Robustness? *The Journal of Supply Chain Management.* Advance online publication. doi:10.1111/jscm.12262

De Wever, S., Lievens, A., Martens, R., & Vandenbempt, K. (2005). Developing capabilities through networks: a step-by-step process. In S. Ron & H. Aime (Eds.), *Competence Perspectives on Managing Interfirm Interactions* (Vol. 8, pp. 71–110). Emerald Group Publishing Limited. doi:10.1016/S0749-6826(04)08004-7

Debono, P. (2019). Transforming Public Procurement Contracts Into Smart Contracts. *International Journal of Information Technology Project Management, 10*(2), 16–28. doi:10.4018/IJITPM.2019040103

Dekker, R., Bloemhof, J., & Mallidis, I. (2012). Operations Research for Green Logistics – an Overview of Aspects, Issues, Contributions and Challenges. *European Journal of Operational Research, 219*(3), 671–679. doi:10.1016/j.ejor.2011.11.010

Delipinar, G. E., & Kocaoglu, B. (2016). Using SCOR model to gain competitive advantage: A Literature review. *Procedia: Social and Behavioral Sciences, 229*, 398–406.

Dell, R., Moseley, P., & Rand, D. (2014). *Towards Sustainable Road Transport*. Academic Press.

Demchenko, Y., Ngo, C., & Membrey, P. (2013). Architecture framework and components for the big data ecosystem. *Journal of System and Network Engineering*, 1-31.

Demidova, O., & Yakovlev, A. (2012). State-Business relations and participation of firms in public procurement in Russia: An empirical study. *Journal of Public Procurement, 12*(4), 547–592. doi:10.1108/JOPP-12-04-2012-B004

Dess, G. G., & Beard, D. W. (1984). Dimensions of organizational task environments. *Administrative Science Quarterly, 29*(1), 52–73. doi:10.2307/2393080

Dess, G. G., & Davis, P. S. (1984). Porter's (1980) Generic Strategies as Determinants of Strategic Group Membership and Organizational Performance. *Academy of Management Journal, 27*(3), 467–488.

Dess, G. G., & Robinson, R. B. Jr. (1984). Measuring organizational performance in the absence of objective measures: The case of the privately-held firm and conglomerate business unit. *Strategic Management Journal, 5*(3), 265–273. doi:10.1002mj.4250050306

Dettmer, H. W. (2014). *The Logical Thinking Process: A Systems Approach to Complex Problem-Solving* (8th ed.). ASQ Quality Press.

Dias, R, Pitassi, C, & Joia, L. (2003). *Integrated management of the supply chain*. Rio de Janeiro: FGV, EBAPE.

Dijkstra, E. W. (1959). A note on two problems in connexion with graphs. *Numerische Mathematik, 1*(1), 269–271. doi:10.1007/BF01386390

Ding, H., Guo, B., & Liu, Z. (2011). Information sharing and profit allotment based on supply chain cooperation. *International Journal of Production Economics, 133*(1), 70–79.

Dolci, P. C., Maçada, A. C. G., & Grant, G. G. (2017). Making Sense of Information Technology Investment on Type of Supply Chain Governance. In Handbook of Research on Technology Adoption, Social Policy, and Global Integration (pp. 258-279). IGI Global.

Domingo, T. (2015).*"Identifying and eliminating the seven wastes or muda*. Godina Nepoznata: Asian Institute of Management. Available from http://rtdbiz.com/BMA/MM/SevenWastes.pdf

Donaldson-Feilder, E., Yarker, J., & Lewis, R. (2008). *Ine management competence: the key to preventing and reducing stress at work*. Emeraldinsight. Available from https://www.emerald.com/insight/content/doi/10.1108/14754390810853110/full/pdf?title=line-management-competence-the-key-to-preventing-and-reducing-stress-at-work

Dong, J.-X., & Song, D.-P. (2012). Quantifying the impact of inland transport times on container fleet sizing in liner shipping services with uncertainties. *OR-Spektrum, 34*(1), 155–180. doi:10.100700291-009-0185-4

Dooley, M. J., Allen, K. M., Doecke, C. J., Galbraith, K. J., Taylor, G. R., Bright, J., & Carey, D. L. (2004). A prospective multicentre study of pharmacist initiated changes to drug therapy and patient management in acute care government funded hospitals. *British Journal of Clinical Pharmacology, 57*(4), 513–521. doi:10.1046/j.1365-2125.2003.02029.x PMID:15025751

Dooner, R. (2014). How supply chain management can help to control health-care cost. *Supply Chain Q. Q., 3*, 50–53.

Doukidis, G. I., Matopoulos, A., Vlachopoulou, M., Manthou, V., & Manos, B. (2007). A conceptual framework for supply chain collaboration: Empirical evidence from the agri-food industry. *Supply Chain Management, 12*(3), 177–186. doi:10.1108/13598540710742491

Dowlatshahi, S. (2000). Developing a theory of reverse logistics. *Interfaces, 30*(3), 143.

Duffy, M., Joakim, V., & Swartout, P. (2016). *Learning DevOps: Continuously Deliver Better Software.* Packt Publishing.

Dugardin, F., Yalaoui, F., & Amodeo, L. (2012). Hybrid multi-objective methods to solve reentrant shops. *International Journal of Applied Logistics, 3*(4), 15–32. doi:10.4018/jal.2012100102

Dupre, K., & Gruen, T. (2004). The use of category management practices to obtain a sustainable competitive advantage in the fast-moving consumer-goods industry. *Journal of Business & Industrial Marketing, 19*(7), 444-459.

Du, T. C., Lai, V. S., Cheung, W., & Cui, X. (2012). Willingness to share information in a supply chain: A partnership-data-process perspective. *Information & Management, 49*(2), 89–98.

Dutta, D. K., & Hora, M. (2017). From Invention Success to Commercialization Success: Technology Ventures and the Benefits of Upstream and Downstream Supply-Chain Alliances. *Journal of Small Business Management, 55*(2), 216–235.

Easterby-Smith, M., Thorpe, R., & Holman, D. (1996). Using repertory grids in management. *Journal of European Industrial Training, 20*(3), 3–30. doi:10.1108/03090599610114138

Eaton, M. (2003). *The Lean Practitioner's Handbook.* Kogan Page.

Ebrahim-Khanjari, N., Hopp, W., & Iravani, S. M. R. (2012). Trust and information sharing in supply chains [Review]. *Production and Operations Management, 21*(3), 444–464. doi:10.1111/j.1937-5956.2011.01284.x

Elmuti, D., Khoury, G., Omran, O., & Abou-Zaid, A. S. (2013). Challenges and opportunities of health care supply chain management in the United States. *Health Marketing Quarterly, 30*(2), 128–143. PMID:23697853

Emerson, C. J., & Grimm, C. M. (1996). Logistics and Marketing Components of Customer Service: An Empirical Test of the Mentzer, Gomes and Krapfel Model. *International Journal of Physical Distribution & Logistics, 26*(8), 29–42. doi:10.1108/09600039610128258

Erb, J., & James, S. (2017). *Global logistics for dummies.* John Wiley & Sons.

Erdmann, J. (2015). SUMO's lane-changing model Modeling Mobility with Open Data. Springer.

Eric, P. J., Thomas, L. P., & Lauren, S. (2010). Reverse logistics capabilities: Antecedents and cost savings. *International Journal of Physical Distribution & Logistics Management, 40*(3), 228–246. doi:10.1108/09600031011035100

Erkip, F., & Ozuduru, B.H. (2015). *Retail development in Turkey: An account after two decades of shopping malls in the urban scene.* Academic Press.

Ertel, D. (1999). Turning Negotiation into a Corporate Capability. *Harvard Business Review, 77*(3), 55–56. PMID:10387578

Etzioni, A. (1964). *Modern organizations.* Prentice Hall.

European Commission. (2020). *EU Transport in Figures 2020.* Author.

Eurostat. (2017). *Road freight transport statistics.* Retrieved from https://ec.europa.eu/eurostat/statistics-explained/index.php/Road_freight_transport_statistics

Eurostat. (2019). *Road freight transport statistics: EU road freight transport continues to grow*. Retrieved from https://ec.europa.eu/eurostat/statistics-explained/index.php/Road_freight_transport_statistics

Faass, J., Greenberg, M., & Lowrie, K. W. (2013). Defending a moving target: H1N1 preparedness training for the transit industry. *Health Promotion Practice*, *14*(1), 24–29. doi:10.1177/1524839911399432 PMID:21460256

Farris, D. R., & Sage, A. P. (1975). On the use of interpretive structural modeling for worth assessment. *Computers & Electrical Engineering*, *2*(2–3), 149–174. doi:10.1016/0045-7906(75)90004-X

Fawcett, S. E., Wallin, C., Allred, C., Fawcett, A. M., & Magnan, G. M. (2011). Information technology as an enabler of supply chain collaboration: A dynamic-capabilities perspective. *The Journal of Supply Chain Management*, *47*(1), 38–59.

Fayezi, S., Zomorrodi, M., & Bals, L. (2018). Procurement sustainability tensions: An integrative perspective. *International Journal of Physical Distribution & Logistics Management*, *48*(6), 586–609. doi:10.1108/IJPDLM-01-2017-0013

Feeny, D. (1988). Creating and Sustaining Competitive Advantage with IT. In Information Management: The Strategic Dimension. Oxford University Press.

Feixas, G., Geldschläger, H., & Neimeyer, R. A. (2002). Content analysis of personal constructs. *Journal of Constructivist Psychology*, *15*(1), 1–19. doi:10.1080/107205302753305692

Field, A. (2003). How to negotiate with a Hard-Nosed Adversary? *Harvard Management Update*, *8*(3), 1–3.

Fisher, M., & Vaidyanathan, R. (2014). A demand estimation procedure for retail assortment optimization with results from implementations. *Management Science*, *60*(10), 2401–2415. doi:10.1287/mnsc.2014.1904

Fisher, R., Ury, W. L., & Patton, B. (2011). *Getting to yes: Negotiating agreement without giving in*. Penguin Books.

Fisher, W., & Ertel, D. (1995). *Getting Ready to Negotiate: The Getting to Yes Workbook*. Penguin Books.

Fisher, W., & Ury, W. (2011). *Getting to Yes: Negotiating agreement without giving in* (3rd ed.). Penguin Books.

Fiske, A. (1990). Relativity within Moose ("Mossi") Culture: Four Incommensurable Models for Social Relationships. *Ethos (Berkeley, Calif.)*, *18*(2), 180–204. doi:10.1525/eth.1990.18.2.02a00040

Ford, J. D., & Schellenberg, D. A. (1982). Conceptual issues of linkage in the assessment of organizational performance. *Academy of Management Review*, *7*(1), 49–58. doi:10.5465/amr.1982.4285450

Forslund, H., & Jonsson, P. (2009). Obstacles to supply chain integration of the performance management process in buyer-supplier dyads: The buyers' perspective. *International Journal of Operations & Production Management*, *29*(1), 77–95.

Fowkes, F. G., Rudan, D., & Rudan, I. (2013). Comparison of global estimates of prevalence and risk factors for peripheral artery disease in 2000 and 2010: A systematic review and analysis. *Lancet*, *382*(9901), 1329–1340. PMID:23915883

Franz, M., Appel, A., & Hassler, M. (2013). Short waves of super- market diffusion in Turkey. *Moravian Geographical Reports*, *21*(4), 50–63. doi:10.2478/mgr-2013-0020

Freitag, D. (1979). History of wheels for off - road transport. *Journal of Terramechanics*, *16*(2), 49–68. doi:10.1016/0022-4898(79)90001-6

Frigo, M. L. (2002). Strategic capabilities of return driven strategy. *Strategic Finance, 83*(12), 6-9.

Friman, M., Gärling, T., Millett, B., Mattsson, J., & Johnston, R. (2002). An analysis of international business-to-business relationships based on the Commitment–Trust theory. *Industrial Marketing Management*, *31*(5), 403–409. doi:10.1016/S0019-8501(01)00154-7

Fynes, B., Voss, C., & de Búrca, S. (2005). The impact of supply chain relationship quality on quality performance. *International Journal of Production Economics*, *96*(3), 339–354.

Galbraith, J. K. (1983). The Anatomy of Power. *The Challenge (Karachi)*, *26*(3), 26–33. doi:10.1080/05775132.1983.11470852

Galia. (2007). *Evalog: Global Evalog frame of reference*. Academic Press.

Galinsky, A. D. (2004). Should you make the first offer? *Negotiation.*, *7*, 1–4.

Galli, B. J. (2021). How to effectively implement continuous improvement for environmental sustainability. *International Journal of Applied Logistics*, *11*(1), 38–51. doi:10.4018/IJAL.2021010103

Gao, S., Rao, J., Kang, Y., Liang, Y., & Kruse, J. (2020). Mapping county-level mobility pattern changes in the United States in response to COVID-19. *SIGSpatial Special*, *12*(1), 16–26. doi:10.1145/3404820.3404824

Gatica, G., Papageorgiou, L. G., & Shah, N. (2003). Capacity planning under uncertainty for the pharmaceutical industry. *Chemical Engineering Research & Design*, *81*(6), 665–678.

Gaukler, G. M., Seifert, R. W., & Hausman, W. H. (2007). Item-level RFID in the retail supply chain. *Production and Operations Management*, *16*(1), 65–76.

Geary, S., Disney, S. M., & Towill, D. R. (2006). On bullwhip in supply chains—Historical review, present practice and expected future impact. *International Journal of Production Economics*, *101*(1), 2–18.

Geerlings, H., & van Duin, R. (2011). A New Method for Assessing Co2-Emissions from Container Terminals: A Promising Approach Applied in Rotterdam. *Journal of Cleaner Production*, *19*(6), 657–666. doi:10.1016/j.jclepro.2010.10.012

Gekara, V., & Chhetri, P. (2013). Upstream Transport Corridor Inefficiencies and the Implications for Port Performance: A Case Analysis of Mombasa Port and the Northern Corridor. *Maritime Policy & Management*, *40*(6), 559–573. doi:10.1080/03088839.2013.776716

General Directorate of Pharmaceutical Inspection. (2010). *breaches of pharmaceutical regulation report Code (No. FM-GID-01 Serial: 00001/ 2009)*. Egypt: Ministry of Health. Retrieved from http://www.mohp.gov.eg/pharmacy/DocLib2/Final%20Inspection%20Report%2030-11-2010.pdf

Gengeswari, K., Bakar, A., & Zaleha, S. (2012). Impact of information technologies (IT) implementation on over\all TSC performance. *Asian Journal of Business and Management Sciences*, *1*(11), 100–108.

Ghadge, A., Dani, S., & Kalawsky, R. (2012). Supply chain risk management: Present and future scope. *International Journal of Logistics Management*, *23*(3), 313–339.

Ghahremani, F., & Tarokh, M. J. (2013). IT-Based classification for supply chain coordination mechanisms. In *Technological Solutions for Modern Logistics and Supply Chain Management* (pp. 148–162). IGI Global.

Gharehgozli, A. H., Roy, D., & De Koster, R. (2016). Sea Container Terminals: New Technologies and or Models. *Maritime Economics & Logistics*, *18*(2), 103–140. doi:10.1057/mel.2015.3

Giannatos, G., & Andrianopoulos, S. (1999). *Logistics, Transport and Distribution*. Tekdotiki.

Gioia, D. A., & Pitre, E. (1990). Multiparadigm perspectives on theory building. *Academy of Management Review*, *15*(4), 584–602. doi:10.5465/amr.1990.4310758

Glock, C. H. (2017). Decision support models for managing returnable transport items in supply chains: A systematic literature review. *International Journal of Production Economics*, *183*, 561–569.

Gobble, M. M. (2013). Big data: The next big thing in innovation. *Research Technology Management*, *56*(1), 64–66.

Golan, M. S., Jernegan, L. H., & Linkov, I. (2020). Trends and applications of resilience analytics in supply chain modeling: Systematic literature review in the context of the COVID-19 pandemic. *Environment Systems & Decisions*, *40*(2), 222–243. doi:10.100710669-020-09777-w PMID:32837820

Goldratt, E. M. (1999). *What Is This Thing Called Theory of Constraints and how should it be implemented?* North River Press.

Goodchild, A. V., & Daganzo, C. F. (2007). Crane Double Cycling in Container Ports: Planning Methods and Evaluation. *Transportation Research Part B: Methodological*, *41*(8), 875–891. doi:10.1016/j.trb.2007.02.006

Gosselin, T. (2007). Practical Negotiating. Tools, Tactics & Techniques. John Wiley & Sons.

Goswami, M. P., & Wettstein, D. (2016). Rational bidding in a procurement auction with subjective evaluations. *International Journal of Industrial Organization*, *44*, 60–67. doi:10.1016/j.ijindorg.2015.10.001

Gough, L. (2011) *Parkinsons's Law.* Infinite Ideas Limited. Available from http://www.infideas.com/books/c-northcote-parkinsons-parkinsons-law/

Graaff, E., & Kolmos, A. (2007) Managemnet of Change. In Management of Change - Implementation of Problem-Based and Project-Based Learning in Engineering. Sense.

Grabara, J., Man, M., & Kolcun, M. (2014). The benefits of reverse logistics. *International Letters of Social and Humanistic Sciences*, (15), 138–147.

Grant, D., Trautrims, A., & Yew Wong, C. (2015). *Sustainable Logistics and Supply Chain Management.* Kogan Page Limited.

Gray, A., & Manasse, H. R. (2012). Shortages of medicines: A complex global challenge. *Bulletin of the World Health Organization*, *90*(3), 158–158A. doi:10.2471/BLT.11.101303 PMID:22461706

Griffiths, J., & Margetts, D. (2000). *Variation in production schedules—implications for both the company and its suppliers. Journal of Materials Processing Technology, 103(1).* https://www.sciencedirect.com/science/article/pii/S0924013600004088

Grimm, C. M. (2006). Strategic paradigms of competitive advantage. Academic Press.

Grochenig, E. (2012). *Elektronische Oszilographie. Nicht invasive Diagnostik angiologischer Krankheitsbilder* (2nd ed.). ABW.

Gu, A., Wertheimer, A. I., Brown, B., & Shaya, T. F. (2011). Drug shortages in the US causes, impacts and strategies. *Innovations in Pharmacy*, *2*(60), 2–6. doi:10.24926/iip.v2i4.243

Guarnieri, P., & Gomes, R. (2019). Can public procurement be strategic? A future agenda proposition. *Journal of Public Procurement*, *19*(4), 295–321. doi:10.1108/JOPP-09-2018-0032

Gulati, R. (1995). Does familiarity breed trust? The implications of repeated ties for contractual choice in alliances. *Academy of Management Journal*, *38*(1), 85–112. doi:10.5465/256729

Gulati, R., & Sytch, M. (2007). Dependence asymmetry and joint dependence in interorganizational relationships: Effects of embeddedness on a manufacturer's performance in procurement relationships. *Administrative Science Quarterly*, *52*(1), 32–69. doi:10.2189/asqu.52.1.32

Gumzej, R., & Gajšek, B. (2011). Introducing Quality of Service Criteria into Supply Chain Management for Excellence. *International Journal of Applied Logistics*, *2*(1), 1–16. doi:10.4018/ijal.2011010101

Gunasekaran, A., & Ngai, E. W. T. (2004). Information systems in supply chain integration and management. *European Journal of Operational Research*, *159*, 269–295.

Gunasekaran, A., Patel, C., & McGaughey, E. (2004). A framework for supply chain performance measurement. *International Journal of Production Economics*, *87*, 333–347.

Gupta, A., Evans, G. W., & Heragu, S. S. (2013). Simulation and optimization modeling for drive-through mass vaccination–A generalized approach. *Simulation Modelling Practice and Theory*, *37*, 99–106.

Gupta, S. M. (Ed.). (2013). *Reverse Supply Chains Issues and Analysis*. Taylor & Francis Group.

Hafeez, K., Hooi Keoy, K., & Hanneman, R. (2006). E-business capabilities model: Validation and comparison between adopter and non-adopter of e-business companies in UK. *Journal of Manufacturing Technology Management*, *17*(6), 806–828. doi:10.1108/17410380610678819

Hair, N., Rose, S., & Clark, M. (2009). Using qualitative repertory grid techniques to explore perceptions of business-to-business online customer experience. *Journal of Customer Behaviour*, *8*(1), 51–65. doi:10.1362/147539209X414380

Hamel, G., & Prahalad, K. C. (1993). Strategy as stretch and leverage. *Harvard Business Review*, *71*(March- April), 75–84. PMID:10124635

Hammami, R. (2006). Deniz Kandiyoti. *Development and Change*, *37*(6), 1347–1354. doi:10.1111/j.1467-7660.2006.00530.x

Hammond, J. S., Keeney, R. L., & Raiffa, H. (2006). The Hidden Traps in Decision Making. *Harvard Business Review*, *84*(1), 1–9. PMID:10185432

Handfield, R., Jeong, S., & Choi, T. (2019). Emerging procurement technology: Data analytics and cognitive analytics. *International Journal of Physical Distribution & Logistics Management*, *49*(10), 972–1002. doi:10.1108/IJPDLM-11-2017-0348

Hands, L. J., Clarke, M., & Mahaffey, W. (2006). An e-health approach to managing vascular surgical patients. *Telemedicine Journal and e-Health*, *12*, 672–680. PMID:17250489

Hansen, K. R. N., & Grunow, M. (2015). Planning operations before market launch for balancing time-to-market and risks in pharmaceutical supply chains. *International Journal of Production Economics*, *161*, 129–139.

Hansen, P., Mladenović, N., & Pérez, J. M. (2010). Developments of variable neighborhood search. *Annals of Operations Research*, *175*(1), 367–407. doi:10.100710479-009-0657-6

Harrington, L. (2015). *Solving the talent crisis: Five alternatives every supply chain executive must consider*. Academic Press.

Harrington, L., Kennerly, D., & Johnson, C. (2011). Safety issues related to the electronic medical record (EMR): Synthesis of the literature from the last decade 2000-2009. *Journal of Healthcare Management*, *56*(1), 31–43. PMID:21323026

Harrison, A., & Hoek, R. (2012). *Logistics Management & Strategy*. Rosili.

Hasani Goodarzi, A., & Hessameddin Zegordi, S. (2016). A Location-Routing Problem for Cross-Docking Networks: A Biogeography-Based Optimization Algorithm. *Computers & Industrial Engineering*, *102*, 132–146. doi:10.1016/j.cie.2016.10.023

Hatten, K. J., & Hatten, M. L. (1985). Some empirical insights for strategic marketers: The case of beer. In H. Thomas & D. M. Gardner (Eds.), *Strategic marketing and management* (Vol. 1, pp. 275–292). John Wiley and Sons Ltd.

Hausman, A., & Johnston, W. J. (2010). The impact of coercive and non-coercive forms of influence on trust, commitment, and compliance in supply chains. *Industrial Marketing Management*, *39*(3), 519–526. doi:10.1016/j.indmarman.2009.05.007

Hawkins, T., Nissen, M., & Rendon, R. (2014). Leveraging strategic sourcing and knowledge management to improve the acquisition of knowledge-based services. *Journal of Public Procurement*, *14*(2), 215–251. doi:10.1108/JOPP-14-02-2014-B003

Hazen, B. T., Overstreet, R. E., Hall, D. J., Huscroft, J. R., & Hanna, J. B. (2015). Antecedents to and outcomes of reverse logistics metrics. *Industrial Marketing Management*, (0). Advance online publication. doi:10.1016/j.indmarman.2015.01.017

Helo, P., & Szekely, B. (2005). Logistics information systems: An analysis of software solutions for supply chain coordination. *Industrial Management & Data Systems*, *105*(1), 5–18.

Hemmelmayr, V. C., Doerner, K. F., & Hartl, R. F. (2009). A variable neighborhood search heuristic for periodic routing problems. *European Journal of Operational Research*, *195*(3), 791–802. doi:10.1016/j.ejor.2007.08.048

Henesey, L. (2004). *Enhancing Container Terminal Performance: A Multi Agent Systems Approach*. Blekinge Institute of Technology Licentiate Dissertation Series, Blekinge Institute of Technology. http://urn.kb.se/resolve?urn=urn:nbn:se:bth-00325

Hensher, D. A. (2020). *What might Covid-19 mean for mobility as a service (MaaS)?* Taylor & Francis.

Heyes, A. (2000). Implementing Environmental Regulation: Enforcement and Compliance. *Journal of Regulatory Economics*, *17*(2), 107.

Hietajärvi, A. M., & Karvonen, I. (2016). Management of Risks in Export Networks: The Role of Collaboration. *International Journal of Applied Logistics*, *6*(1), 47–63.

Hoch, S., & Byung-do Kim, A. L. (1995). Determinants of Store-Level Price Elasticity. *JMR, Journal of Marketing Research*, *32*(February), 17–29. doi:10.1177/002224379503200104

Hoff, A., Andersson, H., Christiansen, M., Hasle, G., & Løkettangen, A. (2010). Industrial aspects and literature survey: Fleet composition and routing. *Computers & Operations Research*, *37*(12), 2041–2061. doi:10.1016/j.cor.2010.03.015

Holweg, M., Disney, S., Holmström, J., & Småros, J. (2005). Supply chain collaboration: Making sense of the strategy continuum. *European Management Journal*, *23*(2), 170–181.

Ho, M. H., Hnaien, F., & Dugardin, F. (2021). Electricity cost minimization for optimal makespan solution in flow shop scheduling under time-of-use tariffs. *International Journal of Production Research*, *59*(4), 1041–1067. doi:10.1080/00207543.2020.1715504

Hood, C. (1995). The new public management in the 1980, s-variations on a theme. *Accounting, Organizations and Society*, *20*(2/3), 93–109. doi:10.1016/0361-3682(93)E0001-W

Horvat, U. (2019). *Prebivalstvo Maribora: razvoj in demografske značilnosti*. Maribor: Univerzitetna založba Univerze v Mariboru.

Hosseini, S., Ivanov, D., & Dolgui, A. (2019). Review of quantitative methods for supply chain resilience analysis. *Transportation Research Part E, Logistics and Transportation Review*, *125*, 285–307. doi:10.1016/j.tre.2019.03.001

Huang, G. Q., Lau, J. S., & Mak, K. L. (2003). The impacts of sharing production information on supply chain dynamics: A review of the literature. *International Journal of Production Research*, *41*(7), 1483–1517.

Huang, J., Wang, H., Fan, M., Zhuo, A., Sun, Y., & Li, Y. (2020). Understanding the impact of the COVID-19 pandemic on transportation-related behaviors with human mobility data. *Proceedings of the 26th ACM SIGKDD International Conference on Knowledge Discovery & Data Mining*. 10.1145/3394486.3412856

Huang, X., Chen, H., Liu, L., & Chen, J. (2020). Robust Optimization Model of Feeder Lines Routing Based on the Hub Port. *Transportation Journal*, *59*(3), 279–303. doi:10.5325/transportationj.59.3.0279

Hudnurkar, M., Jakhar, S., & Rathod, U. (2014). Factors affecting collaboration in supply chain: A literature review. *Procedia: Social and Behavioral Sciences*, *133*, 189–202.

Huete, L. M. (1997). *Servicions & Benefícios*. Ediciones Deusto.

Humang, W. P., Natsir, R., & Fisu, A. A. (2021). Development of a Feeder Port of Tanjung Ringgit Facilities to Support Implementation of Sea Tollway. *Jurnal Penelitian Transportasi Laut*, *23*(1), 1–8. doi:10.25104/transla.v23i1.1699

Hunter, M. G. (1997). The use of RepGrids to gather interview data about information systems analysts. *Information Systems Journal*, *7*(1), 67–81. doi:10.1046/j.1365-2575.1997.00005.x

Hunt, S. D. (2000). *A general theory of competition: Resources, competences, productivity, economic growth*. Sage.

Hunt, S. D., & Arnett, D. B. (2003). Resource-advantage theory and embeddedness: Explaining R-A theory's explanatory success. *Journal of Marketing Theory and Practice*, *11*(1), 1–17. doi:10.1080/10696679.2003.11501928

Hunt, S. D., & Morgan, R. M. (1995). The comparative advantage theory of competition. *Journal of Marketing*, *59*(April), 1–15. doi:10.1177/002224299505900201

Hussein, A. M., Abdullah, K. O., Faraj, K. A., & Hamamin, D. F. (2018). Radon Concentration in the Work Atmosphere of Cement Plants in the Sulaymaniyah Area, Iraq. *ARO-The Scientific Journal of Koya University*, *4*(1), 7–12. doi:10.14500/aro.10329

Hutchinson, D., Singh, J., Svensson, G., & Mysen, T. (2012). Inter-relationships among focal dimensions in relationship quality: A quantitative and exploratory approach. *International Journal of Procurement Management*, *5*(2), 229–252. doi:10.1504/IJPM.2012.045651

Iannone, F., & Thore, S. (2010). An economic logistics model for the multimodal inland distribution of maritime containers. *Rivista Internazionale di Economia dei Trasporti*, *37*(3), 281–326.

Inštitut za politike prostora. (2021). *Mestna občina Maribor spodbuja aktivno in trajnostno mobilnost*. Retrieved from https://ipop.si/2021/03/24/mestna-obcina-maribor-spodbuja-aktivno-in-trajnostno-mobilnost/

Ismail, E., Meltem Nurtanis, V., Funda Sivrikaya, S., Büyüközkan, G., Aras, N., Çakar, N. D., & Aybek, K. (2010). Exploring reverse supply chain management practices in Turkey. *Supply Chain Management*, *15*(1), 43–54. doi:10.1108/13598541011018111

Ittmann, H. W. (2015). The impact of big data and business analytics on supply chain management. *Journal of Transport and Supply Chain Management*, *9*(1), 1–9.

Ivanov, D. (2018). Revealing interfaces of supply chain resilience and sustainability: A simulation study. *International Journal of Production Research*, *56*(10), 3507–3523. doi:10.1080/00207543.2017.1343507

Ivanov, D., Dolgui, A., Sokolov, B., & Ivanova, M. (2017). Literature review on disruption recovery in the supply chain. *International Journal of Production Research*, *55*(20), 6158–6174. doi:10.1080/00207543.2017.1330572

Jääskeläinen, A., & Thitz, O. (2018). Prerequisites for performance measurement supporting purchaser-supplier collaboration. *Benchmarking*, *25*(1), 120–137. doi:10.1108/BIJ-08-2016-0121

Jadrijević, N., & Tomašević, M. (2011). *Feeder service development in Mediterranean ports toward more efficient transport technologies.* 14th International Conference on Transport Science – ICTS, Portoroz, Slovenia.

Jaggi, H. S., & Kadam, S. S. (2016). Integration of Spark framework in Supply Chain Management. *Procedia Computer Science*, 79.

Jain, V., Wadhwa, S., & Deshmukh, S. G. (2009). Revisiting information systems to support a dynamic supply chain: Issues and perspectives. *Production Planning and Control*, *20*(1), 17–29.

Jarmoszko, A. T., D'Onofrio, M., Lee-Partridge, J. E., & Petkova, O. (2013). Evaluating Sustainability and Greening Methods: A Conceptual Model for Information Technology Management. *International Journal of Applied Logistics*, *4*(3), 1–13.

Javna agencija Republike Slovenije za varnost prometa. (2021). *Stanje prometne varnosti 2020 – za petino manj mrtvih in poškodovanih, za petino manj prometnih nesreč*. Academic Press.

Jetly, G., Rossetti, C. L., & Handfield, R. (2012). A multi-agent simulation of the pharmaceutical supply chain. *Journal of Simulation*, *6*, 215–226.

Jin, W.-L. (2010). Macroscopic characteristics of lane-changing traffic. *Transportation Research Record: Journal of the Transportation Research Board*, *2188*(1), 55–63. doi:10.3141/2188-07

Jin, Y., & Hong, P. (2007). Coordinating global inter-firm product development. *Journal of Enterprise Information Management*, *20*(5), 544–561.

Johnson, B. (2015). Intermountain healthcare supply chain. *The 2015 Healthcare Supply Chain Conference*.

Joshi, A. W., & Stump, R. L. (1999). The contingent effect of specific asset investments on joint action in manufacturer-supplier relationships: An empirical test of the moderating role of reciprocal asset investments, uncertainty, and trust. *Journal of the Academy of Marketing Science*, *27*(3), 291–305. doi:10.1177/0092070399273001

Kaakeh, R., Sweet, B. V., Reilly, C., Bush, C., DeLoach, S., Higgins, B., Clark, A. M., & Stevenson, J. (2011). Impact of drug shortages on U.S. health systems. *American Journal of Health-System Pharmacy*, *68*(19), 1811–1819. doi:10.2146/ajhp110210 PMID:21930639

Kabir, M. I. (2013). Reverse Logistics in Pharmaceutical Industry. *International Journal of Supply Chain Management*, *2*(1).

Kalaitzi, D., Matopoulos, A., Bourlakis, M., & Tate, W. (2019). Supply chains under resource pressure: Strategies for improving resource efficiency and competitive advantage. *International Journal of Operations & Production Management*, *39*(12), 1323–1354. doi:10.1108/IJOPM-02-2019-0137

Kaliszewski, A., Kozłowski, A., Dąbrowski, J., & Klimek, H. (2020). Key factors of container port competitiveness: A global shipping lines perspective. *Marine Policy*, *117*, 103896. doi:10.1016/j.marpol.2020.103896

Kamalahmadi, M., & Parast, M. M. (2016). A review of the literature on the principles of enterprise and supply chain resilience: Major findings and directions for future research. *International Journal of Production Economics*, *171*, 116–133.

Kamasak, R. (2017). The contribution of tangible and intangible resources, and capabilities to a firm's profitability and market performance. *European Journal of Management and Business Economics, 26*(2), 252-275. doi:10.1108/EJMBE-07-2017-015

Kantasa-ard, A., Bekrar, A., & Sallez, Y. (2019). Artificial intelligence for forecasting in supply chain management: A case study of White Sugar consumption rate in Thailand. *IFAC-PapersOnLine*, *52*(13), 725–730.

Kaplan, A., & Haenlein, M. (2020). Rulers of the world, unite! The challenges and opportunities of artificial intelligence. *Business Horizons*, *63*(1), 37–50.

Karlaftis, M. G., Kepaptsoglou, K., & Sambracos, E. (2009). Containership routing with time deadlines and simultaneous deliveries and pick-ups. *Transportation Research Part E, Logistics and Transportation Review*, *45*(1), 210–221. doi:10.1016/j.tre.2008.05.001

Karrass, C. (1994). The Negotiation Game: How to get What You Want (7th ed.). Harper Collins Publishers.

Kavakeb, S., Nguyen, T. T., McGinley, K., Yang, Z., Jenkinson, I., & Murray, R. (2015). Green Vehicle Technology to Enhance the Performance of a European Port: A Simulation Model with a Cost-Benefit Approach. *Transportation Research Part C, Emerging Technologies*, *60*(Supplement C), 169–188. doi:10.1016/j.trc.2015.08.012

Kayikci, Y., Stix, V., LeBlanc, L. J., & Bartolacci, M. R. (2014). A Novel Application of a Hybrid Delphi-Analytic Hierarchy Process (AHP) Technique: Identifying Key Success Factors in the Strategic Alignment of Collaborative Heterarchical Transportation Networks for Supply Chains. *International Journal of Applied Logistics*, *5*(1), 52–75.

Kelle, P., Woosley, J., & Schneider, H. (2012). Pharmaceutical supply chain specifics and inventory solutions for a hospital case. *Operations Research for Health Care*, *1*(2-3), 54–63. doi:10.1016/j.orhc.2012.07.001

Kemme, N. (2013). Design and Operation of Automated Container Storage Systems. SpringerLink. doi:10.1007/978-3-7908-2885-6

Khan, M., Hussain, M., & Saber, H. M. (2016). Information sharing in a sustainable supply chain. *International Journal of Production Economics*, *181*, 208–214.

Khan, R. (2013). Business analytics and supply chain performance: An Empirical Perspective. *International Journal of Operations and Logistics Management*, *2*(3), 43–56.

Khosravi, M., Sarvari, H., Chan, D., Cristofaro, M., & Chen, Z. (2020). Determining and assessing the risks of commercial and recreational complex building projects in developing countries: A survey of experts in Iran. *Journal of Facilities Management*, *18*(3), 259–282. doi:10.1108/JFM-02-2020-0010

Kim, C. B. (2016). Impact of exchange rate movements, global economic activity, and the BDI volatility on loaded port cargo throughput in South Korea. *Asian Journal of Shipping and Logistics*, *32*(4), 243–248. doi:10.1016/j.ajsl.2016.12.008

Kim, D., Cavusgil, S. T., & Cavusgil, E. (2013). Does IT alignment between supply chain partners enhance customer value creation? An empirical investigation. *Industrial Marketing Management*, *42*(6), 880–889.

Klipšteter, T. (2020). *Tudi na Dravi javni potniški promet.* Retrieved from https://www.dnevnik.si/1042940324

Klumpp, M. (2018). Automation and artificial intelligence in business logistics systems: Human reactions and collaboration requirements. *International Journal of Logistics Research and Applications*, *21*(3), 224–242.

König, A., & Dreßler, A. (2021). A mixed-methods analysis of mobility behavior changes in the COVID-19 era in a rural case study. *European Transport Research Review*, *13*(1), 1–13. doi:10.118612544-021-00472-8

Kotter, J. (2012) *Leading change.* Available from https://books.google.co.uk/books?id=xpGX1EWL_EMC&printsec=frontcover&dq=Kotter%27s+change+model&hl=en&sa=X&ved=2ahUKEwiVkLb19qLrAhUGi1wKHW4oCJkQ6AEwAHoECAkQAg#v=onepage&q=Kotter's%20change%20model&f=false(Boston)

Kowalski, J. C. (1986). Just-in-time for hospitals – so what's new. *Hospital Materials Management*, *11*(11), 6–9. PMID:10317838

Krajzewicz, D. (2010). Traffic simulation with SUMO–simulation of urban mobility Fundamentals of traffic simulation. Springer.

Krauss, S. (1998). *Microscopic modeling of traffic flow: Investigation of collision free vehicle dynamics*. Universität zu Köln.

Kroll, M., Wright, P., & Heiens, R. (1999). The Contribution Of Product Quality To Competitive Advantage: İmpacts On Systematic Variance And Unexplained Variance İn Returns Strategic Management. *Journal Strat. Mgmt. J.*, *20*, 375–384.

Kros, J. F., Falasca, M., & Nadler, S. S. (2006). Impact of just-in-time inventory systems on OEM suppliers. *Industrial Management & Data Systems*, *106*(2), 224–241.

Kros, J. F., Liao, Y., Kirchoff, J. F., & Zemanek, J. E. Jr. (2019). Traceability in the supply chain. *International Journal of Applied Logistics*, *9*(1), 1–22. doi:10.4018/IJAL.2019010101

Krueger, D. A. (2008). The ethics of global supply chains in China–convergences of East and West. *Journal of Business Ethics*, *79*(1-2), 113–120.

Kulak, O., Polat, O., Gujjula, R., & Günther, H.-O. (2013). Strategies for improving a long-established terminal's performance: A simulation study of a Turkish container terminal. *Flexible Services and Manufacturing Journal*, *25*(4), 503–527. doi:10.100710696-011-9128-x

Kumar, A., Pal, A., Vohra, A., Gupta, S., Manchanda, S., & Dash, M. (2018). Construction of capital procurement decision making model to optimize supplier selection using Fuzzy Delphi and AHP-DEMATEL. *Benchmarking*, *25*(5), 1528–1547. doi:10.1108/BIJ-01-2017-0005

Kumar, & Clemens, & Keller. (2014). Supplier management in a manufacturing environment: A strategically focussed performance scorecard. *International Journal of Productivity and Performance Management*, *63*(1), 127–138. doi:10.1108/IJPPM-12-2012-0137

Kumari, M., Gupta, M., & Ved, C. (2021). Blockchain in Pharmaceutical Sector. In *Applications of Blockchain in Healthcare* (pp. 199–220). Springer.

Kumar, R. S., & Pugazhendhi, S. (2012). Information sharing in supply chains: An overview. *Procedia Engineering*, *38*, 2147–2154.

Kumar, R., Singh, R. K., & Shankar, R. (2015). Critical success factors for implementation of supply chain management in Indian small and medium enterprises and their impact on performance. *IIMB Management Review*, *27*(2), 92–104.

Kumar, S., DeGroot, R. A., & Choe, D. (2008). The impact of package design within US hospital supply chain. *International Journal of Physical Distribution & Logistics Management*, *38*(8), 601–615. doi:10.1108/09600030810915134

Kumar, V., & Karande, K. (2000). The Effect of Retail Store Environment on Retailer Performance. *Journal of Business Research*, *49*(August), 167–181. doi:10.1016/S0148-2963(99)00005-3

Kumar, V., Ramachandran, D., & Kumar, B. (2021). Influence of new-age technologies on marketing: A research agenda. *Journal of Business Research*, *125*, 864–877.

Kundu, A., Jain, V., Kumar, S., & Chandra, C. (2015). A journey from normative to behavioral operations in supply chain management: A review using Latent Semantic Analysis. *Expert Systems with Applications*, *42*(2), 796–809.

Kwateng, K. O., Debrah, B., Parker, D. V., Owusu, R. N., & Prempeh, H. (2014). Reverse logistics practices in pharmaceutical manufacturing industry: Experiences from Ghana. *Global Journal of Business Research, 8*(5), 17–26.

Kwon, I. W., Hamilton, J., & Hong, S. J. (2011). Trust and transaction cost in supply chain cost optimization: an exploratory study. In *Inter-organizational Information Systems and Business Management: Theories for Researchers.* IGI Global.

Kwon, I. W. G., Kim, S. H., & Martin, D. G. (2016). Healthcare supply chain management; strategic areas for quality and financial improvement. *Technological Forecasting and Social Change, 113*, 422–428.

Kwon, I. W. G., & Suh, T. (2004). Factors affecting the level of trust and commitment in supply chain relationships. *The Journal of Supply Chain Management, 40*(1), 4–14. doi:10.1111/j.1745-493X.2004.tb00165.x

Kwon, I. W., & Hong, S. J. (2011). Health care supply chain management in the United States: New paradigm for roles of distributors. *International Journal of Health Management and Information, 2*(2), 73–82.

Kytöjoki, J., Nuortio, T., Bräysy, O., & Gendreau, M. (2007). An efficient variable neighborhood search heuristic for very large scale vehicle routing problems. *Computers & Operations Research, 34*(9), 2743–2757. doi:10.1016/j.cor.2005.10.010

Laeequddin, M., Sahay, B. S., Sahay, V., & Abdul Waheed, K. (2012). Trust building in supply chain partners relationship: An integrated conceptual model. *Journal of Management Development, 31*(6), 550–564. doi:10.1108/02621711211230858

Laganà, I. R., Sharifi, S., Khademi, M., Salimi, M., & Ferrara, M. (2021). Analysis of some incentives on two-echelon reverse supply chain with a strategic consumer: The case of unwanted medications in households. *Journal of Multi-Criteria Decision Analysis*. Advance online publication. doi:10.1002/mcda.1736

Laínez, J. M., Schaefer, E., & Reklaitis, G. V. (2012). Challenges and opportunities in enterprise-wide optimization in the pharmaceutical industry. *Computers & Chemical Engineering, 47*, 19–28.

Lambert, D. M., & Stock, J. R. (1982). *Strategic physical distribution management.* Irwin.

Langan-Fox, J., & Tan, P. (1997). Images of a culture in transition: Personal constructs of organizational stability and change. *Journal of Occupational and Organizational Psychology, 70*(3), 273–293. doi:10.1111/j.2044-8325.1997.tb00648.x

Langfield-Smith, K. (2008). The relations between transactional characteristics, trust and risk in the start-up phase of a collaborative alliance. *Management Accounting Research, 19*(4), 344–364. doi:10.1016/j.mar.2008.09.001

Lauer, C. (2004). Excellence in supply chain management. *Modern Healthcare, 34*(50), 29–32. PMID:15631153

Lau, K. H., & Wang, Y. (2009). Reverse logistics in the electronic industry of China: A case study. *Supply Chain Management, 14*(6), 447–465. doi:10.1108/13598540910995228

Lavie, D. (2006). The competitive advantage of interconnected firms: An extension of the resource-based view. *Academy of Management Review, 31*(3), 638–658.

Lax, D. A., & Sebenius, J. K. (1986). *The Manager as a Negotiator: Bargaining for Cooperation and Competitive Gain.* The Free Press.

Lax, D. A., & Sebenius, J. K. (2003). 3-D Negotiation. Playing the whole game. *Harvard Business Review, 81*(11), 64–74. PMID:14619152

Lee, M., Zhao, J., Sun, Q., Pan, Y., Zhou, W., Xiong, C., & Zhang, L. (2020). *Human mobility trends during the COVID-19 pandemic in the United States*. arXiv preprint arXiv:2005.01215.

Lendaris, G. G. (1980). Structural modeling a tutorial guide. *Systems, Man and Cybernetics, IEEE Transactions on, 10*(12), 807–840.

Leontaris, G., Nápoles, O., Dewan, A., & Wolfert, A. (2019). Decision support for offshore asset construction using expert judgments for supply disruptions risk. *Automation in Construction, 107*, 102903. Advance online publication. doi:10.1016/j.autcon.2019.102903

Leriche, D., Oudani, M., Cabani, A., Hoblos, G., Mouzna, J., Boukachour, J., & El Hilali Alaoui, A. (2015). Simulating New Logistics System of Le Havre Port. *IFAC-PapersOnLine, 48*(3), 418–423. doi:10.1016/j.ifacol.2015.06.117

Letheren, K., & Glavas, C. (2017). Embracing the bots: How direct to consumer advertising is about to change forever. *The Conversation.*

Letmathe, P., & Suares, M. (2020). Understanding the impact that potential driving bans on conventional vehicles and the total cost of ownership have on electric vehicle choice in Germany. *Sustainable Future, 2*, 100018. Advance online publication. doi:10.1016/j.sftr.2020.100018

Liakopoulou, S. (2016). *Cost and pricing in road freight transport: Development of a platform for calculating the cost of transport.* Aristotle University of Thessaloniki Polytechnic School.

Liao, Z., & Rittscher, J. (2007). Integration of supplier selection, procurement lot sizing and carrier selection under dynamic demand conditions. *International Journal of Production Economics, 107*(2), 502–510. doi:10.1016/j.ijpe.2006.10.003

Li, G., Yang, H., Sun, L., & Sohal, A. S. (2009). The impact of IT implementation on supply chain integration and performance. *International Journal of Production Economics, 120*(1), 125–138.

Lin, C., & Lin, M. (2019). The determinants of using cloud supply chain adoption. *Industrial Management & Data Systems.*

Linke, M. (2013). Impact of global hyperconnectivity and increased smartphone usage on the delivery and structure of IT organizsation in transport logistics. *International Journal of Applied Logistics, 4*(2), 18–33.

Lin, M., Lin, C., & Chang, Y. S. (2020). The impact of using a cloud supply chain on organizational performance. *Journal of Business and Industrial Marketing.*

Lin, Y., Wang, X., Hu, H., & Zhao, H. (2020). Research on feeder network design: A case study of feeder service for the port of Kotka. *European Transport Research Review, 12*(1), 61. doi:10.118612544-020-00450-6

Li, Q., Guan, X., Wu, P., Wang, X., Zhou, L., Tong, Y., ... Wong, J. Y. (2020). Early transmission dynamics in Wuhan, China, of novel coronavirus–infected pneumonia. *The New England Journal of Medicine, 382*(13), 1199–1207. doi:10.1056/NEJMoa2001316 PMID:31995857

Li, S., Rao, S. S., Ragu-Nathan, T. S., & Ragu-Nathan, B. (2005). Development and validation of a measurement instrument for studying supply chain management practices. *Journal of Operations Management, 23*(6), 618–641.

Litz, R. A., & Stewart, A. C. (2000). The late show: The effects of after-hours accessibility on the performance of small retailers. *Journal of Small Business Management, 38*(1), 1–26.

Liu, P., Hendalianpour, A., Razmi, J., & Sangari, M. S. (2021). A solution algorithm for integrated production-inventory-routing of perishable goods with transshipment and uncertain demand. *Complex & Intelligent Systems*, 1-17.

Liu, A. M. M., Fellows, R., & Ng, J. (2004). Surveyors' perspectives on ethics in organisational culture. *Engineering, Construction, and Architectural Management, 11*(6), 438–449. doi:10.1108/09699980410570193

Liu, C., Yang, J., Lian, J., Li, W., Evans, S., & Yin, Y. (2014). Sustainable performance oriented operational decision-making of single machine systems with deterministic product arrival time. *Journal of Cleaner Production, 85*, 318–330. doi:10.1016/j.jclepro.2014.07.025

Liu, M., Chu, F., Zhang, Z., & Chu, C. (2015). A Polynomial-Time Heuristic for the Quay Crane Double-Cycling Problem with Internal-Reshuffling Operations. *Transportation Research Part E, Logistics and Transportation Review*, *81*(Supplement C), 52–74. doi:10.1016/j.tre.2015.06.009

Liu, Y., Luo, Y., Huang, Y., & Yang, Q. (2017). A diagnostic model of private control and collective control in buyer-supplier relationships. *Industrial Marketing Management*, *63*, 116–128. doi:10.1016/j.indmarman.2016.11.003

Liu, Y., & Wang, S. (2011). Research on collaborative management in supply chain crisis. *Procedia Environmental Sciences*, *10*, 141–146.

Lopez, P. A., Behrisch, M., Bieker-Walz, L., Erdmann, J., Flötteröd, Y.-P., Hilbrich, R., ... Wießner, E. (2018). Microscopic traffic simulation using sumo. *21st International Conference on Intelligent Transportation Systems (ITSC).*

Lotfi, R., Mehrjerdi, Y. Z., & Mardani, N. (2017). A multi-objective and multi-product advertising billboard location model with attraction factor mathematical modeling and solutions. *International Journal of Applied Logistics*, *7*(1), 64–86. doi:10.4018/IJAL.2017010104

Low, J. M. W. (2010). Capacity Investment and Efficiency Cost Estimations in Major East Asian Ports. *Maritime Economics & Logistics*, *12*(4), 370–391. doi:10.1057/mel.2010.13

Lu, H.-A., Chu, C.-W., & Che, P.-Y. (2010). Seasonal slot allocation planning for a container liner shipping service. *Journal of Marine Science and Technology*, *18*(1), 84–92. doi:10.51400/2709-6998.1868

Lui, S. S., Wong, Y.-y., & Liu, W. (2009). Asset specificity roles in interfirm cooperation: Reducing opportunistic behavior or increasing cooperative behavior? *Journal of Business Research*, *62*(11), 1214–1219. doi:10.1016/j.jbusres.2008.08.003

Luís, R. O., Rossoni, H. A. V., & Duarte, N. F. (2021). Systematic review on reverse logistics of drug residues | Revisão Sistemática De Literatura Sobre A Logística Reversa De Resíduos De Medicamentos. *Fronteiras*, *10*, 339–358. doi:10.21664/2238-8869.2021v10i1.p339-358

Luiz, A. L. B., Eliane, P. Z. B., & Hashiba, L. H. (2014). What type of cooperation with suppliers and customers leads to superior performance? *Journal of Business Research*, *67*(5), 952-959. doi:10.1016/j.jbusres.2013.07.015

Luthra, S., Kumar, V., Kumar, S., & Haleem, A. (2011). Barriers to implement green supply chain management in automobile industry using interpretive structural modeling technique-An Indian perspective. *Journal of Industrial Engineering and Management*, *4*(2).

Luxton, D. D., Kayl, R. A., & Mishkind, M. C. (2012). mHealth Data Security: The Need for HIPAA-Compliant Standardization. *Telemedicine Journal and e-Health*, *18*(4), 284–288.

Lynch, D. (1991). Just-in-time and stockless programs for hospitals: Fad or trend. *Hospital Materiel Management Quarterly*, *12*(4), 17–21. PMID:10110231

Madenas, N., Tiwari, A., Turner, C. J., & Woodward, J. (2014). Information flow in supply chain management: A review across the product lifecycle. *CIRP Journal of Manufacturing Science and Technology*, *7*(4), 335–346.

Malone, D. W. (1975). An introduction to the application of interpretive structural modeling. *Proceedings of the IEEE*, *63*(3), 397–404.

Mandolini, M., Marilungo, E., & Germani, M. (2017). A TCO Model for Supporting the Configuration of Industrial Plants. *Procedia Manufacturing*, *11*, 1940–1949. doi:10.1016/j.promfg.2017.07.339

Manyika, J., Chui, M., Brown, B., Bughin, J., Dobbs, R., Roxburgh, C., & Byers, A. H. (2011). *Big data: The next frontier for innovation, competition, and productivity*. Academic Press.

Manzanero, L. D., & Krupp, K. J. (2009). *Forecasting Container Freight Rates. An Econometric Analysis*. Academic Press.

Manzolillo, B. (2021). Reverse logistics: A solution for medicines disposition at home | Logística inversa: Una solución a la disposición de medicamentos en el hogar. *Gaceta Medica de Caracas*, *129*, 13–21. doi:10.47307/GMC.2021.129.1.3

Marco. (2015). *Marco systems YCM reports Version 2.1 Copyright Marco Ltd.* Available from https://www.marco.co.uk/products/#

Maribor, M. o. (n.d.). *Lega in podnebje*. Retrieved from https://www.maribor.si/povezava.aspx?pid=3794

Marques, C. M., Moniz, S., de Sousa, J. P., Barbosa-Povoa, A. P., & Reklaitis, G. (2020). Decision-support challenges in the chemical-pharmaceutical industry: Findings and future research directions. *Computers & Chemical Engineering*, *134*, 106672.

Marra, M., Ho, W., & Edwards, J. S. (2012). Supply chain knowledge management: A literature review. *Expert Systems with Applications*, *39*(5), 6103–6110.

Martínez-Olvera, C. (2008). Entropy as an assessment tool of supply chain information sharing. *European Journal of Operational Research*, *185*(1), 405–417.

Masoumi, A. H., Yu, M., & Nagurney, A. (2012). A supply chain generalized network oligopoly model for pharmaceuticals under brand differentiation and perishability. *Transportation Research Part E, Logistics and Transportation Review*, *48*(4), 762–780.

Matani, Tripathi, & Matani. (2012). Information Technology Tools uImproving Supply Chain Management Productivity In Food Processing Industries. *International Journal of Advanced Engineering Technology*, *3*(1), 237-238.

Mbang, J. J. A. (2013). Compound Supply Chain Efficiency Model Application in the Gabonese Supply Chain: The Case of Comilog. *International Journal of Applied Logistics*, *4*(1), 60–129.

McAfee, A., Brynjolfsson, E., Davenport, T. H., Patil, D. J., & Barton, D. (2012). Big data: The management revolution. *Harvard Business Review*, *90*(10), 60–68. PMID:23074865

McEvily, B., Zaheer, A., & Kamal, D. K. F. (2017). Mutual and exclusive: Dyadic sources of trust in interorganizational exchange. *Organization Science*, *28*(1), 74–92. doi:10.1287/orsc.2016.1102

Mckone-sweet, K. E., Hamilton, P., & Willis, S. B. (2005). The ailing healthcare supply chain: A prescription for change. *The Journal of Supply Chain Management*, *41*(1), 4–17. doi:10.1111/j.1745-493X.2005.tb00180.x

McLaughlin, M., Kotis, D., Thomson, K., Harrison, M., Fennessy, G., Postelnick, M., & Scheetz, M. H. (2013). Effects on patient care caused by drug shortages: A survey. *Journal of Managed Care Pharmacy*, *19*(9), 783–788. doi:10.18553/jmcp.2013.19.9.783 PMID:24156647

Mehralian, G. H., Rajabzadeh, A., Reza Sadeh, M., & Reza Rasekh, H. (2012). Intellectual capital and corporate performance in Iranian pharmaceutical industry. *Journal of Intellectual Capital*, *13*(1), 138–140. doi:10.1108/14691931211196259

Mehralian, G., Moosivand, A., Emadi, S., & Asgharian, R. (2017). Developing a coordination framework for pharmaceutical supply chain: Using analytical hierarchy process. *International Journal of Logistics Systems and Management*, *26*(3), 277–293.

Mehralian, G., Nazari, J. A., Rasekh, H. R., & Hosseini, S. (2016). TOPSIS approach to prioritize critical success factors of TQM: Evidence from the pharmaceutical industry. *The TQM Journal*, *28*(2), 235–249.

Mehralian, G., Zarenezhad, F., & Rajabzadeh Ghatari, A. (2015). Developing a model for an agile supply chain in pharmaceutical industry. *International Journal of Pharmaceutical and Healthcare Marketing*, *9*(1), 74–91.

Meiler, M., Tonke, D., Grunow, M., & Günther, H. O. (2015). Pattern-based supply network planning in the pharmaceutical industry. *Computers & Chemical Engineering*, *77*, 43–58.

Meisel, F., & Wichmann, M. (2010). Container Sequencing for Quay Cranes with Internal Reshuffles. *OR-Spektrum*, *32*(3), 569–591. doi:10.100700291-009-0191-6

Melnyk, S. A., Closs, D. J., Griffis, S. E., Zobel, C. W., & Macdonald, J. R. (2014). Understanding supply chain resilience. *Supply Chain Manag. Rev*, *18*(1), 34–41.

Melon, L., & Spruk, R. (2020). The impact of e-procurement on institutional quality. *Journal of Public Procurement*. . doi:10.1108/JOPP-07-2019-0050

Mendenhalt, R. W. (1996). Post-Settlement Settlements: Agreeing to Make Resolutions Efficient. *Journal of Dispute Resolution*, 81.

Meng, Q., & Wang, S. (2012). Liner ship fleet deployment with week-dependent container shipment demand. *European Journal of Operational Research*, *222*(2), 241–252. doi:10.1016/j.ejor.2012.05.006

Meng, Q., Wang, T., & Gelareh, S. (2011). A linearized approach for the liner containership fleet planning with demand uncertainty. In E. P. Chew, L. H. Lee, & L. C. Tang (Eds.), *Advances in Maritime Logistics and Supply Chain Systems* (pp. 229–256). World Scientific Publishing. doi:10.1142/9789814329866_0011

Meng, Q., Wang, T., & Wang, S. (2012). Short-term liner ship fleet planning with container transshipment and uncertain container shipment demand. *European Journal of Operational Research*, *223*(1), 96–105. doi:10.1016/j.ejor.2012.06.025

Meng, X. (2015). The role of trust in relationship development and performance improvement. *Journal of Civil Engineering and Management*, *21*(7), 845–853. doi:10.3846/13923730.2014.893923

Meredig, B. (2017). Industrial materials informatics: Analyzing large-scale data to solve applied problems in R&D, manufacturing, and supply chain. *Current Opinion in Solid State and Materials Science*, *21*(3), 159–166.

Merkert, R., Mulley, C., & Hakim, M. (2018). Trade-offs between transaction cost, operation cost and innovation in the context of procurement and asset specificity – The example of the bus industry. *Research in Transportation Economics*, *69*, 173–179. doi:10.1016/j.retrec.2018.07.015

Miao, F., Bao, S., & Li, Y. (2012). *New trends and developments in biometrics: Physiological Signal Based Biometrics for Securing Body Sensor Network*. InTech.

Milan, J. (2007). Modelling the full cost of an intermodal and road freight transport network. *Transportation Research Part D, Transport and Environment*, *12*(1), 33–44. doi:10.1016/j.trd.2006.10.004

Miller. (2020). The innovation impacts of public procurement offices: The case of healthcare procurement. *Research Policy*, *49*(7). . doi:10.1016/j.respol.2020.104075

Ministry of Health and Social Services. (2014). *Annual Report of the Directorate of Tertiary Health Care and clinical support services*. Author.

Miranda, P. L., Morabito, R., & Ferreira, D. (2018). Optimization model for a production, inventory, distribution and routing problem in small furniture companies. *Top (Madrid)*, *26*(1), 30–67.

Mladenović, N., & Hansen, P. (1997). Variable neighborhood search. *Computers & Operations Research*, *24*(11), 1097–1100. doi:10.1016/S0305-0548(97)00031-2

Mnookin, R. H., Peppet, S. R., & Tulumelo, A. S. (1996). The Tension Between Empathy and Assertiveness. *Negotiation Journal*, *12*(3), 217–230. doi:10.1111/j.1571-9979.1996.tb00096.x

Mobarakeh, N. A., Shahzad, M. K., Baboli, A., & Tonadre, R. (2017). Improved Forecasts for uncertain and unpredictable Spare Parts Demand in Business Aircraft's with Bootstrap Method. *IFAC-PapersOnLine*, *50*(1), 15241–15246.

Modgil, S., & Sharma, S. (2017). Information Systems, Supply Chain Management and Operational Performance: Tri-linkage—An Exploratory Study on Pharmaceutical Industry of India. *Global Business Review*, *18*(3), 652–677.

Mohtadi, H. (2008). Information sharing in food supply chains. *Canadian Journal of Agricultural Economics*, *56*(2), 163–178.

Montoya-Torres, J. R., & Ortiz-Vargas, D. A. (2014). Collaboration and information sharing in dyadic supply chains: A literature review over the period 2000–2012. *Estudios Gerenciales*, *30*(133), 343–354.

Moon, J. Y., & Park, J. (2014). Smart production scheduling with time-dependent and machine-dependent electricity cost by considering distributed energy resources and energy storage. *International Journal of Production Research*, *52*(13), 3922–3939. doi:10.1080/00207543.2013.860251

Morgan, R. M., & Hunt, S. D. (1994). The commitment-trust theory of relationship marketing. *Journal of Marketing*, *58*(3), 20–38. doi:10.1177/002224299405800302

Morris, M. H., Schindehutte, M., & LaForge, R. W. (2002). Entrepreneurial marketing: A construct for integrating emerging entrepreneurship and marketing perspectives. *Journal of Marketing Theory and Practice*, *10*(4), 1–19. doi:10.1080/10696679.2002.11501922

Mousazadeh, M., Torabi, S. A., & Zahiri, B. (2015). A robust possibilistic programming approach for pharmaceutical supply chain network design. *Computers & Chemical Engineering*, *82*, 115–128.

Mouzas, S., Henneberg, S., & Naudé, P. (2007). Trust and reliance in business relationships. *European Journal of Marketing*, *41*(9/10), 1016–1032. doi:10.1108/03090560710773327

Moynihan, T. (1996). An inventory of personal constructs for information systems project risk researchers. *Journal of Information Technology*, *11*(4), 359–371. doi:10.1177/026839629601100409

Mukeshimana, M., Zhao, Z., Ahmad, M., & Irfan, M. (2021). Analysis on barriers to biogas dissemination in Rwanda: AHP approach. *Renewable Energy*, *163*, 1127–1137. doi:10.1016/j.renene.2020.09.051

Mullan, R. (2016). The flying squad. *The Caterer*, *206*(4396), 32–36.

Murty, K. G., Liu, J., Yat-wah, W., & Linn, R. (2005). A Decision Support System for Operations in a Container Terminal. *Decision Support Systems*, *39*(3), 309–332. doi:10.1016/j.dss.2003.11.002

Muscatello, J. R., Parente, D. H., & Swinarski, M. (2018). Aligning Supply Chain Logistics Costs via ERP Coordination. *International Journal of Information System Modeling and Design*, *9*(2), 24–43. doi:10.4018/IJISMD.2018040102

Mustaffa, N. H., & Potter, A. (2009). Healthcare Supply Chain Management in Malaysia: A case study. *Supply Chain Management*, *14*(3), 234–243. doi:10.1108/13598540910954575

Nachtmann, H., & Pohl, E. A. (2009). *The state of healthcare logistics: Cost and quality improvement opportunities*. Center for Innovation in Healthcare Logistics, University of Arkansas.

Nahmias, S. (2011). *Perishable inventory systems* (Vol. 160). Springer Science & Business Media.

Najafi, M., & Farahani, R. Z. (2013). New forecasting insights on the bullwhip effect in a supply chain. *IMA Journal of Management Mathematics*, *25*(3), 259–286.

Namibia Statistics Agency. (2011). *Namibia 2011 population and housing Census Main Report*. Author.

Nannestad, P. (2008). What have we learned about generalized trust, if anything? *Annual Review of Political Science, 11*(1), 413–436. doi:10.1146/annurev.polisci.11.060606.135412

Narayana, S. A., Pati, R. K., & Vrat, P. (2012). Research on management issues in the pharmaceutical industry: A literature review. *International Journal of Pharmaceutical and Healthcare Marketing, 6*(4), 351–375.

Nath, T., & Standing, C. (2010). Drivers of information technology use in the supply chain. *Journal of Systems and Information Technology, 12*(1), 70–84.

Navickas, V., & Navikaite, A. (2014) Competitive Advantage Maximization Through Relation Between Trust And Reputation. *Sociálno-Ekonomická Revue, 4.*

Nedaei, M. (2018). Scheduling analysis and strategic service planning for optimum operation of two parallel machines under effect of sequencing: A case study of a manufacturing company in a job-shop environment. *International Journal of Service Science, Management, Engineering, and Technology, 9*(4), 57–72. doi:10.4018/IJSSMET.2018100104

Nelson, R., & S.W. (1982). *An Evolutionary Theory of Economic Change.* Harvard College.

Newton, R. (2020). *The management consultant: Mastering the art of consultancy.* Pearson Education.

Ngai, E. W., Chau, D. C., & Chan, T. L. A. (2011). Information technology, operational, and management competencies for supply chain agility: Findings from case studies. *The Journal of Strategic Information Systems, 20*(3), 232–249.

Nikolaou, I. E., Evangelinos, K. I., & Allan, S. (2013). A reverse logistics social responsibility evaluation framework based on the triple bottom line approach. *Journal of Cleaner Production, 56*(0), 173–184. doi:10.1016/j.jclepro.2011.12.009

Nishant, R., Kennedy, M., & Corbett, J. (2020). Artificial intelligence for sustainability: Challenges, opportunities, and a research agenda. *International Journal of Information Management, 53*, 102104.

Niziolek, L. (2008). *A simulation-based study of distribution strategies for pharmaceutical supply chains* (PhD Thesis). Purdue University.

Nooramin, S., Amir, V. R. A., & Sayareh, J. (2011). A Six Sigma Framework for Marine Container Terminals. *International Journal of Lean Six Sigma, 2*(3), 241–253. doi:10.1108/20401461111157196

Norgen, L., Hiatt, W. R., & Dormandy, J. A. (2007). Inter-society consensus for the management of peripheral arterial disease (TASC II). *International Angiology, 26*, 81–157.

Nouvellet, P., Bhatia, S., Cori, A., Ainslie, K. E. C., Baguelin, M., Bhatt, S., Boonyasiri, A., Brazeau, N. F., Cattarino, L., Cooper, L. V., Coupland, H., Cucunuba, Z. M., Cuomo-Dannenburg, G., Dighe, A., Djaafara, B. A., Dorigatti, I., Eales, O. D., van Elsland, S. L., Nascimento, F. F., ... Donnelly, C. A. (2021). Reduction in mobility and COVID-19 transmission. *Nature Communications, 12*(1), 1090. doi:10.103841467-021-21358-2 PMID:33597546

Nsamzinshuti, A., & Ndiaye, A. B. (2018). Development of a Conceptual Framework for Performance Measurement of Pharmaceutical Supply Chain within Hospital. *International Journal of Applied Logistics, 5*(2), 32–49.

Nyaga, G. N., Whipple, J. M., & Lynch, D. F. (2010). Examining supply chain relationships: Do buyer and supplier perspectives on collaborative relationships differ? *Journal of Operations Management, 28*(2), 101–114. doi:10.1016/j.jom.2009.07.005

O'Malley, L., Patterson, M., & Evans, M. (1995). Retailing applications of geodemographics: a preliminary investigation. Marketing Intelligence & Planning, 13(2). doi:10.1108/02634509510083482

Okano, M. T., & Marins, F. A. (2014). Measuring the Impact of Information Technology (IT) on Supply Chain Management (SCM) Through Indicators: An Exploratory Study. *Journal of Modern Accounting and Auditing, 10*(5).

Oliveira, J. B., Lima, R. S., & Montevechi, J. A. B. (2016). Perspectives and relationships in Supply Chain Simulation: A systematic literature review. *Simulation Modelling Practice and Theory*, *62*, 166–191.

Oliver, N., Lepri, B., Sterly, H., Lambiotte, R., Deletaille, S., De Nadai, M., & Cattuto, C. (2020). *Mobile phone data for informing public health actions across the COVID-19 pandemic life cycle*. American Association for the Advancement of Science.

Ouegnimaoua, L., & Savage, C. J. (2008). Restructuring the pharmaceutical and supply chain: An evaluation of distribution networks in Europe. In *Proceedings of logistics network research conference*. University of Newcastle.

Ouyang, Y. (2007). The effect of information sharing on supply chain stability and the bullwhip effect. *European Journal of Operational Research*, *182*(3), 1107–1121.

Oyegoke, A. S., Dickinson, M., Khalfan, M. M., McDermott, P., & Rowlinson, S. (2009). Construction project procurement routes: An in-depth critique. *International Journal of Managing Projects in Business*, *2*(3), 338–354. doi:10.1108/17538370910971018

Ozcan, G. B. (2000). The transformation of Turkish retailing: Survival strategies of small and medium-sized retailers. *Journal of South-ern Europe and the Balkans, 2*(1), 105–120. http://www.cnu.org/node/1360

Ozkan, M., & Solmaz, B. (2015). The changing face of the employees–Generation Z and their perceptions of work (A Study Applied to University Students). *Procedia Economics and Finance*, *26*, 476–483.

Ozuduru, B. H., & Varol, C. (2011). *Ankara'daki Alisveris Merkezlerinin ve Alisveris Potansiyelinin Mekansal Dagiliminin Pera- kende Yersecim Modelleriyle Analizi, 108K547 nolu 3501 Uusal Genc Arastirmaci Kariyer Gelistirme Programi tarafindan desteklenen proje raporu, Tubitak*. Sobag.

Palombo, D., Mugnai, D., & Mambrini, S. (2009). Role of interactive home telemedicine for early and protected discharge 1 day after carotid endarterectomy. *Annals of Vascular Surgery*, *23*, 76–80. PMID:18809294

Pantano, E., & Viassone, M. (2015). Engaging consumers on new integrated multichannel retail settings: Challenges for retailers. *Journal of Retailing and Consumer Services*, *25*, 106–114. doi:10.1016/j.jretconser.2015.04.003

Pantuso, G., Fagerholt, K., & Hvattum, L. M. (2014). A survey on maritime fleet size and mix problems. *European Journal of Operational Research*, *235*(2), 341–349. doi:10.1016/j.ejor.2013.04.058

Pan, Y., & Zinkhan, G. M. (2006). Determinants of retail patronage: A meta- analytical perspective. *Journal of Retailing*, *82*(June), 229–243. doi:10.1016/j.jretai.2005.11.008

Papageorgiou, L. G. (2009). Supply chain optimization for the process industries: Advances and opportunities. *Computers & Chemical Engineering*, *33*(12), 1931–1938.

Parker, S. G. (2003). Block That Tactic. *Harvard Management Communication Letter*, *6*(9), 3–5.

Park, H., Bellamy, M. A., & Basole, R. C. (2016). Visual analytics for supply network management: System design and evaluation. *Decision Support Systems*, *91*, 89–102.

Partida, B. (2011). Leaders Show Power of Reverse Logistics. *Supply Chain Management Review*, *15*(6), 62–64.

Pauwels, K., Simoens, S., Casteels, M., & Huys, I. (2015). Insights into European drug shortages: A survey of hospital pharmacists. *PLoS One*, *10*(3), e0119322. doi:10.1371/journal.pone.0119322 PMID:25775406

Pazirandeh, A., & Jafari, H. (2013). Making Sense of Green Logistics. *International Journal of Productivity and Performance Management*, *62*(8), 889–904. doi:10.1108/IJPPM-03-2013-0059

Pearce, M. R. (1989). Retailers: How to be different from your competitors. *Business Quarterly, 54*(2), 28-33.

Pedrick, D. (2006). *Green Terminal Design.* Long Beach, CA: CH2M HILL. http://www.fasterfreightcleanerair.com/pdfs/Presentations/FFCACA2006/Andrew %20Pedrick%20-%20Green%20Terminal%20Design.pdf

Penrose, E. (1959). *The Theory of the Growth of the Firm.* Blackwell Publishing.

Pepe, E., Bajardi, P., Gauvin, L., Privitera, F., Lake, B., Cattuto, C., & Tizzoni, M. (2020). *COVID-19 outbreak response: a first assessment of mobility changes in Italy following national lockdown.* MedRxiv; doi:10.1101/2020.03.22.20039933

Pereira, J. V. (2009). The new supply chain's frontier: Information management. *International Journal of Information Management, 29*(5), 372–379.

Permala, A., Rantasila, K., & Pilli-Sihvola, E. (2012). RFID: From closed systems to improving visibility in the manufacturing supply chain. *International Journal of Applied Logistics, 3*(2), 14–24.

Persyn, D., Díaz-Lanchas, J., & Barbero, J. (2019). *Estimating road transport costs between EU regions.* JRC Working Papers on Territorial Modelling and Analysis No. 04/2019, European Commission, Seville, JRC114409.

Peteraf, M. A., & Bergen, M. E. (2003). Scanning dynamic competitive landscapes: A market-based and resource-based framework. *Strategic Management Journal, 24*(10), 1027–1041. doi:10.1002mj.325

Petering, M. E. H., Wu, Y., Li, W., Goh, M., & de Souza, R. (2009). Development and Simulation Analysis of Real-Time Yard Crane Control Systems for Seaport Container Transshipment Terminals. *OR-Spektrum, 31*(4), 801–835. doi:10.100700291-008-0142-7

Pettersen, I. J., Nyland, K., & Robbins, G. (2020). Public procurement performance and the challenge of service complexity – the case of pre-hospital healthcare. *Journal of Public Procurement.* . doi:10.1108/JOPP-01-2020-0002

Pettit, T. J., Croxton, K. L., & Fiksel, J. (2019). The Evolution of Resilience in Supply Chain Management: A Retrospective on Ensuring Supply Chain Resilience. *Journal of Business Logistics, 40*(1), 56–65. doi:10.1111/jbl.12202

Pharco Corporation. (2014). *About Pharco.* Retrieved from https://www.pharco.org/about.aspx

Pharco Pharmaceuticals. (2014). *Pharco Pharmaceuticals.* Retrieved from http://www.pharco.org/Category.aspx?id=711

Pishvaee, M. S., Razmi, J., & Torabi, S. A. (2012). Robust possibilistic programming for socially responsible supply chain network design: A new approach. *Fuzzy Sets and Systems, 206*, 1–20.

Pitta, D. A., & Laric, M. V. (2004). Value chains in health care. *Journal of Consumer Marketing, 21*(7), 451–464. doi:10.1108/07363760410568671

Polat, O., Kulak, O., & Günther, H.-O. (2012). *An adaptive neighborhood search approach for VRPSPDTL.* The 2nd International Conference on Logistics and Maritime Systems, Bremen, Germany.

Polat, L. Ö., & Güngör, A. (2019). Network Design Problems in E-waste Management. In M. N. V. Prasad & M. Vithanage (Eds.), *Electronic Waste Management and Treatment Technology* (pp. 77–102). Butterworth-Heinemann. doi:10.1016/B978-0-12-816190-6.00004-2

Polat, O. (2017a). An Overview of Feeder Services in the Era of Mega Containerships. In S. Laurence & C. Cécile (Eds.), *Global Intermediation and Logistics Service Providers* (pp. 317–339). IGI Global. doi:10.4018/978-1-5225-2133-4.ch016

Polat, O. (2017b). A parallel variable neighborhood search for the vehicle routing problem with divisible deliveries and pickups. *Computers & Operations Research, 85*, 71–86. doi:10.1016/j.cor.2017.03.009

Polat, O., & Günther, H.-O. (2016). The impact of seasonal demand fluctuations on service network design of container feeder lines. *Journal of Transportation and Logistics*, *1*(1), 39–58. doi:10.22532/jtl.237886

Polat, O., Günther, H.-O., & Kulak, O. (2014). The feeder network design problem: Application to container services in the Black Sea region. *Maritime Economics & Logistics*, *16*(3), 1–27. doi:10.1057/mel.2014.2

Poppo, L., Zhou, K. Z., & Ryu, S. (2008). Alternative origins to interorganizational trust: An interdependence perspective on the shadow of the past and the shadow of the future. *Organization Science*, *19*(1), 39–55. doi:10.1287/orsc.1070.0281

Porter, M.E. (1985). *Competitive Advantage: Creating and Sustaining Superior Performance*. Free Press.

Porter, M. E. (1980). *Competitive Strategy: Techniques for Analyzing Industries and Competitors*. Free Press.

Powell, W. W., Koput, K. W., & Smith-Doerr, L. (1996). Interorganizational collaboration and the locus of innovation: Networks of learning in biotechnology. *Administrative Science Quarterly*, *41*(1), 116–145. doi:10.2307/2393988

Powers, T. L., & Reagan, W. R. (2007). Factors influencing successful buyer-seller relationships. *Journal of Business Research*, *60*(12), 1234–1242. doi:10.1016/j.jbusres.2007.04.008

Prajogo, D., & Olhager, J. (2012). Supply chain integration and performance: The effects of long-term relationships, information technology and sharing, and logistics integration. *International Journal of Production Economics*, *135*(1), 514–522.

Puica, E. (2020). Cloud Computing in Supply Chain Management and Economic, Environmental and Social Impact Analysis. *Informações Econômicas*, *24*(4), 41–54.

Pujawan, I. N., Kurniati, N., & Wessiani, N. A. (2009). Supply chain management for Disaster Relief Operations: Principles and case studies. *International Journal of Logistics Systems and Management*, *5*(6), 679–692.

Rafiei, S., Mohammadi-ivatloo, B., Asadi, S., Goldani, S., & Falaghi, H. (2019). Bi-level model for generation expansion planning with contract pricing of renewable energy in the presence of energy storage. *IET Renewable Power Generation*, *13*(9), 1544–1553. doi:10.1049/iet-rpg.2019.0074

Raiffa, H. (1982). *The Art and Science of Negotiation: How to resolve conflicts and get the best out of bargaining*. Harvard Business Press.

Rajeev, A., Pati, R. K., Padhi, S. S., & Govindan, K. (2017). Evolution of sustainability in supply chain management: A literature review. *Journal of Cleaner Production*, *162*, 299–314.

Ramadan, A. (2014). *Egypt's Deadly Medicines* [Press release]. Retrieved from http://en.arij.net/report/egypts-deadly-medicines/

Ramberg, J. (2011). *ICC Guide to Incoterms® 2010: Understanding and Practical Use*. ICC.

RASSD. (2015). *The Problem of Pharmaceutical returns and its effect on patients* [Press release]. Retrieved from https://rassd.com/7-127514.htm

Ravi, V., & Shankar, R. (2005). Analysis of interactions among the barriers of reverse logistics. *Technological Forecasting and Social Change*, *72*(8), 1011–1029. doi:10.1016/j.techfore.2004.07.002

Ravi, V., Shankar, R., & Tiwari, M. K. (2005). Productivity improvement of a computer hardware supply chain. *International Journal of Productivity and Performance Management*, *54*(3–4), 239–255.

Redondo, Y. P., & Cambra Fierro, J. J. (2008). Educational level as moderating element of long-term orientation of supply relationships. *Journal of Marketing Management*, *24*(3-4), 383–408. doi:10.1362/026725708X306158

Reinartz, W., & Kumar, V. (1999). Store-, Market-, and Consumer-Characteristics: The Drivers of Store Performance. *Marketing Letters*, *10*(Winter), 5–22. doi:10.1023/A:1008011622335

Ribeiro, D. P., De Oliveira, U. R., Da Silva César, A., & Aprigliano Fernandes, V. (2021). Evaluation of medicine reverse logistics practices in hospitals. *Sustain.*, *13*. Advance online publication. doi:10.3390u13063496

Richey, R. G., Chen, H., Genchev, S. E., & Daugherty, P. J. (2005). Developing effective reverse logistics programs. *Industrial Marketing Management*, *34*(8), 830–840. doi:10.1016/j.indmarman.2005.01.003

Ritchie, L., Burnes, B., Whittle, P., & Hey, R. (2000). The benefits of reverse logistics: The case of the Manchester Royal Infirmary Pharmacy. *Supply Chain Management*.

Rivard-Royer, H., Landry, S., & Beaulieu, M. (2002). Hybrid stockless: A case study. *International Journal of Operations & Production Management*, *22*(4), 412–424. doi:10.1108/01443570210420412

Roberta Pereira, C., Christopher, M., & Lago Da Silva, A. (2014). Achieving supply chain resilience: The role of procurement. *Supply Chain Management*, *19*(5/6), 626–642.

Rogers & Tibben-Lembke. (1998). Going Backwards: Reverse Logistics Trends and Practices. University of Nevada, Reno: Reverse Logistics Executive Council.

Rogers, D. S., & Tibben-Lembke, R. (2001). An examination of reverse logistics practices. *Journal of Business Logistics*, *22*(2), 129–148.

Rokkan, A. I., Heide, J. B., & Wathne, K. H. (2003). Specific investments in marketing relationships: Expropriation and bonding effects. *JMR, Journal of Marketing Research*, *40*(2), 210–224. doi:10.1509/jmkr.40.2.210.19223

Ronald, S. T.-L., & Dale, S. R. (2002). Differences between forward and reverse logistics in a retail environment. *Supply Chain Management*, *7*(5), 271–282. doi:10.1108/13598540210447719

Rossetti, C. L., Handfield, R., & Dooley, K. J. (2011). Forces, trends, and decisions in pharmaceutical supply chain management. *International Journal of Physical Distribution & Logistics Management*, *41*(6), 601–622.

Rossetti, C., & Choi, T. Y. (2005). On the dark side of strategic sourcing: Experiences from the aerospace industry. *The Academy of Management Perspectives*, *19*(1), 46–60. doi:10.5465/ame.2005.15841951

Rossetti, L. C., Handfield, R., & Dooley, J. D. (2011). Forces, trends, and decisions in pharmaceutical supply chain management. *International Journal of Physical Distribution & Logistics Management*, *41*(6), 601–622. doi:10.1108/09600031111147835

Rotstein, G. E., Papageorgiou, L. G., Shah, N., Murphy, D. C., & Mustafa, R. (1999). A product portfolio approach in the pharmaceutical industry. *Computers & Chemical Engineering*, *23*, S883–S886.

Rugman, A. M., & Verbeke, A. (2002). Edith Penrose's contribution to the resource-based view of strategic management. *Strategic Management Journal*, *23*(8), 769–780. doi:10.1002mj.240

Ruokokoski, M., Solyali, O. G. U. Z., Cordeau, J. F., Jans, R., & Süral, H. (2010). *Efficient formulations and a branch-and-cut algorithm for a production-routing problem*. GERAD Technical Report G-2010-66.

Rustmann, F. W. (2002). *CIA, Inc.: Espionage and the Craft of Business Intelligence*. Brassey´s, Inc.

Ryciuk, U., & Nazarko, J. (2020). Model of trust-based cooperative relationships in a supply chain. *Journal of Business Economics and Management*, *21*(5), 1225–1247. doi:10.3846/jbem.2020.12829

Rycroft, R. W., & Kash, D. E. (2004). Self-organizing innovation networks: Implications for globalization. *Technovation*, *24*(3), 187–197. doi:10.1016/S0166-4972(03)00092-0

Ryu, J. H., & Pistikopoulos, E. N. (2007). Multiperiod planning of enterprise-wide supply chains using an operation policy. *Industrial & Engineering Chemistry Research*, *46*(24), 8058–8065.

Ryu, S. J., Tsukishima, T., & Onari, H. (2009). A study on evaluation of demand information-sharing methods in supply chain. *International Journal of Production Economics*, *120*(1), 162–175.

Sadraoui, T., & Mchirgui, N. (2014). Supply Chain Management Optimization within Information System Development. *International Journal of Econometrics and Financial Management.*, *2*(2), 59–71.

Saeed, N., & Larsen, O. I. (2016). Application of Queuing Methodology to Analyze Congestion: A Case Study of the Manila International Container Terminal, Philippines. *Case Studies on Transport Policy*, *4*(2), 143–149. doi:10.1016/j.cstp.2016.02.001

Saha, S. K., & Jha, A. (2018). Role of Information Technology on Supply Chain Management of Pharmaceutical Industry. *International Journal of Applied Logistics*, *8*(2), 39–68. doi:10.4018/IJAL.2018070103

Sahay, B. S. (2003). Understanding trust in supply chain relationships. *Industrial Management & Data Systems*, *103*(8), 553–563. doi:10.1108/02635570310497602

Sahay, B. S., & Ranjan, J. (2008). Real time business intelligence in supply chain analytics. *Information Management & Computer Security*, *16*(1), 28–48.

Sahin, F., & Robinson, E. P. Jr. (2005). Information sharing and coordination in make-to-order supply chains. *Journal of Operations Management*, *23*(6), 579–598.

Sako, M., & Helper, S. (1998). Determinants of trust in supplier relations: Evidence from the automotive industry in Japan and the United States. *Journal of Economic Behavior & Organization*, *34*(3), 387–417. doi:10.1016/S0167-2681(97)00082-6

Salam, M. (2019). Analyzing manufacturing strategies and Industry 4.0 supplier performance relationships from a resource-based perspective. *Benchmarking: An International Journal.* . doi:10.1108/BIJ-12-2018-0428

Samaddar, S., Nargundkar, S., & Daley, M. (2006). Inter-organizational information sharing: The role of supply network configuration and partner goal congruence. *European Journal of Operational Research*, *174*(2), 744–765.

Sambharya, R., & Lee, J. (2014). Renewing Dynamic Capabilities Globally: An Empirical Study of the World's Largest MNCs. *MIR. Management International Review*, *54*(2), 137–169. doi:10.100711575-013-0199-7

Samir, K. S., & Rajiv, K. S. (2006). Managing product returns for reverse logistics. *International Journal of Physical Distribution & Logistics Management*, *36*(7), 524–546. doi:10.1108/09600030610684962

Sanchez, R., Heene, A., & Thomas, H. (1996). *Introduction: Towards the Theory and Practice of Competence-based Competition*. Pergamon Press. doi:10.4000/books.pur.47926

Sander, F. A. (2004). *How to break a stalemate*. Academic Press.

Sanders, N. R., & Premus, R. (2002). IT applications in supply chain organizations: A link between competitive priorities and organizational benefits. *Journal of Business Logistics*, *23*(1), 65–83.

Sarac, A., Absi, N., & Dauzère-Pérès, S. (2010). A literature review on the impact of RFID technologies on supply chain management. *International Journal of Production Economics*, *128*(1), 77–95.

Sarhani, M., & El Afia, A. (2014). Forecasting Demand with Support Vector Regression Technique Combined with X13-ARIMA-SEATS Method in the Presence of Calendar Effect. *International Journal of Applied Logistics*, *5*(2), 74–86.

Sarkar, M., Aulakh, P. S., & Cavusgil, S. T. (1998). The strategic role of relational bonding in interorganizational collaborations: An empirical study of the global construction industry. *Journal of International Management*, *4*(2), 85–107. doi:10.1016/S1075-4253(98)00009-X

Sazvar, Z., Mirzapour Al-e-Hashem, S. M. J., Baboli, A., & Jokar, M. A. (2014). A bi-objective stochastic programming model for a centralized green supply chain with deteriorating products. *International Journal of Production Economics*, *150*, 140–154. doi:10.1016/j.ijpe.2013.12.023

Schapranow, M. P., Zeier, A., & Plattner, H. (2011, January). A formal model for enabling RFID in pharmaceutical supply chains. In *System Sciences (HICSS), 2011 44th Hawaii International Conference on* (pp. 1-10). IEEE.

Schewdhelm, A., Li, W., Harms, L., & Adriazola-Steil, C. (2020). *Cycling during COVID-19 | world resources institute. Biking Provides a Critical Lifeline During the Coronavirus Crisis.* Retrieved from https://www.wri.org/blog/2020/04/coronavirus-bikingcritical-in-cities

Schlosser, F., Maier, B. F., Jack, O., Hinrichs, D., Zachariae, A., & Brockmann, D. (2020). COVID-19 lockdown induces disease-mitigating structural changes in mobility networks. *Proceedings of the National Academy of Sciences of the United States of America*, *117*(52), 32883–32890. doi:10.1073/pnas.2012326117 PMID:33273120

Schmidt, A. P., Schmidt-Weitmann, S. H., Lachat, M. L., & Brockes, C. M. (2014). Teleconsultation in vascular surgery: A 13-year single centre experience. *Journal of Telemedicine and Telecare*, *20*, 24–28. PMID:24352901

Schmidt, C. G., & Wagner, S. M. (2019). Blockchain and supply chain relations: A transaction cost theory perspective. *Journal of Purchasing and Supply Management*, *25*(4), 100552. doi:10.1016/j.pursup.2019.100552

Schneller, E. S., & Smeltzer, L. R. (2006). *Strategic Management of the Health Care Supply Chain* (1st ed.). Wiley.

Schulze, P. M., & Prinz, A. (2009). Forecasting container transshipment in Germany. *Applied Economics*, *41*(22), 2809–2815. doi:10.1080/00036840802260932

Schwartz, P. (1996). *The Art of the Long View: Planning for the Future in an Uncertain World.* Doubleday.

Sebenius, J. K. (2002). Six Habits of Merely Effective Negotiators. *Harvard Business Review*. PMID:11299696

Seif, E., Tharwat, B., Naser, A., & Madiha, A. (2010) *The Problem of Pharmaceutical Returns: The Gate for Fake Drugs/ Interviewer: M. Reem.* Our country, ON-TV, Egypt.

Selviaridis, K. (2020). Effects of public procurement of R&D on the innovation process: evidence from the UK small business research initiative. *Journal of Public Procurement*. . doi:10.1108/JOPP-12-2019-0082

Seth, A., & Thomas, H. (1994). Theories of the firm: Implications for strategy research. *Journal of Management Studies*, *31*(2), 165–191. doi:10.1111/j.1467-6486.1994.tb00770.x

Seth, D., & Rastogi, S. (2019). Application of vendor rationalization strategy for manufacturing cycle time reduction in engineer to order (ETO) environment: A case study. *Journal of Manufacturing Technology Management*, *30*(1), 261–290. doi:10.1108/JMTM-03-2018-0095

Shabani, A., Visani, F., Barbieri, P., Dullaert, W., & Vigo, D. (2019). Reliable estimation of suppliers' total cost of ownership: An imprecise data envelopment analysis model with common weights. *Omega*, *87*, 57–70. doi:10.1016/j.omega.2018.08.002

Shahabadkar, P. (2012). Deployment of Interpretive Structural Modelling Methodology in Supply Chain Management–An overview. *International Journal of Industrial Engineering & Production Research*, *23*(3), 195–205.

Shah, N. (2004). Pharmaceutical supply chains: Key issues and strategies for optimization. *Computers & Chemical Engineering*, *28*(6-7), 929–941.

Shah, N. K., & Ierapetritou, M. G. (2012). Integrated production planning and scheduling optimization of multisite, multiproduct process industry. *Computers & Chemical Engineering*, *37*, 214–226.

Shannon, R. E. (1975). *Systems Simulation – The Art and Science*. Prentice-Hall.

Shao, X. F., Liu, W., Li, Y., Chaudhry, H. R., & Yue, X. G. (2021). Multistage implementation framework for smart supply chain management under industry 4.0. *Technological Forecasting and Social Change*, *162*, 120354. PMID:33041379

Sharfman, M. P., & Dean, J. W. Jr. (1991). Conceptualizing and measuring the organizational environment: A multidimensional approach. *Journal of Management*, *17*(4), 681–700. doi:10.1177/014920639101700403

Shaurabh, S., Saurabh, B., & Moti, K. (2013). Strategic Framework for Reverse Logistics in Pharmaceutical Industry. *Asian Research Journal of Business Management, 1*(1).

Shell, R. (1991). When is it legal to lie in negotiations? *Sloan Management Review*, *32*(3), 93–101.

Shell, R. (2000). *Bargaining for Advantage: Negotiation Strategies for Reasonable People*. Penguin Publishing Group.

Shi, K., De Vos, J., Yang, Y., & Witlox, F. (2019). Does e-shopping replace shopping trips? Empirical evidence from Chengdu, China. *Transportation Research Part A, Policy and Practice*, *122*, 21–33. doi:10.1016/j.tra.2019.01.027

Simatupang, T. M., & Sridharan, R. (2002). The collaborative supply chain. *International Journal of Logistics Management*, *13*(1), 15–30.

Simatupang, T. M., & Sridharan, R. (2005). The collaboration index: A measure for supply chain collaboration. *International Journal of Physical Distribution & Logistics Management*, *35*(1), 44–62.

Simon, H. A. (1947). *Administrative behaviour*. Free Press.

Simpson, L. (2003, April). Get around resistance and win over the other side. *Harvard Management Communication Letter*, 1–5.

Simulation of Urban Mobility. (2019). Retrieved from http://sumo.sourceforge.net/userdoc/Sumo_at_a_Glance.html

Singer, A. E. (1997). Game theory and the evolution of strategic thinking. *Human Systems Management*, *16*(1), 63–75. doi:10.3233/HSM-1997-16108

Singh, R., & Modgil, S. (2020). Supplier selection using SWARA and WASPAS – a case study of Indian cement industry. *Measuring Business Excellence*, *24*(2), 243–265. doi:10.1108/MBE-07-2018-0041

Šinko, S., & Gumzej, R. (2021). Towards Smart Traffic Planning by Traffic Simulation on Microscopic Level. *International Journal of Applied Logistics*, *11*(1), 1–17. doi:10.4018/IJAL.2021010101

Sirkeci, I., & Yucesahin, M. M. (2020). Coronavirus and migration: Analysis of human mobility and the spread of COVID-19. *Migration Letters: An International Journal of Migration Studies*, *17*(2), 379–398. doi:10.33182/ml.v17i2.935

Smith A, (2009). Internet retail banking A competitive analysis in an increasingly financially troubled environment. *Information Management & Computer Security, 17*(2), 127-150. doi:10.1108/09685220910964009

Smith, S. (2014). Muda, muri and mura. *Lean & Six Sigma Review, 13*(2), 36-37.

Sodhi, M. S., & Tang, C. S. (2020). Supply Chain Management for Extreme Conditions: Research Opportunities. *The Journal of Supply Chain Management.*

Sohn, S. Y., & Lim, M. (2008). The effect of forecasting and information sharing in SCM for multi-generation products. *European Journal of Operational Research, 186*(1), 276–287.

Song, J., Wu, Y., Xu, Z., & Lin, X. (2014). Research on car-following model based on SUMO. *The 7th IEEE/International Conference on Advanced Infocomm Technology.* 10.1109/ICAIT.2014.7019528

Soni, U., & Jain, V. (2011, December). Minimizing the vulnerabilities of supply chain: A new framework for enhancing the resilience. In *Industrial Engineering and Engineering Management (IEEM), 2011 IEEE International Conference on* (pp. 933-939). IEEE.

Soroor, J., Tarokh, M. J., & Shemshadi, A. (2009). Initiating a state of the art system for real-time supply chain coordination. *European Journal of Operational Research, 196*(2), 635–650.

Sousa, C. M. P., Martínez-Lopez, F. J., & Coelho, F. (2008). The determinants of export performance: A review of the research in the literature between 1998 and 2005. *International Journal of Management Reviews, 10*(4), 343–374. doi:10.1111/j.1468-2370.2008.00232.x

Sparmann, U. (1979). The importance of lane-changing on motorways. *Traffic Engineering & Control, 20*(6).

Spekman, R. E., & Carraway, R. (2006). Making the transition to collaborative buyer-seller relationships: An emerging framework. *Industrial Marketing Management, 35*(1), 10–19. doi:10.1016/j.indmarman.2005.07.002

Spekman, R. E., Kamauff, J. W. Jr, & Myhr, N. (1998). An empirical investigation into supply chain management: A perspective on partnerships. *Supply Chain Management, 3*(2), 53–67.

Spiekermann, M., & Urban, W. (2013). *Overview of Country Transport Models.* Regional Section Research Lindemannstrasse.

Srivastava, Shervani, & Fahey. (1998). Market-based Assets and Shareholder Value: a Framework for Analysis. *Journal of Marketing, 62*(1), 2-18.

Ssengonzi, R., & Oginski, P. (2012). *Effective adaptation to global humanitarian challenges* (Master's thesis). Jönköping International Business School, Torpa, Sweden.

Stadtler, H. (2005). Supply chain management and advanced planning Basics, overview and challenges. *European Journal of Operational Research, 163*(3), 575588. doi:10.1016/j.ejor.2004.03.001

Stahlbock, R., & Voß, S. (2008). Operations Research at Container Terminals: A Literature Update. *OR-Spektrum, 30*(1), 1–52. doi:10.100700291-007-0100-9

Stecca, G., Baffo, I., & Kaihara, T. (2016). Design and operation of strategic inventory control system for drug delivery in healthcare industry. *IFAC-PapersOnLine, 49*(12), 904–909.

Stenger, A., Vigo, D., Enz, S., & Schwind, M. (2013). An adaptive variable neighborhood search algorithm for a vehicle routing problem arising in small package shipping. *Transportation Science, 47*(1), 503–527. doi:10.1287/trsc.1110.0396

Stevens, J. (1989). Integrating the supply chain. *International Journal of Physical Distribution & Materials Management, 19*(8), 3–8. doi:10.1108/EUM0000000000329

Stevenson, W. J., & Hojati, M. (2007). *Operations management* (Vol. 8). McGraw-Hill/Irwin.

Stojčića, N., Srhoja, S., & Coad, A. (2020). Innovation procurement as capability-building: Evaluating innovation policies in eight Central and Eastern European countries. *European Economic Review*, *121*, 103330. Advance online publication. doi:10.1016/j.euroecorev.2019.103330

Stopford, M. (2009). Maritime economics (3rd ed.). Routledge.

Strandskov, J. (1999). *Sources of competitive advantage and business performance in the European meat processing industry*. MAPP Working Paper no. 63, Aarhus: Aarhus School of Business.

Strawn, G. O. (2012). Scientific Research: How Many Paradigms? *EDUCAUSE Review*, *47*(3), 26.

Subiyanto, E. (2020). Assessing Total Logistics Costs: Case Study during the Execution of Cement Projects in Indonesia. *International Journal of Applied Logistics*, *10*(2), 45–61. doi:10.4018/IJAL.2020070103

Subiyanto, E. (2021). Investigating the logistics costs model: Recent update in Indonesia. *Journal of Science and Technology Policy Management*, *12*(2), 331–350. doi:10.1108/JSTPM-03-2020-0034

Subiyanto, E., & Rini, H. P. (2020). Developing Model of Logistics Costs in Indonesia's Cement Projects: A Literature and Empirical Study Approach. *Journal of Economics and Business*, *3*(2), 697–718. doi:10.31014/aior.1992.03.02.232

Subiyanto, E., & Suyoto, Y. T. (2020). Determining Value of Logistics Costs in Projects; Empirical Findings based-on Executing Several Cement Projects in Indonesia. *Heliyon*, *6*(7), e04352. Advance online publication. doi:10.1016/j.heliyon.2020.e04352 PMID:32695900

Sumo. (2019a). *Definition of Vehicles, Vehicle Types, and Routes*. Retrieved from https://sumo.dlr.de/docs/Definition_of_Vehicles,_Vehicle_Types,_and_Routes.html

Sumo. (2019b). *Pedestrian Simulation*. Retrieved from https://sumo.dlr.de/docs/Simulation/Pedestrians.html

Sundarakani, B., Kamran, R., Maheshwari, P., & Jain, V. (2019). Designing a hybrid cloud for a supply chain network of Industry 4.0: A theoretical framework. *Benchmarking*.

Suresh, M., & Nathan, A. (2020). Readiness for lean procurement in construction projects. *Construction Innovation*, *20*(4), 587–608. doi:10.1108/CI-07-2019-0067

Susarla, N., & Karimi, I. A. (2012). Integrated supply chain planning for multinational pharma-ceutical enterprises. *Computers & Chemical Engineering*, *42*, 168–177.

Sutanto, S. H. (2021). The characteristic, performance, accessibility, and prediction of cargo handling in Probolinggo New Terminal Port. *IOP Conference Series. Earth and Environmental Science*, *649*(1), 012045. doi:10.1088/1755-1315/649/1/012045

Svensson, G. (2000). A conceptual framework for the analysis of vulnerability in supply chains. *International Journal of Physical Distribution & Logistics Management*, *30*(9), 731–750. doi:10.1108/09600030010351444

Swafford, P. M., Ghosh, S., & Murthy, N. (2008). Achieving supply chain agility through IT integration and flexibility. *International Journal of Production Economics*, *116*(2), 288–297.

Syahrir, I., & Vanany, I. (2015). Healthcare and disaster supply chain: Literature review and future research. *Procedia Manufacturing*, *4*, 2–9.

Syntetos, A. A., Babai, Z., Boylan, J. E., Kolassa, S., & Nikolopoulos, K. (2016). Supply chain forecasting: Theory, practice, their gap and the future. *European Journal of Operational Research*, *252*(1), 1–26.

Tajima, M. (2007). Strategic value of RFID in supply chain management. *Journal of Purchasing and Supply Management, 13*(4), 261–273.

Tan, E. N., Smith, G., & Saad, M. (2006). Managing the global supply chain: A SME perspective. *Production Planning and Control, 17*(3), 238–246.

Tan, F. B., & Hunter, M. G. (2002). The Repertory Grid Technique: A Method for the Study of Cognition in Information Systems. *Management Information Systems Quarterly, 26*(1), 39–57. doi:10.2307/4132340

Tan, K. C. (2002). Supply chain management: Practices, concerns, and performance issues. *The Journal of Supply Chain Management, 38*(4), 42–53. doi:10.1111/j.1745-493X.2002.tb00119.x

Tanskanen, K., & Aminoff, A. (2015). Buyer and supplier attractiveness in a strategic relationship—A dyadic multiple-case study. *Industrial Marketing Management, 50*, 128–141. doi:10.1016/j.indmarman.2015.04.011

Tat, R., Heydari, J., & Rabbani, M. (2020). A mathematical model for pharmaceutical supply chain coordination: Reselling medicines in an alternative market. *Journal of Cleaner Production, 268*, 121897.

Tat, R., Heydari, J., & Rabbani, M. (2021). Corporate social responsibility in the pharmaceutical supply chain: An optimized medicine donation scheme. *Computers & Industrial Engineering, 152*, 107022.

Technology, P. (2021). *Ictsi Orders Rtgs from Mitsui for $80 Million Upgrade*. Accessed April 11, 2021, https://www.porttechnology.org/news/ictsi_orders_rtgs_from_mitsui_for_80_million_upgrade

Teece, Pisano, & Shuen. (1997). Dynamic Capabilities and Strategic Management. *Strategic Management Journal, 18*(7), 509-533.

Teller, C., Kotzab, H., & Grant, D. (2006). The consumer direct services revolution in grocery retailing: an exploratory investigation. *Managing Service Quality, 16*(1), 78-96. doi:10.1108/09604520610639973

Tendera, M., Aboyans, V., & Bartelink, M. L. (2011). ESC guidelines on the diagnosis and treatment of peripheral artery diseases. *European Heart Journal, 32*, 2851–2906.

Terreno, S., Asadi, S., & Anumba, C. (2019). An Exploration of Synergies between Lean Concepts and BIM in FM: A Review and Directions for Future Research. *Buildings, 9*(147), 147. Advance online publication. doi:10.3390/buildings9060147

Tetteh, G. (2005). *Finalization and Dissemination of the Rapid Assessment of Antimalarial Drug Availability and Use in Nigeria: Rational Pharmaceutical Management Plus program*. Retrieved from http://pdf.usaid.gov

The SCM Journal List. (n.d.). http://www.scmlist.com/

The World Bank. (2017). *Listed domestic companies*. https://data.worldbank.org/indicator/CM.MKT.LDOM.NO?end=2015&start=1990

Theodoropoulou, R., & Kasoli, M. (2014). *Transport and Logistics*. Hellenic General Secretariat for Research and Technology.

Thompson, J. D. (1967). *Organizations in action*. McGraw-Hill.

Tibben-Lembke, R. S. (2002). Life after death: Reverse logistics and the product life cycle. *International Journal of Physical Distribution & Logistics Management, 32*(3–4), 223–244.

Ting, S., Chen, C., & Bartholomew, D. E. (2007). An integrated study of entrepreneurs' opportunism. *Journal of Business and Industrial Marketing, 22*(5), 322–335. doi:10.1108/08858620710773459

Tirole, J. (1988). *The theory of industrial organization*. MIT Press.

Tjitemisa, K. (2014, June 4). A shortage of essential drugs used in surgery at both public and private pharmacies has sparked panic at leading hospitals in the country. *The Namibian*. Retrieved from http://www.namibian.com.na

Tokatli, N., & Boyaci-Eldener, Y. (2002). Globalization and the changing political economy of distribution channels in Turkey. *Environment & Planning A*, *34*(2), 217–238. doi:10.1068/a34113

Tokatli, N., & Boyaci, Y. (1998). The changing retail industry and retail landscapes: The case of post-1980 Turkey. *Cities (London, England)*, *15*(5), 345–359. doi:10.1016/S0264-2751(98)00030-4

Tokatli, N., & Boyaci, Y. (1999). The changing morphology of commercial activity in Istanbul. *Cities (London, England)*, *16*(3), 181–193. doi:10.1016/S0264-2751(99)00015-3

Toorajipour, R., Sohrabpour, V., Nazarpour, A., Oghazi, P., & Fischl, M. (2021). Artificial intelligence in supply chain management: A systematic literature review. *Journal of Business Research*, *122*, 502–517.

Touboulic, A., McCarthy, L., & Matthews, L. (2020). Re-imagining supply chain challenges through critical engaged research. *The Journal of Supply Chain Management*, *56*(2), 36–51. doi:10.1111/jscm.12226

Tung, R. L. (1979). Dimensions of organizational environments: An exploratory study of their impact on organization structure. *Academy of Management Journal*, *22*, 672–693.

Turner, J. R. (2004). Farsighted project contract management: Incomplete in its entirety. *Construction Management and Economics*, *22*(1), 75–83. doi:10.1080/0144619042000186077

U.S. Department of Health and Human Services. (2017). *Health Information Privacy*. https://www.hhs.gov/hipaa/for-professionals/index.html

Umarusman, N. (2021). Fuzzy goal programming with interval type-2 for solving multi-objective sustainable supplier selection problems. In G. Aytekin & Ç. Doğru (Eds.), *Handbook of Research on Recent Perspectives on Management, International Trade, and Logistics* (pp. 164–197). IGI Global. doi:10.4018/978-1-7998-5886-7.ch010

Uzzi, B. (1996). The Sources and Consequences of Embeddedness for the Economic Performance of Organizations: The Network Effect. *American Sociological Review*, *61*(4), 674–698. doi:10.2307/2096399

Van den Broeck, E., Zarouali, B., & Poels, K. (2019). Chatbot advertising effectiveness: When does the message get through? *Computers in Human Behavior*, *98*, 150–157.

van Hoek, R. I. (1999). From reversed logistics to green supply chains. *Supply Chain Management*, *4*(3), 129.

van Weele, A. J., & van Raaij, E. M. (2014). The future of purchasing and supply management research: About relevance and rigor. *The Journal of Supply Chain Management*, *50*(1), 56–72. doi:10.1111/jscm.12042

Varbanova, A. (2011). Current iIssues in operational planning of general cargo transportation on container feeder lines in the Black Sea region. *The International Virtual Journal for Science, Techniques and Innovations for the Industry Machines, Technologies, Materials*, *2011*(3), 35–38.

Ventola, L. S. (2011). The Drug Shortage Crisis in the United States. Causes, Impact, and Management Strategies. *Supply Chain Management*, *36*(11), 189–190. PMID:22346307

Verdecho, M. J., Alfaro, J. J., & Rodriguez-Rodriguez, R. (2009). Foundations for collaborative performance measurement. *Production Planning and Control*, *20*(3), 193–205. doi:10.1080/09537280902721001

Verdouw, C. N., Beulens, A. J., Reijers, H. A., & van der Vorst, J. G. (2015). A control model for object virtualization in supply chain management. *Computers in Industry*, *68*, 116–131.

Vereecke, A., & Muylle, S. (2006). Performance improvement through supply chain collaboration in Europe. *International Journal of Operations & Production Management*, *26*(11), 1176–1198.

VHSS. (2013). *Containership time-charter-rates.* Retrieved 15.06.2012 from http://www.vhss.de/contex_new.php

Vibert, C. (2004). *Theories of macro-organizational behavior: A handbook of ideas and explanations.* M.E. Sharpe.

Vibert, C., & Hurst, D. (2004). Radical humanist and structuralist perspectives. In C. Vibert (Ed.), *Theories of macro-organizational behavior: A handbook of ideas and explanations.* M.E. Sharpe.

Vila-Parrish, A. R., & Ivy, J. S. (2013). Managing supply critical to patient care: an introduction to hospital inventory management for pharmaceuticals. In *Handbook of Healthcare Operations Management* (pp. 447–463). Springer.

Vitzthum, C. (2001, May 18). Just-in-time fashion: Spanish retailer Zara makes low cost lines in weeks by running its own show. *Wall Street Journal*, p. B1.

Vorhies, D. W., & Morgan, N. A. (2005). Benchmarking marketing capabilities for sustainable competitive advantage. *Journal of Marketing*, *69*(1), 80–94. doi:10.1509/jmkg.69.1.80.55505

Wade & Hulland. (2004). Review: The Resource-Based View and Information Systems Research: Review, Extension, and Suggestions for Future Research. *MIS Quarterly, 28*(1), 107-142.

Waller, M. A., & Fawcett, S. E. (2013). Data science, predictive analytics, and big data: A revolution that will transform supply chain design and management. *Journal of Business Logistics*, *34*(2), 77–84.

Wamba, S. F., Akter, S., Edwards, A., Chopin, G., & Gnanzou, D. (2015). How 'big data'can make big impact: Findings from a systematic review and a longitudinal case study. *International Journal of Production Economics*, *165*, 234–246.

Wamba, S. F., Lefebvre, L. A., Bendavid, Y., & Lefebvre, É. (2008). Exploring the impact of RFID technology and the EPC network on mobile B2B eCommerce: A case study in the retail industry. *International Journal of Production Economics*, *112*(2), 614–629.

Wang, S. J., Liu, S. F., & Wang, W. L. (2008). The simulated impact of RFID-enabled supply chain on pull-based inventory replenishment in TFT-LCD industry. *International Journal of Production Economics*, *112*(2), 570–586.

Wang, T., Meng, Q., & Wang, S. (2012). Robust Optimization Model for Liner Ship Fleet Planning with Container Transshipment and Uncertain Demand. *Transportation Research Record: Journal of the Transportation Research Board*, *2273*(1), 18–28. doi:10.3141/2273-03

Wang, Y., Wallace, S. W., Shen, B., & Choi, T. M. (2015). Service supply chain management: A review of operational models. *European Journal of Operational Research*, *247*(3), 685–698.

Warfield, J. N. (1974). Developing Interconnection Matrices in Structural Modeling. *Systems, Man and Cybernetics, IEEE Transactions on*, *SMC-4*(1), 81–87. doi: . doi:10.1109/TSMC.1974.5408524

Warfield, J. N., & Cárdenas, A. R. (1994). *A handbook of interactive management* (2nd ed.). Iowa State University Press Ames.

Welker, G. A., van der Vaart, T., & van Donk, D. P. (2008). The influence of business conditions on supply chain information-sharing mechanisms: A study among supply chain links of SMEs. *International Journal of Production Economics*, *113*(2), 706–720.

Weraikat, D., Zanjani, M. K., & Lehoux, N. (2016). Coordinating a green reverse supply chain in pharmaceutical sector by negotiation. *Computers & Industrial Engineering*, *93*, 67–77.

Wernerfelt, B. (1984). A Resource-based View of the Firm. *Strategic Management Journal*, *5*(2), 171–180. doi:10.1002mj.4250050207

White, A. D., & Mohdzain, M. B. (2008). An innovative model of supply chain management: A single case study in the electronic sector. *International Journal of Information Technology and Management*, *8*(1), 69–84. doi:10.1504/IJITM.2009.022271

WHO. (2020). WHO *Director-General's opening remarks at the media briefing on COVID-19 - March 11 2020*. Retrieved from https://www.who.int/dg/speeches/detail/who-director-general-s-opening-remarks-at-the-media-briefing-on-covid 19

Wicher, P., & Lenort, R. (2012). The ways of creating resilient supply chains. *Proceedings of CLC: Carpathian Logistics Congress*, 688–694.

Wieland, A. (2021). Dancing the supply chain: Toward transformative supply chain management. *The Journal of Supply Chain Management*, *57*(1), 58–73.

Wiengarten, F., & Ambrose, E. (2017). The role of geographical distance and its efficacy on global purchasing practices. *International Journal of Operations & Production Management*, *37*(7), 865–881. doi:10.1108/IJOPM-09-2015-0556

Wijnolst, N., Waals, F., Bello, F., Gendronneau, Y., & Kempen, D. v. (2000). *Malacca Max (2) Container Shipping Network Economy*. Delft University Press.

Williamson, O. E. (1976). *Markets and hierarchies: Analysis and anti-trust implications*. Free Press.

Williamson, O. E. (1988). Corporate finance and corporate governance. *The Journal of Finance*, *43*(3), 567–591. doi:10.1111/j.1540-6261.1988.tb04592.x

Wilson, J. W., Cunningham, W. A., & Westbrook, K. W. (1992). Stockless inventory systems for the health care provider: Three successful applications. *Journal of Health Care Marketing*, *12*(2), 39–45. PMID:10119212

Wollenberg, E., Edmunds, D., & Buck, L. (2000). Using scenarios to make decisions about the future: Anticipatory learning for the adaptive co-management of community forests. *Landscape and Urban Planning*, *47*(1-2), 65–77. doi:10.1016/S0169-2046(99)00071-7

Wood, L. C., & Wang, J. X. (2018). The Event Study Method in Logistics Research: Overview and a Critical Analysis. *International Journal of Applied Logistics*, *8*(1), 57–79. doi:10.4018/IJAL.2018010104

Woolliscroft, P., Caganova, D., Cambal, M., Holecek, J., & Pucikova, L. (2013). Implications for optimization of the automotive supply chain through knowledge management. *Procedia CIRP*, *7*, 211–216.

World Health Organization. (2016). *Pharmaceutical products*. Retrieved from: http://www.who.int

World Shipping Council. (2021). *Top 50 World Container Ports*. Accessed April 01, 2021, https://www.worldshipping.org/about-the-industry/global-trade/top-50-world-container-ports

Wright, D., & Yuan, X. (2008). *Mitigating the bullwhip effect by ordering policies and forecasting methods. International Journal of Production Economics, 113(2).* https://www.sciencedirect.com/science/article/pii/S0925527308000340

Wright, R. P., & Cheung, F. K. K. (2007). Articulating appraisal system effectiveness based on managerial cognitions. *Personnel Review*, *36*(2), 206–230. doi:10.1108/00483480710726118

Wu, H., Cao, J., Yang, Y., Tung, C. L., Jiang, S., Tang, B., . . . Deng, Y. (2019, July). Data management in supply chain using blockchain: Challenges and a case study. In *2019 28th International Conference on Computer Communication and Networks (ICCCN)* (pp. 1-8). IEEE.

Wu, J., & Haasis, H. D. (2013). Integration of Knowledge Management Approach to the Planning Stage of Freight Villages: Towards Sustainable Development. *International Journal of Applied Logistics*, *4*(2), 46–65.

Wu, Y. N., & Cheng, T. E. (2008). The impact of information sharing in a multiple-echelon supply chain. *International Journal of Production Economics*, *115*(1), 1–11.

Xie, Y., & Breen, L. (2012). Greening community pharmaceutical supply chain in UK: A cross boundary approach. *Supply Chain Management*, *17*(1), 40–53.

Yang, C. H., Choi, Y. S., & Ha, T. Y. (2004). Simulation-Based Performance Evaluation of Transport Vehicles at Automated Container Terminals. *OR-Spektrum*, *26*(2), 149–170. doi:10.100700291-003-0151-5

Yang, C., Wu, L., Cai, W., Zhu, W., Shen, Q., Li, Z., & Fang, Y. (2016). Current Situation, determinants, and Solutions to drug shortages in Shaanxi Province, China: A Qualitative Study. *PLoS One*, *11*(10), e0165183. doi:10.1371/journal.pone.0165183 PMID:27780218

Yang, J., & Xie, S. J. (2012). *New Trends and Developments in Biometrics*. InTech.

Yang, Y.-C. (2017). Operating Strategies of Co2 Reduction for a Container Terminal Based on Carbon Footprint Perspective. *Journal of Cleaner Production*, *141*(Supplement C), 472–480. doi:10.1016/j.jclepro.2016.09.132

Yang, Y.-C., & Lin, C.-L. (2013). Performance Analysis of Cargo-Handling Equipment from a Green Container Terminal Perspective. *Transportation Research Part D, Transport and Environment*, *23*(Supplement C), 9–11. doi:10.1016/j.trd.2013.03.009

Yan, J., Xin, S., Liu, Q., Xu, W., Yang, L., Fan, L., ... Wang, Q. (2014). Intelligent supply chain integration and management based on cloud of things. *International Journal of Distributed Sensor Networks*, *10*(3), 624839.

Yellowlees, P., Shore, J., & Roberts, L. (2010). Practice guidelines for videoconferencing-based telemental health. *Telemedicine Journal and e-Health*, *16*(10), 1074–1089.

Yildirim, M. B., & Mouzon, G. (2011). Single-machine sustainable production planning to minimize total energy consumption and total completion time using a multiple objective genetic algorithm. *IEEE Transactions on Engineering Management*, *59*(4), 585–597. doi:10.1109/TEM.2011.2171055

Yongqiang, S., Yang, X., He, Q., Li, Q., & Xu, Q. (2010). Anylogic- Based Simulation Analysis of Queuing System at Container Terminals. *The 2nd International Conference on Information Science and Engineering*. 10.1109/ICISE.2010.5689971

Yoon, J., & Moon, J. (2019). The moderating effect of buyer purchasing strategy on the relationship between supplier transaction-specific investment and supplier firm performance. *Journal of Business Research*, *99*, 516–523. doi:10.1016/j.jbusres.2017.08.022

Yuchtman, E., & Seashore, S. E. (1967). A system resource approach to organizational effectiveness. *American Sociological Review*, *32*(6), 891–903. doi:10.2307/2092843

Yu, M. M., Ting, S. C., & Chen, M. C. (2010). Evaluating the cross-efficiency of information sharing in supply chains. *Expert Systems with Applications*, *37*(4), 2891–2897.

Yu, X., Li, C., Shi, Y., & Yu, M. (2010). Pharmaceutical supply chain in China: Current issues and implications for health system reform. *Health Policy (Amsterdam)*, *97*(1), 8–15. PMID:20307912

Zachcial, M., & Lemper, B. (2006). Container shipping: An overview of Development Trends. In C. Heideloff & T. Pawlik (Eds.), Handbook of Container Shipping Management (pp. 23-37). Institute of Shipping Economics and Logistics (ISL).

Zaharudin, A. A., Wong, C. Y., Agarwal, V., McFarlane, D., Koh, R., & Kang, Y. Y. (2006). *The intelligent product driven supply chain.* Tech. Rep. 05, AUTO-ID LABS.

Zawislak, P. A., Cherubini Alves, A., Tello-Gamarra, J., Barbieux, D., & Reichert, F. M. (2012). Innovation capability: From technology development to transaction capability. *Journal of Technology Management & Innovation*, *7*(2), 14–27. doi:10.4067/S0718-27242012000200002

Zeddam, B., Belkaid, F., & Bennekrouf, M. (2020). An efficient approach for solving integrated production and distribution planning problems: Cost vs. Energy. *International Journal of Applied Logistics*, *10*(2), 25–44. doi:10.4018/IJAL.2020070102

Zeng, Q., & Yang, Z. (2009). Integrating Simulation and Optimization to Schedule Loading Operations in Container Terminals. *Computers & Operations Research*, *36*(6), 1935–1944. doi:10.1016/j.cor.2008.06.010

Zeng, Q., Yang, Z., & Chen, C. (2010). Robust optimization model for resource allocation of container shipping lines. *Tsinghua Science and Technology*, *15*(5), 586–594. doi:10.1016/S1007-0214(10)70105-X

Zhang, X., Zeng, Q., & Yang, Z. (2016). Modeling the Mixed Storage Strategy for Quay Crane Double Cycling in Container Terminals. *Transportation Research Part E, Logistics and Transportation Review*, *94*(Supplement C), 171–187. doi:10.1016/j.tre.2016.08.002

Zhang, Z., Luo, Z., Baldacci, R., & Lim, A. (2021). A benders decomposition approach for the multivehicle production routing problem with order-up-to-level policy. *Transportation Science*, *55*(1), 160–178. doi:10.1287/trsc.2019.0964

Zheng, H. Y., & Wang, L. (2015). Reduction of carbon emissions and project makespan by a Pareto-based estimation of distribution algorithm. *International Journal of Production Economics*, *164*, 421–432. doi:10.1016/j.ijpe.2014.12.010

Zhou, G., Fei, Y., & Hu, J. (2016). The analysis of vertical transaction behavior and performance based on automobile brand trust in supply chain. *Discrete Dynamics in Nature and Society*, *2016*, 1–13. Advance online publication. doi:10.1155/2016/4793851

Zhou, H., & Benton, W. C. Jr. (2007). Supply chain practice and information sharing. *Journal of Operations Management*, *25*(6), 1348–1365.

Zhu, X., Mukhopadhyay, S. K., & Yue, X. (2011). Role of forecast effort on supply chain profitability under various information sharing scenarios. *International Journal of Production Economics*, *129*(2), 284–291.

Zurheide, S., & Fischer, K. (2011). A Simulation study for evaluating a slot allocation model for a liner shipping network. *Lecture Notes in Computer Science*, *6971*, 354–369. doi:10.1007/978-3-642-24264-9_26

Zurheide, S., & Fischer, K. (2012). A revenue management slot allocation model for liner shipping networks. *Maritime Economics & Logistics*, *14*(3), 334–361. doi:10.1057/mel.2012.11

Zveza potrošnikov Slovenije. (2020). *Strah pred okužbo s COVID-19 bo zaznamoval mobilnost.* Retrieved from https://www.zps.si/okolje-topmenu-320/trajnostna-mobilnost/10708-strah-pred-okuzbo-s-covid-19-bo-zaznamoval-mobilnost

About the Contributors

Lincoln C. Wood, PhD, is an Associate Professor in the Department of Management at the University of Otago (New Zealand) and an Adjunct Research Fellow at Curtin University (Western Australia). His research has been recognised with an award from the CSCMP and his focus on education in operations and logistics resulted in leading an Office of Learning and Teaching government grant in Australia. Working closely with industry partners on a range of projects, Dr Wood's core research focus is on two broad themes. First, sustainable and consumer-focused outcomes through supply chain practices, with a particular focus on applications in the construction sector. This includes examining a range of sustainable supply chain practices and consideration of ethical and privacy issues when using supply chain technologies. Second, logistics relationships, dynamics, and the use of technology with a focus on 3PLs and logistics service providers.

Linh N. K. Duong, PhD is a Senior Lecturer in Operations Management at Bristol Business School, the University of the West of England, UK. His current research interests focus on sustainable and resilient supply chain management with the link to digital transformation, innovation, and collaboration among supply chain partners. He focuses on vulnerable contexts such as the agri-food industry, tourism industry, or small and medium enterprises (SMEs). His papers relating to supply chain resiliency and sustainable innovation were published in the International Journal of Production Research (ABS: 3, JIF: 3.199), Journal of Macromaketing (ABS: 2, JIF: 1.952), and Trends in Food Science and Technology (JIF: 11.077). He has previously worked at the University of Lincoln (UK), New Zealand Forest Research Institute (Scion) and Auckland University of Technology (NZ). Prior to this, he worked in the Supply Chain Management field since 2007 for dairy and pharmaceutical companies. He also joined projects on Distribution Management Systems, Inventory Management, and Production Management.

* * *

Alaa Abdelsalam is an Assistant Lecturer in College of International Transport and Logistics (CITL), Arab Academy for science, Technology and Maritime Transport (AASTMT) a Masters' Degree holder in Industrial Logistics and Supply Chain Management, Molde University College, Molde, Norway. a PhD candidate in Minho University in Portugal, my research field is Risk Management and Resilient Supply Chain Teaching for Bachelor Degree students subjects related to Risk Management, Resilient Supply chain, Logistics Information Systems.

Pedro B. Água is a Professor of General Management at the Portuguese Naval Academy. He has authored several articles and book chapters, while continuing his research in the field of cutting-edge technology, industrialization, innovation and business policy. Professor Água has over twenty-five years of experience across high technology endeavours, from defence to telecommunications and oil and gas industry, combining his extensive professional and business background with teaching. Professor Água holds an MBA from IESE Business School and a Ph.D. in Management and Engineering awarded by the University of Lisbon.

Bülend Avcı, PhD is Head Of Store & Technical Operations at METRO/MAKRO Cash and Carry.

Neeta Baporikar is currently Professor (Management) at Harold Pupkewitz Graduate School of Business (HP-GSB), Namibia University of Science and Technology, Namibia. Prior to this, she was Head-Scientific Research, with the Ministry of Higher Education CAS-Salalah, Sultanate of Oman, Professor (Strategic Management and Entrepreneurship) at IIIT Pune and BITS India. With more than a decade of experience in the industry, consultancy, and training, she made a lateral switch to research and academics in 1995. Prof Baporikar holds D.Sc. (Management Studies) USA, Ph.D. in Management, the University of Pune INDIA with MBA (Distinction) and Law (Hons.) degrees. Apart from this, she is an external reviewer, Oman Academic Accreditation Authority, Accredited Management Teacher, Qualified Trainer, FDP from EDII, Doctoral Guide, and Board Member of Academic and Advisory Committee in accredited B-Schools. She has to her credit many conferred doctorates, is a member of the international and editorial advisory board, reviewer for Emerald, IGI, Inderscience, etc, published numerous refereed papers, and authored books in the area of entrepreneurship, strategy, management, and higher education.

Carl Baxter is a Programme Leader and a Senior Lecturer in Food Operations, Manufacturing, and Supply Chain Management in College of Science. Carl leads the Degree Apprenticeship programmes in: Food Science and Technology; Food and Drink Operations and Manufacturing; Supply Chain; Agri-Produce; and the Senior Leader Master's. Carl is a personal tutor, supporting apprentices in Industry, and delivers modules throughout the programmes at the NCFM. He is also active in providing outreach support to industry through a variety of funding streams. Carl has over 30 years experience of working in the food industry. His specialist areas are Operations and Supply Chain management, especially around product development, process development, change processes, business IT solutions, and automation.

Fayçal Belkaid is currently an associate professor at university of Tlemcen and member of the Manufacturing Engineering Laboratory of Tlemcen (MELT). He obtained his Doctorate degree in Manufacturing Engineering from University of Tlemcen in 2014 and his accreditation to supervise research (HDR) in Manufacturing Engineering from the same University in 2017. He advised several master's and doctorate thesis. His research interests concern the planning and scheduling problems, optimization methods (metaheuristic…), optimization of logistic and production systems and supply chain management. He is author or co-author of more than 50 contributions with 2 book chapters and several publications. He is a member of several international conference committees and international journal boards. He is reviewer of many international journals.

Mohammed Bennekrouf is a PhD full associate professor in Higher School of Applied Sciences in Tlemcen (Algeria). He is responsible for several educational units in logistics, production and measuring the performance in the supply chain. He has supervised several doctoral students and master students in different themes that are related to operational research, decision support in the integrated supply chain planning development at multi-levels strategic-tactical and operational horizons. In particular, his research is focused on the management of logistics operations for the sustainable development both in the closed supply chain and agrifood supply chain. During his 13 years of research, he has contributed in the publication of several indexed journal articles and conference papers.

Anacleto Correia (M) is an Associate Professor and lecturer of Management and Information Systems at the Portuguese Navy Academy. He holds a Ph.D. in Computer Science, an M.Sc. in Statistics and Information Management, a B.Sc. degree in Management, and also a B.Sc. at Portuguese Naval Academy. His research interests are focused on requirements engineering, software engineering, process modeling, data mining, machine learning, and business engineering. He has also more than 20 years of experience in industry-leading projects and architecting large software development projects and is the author of several scientific papers in journals and conference proceedings.

Guy Coulthard is Product Manager at Richard Hochfeld Ltd. He has completed his studies at the University of Lincoln, United Kingdom.

Chehab Elbelehy is an Assistant Lecturer in College of International Transport and Logistics (CITL), Arab Academy for Science, Technology and Maritime Transport (AASTMT). a Masters' Degree holder in Transportation in Supply Chain Management Major, Molde University College, Molde, Norway. a PhD candidate in Minho University in Portugal, my research field is Supply Chain Sustainability, Reverse Logistics, Green supply chain. Teaching for Bachelor's degree students basics of logistics management, applied statistics, reverse logistics and sustainable supply chain, humanitarian logistics.

Dimitris Folinas is a Professor at International Hellenic University. He holds a Ph.D. in Applied Informatics from the University of Macedonia, Thessaloniki, Greece and a Master of Information Systems from the same Institution. He has held various teaching posts teaching mainly Information Systems, Enterprise Information Systems and Logistics and Supply Chain Management. He is the author and co-author of over 280 research publications, 10 books, and as a researcher, he has prepared, submitted, and managed a number of projects funded by National and European Union research. His research interests and working experiences refer to information systems, logistics and supply chain management, and technologies.

Lidija Fošnarič is working in General hospital Trbovlje as leading nurse of surgery department. Lidija completed undergraduate studies at the Faculty of Health Sciences, University of Maribor. Later, she continued my postgraduate studies at the same university, which she has completed in 2010 with a master's degree. She is continuing her PHD studies at the Faculty of Logistics of the University of Maribor. Her fields of research are logistic, telemedicine and nursing in vascular surgery.

Armindo Frias is a Military Professor of Logistics, Management and Administration at the Portuguese Naval Academy. He holds a PhD in Management, an MSc in Business Sciences, a BSc in Naval Military Sciences - branch of Naval Administration. He has more than thirty years of experience in Naval Logistics, Public Administration and Budgeting. Armindo Frias is the author of several scientific papers in journals and conference proceedings, his main research interests are procurement, negotiation, naval and maritime logistics, integrated logistics support, systems engineering and decision making.

Roman Gumzej received a doctorate degree in computer and information science from the University in Maribor in 1999. He was elected assistant professor at the Faculty of electrical engineering and computer science at University of Maribor in 2004 and associate professor at the Faculty of logistics, University of Maribor in 2014. He conducted several international research projects as visiting researcher at INSA de Lyon, France in 1998 and ifak e.V. Magdeburg, Germany in 2002. He gave lectures as a guest professor at the Faculty of Mathematics and Computer Science, Fernuniversität in Hagen, Germany in 2011, 2012 and 2013, as well as at the Faculty of Maritime studies, University of Rijeka, Croatia in 2018. He has authored or co-authored two patents, two books, three textbooks, several refereed book chapters, as well as many journal and conference articles. He is a member of several international professional organizations as well as editorial boards and program committees of international journals and conferences.

Adil Hammadi, PhD is a Lecturer at the School of Management, Curtin University. Adil does research in trust, risk and reputation assessment in supply chain.

Ajeya Jha is a Professor at the Department of Management Studies at Sikkim Manipal Institute of Technology (SMIT) since February 2000. In addition to having post-graduate and doctoral degrees in Business Administration, he possesses graduation and post graduation in Pharmaceutical Sciences also. fellow of International Society of Management.Has a rich and diverse industrial experience of 15 years (includes launching two green-field projects), teaching 22 years and with NGO 8 months. He is the founder Chief coordinator of Entrepreneurship Development Cell (EDC) at SMIT established with support from Department of Science and Technology, Government of India.

Panagiotis Kotsios is a freelance economist providing economic analysis, data analytics and marketing services to private and public entities in Greece and abroad. He holds a Ph.D. with distinction in Industrial Economics from the University of Macedonia's (Greece) Department of International and European Studies (2010). He teaches as a contract lecturer in the Hellenic Open University (Patra) and the International Hellenic University (Katerini). His is a member of the Labour Market Diagnosis Mechanism (LMD) and has participated in several European projects. He is the author of the book Entrepreneurship and Innovation: Conception, Planning, Implementation and Operation, which is used as a textbook in 11 Greek universities.

Daniel Londono-Bernal is a Master of Commerce in Supply Chain Management and Industrial Engineer with experience in mining, coffee, textile, automobile, plastics and furniture production companies, within their HR, production, logistics or Information Systems departments. He has strong leadership style and is able to work under pressure with attention to detail.

Olcay Polat received his Industrial Engineering PhD degree from the Technical University of Berlin (Germany) with the scholarship of German Academic Exchange Service (DAAD) in 2013. He has been working as an Associate Professor in the Department of Industrial Engineering at Pamukkale University (Turkey). He has a special interest in supply chain management, logistics and transportation optimization, production management and risk management. He has been published more that 90 papers in respected journals, conference proceedings and books.

Torsten Reiners, PhD is Senior Lecturer in Logistics and Supply Chain Management at the Curtin University, Australia. His research and teaching experiences are in the areas of operations research (i.e., modelling, algorithm development, meta-heuristics, and simulation), fleet and maritime logistics, supply chain, information systems, and emerging technologies. His interests include instructional design, development of adaptive learning environments, distant collaboration and mobile learning, which is also manifested in his PhD Thesis about adaptive learning material in the field of operations research. He participated in multiple projects to use 3D spaces for learning support. He coordinated multiple industry projects in Germany (with e.g., Avis, HHLA, Lufthansa Technik, and Airbus). He participated in multiple projects to use 3D spaces for learning and training support; i.e. to improve the authenticity of learning in classes about production and simulation as well as developing a theoretical framework for authentic and immersive education with gamified elements.

Bojan Rupnik received his PhD in computer science at the Faculty of Electrical Engineering and Computer Science, University of Maribor in 2016. He is currently employed at the Faculty of logistics, University of Maribor as a teaching assistant. His research areas include geographic information systems, logistic information systems, simulation, system dynamics, and optimization algorithms.

Saibal Kumar Saha (UGC NET Qualified) holds a first class Master's degree in MBA and a first class Bachelor's Degree in Electronics and Communication Engineering. He has 10+ years of experience and has worked in MNCs like Cognizant Technology Solutions and Tata Aig Life. He has served National Institute of Technology - Silchar, Jyotirmoy School of Business – Kolkata, University of Technology and Management - Shillong and is presently working as Assistant Professor at Sikkim Manipal Institute of Technology - Majitar, India.

Sangita Saha is an MBA master from Sikkim Manipal Institute of Technology and BCA graduate from Indira Gandhi National Open University. She has specialized in Human Resource and Marketing. She has active interest in academic research and her area of interest includes motivation, consumer behaviour, tourism, and digital technologies.

Simona Sinko received her B.Sc and M.Sc degree from the Faculty of Logistics, University of Maribor in 2016 and 2018, where is a currently teaching assistant and Ph.D. student. Her main research area is quantitative modelling in logistics.

Effnu Subiyanto is a professional in PT Semen Indonesia (Persero) Tbk, one of the biggest State-owned cement corporations in Indonesia for over than 25 years. He earned bachelor in electrical engineering, master degree in business strategic and doctoral degree in economics. His area of expertise is logistics and transportation, economics, public policies, infrastructure and various related. He is now serving as a post-graduate lecturer at the Widya Mandala Surabaya Catholic University in Indonesia.

Binh Tu Van is an Associate Professor at the University of Economics Ho Chi Minh City and CFVG. His research mostly concerns enterprise behaviour and the marketing of SMEs.

Kripanshu Vora is a Master of International Business from the University of Otago. He has worked for the Ministry of External and Overseas Affairs of India and hails from a french colonial town called Pondicherry, India. He is an alumnus of the Sri Aurobindo International Centre of Education (SAICE), also known as the 'Ashram School'.

Besma Zeddam is currently a PhD student at university of Tlemcen and member of the Manufacturing Engineering Laboratory of Tlemcen (MELT). She received her License (2016) in Industrial Engineering and her Master (2018) in Industrial Engineering also from the University of Tlemcen. She prepares her Doctorate degree since October 2018 in Industrial Engineering from the University of Tlemcen. Her research interests concern supply chain management, optimization methods (metaheuristic …), production and transportation optimization, multi-criteria decision making methods and other related fields.

Index

S

T

U

V

W

Z

www.ingramcontent.com/pod-product-compliance
Lightning Source LLC
LaVergne TN
LVHW062113300926
849161LV00010B/2448